WINDOWS NT SERV...
NO EXPERIENCE RE...

ROBERT COWART AND BOYD WATERS

ISBN: 0-7821-2081-4
512 pages; 7.5" × 9"
$29.99 U.S.

Here is the quickest and easiest way for consultants and IS personnel to get up to speed with Windows NT networks. This step-by-step guide to installing, configuring, and administering NT Server gives readers all of the essential skills and practical knowledge that they need when first booting up a new network. Learn—with real-world examples—how to install, design, and control any size network; integrate NT Server with NetWare and other existing networks; and manage applications, disks, printer services, and much more.

EXPERT GUIDE TO WINDOWS NT 4 REGISTRY

PETER D. HIPSON

ISBN: 0-7821-1983-2
816 pages; 7.5" × 9"
$44.99 U.S.

This is the essential, objective look at the Windows NT Registry that Microsoft dares not publish! Strengths and weaknesses are examined in the same thorough fashion. You'll find explanations, warnings, notes, tips, and examples for every key and every parameter. Understand why the Registry is the single most important structure in Windows NT, and how one incorrect or corrupted entry can jeopardize an entire network.

Windows NT® 4
Complete

SYBEX® SAN FRANCISCO ‣ PARIS ‣ DÜSSELDORF ‣ SOEST ‣ LONDON

Associate Publisher: Gary Masters

Contracts & Licensing Manager: Kristine O'Callaghan

Acquisitions & Developmental Editor: Tracy Brown

Project Editor: Emily K. Wolman

Compilation Editor: Marilyn Smith

Editors: Davina Baum, Pat Coleman, Nancy Conner, Dana Gardner, Ben Miller, Valerie Perry, Lee Ann Pickrell, Doug Robert, Marilyn Smith, June Waldman, and Sharon Wilkey

Compilation Technical Editor: Donald Fuller

Technical Editors: Jeffrey A. Bankston, Dave Conners, Mark Edwards, Robert Gradante, Rob Hill, Doug Langston, Jim Polizzi, Ron Reimann, Rob Sanfilippo, John Savill, John Schroeder, and Kevin Summers

Book Designer: Maureen Forys, Happenstance Type-O-Rama

Graphic Illustrator: Tony Jonick

Electronic Publishing Specialist: Robin Louise Kibby

Project Team Leader: Lisa Reardon

Proofreaders: Susan Berge and Bonnie Hart

Indexer: John S. Lewis

Cover Designer: DesignSite

Cover Photographer: Mark Johann

Library of Congress Card Number: 99-61817
ISBN: 0-7821-2470-4

Manufactured in the United States of America

10 9 8 7 6 5 4 3 2 1

ACKNOWLEDGMENTS

This book incorporates the work of many people, inside and outside Sybex.

Gary Masters and Tracy Brown defined the book's overall structure and contents. Marilyn Smith compiled and adapted all the material for publication in this book.

A large team of editors, developmental editors, project editors, and technical editors helped to put together the various books from which *Windows NT 4 Complete* was compiled: Tracy Brown handled developmental tasks; Raquel Baker, Davina Baum, Pat Coleman, Nancy Conner, Brenda Frink, Dana Gardner, Malka Geffen, Dann McDorman, Ben Miller, Alison Moncrieff, Gemma O'Sullivan, Valerie Perry, Lee Ann Pickrell, Doug Robert, Marilyn Smith, June Waldman, Sharon Wilkey, and Kim Wimpsett all contributed to editing or project editing; and Jeffrey A. Bankston, Dave Conners, Mark Edwards, Donald Fuller, Robert Gradante, Rob Hill, Doug Langston, Jim Polizzi, Ron Reimann, Rob Sanfilippo, John Savill, John Schroeder, and Kevin Summers provided technical edits. Marilyn Smith and Donald Fuller deserve particular thanks for their help in shaping the book's outline and updating material, as does Emily Wolman, who tied it all together.

The *Windows NT 4 Complete* production team of electronic publishing specialist Robin Kibby and project team leader Lisa Reardon worked with speed and accuracy to turn the manuscript files and illustrations into the handsome book you're now reading. Ellen Bliss and Dan Schiff also helped in various ways to keep the project moving.

Finally, our most important thanks go to the contributors who agreed to have their work excerpted in *Windows NT 4 Complete*: James Chellis, J. Scott Christianson, Robert Cowart, Lisa Donald, Peter Dyson, Ava Fajen, Barry Gerber, Peter D. Hipson, Todd Lammle, Mark Minasi, Charles Perkins, Chris Russel, Matthew Strebe, and Boyd Waters. And thanks to Todd Phillips, who wrote Chapters 29 and 30 specifically for this book. Without their efforts, this book would not exist.

CONTENTS AT A GLANCE

TABLE OF CONTENTS

Part III ▸ Certification   723

Chapter 24 □ Why Become Certified?   725

Chapter 25 □ Choosing the Right Certification for You   737

INTRODUCTION

Windows NT 4 Complete is a one-of-a-kind computer book—valuable both for the breadth of its content and for its low price. This thousand-page compilation of information from fifteen Sybex books, plus reference material written for this book, provides comprehensive coverage of Windows NT Workstation 4 and Windows NT Server 4. This book, unique in the computer book world, was created with several goals in mind:

- Offering a thorough guide that covers the features of Windows NT Workstation 4 and NT Server 4 at an affordable price

- Helping you become familiar with the essentials of Windows NT 4 so you can choose an advanced Windows NT book with confidence

- Acquainting you with some of Sybex's best authors—their writing styles and teaching skills, and the level of expertise they bring to their books—so you can easily find a match for your interests as you delve deeper into Windows NT

Windows NT 4 Complete is designed to provide all the essential information you'll need to get the most from Windows NT, while at the same time inviting you to explore the even greater depths and wider coverage of material in the original books.

If you've read other computer "how-to" books, you've seen that there are many possible approaches to the task of explaining how to use software and hardware effectively. The books from which *Windows NT 4 Complete* was compiled represent a range of the approaches to teaching that Sybex and its authors have developed—from the quick, concise *ABCs* style to the exhaustively thorough *Mastering* style. As you read through various chapters of *Windows NT 4 Complete*, you'll see which approach works best for you. You'll also see what these books have in common: a commitment to clarity, accuracy, and practicality.

You'll find in these pages ample evidence of the expertise of Sybex's authors. Unlike publishers who produce "books by committee," Sybex encourages authors to write in their individual voices that reflect experience with the software at hand and with the evolution of today's personal computers. Nearly every book represented here is the work of a single writer or a few close collaborators, and you are getting the benefit of each author's direct experience.

In adapting the various source materials for inclusion in *Windows NT 4 Complete*, the compiler preserved these individual voices and perspectives. Chapters were edited only to minimize duplication and to add sections, so that you get coverage of cutting-edge developments.

WHO CAN BENEFIT FROM THIS BOOK?

Windows NT 4 Complete is designed to meet the needs of a wide range of computer users. Therefore, while you *could* read this book from beginning to end, you may not *need* to read every chapter. The table of contents and the index will guide you to the subjects you're looking for.

Beginners   Even if Windows NT is new to you, this book will get you up and running with both Windows NT Workstation and Windows NT Server.

Intermediate users   Chances are, you already know how to perform routine operations with Windows NT. You also know that there is always more to learn about working effectively, and you want to get up to speed on new features in Windows NT 4. Throughout this book, you'll find instructions for just about anything you want to do.

Advanced users   If you've worked extensively with Windows NT, you'll appreciate this book as a reference and as a guide to further work with NT Workstation 4 and NT Server 4.

HOW THIS BOOK IS ORGANIZED

Windows NT 4 Complete has 30 chapters and one appendix.

Part I: NT Workstation   In the first ten chapters, you'll learn about Windows NT Workstation 4. The chapters in this part cover installing NT Workstation, setting up your work environment, printing, sharing data among applications, using Internet Explorer 4, and troubleshooting.

Part II: NT Server The next thirteen chapters are your guide to setting up and running a network with Windows NT Server 4. The chapters in this part provide the information you need to plan your network and design your server, as well as install and run NT Server. You'll also learn how to work with the Registry, manage user accounts, and handle security for your network. And because NT Server is designed to work with other systems in your network, you'll find information about Microsoft Exchange Server 5.5 and Microsoft Internet Information Server, including a chapter on developing intranet systems. The final chapter in this part covers network protection and disaster recovery.

Part III: Certification If you're considering becoming a certified computer professional (or adding to your current certification), this part is for you. The first two chapters explain the benefits of certification and the types of certification available. The next three chapters deal with MSCE (Microsoft Certified Engineer) certification, specifically the Windows NT Workstation 4 and NT Server 4 exams. You can test yourself on the sample study questions presented in this part.

Part IV: Reference The two chapters here provide a handy reference guide to Windows NT. The first chapter is a succinct summary of essential operations. The second chapter is a complete Windows NT command reference.

Appendix To see how you did on the sample study questions in Part III, turn to this appendix. You'll find the answers here.

A Few Typographical Conventions

When an operation requires a series of choices from menus or dialog boxes, the ➤ symbol is used to guide you through the instructions, like this: "Start ➤ Programs ➤ Accessories ➤ ClipBook Viewer." The items the ➤ symbol separates may be menu names, toolbar icons, checkboxes, or other elements of the Windows NT interface—anyplace you can make a selection.

`This typeface` is used to identify filenames and paths, Internet URLs, and program code. **Boldface type** is used whenever you need to type something into a text box.

You'll find these types of special notes throughout the book:

TIP

You'll see a lot of these—quicker and smarter ways to accomplish a task, which the authors have based on their experience using Windows NT 4.

NOTE

You'll see these types of notes, too. They usually represent alternate ways to accomplish a task or some additional information that needs to be highlighted.

WARNING

In a few places, you'll see a warning like this one. When you see a warning, pay attention to it!

YOU'LL ALSO SEE "SIDEBAR" BOXES LIKE THIS

These boxed sections provide added explanation of special topics that are noted briefly in the surrounding discussion, but that you may want to explore separately. Each sidebar has a heading that announces the topic, so you can quickly decide whether it's something you need to know about.

FOR MORE INFORMATION...

See the Sybex Web site, www.sybex.com, to learn more about all of the books that contributed to *Windows NT 4 Complete*. On the site's Catalog page, you'll find links to any book you're interested in.

We hope you enjoy this book and find it useful. Happy computing!

PART i

INTRODUCING WINDOWS NT

Chapter 1

INTRODUCING WINDOWS NT

Windows NT is the foundation upon which Microsoft's networking strategy rests. Microsoft intends to provide a networking environment that is unified from bottom to top, serving desktop clients to industrial-strength enterprise servers. Windows NT is the operating system that makes this strategy possible.

Windows NT's main competitor, Novell NetWare, provides powerful enterprise networking capabilities, but it is not useful as a desktop operating system. NT Server and NT Workstation are essentially the same software, with Server providing additional functionality and control for network environments.

Windows has established itself as a major contender to Novell NetWare's dominance in the network operating system market. Considering its more robust architecture, its flexibility, and its

Adapted from *MCSE: NT® Workstation 4 Study Guide,*
Second Edition by Charles Perkins and Matthew Strebe
with James Chellis

ISBN 0-7821-2223-X   752 pages $49.99

ability to support important fundamental improvements like multi-processing, Windows NT may eclipse NetWare in the near future.

Choosing an Operating System

Windows NT Workstation is a very demanding operating system. It does not support the broad range of legacy hardware supported by Windows 95/98, and running Windows NT requires a bit more RAM and hard disk space than you need for Windows 95/98. Windows NT Workstation's security and multitasking scheduling puts more of a burden on the computer, causing noticeably slower performance for desktop applications compared to their performance on Windows 95/98.

Two primary considerations come into play when you select an operating system: what you have and what you want. What you have is the computer in which you will be installing an operating system. What you want is fulfillment of your computing requirements.

Operating System Hardware Requirements

Table 1.1 shows the official Microsoft minimum standards for its various operating systems.

TABLE 1.1: Minimum Hardware Requirements for Windows NT

COMPONENT	INTEL	RISC
Microprocessor	80486/33/DX or higher at minimum; Pentium or higher is preferable	MIPS, PowerPC, or Digital Alpha will provide acceptable performance
Disk storage	125MB	160MB
Memory	12MB (16MB for NT Server; 16MB is the recommended minimum for NT Workstation; 24MB will reduce virtual memory usage and provide acceptable performance; 48MB will increase performance)	16MB (24MB for a small network; 32MB will reduce virtual memory usage and provide acceptable performance; 64MB will increase performance)
Display	VGA or higher resolution video display adapter	VGA or higher resolution video display adapter
Required additional drive	CD-ROM or access to files from a networked CD-ROM	SCSI CD-ROM drive or access to files from a networked CD-ROM

The minimum standards are the minimum requirements to load and run the operating system alone. Many users will actually want to use additional software. Use the criteria shown to determine which Microsoft operating system will be the best fit for your computer.

Validating Your Hardware for Windows NT

Prior to Windows NT 4, the only way to find out about a hardware incompatibility problem was to attempt to install the operating system and fail. This involuntary method takes a bit of time, is very frustrating, and usually doesn't give you much information about what exactly is wrong.

Microsoft has remedied this problem with the Windows NT Hardware Qualifier (NTHQ), a program that runs under DOS and inspects your computer for hardware incompatibilities without actually installing the operating system.

To use NTHQ, you must first create the NTHQ disk, as shown in Exercise 1.1. You can run this program from any operating system that can run MS-DOS programs.

EXERCISE 1.1: CREATING THE WINDOWS NT HARDWARE QUALIFIER (NTHQ) DISK

1. Boot to MS-DOS or open an MS-DOS session in any operating system that supports running MS-DOS programs.

2. Insert the Windows NT Workstation CD-ROM.

3. Insert a formatted 1.44MB floppy disk into the A drive.

4. Change drives to your CD-ROM.

5. Type **CD \SUPPORT\HQTOOL**.

6. Type **makedisk** and press Enter.

7. Remove the floppy disk and label it *NT Hardware Qualifier*.

After creating the NTHQ disk, you are ready to use it to validate your computer. Exercise 1.2 shows how to use the NTHQ disk.

EXERCISE 1.2: USING THE WINDOWS NT HARDWARE QUALIFIER (NTHQ) DISK

1. Boot the NTHQ floppy you created in Exercise 1.1.

2. Click Yes to continue at the query tool screen.

3. Click Yes for comprehensive detection. If this process locks up your computer, start over at step 1 and click No at step 2.

4. Note the information detected about your computer.

5. Click the compatibility button.

6. Review each device listed as not compatible.

7. Ensure that you have third-party drivers for each device in this list or remove the device before attempting to install Windows NT.

Once you have installed Windows NT, you can attempt to reinstall any devices you removed for incompatibility reasons.

Operating System Features

Determining if an operating system will run on your computer is only the first step. You must also determine whether the operating system fulfills your computing requirements.

Your requirements will be determined by:

▶ Your hardware

▶ Your need for security

▶ The software you currently use

▶ The software used by others in your organization

▶ The software you want to use

▶ Your need for reliability and fault tolerance

▶ How responsive you want your computer to be

▶ The type of user interface you want to use

You are not likely to find an operating system that will meet all of your needs. Prioritize your requirements to find the best operating system for you. For instance, if you must have fault tolerance, but you would like to support an old printer that Windows NT doesn't support, ask yourself how important that printer really is. If you can live without it (or upgrade it), you should use Windows NT.

You may find that your requirements cannot be fulfilled by the computer you currently own because it can't run the operating system you've decided will work best for you. Your best option in this case is to upgrade your computer. Use Table 1.2 to decide which operating system comes closest to fulfilling your requirements.

TABLE 1.2: Operating System Features

Requirement	MS-DOS	Win 3.11	OS/2 Warp	Win 95/98	NT WS	NT Server
DOS software	√	√	√	√	1	1
Win16 software		√	√	√	√	√
Win32 software				√	√	√
Plug and Play				√		
Power management			√	√		
File-level security			√		√	√
RAID						√
Preemptive			√	2	√	√
Multiprocessing					√	√
RISC CPU					√	√
Peer networking		√	√	√	√	√
Network server						√
Win16 drivers		√		√	√	√
DOS drivers	√	√	3	√		
POSIX compliance					√	√
Peer Web services				4	√	
Internet host						√
Runs OS/2 1.3			√		√	√
Runs OS/2 2.0 PM			√			

1. Windows NT will not allow hardware access. DOS programs requiring such access will not run.

2. Windows 95/98 preemptive multitasking is not as fault tolerant as Windows NT.

3. OS/2 does not support all DOS mode drivers.

4. Available to Windows 95/98 is the Personal Web Server product. It is, in function, similar to Peer Web Services but does not include all of the same features.

What Is Windows NT?

Windows NT is a 32-bit, preemptive, multitasking operating system that belongs to the Microsoft Windows family of operating system products.

It comes in two versions:

Windows NT Workstation   Designed to work as member of a Windows NT Workstation workgroup, as a client of a Windows NT Server domain, as a Novell NetWare client, or on a stand-alone workstation. It is aimed toward users who need a reliable operating system with a high level of security.

Windows NT Server   Essentially the same as Windows NT Workstation but with added features that enable it to work as a network operating system.

NOTE

Windows NT Workstation comes with client software for NT Server and Novell NetWare.

Because these two products have so much in common, we'll look at their shared features first and then explore their differences.

Windows NT Features

Windows NT is a secure computer operating system with a graphical interface. It is not a revision of any of the other Windows operating systems such as Windows 3.x or Windows for Workgroups 3.x, but rather an entirely new operating system.

NOTE

Unlike previous versions of Windows, Windows NT really is a complete, true operating system in itself, not relying on DOS for lower-level functions. When a computer with Windows NT starts up, it starts immediately in Windows NT.

Earlier versions of Windows NT used the graphical interface from Windows 3.x and Windows for Workgroups, but Windows NT 4 uses the Windows 95 graphical interface. Figure 1.1 shows the face of Windows NT 4.

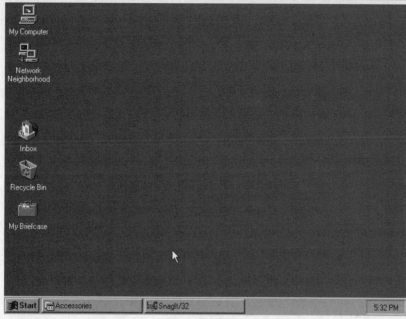

FIGURE 1.1:   The Windows NT 4 graphical interface

With Windows NT, Microsoft was able to go beyond the 16-bit limitations imposed by the MS-DOS operating system while maintaining support for MS-DOS applications (as well as Win16, Win32, OS/2, and POSIX environments). Windows NT Workstation supports existing file structures, in addition to the new file structure it introduces.

Windows NT has many features that we'll cover in detail in later chapters, but a few that are especially noteworthy are described in the following sections.

Portability

Unlike most operating systems, Windows NT can run on a variety of platforms. This flexibility can be a great advantage when implementing a computer strategy for an organization because it can free you from being tied to a narrow selection of hardware platforms. Whereas DOS, for example, was written for the Intel 8086/8088 family of microprocessors, Windows NT was designed to support Intel 80486 and Pentium-based computers, as well as Reduced Instruction Set Computers (RISC) computers. Windows NT supports the following microprocessors:

▶ IBM PowerPC

▶ MIPS R4x00

▶ DEC Alpha AXP

▶ 80486 DX 33 and Pentium class

NOTE

Microsoft is able to port Windows NT easily to a variety of platforms because of the modular nature of Windows NT architecture. The hardware-specific components of NT architecture are stored apart from the rest of the operating system in a special module called the Hardware Abstraction Layer (HAL). This architecture enables NT developers to adapt Windows NT to various platforms simply by making changes to the HAL, rather than to an entire, monolithic operating system.

Multitasking Operations

From the perspective of the end user, *multitasking* means that different types of applications can run simultaneously. While the user is working on one application, another application can be running in the background.

An operating system achieves this effect by rapidly switching tasks, not—as it seems—by scheduling the microprocessor to work on more than one task at the same time. The microprocessor alternates so quickly from task to task that the user might think the machine is processing several different tasks at the same time. Windows NT actually supports two kinds of multitasking: preemptive and cooperative.

Preemptive Multitasking   Under previous versions of Windows, poorly written applications could seize control of a computer's processor and cause it to hang. Windows NT corrects this problem with *preemptive multitasking.* This type of multitasking allows the operating system to manage the processing of application *threads* in separate sessions without surrendering control of the processor.

Cooperative Multitasking   Some multiple 16-bit Windows applications share the same processing session. In this case, Windows NT relies on *cooperative multitasking* (rather than preemptive multitasking) under which the sharing of the session time is not managed by the operating system. Instead, each 16-bit Windows application must cooperate by releasing control of the processor so that the other applications can use it. Consequently, a poorly written application may be able to hang the other 16-bit applications running in the same 16-bit session, but it will not be able to affect the operation of Windows NT or other 32-bit processes. Windows NT is never hobbled by its ability to run cooperative multitasking applications.

Multithreading Operations

While running on a Pentium or RISC-based processor, Windows NT can actually execute multiple pieces of code—or *threads*—from a single application simultaneously. This capability is called *multithreading*. It helps to speed up applications and allows them to be executed more smoothly.

NOTE

A *thread* is the most basic unit of code that can be scheduled for execution. A *process* is composed of one or more threads.

For example, under Windows 3.*x* you may have had the experience of running a multimedia application that was unable to produce smooth video while sound was playing. This situation could have been caused by Windows 3.*x* failing to process the application's video and audio threads in the correct distribution. If Windows 3.*x* had been able to multithread, as Windows NT does, it could have executed both the video and the audio threads smoothly.

File Systems

Windows NT supports a variety of file systems, including FAT, NTFS, and VFAT:

File Allocation Table (FAT)   The file system used with DOS

New Technology File System (NTFS)   The file system introduced by Windows NT

Virtual File Allocation Table (VFAT)   The file system introduced by Windows 95

Windows NT supports filenames of up to 256 characters, thus offering the "long filenames" feature that is a popular part of Windows 95/98.

NOTE
Previous versions of Windows NT supported HPFS, but this feature was eliminated in the first release of NT 4.

Security

Microsoft designed Windows NT with security in mind. Windows NT's security features, such as a mandatory logon procedure, memory protection, auditing, and limited network access, have been developed so that Windows NT can be used in accordance with the U.S. Department of Defense's Class C2 security specification.

Support for Many Clients

The following clients can serve as workstations on a Windows NT network:

- Windows 3.*x*
- Windows for Workgroups
- MS-DOS
- Windows 95/98
- Macintosh
- OS/2
- Windows NT Workstation

Because Windows NT Workstation is designed to work well with Windows NT Server, it is excellent as a client on a Windows NT network.

In addition, Windows NT has been designed to operate well on the same network as Novell NetWare and Unix file, print, and application servers. Windows NT includes a suite of tools to provide seamless connectivity to NetWare servers.

Multiprocessor Support

Windows NT has the scalability to run on computers with multiple microprocessors, thereby enabling multiprocessing applications to run on more than one processor. This feature is referred to as *scalability* because the number of processors can be scaled to the demands of the task. When running on multiple processors, the Windows NT operating system manages the microprocessors as well as the memory, which they share.

The two main multiprocessing techniques are asymmetrical and symmetrical:

Asymmetrical multiprocessing (ASMP)   One processor is typically reserved for the operating system and the I/O devices, while the other processor(s) can run application threads and other tasks. The problem with this approach is that it can be an inefficient way to use microprocessor resources, since one processor can end up being busier than another.

Symmetrical multiprocessing (SMP)   The available processors share all tasks, including operating system tasks, user processes, and application threads. This approach is the most efficient way to do multiprocessing, but designing an operating system to handle SMP is difficult. Fortunately, Windows NT was designed to support this type of multiprocessing.

NOTE

To truly exploit the advantages of a multiprocessing operating system, an application must be specifically designed to execute multiple threads of code simultaneously.

Compatibility with Applications

Windows NT can run the following types of applications:

- ► DOS 16-bit applications

- ► Windows 3.x 16-bit (Win16) applications

- ► POSIX-compliant (POSIX is a Unix implementation) applications

- ► OS/2 1.x character-based programs (and OS/2 1.x Presentation Manager applications if you obtain a special add-on package from Microsoft)

- ► New 32-bit (Win32) applications

Windows NT's compatibility with a variety of applications is critical to its success in the marketplace. For example, corporate MIS departments can switch to NT without needing to purchase new applications, which means they can avoid large expenditures and massive retraining.

Storage Space

Windows NT supports a virtually limitless amount of memory and hard disk space. The specific numbers are as follows:

RAM   Windows NT supports 4 gigabytes (GB).

Hard disk space   Windows NT supports 16 exabytes.

Networking Connectivity

Windows NT supports the following network protocols:

- ▶ TCP/IP
- ▶ DLC
- ▶ NetBEUI
- ▶ AppleTalk
- ▶ NWLink (Microsoft's 32-bit Windows NT IPX/SPX)

Because Windows NT was designed to be an operating system within an existing network, its developers provided support for the following network operating environments:

- ▶ AppleTalk networks
- ▶ Banyan Vines
- ▶ DEC Pathworks
- ▶ IBM LAN Server
- ▶ IBM SNA networks
- ▶ Microsoft LAN Manager
- ▶ Microsoft Windows 95/98 Peer Networking
- ▶ Microsoft Windows for Workgroups
- ▶ Novell NetWare
- ▶ TCP/IP networks

WINDOWS NT ARCHITECTURE

Before we head further into the services and features offered by Windows NT, and the differences between Windows NT Workstation and Windows NT Server, let's quickly detour into the guts of the Windows NT operating system. Figure 1.2 diagrams the Windows NT architecture.

TIP

A good understanding of the Windows NT architecture is crucial to understanding its inner workings.

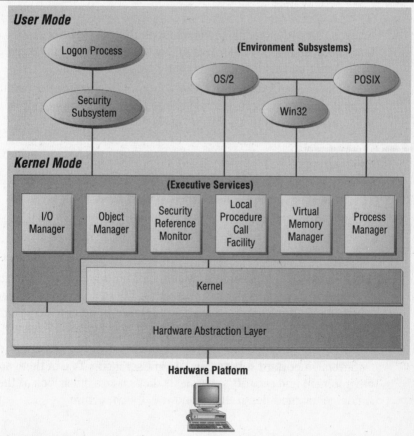

FIGURE 1.2: The Windows NT architecture is composed of several separate modules.

Windows NT is based on a *modular* operating system. Rather than weaving all of the different components of the operating system into a complex, monolithic system, the designers of Windows NT decided to separate different operating system functions into independent components that work together to provide the complete functionality of a network operating system.

NOTE

The Windows NT operating system uses objects. The word *objects* here is a general term that describes combinations of data and functions representing a service that can be shared by more than one process. These objects can be of different types, can be given different attributes, and can be protected by NT's security system.

Each component, while integrated with the rest of the operating system, is still distinct and has unique functionality. In fact, the modules are so distinct that they do not even share any code.

As you can see in Figure 1.2, the Windows NT system architecture is divided into two modes: User and Kernel. Let's begin by looking at the mode that is closest to us, the end users of NT.

NOTE

Dave Cutler headed the Windows NT design team. Cutler also designed the VMS operating system that runs on the DEC VAX system.

The User Mode

The *User mode* is the operating system mode in which user applications and environment subsystems are executed. It is a nonprivileged mode in which applications must call executive services in order to access memory and hardware. You'll learn more about executive services in just a few moments.

Several important subsystems run in User mode. Two of them are the environment and security subsystems. Let's take a quick look at these fundamental modules of the Windows NT architecture.

Environment Subsystems

As we mentioned earlier, Windows NT can run applications that are native to other operating systems. For example, Windows NT can run POSIX or OS/2 applications. Windows NT is able to do this because of the *environment subsystems* that reside in User mode.

The environment subsystems are:

Win32   This is the Windows NT 32-bit subsystem, which supports Windows NT, DOS, and Windows applications.

POSIX   This subsystem supports POSIX.1 applications, but these applications have limited functionality.

OS/2   This subsystem provides limited support for OS/2.

Each of these subsystems contains an Application Programming Interface (API) that allows applications to run by emulating their native operating system. The Win32 subsystem, however, has a unique role in that it also controls the user interface.

NOTE
The environmental subsystems are referred to as *server objects*; the applications are referred to as *client objects*.

Security Subsystem

The security subsystem handles the logon process. It works directly with the security reference monitor in the Kernel mode to verify the password. Here's how the security subsystem works: A user enters a username and password. The security subsystem builds and sends an authentication package into the Kernel mode, then to the security reference monitor, where it is checked against the security account database. If the username and its password are correct, the security reference monitor builds and sends an access token back to the security subsystem.

NOTE
One of the first things you may have noticed about Windows NT is that you log on by pressing Ctrl+Alt+Del. This key combination directly invokes the Windows NT logon routine, which resides in a secure area of the Windows NT architecture that cannot be manipulated by would-be hackers.

Kernel Mode

The *Kernel mode* is also called the privileged processor mode. It is the inner core of the operating system. Unlike the User mode, this mode has execution priority over all User mode processes and cannot be swapped out to disk by the virtual memory manager (described later in this chapter).

User applications cannot access machine resources directly. To access system hardware and data, User mode applications make requests to the Kernel, then the Kernel executes the request and returns the resulting data. This method prevents a badly written program from destroying system resources or leaving the computer in an unstable state. Think of the Kernel as the teller in a bank. When you go into a bank to retrieve your money, the bank won't just let you walk into the vault. Instead, you must make a request to a teller, who enters the vault, retrieves your valuables, and returns them to you. The teller also makes a record of the transaction, which can be reviewed in a future audit. In this way, the bank protects itself from both innocent and malicious loss and also keeps a record of all important accesses.

The Kernel mode is composed of three modules:

▶ The NT Executive

▶ The Kernel

▶ The HAL

These three modules are often called the *Executive services*. They are responsible for the fundamental functions of the operating system, including processing by the microprocessor, as well as access to memory, hard disks, printers, and so on.

Executive

The NT Executive serves as the interface between the Kernel and the environmental subsystems in the User mode. It provides a set of services to support the native mode environments and contains nine modules:

Object manager   Provides the rules for the retention, naming, and security of objects. It allocates objects, tracks their use, and removes them when they are no longer required.

Security reference monitor   Is responsible for handling the logon process and the security protected subsystem (which is in User mode).

Process manager   Creates and deletes processes and is also responsible for tracking process objects and thread objects.

Local procedure call facility   Provides a client/server relationship between applications and the environmental subsystems.

Virtual memory manager   Maps virtual addresses to physical pages in memory and makes sure that virtual memory is used efficiently.

I/O manager   Handles all input and output (I/O) for the operating system. When the I/O manager receives a request for an I/O service from an application, it determines which driver should be used and then sends a request to the driver.

Hardware device drivers   A program that enables a specific piece of hardware (device) to communicate with Windows NT. Although a device may be installed on your system, Windows NT cannot recognize the device until you have installed and configured the appropriate driver. If a device is listed in the Hardware Compatibility List (HCL), a driver is usually included with Windows NT. Drivers are installed when you run the Setup program (for a manufacturer's supplied driver) or by using Devices in Control Panel.

Win32k window manager and GDI   Consists of functions in Win32k.sys that display graphics on the computer monitor and printers. GDI provides a set of standard functions that let applications communicate with graphics devices, including displays and printers, without knowing anything about the devices. It effectively reduces the required memory, allowing for improved graphics handling and performance.

Graphics device drivers   Programs that enable a specific piece of hardware (graphics device) to communicate with Windows NT.

Kernel

The nucleus of the entire operating system is the *Kernel*. The Kernel schedules all system activities (threads) for optimum performance. The Kernel queues data, channels it to the microprocessor, and the processed data directs it into the appropriate route. Windows NT has 32 thread-priority levels—the Kernel enforces and manages execution according to thread priority.

NOTE

The Kernel is responsible for synchronizing multiple microprocessors.

Because the Kernel is responsible for the flow of activity in the microprocessor, it cannot be paged out to virtual memory (you'll learn more about virtual memory and paging soon).

Hardware Abstraction Layer (HAL)

As mentioned earlier, one of the major features of Windows NT is its portability. The designers of Windows NT facilitated portability by creating the *Hardware Abstraction Layer* to hide the individual differences between different types of hardware platforms. The HAL effectively makes the hardware transparent to the rest of the operating system.

When NT is ported to a new platform, the HAL is rewritten, but most of the rest of the operating system is left untouched. Because the HAL is separate from the rest of the operating system, rewriting it is relatively easy.

WINDOWS NT MEMORY ARCHITECTURE

The following features are the most important aspects of the Windows NT memory model:

▶ Virtual memory

▶ Demand paging

▶ 32-bit, flat, linear address space

Let's take a closer look at these features.

Virtual Memory and Demand Paging

If typical computers had hundreds of megabytes of RAM, virtual memory would probably not be an issue. But because most workstations have a limited amount of memory, virtual memory compensates for this shortfall.

Virtual memory refers to the practice of using the hard drive to fool the operating system and applications into behaving as if there were more

RAM than actually exists. By using a local, physical disk as an extension of physical memory, Windows NT is able to create virtual memory. When actual RAM fills up, virtual memory is created on the hard drive.

When Windows NT runs out of physical memory, the virtual memory manager chooses sections of memory that have not been recently used and are of low priority and writes their contents to the virtual memory file, thus freeing that RAM for use by other processes. When that information is needed again, the same process occurs to make room for it in RAM, and the original information is restored from the virtual memory disk file. This disk file is also known as the *swap file*.

All of this activity is hidden from the application, which sees both virtual and actual memory as the same memory system. By centrally managing the memory addresses, Windows NT can keep memory used in one application separate and protected from interference by other applications. This arrangement provides greater stability for applications.

Each application running under Windows NT is given a unique virtual address space composed of equal blocks called *pages. Demand paging* refers to the process of moving data into paging files and then paging it back into physical memory when the application needs it.

The downside of virtual memory is that it is much slower than physical memory, because hard drives are far slower than RAM.

NOTE

When you run Windows NT on a machine with insufficient RAM, the amount of paging to the hard drive will become very noticeable, and the computer will run very slowly.

32-bit, Flat, Linear Addressing

Windows NT treats memory as one large contiguous block—there are no physical or logical divisions, and Windows NT can address up to 4GB of RAM at one time. This type of memory architecture is called a *flat* or *linear address space*, without the divisions of conventional, upper, expanded, and extended used in DOS and previous operating systems. Windows NT does use 2GB of this memory space for User mode applications, and it protects 2GB for Kernel mode processes.

If you are familiar with the Windows for MS-DOS memory architecture, you will know that memory is broken into segments with a maximum length of 64KB. This division presents major challenges to programmers who write large applications for Windows. The contiguous block of memory in Windows NT makes the programmer's job much easier.

NT SERVER AND WORKSTATION DIFFERENCES

Windows NT Server is essentially Windows NT Workstation with enhanced features that allow it to function as a network operating system. Here's a brief look at the chief differences between the two products:

▸ Server allows unlimited inbound client sessions; Workstation allows only 10.

▸ Server can support four processors (out of box); Workstation can support only two (out of box). OEM-manufactured versions of NT products can support up to 32 processors.

▸ Server allows up to 256 simultaneous sessions through Remote Access Service (RAS, which allows users to dial in across a modem); Workstation allows only one.

▸ Server can import and export directory replication, but Workstation can only import it.

▸ Server offers services for Macintosh, logon validation, and disk fault tolerance. Workstation offers none of these.

NOTE
For a detailed exploration of Windows NT Server, see the companion book *MCSE: NT Server 4 Study Guide*, also published by Sybex (1998).

WHAT'S NEXT?

In this chapter, we presented an overview of Windows NT Workstation, including its major features, modular design, and memory system. The next chapter covers the procedures for installing NT Workstation. It also explains how to set up a dual-boot system, upgrade to NT Workstation 4, and configure NT Workstation in a large, wide-scale deployment.

Chapter 2

INSTALLATION AND CONFIGURATION

In this chapter, I cover installing NT Workstation in different ways on an Intel platform and show you how to use different operating systems in the same machine simultaneously. In addition, I demonstrate how to remove and upgrade in various situations, as well as how to install and configure NT Workstation in a large, wide-scale deployment. I also explore in detail how to configure, install, and remove different hardware devices in an NT Workstation machine.

Adapted from *MCSE Test Success™: NT® Workstation 4* by Todd Lammle and Lisa Donald
ISBN 0-7821-2149-7   384 pages $24.99

INSTALLING WINDOWS NT WORKSTATION

Windows NT Workstation will not function properly if it is installed onto a computer that does not have compatible components.

You can get a list of these components from the NT Hardware Compatibility List (HCL). The Windows NT HCL is part of the Windows NT documentation package that comes with Windows NT. It lists the hardware that Microsoft has tested and found to be compatible with Windows NT. It gives information on:

- Storage devices, including SCSI and RAID I/O subsystems

- Monitors, modems, network adapters, CD-ROMs, UPS systems, keyboards, and pointing devices

- CPUs

Before you install Windows NT Workstation, you should make sure your system meets the minimum requirements to run NT. (See Table 1.1 in Chapter 1.)

NOTE

Microsoft's Windows NT Hardware Qualifier (NTHQ) is a utility provided by Microsoft to inspect your computer and provide a detailed report of any suspected incompatibility problems. See Chapter 1 for details.

Some of the common installation methods are listed below:

- Boot from floppies and install from a CD-ROM. No operating system on the computer is required. By using the boot floppies, you are actually launching WINNT.EXE with no parameters.

- Connect to a network share containing i386 installation files. Typically, it's faster to install NT by connecting to a server and downloading the installation from there. An operating system is required to attach to the server with the distribution files.

- Boot from a network installation startup disk and run from the network share. If no operating system is present on the system, you can create a boot/install disk from the NT CD-ROM. This will create a DOS boot disk with networking capabilities, allowing the workstation to connect to a server network share.

▶ Install from an existing operating system by accessing the NT Workstation CD-ROM. If you can access the CD-ROM, but the CD-ROM drive is not HCL-compatible, you can copy the distribution files to the hard drive and start the installation with the /B switch to skip creating boot floppies. If installing NT Workstation on a computer that has an HPFS partition, convert the partition to NTFS by using either CONVERT.EXE or ACLCONVERT.EXE. (CONVERT.EXE does not retain the file system security attribute information.)

TIP

Why not use the Autoplay Screen Install button on the CD-ROM to start the NT Workstation install? You can, in fact, use this method to start the install. Bear in mind that it is the typical install path. You can't control your installation in a special way if you use this method. However, it's fine for a straightforward, simple installation.

Installing Windows NT by Using WINNT.EXE

The Setup program for 16-bit operating systems (WINNT.EXE) is capable of performing the following:

▶ Creating a set of the three Setup boot disks for Intel-based systems by using the /o or /ox switches. The /x switch prevents the floppy set creation if an existing set of disks are to be used.

▶ Creates a temporary folder called Win_nt.~ls and copies the Workstation files to this folder. If the floppy disk boot files are to be loaded to the system hard drive from the CD-ROM or network share service using the disks, the /b switch is used.

▶ Prompts the user to restart the computer from the first Setup disk.

Table 2.1 explains the switches that can be used with WINNT.EXE to control the setup process.

TABLE 2.1: Switches to Control the Installation Process

Switch	Explanation
/b	Installs without creating installation boot floppies.
/c	Skips free space check on installation boot floppies.
/f	Copies files from the boot floppies without verifying the copies.
/II	Specifies the filename (but not the path) of the setup information file. The default is dosnet.inf.
/o	Creates boot floppies only.
/ox	Creates boot floppies for CD-ROM–based installation.
/s	Specifies the source location of Windows NT setup files. Must be in the form WINNT /s: <Path>.
/t	Specifies the drive to contain the temporary setup files.
/u	Specifies unattended operation and an optional script file.
/udf	Specifies tailored, unattended installation for installation on multiple machines.

WINNT32.EXE is very similar to WINNT.EXE, except that it can be used only on a computer already running NT (a true 32-bit operating system). This is used to upgrade or install NT into a different directory to allow dual-booting of NT operating systems.

System and Boot Partitions

Differentiating between the system and boot partitions can be confusing because the names seem to be backwards. The actual files used to boot the system are on the system partition where the WINNT or %*systemroot*% resides, and the system files used to run NT are stored on the boot partition.

System Partition

The system partition contains the files NT uses to start itself: NTLDR, BOOT.INI, BOOTSECT.DOS, NTDETECT.COM, and, if the system is SCSI-based, NTBOOTDD.SYS. These must be in the root of the startup disk or partition—usually the C drive.

Boot Partition

The boot partition contains key files that make up NT (NTOSKRNL.EXE and HAL.DLL), which are found in the %*systemroot*%\System32 directory (default = C:\WINNT\System32).

Therefore, if you choose to install NT on a non-default drive such as D, you can create a situation where NT "boots" or starts from its system partition on C and runs from its boot partition on D.

Dual-Boot Systems

Dual-boot systems are computers that have more than one operating system installed on the same computer.

Windows NT will coexist happily with other operating systems on the same computer, and Windows NT can be installed in its own partition using NTFS or with other operating systems in a FAT partition. The boot loader (BOOT.INI) decides which operating system starts by default or allows the user to select an operating system at startup.

File Systems and Dual-Boot Configurations

You can install and run NT with the NTFS file system. However, Windows 95/98, Windows for Workgroups, and DOS use the FAT file system. If you want to share files between your NT operating system and any other operating system, you must format or retain at least one FAT partition in addition to the NT operating system. However, if you want to have security on your NT operating system, you must format or convert all partitions to NTFS.

Common Dual-Boot Configurations

Dual-boot configurations are common because most people like to keep their old operating system when upgrading to NT for legacy applications. If you want to dual-boot with your old operating system—for example, Windows for Workgroups—then you must install NT in its own directory. This is C:\WINNT by default. If you wanted to upgrade from Windows for Workgroups or Windows 95/98, then installing NT in the C:\Windows directory will upgrade the current operating system to NT.

Some of the common dual-boot configurations are DOS and NT Workstation, Windows for Workgroups and NT, and Windows 95/98 and NT.

There is not limit to the number of operating systems on your computer. The only limiting factor is your disk space.

NOTE

It is not a good idea to load NT and then load Windows 95, as Windows 95 has its own boot loader and can effectively disable a Windows NT boot loader.

Configuration of Applications in a Dual-Boot System

One of the problems with installing NT and Windows 95/98 as a dual-boot system is that each application must be installed for each operating system. If, for example, you have Microsoft Word installed in Windows 95, and set up your system to dual-boot with Windows NT, you must reinstall Microsoft Word while the Windows NT operating system is loaded to be able to run that application in NT and Windows 95.

NOTE

OS/2 has its own boot manager. When installing NT on the same machine as OS/2, the boot manager for OS/2 is disabled in favor of NT's boot manager. To enable the OS/2 boot manager, you can go to Disk Administrator and set active the OS/2 boot partition.

REMOVING WINDOWS NT WORKSTATION

If you need to remove NT, you must first consider what operating systems will be left on the computer:

- ▶ If NT 4 is the only operating system, then a replacement system should be installed before NT's removal.

- ▶ If another NT version will still be resident on the machine, you only need to delete several directories and modify the BOOT.INI file to reflect the removal of NT 4.

▶ If another installed system will be used as the primary operating system, then several directories and files must be removed. Also, the master boot record of the hard drive primary partition must be present to bypass the NTLDR, which starts the NT boot process.

Because Windows NT doesn't have a specific uninstall routine, you need to use a few tricks to remove it. Then you need to reinstall the previous operating system. Follow these three steps:

▶ Remove the NTFS volume if necessary.

▶ Change the bootstrap routing.

▶ Delete the Windows NT directories and files.

Removing Windows NT by Deleting the NTFS Partition

Removing an NTFS volume can indeed be difficult. Why? Because some versions of the MS-DOS FDISK program can't delete an NTFS volume, and none of the versions can remove an NTFS logical drive in an extended MS-DOS partition.

The easiest way to delete an NTFS partition is to follow these steps:

▶ Boot the three floppy disks that come with NT.

▶ When prompted to create or choose a partition, select the NTFS partition where the Windows NT files are located.

▶ Press D to delete the partition, then exit Setup.

NOTE

You can use Disk Administrator to delete NTFS partitions, but not the boot partition. That must be done with the FDISK DOS utility.

Removing Windows NT from a FAT Partition

To remove NT from a FAT partition, boot from a Windows 95/98 emergency boot disk or from a DOS disk and run the SYS.COM command by typing **sys c:**. This resets the hard disk master boot record and bypasses NTLDR.

Restart the computer, then delete the following files:

- ▶ PAGEFILE.SYS (the swap file that allows NT to use more memory than is physically installed in the system)

- ▶ BOOT.INI

- ▶ NT*.* (this removes NT startup files NTLDR, NTDETECT.COM, and NTBOOTDD.SYS)

- ▶ BOOTSECT.DOS

- ▶ %*systemroot*% directory (the installation directory, which is C:\WINNT by default)

- ▶ C:/PROGRAM FILES/WINDOWS NT (the directory that contains various utility files installed by NT 4)

INSTALLING, CONFIGURING, AND REMOVING HARDWARE COMPONENTS

The general procedure for installing a hardware device is described below:

1. Determine the hardware settings.

2. Verify the required hardware resources are unused on the workstation.

3. Configure and install the hardware using jumpers or software utilities.

4. Boot the NT Workstation computer and add the NT driver.

5. Reboot the system.

The general procedure for removing a hardware device is described below:

1. Uninstall the device driver.

2. Power down the computer.

3. Remove the device.

4. Restart the computer.

Remember to check the HCL and verify the latest drivers. Again, Windows NT doesn't support Plug and Play, so hardware designed for both NT and 95/98 operating systems may have separate configuration methods.

In the following sections, I describe some specific hardware components and how to work with them.

Network Adapter Drivers

Installing a network adapter is simple. Typically, the driver is included within Windows NT. If it's not, make sure you have a driver from the manufacturer. Remember that any changes to the Control Panel ≻ Network usually require access to the original NT installation source, so have your CD-ROM or network share to the NT distribution files accessible.

To install a network adapter:

1. Install the network interface card.

2. Boot NT Workstation, then open the Control Panel and click Network.

3. Select the Adapters tab, and click Add.

4. Select the driver listed or click Have Disk.

5. Click Close and reboot the system.

To remove a network adapter:

1. Open the Control Panel, click Network, and select the Adapter tab.

2. Highlight the adapter you want to remove.

3. Click Remove.

4. Shut down and remove the network interface card.

SCSI Devices

SCSI stands for Small Computer Systems Interface. These adapters are used to connect devices such as hard drives, CD-ROM players, and printers.

Installing a SCSI adapter properly can be the most difficult portion of a Windows NT installation. You can minimize potential glitches by following these guidelines:

▸ Use only SCSI controllers that are listed in the HCL and that are marked as NT-compatible.

▶ Search the Microsoft Windows NT Knowledge Base at `http://` `www.microsoft.com`. Search for the key "SCSI" to identify any compatibility issues associated with the particular SCSI controllers you're considering using with NT.

▶ Make sure the SCSI card is terminated properly. Boot the computer once with no devices installed to ensure that the driver loads correctly.

▶ If installing NT on an existing system that has a SCSI interface, use the NTHQ program to identify and resolve SCSI adapter issues before attempting to install NT.

▶ Disable the Plug-and-Play BIOS on your computer and manually assign interrupts to PCI slots.

▶ Enable the SCSI BIOS to boot the hard disk attached to SCSI ID 0, then install NT in the first primary partition of that disk.

Tape Device Drivers

Adding tape drives to Windows NT is fairly easy for most tape devices. Open the Control Panel, click Tape Devices, then click the Detect button. NT loads each tape driver it knows about and scans for the presence of a supported device, then automatically installs the driver. You can also add and remove device drivers by using the Add and Remove buttons located on the Drivers tab. You don't even need to restart NT to add or delete tape devices.

When installing IDE and SCSI tape devices, make sure to set the correct Master/Slave setting on your IDE devices and the correct SCSI number and terminators for your SCSI tape devices.

UPSs

Uninterruptible power supplies, or UPSs, provide power to your computer in the event of a conventional power loss. Advanced UPSs can communicate with your computer through a serial port using a standard RS-232 serial cable.

You should test the UPS unit after it has been configured. Upon startup of Intel-based computers, `ntdetect.com` sends test messages to all serial ports to determine whether or not a serial mouse is attached. Some UPS units misinterpret these test messages and respond by shutting down. If this happens, you can prevent your UPS unit from doing this by adding the /NoSerialMice switch to the entries in the operating system section of the BOOT.INI file.

UPS settings are controlled through the UPS program in the Control Panel, as shown in Figure 2.1.

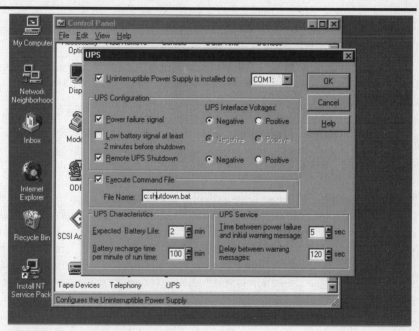

FIGURE 2.1:   UPS in the Control Panel

Multimedia Devices

Multimedia device drivers are added and configured from the Multimedia Control Panel applet. Multimedia devices include MIDI instruments and sound cards. The Control Panel also has a Devices applet, with which you can view information on all the multimedia devices and drivers installed on your system.

You can't configure sound cards during an unattended installation. You can do this only after a successful installation has taken place.

Display Drivers

The initial display driver is installed when Windows NT is installed—a display driver must be present for Windows NT to operate. You can change display drivers through the Display Type button on the Settings tab of the Display Control Panel applet. The Settings tab also lets you choose options for your display:

Color Palette   Lists color options for the display adapter.

Desktop Area   Configures the screen area used by the display.

Display Type   Allows installation of new drivers and displays options about the display device driver.

Font Size   Configures color and Desktop options.

Refresh Frequency   Sets the screen refresh rate for high-resolution drivers.

Test   Tests changes to screen choices.

Because NT must have a display driver to operate correctly, you should remove your old driver and install the new one prior to shutting down your computer and swapping display cards. You should also set your display resolution to VGA to ensure that you can see the screen when you reboot for the first time following the installation of a new display driver. Once proper operation is verified, adjust display settings as required.

If the display driver installed on NT Workstation is not compatible with your device, the workstation will go directly to Display setup when you boot the computer. Change your driver to the correct video driver and reboot.

Keyboard Drivers

You can change keyboard drivers through the General tab of the Keyboard applet in the Control Panel. The Keyboard Properties dialog box has three tabs:

Speed   Lets you control repeat character delay, character repeat rate, and cursor blink speed.

Input Locales   Specifies international keyboard layout.

General   Allows you to view or change the keyboard driver.

Mouse Drivers

You can change your mouse drivers to change the behavior of your mouse through the General tab of the Mouse Control Panel program. The Mouse Properties dialog box has four tabs:

Buttons   Lets you configure the mouse for right- or left-handed operation, as well as the speed of double-clicks.

Pointers   Provides a selection of pointer shapes.

Motion   Allows you to control pointer speed and specify whether you want the mouse pointer to snap to the default button in dialog boxes.

General   Lets you change or update the mouse driver.

USING THE CONTROL PANEL TO CONFIGURE AN NT WORKSTATION COMPUTER

In the previous section, I explained how to view and change many settings from the Control Panel. This section shows you how to change the environment of each individual user to match that user's preferences. You can change the following items through the Control Panel on a per-user basis:

▶ Display

▶ Keyboard

▶ Mouse

▶ Regional settings

▶ Sounds

Display

The Display Properties dialog box, shown in Figure 2.2, has five sections, represented by the tabs at the top.

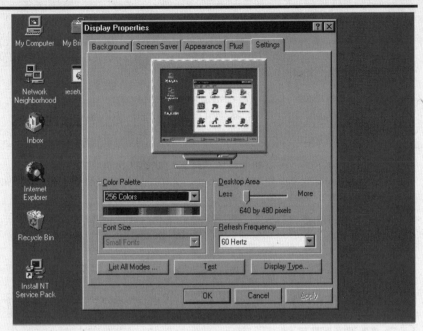

FIGURE 2.2: The Display Properties dialog box

Background   Allows you to set the pattern or image that will appear in the background of your computer screen.

Screen Saver   Allows you to select the particular screen saver you want to appear when your computer has been inactive for a period of time.

Appearances   Configures the colors and sizes of NT screen elements, such as border windows, icons, and the Desktop. You can also create and manipulate schemes. These contain predefined or user-defined settings for the screen elements.

Plus!   Allows you to choose the type of icons designating certain Desktop elements. It also lets you change certain characteristics of the NT Desktop, such as the size of icons, whether windows should appear as solid or as outline shapes when you move them, and whether icons should be shown in all possible colors or not.

Settings Lets you configure the hardware settings of the display, such as the resolution, the number of colors, and the refresh rate. This is also where you configure the device driver that NT uses to talk to your video card. These settings apply to every user.

Keyboard

The Keyboard Properties dialog box is where you configure the keyboard speed and layout. The Speed tab allows you to set the cursor repeat delay, rate, and blink rate. The Input Locales tab provides multiple key mappings so you can remap the keyboard for other languages or preferred key placements. The General tab is a system configuration tab. You'll most likely accept the default PC/AT Enhanced Keyboard settings, but if you have an unusual keyboard attached to your computer, this is where to configure it.

Mouse

The Mouse Properties dialog box is where you configure the buttons, pointers, and motion of the mouse. You can use the General tab to select the type of mouse attached to your computer.

Regional Settings

The Regional Settings dialog box lets you set the default language, time zone, number currency, and time representations from predefined lists or by creating your own specifications. You can also input locales for the current user.

Sounds

The Sounds Properties dialog box, shown in Figure 2.3, allows you to associate sounds with system events, such as a window opening or the system shutting down. You can associate individual sounds with individual events, or you can select or even create a sound scheme that associates sounds with events important to you.

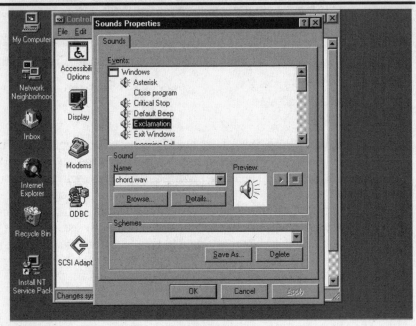

FIGURE 2.3: The Sounds Properties dialog box

UPGRADING TO NT WORKSTATION 4

After you've prepared your hardware for Windows NT by making sure you have met the minimum requirements, and after you have determined that the hardware you are using is in the HCL, it's time to decide whether you'll upgrade an existing Windows operating system to NT Workstation 4 or perform a fresh installation of the NT operating system.

If your computer already has Windows 3.x, Windows for Workgroups, or an earlier version of Windows NT, you might want to upgrade to NT Workstation 4. Windows 95 does not support a direct upgrade path, due primarily to Registry differences, but it can be adapted manually from a fresh installation. The difference between installing and upgrading is that when you upgrade, many of the old settings for the existing version of Windows are simply copied and used in the new NT Workstation 4 configuration.

If you are upgrading from an NT installation, you need to use the 32-bit installation version of the Setup program, WINNT32.EXE, as explained earlier.

You may wish to upgrade when the following situations exist:

▶ You want to transfer Desktop settings, such as the wallpaper or sound settings.

▶ You want to transfer password files.

▶ You don't need to boot to the other version of Windows.

You may wish to install when the following situations exist:

▶ You want to be able to boot to other versions of Windows and even DOS.

▶ You're installing to a large number of computers, and you want all of the computers to be the same.

The upgrade process doesn't transfer all settings from your current Windows operating system to your NT Workstation computer because some of the current settings don't apply to NT Workstation 4. The settings that are transferred also vary from one original operating system to another. For instance, almost all of the Windows NT 3.51 settings, including security and user accounts, are transferred when you upgrade. Since NT 3.51 contains most of this data in the Registry, it can be easily utilized by NT 4. Much less configuration information is transferred when you upgrade to NT 4 from Windows or Windows for Workgroups, since NT can't look for all configuration files created by applications.

Upgrading from Windows 95 requires the following steps:

1. Check to see that all Windows 95 hardware and software will run under NT.

2. Install NT 4 in a separate directory to create a dual-boot system.

3. Reinstall all application software.

4. Delete the Windows 95 directory C:\Windows.

CONFIGURING SERVER-BASED INSTALLATION FOR WIDE-SCALE DEPLOYMENT

You can install NT Workstation on a number of computers using a server-based installation. There are several ways to do this:

- ▶ Use Microsoft Systems Management Server (SMS). This method provides the most extensive control and speed.
- ▶ Modify logon scripts on user accounts so that the unattended setup runs when the user logs on to the computer.
- ▶ Create a .BAT file to run the unattended setup from the Desktop. The .BAT file can be sent as an embedded link in an e-mail.
- ▶ Administrators can initiate the unattended setup from the workstation.

Regardless of the implementation method, the server-based installation combines a network installation with an automated installation. It requires several steps:

1. Decide what parts of the operating system and application software will be installed on each computer.
2. If required, install the operating system on one computer and use the SYSDIFF utility to take a snapshot of the computer using the /SNAP switch.
3. If required, install the application software on the prototype computer and create a difference file with SYSDIFF using the /DIFF switch.
4. Copy the operating system and application software installation files to a network share.
5. Create the unattended installation text files for each different configuration type (UNATTEND.TXT).
6. Create a uniqueness database file (UDF) having an individual section for unique data required for each computer.
7. Run SYSDIFF/APPLY as part of the unattended setup to apply the difference file and install the software.
8. Connect the target computer to the network, access the network share, and start the automated setup.

Copying Installation Files

There are no special considerations for copying the installation files. You can simply copy the contents of the directory for your hardware platform to a shared directory on your network. For Intel-based machines, this is the i386 directory on the CD-ROM. All application software and any other items that are to be loaded as part of the automated installation must be placed in the OEM directory structure.

NOTE

The OEM directory structure is an important topic in large, complex automated installs. It is discussed in detail in the Windows NT Workstation Resource Kit.

Creating Unattended Installation Files

You should create an unattended installation file for each specific configuration type you need to install. You can either edit the UNATTEND.TXT file sample supplied on the NT Workstation CD-ROM or, if you have the Windows NT 4 Workstation Resource Kit, you can use the SETUPMGR tool to build your unattended installation file. Copy the unattended installation files to the same shared directory on your network.

Creating a UDF

A UDF allows you to create a file having sections that customize the installation of each individual computer. The UDF is used together with an unattended installation file to replace certain sections of the answer file with the information for the specific computer. You need to create a single UDF for all the computers on which you automate the installation of NT Workstation. Copy the UDF files to the same shared directory on your network.

Connecting to and Accessing the Network

If you have no other operating system on the computer, or you cannot access the network share from the existing operating system, you must create a network installation boot disk. A network installation boot disk is a bootable DOS disk you can use to start your system and connect to your network share (the location of the installation files). Since it's a

DOS system disk, you need to create it on a DOS system using the command FORMAT A: /S, or by using the SYS command on a disk that was formatted for DOS previously. Go to your Windows NT Server computer and double-click the Network Client Administrator Utility in the Network Administration program group. This loads the files you need onto your DOS system disk. The network driver you need is specific to your client (target) system. You may need to copy driver files for your network interface card.

TIP

Running SMARTDRV.EXE in the AUTOEXEC.BAT file on your network installation boot disk will greatly speed up the installation over the network.

Automating the Installation

Now that you have your network installation boot disk, you can edit the CONFIG.SYS and AUTOEXEC.BAT files to fully automate the installation. For example, assume that you've copied the installation files (from the \i386 directory) to a directory named SHARE on a computer named SERVER. You've created an unattended configuration file named CONFIG.TXT and a UDF for this specific computer named SYSTEM3.UDF. You want the disk to boot your target computer, connect to the SHARE directory on SERVER, and begin the automated installation. To do this, you can add the following commands to the AUTOEXEC.BAT file on your floppy:

```
NET USE Z:\\SERVER\SHARE
CD Z:
WINNT /U:CONFIG.TXT /UDF:id2,SYSTEM3.UDF /B
```

Let's examine these commands:

- ▶ NET USE instructs the computer to assign the logical drive letter Z to the SHARE (shared) directory on the SERVER computer. This form of notation is known as a Universal Naming Convention, or UNC, name.

- ▶ CD Z: instructs the computer to change to the Z drive, where you execute your next command.

- ▶ With the WINNT command, the /U switch specifies the unattended configuration filename.

▶ /UDF:id2,SYSTEM3.UDF specifies using the id2 data section from the system3.udf uniqueness database file for this computer.

▶ The /b switch suppresses the creation of the three NT installation disks.

What's Next?

Now that you have NT 4 installed and configured, you're ready to start working with it. One of the first things you may need to do is to organize your files and programs. The next chapter covers using the Start menu, Taskbar, and Windows Explorer to manage your Desktop, folders, and files.

Chapter 3

ORGANIZING PROGRAMS AND DOCUMENTS

An operating system is like your desk. Or more accurately, it's like your whole office. If your office is cluttered, you will find it harder to find things and to be as productive as you like. The same goes for your operating system.

Like other operating systems, NT Workstation not only offers its own filing system, it pretty much forces you to use it. However, just as you might be in the habit of keeping stacks of mail in a drawer of your office filing cabinet because you never seem to get around to buying those special hanging folders, you can misuse (or under-use) NT Workstation's file system and not capitalize on its strengths. Fortunately, NT Workstation has numerous tools, tricks, and enhanced usability features to keep you organized.

• •

Adapted from Mastering™ Windows® NT® Workstation 4 by Mark Minasi and Todd Phillips

ISBN 0-7821-2491-7   1152 pages $49.99

Under Windows 3.*x*, you had only two choices for organizing the contents of your hard drive: File Manager and Program Manager. Program Manager merely enabled you to arrange shortcuts to your programs. You could store files there as well, but almost nobody ever did. File Manager, on the other hand, enabled you to create and delete directories, to organize your files by means of those directories, and to launch or open programs and files by double-clicking them. NT Workstation 4, using the Windows 95 GUI, has taken the best features of Program Manager and File Manager and has modified them to integrate them with the Desktop. In this chapter, you'll see the usefulness of this approach as exemplified by the Start menu, which you can think of as an always-available list of shortcuts, and by Windows NT Explorer.

USING THE START MENU

Clicking the Start button brings up the Start menu, which, as its name implies, is the place to go first. From the Start menu, you can find anything you need or want on your system—and that includes anything on any machines that you have been given rights to, through a shared or network arrangement. The Start menu is highly customizable insofar as *you* can decide what to list on it. You can easily modify it to present shortcuts to any program, file, or resource (such as a printer or an external tape drive). By default, it already offers a fast way to access the Help system, a command for opening the Control Panel (to change your computer's settings), commands for launching tools such as Find and Explorer (to find, analyze, or launch any file on your system), and the command for shutting down the system. The Start menu appears below.

TIP

The Start menu can be accessed no matter what application you're using, so you'll always have instant access to the "controls" for your computer. If you have a Windows 95/98/NT keyboard, you can quickly access the Start menu by pressing the special Windows key; otherwise, you can press Ctrl+Esc.

Adding Your Favorite Programs to the Start Menu

If you copy any file, program, or system object (such as a printers or hard drive object) to the Start menu, NT Workstation automatically creates a shortcut to that item—and because it's on the Start menu, you can access that shortcut anytime, no matter what other programs you are running.

To create a shortcut on the Start menu, drag the file you want onto the Start button. The next time you click the Start button, the shortcut to that file will appear at the top of the Start menu.

NOTE

If a shortcut is damaged or accidentally deleted, it won't affect the file that it points to.

Arranging Open Windows with the Taskbar

Like most objects you can click in the NT Workstation environment, the Start menu and Taskbar offer right-click menus that enable you to set options for controlling their behavior and appearance. (The general topic of right-click menus is presented in depth in Chapter 4, "Setting Object Properties." In this chapter, you get to see some of the most immediate advantages of using them.)

You can quickly change the size and position of all open applications on the Desktop by making choices from the Taskbar's right-click menu. Simply right-click anywhere on the Taskbar to bring up a menu with the following choices:

Cascade Windows   Places each of your open applications across your Desktop, one almost on top of another. Your windows look somewhat like a deck of cards spread across a dealer's table.

Tile Windows Horizontally and **Tile Windows Vertically**
Arranges your current applications in equal-sized windows so
that you can see some contents of every window at once.

Minimize All Windows   Minimizes all your open applications
to the Taskbar. This is probably the fastest way to clear the
Desktop when it is cluttered.

TIP

When you click a program that has been minimized (shows up as a button on
the Taskbar), it returns to its former size and position on the Desktop.

Undo Tile and **Undo Minimize All**   Undoes whatever Taskbar
action you last performed. The first time you access the
Taskbar properties, these commands do not appear.

Properties   Brings up the Taskbar properties sheet, a tabbed
dialog box with various pages of options that not only let you
arrange items on the Start menu and the Taskbar, but also permit you to specify the opening and closing behaviors of those
items.

Customizing the Start Menu and Taskbar with the Taskbar's Properties Sheet

Right-clicking the Taskbar and choosing Properties from the menu that
pops up displays the Taskbar's *properties sheet*, shown in the following
illustration. This sheet (a dialog box, really) contains two tabs: Taskbar
Options and Start Menu Programs. The latter one might better have been
entitled Programs on the Start Menu, to reduce the confusion you might
have when you first see it ("Hmm, so is this where I go to start all my
menu programs? I thought that was what the Start menu was designed
for!"). But now that we've made a point about it, you'll never be confused
again. Let's take the tabs one at a time.

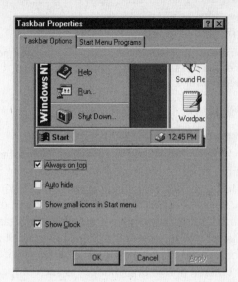

The Taskbar Options Tab

The Taskbar Options tab of the Taskbar's properties sheet lets you set a few basic options for the Taskbar and the Start menu, as follows:

Always on Top   Keeps the Taskbar visible at all times. This is the default setting. (Screen saver programs ignore this setting, however, because they blank the entire screen.)

Auto Hide   Makes the Taskbar disappear until such time as you move your mouse pointer to where the Taskbar is hidden. AutoHiding the Taskbar is useful if you have limited screen space or if you just don't like the look of the Taskbar.

Show Small Icons in Start Menu   Shrinks the size of the icons on the Start menu and removes the Windows NT Workstation label that appears along the left side of the Start menu. If you have limited screen space or just want to reduce the size of the Start menu, use this option.

Show Clock   Removes the clock that by default is displayed at the far end of the Taskbar. NT Workstation 4 also has another Clock program in the Accessories group on the Start menu if it was installed during Setup.

TIP

Remember, you don't have to set any options to reposition the Taskbar. At any time, you can simply click the Taskbar and drag it to whichever edge of the screen you like.

The Start Menu Programs Tab

The second tab on the Taskbar properties sheet, Start Menu Programs, affords more advanced options for configuring the Start menu. Although we wouldn't suggest using it to *add* programs to your Start menu (it is no match for the ease of the drag-and-drop approach outlined at the beginning of the chapter), the options offered by the Start Menu Programs tab are the fastest way to *remove* programs from the Start menu. Moreover, this tab offers more control over the appearance of the items listed on your Start menu, permitting changes to such properties as the following:

▶ The icon that appears next to an item on the Start menu

▶ The order of the items on the Start menu

▶ The size of an item's window after it is opened

▶ Other options, depending on your system configuration

OF WIZARDS AND MINI-EXPLORERS

The route you'll follow to change settings in NT Workstation will often take you to one or more of the following types of assistant programs:

▶ A wizard, which is a series of dialog boxes and folders programmed specifically to prompt you for additional information relating to the option you initially chose

▶ A mini-Explorer (or sometimes Explorer itself), which knows from the context of what you're doing to open folders and menus from which you can make appropriate selections

You'll see a couple of minor examples of these assistants in the following discussions. If you haven't yet mastered Explorer, don't worry; you'll just get a taste of what it can do in these next few paragraphs. The more extensive presentation of how you can make full use of Explorer takes up most of the remainder of the chapter.

Removing Programs from the Start Menu

Follow the directions below to remove programs from the Start menu.

1. Right-click the Taskbar and choose Properties.

2. Click the Start Menu Programs tab.

3. Click the Remove button. A mini-Explorer opens, showing the items on the Start menu arranged hierarchically like files in a folder, because that is essentially what they are.

4. From the mini-Explorer window, click the item you want to remove. If you had to go to a fly-out menu (such as Programs) when you used the Start menu to access the item, the item will be in a subfolder in the mini-Explorer window now.

5. Click the Remove button.

6. A dialog box asks if you are sure you want to delete the program. (Are you? Click OK if you are sure.)

7. Click the Close button to finish the process.

The Advanced Button and Explorer

You might recall that in previous versions of Windows the File Manager offered a View menu that, among other things, let you rearrange the order of the files it was listing for you. The approach to rearranging the items on the Start menu is similar in NT Workstation 4: If you go to Explorer, you can use *its* View menu to rearrange the items in the Start Menu folder (or any of its subfolders).

You can go to Explorer any way you like, but if you don't remember where your Start Menu folder lies in the hierarchy of your hard drive, you may have to hunt for it. (In fact, your computer may have a confusing multitude of Start Menu folders. Remember that because NT Workstation is a multi-user environment, you may elect to have different Start menus for the different types of work you do. Also, all other users who log on to your system have their own profile, and that profile includes their individual folder of Start menu items.) NT Workstation can help you make short work of this confusion by taking you directly to your own current Start Menu folder.

When you click the Advanced button on the Start Menu Programs tab, you are led to an Explorer window that automatically opens with your Start Menu folder open, the Start menu's items listed, and the commands and buttons for rearranging, renaming, and copying those items right at hand. While you're there, you can continue to use Explorer to do just about anything else you might normally want to do with Explorer, just as you would if you had run Explorer by itself. Unlike the mini-Explorer, which usually displays an incomplete set of Explorer features, you don't have to go straight back to the tab that gave rise to it.

Using Explorer

Program Manager and File Manager from Windows 3.1 have been combined into a new animal called Explorer. Explorer could almost *be* your Desktop, really, because anything you might want to do to a file or program, and any configuration changes you want to make to your operating environment, can be done right from Explorer.

Opening vs. Exploring

One thing you'll notice right away when you use Explorer is a difference between *opening* a Desktop object and *exploring* a Desktop object. Figure 3.1 shows the difference. Opening simply opens a window that shows only the contents of the object or the folder.

When you open the program called My Computer, for example, you'll see its contents, but nothing else: no toolbar or double panes. However, if you explore the same program (that is, if you right-click the My Computer icon, either on the Desktop or in a file list where it appears) and choose Explore from the menu that pops up, the window that opens proudly displays a toolbar full of useful buttons and a right pane for displaying the contents of whatever you select in the left pane. These are the telltale features of Explorer. If you already know where you want to go—that is, the location of the file or object you want to access—Open is the way to get there. But, as the name suggests, Explorer is best when you want to, er, explore what file or application you want to use.

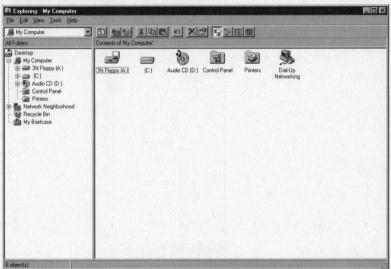

FIGURE 3.1: Opening My Computer produces a single window (top); Exploring My Computer opens the entire Explorer window (bottom) for the same set of objects.

Branches

The best way to look at Explorer is as a file system with many levels or branches. The top level lets you look at the fundamental pieces of your system, which includes all the storage devices connected to your computer. The simplest way to access this top level of Explorer is to right-click the My Computer icon on your Desktop and choose Explore from the menu that pops up. In Explorer, you'll notice two panes: on the left, a hierarchical listing of the contents of your computer; on the right, a group of icons representing the components installed in the item that is selected in the left pane. The following illustration shows Explorer's left pane, used to view folder branches.

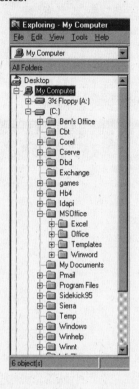

When you first open Explorer this way there is no highlight to show you what's selected in the left pane. This changes as soon as you click something in the left pane to change the view in the right pane. (There's a line at the top of the right pane that displays the name of the selected folder, but it's not always intuitive to use that.)

TIP

You can consider each of the items that appear in Explorer as separate objects. Each has its own properties, many of which you can easily change to fit the particular environment or configuration you are working in. This applies to files, folders, programs, networked computers, or anything else that makes up your computing environment. Although you can look at Explorer as a means of finding, accessing, and organizing the contents of My Computer, it is perhaps more correct to view it as the glue that holds the disparate elements of the operating system together.

Views

There are a lot of ways to arrange how the objects appear in Explorer, all of which are called *views*. The View menu not only controls how the objects in the right Explorer pane appear, but also how Explorer itself can be configured to work best for you.

The view that you choose affects only the right Explorer pane. The left pane always looks the same—an expandable list of the folders and files on your computer.

There are four views you can choose from to display icons in Explorer and five ways to arrange the icons after you've chosen your view. The Large Icon view (Figure 3.2) is probably the one you're most familiar with. In this view, the icons are large and easily recognizable. Depending on how many files you have in a particular folder, the icons can take up most if not all the space in the right Explorer pane.

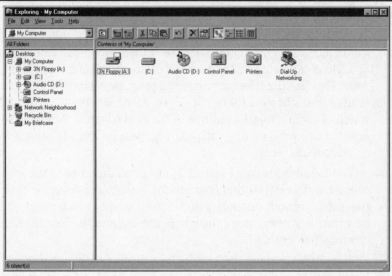

FIGURE 3.2:   This is the Large Icon view, which is Explorer's default view.

The Small Icon view (see Figure 3.3) shrinks the size of the icons on the right Explorer pane. This makes it significantly easier to see all of the files in a folder, particularly if there are a lot of them, as in the Windows folder.

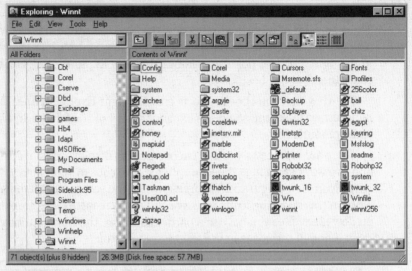

FIGURE 3.3: This is the Small Icon view.

The List view (see Figure 3.4) takes those same small icons of the Small Icon view and lists them up and down instead of across the Explorer pane. This has the effect of putting all your folders into the leftmost column of the right pane (of course, if you have more than one column's worth of folders, they'll continue in the next column). After you've selected this view, sorting and ordering the files/icons to meet your search criteria is easy.

The Details view (see Figure 3.5) moves all the icons to the leftmost column and uses the other columns for file/object information related to the icons. This information includes the file type (which is determined by how the file is associated), the size of the file, and the date the file was last modified or saved.

Sometimes, you may be looking for a file and, although you may not know the name of it, you know what *type* of file it is. On other occasions, you may remember only that you created the file on October 11 or 12, but you have no idea what its name is. Sorting can help you find files when you can barely remember where to look. With Explorer, you can arrange the items in the right pane so that they are sorted or organized by name, size, date, or file type. This makes it easier for you to better comprehend in a single glance what is and isn't inside the folder.

FIGURE 3.4: This is the List view.

FIGURE 3.5: This is the Details view.

To rearrange the order of your files in Explorer's right pane, go to the View menu and click Arrange Icons. When you click there, one of those great little fly-out menus does just that (flies out, that is) and presents you with sorting options. Name and Date are self-explanatory; Type refers to the three-character extension at the end of the filename (for example, this book was written as a .doc file); and Size refers to the size of the file in bytes, kilobytes, or megabytes as appropriate.

Toolbar

One of the great inventions of the modern computing world, toolbars take all the most commonly used tasks from a specific application and put them in easy reach. This has been true for most Windows applications for quite a while, but it is relatively new to the process of file management. Sure, there was a toolbar in File Manager, but that was a little on the anemic side. Finally, Explorer gives you the toolbar you've always wanted—see Figure 3.6.

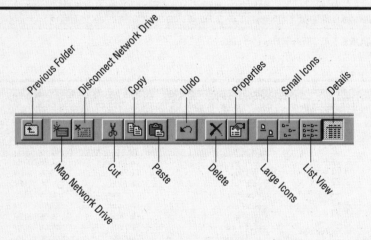

FIGURE 3.6:   The Explorer Toolbar brings common commands to your fingertips.

From left to right, here's what each of the toolbar buttons do for you:

Previous Folder   Takes you to the folder above the one you are in. If you are in a folder located at the root of your hard drive, clicking this button takes you up to the next level, which is My Computer. Up one level from there it takes you to the Desktop. From there, you can't go any further.

Map Network Drive   Creates a network connection to a shared folder on a server and assigns it a drive letter. This works pretty much the same as the Connect Network Drive button on the File Manager toolbar.

Disconnect Network Drive   Disconnects you from the network drive you specify (the opposite of the preceding button).

Cut   Cuts or deletes a selected file or folder from your hard drive. This works just like it does in any other Windows application (which is true of the following Copy, Paste, Undo, and Delete buttons as well). You can also use Ctrl+X on the keyboard or choose Cut from the Edit menu.

Copy   Copies a selected file or folder from your hard drive. You can also use Ctrl+C on the keyboard or choose Copy from the Edit menu.

Paste   Adds a selected file or folder from your hard drive. You can also use Ctrl+V on the keyboard or choose Paste from the Edit menu.

Undo   Reverses the last activity you performed. You can also use Ctrl+Z on the keyboard or choose Undo from the Edit menu.

Delete   Moves any files or folders you've selected to the Recycle Bin. It's almost the same as the Cut button, except after you've deleted a file, you can't paste it somewhere else.

Properties   Opens the properties sheet for the item you've selected. You can also use Ctrl+Enter on the keyboard or choose Properties from the File menu. If you have a Windows 95/98 keyboard, you can also use the Context Menu key, which depicts an arrow pointing to a small menu. Pressing this key gives you the equivalent of clicking the right mouse button.

Large Icons, Small Icons, List View, and **Details**   Set the different views for Explorer's right pane. These buttons were described earlier in this chapter (in the "Views" section).

USING EXPLORER'S MAIN MENUS AND RIGHT-CLICK MENUS

With Explorer, you get a lot more menu for your money. This section briefly describes all the main menu options and then provides an overview of the right-click menu options in Explorer.

File

The File menu contains commands for opening files and creating and administering folders. You can also access properties sheets from the File menu.

Open   (Only present when you have a file selected.) Opens your selected file using its associated application. If the file you have selected does not have an associated application, the command changes to Open With and prompts you for the application to open the file.

NOTE

Not all files can be opened. Many of the files you see in Explorer are system files that are used by the operating system or by applications. As a rule, files that can be opened have the extension .exe or are represented by easily recognizable icons.

New   Creates a new folder or shortcut in your current directory. The new item is given the default name New Folder or New Shortcut.

Send To   (Only present when you have a file selected.) Sends your selected file to any of the locations you have placed in your Send To folder. Default choices are Floppy Disk, Printer, Mail Recipient, and My Briefcase.

Create Shortcut   (Only present when you have a file selected.) Creates a shortcut to the selected file in the current folder.

Delete   (Only present when you have a file selected.) Sends selected files and folders to the Recycle Bin.

Rename   (Only present when you have a file selected.) Highlights the name of the selected file or folder. Type your new name for the file or folder and press Enter to accept it.

WARNING

Do not rename program or system files. For example, leave `excel.exe` and `system32.dll` alone. As a rule, only rename files and folders that you have created.

Properties   (Only present when you have a file selected.) Displays the properties sheet for the file or folder. For more information on properties, please see Chapter 4.

Close   Closes the active Explorer window.

Edit

The Edit menu contains all the commands you would expect to find in the Edit menu of a Windows application. These include:

Undo   Reverses or undoes the last action you completed. Even if you send a file to the Recycle Bin, Undo restores it to the folder you deleted it from.

Cut   Removes files and folders from their current location. You can paste them into a new folder or use Cut as a means of deleting them.

Copy   Copies selected files and folders so you can paste them elsewhere.

Paste   Pastes or inserts files and folders you have cut and copied from other folders into the currently open folder.

NOTE

Cut, Copy, and Paste work just like they do in a word processor or spreadsheet.

Paste Shortcut   Takes a file you've copied and pastes a shortcut to the file (or folder) in the active folder.

Select All   Selects (highlights) the contents of a folder or drive.

Invert Select   Reverses the number of items selected in a folder. If you have two items selected, Invert Select will select all but the two files you originally selected.

Tools

The Tools menu offers commands for finding files and mapping and disconnecting network drives. The menu also has a Go To command that enables you to make a quick jump to any other folder. The Tools menu commands are:

Find   Enables you to locate files or a computer on your network.

TIP

As with any Find command, the Tools menu's Find command lets you find files not just on your computer, but on any computer connected to your network.

Map Network Drive   Assigns a drive letter to a network drive. If you check the Reconnect at Logon box, any drive you have mapped is automatically assigned the same drive letter each time you restart NT Workstation. You can use any letter from *A* to *Z* that hasn't already been assigned to a local or network drive.

Disconnect Network Drive   Removes a drive letter assignment from a network drive that you have previously mapped.

Go To   Automatically takes you to the drive or folder you indicate. In the text field, enter the path of the drive and/or folder you want to go to and click OK or press Enter. (For example, type **C:\winnt** and press Enter). As a bonus, Go To keeps a list of folders you have gone to previously. To access one of those destinations again, click the drop-down list and choose the path. You can also access Go To by using Ctrl+G when you are in Explorer.

TIP

The Go To command looks just like the Start menu's Run command. If you scroll through its drop-down list, you will even see the history of programs that you have previously entered into the Run command line. However, you won't be able to access them, because Go To is for folder names only.

Help

As you might expect from the name, the Help menu opens Explorer's Help file. This menu also provides access to overall Windows NT Help, too.

TIP

You can press F1 from any Explorer window or the NT Workstation Desktop to open Windows NT Help.

Right-Click Menus

Thanks to NT Workstation's context-sensitive right-click menus, you probably don't need to use the main Explorer menus too often. In fact, the context-sensitive menus give you more options then the main menus do. By context-sensitive, we mean that the commands available on the right-click menu change depending on such factors as your current folder's location, the current file or folder type, user privileges, and the existence of other programs installed on your computer.

Here are some of the most common commands that appear on right-click menus:

- New (for example, to create a new file or folder)
- Cut, Copy, and Paste
- Map Network Drive
- Send To
- Rename
- Delete
- Create Shortcut
- Properties

Of these commands, most are equivalent to what you would find on the application's File or Edit menu. The Properties choice, which usually appears at the bottom of a right-click menu, generally takes you to the object's properties sheet, a topic we discuss in more detail in Chapter 4.

Part i

ORGANIZING YOUR FILES AND FOLDERS

Managing your files in NT Explorer is easy and logical. After you learn a few commands, you can use these commands over and over for a variety of tasks. After a short time using Explorer, you'll wonder how you ever did it any other way.

Creating New Folders

To create a new folder, do the following:

1. Choose where you want to create a new folder. You can create a folder on the Desktop, at the root of a hard drive or floppy drive, or inside another folder.

2. If you are in Explorer, choose New Folder from the File menu, or, from the right-click menu, choose New and then Folder. Similarly, If you are creating a folder on the Desktop, choose New and then Folder from the right-click menu.

3. The folder is created with the default name New Folder. By default, the name is be highlighted. If you want to give a new name to the folder you've just created, type it now. You can always rename a folder by choosing Rename from the File menu or the right-click menu and typing in a new name. (Refer to the more detailed renaming instructions in the "Renaming Documents and Folders" section later in this chapter.)

Moving Items

Files and folders can be moved anywhere on your computer or over the network you are attached to. To move a file or folder, do the following.

1. Select the file or folder you are going to move. If you want to select more than one object, use the mouse to highlight all the objects you want to move or copy. (Ctrl+click different objects in the same pane to select multiple objects one at a time, or simply Shift+click the first and last objects if they all appear in one uninterrupted series.)

2. To perform the actual move, you can follow two methods. One is to choose Cut and then Paste from the Edit menu (the keyboard equivalents are Ctrl+X and then Ctrl+V). The other is to drag the items from one place to another. There are various drag destinations:

    ▶ Drag from the right Explorer pane to the left.

    ▶ Drag from either Explorer pane to another Explorer or Explorer-type window.

    ▶ Drag from either Explorer pane to the Start button. (Actually, this doesn't *move* the item; instead, it creates a shortcut on the Start menu.)

    ▶ Drag from either Explorer pane to the Desktop. (Optionally, if you hold down the right mouse button while you drag, you're given an option to create a shortcut or shortcuts on the Desktop for the object or objects you are dragging.)

    ▶ Drag from the Desktop to an Explorer folder.

TIP

If you drag a folder from the right Explorer pane to the left on a *different* drive, NT Workstation defaults to *copying* the file instead of *moving* it. (As long as you are dragging the object to the *same* drive, NT moves the file or folder by default.) If you don't want NT to copy the file that you want to move, hold down the Shift key while you drag the object to another drive. That way it will be moved, not copied.

Copying Items

Files and folders can also be copied anywhere on your computer or the network you are attached to. To copy a file or folder, do the following.

1. Select the file or folder you are going to copy. If you want to select more than one object, use the mouse to highlight all the objects you want to copy. As with the instructions above for moving objects, you can Ctrl+click to select multiple objects one at a time or Shift+click the first and last objects if they're all in one uninterrupted series.

2. To perform the actual copy, you can follow two methods. One is to choose Copy and then Paste from the Edit menu (the keyboard equivalents are Ctrl+C and then Ctrl+V). The other is to drag the items from one place to another, as described earlier in the move instructions, with one difference: To ensure that the objects you are dragging are copied and not moved, you should hold down the Ctrl key while you are dragging.

TIP

If you drag a folder from the right Explorer pane to the left on the *same* drive, NT Workstation defaults to *moving* the file instead of *copying* it. (As long as you are dragging the object to a *different* drive, NT copies the file or folder by default.) If you don't want NT to move the file that you want to copy, hold down the Ctrl key while you drag the object to another drive. It will be copied, not moved.

Saving Files and Folders to the Desktop

NT Workstation enables you to keep files on your Desktop for quick and easy access. To store files and folders on the Desktop, do one of the following:

▶ Drag a file from Explorer to the Desktop.

▶ If you are saving the file from within an application, scroll to Desktop (it's at the very top of your local drive hierarchy) in the application's Save As dialog box and then save your file.

Dragging with the Right Mouse Button

When you drag files with the right mouse button and then release the button, a menu pops up offering a special set of options to help you decide how to move the file or folder. Use the following steps to move a file or folder:

1. Select the file or folder you want to move to the Desktop.

2. Click with the right mouse button and drag the object to the Desktop.

3. When you drag the object to the Desktop and release the right mouse button, a menu appears giving you these options:

Move Here   Moves the file to the new location.

Copy Here   Copies the file to the new location.

Create Shortcut(s) Here   Creates a shortcut to the file at the new location. As we've discussed, a shortcut is a pointer to the real file or folder, and can be stored anywhere on your computer. You can double-click a shortcut wherever you find it, and it will run or open the object regardless of where it is located. (Shortcuts are what make the Start menu so customizable.)

Cancel   Cancels the operation.

TIP

If you are new to NT or are confused about when to use Ctrl+Shift when moving or copying files, the safest way is to drag the file with the right mouse button. This way, you are always presented with a choice of whether to move or copy the file.

Renaming Documents and Folders

NT Workstation enables you to quickly and easily rename files and folders. Because NT Workstation keeps track of file associations for you, you don't have to worry about including the three-character file extensions that you did in Windows 3.x. To rename a file or folder, do the following:

1. Select the file or folder you want to rename.

2. Choose Rename from the File menu or Rename from the right-click menu.

3. When only the name of the file (the text associated with the icon) becomes highlighted, do one of the following:

   ▶ If you want to simply replace the entire name, then while the whole name is still highlighted, start typing the new name; the old name disappears the moment you start typing.

▶ If you want to make just a correction or two to the existing name, then while the whole name is still highlighted, use your cursor-movement keys (the arrow keys) on your keyboard to move to specific characters within the existing name. The highlight disappears the moment you start moving within the name, enabling you to insert or delete specific characters without deleting the entire name.

4. Press Enter to accept the new name, or Esc if you made a mistake.

TIP

You can also rename files and folders by single-clicking twice (but not so fast that NT interprets it as a double-click) on the name of the object so that it is highlighted, and then type the new name as described in step 3 above. Again, press Enter when you are finished (or Esc if you made a mistake).

Deleting Files and Folders

If you decide you don't want a file or a folder anymore, you can easily delete it. By default, when you delete a file in NT, the file is not actually deleted: instead, it is compressed and sent to a folder called the Recycle Bin. When a file has been moved to the Recycle Bin, it hasn't been removed from your hard drive, only placed on inactive duty, so to speak. (You can periodically delete items within the Recycle Bin to *actually* remove them entirely from existence, or even empty the entire Recycle Bin to delete everything in it.)

The Recycle Bin is a good intermediate place to keep files you're pretty sure you want to delete, because if you change your mind after "deleting" them to the Recycle Bin, you can always open the Recycle Bin and use its Restore option to resurrect the object. Mutter your apologies for treating the item so shabbily, and it's ready for use once more.

TIP

If you're the kind of person who hates being pestered by second thoughts, and you would prefer to avoid the nice little safeguard of the Recycle Bin, you can *really* delete an item by selecting it and pressing Shift+Delete.

Sending Items to the Recycle Bin

There are several ways to send a file to the Recycle Bin:

▶ Press the Delete key on your keyboard.

▶ Choose Delete from the File menu.

▶ Choose Delete from a right-click menu.

▶ Drag-and-drop the item on the Recycle Bin icon.

Emptying the Recycle Bin

After a file has been sent to the Recycle Bin, it can be kept there indefinitely until such time as you decide to delete it from the Recycle Bin. After a file has been deleted from the Recycle Bin, the file is removed from your hard drive and is gone forever. To empty the Recycle Bin, do one of the following:

▶ Right-click the Recycle Bin icon on your Desktop and choose Empty Recycle Bin.

▶ Open the Recycle Bin in Explorer (it can be opened and otherwise treated like any other folder, except that the Recycle Bin itself cannot be deleted) and choose Empty Recycle Bin from the File menu.

WARNING

When a file is deleted in NT Workstation, it is really deleted. Other operating systems, such as MS-DOS or Windows 95/98, delete only the first byte from a file and mark the space as available. NT is much more thorough because of its secure nature. When you delete a file in NT, all the bytes in the file are set to a zero value. This is like formatting the space where the file was so it can be reclaimed.

Restoring Items from the Recycle Bin

To restore items from the Recycle Bin, you can do one of three things:

▶ Open the Recycle Bin and drag the file you want to restore to the folder of your choice.

▶ Open the Recycle Bin, select the file you want to restore, and choose Restore from the File menu or the right-click menu.

► Right-click the location you deleted the file from and select Undo delete from the context menu.

NOTE

NT Workstation goes further to protect your data when using the Recycle Bin. There is a Recycle Bin folder on every hard drive that contains the files or folders that have been deleted from that drive. If the drive has been formatted with NTFS, a folder called the Recycler contains a Recycle Bin for every user of the computer, named by the user's Security Identifier (SID).

UNDERSTANDING NT AS A MULTI-USER ENVIRONMENT

From the ground up, NT Workstation is designed as a multi-user networking environment. Because security is so integral to the way that NT operates, it is possible for two or more users to use the same workstation without stepping on each other's feet. User 1 can log in and do the work he or she wants to do without necessarily knowing who else has access to the computer and without having access to another user's files.

NOTE

For multi-user access to work the way it should, the system administrator needs to set up the appropriate accounts in the User Manager utility.

User Profile Folders

When a user logs on to an NT Workstation computer, the operating system assigns that user a security token. Security tokens are managed by the NT Security Manager portion of the NT Executive. Each time that user attempts to do something in NT—such as opening a file, sending e-mail, or changing the way the Desktop looks—the Security Manager checks that person's token to see if the user has the rights and permissions to perform the requested task.

As a result of the token-based security system, NT Workstation administers multi-user environments logically. In the WINNT folder (or wherever you installed NT Workstation), there is a folder called Profiles.

Inside the Profiles folder is a folder for each user that logs in to a workstation (see Figure 3.7), and inside each user's folder is a set of folders that customize the NT environment for that user.

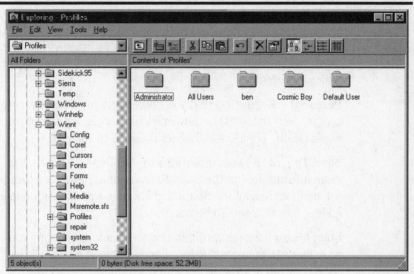

FIGURE 3.7: Inside the Profiles folder is a separate folder for each user that logs on to a specific NT workstation.

The folders within your user folder are:

Application Data   Contains information about how you configure your applications. This folder contains settings describing whether you run programs in full windows, what recent documents you have used, and other pertinent information. This relieves other users from having to see your preferences when they use your machine. For example, many programs list the files you have most recently opened at the bottom of their File menu. With NT's multi-user system, the recently opened files for one user do not appear when another user runs the same application.

Desktop   Contains any files that you store on the Desktop. This does not include My Computer, Network Neighborhood, or the Recycle Bin.

Favorites   Stores your favorite programs, files, and Web sites. From the outside, Favorites looks like just another folder. You can add files to it and delete files from it as you would with any other folder. The difference is that "Designed for Windows 95/98" programs often have an option on their File ➤ Open dialog boxes to open files directly from the Favorites folder. Additionally, these same dialog boxes have options to *add* files and folders to the Favorites folder so you don't have to navigate to the Favorites folder manually. Microsoft's Internet Explorer also automatically stores Web page bookmarks in the Favorites folder by default.

Personal   Keeps files that you don't want any other users to access, even though the users may share other aspects of your workstation. The Personal folder is empty by default.

Send To   Stores customizations to your Send To menu. For more information on the Send To command, please see Chapter 4. The Favorites folder mentioned above is a good candidate for adding to your Send To menu.

Start Menu   Stores configurations and customizations you have made to your Start menu. For example, it shows all the shortcuts you have added to your Start menu.

The Windows NT Folder

Your Windows NT folder (or WINNT folder, if you use the default name when installing it) contains several subfolders that perform specific functions for the operating system. By learning how these folders are structured, you'll not only understand how NT Workstation works, but also how to make it work for you.

The Windows NT folder is divided into the following folders:

Config   Contains the NT Registry. Every file in this folder is vital to NT's continued health and well-being. This provides information on all the hardware devices connected to your machine, directly or indirectly (that is, via a network).

Cursors   Stores NT's animated mouse cursors. This folder may be empty if you did not choose to install all the cursors during NT Workstation Setup.

Fonts Contains all your installed fonts.

Forms Stores forms if you are using forms with Microsoft Exchange. By default, only basic form templates are stored here.

Help Contains all NT's Help files. In addition to being called from individual applications or from Explorer, Help files can be launched by double-clicking them, as though they were any other program. Help files for nonoperating system programs (such as Microsoft Word and Excel) are not stored here.

Media Stores system sound files. When you assign system sounds to different operating system events (for instance, NT Workstation startup or new mail), you call files from this folder. You can store any .wav file in this folder and make it available to NT.

Profiles Holds a hierarchy of personal folders for each user who uses your system. These are the folders we discussed in the preceding section, "User Profile Folders."

Repair Contains backup copies of some essential system files, so that you can restore them in the case of a system crash. The file called setup.txt offers a map of where all of NT Workstation's essential system files were installed during installation. Use this file as a guide if you need to make NT repairs.

TIP

The files in the Repair folder have been compressed. You can determine this by the underscore character after the period in the filename. If you ever need to decompress the files, go to a command prompt and type **expand system._ system**. This should never be necessary, however, because the NT Repair process automatically restores these files to their correct location. You can get more information about the expand command in Online Help or by typing **expand /?** at the command prompt.

System Stores 16-bit system files if you installed NT Workstation over Windows 3.1. It also provides some backward compatibility for 16-bit Windows applications that really want to see a System folder.

System32   Contains most of the files and program code that make NT operate. This is the most important folder in NT Workstation. In addition to essential system files, System32 contains many of NT's applets and utilities. As a rule, you should not manually move or change files in this folder except as instructed by your Management Information Service (MIS) department or a technical support representative.

WHAT'S NEXT?

In this chapter, you learned about the Start menu, Explorer, and the multi-user environment of NT Workstation. We briefly mentioned properties, with a promise that they would be covered in Chapter 4. Coming up next, you'll learn the details of accessing and using properties sheets.

Chapter 4

SETTING OBJECT PROPERTIES

n this chapter, we discuss properties sheets in more detail. Also, because one of the easiest ways of revealing an object's properties is via a right-click of your mouse, we present a comprehensive summary of the other things you can do with a right-click to get your work done faster. You've already had the opportunity to use these features in Chapter 3. This time around, though, we get into the essentials. Let's start with a brief recap of right-clicking.

Adapted from Mastering™ Windows® NT® Workstation 4 by Mark Minasi and Todd Phillips

ISBN 0-7821-2491-7   1152 pages $49.99

RIGHT-CLICKING AROUND WINDOWS

Right-clicking objects throughout the NT interface brings up a shortcut menu with options pertaining to the objects at hand. The same options are typically available from the main menus but are more conveniently reached with the right-click.

The "rightness" and "leftness" of these clicks will, of course, be reversed if you have reversed the mouse buttons (because you're left-handed, for example, or for some other reason). If you have a trackball, a GlidePoint, or other non-mouse pointing device, your right-click button may be somewhere unexpected. You may have to refer to your pointing device's Help files to find out how to trigger the right-click event. In addition, if you have a special Windows 95/98/NT keyboard, there is a special "right menu" key (next to the Windows key) that you can press to trigger the right-click for whatever screen object has the current focus.

Right-clicking doesn't belong only to the Windows 95/98 and NT interface—it has been incorporated into recently written Windows programs, too. For example, Microsoft Office programs such as Word and Excel have had right-click menus for some time. Most of the accessory programs supplied with NT have context-sensitive right-click menus, too. In general, the contents of the right-click menus change depending on the type of object. Options for tables differ from those for spreadsheet cells, frames, text, graphics, and so on.

As a rule, we suggest you start using the right-click button whenever you can. You'll learn through experimentation which of your programs do something with the right-click and which don't. Many NT 3.51 (and 16-bit Windows) programs won't even respond to the click; others may do the unexpected. But in almost every case, right-clicking results in a pop-up menu. Incidentally, as with any menu in Windows, you can close the pop-up menu by clicking elsewhere or by pressing Esc, so don't worry about doing anything dangerous or irreversible.

A good example of a right-clickable item is the Taskbar. Right-click an empty place on the Taskbar, and you'll see this menu:

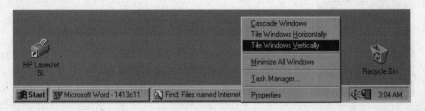

Now right-click the Start button, and you'll see the following menu:

Other right-click menus often have Cut, Copy, Paste, Open, Print, and Rename choices on them. Here are a few other right-clicking experiments to give you a feel for the usefulness of this facility:

▶ Right-click My Computer and notice the menu options. You'll see different right-click menus depending on whether you right-click the My Computer icon on the Desktop or if you right-click the My Computer window after it's open. In fact, you'll get different right-click menus within the open window depending on which part of the window you click—for example, the title bar, the list area of the window, and an object highlighted within the list will each pop up a different right-click menu.

▶ Right-click a program file (a file with an .exe extension). If a Quick View option is on the menu, select it to read information about the program, such as how much memory it requires to run and when it was created. (Quick View is not part of a typical NT Workstation installation, so there's a chance it might not be installed on your system. If the Quick View option does not appear on any of your right-click menus, use the Add/Remove Programs icon in the Control Panel, as described in Chapter 7.)

▶ When you right-click a printer in the Printers folder, you can quickly set the printer to be the default printer or to work offline. Printing offline is handy when the printer you want to use is not connected (or is turned off), because the result of offline printing is that your print jobs are queued up, ready and waiting until your printer is reconnected and ready to print. To begin printing again, simply right-click the printer and select Work Online, and all the print jobs in your queue are sent to the printer. (Work Offline and Work Online appear on a printer's right-click menu only if the printer is located on a network.) (See Chapter 5 for more information about printing.)

▸ Right-click the Desktop to see options for setting the screen colors, wallpaper, screen saver, and so forth.

▸ Right-click any program's title bar and notice the options for resizing the window or closing the application. This menu is the same as the program's System menu.

▸ Right-click a minimized program's button in the Taskbar. This gives the same result as clicking the same program's title bar: It pops up the program's System menu, which offers options for restoring the application (i.e., restoring it to its former size and position on the Desktop), resizing the application window, or closing the application.

Many objects, such as folders, printers, Network Neighborhood, and Inbox, have a right-click menu option called Explore that brings up the item in Explorer's format (two vertical panes). This is a super-handy way to check out the object in a display similar to the NT 3.*x*/Windows 3.*x* File Manager. You'll have the object in the left pane and its contents listed in the right pane. In some cases, the contents are print jobs; in other cases, they are fonts, files, folders, disk drives, or computers on the network. Explorer is covered in Chapter 3, "Organizing Programs and Documents."

Sharable items, such as printers, hard disks, and fax modems, have a Sharing option on their right-click menu. The resulting box lets you declare how an object is shared by other users on the network. Sharing a printer is covered in Chapter 8, "Sharing Data between Applications," and those general rules apply here.

Using Properties Sheets

Just as most objects have right-click menus, many also have properties sheets. Properties pervade all aspects of the NT Workstation 4 interface, providing you with a simple and direct means for setting everything from how the screen looks to whether a file is hidden or what a shared printer is named.

Virtually every object in NT Workstation 4—whether a printer, modem, shortcut, hard disk, folder, networked computer, or hardware driver—has a *properties sheet* containing its settings. These settings affect how the object works and, sometimes, how it looks. And properties sheets not only *display* the settings for the object, but also usually enable you to easily *alter* the settings.

You've probably noticed that many right-click menus have a Properties choice at the bottom. This choice is often the quickest path to an object's properties sheet—not that there aren't other ways. Many dialog boxes, for example, have a Properties button that brings up the object's settings when clicked. The Control Panel also can be used for setting numerous properties. Still, as you become more and more comfortable with NT, you'll find the right-click approach most expedient.

Deciding Whether You Need to Use Properties Sheets

The majority of NT Workstation users will rarely bother viewing or changing properties sheet settings because NT is well-behaved enough to govern itself (for example, repairing shortcuts when the target file or folder has been moved) and to prompt you when necessary for details about objects. As a case in point, when you install NT Workstation for the first time, or when you add new hardware or create a new printer, wizards conscientiously assume the responsibility of setting up properties appropriately. The upshot is that tweaking NT Workstation 4's internals and objects isn't nearly as necessary as it was in earlier versions of NT or in Windows 3.*x*. And in those rare instances when it is, unearthing the required dialog box for the job isn't an exercise reminiscent of dismantling a Chinese box puzzle.

Certainly, any self-respecting power user will want to know all about properties for easily performing tasks such as sharing a folder on the network, changing the name of a hard-disk volume, checking the status of the computer's ports, displaying a font or other file's technical details, or checking the amount of free disk space on a hard disk.

TIP

To see an object's properties even more quickly, highlight the object and press Alt+Enter. Other alternatives are to hold down the Alt key and double-click the object, or press the right-menu key on a Windows 95/98/NT keyboard and choose Properties.

Trying Out a Few Properties Sheets

The Properties option is always the last command on a right-click menu. For example, if you right-click the My Computer icon on the Desktop, you'll see this menu:

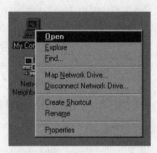

Or right-click the clock in the Taskbar, and you'll see this:

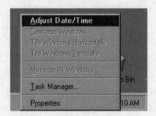

Just choose the Properties command to easily set the time, date, and time zone for your computer, ensuring that all your files are properly dated and time-stamped and that your Taskbar displays the time correctly.

Here's another everyday example. Suppose you're browsing through some folders using Explorer and you come across an item identified as a Word document. Wondering what it is, when it was created, and who created it, you right-click and choose Properties. The file's properties sheet pops up, as shown in Figure 4.1. Notice that several tab pages are on the sheet. That's because Word stores its property information in several locations. Other applications might pop up only a single-tabbed properties sheet.

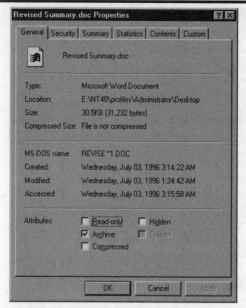

FIGURE 4.1:   A typical properties sheet for a document file. This one is for a Word 6 file, so it has several pages listing its editing history, who created it, keywords, title, and so forth.

As you might guess, properties sheets for other kinds of files may have more or less information than the one shown in Figure 4.1. In fact, most documents' properties sheets are truly useful only if you want to examine the history of the file or set its attributes, such as whether it should be read-only (to prevent others from changing it) or hidden from view in folders, or whether its archive bit should be set. (A check mark in the Archive box means the file hasn't been backed up since it was last altered or since it was created.) The point is that you can usually only view the status of the document, not alter it.

Properties sheets for objects *other* than documents, however, often let you make more substantive changes to them. A shortcut's properties sheet, for example, lets you adjust some goodies about how the shortcut works, the file it points to, and so on, as shown in Figure 4.2.

FIGURE 4.2: Shortcuts have properties sheets with a second tab page listing the particulars of the shortcut and allowing modification. Here you can change settings that control how the document or program will run when the shortcut is double-clicked.

TIP

There is now a way to ensure that a program defaults to a certain directory. In the dialog box shown in Figure 4.2, you can use the Start In field to set the default directory for a program. When you start the application from the shortcut, the File ≻ Open and File ≻ Save As commands then default to this directory. In Windows 3.x, setting this variable was only possible for DOS programs—now it's possible for Windows programs (both 16-bit and 32-bit) also.

A shortcut's properties sheet is somewhat similar to the .pif files in NT 3.x and Windows 3.x, although those affected the running of only DOS programs. These properties sheets can affect any program or document. You can use the ? button (found in the upper right of most sheets and dialog boxes) for help on any of the options. We'll just say that the two handiest items here are Shortcut Key and Run. Shortcut Key lets you assign a key combination that will run the shortcut from anywhere. For example, to jump to My Computer without having to first minimize all your other windows:

1. Get to the Desktop. Then right-click My Computer and choose Create Shortcut. This creates a new shortcut on the Desktop called Shortcut to My Computer.

2. Right-click the new shortcut and choose Properties.

3. In the Properties dialog box, click the Shortcut tab, then click in the Shortcut Key field.

4. Press Ctrl+Alt+C to assign the shortcut key of Ctrl+Alt+C.

5. Click OK to finish.

Now, whenever you want to open My Computer, just press Ctrl+Alt+C. It takes a little manual dexterity, but it's quick. Use the same trick for any object you use regularly and have to fish around to open.

The Run field in a shortcut's properties sheet determines whether the object opens in a maximized, minimized, or normal (floating) window.

Making Properties Settings from My Computer

Probably the most powerful of the properties sheets can be reached directly from My Computer. Clicking the My Computer icon on the Desktop and choosing Properties brings up the System properties sheet, shown in Figure 4.3.

Examine the six tab pages here. The General page tells you some useful information about the version of NT you are running, how much memory your computer has, and what type of CPU chip is in your machine. This will come in handy the next time someone asks you what's in the computer you're running. Instead of drumming your fingers on the desk and feeling like a dufus, you can open this box and read what it says.

The Performance page lets you set to what degree the foreground application gets extra processor priority (that is, it tailors the responsiveness) and also lets you adjust the system's virtual memory settings. Unless you know what you're doing, it's best to keep the default settings and let NT automatically handle the paging file and virtual memory management.

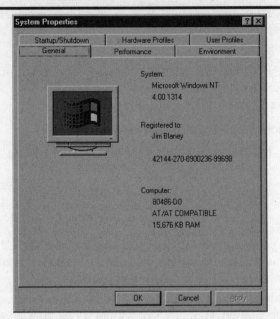

FIGURE 4.3:   A grand overview of your computer's attributes is available by right-clicking My Computer and choosing Properties. Use some caution with these settings. This box is also available from the System icon in the Control Panel.

The Environment page lets you adjust or add system-environment variables as well as user-environment variables. One such environment variable accessible here is the system path, which from time to time you might need to adjust or add to.

On the Startup/Shutdown page you can select a different operating system to use on restart (assuming there's more than one installed), as well as what to do with serious errors (for example, you can have NT log the error messages to a file, send an alert, and/or automatically restart the system).

The Hardware Profiles page provides a convenient way to create a "snapshot" of your current driver configuration, then add some other hardware and/or drivers and take a second snapshot (create a second profile). With two profiles, you can choose which configuration to use at system startup. This is useful when you want to add or remove hardware and would like to test your new configuration against your old one.

Finally, the User Profiles page lets you save different configurations of your Desktop *appearance*, including which items appear on your Start menu and other interface settings, so that different Desktop appearances can be associated with different users logging in to the system. You can also specify a "roaming" configuration, which permits your Desktop appearance to be available to every machine on your network, so that you can work at other machines using your own familiar interface.

WARNING

As a rule, don't mess with the settings in the My Computer's System properties sheet unless you know what you're doing. Adjusting the virtual memory settings, for example, will more likely negatively impact your system's performance than accelerate it. Examining all the pages is fine if you click Cancel after viewing the information.

WHAT'S NEXT?

In this chapter, you learned how to adjust properties for many of the objects in NT Workstation. The next chapter is about printing. It covers NT Workstation's powerful printing features, including local and network printing, print job monitoring and forwarding, printer security, and support for operating systems such as Macintosh and Unix.

Chapter 5

PRINTING

Windows NT Workstation gives you flexible and powerful printing support. You can attach printers directly to your computer, or you can print to printers over the network. NT supports many different types of printers from many different printer manufacturers. Some of the printing features of NT include local and remote printing, print spooling with print job monitoring and forwarding, printer security, and foreign client support for operating systems such as Macintosh and Unix.

This chapter will introduce the basic concepts of local and network printing and describe the NT print model. Then it will show you how to use the Print Manager, set up printers, and troubleshoot common printer problems.

Adapted from *MCSE: NT® Workstation 4 Study Guide* by Charles Perkins and Matthew Strebe with James Chellis
ISBN 0-7821-2223-X   752 pages $49.99

INTRODUCTION TO PRINTING

Many companies manufacture printers, and each manufacturer makes printers that are a little different from all of the others. There are many ways of making marks on paper, which is, after all, what printers do. Some manufacturers introduce new technologies to increase the resolution, color capacity, or pages per minute of their printers. Other manufacturers wait a while to see which technologies will prove to be popular and then implement the features that are most cost effective in their niche of the printer market. The end result is that almost any printing technology is implemented on some manufacturer's printer.

Any operating system's printing system has three components: the printing devices themselves and how they are attached to the computers, the printing software that translates print requests from application software into a form the printing devices will understand, and the way the operating system accomplishes printing over networks.

Printing Devices

Printing devices are the physical parts of the printing system, the components that actually make the black or colored marks on the paper. These units are commonly called *printers,* but in NT terminology, they are called *printing devices* because application software never directly communicates with a printing device. The "printer" that a Windows application sees is a software construct that translates print requests and forwards the resulting print job to the appropriate printing device.

NOTE

A printing device is usually connected to a computer via a serial or parallel cable, but printing devices can be connected to computers in other ways, such as directly via the computer's expansion bus or through a SCSI interface. Sometimes printers are connected directly to a network without an intervening general-purpose computer.

Some printing devices do not print directly to paper. For instance, a PostScript slide maker will print directly to 35mm slides for use in presentations. A fax modem, connected via a serial cable or installed in an expansion slot in your computer, can be configured as a printer, making it possible for you to print directly from your word processor or other application to a fax machine anywhere in the world. If the device you are "printing to" is actually a fax modem, the document may never actually be printed. Figure 5.1 illustrates several printing devices.

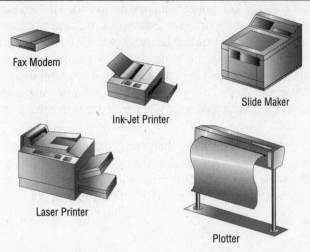

FIGURE 5.1: Laser printers, ink-jet printers, fax modems, slide makers, and plotters are all printing devices.

Printing Software

You cannot expect your word processor or spreadsheet to understand the printing languages and features of every printing device you can attach to your computer, because the variety of printing devices and printing languages is too great. If the routines for accessing printing devices were contained in the applications, you would need to update your applications whenever you attach a new printer with new options to your computer. (This unwieldy technology was used in early operating systems such as MS-DOS.)

NT, like many other modern operating systems, frees the application from having to speak the printer's native printing language. A layer of software between the printing device and the application software converts the application's print requests into a form that the user's printer can understand. This middle layer in NT is the set of software components described in the "NT Print Model" section later in this chapter.

The printer, in NT terminology, is a software component, not the physical device that produces documents on paper. When you select a printer from within an application, you are selecting the software component that will translate the application's print requests into a form that the printing device can understand. If your printing device is versatile, you might have several printer software components for one device, one for each mode of printing that the device supports. For instance, if you have a printer that supports both the HPGL/2 printing language and the PostScript printing language, you might have two printer icons and two printer options within your application but only one physical printer. Or if you have two printers that are the same, you might have just one printer (software component) that operates both of the printing devices; whichever one is free will print the current document.

When one printer services more than one printing device, the printing devices form a *printer pool*. All the printing devices in the printer pool must be of the same type, and the printer will assign documents to be printed to whichever printing device is free in the printer pool.

NOTE

Some network operating systems (NetWare, for example) use the term *queue* to refer to what Windows NT calls *printers*.

Figure 5.2 shows the relationship between applications, printers, and printing devices.

Printing and Networks

One of the most common uses of a network is to share a printer. In the NT print model, an application program doesn't care whether a printing device is connected directly to the computer the application is running on or resides elsewhere on the network.

If the printing device is attached to another computer over the network, the networking software will redirect the print request to the computer to which the printing device is attached. That computer will present the print request to its printing device.

One computer can provide printing services for many different types of computers. For instance, NT Workstation can provide printing services for Windows, Unix, Apple Macintosh, and MS-DOS computers.

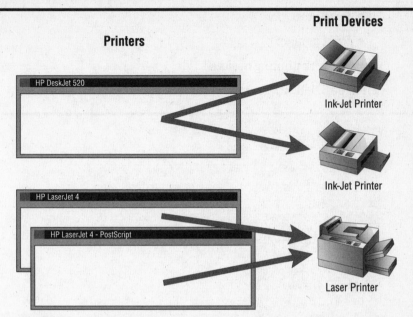

Printers

Print Devices

Ink-Jet Printer

Ink-Jet Printer

Laser Printer

HP DeskJet 520

HP LaserJet 4

HP LaserJet 4 - PostScript

FIGURE 5.2:   A printing device may be associated with more than one printer (application visible software component), and a printer may be associated with more than one printing device.

NT PRINT MODEL

NT has a modular print architecture. Each portion of the NT printing system has a specific purpose and well-defined interfaces to other components of the system. The modular architecture makes NT printing flexible; different versions of the modules can be installed for different purposes, and only the versions of the modules that are needed must be loaded. The software and hardware components that make up the print model are as follows:

- ▶ Graphics device interface (GDI)
- ▶ Print driver
- ▶ Print router
- ▶ Print provider (spooler)

- ▶ Print processor
- ▶ Print monitor
- ▶ Network printing devices

Figure 5.3 illustrates the NT print model.

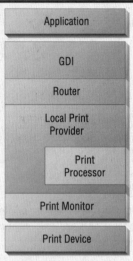

FIGURE 5.3:   Software components in the Windows NT print model cooperate to provide a sophisticated and powerful printing system.

Graphics Device Interface

The graphics device interface (GDI) provides Windows programs with a single unified system for presenting graphical information to the user. Therefore, the program can ignore the specific details of a device's resolution, color depth, coordinate system, bits per pixel, available fonts, and so on. The GDI will translate the generic print requests of the application into device driver requests that are specific to the printing characteristics of that device.

The GDI does not make a special case of either drawing on the screen or printing to a printer; both are merely graphical devices that vary somewhat in characteristics. The screen, for instance, is usually a much lower-resolution printing device than a printer, but the screen usually supports many more colors.

The GDI takes application print requests and translates them into device driver interface (DDI) calls. DDI calls are specific to the drawing characteristics of a printer, but they are not specific to an individual printing device.

When an application prints a document using the GDI interface and the device driver for the printer, the GDI and device driver produce a file called a print job. The *print job* contains either the sequence of instructions for the printer that will produce the printed document, in which case it is called a *raw print job*, or a list of the DDI calls that will produce a raw print job, in which case the print job is called a *journal file print job*.

The GDI produces a journal file print job when the printing device is local (directly connected to the computer instead of over the network). GDI produces a journal file more quickly than it produces a raw print job, which means that the GDI can return control to the application more quickly. The DDI calls stored in the print job must still be performed in order for the document to be printed. However, the print processor (described in the "Print Processor" section) will perform each DDI call in order, in the background, producing the raw print job that will be sent to the printing device.

Print Driver

The print driver is the software component that translates the printer-generic DDI calls into the printer-specific commands that will be passed on to the actual printer. You must have a print driver for the type of printer your workstation is connected to when you print. The print driver may be downloaded from a remote print server automatically. The printer manufacturer usually supplies the print driver software.

The print driver consists of three parts:

Printer Graphics Driver   This part of the print driver does the actual DDI-to-printer-language conversion. The three printer graphics drivers included with Windows NT are PSCRIPT.DLL (for PostScript printers), RASDD.DLL (for raster-based printers), and PLOTTER.DLL (for HPGL/2-based printers).

Printer Interface Driver   This component provides the Print Manager user interface in which you configure the printer. The printer interfaces for the above-mentioned printer graphics drivers are PSCRIPTUI.DLL, RASDDUI.DLL, and PLOTUI.DLL.

Characterization Data File or Minidriver This file isolates the make- and model-specific characteristics of a printer for the printer graphics driver.

Printer manufacturers can supply all three components of the print driver; however, often the only part that the manufacturer needs to provide is a mini-driver for one of the three Microsoft-supplied printer graphics and printer interface drivers.

Print Router

The print router directs the print job to the appropriate print provider. The router can also download a print driver for the printer if the printer is on a remote computer and the remote computer is configured to provide a print driver for the type of computer the router is running on.

Print Provider (Spooler)

Each printing device configured for use in your Windows NT workstation has a print provider. A print provider may accept print jobs from the router for a local printer, or it may accept print jobs to be printed on a remote printer. An application sees this printer when it prints.

A print provider for a local printer accepts print jobs from the router, calls the print processor to perform any final modifications to the print jobs, and then transfers the jobs one by one to the print monitor. Print providers can accept print jobs while a print job is printing; print jobs that are waiting to be printed are stored in memory or on disk as spool files.

The print provider also adds separator pages to print jobs if the user has requested them in the Print Manager.

A print provider for remote printers locates the network print server that is the destination of the print job and transfers the print job to that print server. Remote print providers do not spool the print job—they transfer the print job to the destination where it may be spooled.

Print Processor

The print processor performs any modifications to the print job before passing the print job to the print monitor. NT supplies two print processors: the Windows print processor and the Macintosh print processor.

In the Windows print processor, if the print job is a journal file, the print processor creates the raw type of print job by performing each of the DDI print driver calls.

The print processor may perform print processing on a raw print job if it is of one of two types: Raw FF Auto or Raw FF Appended. In the first case, the print processor always appends a form feed to the print job, which will cause the printer to eject the printed page. The second case appends a form feed if one is not already present. These two options are useful for older programs that send ASCII text to the printer, never or seldom appending a form-feed character.

The print processor does not change a normal raw print job (the kind of print job produced by Windows programs when they do not produce journal files).

The Windows print processor handles all print jobs from Macintosh computers to PostScript printers attached to a Windows NT computer and from Unix, Windows 95/98, older versions of Windows, and DOS.

The Macintosh print processor processes print jobs that a Macintosh computer sends to a non-PostScript printer connected to a Windows NT computer. The Macintosh print processor interprets the PostScript language in the Macintosh PostScript print job and prepares a raw print job for non-PostScript printers.

Print Monitor

The print monitor is the software component that transmits the print job (by now transformed into the language of the printer) to the printing device. Windows NT supplies several print monitors, the most important of which are LOCALMON.DLL, HPMON.DLL, and LPRMON.DLL.

The local print monitor communicates with the printing device through serial and parallel ports, remote print shares, and named pipes and can store the print job in a file instead of sending it to a printer.

The HP print monitor sends the print jobs to an HP printer that is connected directly to the network instead of attached through a computer.

The LPR (line printer) print monitor sends the print job to a Unix LPD (line printer daemon) print server.

The print monitor can also report the condition of the printing device (busy, offline, ready, out of paper or toner, and so on), detect printing errors, and restart a print job if necessary.

MANAGING PRINTERS

From the Printers window (opened by selecting Start ➤ Settings ➤ Printers), you can perform local and network printer administrative tasks, such as creating and attaching to printers; configuring printers; setting print permissions; starting, stopping, and redirecting print jobs; and auditing printer use.

This section will show you how to:

▸ Manage print jobs

▸ Create local printers

▸ Attach to remote printers

Configuring printers is a complex task and is covered in the "Printer Configuration" section later in this chapter.

Managing Print Jobs

Within the Printers folder is an icon for each of the printers you have installed or connected to your workstation. Opening the icon for a printer (double-clicking the icon) shows you the status of the printer (see Figure 5.4). Each printer has a separate window, showing only print jobs for that printer.

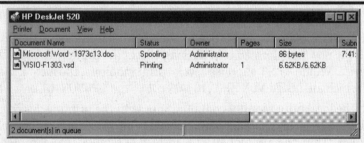

FIGURE 5.4:   Opening the Printer icon will show you the jobs in that printer's queue and allow you to control the printer and manage those jobs.

Print job entries will appear in the list in the middle of the window and will persist until the document is printed or until the print job is removed from the queue. You can modify a print job's status while it is in the queue.

If you have sufficient permission, you can pause, resume, restart, and cancel print jobs. You perform any of these actions by clicking once on the print job name and then selecting the operation (pause, etc.) from the Document menu in the Printers window.

From the Printer menu in the Printers window, you can pause all printing for that printer, cancel all of the print jobs on that printer, set the printer to be the default printer, start and stop sharing of the printer, select the default document properties (page size, paper tray, and so on), and reach the properties sheet for that printer. (The properties sheet is described in the "Printer Configuration" section later in this chapter.)

Follow the steps in Exercise 5.1 to create a print job, pause the job, and then cancel the job.

EXERCISE 5.1: CREATING, PAUSING, AND STOPPING A PRINT JOB

1. Log on as an administrator.

2. Select Start ➤ Settings ➤ Printers.

3. Double-click a printer installed in your computer.

4. Select Properties from the Printer menu.

5. Position the Properties window so that you can see both the Properties window and the Printers window.

6. Click the Print Test Page button in the Properties window. As soon as the test page appears in the Printers window, click once on the test page print job (highlighting the test page print job) and then select Document ➤ Pause. (The test document is small and your printer may be quick, so you may need several tries to do this step. If you are quick enough, the status of the test print job will change to paused.)

7. Select Document ➤ Cancel. The print job will disappear from the list.

Creating a Local Printer

Before you can use a printer that is directly attached to your computer, you must create a printer within Print Manager. Exercise 5.2 outlines the steps for creating a printer.

EXERCISE 5.2: CREATING A LOCAL PRINTER

1. Log on as an administrator.

2. Select Start ➢ Settings ➢ Printers to display the Printers window (see Figure 5.5).

3. Open the Add Printer icon by double-clicking it. This step starts the Add Printer Wizard.

4. Make sure that the My Computer option is checked.

5. Click the Next button at the bottom of the window. The Add Printer Wizard window now shows a list of available ports (see Figure 5.6).

6. Select the port that the printer is attached to (a parallel printer will most likely be attached to LPT1:) and then click the Next button at the bottom of the window.

7. Select the manufacturer of your printer from the first list and then select your printer model from the other list. Click Next.

8. Enter a name for the printer. If you wish this printer to be the default printer for use with Windows programs, select the Yes option; otherwise, select No. Click Next when you are ready to continue.

9. Select the Shared option and enter a name for the printer to be recognized by on the network if you wish to allow other computers on the network to print to this printer. If it will be a shared printer, also select the types of clients that will connect to the printer (see Figure 5.7). Click Next when you are ready to continue.

10. The Add Printer Wizard window will allow you to print a test page. Select Yes to print a test page and then click Finish.

11. Insert the operating system installation media (the Windows NT CD-ROM) if you are asked to do so. Follow the instructions in the dialog boxes so NT can load the drivers it needs to control the printer.

12. Notice that a new icon appears in the Printers window. In addition, the Properties window for the icon will open in order for you to configure the printer you have just installed. Click OK to close the window.

FIGURE 5.5: The Printers window shows you the printers you have configured in your workstation.

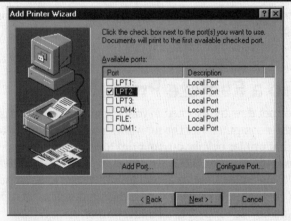

FIGURE 5.6: You can select one or more local ports for the printer to send documents to. If you select more than one, the printing devices on each port must be of the same type.

Creating a printer installs the printer driver for the printer and configures NT applications and the NT operating system to be able to print to the printer.

When you install the printer, you can also select the drivers for other operating systems that your computer can download to a remote printer so that it can print your job.

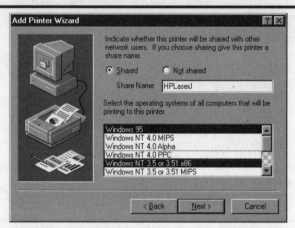

FIGURE 5.7:   When you share a printer, you may also select which network clients to provide downloadable print drivers for.

Connecting to a Remote Printer

When a printer is not directly attached to your computer, but is instead attached to another computer over the network, you must connect your workstation to that printer before you can print to it. The printer attached to a computer over the network is called a *remote printer*. To the other computer, however, the remote printer is a local printer. (Refer to Exercise 5.2 for instructions on creating a local printer for the remote computer.) Exercise 5.3 shows you how to connect to a remote printer.

EXERCISE 5.3: CONNECTING TO A REMOTE PRINTER

1. Log on as an administrator.

2. Select Start ➤ Settings ➤ Printers to display the Printers window.

3. Open the Add Printer icon by double-clicking it. This step will start the Add Printer Wizard and display a network browser window.

4. Make sure that the Network Printer Server option is checked.

5. Browse the network to find the printer that you wish to attach to. Figure 5.8 shows a remote printer being selected.

CONTINUED ➤

6. Select the printer you want to attach to and click OK in the Connect To Printer window. You will be asked if this printer should be the default printer for use with Windows programs.

7. Select the Yes option to make it the default printer; otherwise, select No. Click Next when you are ready to continue.

8. Click Finish to allow Windows NT to complete the installation of the remote printer in your workstation.

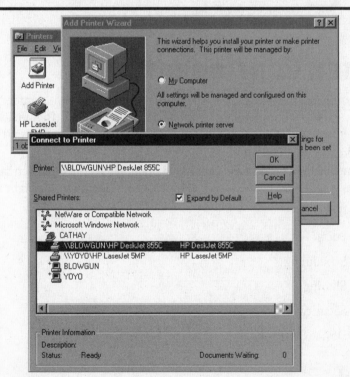

FIGURE 5.8:   The Add Printer Wizard will help you connect to remote printers.

TIP

Exercise 5.3 explains the preferred method of connecting to a remote printer. You can also connect to a remote printer by creating a local printer of the same type as the remote printer and then changing the port setting of the printer to point to the remote location, rather than to LPT1, as follows: *remote_computer_name**printer_name*. This statement will cause the print job to be spooled locally as well as on the remote computer.

NOTE

In order for a DOS application to print to a remote printer, the UNC printer share must be mapped to a local LPT port. The syntax for this command is NET USE LPTx *computer_name**share_name*.

PRINTER CONFIGURATION

You configure the printer from the properties sheet for that printer. You can reach the properties sheet from the Printers window. (Right-click the Printer icon and then select Properties, or click the Printer icon and then select File ➣ Properties.)

The printer's properties sheet has six tabs across the top. Each tab allows you to modify one aspect of the printer's operation. The tabs are:

- ▶ General
- ▶ Ports
- ▶ Scheduling
- ▶ Sharing
- ▶ Security
- ▶ Device Settings

General

From the General tab, you can enter a comment about the printer, describe the location of the printer, and select the print driver for the printer (see Figure 5.9).

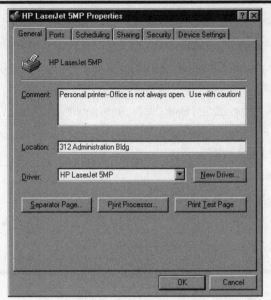

FIGURE 5.9: The Properties window for your printer has six tabs. The General tab allows you to describe the printer to network users, print a test page, and set the separator page and print processor options.

Across the bottom of the General tab are three buttons:

Separator Page   Allows you to place a separator page between each document printed on the printer. Exercise 5.4 outlines the steps for selecting a separator page for a printer.

Print Processor   Allows you to select a print processor for this printer. When a printer has a print processor, it can accept print jobs from other operating systems, such as Unix or Macintosh. (Refer to the section on Windows NT printing architecture earlier in this chapter.)

Print Test Page   Prints a test page so that you can be sure the settings for the printer are correct.

EXERCISE 5.4: SELECTING A SEPARATOR PAGE

1. Log on as an administrator.

2. Select the printer from the Printers window (click the printer one time).

3. Select File ➤ Properties from the Printers window.

4. Make sure that the General tab is selected and then click the Separator Page button.

5. Click Browse.

6. Select the file SYSPRINT.SEP and then click Open.

7. Click OK.

8. Click OK to close the printer's properties sheet.

Ports

The Ports tab shows a list of ports that this printer selection can print to. If you can have more than one printing device attached to your computer, configure this printer selection to print to whichever is not busy. As explained earlier, several printing devices that work together are called a print pool. All of the printers in a print pool must be of the same type.

The buttons at the bottom of the window allow you to add, delete, and configure ports. You can also enable bidirectional printing if your printer supports it.

TIP

You can redirect the output of the printer to a file, which you might do if you needed a file containing the printing device-specific commands, for example, to send output for printing on a large or high-resolution printing device.

Exercise 5.5 shows how to redirect printer output to a file.

EXERCISE 5.5: REDIRECTING PRINTER OUTPUT TO A FILE

1. Log on as an administrator.

2. Select the printer from the Printers window (click the printer one time).

3. Select File ➤ Properties from the Printers window.

4. Select the Ports tab.

5. Remove the check mark from the currently checked ports.

6. Click Add Port and then select Local Port from the Printer Ports window.

7. Click the OK button at the bottom of the window. In the Port Name window, enter the path and filename that this printer will print to. Click OK and then click Close. The name you entered will appear in the Ports list.

8. Click the checkbox for that entry to enable printing to the file.

9. Click the OK button at the bottom of the window.

Scheduling

The Scheduling tab (see Figure 5.10) controls when the printer is available and how print jobs are presented to the printer. You can set the printer to be always available or to be available for certain hours of the day. If you limit the availability of the printer, you must enter the start time and stop time of the printer's operation. Exercise 5.6 shows how to limit the hours of operation of a printer.

You can set the priority of print jobs from this printer (represented by an icon) in the Priority section of the window. If you have created more than one printer icon for one printing device, and therefore more than one logical printer, the print jobs from the printer with the highest priority print first. The priority for this printer can be set to any number from 1 to 99, with 99 as the highest priority.

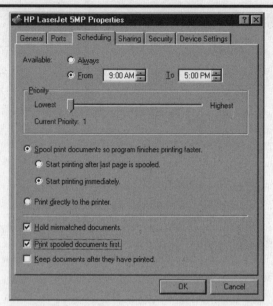

FIGURE 5.10: The Scheduling tab governs the availability of the printer and its print spooling characteristics.

EXERCISE 5.6: LIMIT THE HOURS OF OPERATION OF A PRINTER

1. Log on as an administrator.

2. Select the printer from the Printers window.

3. Select File ➤ Properties from the Printers window.

4. Select the Scheduling tab.

5. Go to the top of the window. Under Available, select the From option. Enter the start time (9:00 A.M., for example) and the end time (5:00 P.M.).

6. Click the OK button at the bottom of the window.

The spooling options in the middle of the window allow you to set the printer either:

▶ Not to spool (*spooling* is storing print jobs on the hard disk until the print monitor is ready to accept them)

▶ To spool the jobs to disk

If you enable spooling, you can set the spooler either:

▶ To begin sending the print job to the print monitor immediately

▶ To send the print job when the whole job has been received by the spooler

The three checkboxes at the bottom of the window allow you to:

▶ Specify that the spooler hold mismatched jobs (which checks to ensure that the type of print job matches the type of printer, or holds the document otherwise)

▶ Print spooled jobs first (which gives documents that have been spooled to disk priority)

▶ Keep documents after they have been printed (which you might enable if you need an electronic copy of every document printed on a printer)

Sharing

From the Sharing tab, you control the availability of your printer on the network. By selecting the Not Shared option, you restrict printing to that printer to your computer.

If you enable sharing by selecting the Shared option, you must give a network name for the printer in the Share Name field.

You may also wish to configure your workstation to automatically download print drivers to computers that access your printer over the network. The remainder of the window allows you to select the client operating systems for which your workstation will provide print drivers.

Security

The Security tab contains three buttons: Permissions, Auditing, and Ownership.

Clicking the Permissions button displays a window from which you set user permissions for printing and managing documents. Exercise 5.7 leads you through the process of restricting a printer so that only administrators can print to it.

EXERCISE 5.7: RESTRICTING ACCESS TO A PRINTER

1. Log on as an administrator.

2. Select the printer from the Printers window.

3. Select File ➤ Properties from the Printers window.

4. Select the Security tab and then click the Permissions button to display the Printer Permissions window.

5. Click once on the Everyone item in the Name list.

6. Click Remove.

7. Click once on the Power Users item in the Name list.

8. Click Remove.

9. Click the OK button in the Printer Permissions window and then click OK in the printer's properties sheet.

The Auditing button displays an auditing window, which allows you to track the printing activities of users and groups for this printer.

With the Ownership button, you can take ownership of the printer, although we do not recommend this step.

Device Settings

The Device Settings tab contains a hierarchical view of device-specific settings such as the default tray assignment, loaded printer fonts, available printer memory, and so on. Although you can change device settings from this tab, the printer's properties sheet (available from within the Print dialog box by clicking Properties when you print from an application) is a better place from which to change these settings.

PRINTER TROUBLESHOOTING

The many different printer types and configurations make the job of troubleshooting printing problems difficult. No set of guidelines can solve every printing problem. However, you can resolve many printing problems by checking a few basic failure points of printers and printing systems.

Follow the steps outlined in Exercise 5.8 if you have difficulty printing to your printer. Each of the steps checks a potential printing problem.

EXERCISE 5.8: RESOLVING SIMPLE PRINTING PROBLEMS

1. Make sure that the printer is plugged in to the wall and that the printer is turned on.

2. Make sure that the printer is online. If the printer is not online and is reporting an error condition, consult the printer manual to determine the cause of the error and then fix the problem.

3. Make sure that the printer cable is attached securely to both the printer and the computer.

4. Check the print driver. Is it installed properly? Is it the correct version for the printer? If not, install the correct print driver.

5. Make sure that when you attempt to print, you are selecting the print driver you verified in step 4.

6. Check to see if you have sufficient hard disk space for the print driver to create temporary print files. Without sufficient space, the print driver will not be able to create a print job to send to the printer. If space is low, delete some files, archive some files to floppy or backup tape, or add hard disk space.

7. Check to see if you can print from other applications within NT. If so, you may need to troubleshoot the printing options of the application you are using. If you can print from Win32 based applications but not from a DOS, Win16, or POSIX application, you may need to troubleshoot that subsystem of your NT operating system configuration.

8. Print to a file and then copy the output of the file to the printer port. If you get a printed document using this method, then the problem may lie with the spooler or data transmission. Otherwise, the problem probably lies with the driver or application.

Part i

Printing Problems

Occasionally, the print jobs are transferred to the spooler but fail to print. You can usually solve this problem by stopping and restarting the print spooler, following the instructions in Exercise 5.9.

EXERCISE 5.9: STOPPING AND RESTARTING THE PRINT SPOOLER

1. Select Start ➤ Settings ➤ Control Panel.

2. Double-click the Services Control Panel.

3. Select Spooler in the Services list box.

4. Click Stop.

5. Answer Yes to confirm.

6. Click Start. Your stuck print jobs should print.

WHAT'S NEXT?

In this chapter, you learned about NT's flexible and powerful printing system, as well as how to configure printers and troubleshoot printer problems. The next chapter explores the multimedia capabilities of NT. It covers the CD Player, Media Player, and Sound Recorder built into NT Workstation.

Chapter 6

SIGHTS AND SOUNDS

The multimedia capabilities built into many computers and now implemented by NT Workstation may strike you as more of a toy than anything useful. People who use computers as intensely as writers, accountants, and computer consultants do are not looking for more ways to get distracted but for ways to remove distractions. Who needs moving pictures or music to get a book written?

Turns out that's the wrong question. The fact is publishing is different in the age of the computer, as are accounting and data crunching. Books can be published online with animation, pictures, or music. Spreadsheets can include pictures of products or factories to make data more concrete. Databases can include pictures of clients and employees to make information more personal.

Adapted from *The ABCs of Windows® Workstation® 4* by Charlie Russel
ISBN 0-7821-1999-9   384 pages $19.99

This chapter examines the CD Player, Media Player, and Sound Recorder built into NT Workstation. The first can be used for your private enjoyment or to accompany a presentation with a soundtrack. The second and third can be used to display and enhance multimedia presentations.

You'll find all the multimedia applications by clicking the Start button and proceeding through Programs ➤ Accessories ➤ Multimedia.

CAN'T FIND MULTIMEDIA?

You won't have a Multimedia option on your Accessories menu if the Multimedia applications weren't installed at the time NT Workstation was installed. If this is the case, it's easily remedied:

1. Go to the Control Panel and click Add/Remove Programs.

2. Click the Windows NT Setup tab at the top of the Add/ Remove Programs Properties dialog box.

3. Scroll through the list of options in the dialog box until you locate Multimedia.

4. Double-click Multimedia to see a list of multimedia programs available.

5. Click the checkboxes next to as many programs as you want to install. (For the purposes of this chapter, make sure CD Player, Media Player, Sound Recorder, and Volume Control are selected.)

6. OK your way out, and insert your NT Workstation disk as requested to complete the installation.

NOTE
You can associate sounds with different events—for example, a program opens and a particular sound plays. Chapter 7 covers how to do this.

THE CD PLAYER

The CD Player lets you play audio CDs using your CD-ROM drive, sound card, and speakers. You can plug speakers or headphones into the sound card or into the jack on the front of the CD-ROM drive.

To open the CD Player, follow these steps:

1. Click the Start button on the Taskbar.

2. Select Programs.

3. Select Accessories in the Program menu.

4. Select Multimedia in the Accessories menu to open the Multimedia menu.

Depending on the programs you selected when you installed NT Workstation, you'll probably have several applications on this menu.

Starting It Up

To start the CD Player, follow these steps:

1. Locate CD Player among the programs in the Multimedia menu.

2. Click the CD Player option to start the program. You will see the window shown in Figure 6.1.

FIGURE 6.1:   The CD Player window

All you have to do is supply a music CD. The CD Player will play it through your sound card and speakers (plugged into the audio jacks on the back of the sound controller) or through the headphone jack in the front of your CD-ROM drive.

TIP

Windows NT Workstation 4 has an automatic play feature for the CD-ROM drive. Put a music CD in the drive and close it. The CD Player will start up. Similarly, when you put a data CD in the drive, NT will show the opening screen.

How It Works

Just as a demonstration, I popped a music CD in the drive and clicked on the large triangle next to the digital read-out (the Play button). The CD Player (with Disc/Track Info enabled from the View menu) can be seen in Figure 6.2.

FIGURE 6.2: Here's what the CD Player at work looks like.

Notice that several of the buttons that were gray and unavailable in Figure 6.1, when there wasn't a CD in the drive, are now black and available in Figure 6.2.

Play   At the top, the large triangle is gray because the CD is playing. (There's no reason to click the Play button when the CD is playing, but if you do, no harm is done.)

Pause   Next to the Play button is a button with two vertical bars. This is the Pause button. Click it to hold your playback while you run to answer the door or the phone.

Stop   The last button at the right end of the top tier is the Stop button. Click it when you're tired of listening to the music or when the boss walks into your office. It will stop playback dead.

Previous Track   The first button at the left end of the second tier of buttons looks like a double arrowhead pointing left toward a vertical line. Click once to move to the beginning of the current piece; click twice to move to the previous track on the CD.

Skip Backwards   The second button on the second tier looks like a double arrowhead pointing left. This is the Skip Backwards button. Each time you click it, you move back one second in the music.

Skip Forwards The third button on the second tier is the Skip Forwards button. It looks like a double arrowhead pointing to the right. Each time you click it, you move one second forward in the music.

Next Track The fourth button on the second tier is the Next Track button. It looks like a double arrowhead pointing right toward a vertical bar. It will instantly take you to the next song.

Eject The final button at the right end of the second tier of buttons looks like an arrow pointing upward. Click it to pop open the CD-ROM drive.

Setting Time and Play Options

Is that all there is? Certainly not. If you're an information freak, click the digital readout. Before you click, the readout will tell you the current track number and the elapsed time for that track. The first time you click, you'll see the track number and the time remaining on the track. The second click will display the time remaining for the whole CD (shown in Figure 6.3).

FIGURE 6.3: Getting instant information about the play time remaining on the whole CD

If you want to set these without clicking the digital display, pull down the View menu and select from these options:

▶ Track Time Elapsed

▶ Track Time Remaining

▶ Disc Time Remaining

The Options menu lets you opt for Continuous Play, Random Play, or Intro Play. Select the Preferences option. It allows you to set the font size for the digital readout as well as the length of intro play (ten seconds is the default).

Part i

TIP

Want a shortcut to the CD Player or Media Player on your Desktop? Open the WINNT folder, then open the System32 folder and look for the file CDPLAYER.EXE or MPLAY32.EXE. Right-click and drag the file to the Desktop. Release the right mouse button, and select Create Shortcut(s) here.

Editing the Play List

And if that's not enough, there's an entire layer of the CD Player we haven't even touched yet. Here's how to access it:

1. Pull down the Disc menu.

2. Select Edit Play List. You will see the dialog box shown in Figure 6.4.

Using this dialog box, you can do something owners of CD players often never get the hang of—programming your player to play specific songs in a specific order.

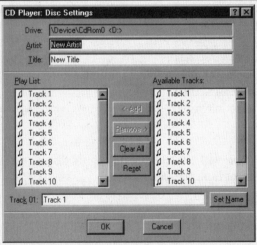

FIGURE 6.4: The Disc Settings dialog box lets you program a play list.

By Track Number

As an example, let's set up the CD Player to play Tracks 5, 12, and 3 on this particular disc. Here's how:

1. Click the Clear All button to clear all the entries on the Play List.

2. Double-click Track 5 in the Available Tracks list box. It will appear in the Play List.

3. Double-click Track 12, then double-click Track 3 in the Available Tracks list box.

By Track Name

If you'd rather deal with track names than track numbers, you can insert names for each of the tracks (or just the ones you care about), as follows:

1. Click a track—for this example, we'll click Track 3 in the Available Tracks list.

2. Click the text box next to the Set Name button.

3. Refer to your CD packaging to get the name of the third song on the CD.

4. Type the name in the text box. (You can type it next to Track 3 or delete the track and type the name instead.)

5. Click the Set Name button. In the Available Tracks list and in the Play List, Track 3 will be replaced with the name you just typed.

6. Just for the sake of completeness, click the text box marked Artist and type the performer(s) name.

7. Highlight the text box marked Title and type the CD's title.

8. Click the OK button.

Once you've supplied the CD Player with this information, the program will remember it, recognize the CD, and follow your programmed instructions every time you play it.

TIP

If you have a CD-ROM player capable of playing multiple discs, Multidisc Play will be an option on the Options menu. Select it, and when you click the downward-pointing arrow at the right end of the Artist box, you will see each of the CDs available to you. Select the CD you want to play.

THE MEDIA PLAYER

These days, the word *media* conjures up more talk-show blather about how everything's the fault of the media—whoever they are.

Not this media. The media in this section are fun—never trouble.

Let's begin, as always, by first opening the program:

1. Click the Start button on the Taskbar.

2. Select Programs.

3. Select Accessories from the Programs menu.

4. Select Multimedia from the Accessories menu.

5. Select Media Player from the Multimedia menu.

You should see something similar to the window shown in Figure 6.5.

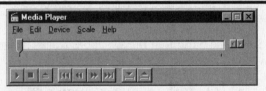

FIGURE 6.5: The Media Player window

The Media Player will play Video for Windows animated files (.AVI), sound files (.WAV), MIDI files (.MID and .RMI), or your audio CD. Yes, that's right. You can use the Media Player to play your music CDs. It's just like the CD Player, except that the Media Player offers fewer customization options.

Playing Files

NT Workstation comes with a variety of multimedia files, especially on the CD-ROM version. To play a file, follow these steps:

1. Pull down the Media Player Device menu and select the type of file you want to play.

2. Locate the file you want to play, double-click or highlight it, and select Open.

3. Click the single right-pointing arrow (the Play button).

You can select sections of animation or movies in the same way that you select recorded music tracks (see the CD Player section earlier in this chapter). Although the buttons are in different places than the ones on the CD Player, you should be able to identify them by their icons (see the "How It Works" section).

Copying and Pasting Files

You can copy and paste sound, animation, or movie files using the Select buttons, which look like tiny arrows above a horizontal bar pointing down (Begin Selection) and up (End Selection).

Selecting a Piece of the File

To select a section of either an audio or a video file:

1. Listen (or watch) until you reach the point where the section begins.

2. Click the Begin Selection button.

3. Continue listening or watching until you reach the end of the section.

4. Click the End Selection button.

5. Pull down the Edit menu and select Copy Object. (The piece you have selected will be placed on the Clipboard for pasting into any document that supports sound or video files.)

Getting Looped

If you want a piece of music, film, or animation to repeat continuously, pull down the Edit menu and select Options. Click the option marked Auto Repeat. Your media file will play over and over until:

1. The end of time

2. You turn off the Media Player

3. You lose your mind and destroy your computer with a fire ax

THE SOUND RECORDER

If you have an audio input device on your computer (either a microphone or a CD-ROM player), you can use the Sound Recorder to make a .WAV file that you can associate with a Windows event or send in a message.

Making .WAV Files

Here's how to make a .WAV file with the Sound Recorder:

1. Open Sound Recorder in the Multimedia menu under Accessories.

2. To begin recording, click the button with the dark red dot.

3. Start the CD or start speaking into the microphone.

4. Click the button with the black square to stop recording.

5. Select Save from the File menu to save the sound clip, then enter a name for the file in the Save dialog box that appears.

Figure 6.6 shows the Sound Recorder recording from a CD being played in the Media Player.

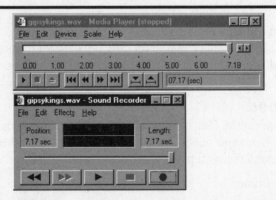

FIGURE 6.6: Make your own .WAV files from a CD-ROM with the Sound Recorder.

The Sound Recorder also lets you play other types of sound clips in the Media Player and record them as .WAV files. The .WAV files you make can be played back with the Sound Recorder or the Media Player.

TIP

To easily associate a .WAV file with an event in NT Workstation, move the file to the Media folder (inside the Windows folder). See Chapter 7 for the specifics on how to use sound files in this way.

Special Effects and Editing

Use the Effects menu to change some of the sound's qualities—to add an echo or decrease the speed, for example. The sound can also be edited using the menu controls.

VOLUME CONTROL

The Volume Control panel lets you not only adjust the sound level, but also individually tune levels for different types of files. The best way to reach the Volume Control panel is to open it from the Multimedia menu under Accessories. Figure 6.7 shows the Volume Control panel.

FIGURE 6.7: The Volume Control panel lets you make adjustments in your sound files.

Tone Controls

For tone controls (bass and treble), select Advanced Controls from the Options menu. This will put an Advanced button at the bottom of the

Volume Control panel. Click this button to open the dialog box shown in Figure 6.8.

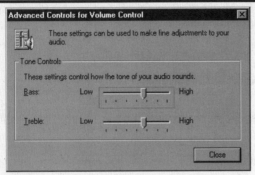

FIGURE 6.8: Use the slider controls to adjust tone.

Use the slider controls to increase or decrease the treble and bass tones. These settings will affect all the sound files you play.

NOTE

If Advanced Controls is dimmed on your screen, it means your hardware doesn't support these functions.

Setting the Volume Control Display

Figure 6.7 shows the default settings for Volume Control, but you can decide which devices you want to show on the Volume Control panel. Open Volume Control and select Properties from the Options menu. This will open the Volume Control dialog box.

Select Playback and check the devices you want shown on Volume Control. Similarly, you can display recording levels. The choices will probably differ based on your specific computer hardware.

MORE MULTIMEDIA SETTINGS

There's also a Multimedia icon in the Control Panel that contains mostly advanced settings, but some basic ones, too.

Double-click this icon to open the Multimedia Control Panel. Then you can poke around, right-clicking anything you don't understand to get an explanation box. There are a lot of terms here that will be unfamiliar to anyone who's a novice at computer-based sound and video. Experiment but also take care not to remove a device unintentionally.

Multimedia

Part I

NOTE

The Multimedia Control Panel is the place you go to install a sound card or other audio/video devices.

WHAT'S NEXT?

This chapter hasn't exhausted all the features for the eyes and ears. In the next chapter, we'll go on to some neat functions in the Control Panel that also affect how your computer looks and sounds, and you'll learn how to customize settings to make your computer truly your own.

Chapter 7

IN THE CONTROL PANEL

I f you've fiddled around with the Control Panel at all, you can see that it acts as a sort of "mission central" for NT Workstation. Some of the settings behind the icons can be reached from other directions, but others can be reached only by way of the Control Panel. Most of the items in the Control Panel help you customize your NT Workstation even further.

You'll find a heading in this chapter for all the usual icons in the Control Panel (listed alphabetically). If the settings behind an icon are detailed elsewhere, you'll be pointed to the correct location.

Adapted from *The ABCs of Windows® Workstation® 4* by Charlie Russel

ISBN 0-7821-1999-9   384 pages $19.99

ACCESSIBILITY OPTIONS

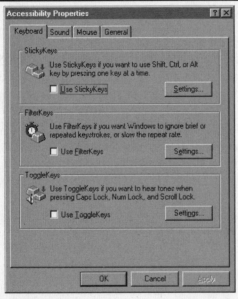

The Accessibility Options are installed automatically when NT Workstation is installed. If they're not on your system, you can use Add/Remove Programs to add them.

Double-click the Accessibility Options icon, and you'll find options for adding sound to the usual visual cues, adding visual cues to the sound cues, and making the keyboard and mouse easier to use for those of us with dexterity problems (see Figure 7.1).

FIGURE 7.1:   Here's where you can add sounds to visual cues and visual cues to sound.

Not all the settings are obvious, so when you come across one that's unclear, right-click the text and then click the What's This? button for more information.

After you've made your settings, don't leave until you click the General tab to check the Automatic Reset section. Put a check mark next to Turn Off Accessibility Features After Idle to turn off the options if the computer isn't used for the period specified in the Minutes box. Clear the checkbox if you want to make the selected options permanent.

TIP

The Toggle Keys option on the Keyboard page is of great help if you often hit the Caps Lock key inadvertently and find your text looking like "cALL mR. jAMES IN cAPE vERDE." With Toggle Keys on, you'll hear a quiet but distinct warning beep when Caps Lock is switched on.

ADD/REMOVE PROGRAMS

Add/Remove Programs

NT Workstation provides a good deal of aid and comfort when it comes to adding or removing programs from your system, especially adding and removing parts of NT Workstation itself. Double-click the Add/Remove Programs icon in the Control Panel.

The Add/Remove function has two parts, one on each tab:

▶ Installing or uninstalling software applications

▶ Installing or removing portions of NT Workstation

Install/Uninstall

A software producer who wants the right to put a Windows NT (or Windows 95/98) logo on a product is supposed to make sure the program can uninstall itself. This capability is to correct a problem that made it difficult to completely remove a program and all of its associated files in previous versions of NT Workstation.

Programs written for previous versions of Windows don't have this uninstall capability. And some programs actually written for NT and Windows 95 can be uninstalled but still leave bits of themselves cluttering your hard disk (although this is less of a problem for recent versions of software). How the major programs written for NT handle the Add/Remove function varies widely. Some will just uninstall themselves without a fuss; others will give you the option of removing all or just parts of the program. You'll have to select the program and click Remove to see what happens. *Nothing* will be uninstalled without your OK.

Add/Remove is an easy-to-use tool for installing new programs. Just put the program's first floppy disk in the drive (or if the program came on a CD, insert the CD in the proper drive), click the Install/Uninstall tab, and then click the Install button.

The program searches for an install routine first in drive A, then in drive B (if you have one), and finally in the CD drive. Figure 7.2 shows the result of one search. Click Finish to continue. After this, the program's install routine takes over.

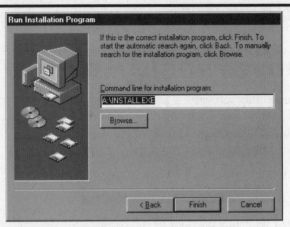

FIGURE 7.2:   NT's installation program finds the INSTALL or SETUP file and proceeds to install the program.

Windows NT Setup

Click the Windows NT Setup tab to add or remove a component of NT Workstation. The various parts are organized by groups (see Figure 7.3). For certain groups, you can highlight the group and click Details to see the individual components.

As you click each item in a group, a description of the item's function is displayed at the bottom of the page. The rules are simple:

▶ If an item is checked, it's installed. Remove the check mark, and it will be removed.

▶ If an item is not checked, it's not currently installed on your system. Put a check mark next to it, and it will be installed.

▶ If the checkbox is gray, a part of the component is selected for installation. Click the Details button to specify which parts you want.

Click OK once or twice until the window closes. You'll be prompted to put the NT Workstation CD in the CD drive.

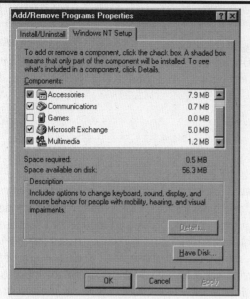

FIGURE 7.3:   Here's where you can install or uninstall various parts of NT Workstation.

CONSOLE

When you want to run a DOS session from NT, you open a command prompt window (by choosing Start ➤ Programs ➤ MS-DOS Prompt). The command prompt window in NT is not DOS, but rather a full 32-bit program that understands DOS commands. You can set options for the command prompt window through the Console program. Double-click the Console icon to set the display as window or full screen and adjust other settings, such as the font, colors, and the cursor size.

CSNW

If you have this icon, it means that Client Services for NetWare is installed on your computer. This service allows you to use the printers and drives of a NetWare server on your NT Workstation. If you need to change something here, call your system administrator.

DATE/TIME

 Unless you're logged in using an account with administrative privileges, this Control Panel option is unavailable to you, which makes sense since you don't have permission to change the system date and time.

DEVICES

 If you double-click the Devices icon in the Control Panel, you'll see a mysterious-looking list of items. What you have in front of you is actually an inventory of devices on your system, which includes basic things, such as your keyboards, ports, and mouse, but also more complicated things, such as hardware and software drivers. My advice on this one is *don't touch!* You'll probably never need to change any of the settings behind the Devices icon, and if you do, it's probably best to call your trusty system administrator, whose job it is to know more about such arcane matters than you do.

DIAL-UP MONITOR

 If you have Dial-Up Networking or Remote Access Service installed, you may have an icon for the Dial-Up Networking Monitor, which lets you keep tabs on your modem network connection.

DISPLAY

Behind the Display icon are all the settings that affect your screen display, including colors, screen savers, the appearance of windows and dialog boxes, and resolutions. These settings are discussed in Chapter 2.

FONTS

TrueType fonts are managed in NT Workstation in a clear and understandable way. To see the list of fonts on your computer, double-click the Fonts icon in the Control Panel.

Selecting and Viewing Fonts

The Fonts folder is a little different from the usual run of folders in that the menus show some new items. In the View menu, in addition to the choices for viewing icons and lists, you'll find an option called List Fonts By Similarity (see Figure 7.4).

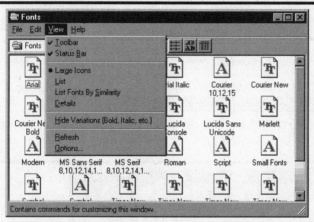

FIGURE 7.4:   The View menu is a little different in the Fonts folder.

TIP

If your font list is very long and unwieldy, select View ➤ Hide Variations. This option conceals font variations, such as bold and italic, and makes the list easier to look through.

If you select the List Fonts By Similarity option and then select a font in the drop-down box at the top of the Fonts folder, the other fonts will line up in terms of their degree of similarity (see Figure 7.5). Before you make a commitment, you can right-click any of the font names and select Open (or just double-click). A window will open with a complete view of the font in question.

TrueType fonts that you may have located elsewhere can be moved into this folder. Figure 7.6 shows a newly acquired font being dragged into the folder.

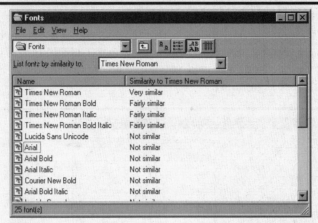

FIGURE 7.5:   Fonts can be listed in terms of their resemblance to one another.

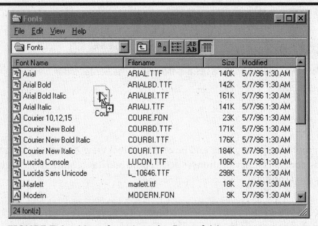

FIGURE 7.6:   Move fonts into the Fonts folder just as you move any object—drag and drop or cut and paste.

Fonts don't have to be physically located in the WINNT/Fonts folder to be recognized by NT Workstation. You can make a shortcut to a font in another folder and put the shortcut in the Fonts folder. The shortcut is all you need for the font to be installed.

Fonts that are identified with an icon containing the letter *A* are not TrueType fonts. They're not *scaleable*, which means they tend to look quite crummy at large point sizes (see Figure 7.7). Many of these fonts can be used only in certain limited point sizes.

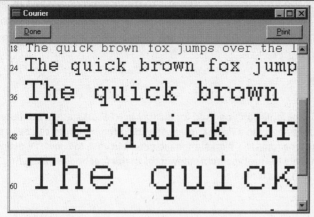

FIGURE 7.7: The non-True Type fonts are not much to look at in the larger sizes.

Installing New Fonts

Installing new fonts is a pretty easy project. Just double-click the Fonts icon in the Control Panel and select Install New Font from the File menu. In the Add Fonts dialog box (see Figure 7.8), you can specify the drive and directory where the font(s) resides. If there's one or more TrueType or PostScript fonts at the location you specify, they'll show up in the List Of Fonts box.

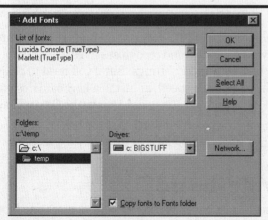

FIGURE 7.8: Here's where you add fonts to the Fonts folder.

Highlight the font or fonts you want to install and click the OK button. Packages like Microsoft's TrueType Fonts for Windows may need to be installed like other programs. Use Add/Remove Programs, described earlier in this chapter.

NOTE

PostScript fonts can't be used for display in NT Workstation, but they can be used for printing to a PostScript-compatible printer, or they can be converted to TrueType fonts. NT Workstation includes a license to convert existing Post-Script fonts to TrueType from many of the major font houses, including Adobe, Bitstream, and others.

INTERNET

If your favorite NT Workstation is connected to the Internet, you can use the Internet icon in the Control Panel to specify a *proxy server*. If you're not sure what a proxy server is and you've never needed one before, chances are you won't have to bother changing these settings. Should the need for a proxy server ever arise, consult your system administrator, who should be able to tell you what the correct settings are.

KEYBOARD

The installation routine of NT Workstation finds the keyboard plugged into your computer and recognizes it, so you normally don't need to fuss with these settings. But if you need to change keyboards, adjust the keyboard's speed, or install a keyboard designed for another language, double-click the Keyboard icon in the Control Panel.

The three tabs on the Keyboard Properties dialog box cover these different types of settings and are explained in the following sections.

Changing Your Keyboard

If you're changing keyboards or NT Workstation recognizes one type of keyboard when in fact you have a different kind, go directly to the General tab. The Keyboard Type box shows what NT Workstation thinks is your keyboard. If it's wrong, click the Change button and follow these steps:

1. On the Select Device page, click Show All Devices.

2. Select the correct keyboard from the list shown. If you have some special installation software, click Have Disk.

3. Click OK. NT Workstation will install the correct keyboard either from your disk or from its own set.

You *may* have to shut down and restart your computer for the keyboard to be completely recognized.

Adjusting Your Keyboard's Speed

Click the Speed tab to adjust keyboard rates. Here are the available settings:

Repeat Delay   Determines how long a key has to be held down before it starts repeating. The difference between the Long and Short settings is only about a second.

Repeat Rate   Determines how fast a key repeats. Fast means if you hold down a key you almost instantly get vvvvvvvvvvvvery long streams of letters. (Click in the Practice area to test this setting.)

Cursor Blink Rate   Makes the cursor blink faster or slower. The blinking cursor on the left demonstrates the setting.

Keyboard Languages

If you need multiple-language support for your keyboard, choose the Input Locales tab. Click the Add button to select languages from Afrikaans to Ukrainian—including 15 varieties of Spanish.

If you have more than one language selected, the settings on the Input Locales tab let you choose a keyboard combination to switch between languages (see Figure 7.9). Highlight the language you want to be the default (the one that's enabled when your start you computer) and click the Set As Default button.

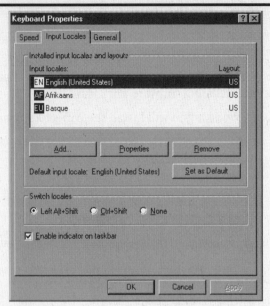

FIGURE 7.9:   Set up your keyboard for more than one language.

Check Enable Indicator On Taskbar, and an icon will appear on your Taskbar. Click the Taskbar icon to instantly switch between languages.

MAIL

The Mail icon will appear in the Control Panel if you opted to install mail services when you installed NT Workstation.

Mail

MICROSOFT MAIL POSTOFFICE

The Microsoft Mail Postoffice icon will appear in the Control Panel if you opted to include Microsoft Mail when you installed mail services. If you have this icon, you can use it to administer

Microsoft Mail
Postoffice

or create a Microsoft Mail Workgroup postoffice. Don't—save this job for your system administrator, who gets paid the big bucks.

MODEMS

Modems

Double-clicking the Modems icon launches the Wizard. You can use it to set up your modems.

MOUSE

Mouse

You can use the Mouse icon to configure the buttons, pointers, and motion of your mouse. The General page lets you select the type of mouse attached to your computer.

MULTIMEDIA

Multimedia

Read Chapter 6 for information about the multimedia applications that come with NT Workstation and how to set them up. The settings behind this icon are covered there as well.

NETWORK

Network

Fortunately or unfortunately, the majority of options that the Network icon offers are unavailable to you unless you're logged on to an account with administrative privileges. These things really *are* the business of the system administrator, whose job it is to keep the network up and running. If other users were allowed to muck around with network settings, the poor system administrator's job would be that much harder, so it's really a good thing that we plain-old users can't put our grubby paws where they don't belong.

If you double-click the Network icon just because you're curious, you'll see the Network pages in *viewing* mode, which means all the buttons that do anything are grayed out. On the Identification page, you'll see the name of your computer and the domain to which it belongs. On the Services, Protocols, and Adapters pages, you'll see a whole lot of arcane settings, so be glad you're not the person who is supposed to know what they all mean.

NOTE

Installing a network adapter is discussed in Chapter 2.

ODBC

The ODBC icon will appear in the Control Panel if you have any database applications installed that provide ODBC (Open Database Connectivity) drivers. If you do, follow the instructions provided with the application or contact your system administrator for more information.

PC CARD

The PC Card icon in the Control Panel enables PCMCIA sockets and allows you to change PC Card settings. This option is relevant only if you have a laptop with a PC Card installed. Chances are if the card was already in the machine when you installed NT Workstation, you'll never have to bother with these settings.

PORTS

The Ports box (see Figure 7.10) displays which ports are currently installed on your NT Workstation, and it lets you view and/or change the settings for a given port. Here, you can also add or delete a port, but consult your system administrator before doing this, since he or she usually knows best about this kind of hardware issue.

PRINTERS

The Printers icon in the Control Panel is a shortcut to your Printers folder (also seen in My Computer and the Explorer). Details on how to install, remove, or change the settings of printers are in Chapter 5.

FIGURE 7.10:   Here's where you can add or delete a port.

REGIONAL SETTINGS

The Regional Settings icon in the Control Panel lets you set the variations in how numbers and the time and date are formatted in different parts of the world. For example, if you're using a program that supports international symbols, changing the Regional Settings can affect how the program displays currency, time, and numbers.

First select the geographic area you want to use on the Regional Settings tab, then confirm or change the individual settings on the other tabs. Your system will have to be rebooted for the settings to take effect system-wide.

SCSI ADAPTERS

This SCSI Adapters icon in the Control Panel lets you add or remove a SCSI adapter and view the properties of any and all SCSI adapters installed in your system. If you double-click the SCSI Adapters icon, highlight the adapter whose properties you want to view, and then click the Properties button, you should see something that looks like Figure 7.11. The settings on these tabs won't mean much to most of us; what's important is that you make sure there's a message on the CardInfo tab that says, "The device is working properly."

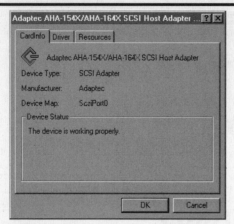

FIGURE 7.11: Viewing the properties of your SCSI adapter

If the device *isn't* working properly, it's time to yell for your system administrator, whose job it is to help you with just this sort of problem. If you notice the buttons on the Driver tab are grayed out, don't panic—this is so you can't accidentally modify the device driver for your SCSI adapter. If you ever need to fiddle with the device driver, contact your system administrator (or anyone else who has the proper administrative privileges).

SERVER

Unless you're logged in using an account with administrative privileges, this Control Panel option is unavailable to you, which makes sense since you don't have permission to view Server properties.

SERVICES

The Services icon on the Control Panel, like the Server icon, shouldn't really concern mere mortals who just happen to be using a networked NT Workstation. These settings are the exclusive purview of the system administrator, who should know better than anyone else how to change them when necessary.

SOUNDS

Sounds

What with NT Workstation's emphasis on multimedia, it's no surprise that using sound with your computer is easier than ever. Double-click the Sounds icon in the Control Panel to set and change sound schemes. (See Chapter 6 for more on sounds.)

NOTE

To play the sounds that come with NT Workstation, you'll need a sound card and speakers (or you'll have to wear headphones all the time).

A Sheet Full of Sounds

The Sounds properties sheet is shown in Figure 7.12. The Events box lists everything on your system associated with a sound. Most are NT Workstation events. For example, opening a program can cause a sound, as can maximizing or minimizing a window and many other actions.

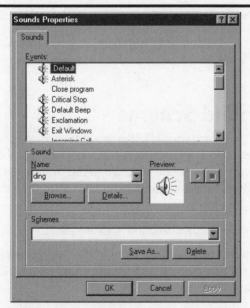

FIGURE 7.12:   Use the Sounds Properties sheet to associate a sound with an event.

Many of the new programs coming out now also include sound capabilities. Their sounds may not end up in the list shown on this sheet because they're configured in the program.

If there's a Speaker icon next to the event, a sound is associated with it. Highlight the event—the name of the sound file will appear in the Name text box—and click the button next to the Preview box to hear its sound.

Sound schemes are included with NT Workstation, and you can choose one of them from the drop-down list.

TIP

If sound schemes don't appear in the Schemes drop-down list, you'll need to install them. Double-click the Add/Remove Programs icon in the Control Panel. In the Windows NT Setup page, double-click Multimedia and select the sound schemes you want. Select OK twice, and then follow the instructions.

Customizing a Sound Scheme

All the sound schemes that come with NT Workstation are nice enough, but none of them is perfect. There are either too many sounds or not enough, or maybe the wrong sounds are attached to the wrong events. Fortunately, there's a way to make as many customized sound schemes as you like. Here's how:

1. Double-click the Sounds icon in the Control Panel.

2. If there's a sound scheme that's close to the one you want, select it from the Schemes drop-down list. Otherwise, select Windows default.

3. In the Events list, select an item that you want a sound associated with.

4. Select a file from the Name drop-down list. To make sure it's the one you want, click the Preview button to hear it.

5. Select (none) from the Name drop-down list for events you want to keep silent.

6. Repeat steps 3–5 until you've completed the list.

7. Select Save As to save this particular assortment of sounds under a specific name. (The new scheme will appear in the Schemes drop-down list.)

TIP

NT Workstation stores all its sound files in the WINNT\Media folder. You'll probably want to move any additional sound files you acquire to that folder. Using a single location makes setting up and changing sound schemes much easier.

SYSTEM

The properties sheet that opens when you double-click the System icon in the Control Panel can also be accessed by right-clicking My Computer and choosing Properties. You won't use most of the settings if your computer is working properly. It's only when things go awry that you need to be changing anything here.

Environment

The Environment page displays information about system and user variables on your NT Workstation. Unless you really know what you're doing, you should never attempt to change any of the settings here. Who knows what might happen if you do?

General

The General page tells you which version of NT Workstation you're using, the registered owner, and a little bit about the type of computer. You'll find the main computer information on this page of the properties sheet.

Hardware Profiles

Hardware profiles are something you may need if you're using a portable computer with a docking station. In a limited number of circumstances, you may need to configure alternate setups when the hardware on your system changes. If you think this might be your situation, consult the NT Workstation Help files and/or your system administrator for instructions.

Performance

On this page, you'll see two entries (see Figure 7.13). The first is for Application Performance. By default, the slider is set to Maximum, which means the active application (the foreground application) will get the most attention from the processor. You can move the slider to the left to get more processor power for any background applications, but be aware that it may slow down the program you're actually working in.

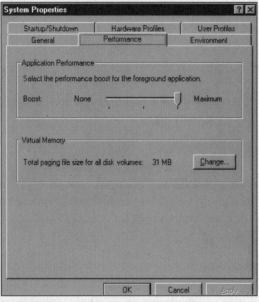

FIGURE 7.13:   The Performance tab lets you adjust the amount of time your active application gets from the processor.

The second setting is for Virtual Memory. Don't mess with this unless you're sure you know what you're doing or if the operating system tells you to change the setting. NT Workstation is very good at determining how much virtual memory it needs. It's a losing game to try to outsmart the system.

Startup/Shutdown

The Startup/Shutdown page allows you to specify startup and shutdown options, such as which operating system should be the default when you boot up your computer and what should happen in case you experience a dreaded STOP error (most of us just call our friendly neighborhood system administrator; that's what he or she is there for!).

NOTE

This Startup/Shutdown page won't be present in your Control Panel unless you're running multiple operating systems on one computer.

User Profiles

The User Profiles tab lets you switch between two different types of user profiles, which are files that contain Desktop settings and other information related to your NT Workstation logon. Just in case you're wondering, a user profile is created for you when you log on to your favorite NT Workstation computer for the first time. If you often use different computers, a different (local) user profile can be created on each computer you use, or you can set up what's called a *roaming user profile* that is the same on every computer you use. By default, a *user profile* is a local profile. If you'd like to try using a roaming profile, ask your system administrator to arrange this for you.

TAPE DEVICES

Tape Devices   The Tape Devices icon on the Control Panel displays information about any tape device(s) installed on your system and the drivers that run them. Since your system administrator is presumably the one who is responsible for hardware and any problems therewith, it's a good idea here (as elsewhere) to look but not touch.

NOTE
Adding tape devices is discussed in Chapter 2.

TELEPHONY

Telephony

Double-clicking the Telephony icon on the Control Panel leads you to two pages whose contents relate to your modem's dialing properties and the drivers it uses to communicate with other computers.

UPS

Unless you're logged in using an account with administrative privileges, this Control Panel option is unavailable to you, which makes sense since you don't have permission to configure a UPS, or *uninterruptible power supply*, in case you were wondering what the initials stand for!

NOTE
UPS settings are discussed in Chapter 2.

WHAT'S NEXT?

This chapter provided a tour of the Control Panel. The next chapter covers data sharing on the NT platform. You'll learn the techniques for using the Clipboard, the ClipBook, and OLE.

Chapter 8

SHARING DATA BETWEEN APPLICATIONS

As you know, you can run several applications at one time and switch between them with a click of the mouse or a press of Alt+Tab. You may also know that you can cut, copy, and paste information between programs and documents, embedding bits and pieces of information, graphics, sound, and video from multiple sources into a single destination source to create complex documents. Previously disparate types of information are beginning to merge into a new synthesis, evidenced by products such as CD-ROM-based interactive encyclopedias, in-car electronic guidance (map) systems, and voice-controlled telephone systems. All these capabilities are outgrowths of the desire to mix and match heretofore unrelated kinds of data.

As a result of the standardization of the Windows interface and API, users have become accustomed to being able to cut,

Adapted from *Mastering™ Windows® NT® Workstation 4* by Mark Minasi and Todd Phillips
ISBN 0-7821-2491-7   1152 pages $49.99

copy, and paste not only within a given program but between Windows programs. Nowadays, thousands of applications can easily share data with one another through these commands that use the Windows Clipboard.

But we still have the problem of proprietary file and data formats—the kind of thing that makes a WordPerfect file different from a Word for Windows file or a Microsoft Excel file different from a Lotus 1-2-3 file. These proprietary formats often seem to be promoted by software developers as a means of pushing their programs by locking users into a particular file format. Unfortunately, the proprietary-file-formats marketing strategy has backfired, leaving users grumbling and feeling held hostage by a particular brand of program.

For example, just try printing, say, a JPEG graphics file from your favorite word processor or desktop publishing program. The situation becomes even thornier when multimedia files are thrown in. We are now seeing competing formats for live-motion video, audio recording, MIDI files, and the like.

Software developers have finally figured this out, and they have made working with "foreign" file formats much easier. With each new month, more applications have built-in file-format converters to enable applications to share files. For example, Word for Windows 6 and 7 can read and write a whole gaggle of text and graphics file formats. Ditto for PageMaker, Ventura Publisher, Microsoft Access, and many others. Standards such as Rich Text Format (RTF), Windows Metafiles, and others are now emerging to facilitate data transfers between programs. Embedded TrueType fonts and utility programs such as Adobe Acrobat even enable people to see and edit documents containing fonts that are not in their systems.

In this chapter, we look at data sharing on the NT platform, paying particular attention to the techniques you can use to create complex documents, including the latest in Windows data sharing: OLE version 2.

EXCHANGING DATA WITH NT

Actually, much more interesting than simply being able to use one program's document in another program is the ability to mix and match a great variety of document types, such as text, sound, graphics, spreadsheets, databases, and so forth. This mixing and matching lets you construct complex documents previously requiring physical cutting and pasting and possibly the aid of an art department. Such operations are dependent on the operating system's capacity to exchange data between dissimilar applications, such as between spreadsheets and word processors.

NT offers three internal vehicles for exchanging data between programs: the Windows Clipboard (and ClipBook, which is an extension of Clipboard), Dynamic Data Exchange (DDE), and Object Linking and Embedding (OLE). In this chapter, we explain each of them, discuss how NT's treatment of them differs from other versions of Windows, and then describe some special considerations for data sharing across the network.

If you're new to Windows applications, you may want to read only the portion about the Clipboard and the Cut, Copy, and Paste commands. You'll use these commands much more often than the other techniques covered here. If you're using a network and want to share little bits of information with other people, then read about the ClipBook, too. If you want to take full advantage of what OLE has to offer under Windows, read the entire chapter. Using OLE, you can construct complex documents by putting, say, a portion of a spreadsheet or a fancy chart into a word processor document.

NOTE

Many of the examples in this chapter refer to Microsoft products. This isn't necessarily an endorsement of Microsoft products over other competing products! We're just using the most common examples to reach the widest audience, and the most commonly used products just happen to be Microsoft products.

USING THE CLIPBOARD

Although the Clipboard is not capable of converting data files between various formats (such as .xls to .wk3 or .rtf to .doc), it is great for many everyday data-exchange tasks. Just about all Windows programs support the use of the ubiquitous Cut, Copy, and Paste commands, and it's the Clipboard that provides this functionality for you.

The Clipboard makes it possible to move any kind of material—whether it's text, data cells, graphics, video, or audio clips—and OLE objects between documents and, with NT, between folders, the Desktop, Explorer, and other portions of the interface. The form of the source data doesn't matter that much. The Clipboard and Windows together take care of figuring out what's being copied and where it's being pasted, making adjustments when necessary or providing just a few manual options for you to adjust. The Clipboard can also work with non-Windows (DOS) programs, albeit with certain limitations that we explain later.

Understanding How the Clipboard Works

How does the Clipboard work? It's simple. The Clipboard is built into NT and uses a portion of the system's internal resources (RAM and virtual memory) as a temporary holding tank for material you're working with. For example, suppose you cut some text from one part of a document in preparation for pasting it into another location. NT stores the text on the Clipboard and waits for you to paste it into its new home.

The last item you copied or cut is stored in this no-man's-land somewhere in the computer until you cut or copy something else, exit NT, or intentionally clear the Clipboard. As a result, you can paste the Clipboard's contents any number of times.

You can examine the Clipboard's contents using the ClipBook utility supplied with NT. If you've used Windows for Workgroups or an earlier version of Windows NT, you'll be familiar with this application. You can also use this application to save the Clipboard's contents to disk for later use or to share specific bits of data for use by others on your network.

Selecting, Copying, and Cutting in Windows Applications

In NT, the earlier Windows standards and procedures for copying, cutting, and pasting apply, because NT supports all the Windows calls for these services. Even if you're mixing and matching 16-bit and 32-bit applications, the Clipboard works just fine, because in the internals of NT, the 16-bit subsystem shares the same Clipboard as the 32-bit section.

When running NT, you simply use each application's Edit menu (or the Edit menu's shortcut keys) for copying, cutting, and pasting. These tasks work just as they did in earlier versions of Windows. Figure 8.1 illustrates copying and pasting in a Windows program.

Select an item and
choose Cut or Copy

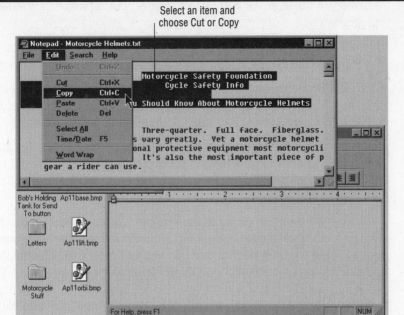

Move to a destination
and choose Paste

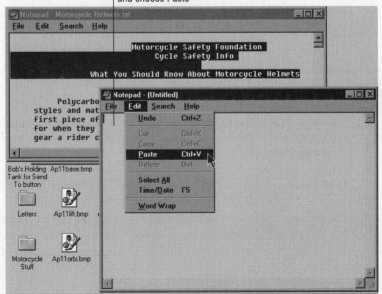

FIGURE 8.1: Copying and pasting in a Windows program using Edit menu
commands

Here are the steps for cutting, copying, or pasting within a Windows program:

1. Arrange the windows on the screen as necessary, particularly so you can see the window containing the source information.

2. Select the information you want to copy or cut, such as text, a graphic, spreadsheet cells, or whatever. In many programs, simply clicking an object, such as a graphic, selects it.

3. Open the application's Edit menu and choose Copy or Cut, depending on whether you want to copy the material or delete the original with the intention of pasting it into another location.

4. Position the cursor at the location where you want to insert the item in the destination document (which may or may not be in the source document) you're working in. This might mean scrolling the document up or down, switching to another application using the Taskbar, or switching to another document within the same application via its Window menu.

5. Open the Edit menu and choose Paste. Whatever material was on the Clipboard is now dropped into the new location. Normally, this means any preexisting material, such as text, is moved down to make room for the item you just pasted.

NOTE

In Windows applications, the standard shortcut keys are Ctrl+X, Ctrl+C, and Ctrl+V for cutting, copying, and pasting, respectively. Some programs may have other shortcuts, which you can find in the manual or Help screens supplied with the program.

When pasting graphics, you'll typically need to reposition the graphic after pasting, rather than before. For example, Figure 8.2 shows a graphic (a picture of the Earth as taken from the moon on the Apollo 11 mission) just after it was pasted into the Paint window from which it was copied. It appears in the upper-left corner, waiting to be dragged to its new home.

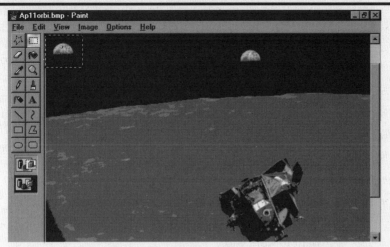

FIGURE 8.2:   Graphics applications typically accept pasted information into their upper-left corner, where it waits to be repositioned.

Copying Text and Graphics from a DOS Box

With NT, you can also copy selected graphics from DOS programs. This is a pretty nifty trick for lifting material out of your favorite DOS program and dropping it into a Windows document. There's only one caveat: The DOS program must be running in a window, not full-screen.

When you cut or copy selected material from the DOS box, it gets dumped into the Clipboard as text or graphics, depending on which mode NT determines the DOS box (*box* means window) was emulating. NT knows whether the application is running in character mode or graphics mode and processes the data on the Clipboard accordingly. If text mode is detected, the material is copied as characters that could be dropped into, say, a word processor document. If the DOS application has set up a graphics mode in the DOS box (because of the application's video requests), you'll get a bitmapped graphic in the destination document when you paste.

As you may know, some fancy DOS programs may look as though they are displaying text when they're really running in graphics mode. For example, WordPerfect for DOS and Microsoft Word for DOS can both run in a graphics mode that displays text attributes such as underline, italics, and bold, rather than as boring block letters displayed in colors that indicate these attributes. When you copy text from such a program and then paste it into another document, you'll be surprised to find you've pasted a graphic, not text. This means you can't edit it like text because it's being treated like a bitmapped graphic. The solution is to switch the DOS application back to text mode and try again. (Refer to your DOS program manual for help.)

The procedure for copying from a DOS box (also known as a command prompt window) under NT is simple, once you know where the Edit ➢ Copy and Edit ➢ Paste menu options are located. Unfortunately, NT doesn't have a toolbar on DOS boxes (as does Windows 95). To access the Edit menu options, *single*-click the upper-left corner icon or press Alt+spacebar.

Here are the steps to copying in a DOS box:

1. Switch to the DOS application and display the material you want to work with.

2. Make sure the application is running in a window, rather than running full-screen. If it's not, press Alt+Enter. (Each press of Alt+Enter toggles any DOS window between full and windowed view.)

3. Open the DOS box's System menu by single-clicking the upper-left corner icon or by pressing Alt+spacebar. The following graphic shows the icon being clicked.

4. Select Edit from the System menu. This pops up a side menu of Edit choices; choose Mark from this menu. As soon as you choose it, the DOS box's title bar changes to read *Mark*. Once you start marking the selection, the word *Select* precedes the program's name in the title bar, indicating that you're in select mode. Pressing the Enter key (or Esc to cancel) terminates the selection process.

NOTE

Notice that there isn't a Cut option for the DOS box. This is because you can't cut from a DOS application in this way. You cut using the DOS program's editing keys, and the DOS program won't interact with the NT Clipboard.

Part i

5. Hold down the mouse button and drag the pointer over the desired copy area, dragging from upper left to lower right. As you do so, the color of the selection changes to indicate what you're marking.

6. Release the mouse button. The selected area stays highlighted.

7. Press the Enter key. The information is now on the Clipboard.

That's all there is to copying information from an application that's running in the DOS box. Of course, the standard procedure applies to pasting what was just copied. You just switch to the destination application (which, incidentally, can be a DOS or a Windows program), position the cursor, and choose Edit ➤ Paste to paste the Clipboard's contents at the cursor position. (For a DOS application as the destination, you use the Paste option on the DOS box's Edit submenu, as explained later in this chapter.)

TIP

One rather unique advantage of the way a DOS box lets you drag a selection rectangle is that it lets you copy *columns* of text without automatically including text to the left of your text block. Interestingly, not many Windows word processors let you access columns of text this easily; almost all of them select text in a wrap-around fashion, automatically extending the selection rectangle out to both margins as you drag downward. (Programmers out there, take note!)

Capturing Screens with the Clipboard

As in earlier versions of Windows and NT, you can capture all or part of a screen image while running an application. Screen captures are useful for creating program documentation, software education materials, or promotional material about software.

The Clipboard is handy for capturing screen images in lieu of purchasing a special-purpose screen-capture program. The price is right, and it works, albeit with some limitations.

Although you can't edit your files or make changes such as adding borders when using this economy approach to captures, you can save a file to disk for later use. The Clipboard and the ClipBook both let you save files to disk. See the "Storing the Clipboard's Contents in a File" and "Using the ClipBook Instead of the Clipboard" sections later in this chapter for more information.

TIP

Professional programs designed for screen capture help you organize, crop, and edit your screen captures, among other things. If you regularly do screen captures, you might want to check these programs out. We used Collage Complete for the screens in this book. Other programs you might want to explore are Tiffany, PixelPop, Hotshot, and Hijaak. These programs give you a lot of latitude with capture techniques, file formats, color settings, grayscaling, and so forth, which the Clipboard doesn't allow.

With the Clipboard, you have just two options when capturing: You can capture the entire screen or just the active window. Whether you're capturing a DOS or Windows-based application, the capture is converted to bitmapped format for pasting into graphics programs, such as Page-Maker and Paint.

To copy the active window's image onto the Clipboard, do the following (note that if a dialog box is open, this is usually considered the *active* window):

1. With the application whose screen you want to capture open and running in a window, adjust and size the window as desired.

2. Press Alt+Print Screen. The image of the active window is copied to the Clipboard.

NOTE

Most computers work with the Alt+Print Screen key combination. However, some older PC keyboards use slightly different codes, requiring the user to press Shift+Print Screen instead.

Instead of copying the active window, you might want to capture a picture of the entire screen. To do this, set up the screen as described above, and then press Print Screen (instead of Alt+Print Screen). The image will be copied to the Clipboard. (See the following discussion about pasting the Clipboard contents.)

Using the Paste Command

After you have some information on the Clipboard, NT offers you several options for working with it. (In Windows 3.x, only two of these were possible, but NT incorporates the ClipBook facility that was previously part of Windows for Workgroups, so now there are three.) Here are the three routes you can take:

- ▶ Paste the information into a document you're working with (or that you open subsequently).

- ▶ Save it to a Clipboard (.clp) file that you can use later.

- ▶ Save it on a ClipBook page for later use or for sharing over the network.

The last two choices are described later in this chapter. For standard pasting, there are two options:

- ▶ You can paste information into Windows applications.

- ▶ You can paste into DOS applications (when they are in a window rather than running full-screen).

Let's look at these two individually because they require distinctly different techniques.

Pasting into Windows Applications

As you are probably aware, the great majority of Windows applications' Edit menus include a Paste command. As the name implies, this is the command you use to paste material from the Clipboard into your documents. Of course, this command isn't available unless something is already on the Clipboard that can be accepted by the document you're working with at the time.

NOTE

To accommodate proprietary data types and large amounts of data, some heavier-duty programs have their own internal Clipboard that's not connected at all to the system's Clipboard. Word for Windows, for example, has its own large Clipboard that it uses when you cut or copy a large bulk of material. In such an application, data you thought you were making available to the entire NT system might *not* be. But this caveat applies less to 32-bit applications than it does to 16-bit ones. We can expect the 32-bit internals of NT—along with more intelligent memory management—to render its system-wide Clipboard both more intelligent and larger in capacity than its predecessor's Clipboard.

Here's the basic approach for pasting information from the Clipboard (there may be some variation from application to application, but the basic procedure is the same), after you have cut or copied material there:

1. Switch to the destination program or document—the one that will receive the information.

2. Position the cursor or insertion point. In a text-based program this means position the I-beam cursor where you want it and click the primary mouse button.

3. Choose Edit ➤ Paste or (in most programs) press Ctrl+V. The Clipboard's contents appear in the destination window.

The Clipboard's contents remain static until you copy or cut something new, so repeated pasting of the same material is possible. Just keep selecting insertion points and choosing Edit ➤ Paste or pressing Ctrl+V.

Pasting into a DOS Box

As weird as this seems, you can also paste into DOS applications—weird because most DOS applications were invented way before the Windows Clipboard was even a twinkle in Bill Gates' eye. There are certain limitations to this technique, such as pasting only text (no graphics). This is for obvious reasons—pasting graphics into a DOS application would be a nightmare. It simply wouldn't work because there is no standard agreement among DOS applications as to the treatment of on-screen graphics. Even with text, the results of pasting may be less than expected, because all DOS applications don't accept data the same way.

You should be aware that all text formatting will be lost when you paste text into a DOS document. This is because formatting (bold, italics, fonts, bullets, and so forth) is application-specific information (specially coded for each program), and most applications just don't speak the same language at this point.

TIP

Although you can't paste graphics directly into DOS applications, here's a way to work around that: Simply paste the graphic into a Windows-based graphics program such as Paint or Corel Draw. Then save the graphic in a file that's readable by the DOS graphics program. Most DOS programs can read .bmp or .pcx files, and most Windows graphics programs can save files in these formats.

When it comes time to do the pasting into a DOS application, here are the steps:

1. Put the desired text on the Clipboard by cutting or copying it from somewhere.

2. Toggle the destination DOS application so it's a window (it won't work if the DOS box is full-screen size).

3. Position the DOS application's cursor at the location where you want to insert the Clipboard's material. This *must* be the location where you would next type text into the DOS document.

4. Open the DOS box's System menu (press Alt+spacebar), and select Edit ➤ Paste.

Figure 8.3 shows an example in which we're about to insert Clipboard text into a DOS text-based program (my apologies to H.W. Longfellow).

The process of pasting into a DOS box is interesting. The text on the Clipboard is sent to the portion of the operating system that's responsible for buffering keyboard data entry. When you paste, the application thinks you have typed in the new text from the keyboard. For the procedure to work correctly, however, the recipient program must be written in such a way that it doesn't balk at receiving information at the speed a supernormal typist could enter it.

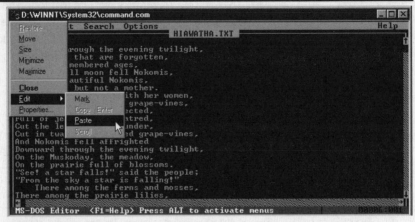

FIGURE 8.3: To paste text into a DOS application running in a window, select Edit, then Paste from the DOS box's System menu.

TIP

If you use the DOS box (command prompt) often, consider using the Edit ➤ Copy command to copy long and unwieldy pathnames from the DOS prompt to the Clipboard. You can then paste these into a File Save, Start Run, or Create Shortcut dialog box and spare yourself some typing.

Using Right-Click Shortcuts for Cut, Copy, and Paste

As mentioned earlier, the cut, copy, and paste scheme is implemented throughout NT, even on the Desktop, in Explorer, in folder windows, and so forth. This is done using right-mouse-button shortcuts. Some applications are also starting to offer this feature.

For example, right-clicking a file in a folder window and choosing Copy puts a pointer to the file on the Clipboard. Right-clicking another location, such as the Desktop, and choosing Paste drops the file there (on the Desktop). This shortcut is being pushed by Microsoft and is included in some of its applications such as Word and Excel. Expect to see it included in applications from other makers, particularly 32-bit NT applications.

Try right-clicking icons or selected text or graphics in applications to see if there is a shortcut menu. Figure 8.4 shows an example of copying some text from a Word for Windows document using this shortcut.

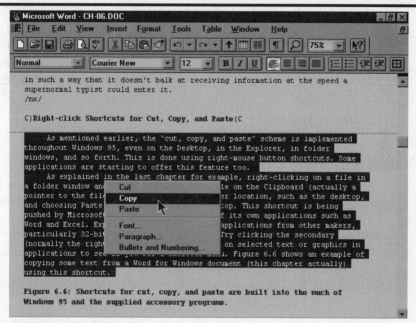

FIGURE 8.4:   Shortcuts for Cut, Copy, and Paste are built into NT via the right-click menu. Windows applications are beginning to implement this feature, too, as you see here in Word for Windows.

WORKING WITH THE CLIPBOARD VIEWER

After data is on the Clipboard, you might not want to paste it immediately, or you might want to see what's there. Two programs supplied with NT Workstation make this easy. One is called Clipboard Viewer, and the other is ClipBook Viewer. You can find one or both in the Accessories folder (choose Start ➤ Programs ➤ Accessories ➤ ClipBook Viewer or

Clipboard Viewer). These programs let you do some useful Clipboard-related tasks, such as:

▶ View the Clipboard's contents.

▶ Save and retrieve the Clipboard's contents to or from a file.

▶ Clear the Clipboard's contents.

▶ Set up pages of the Clipboard, with each page storing information you plan to use later or want to make available to networked colleagues.

Let's look at each of these simple tasks in order.

Viewing the Clipboard's Contents

You may simply forget what information is on the Clipboard; you don't remember what you cut or copied last. Before you go ahead and paste it into an application (especially if that application doesn't have an Undo command), you might want to check out what will be inserted. Viewing the Clipboard's contents is also useful when you've tried to get a particular item into the Clipboard and don't know how successful you've been. Bringing up the Viewer and positioning it off in the corner of the screen can give you instant feedback as you cut and copy.

NOTE

Both the Clipboard Viewer and ClipBook Viewer let you see the Clipboard's contents. You may have both programs in your Accessories folder. The procedure below explains the ClipBook approach. If you have only the Clipboard Viewer, the steps are quite similar. Simply run Clipboard Viewer instead of ClipBook Viewer and skip step 2.

Here's how to view the Clipboard's contents:

1. Click the Start button and choose Programs ➤ Accessories ➤ ClipBook Viewer to open the ClipBook Viewer window.

2. Double-click the Clipboard icon in the bottom-left corner of the window or open the Window menu and choose Clipboard. The ClipBook icon turns into a window, displaying the Clipboard's current contents. Figure 8.5 shows typical Clipboard contents, in this case, a portion of an image just copied from the Paint program.

FIGURE 8.5:   The Clipboard's contents (in this case an image) can be displayed in a window within the Clipboard Viewer or within the ClipBook Viewer. The views are virtually the same; here we're using the Clip-Book Viewer.

Changing the View Format

It's possible that the contents of the Clipboard will look different in the Viewer window than they do in the application you copied or cut it from. For example, graphics may appear mottled or distorted, and text may appear with incorrect line breaks, fonts, and so forth. Graphics and text can contain substantial amounts of formatting, such as font type and size, indents, colors, resolution settings, grayscaling, and so on. But there are some limitations to the amount of information that will be transferred through the Clipboard. It's the job of the source application to inform NT, and thus the Clipboard, of the nature of the material. The Clipboard tries its best to keep all the relevant information, but it doesn't necessarily display it all in the Viewer window.

Let's take an example. A Paint picture can be passed onto another application as what NT calls a bitmap, a picture, or a Windows Enhanced Metafile. (In addition to this, there can be information that pertains to OLE, but these aspects don't appear in the Viewer window.) When you first view the Clipboard's contents, the Viewer does its best to display the contents so they look as much as possible like the original. However, this isn't a fail-safe method, so there may be times when you'll want to try changing the view. To do this:

1. Open the View menu (or the Display menu in Clipboard Viewer).

2. Check out the available options. They'll vary depending on what you have stored on the Clipboard. Choose one and see how it affects the display. None of the options affect the Clipboard contents—only its display. The Default setting (called Default Format) returns the view to the original display format.

NOTE

When you paste into another Windows application, the destination program tries to determine the best format for accepting whatever is on the Clipboard. If the Edit menu on the destination application is grayed out, you can safely assume that the contents are not acceptable. Changing the Clipboard's view format as described above won't rectify the situation; it doesn't have any effect on how material is pasted.

Storing the Clipboard's Contents in a File

When you place new material onto the Clipboard, reboot, or shut down the computer, the Clipboard contents are lost. Also, because the Clipboard itself is not *network-aware* (meaning it can't interact with other workstations on the network), you can't share the Clipboard's contents with other network users. You'll want to take advantage of ClipBook pages for that, as described later in the chapter. However, you can save the Clipboard's contents to a disk file. Clipboard files have the extension .clp. After the Clipboard's contents are stored in a disk file, it's like any other disk file—you can later reload the file from disk. If you do a lot of work with clip-art and bits and pieces of sound, video, text, and the like, this technique can come in handy. Also, if you give network users access to your .clp file directory, they can, in effect, use your Clipboard.

TIP

The Clipboard .clp files use a proprietary file format; no other popular programs can use these files. So, to use a .clp file, you *must* open it in Clipboard before pasting it where you want it to appear. If this is a hassle for you, then you're a prime candidate for using the Clip*Book* instead, because its way of archiving little things that you'll regularly want to paste is more convenient. The ClipBook is discussed in detail a little later, in the section "Using the Clip-Book Instead of the Clipboard."

Here's how to save a Clipboard file:

1. Make sure you have run the ClipBook Viewer or Clipboard Viewer, as explained in the previous section.

2. Activate the Clipboard window within the ClipBook Viewer. The easiest way to do this is to choose Clipboard from the Window menu. You can also double-click the Clipboard icon if you see it at the bottom of the ClipBook Viewer window.

3. Choose File ➤ Save As. A standard Save As dialog box appears.

4. Enter a name. As usual, you can change the folder, name, and extension. Leave the extension as .clp, because Clipboard uses this as a default when you later want to reload the file.

5. Click the OK button, as you see in the following dialog box. The file is saved and can be loaded again.

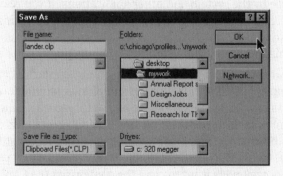

Retrieving the Contents of a Stored Clipboard File

After the . c l p file is on disk, you can reload it. However, you should be aware that when you reload a . c l p file, anything currently on the Clipboard will be lost.

Follow these steps to open your saved Clipboard file:

1. Run ClipBook Viewer.

2. Choose Clipboard from the Window menu.

3. Choose File ➤ Open. The Open dialog box appears.

4. Select the file you want to pull onto the Clipboard. (Only legitimate . c l p files can be opened.)

5. If there's something already on the Clipboard, you are asked if you want to erase it. Click the OK button.

6. Change the display format via the View menu if you want to (assuming there are options available on the menu).

7. Paste the contents into the desired destination.

Clearing the Clipboard to Save Resources

While you're using the Clipboard, keep in mind that the information you store there, even temporarily, can affect the amount of memory available for use by the system and other applications. If you're cutting and pasting small bits of text and graphics as most people do during the course of a workday, this shouldn't be a concern, especially because NT's new memory management is more efficient than its predecessor's.

But some items you might place on the Clipboard can be large. For example, graphics, video, sound samples, or large amounts of formatted text take up considerable space on the Clipboard. Some items are stored in a number of formats for pasting into different kinds of destinations and thus may be more memory-hogging than you might expect. The moral of the story is that if you're running into memory shortages, you may occasionally want to clear the contents of the Clipboard using the technique described here.

NOTE

In Windows 3.1 or NT 3.x, you could get an idea of how much system memory an item on the Clipboard was occupying by switching to Program Manager or File Manager and choosing Help ➤ About. The dialog box told you how much memory and user resources were available. NT isn't as informative. Many of the About dialog boxes that reported free memory under Windows 3.x now simply report the total amount of RAM your system has. NT utility programs that monitor and report memory usage will probably begin to appear on the market. In the meantime, you can run the Task Manager (right-click an empty region of your Taskbar) if you really need to keep track of memory usage.

To clear the Clipboard, follow these steps:

1. From ClipBook Viewer, select the Clipboard view by double-clicking the Clipboard icon or clicking its window.

2. Click the X in the toolbar or choose Edit ➤ Delete.

3. Click the OK button in the dialog box that appears to clear the Clipboard. The Clipboard's contents are deleted.

USING THE CLIPBOOK INSTEAD OF THE CLIPBOARD

Although it's very handy, the Clipboard does have several drawbacks. The most obvious of these are:

▶ Sharing information on the Clipboard with network users can't be done easily.

▶ Copying or cutting a new item erases the previous one, so you're limited to one item on the Clipboard at a time.

▶ Saving and retrieving Clipboard files is a hassle. Accessing, say, several small sound clips or clip-art pictures requires giving each one a .clp filename and later remembering their names so you can reload them.

So, what to do? Well, as we mentioned earlier, there's an application called the ClipBook that works much like the Clipboard, but it has more features. The ClipBook first made an appearance in Windows for Workgroups. Then it came out in 32-bit form in NT, and now it's in Windows NT Workstation 4. The ClipBook offers the following advantages over the Clipboard:

▸ You can store Clipboard memory on *pages* within the ClipBook. There can be as many as 127 of these pages, each one acting like a separate Clipboard.

▸ You can give each ClipBook page a description to help you remember what it contains. The description can be up to 47 characters long. This means you can give a page a name such as "Joe's logo version 10."

▸ You can share all or selected pages of your ClipBook for use by colleagues at other network workstations.

▸ You can display thumbnail representations of each page so you can visually scan many pages of your ClipBook at once to find the one you want.

Running the ClipBook

If you've been following the steps in this chapter, you already know how to run the ClipBook Viewer. This program is your connection to the ClipBook, just as it is to the Clipboard. The only difference is that you select the ClipBook window rather than the Clipboard window. Do this from the Window menu by choosing Local ClipBook.

Figure 8.6 identifies the buttons available to you on the ClipBook Viewer's toolbar, and the following list describes their use.

Connect   Connects to a ClipBook on a remote (networked computer).

Disconnect   Disconnects from a ClipBook on a remote (networked) computer.

Share   Shares a page of your ClipBook for network users to access.

Stop Sharing   Stops sharing a page.

Copy   Pastes a selected ClipBook page to the Clipboard.

Paste   Pastes the contents of the Clipboard to the ClipBook.

Delete   Deletes the contents of a selected page (or of the Clipboard if it's showing).

Table of Contents   Lists the named pages in the ClipBook.

Thumbnails   Displays thumbnails of the ClipBook's pages.

Full Page   Displays a selected ClipBook page.

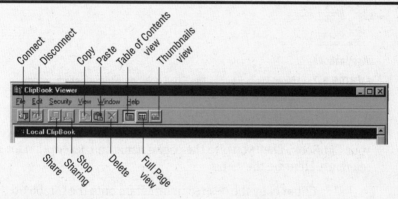

FIGURE 8.6:   The buttons available on the ClipBook Viewer's toolbar

Pasting Items into the ClipBook

The ClipBook doesn't replace the Clipboard; it simply works in concert with it. In NT, cutting, copying, and pasting within and between your various applications is still orchestrated by the Clipboard. The ClipBook supplies a convenient repository for Clipboard items—items that would normally be wiped out of the Clipboard when you shut down Windows or when you copy something new onto the Clipboard. Figure 8.7 illustrates the relationship of the Clipboard to the ClipBook.

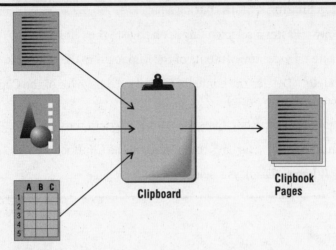

Applications

FIGURE 8.7:   Items are added to the ClipBook by pasting them from the Clipboard.

To use the ClipBook, you paste an item onto one of the 127 pages in your ClipBook. Then you give the page a name and description for later reference. Here are the steps:

1. Cut or copy the desired information onto the Clipboard.

2. Run or switch to the ClipBook Viewer.

3. At this point, it doesn't matter whether the Clipboard or Local ClipBook window is the active window. Choose Edit ➢ Paste from within the ClipBook Viewer. A Paste dialog box appears, asking for a name for the new page. Each time you paste into the ClipBook, you need to name the page. You can name the page anything you like, using up to 47 characters. So you could name a page "This is a silly picture of an elephant." The Paste dialog box is shown below.

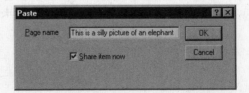

4. If you want to make the new ClipBook page immediately available to other users on the network (if you're on a network), click the Share Item Now box to turn it on. This brings up another dialog box, which asks how you want to share the item. See the upcoming section, "Sharing Your ClipBook Pages with Network Users," for details.

After you've stowed away your items on ClipBook pages, how do you use them again? No problem. You can easily paste them into documents or share them for use by others on your network. Let's take these two situations separately.

Pasting Items from the ClipBook

Here's how to paste something from the ClipBook into a document you're working on. Suppose you've saved a piece of clip-art on a page and now you want to paste it:

1. Run ClipBook Viewer (or switch to it, if it's already running).

2. Display the Local ClipBook window by double-clicking it or by opening the Window menu and choosing Local ClipBook. You can change the display from Thumbnail view to List view (whoops, I mean Table of Contents) from the View menu or from the toolbar. Figure 8.8 shows a typical view of pages.

3. Select the page containing the information you want by clicking its thumbnail or name.

4. Within ClipBook Viewer, click the Paste button, or choose Edit ➤ Copy. This copies the particular ClipBook page onto the Clipboard.

5. Switch to the application you want to paste into. Position the cursor or do any setup in that application that might be necessary, and then choose Edit ➤ Paste from that application. Windows should now paste in the item.

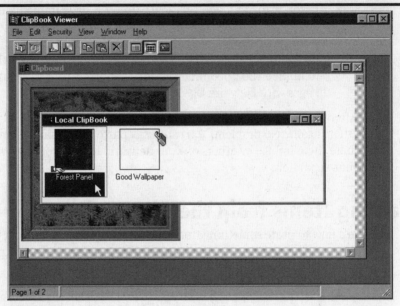

FIGURE 8.8: To paste a ClipBook page, start by clicking it to select it. You can then copy and paste it into the destination application. The Clipboard is used as an intermediary.

Sharing Your ClipBook Pages with Network Users

When you want to share a ClipBook page so others on the network can link or copy it into their documents, do the following:

1. Run or switch to ClipBook Viewer.

2. View the Local ClipBook (via the Window menu).

3. Select the item you want to share. If you want to examine the item before sharing it, click the Full Page button.

TIP

You can quickly toggle between Full Page and Thumbnail or Table of Contents view by double-clicking an item.

4. Choose File ➤ Share. You'll see the following dialog box with
    options for sharing.

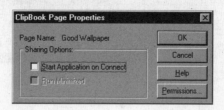

5. Note the Start Application on Connect checkbox. You need
    to check this box if the data on the ClipBook page is anything
    more complex than a bitmap or unformatted text. If you
    don't, network users won't be able to access the data. When
    the option is selected, the source application will run when
    a remote user accesses the specific page. If you don't want
    the running of the application to interrupt your work by
    opening a window on the serving workstation, check the Run
    Minimized box.

TIP

If you're in doubt about whether to turn on the Start Application on Connect
option, share the page with the setting turned off and let others try to use it. If
this doesn't work, turn the setting on.

6. Unless you specify otherwise, pages are shared with a type of
    Full Control permission. This means other people can erase
    or edit the page as well as copy it. If you want to prevent oth-
    ers from editing or erasing the page, click the Permissions
    button. You can specify users and user groups who will have
    access, and set whether they have read-only, read-and-link,
    or change permission, as shown in Figure 8.9. You can even
    enable auditing of ClipBook pages and have specific page
    accesses (and attempted accesses) logged, as shown in Fig-
    ure 8.10.

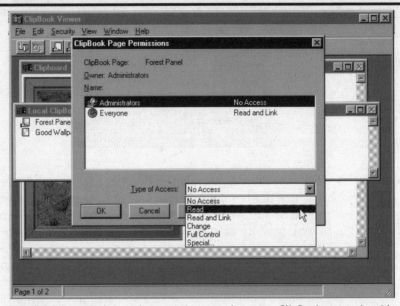

FIGURE 8.9: NT's heavy-duty security extends even to ClipBook pages. As with files, printers, and so on, you can specify which users and groups have access to your pages, and how extensive this access should be.

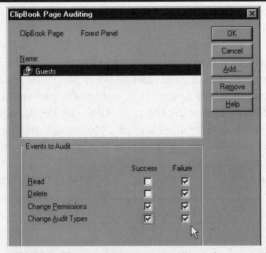

FIGURE 8.10: In addition to controlling who can access your ClipBook pages, NT's auditing lets you keep a log of who has accessed (or tried to access) your pages.

Connecting to a Shared ClipBook Page

So much for creating your own ClipBook pages, using them locally (that means on your computer), and sharing them with other network users. What about connecting to another network station's ClipBook to use those pages? And by the same token, how do other users connect to your ClipBook pages after you've shared them?

It's a relatively straightforward process. You simply use the File ➢ Connect command in the ClipBook Viewer to browse the network and connect to the desired station and page. Then you use the pages as if they were your own. Here are the steps:

1. Run ClipBook Viewer and open the local ClipBook window.

2. Open the File menu and click Connect.

3. Browse to select the computer whose ClipBook has the information you want, or type in its name.

4. Click the OK button. If a password is required for the remote ClipBook, you are prompted to enter it. The newly available page(s) now appear in a new window within your ClipBook Viewer. When you attempt to access one of its pages, you may be prompted for a password.

5. When you're finished using another person's ClipBook, you may want to disconnect from it. Simply activate the particular remote ClipBook's icon or window within your ClipBook Viewer and choose File ➢ Disconnect.

USING OLE

The ability to run numerous programs, simultaneously switching between them at will and copying data between documents, marked a major advance in desktop computing, especially on the PC. Merely for its task-switching capabilities, Windows has been embraced by thousands of DOS diehards who don't even like Windows. They use Windows just to switch between multiple DOS programs!

However, the Clipboard and ClipBook impose severe limitations to the idea of truly "transparent" data sharing between applications. If you've been following Windows developments over the past several years, you'll know that post-Windows 3 products (3.1, Windows for Workgroups,

Windows 95/98, Windows NT 3.*x*, and now NT Workstation 4) have taken data sharing several steps further with schemes called Dynamic Data Exchange (DDE), Network DDE, and Object Linking and Embedding (OLE).

If you read the computer magazines at all, you've likely been as inundated as we have on the topic of OLE 2, the latest and greatest of data-sharing schemes, which is incorporated into NT. In fact, you may already be familiar with its predecessor, OLE 1, and know that you can use it to create fancy documents combining bits and pieces of data from a variety of programs scattered on your hard disk or across your company's network.

On the other hand, many veteran Windows users have only the barest awareness of OLE and consider it some kind of black art (along with, unfortunately, such simple tasks as using a modem or getting their printer to work). So why should they care about OLE? The vast majority of folks don't understand OLE's nuances and stick instead with the tried-and-true Clipboard when it comes to passing data between applications. (Want a chart in that report? Paste it in!)

And for good reason. *Live* data sharing such as that offered by Windows OLE and DDE are the stuff computer-science conventions are made of. There are some highly technical distinctions between DDE and OLE that are a bit difficult to grasp, not to mention that not all Windows applications are OLE-aware or implement OLE in the same way when they are. Add to this some confusion concerning OLE's use over a PC network, and you've got a topic in need of clarification!

In hopes of dispelling some of the confusion, we offer in this section a brief OLE and DDE primer. This section fills you in on why you won't be using DDE, why you'd want to use OLE, and how easy OLE 2 makes creating flashy documents that take advantage of all that power your computer has under its hood.

WHAT IS DDE?

OLE is getting all the attention these days, but you might run into another term while reading about data-sharing methods in Windows. An older and less ambitious means for intercommunication between applications is called Dynamic Data Exchange (DDE), and it is also included in NT. Some older applications used DDE to achieve some of the same results you get nowadays with OLE.

CONTINUED ➡

NT Workstation 4, Windows for Workgroups, and Windows 95/98 have included an updated network version of DDE called NetDDE that enables applications to talk to one another over the network as well as on the same machine. And actually, OLE uses DDE as its communications link between programs.

The downside of DDE is that although it provides a way for applications to share information in a *live* way as OLE does (meaning that altering one document updates any linked documents, too), how you, the user, set up the link varies considerably from program to program. Another problem inherent in DDE is that the links it sets up between documents are too easy to sever. Simply moving a file to a new location or upgrading one of the source applications could result in a document losing one of its objects.

Since OLE's debut (with Windows 3.1), the bulk of serious Windows applications support OLE rather than DDE for user-created data sharing. Few programs used DDE internally to communicate between modules of a program or between multiple documents running under the same program. DDE has essentially been left to the domain of hackers working with such tools as Excel macros — one of the few DDE-enabled tools.

Advantages of OLE

Just to give you an idea of what we're talking about here, consider an example when the regular old Clipboard doesn't cut the muster, and when you might want to use OLE instead.

NOTE

The Clipboard in NT is an OLE application, as cutting and pasting are essentially OLE functions. But the Clipboard only facilitates cutting and pasting; it usually does not get directly involved in linking and embedding.

Let's assume you're applying for a grant from an arts council and the board members want to see a professional-looking, attractive business plan as part of your application. You'll be using a Windows word processor such as WordPerfect, Word, or AmiPro to write the text, and you'll also need to incorporate financial projections for your project using data taken from a spreadsheet. Got the picture?

You could copy numbers from the spreadsheet into your text document. But there's a problem—your projections are changing daily as you update and refine your spreadsheet. What to do? Well, you could paste in the cells at the last minute before printing the grant application, but there's a more elegant solution. You can *link* the relevant cells from the live spreadsheet directly to the document. Then, whenever you alter any numbers in the spreadsheet, they'll be automatically updated in your grant application. Figure 8.11 shows an Excel spreadsheet linked to a Word for Windows document.

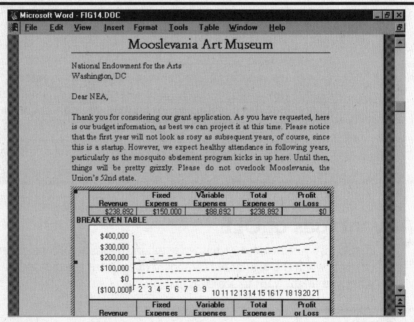

FIGURE 8.11:   With OLE, you can link data between an Excel spreadsheet on one user's hard drive and a Word for Windows document on yours. If the other user changes the spreadsheet, you'll see the changes when you view your Word document.

This is basically what OLE is all about: splicing pieces of documents (called *objects*) from different applications into a single *compound* document. And this splicing (called *linking*) keeps the documents connected so that editing one affects any other documents that are linked to it.

There's one other major nicety of OLE: You can edit a linked addition to a document just by double-clicking it. In our example, this means if you wanted to enter new figures in the spreadsheet, there's no need to run Excel and open the source spreadsheet file. You just double-click the portion of the spreadsheet that's in your word processor document. NT knows that Excel created this portion of the document and dishes up the correct tools for you to edit with, as you can see in Figure 8.12. After you've entered your changes, you save them, and you're dumped back into your word processor document. NT takes care of updating any related documents.

NOTE

Technically, in the example here, Excel becomes the active application, not Word. Excel runs and takes over the active window, changes the menus, and accepts the edits. After you exit, the window returns to Word. To the user, it looks as though only the menus and toolbars have changed.

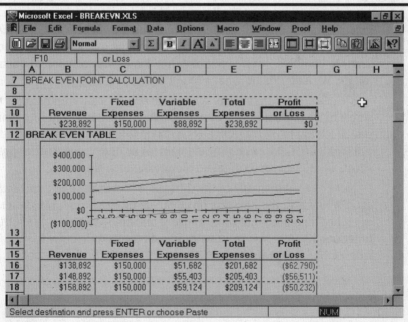

FIGURE 8.12:   If you want to edit a linked object within a compound document (in this example, the Excel spreadsheet within the Word document shown in Figure 8.11), just double-click the object and that object is reopened with the tools you need to make changes to it.

The catch is that programs must be intentionally designed with OLE. But more and more of them are these days, so you shouldn't have trouble finding chart, graphics, sound, and even video programs that'll all work together. For example, you might want to add a chart from that same spreadsheet program to your business plan to communicate the numeric information graphically or a sound clip that, when clicked, explains a concept in the author's voice. And because NT supports networks so well, linked documents can be spread all over the network. The art department's latest version of the corporate logo could be loaded into the annual report you're about to print, and you don't even need to call the artist first.

Basic OLE Concepts

It's important that you have a working understanding of OLE terms and concepts before you try creating documents with OLE. Also, it's important that you understand that differences exist between OLE 1 and OLE 2. As of this writing, only a handful of applications are OLE 2-enabled. Although OLE 2 is backward-compatible with OLE 1, meaning you can mix and match the two, the techniques you'll use to create compound documents differ somewhat. In this section, we explain all you need to know to use OLE 1 or 2 to put together some fancy compound documents. We also explain what's so great about OLE 2.

So let's start with objects. What is an object, really? An *object* is any single block of information stored as a separate bundle but incorporated into a document. An object can consist of as little as a single spreadsheet cell, database field, or graphic element; or as much as an entire spreadsheet, a database, or a complete picture or video clip.

Next, there's the issue of the differences between *linking* and *embedding*. With OLE, you have the option of using either one. You either link *or* embed an object—not both. Linking and embedding are different in functionality. Also you work with linked objects differently than you do with embedded ones. Study the images in Figure 8.13 for a moment.

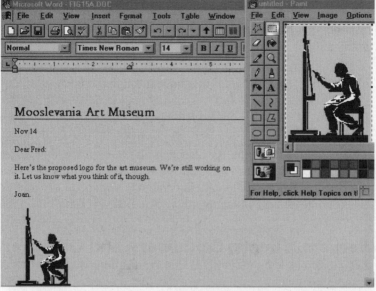

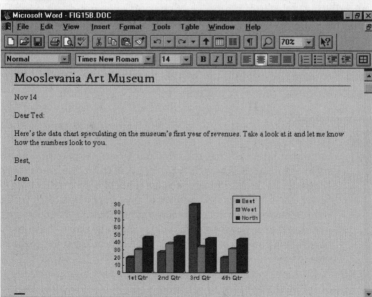

FIGURE 8.13:   Linked files have a life outside the combined document (top), but embedded files do not (bottom).

In the case of linking, two separate files exist: In the top part of Figure 8.13, the files are a Paint image and a Word file. The image can be edited either from within the Word document or separately in the Paint application.

By contrast, the bottom part of Figure 8.13 displays an *embedded* object. The embedded graphic is more intimately connected to the word processor document. In fact, it is contained *within* the word processing file itself. Although the embedded picture can still be edited, it doesn't have a life outside the word processing document that contains it.

Regardless of whether the objects in the word processing document are linked or embedded, the resulting larger document is called a *compound* document. A compound document is any document composed of two or more dissimilar document types joined via OLE.

Servers, Clients, Containers, and Other Terms

Let's look a little more closely at how applications work together to create compound documents. First, consider that programs play two separate and distinct roles in the process of sharing information through OLE. One program originates the object that is to be embedded or linked. This is referred to as the OLE *server*. The other program accepts the object. This is referred to as the OLE *client*. For example, in Figure 8.13, Paint and Excel are the originating (server) programs and, in both cases, Word is the accepting (client) program.

NOTE

To be absolutely precise, the terminology varies somewhat depending on whether you're speaking of OLE 1 or OLE 2. In OLE 2, the overall design model suggests the terms *container* and *component object* rather than *client* and *server*. The container is the receiver of any component object. For example, a word processor document containing a graph would be the container; the graph would be the component object. You'll probably be seeing these terms bandied about in the trade press, so the discussion here incorporates these terms from time to time.

Sophisticated Windows applications usually will work both as OLE servers and as clients. As an example, consider a spreadsheet program such as Excel. This program can supply charts and worksheet objects to a word processor or desktop publishing program, acting as an OLE server. Excel can also accept embedded database objects from, say, Access or Q&E.

This bidirectionality isn't always the case, however. For example, Windows Write, WordPad, and Cardfile can function only as clients. Programs such as Paint, Media Player, and Sound Recorder can behave only as servers.

Two final terms you need to know are *source* and *destination*. The *source document* (a close kin of the OLE server program) is the one in which an object is originally created. A *destination document* (similarly, this one is kin to the OLE client program) is the one into which you place the object.

Object Packages

In addition to the two basic OLE options of linking and embedding, there is a third variation of OLE called *packaging*. Packaging is a technique you can use to wrap an object into a cute little bundle represented by an icon. Then you drop the icon into the destination document. For example, you might want to drop a sound clip or video clip into a document in this way. When the reader of the container document comes across the icon, he or she just double-clicks it, and it unwraps, so to speak. The video clip runs in a window, a sound clip plays, and so forth. Of course, this is useful only if the document is being viewed on a computer, because nothing happens when you double-click a piece of paper! It's particularly useful when sending e-mail messages because it keeps the messages smaller. Figure 8.14 shows an example of a WordPad document with a sound-file package embedded in it.

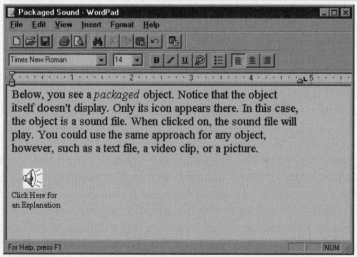

FIGURE 8.14: Packaging a document "iconifies" it for later replay.

You can add a package to a document using Explorer, the File Manager, or the Object Packager program.

OLE 2 versus OLE 1

OLE 1 represented a great stride forward in application integration when it was introduced with Windows 3.1. However, it still left much to be desired. For starters, creating and moving objects between applications was awkward, requiring use of the Clipboard. With OLE 2, you can use the ubiquitous drag-and-drop approach. By Ctrl-dragging, you can copy the object.

Editing embedded objects is also much easier. In OLE 1, editing embedded objects confused users because double-clicking an object brought up its source application in another window on the screen with the object loaded into that window. You would use the other application's window to change the data, then exit that application. This returned you to the original application with the data updated. This process was not particularly intuitive, because you felt as though you had left the report you were working on.

In contrast, with OLE 2 another window does *not* appear. You are still in the window you began in. The two participating applications negotiate an arrangement whereby the menus, toolbars, menu commands, and palettes on the menus within the primary document's application window change. An example of this was shown in Figure 8.12, earlier in the chapter.

This convenient arrangement has been dubbed *visual editing*, and it is much more intuitively obvious for users. Note, however, that it applies to editing only embedded objects, not linked ones, and works only if both applications are OLE 2-enabled. Linked objects are edited in separate windows, just as with OLE 1.

The other primary problem with OLE 1 was that moving any of the linked object files would break the link, resulting in an error message when the compound document was opened. OLE 2 solves this problem by enabling you to move files to other drives or directories at will. As long as all the linked files are present in the directory, the compound document will still be intact. As another way around having to deal with multiple files in compound documents composed of many objects, OLE 2 enables you to easily convert all the links in a compound document to embedded objects. This, in essence, takes all the relevant data that was previously stored in separate files and squishes it into a single (albeit a larger) one. With OLE 1, breaking the link meant losing the object altogether and needing to reestablish it.

Another interesting feature of OLE 2 is that it conforms to a *transaction-based* I/O model. Thus, an OLE 2-enabled application can undo changes that were made to a compound document. For example, if you cut an embedded object, the application can undo the cut, reestablishing the presence of the object in the file.

Next, OLE 2 specifies a new type of file format called the Compound File Format. This new format helps the operating system more efficiently store and edit complex documents that contain numerous objects. One advantage to this is that you can now edit a compound document object on an *incremental* basis rather than editing the entire object. For example, say you double-click a series of spreadsheet cells embedded in your text-based report and start editing the cells. Only the cells you alter will be updated, rather than the whole series of cells. This makes for faster updating and overall performance.

Finally, the expanded OLE 2 specification not only enables document objects such as charts, pictures, video, and sound to communicate, but it also works with program modules. As you may know, many applications are composed of separate modules (each one usually stored in separate .dll files). A .dll file typically performs a specific function, such as spell checking, within a word processor program. OLE 2 supplies a standard by which program modules can communicate with one another. As applications are written to comply with this standard, you'll have the option of mixing and matching your favorite program modules to create the "perfect" application. For example, you could buy a replacement spell checker for your favorite word processor, a favorite macro organizer for your spreadsheet, or some flashy graphics-manipulation tools for your favorite image-processing program.

OLE Inconsistencies

Developers, keen on building OLE compatibility into their products, are complying more and more with OLE conventions. However, there's been some leeway in the interpretation of how an application will incorporate OLE, and idiosyncrasies and slight variations arise in the way you work with OLE in different applications. Drag-and-drop isn't implemented everywhere, so it's not as simple as Microsoft might have you believe. You may need to do a little snooping in an application's manual, use online Help, or check out an application's menus to determine how to import or edit OLE items in your application.

For example, in the Windows 3.*x* Cardfile, you don't need to click a linked picture before you edit it, because Cardfile knows the picture is in the upper-left corner. Similarly, because you place a linked or embedded sound object in a destination document by double-clicking the Sound Recorder icon, you can't use the double-click method to edit the object as you would in the case of, say, an embedded section of an Excel spreadsheet. Instead, you must use the Edit menu's Sound Object command.

As a general rule, one consistency you can usually count on is that an OLE-aware application has a Paste Special command on its Edit menu. If it's there, the application knows about OLE, and you'll almost certainly be able to use this command to embed and link objects into your documents.

Some applications (such as Word and WordPad) also have an Insert dialog box that lets you create and embed all kinds of objects, as shown in Figure 8.15. As you can see, this latter approach breaks down the distinction between running different applications to create different types of objects; you can create spreadsheets, images, and even animations all from within your word processor application!

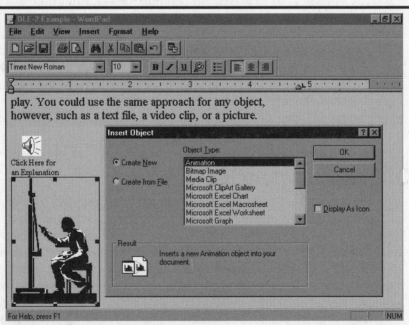

FIGURE 8.15: WordPad has an Insert dialog box for creating and embedding objects of different types (even non–word-processor objects) on the fly while still in WordPad.

You may have found the previous discussion a bit daunting, what with all the hairy terms and such. Don't panic! OLE is a little confusing to everyone, especially because it's a scheme that's in flux. After you experiment with embedding and linking a bit, you'll figure it out.

Now let's discuss the procedures for embedding, linking, and packaging objects in NT. We'll also discuss some networking and security issues that pertain to linked objects.

EMBEDDING OBJECTS

The difference between linking and embedding throws people sometimes, so let's talk about that for a minute. It might help to think of embedding an object as almost identical to pasting a static copy of it from the Clipboard in a regular old non-OLE document. This is because neither embedding nor pasting involves a link to external files. After a chart is embedded into your word processor file, it becomes part of that file. The only difference between standard Clipboard cut-and-paste and OLE embedding is that once embedded, an object can easily be edited by double-clicking it or via some other command. Even though the object (let's say a graph) isn't something the container application (let's say Word) knows how to edit, the object contains a pointer to a program that can edit it.

You might want to experiment using some OLE applications, such as Word, Excel, Word Pro, 1-2-3, WordPad, or Sound Recorder, just to name a few. Here are the basic steps:

1. Open the source application and document. (The application must be able to perform as an OLE server.)

2. Select the portion of the document you want to embed in another.

3. Switch to the destination application and document. Position the insertion point and choose Paste Special. When you do so, you may see a dialog box giving you some choices about what you want to do. For example, here are two Paste Special boxes, one from Word and one from Excel, respectively.

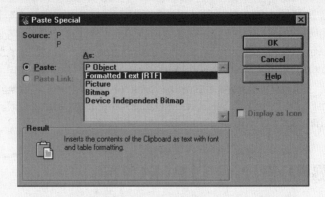

You might have to do a little head scratching to figure out which option to choose. As a rule, if the option says just plain Paste, that won't get you anything more than a normal paste job, which isn't what you want. You want a choice that does not say Link but does say something about an *object*. So, for example, in Word's dialog box you would choose the first option and click OK. In the Excel box you would choose Object and click Paste (not Paste Link, because that links the object rather than embeds it). Some dialog boxes let you choose to display the pasted information as an icon rather than as the item itself. For example, an embedded video clip typically appears in a box that displays the first video frame of the clip.

After doing the Paste operation, and assuming both applications are OLE-aware, you might get what looks like a static copy of the material (such as a bitmap); but the destination application knows the source application for the object, and thus the object can be edited easily. Figure 8.16 shows an example of a Microsoft Graph file embedded in a Word document.

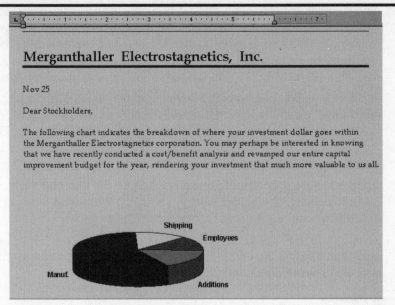

FIGURE 8.16: After pasting a graph object into Word, the graph appears in the container document.

With some OLE applications you can embed an object using a command choice, such as Insert ➤ Object. This leads to a dialog box that enables you to choose the type of object (all the OLE-aware programs on your system are listed). When you choose, the source application runs, and you can then create the object and exit. When you exit, the object is placed in the container document you were previously working in.

Editing an Embedded Object

Now assume that you have an object embedded in a document—anyone viewing the document can see it, you can print it out, and so forth. If it's a video clip or sound clip, double-clicking it brings up a suitable program (such as Sound Recorder or Media Player) that runs the clip and enables the reader of the document to pause, stop, rewind, and replay the clip as needed. For other types of objects, double-clicking makes the object easy to edit.

For example, say you have a graph in your Word document. To edit it, double-click the embedded item. The resulting scenario depends on whether the applications involved are OLE 1 or OLE 2. If both applications are OLE 2-aware, what ideally happens is that the toolbar, menus, and commands in the application you're working with (the container application) change to those of the object's. Use them just as if you were working in whatever program created the object. If one or both of the applications are only OLE 1-aware, the object's source application runs in its own window, and the object is loaded into it. Edit as you normally would.

In some cases, such as with a sound or video clip, double-clicking an object will "play" the object rather than enable you to edit it. You'll need to edit it via another means, such as right-clicking it and choosing Edit or by selecting it, opening the File menu, and choosing Edit Object or some similar command.

In other cases, double-clicking an embedded file won't have any effect until you change modes. For example, with the Windows 3.*x* version of Cardfile, you need to choose Edit ➤ Picture first.

After you've finished editing the embedded object, choose File ➤ Update and then File ➤ Exit, or just choose File ➤ Exit and then answer Yes to any dialog boxes about updating.

TIP

As an alternative to the techniques described above, check to see if the compound document has an Edit menu option for editing the object. Select the object first, then check the Edit menu.

LINKING OBJECTS

Recall that linking an object is similar to embedding it, but there's one important difference! When linking, the object and the container both "live" in separate files on a hard disk somewhere. However, a connection exists between the linked document and the container it's linked to. This connection is called, not surprisingly, the *link*. So, instead of copying the object's data to the destination document, the link tells the destination application where to find the original source file.

As long as the link isn't broken, the link is kept live by NT, even between sessions. You can edit the linked object by double-clicking it in the container document, just as you can an embedded object. However, the object opens in a separate window for editing—even if both the server and client applications are OLE 2-aware.

You can also edit the object separately using the program that created it, even if the container document isn't open. For example, if the linked item is a spreadsheet file, editing the spreadsheet file at its source (say by running 1-2-3, opening the file, editing the spreadsheet, and saving it) will still work. What's more, any changes you make to the file independently show up in any and all linked files. Because of this, linking is the technique to use when you want to use data that must always be identical in two or more documents.

To link two files, follow these steps:

1. Create or find the server document you want to link (the source document). For example, you could open Paint and draw something.

NOTE

Before a file can be linked, it has to be given a name and saved on disk. Windows won't let you link a file that's still called Untitled (the default name of many documents before they are saved).

2. Select the portion of the document you want to pull into the container document.

3. Choose Edit ➤ Copy to put it onto the Clipboard.

4. Switch to the destination document.

5. Move the insertion point to the place where you want to insert the linked item.

6. Open the container's Edit menu and choose Paste Link (not Paste). If there isn't a Paste Link command, look for Paste Special and the relevant linking option. You'll likely see a dialog box something like one of these two (from Word and Excel, respectively):

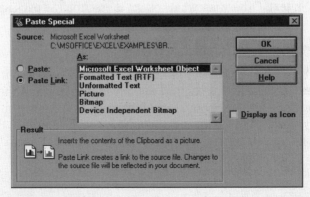

NOTE

Some friendlier Paste Special dialog boxes explain what effect the various format options have when you paste the link. The default choice (the one that comes up highlighted when the box first appears) is usually your best bet. However, you might prefer one of the other choices, particularly if you want the linked material to have the exact same look as the source. When linking to a spreadsheet, for example, if you want the headings, grid, and exact font in which the spreadsheet is displayed, you would choose Bitmapped Picture. But be aware that linking data as a picture rather than text takes up much more room on the disk, making your file much larger. Importing data as formatted text is more space efficient.

7. If you want to establish a second link, repeat steps 4 through 6 but select a different destination document in step 4.

The linked item should now be added to the container document in the correct position. If everything went as planned, the object appears in its original form; that is, a graphic looks like a graphic, cells look like cells, and so forth. In some cases, when OLE applications aren't communicating properly, you'll see the source application's icon instead. This can occur with older applications such as Windows 3.x's Write and Word for Windows 2. If this happens, you're better off pasting in the text as plain text. Otherwise, what you get is essentially a packaged object.

Editing a Linked Object

After you've successfully linked some object(s) into a container document, you can check out how well the linking works. Adjust both windows so you can see both sets of the same data (source and destination). Try altering the source and notice how, in a few seconds, the linked version of the data (stored in the container document) is updated as well.

But what about editing the linked stuff right from the container document? No problem. Just as with editing embedded objects, you simply double-click. The result, however, is different, because changes you make to a linked object appear in all the documents you've linked it to.

Here's the basic game plan for editing a typical linked object:

1. In any of the documents the object has been linked to, double-click the object. The source application opens in a window, with the object loaded. For example, Figure 8.17 shows some linked spreadsheet cells that opened in Excel when double-clicked from a WordPad document.

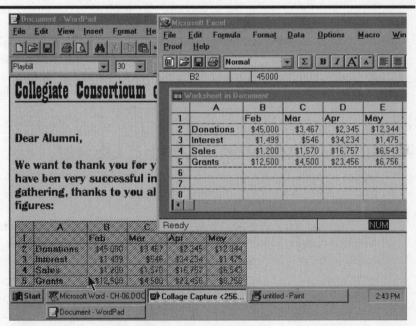

FIGURE 8.17: Editing a linked object is usually as easy as double-clicking it.

TIP

As an alternative to double-clicking to bring up the source application, check the compound document's Edit menu. If you click the object once and open the Edit menu, it may list an option such as Edit Object. Many NT applications are also now supporting the right-click approach to editing. Click the item, then click the right mouse button. You're likely to see an option such as Edit Lotus 1-2-3 Worksheet Link.

2. In the source application's window, make your edits.

3. Choose File ➢ Save, then File ➢ Exit. Changes you made should appear in all destination documents containing links to this source material.

MAINTAINING YOUR OLE LINKS

Although NT Workstation 4 can usually maintain a link between the server and client documents, largely because of improvements in OLE 2, at times a link may be broken for some reason. A traditional example is an application crashing before its links can be recorded properly. And although OLE 2 is intelligent about keeping your links in working order, it's not impossible to mislead it by copying source and destination files from folders, erasing folders, and so forth. A broken link typically manifests as a hole where data was to appear in a document or as data that isn't up to date. In the next few sections we explain how to manually make changes to a link to modify its properties.

Manually Updating a Linked Object

Under normal circumstances, when you make changes to a server document (that is, a source document), your changes appear immediately in any other documents that contain copies of that object. Actually, *immediate* updating requires that the other destination documents be open. If they aren't open, destination documents are updated the next time you open them.

In any case, there are times when you might want to delay the updating of objects linked to other documents. You can stipulate that a given link will update destination documents only when you manually execute an update command. This might be useful when your source document is undergoing repeated revision that would cause the destination document to read inaccurately or appear unfinished, or if the source document is linked to many destination documents and the automatic updating process slows your computer too much, ties up the network (in the case of links to documents across the network), or is otherwise annoying.

To deal with this, just set up your link for manual updating. Here's how:

1. Open the destination document.

2. Click the object to select it.

3. Choose Edit ➤ Links. You'll see a Links dialog box similar to the one shown in Figure 8.18. (The box may vary somewhat depending on the application you're running.)

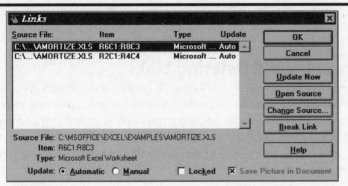

FIGURE 8.18: Use the Links dialog box to change the details of a link.

NOTE

If the Links dialog box lists two or more links, you can select multiple consecutive links by holding down the Shift key while you click with the mouse. You can also select multiple links that don't appear consecutively by pressing Ctrl while you click.

4. The Links dialog box lists all the links in your document, identifying each link by the source-document filename. Select the link whose automatic updating you want to turn off.

5. Click the Manual button (at the bottom of the box), then choose OK. The button should have an X or dot in it, indicating the setting is turned on.

If later you want to reset the updating to the automatic mode, open this box again and click Automatic.

Note that after you've set a linked object to manual updating, no changes you make to the source document will be reflected in the destination until you manually update it. You'll need to open the Links dialog box, highlight the link in question, and choose Update Now.

Completing Other Link-Management Tasks

You probably noticed that there are other buttons in the Link dialog box that suggest other possible link-related tasks. For example, you might want to break, delete, reestablish, or alter existing links to refer to different source documents. Here's the rundown on each of these activities.

Canceling and Deleting Links

In certain circumstances, you'll want to break a link between two documents. When you break a link, the data continues to appear in the destination document; it just can no longer be edited from within that document. If the destination application is capable of displaying the data, you will still see it. If it's not capable of displaying it, you will see an icon representing the material.

TIP

In most cases, double-clicking an object whose link has been broken doesn't have any effect; that is, it doesn't bring up the source application or enable you to edit the object. But here's another method: Select the object, copy it to the Clipboard, and paste it back into the originating program. Then edit it as you need to, copy it onto the Clipboard again, and paste it back into the destination.

But now for the obvious question. Why would you want to break a link? You would break a link if having the link is more of a hassle than it's worth, such as when you are going to separate the source and destination documents. For example, suppose you want to copy the destination document onto a floppy disk to send to someone. When the recipient opens the document, he or she would see empty sections in the document and a dialog box saying that parts of the document are missing. So, breaking the link keeps the data in the document, with the only downside being that it can no longer be edited.

What about deleting a link? Deleting a link wipes out the linked material in the destination document. The source document is left intact, of course, but the previously linked object is purged from the destination document.

How do you break or delete a link? Use the Links dialog box, as follows:

1. Open the document containing the object with the link you want to break or delete.

2. Select the object and choose Edit ➤ Links to bring up the Links dialog box. (In some applications, such as Word, you don't need to select the object, because all linked objects appear in the Links dialog box.)

3. In the list of links, highlight the one whose connection you want to break or delete.

4. To cancel the link, click the Cancel Link (or Break Link) button. To delete the link, choose Delete.

5. Click the OK button in the dialog box.

Fixing Broken Links

As mentioned earlier, links can be broken inadvertently, especially on a network. Links made from within NT are robust and can survive even when you move source and destination documents between directories or rename files. However, links are still sometimes broken, especially in the case of documents composed of information on different workstations across the network. When a destination document can't find the filename and path name to locate a linked object, the application gets confused and breaks the link. The data may still appear in the destination document, but you won't be able to edit it, and the connection will no longer be live.

Here's how to reestablish a link so the source and destination documents are once again connected:

1. Open the document containing the object whose link is broken.

2. Select the object and choose Edit ➤ Links. The Links dialog box appears with the object already highlighted in the list of links.

TIP

You can also use Change Link to replace one link with a completely different one. Just select a different filename for the source document.

3. Click the Change Link (possibly called Change Source) button. The Change Link or Change Source dialog box appears, as shown in Figure 8.19.

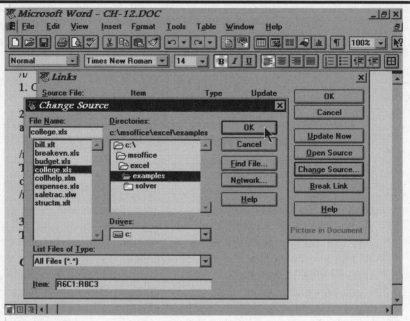

FIGURE 8.19:   You can use the Change Source dialog box to reestablish links.

4. Select the computer, drive, directory, and file as necessary to select the filename of the source document that contains the source material. Click the OK button. The Links dialog box then reappears listing the updated location and name of the source document. If the source is on a workstation across the network, look for a Network button to click.

5. Click the OK button to finalize the new link information. When the box closes—and assuming the link is set for automatic updating—the current version of the linked object appears in the destination document.

What's Next?

This chapter explained how to share data between applications using the Clipboard, ClipBook, and OLE. The next chapter takes you to the World Wide Web. You'll learn how to use Internet Explorer, as well as get some tips on searching the Web.

Chapter 9

Browsing the World Wide Web with Internet Explorer 4

Internet Explorer is your window not only to your own computer and network, but also to the World Wide Web and all you'll find there. Although it's really "just a browser," you'll see in this chapter that Internet Explorer does a lot more than simply display pages from the Web. In fact, you'll find that Internet Explorer is now an integral part of Windows, just as the worldwide network called the Internet is now an integral part of our lives.

Adapted from *Mastering*™ *Windows*® *98*
by Robert Cowart
ISBN 0-7821-1961-1   1200 pages $34.99

INSIDE INTERNET EXPLORER

You'll find that Internet Explorer has many similarities to other Windows programs you have used, especially those in Microsoft Office (Word, Excel, Access, and so on). The primary difference between Internet Explorer and other programs you use is that you use it for viewing files, not editing and saving them. Let's begin by seeing how you can start Internet Explorer.

Starting Internet Explorer

Like just about all Windows programs, Internet Explorer can be started in many ways. You can also run more than one copy of the program at a time, which allows you to view the pages from multiple Web sites or different sections of the same page.

To start Internet Explorer at any time, simply choose it from the Start menu. In a standard installation, choose Start ➢ Programs ➢ Internet Explorer ➢ Internet Explorer. The program will start and open its *start page*, which is the page Internet Explorer displays first whenever you start it in this way.

NOTE
To specify a different start page for Internet Explorer, choose View ➢ Internet Options, choose the General tab. Enter the URL to the start page in the Address field. You can instead click Use Current to use the URL currently displayed in Internet Explorer, or click Use Blank to display a blank page each time Internet Explorer starts.

If the start page is available on a local or networked drive on your computer or if you are already connected to the Internet, Internet Explorer opens that page immediately and displays it.

If you use a modem to connect to the Internet, however, and the start page resides there but you're not currently connected, Internet Explorer opens your Dial-Up Networking connector to make the connection to the Internet.

Here are some ways you can start Internet Explorer:

▶ Open a GIF or JPEG image file, which is associated with Internet Explorer, unless you have installed another program that takes those associations.

▶ While in another program, click (activate) a hyperlink that targets an HTML file to open that file in Internet Explorer. For example, while reading an e-mail message you have received in Outlook Express (as shown below), click a hyperlink in the message that targets a Web site, and that site will be opened in Internet Explorer.

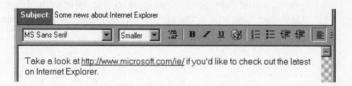

To close Internet Explorer, choose File ➤ Close as you would in many other programs. Unlike a word processor or spreadsheet program, when you have been viewing sites on the Web in Internet Explorer, there are normally no files to save before exiting the program.

MAKING INTERNET EXPLORER YOUR DEFAULT BROWSER

If you have installed another browser since installing Internet Explorer, Internet Explorer may not be set as your default browser, and that other browser will be called upon to open any Web pages you request. If you want to make Internet Explorer your default browser and keep it that way, here's how to do it.

In Internet Explorer, choose View ➤ Internet Options. On the Programs tab, you'll find an option called "Internet Explorer should check to see whether it is the default browser." Select this option, and close the Internet Options dialog box.

Now whenever you start Internet Explorer, it will check to see if it is still the default browser. If it finds that it isn't, it will ask if you want it to become the new default browser. If you choose Yes, it will change the Windows settings to make it the default. Now when you open an HTML file—for example, by clicking a hyperlink in a Word document that targets a Web page—Internet Explorer will be the program that opens it. You'll also get the "e" icon on your Desktop for starting Internet Explorer with a single click.

If you later install another browser that makes itself the default, the next time you start Internet Explorer, it will check to see if it is the default and prompt you accordingly.

NOTE

When you started Internet Explorer, it may have caused Dial-Up Networking to make the Internet connection. In that case, when you later exit Internet Explorer, you will be asked if you want to disconnect from the Internet. You can choose to stay connected if you want to work in other Internet-related programs. In that case, don't forget to disconnect later by double-clicking the Dial-Up Networking icon in the system tray of the Windows Taskbar. Then click the Disconnect button in the dialog box.

The Components of Internet Explorer

Now we'll look at the features and tools that make up Internet Explorer. Figure 9.1 shows Internet Explorer while displaying a Web page. As you can see, the Internet Explorer window contains many of the usual Windows components.

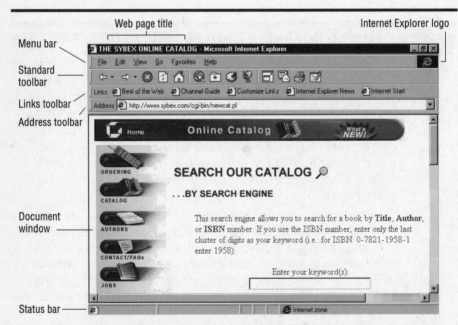

FIGURE 9.1: The Internet Explorer program window contains many components that are common to other Windows programs.

NOTE

A company or an Internet service provider (ISP) can customize Internet Explorer to make it look and act as though it were their own browser and then distribute it to employees or customers. So if your ISP or your employer gives you a copy of Internet Explorer, it may not look exactly like the one shown in Figure 9.1.

Part i

When you want to show as much of the Web page as possible, try the View ➤ Full Screen command, or click the Full Screen button on the toolbar. Internet Explorer will be maximized to occupy the entire screen; it will lose its title bar, status bar, two of its toolbars, and even its menu bar. (You can right-click a toolbar and choose Menu Bar to display it again.)

NOTE

To view or adjust the various options and settings for Internet Explorer, choose View ➤ Internet Options. For example, if you want to have Internet Explorer always start in its full-screen mode, select the Advanced tab in this Internet Options dialog box and then select the option called "Launch browser in full screen window."

You can switch back to the normal view by choosing the Full Screen command again. The full-screen mode is the default when you open a channel from the Desktop, when it's formally called the Channel Viewer.

Here are the parts of Internet Explorer that are labeled in Figure 9.1:

Title bar   At the top of the window is the usual title bar. It displays either the title of the Web page you are viewing or the document's filename, if it is not a Web page. On the right side of the title bar are the Minimize, Maximize/Restore, and Close buttons; on the left side is the System menu.

Menu bar   Beneath the title bar is the menu bar, which contains almost all the commands you'll need in Internet Explorer. Keyboard shortcuts are shown next to those commands that have them. For example, you can use the shortcut Ctrl+O instead of choosing the File ➤ Open command.

Toolbars   By default, the toolbars appear beneath the menu bar and contain buttons and other tools that help you navigate the Web or the files and other resources on your computer. The three toolbars are Standard, Links, and Address (top, middle, and bottom in Figure 9.1). The Internet Explorer logo to the right of the toolbar is animated when the program is accessing data.

Document window   Beneath the menu and toolbars is the main document window, which displays a document such as a Web page, an image, or the files on your computer's disk. If Internet Explorer's program window, which encompasses everything you see in Figure 9.1, is smaller than full-screen, you can resize it by dragging any of its corners or sides. The paragraphs in a Web page generally adjust their width to the size of the window.

NOTE
You cannot display multiple document windows in Internet Explorer. Instead, you can view multiple documents by opening multiple instances of Internet Explorer (choose File ➤ New ➤ Window). Each instance of the program is independent of the others.

Explorer bar   When you click the Search, Favorites, History, or Channels button on the toolbar (or choose one of those commands from the View ➤ Explorer Bar menu), the Explorer bar will appear as a separate pane on the left side of the window. This useful feature displays the contents for the button you clicked, such as the search options shown in Figure 9.2. This allows you to make choices in the Explorer bar on the left, such as clicking a link, and have the results appear in the pane on the right. To close the Explorer bar, repeat the command you used to open it or choose another Explorer bar.

Scroll bars   The horizontal and vertical scroll bars allow you to scroll the document window over other parts of a document that is otherwise too large to be displayed within the window.

Status bar   At the bottom of the Internet Explorer window is the status bar. It displays helpful information about the current state of Internet Explorer, so keep an eye on it. For example, when you are selecting a command from the menu bar, a description appears on the status bar. When you point to a hyperlink on the page (either text or an image), the mouse pointer changes to a hand, and the target URL of the hyperlink is displayed on the status bar. When you click a hyperlink to open another page, the status bar indicates what is happening with a progression of messages. Icons that appear on the right side of the status bar give you a status report at a glance. For example, you'll see an icon of a padlock when you have made a secure connection to a Web site.

TIP

You can use the Toolbars and Status Bar commands on the View menu to toggle on or off the display of the toolbars and status bar.

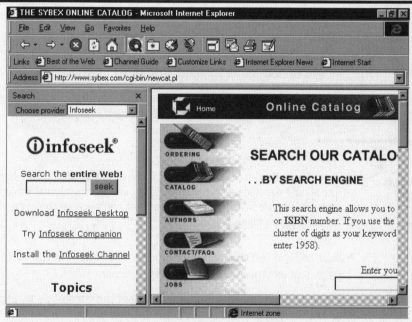

FIGURE 9.2:   When you click the Search, Favorites, History, or Channels button on the toolbar, the Explorer bar opens as a separate pane on the left side of the window, where you can make choices and see the results appear in the right pane.

Some Commands You'll Use Frequently

Here's a short list of the Internet Explorer commands that you'll use on a regular basis, or would use if you knew they existed:

▶ File ≻ Open opens an existing file (an HTML file on your hard disk) in the current Internet Explorer window.

- File ➤ New ➤ Window opens an existing file in a new Internet Explorer window, while leaving the first window open. You can switch between open windows in the usual ways, such as by pressing Alt+Tab.

- File ➤ Save As lets you save the current document to disk as an HTML file.

- File ➤ Properties displays the Properties dialog box for the current document.

- File ➤ Work Offline lets you browse without being online, as data is opened from your Internet Explorer cache on your local disk.

- Edit ➤ Cut/Copy/Paste lets you copy or move selected text or images from Internet Explorer to another program.

- Edit ➤ Page opens the current page for editing in your default HTML editor, such as FrontPage Express if it is installed.

TIP

Don't forget that you can access some of these commands from the buttons on the Standard toolbar. Also, try right-clicking an object in Internet Explorer, such as selected text, an image, or the page itself, and see what choices are offered on the shortcut menu.

- Edit ➤ Find (on this page) lets you search for text in the current page, just as you can do in a word processor.

- View ➤ Stop cancels the downloading of the current page (same as the Esc key).

- View ➤ Refresh updates the contents of the current page by downloading it again (same as the F5 key).

- View ➤ Source displays the HTML source code for the current page in your default text editor, such as Notepad, which is a great way to see the "inner workings" of a page and learn more about HTML, the HyperText Markup Language.

- View ➤ Internet Options lets you view or change the options for Internet Explorer (the command is called View ➤ Folder Options when you are displaying the contents of your local disk).

- Go ➤ Back/Forward lets you move between the pages you've already displayed (also available on the toolbar).

- ▶ Favorites lets you open a site that you have previously saved as a shortcut on the Favorites menu.

- ▶ Favorites ➤ Add to Favorites lets you add the current URL to the this menu and establish a subscription to the site, if you wish.

- ▶ Favorites ➤ Organize Favorites opens the Favorites folder so you can rename, revise, delete, or otherwise organize its contents.

Using the Toolbars

The three toolbars in Internet Explorer (Standard, Links, and Address) are quite flexible. You can change the size or position of each one in the trio, or you can choose not to display them at all. In fact, the menu bar is also quite flexible and can be moved below one or more toolbars or share the same row with them.

- ▶ To hide a toolbar, choose View ➤ Toolbars and select one from the menu; to display that toolbar, choose that command again. Or right-click any of the toolbars or the menu bar and select a toolbar from the shortcut menu.

- ▶ To hide the descriptive text below the Standard toolbar buttons, choose View ➤ Toolbars ➤ Text Labels or right-click a toolbar and choose Text Labels. Choose the command again to display the text.

- ▶ To change the number of rows that the toolbars use, point to the bottom edge of the bottom toolbar; the mouse pointer will change to a double-headed arrow. You can then drag the edge up to reduce the number of rows or drag it down to expand them.

- ▶ To move a toolbar, drag it by its left edge. For example, drag the Address toolbar onto the same row as the Links toolbar, as shown below.

- ▶ To resize a toolbar when two or more share the same row, drag its left edge to the right or left.

NOTE

Remember that you'll also find these three toolbars when you are browsing the files and folders on your local computer. The Address and Links toolbars are also available on the Windows Taskbar.

Standard Toolbar

The buttons on the Standard toolbar in Internet Explorer (the toolbar just beneath the menu bar in Figures 9.1 and 9.2) are shortcuts for the more commonly used commands on its menus. For example, you can click the Stop button to cancel the downloading of the current page instead of using the View ➤ Stop command, or you can click the Home button as a shortcut for the Go ➤ Home Page command.

Point at a button to see its name appear in a ToolTip. You can also have each button's name displayed beneath it in the toolbar by choosing View ➤ Toolbars ➤ Text Labels.

Links Toolbar

Each of the buttons on the Links toolbar is a hyperlink to a URL (you can also access these links from the Links command on the Favorites menu). By default, they all target Microsoft Web sites that serve as gateways to a wealth of information on the Web (if you received a customized version of Internet Explorer, these hyperlinks may point to other locations).

For example, the Best of the Web button displays a useful collection of links to reference-related Web sites, where you might look up a company's phone number, find an e-mail address of a long-lost relative, or find sites that will help you with travel arrangements or personal finance. All the Links buttons are customizable:

▶ To modify a button's target, right-click it, choose Properties from the shortcut menu, and then choose the Internet Shortcut tab.

▶ To change any aspect of a button, including its display text, choose Favorites ➤ Organize Favorites and then open the Links folder, where you'll see the names of all the buttons on the Links toolbar. Rename a button just as you rename any file in Windows, such as by selecting it and press F2. Delete a button by selecting its name and pressing Delete.

▶ To add a new Links button, simply drag a hyperlink from a Web page in Internet Explorer onto the Links toolbar. When you release the mouse button, a new button will be created that targets the same file as the hyperlink.

▶ To rearrange the buttons, drag a button to a new location on the Links bar.

Once you've tried these buttons and have a feeling for the content on each of the sites, you can revise the buttons or create new ones that point to sites that you want to access with a click. An example is shown below.

Address Toolbar

The Address toolbar shows the address of the file currently displayed in Internet Explorer, which might be a URL on the Internet or a location on your local disk. You enter a URL or the path to a file or folder and then press Enter to open that Web site or file.

NOTE

When you are entering a URL that you have entered once before, Internet Explorer's AutoComplete feature recognizes the URL and finishes the typing for you. You can either accept the URL or continue to type a new one. Or right-click in the Address toolbar, choose Completions from the shortcut menu, and then select one of the possibilities from the menu.

To revise the URL, click within the Address toolbar and use the normal Windows editing keys. Then press Enter to have Internet Explorer open the specified file. The arrow on the right side of the Address toolbar opens a drop-down list of addresses that you've previously visited via the Address toolbar. They're listed in the order you visited them. Select one from the list, and Internet Explorer will open that site.

Getting Help

Internet Explorer offers the usual variety of program help, with a few touches of its own. Choose Help ➤ Contents and Index to display its

Help window, where you can browse through the topics in the Contents tab, look up a specific word or phrase in the Index tab, or find all references to a word or phrase in the Search tab.

To see if there is a newer version of any of the Internet Explorer software components, or to add new components, choose Help ➤ Product Updates, which is an easy way to keep your software current.

To work through a basic online tutorial about browsing the Web, choose Help ➤ Web Tutorial. Internet Explorer goes online to a Microsoft Web site and opens the tutorial page, where you can click your way through the lessons.

To find answers to your questions or problems, choose Help ➤ Online Support. This will open Microsoft's online support page for Internet Explorer. It's packed with tips, troubleshooting guides, answers to common questions, and much more. It's a great place to go for up-to-the-minute solutions and fixes.

The items under Help ➤ Microsoft On The Web each take you online to the Internet and should prove to be quite valuable. For example, the Best Of The Web command displays Microsoft's Exploring page, which offers a wide variety of links to interesting and useful sites. The Send Feedback command lets you post a comment about Internet Explorer for Microsoft. You can report a bug or send in a request for a special feature you would like to see in the program. The Microsoft Home Page command takes you to Microsoft's ever-so-humble home page for Internet Explorer, where you can catch up on the latest Microsoft news, read about products, and link to other Microsoft sites.

NOTE

The Microsoft Home Page command is *not* the same as the Go ➤ Home Page command (or the Home button on the toolbar), which opens your chosen start page.

MOVING BETWEEN PAGES

The feature that perhaps best defines the whole concept of browsing in Internet Explorer is your ability to move from page to page, winding your way through the Web. The most common way to do so is by clicking a hyperlink, but this section will also show you some other ways to jump to another page.

Making the Jump with Hyperlinks

You can click an embedded hyperlink (either a text link or a graphic image link) in a page on the Web or on your intranet to open the target file of that link. The target can be anywhere on the Web or your local computer. Clicking a link in a page that's on a server in Seattle might open a page on the same server or on a server in London, Tokyo, Brasilia—or maybe next door.

When you point to a text or to an image link with your mouse in Internet Explorer, the pointer changes to a small hand. Click here to jump to the link destination. Clicking a hyperlink with your mouse is the usual way to activate a link, but you can activate a link in Internet Explorer in several other ways.

▶ Press Tab to move to the next hyperlink in the page; you'll see a dotted outline around the currently selected link. Press Enter to activate the selected link.

▶ Right-click a hyperlink and choose Open from the shortcut menu.

▶ Choose Open in New Window to open the target in a new Internet Explorer window.

▶ Choose Save Target As to save the target of the link to disk (you will be prompted for a location). In this case, Internet Explorer will not display the target.

▶ Choose Print Target to print the target of the link without opening it.

You can use any of these methods to open the target of a hyperlink, whether the link is text, an image, or an image map.

In many cases, the target of a hyperlink will be another Web page, which will probably have hyperlinks of its own. Sometimes, however, the target will be another kind of resource, such as an image file or a text file that contains no links of its own. You'll have to use the Back button to return to the previous page.

Another type of target uses the *mailto* protocol. For example, many Web pages have a link via e-mail to the Webmaster, who is the person

Part I

who created or maintains the site. The link target might look like the one shown here on the status bar, where the target uses the mailto protocol.

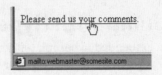

When you click such a link, your e-mail program, such as Outlook Express, opens a new message with the address of the target already entered in the recipient field. You can then fill out the subject and body of the message and send it in the usual way.

Other Ways to Move between Pages

Although clicking a hyperlink in Internet Explorer is the usual way to open another resource (a file, such as a Web page or an image), you'll undoubtedly use other means on a regular basis.

Using the Back and Forward Commands

Once you jump to another page during a session with Internet Explorer, you can use the Back and Forward commands to navigate between the pages you've already visited. You can either use those commands on the Go menu or click the Back and Forward buttons on the toolbar.

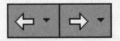

You can right-click either button or click the down-arrow to its right to see a menu of the places that button will take you. The first item on the menu is the site you would visit if you simply click the larger button. Select any site from the menu to go directly to that site.

NOTE

The Back and Forward buttons work exactly the same when you are browsing your local or network drive in an Explorer window. As you display various folders, you can use these buttons to open folders that you have already visited.

Using the Address Toolbar

As mentioned earlier, you can also jump to another page by entering its URL into the Address toolbar and pressing Enter. Keep the following in mind when you do:

- Spelling counts! The bad news is that if you do not type in the address exactly right, Internet Explorer will not be able to open the site and will display an error message to that effect. The good news is that the URL you typed might take you to some new and exciting place on the Web. Good luck!

- If you're entering a complete URL including a filename with a trailing filename extension, watch that extension. Some Web sites use the traditional four-letter extension for a Web page, HTML. Other sites may have adopted the three-letter extension, HTM.

TIP

One way to take advantage of the Address toolbar is by also taking advantage of the Windows Clipboard. For example, you can copy a URL from a word processing document and paste it into the Address toolbar—after that, all you need to do is press Enter to go to that site.

Choosing from Your Favorites Menu

In Internet Explorer, you can create a list of your favorite Web sites or other destinations, such as folders on your local disk, by adding each one to the appropriately named Favorites menu. You don't need to remember a site's URL in order to return to that site—simply select it from the Favorites menu.

Digging into the History and Cache Folders

Internet Explorer keeps track of both the URLs you visit and the actual files that are downloaded:

History   It keeps a list of the URLs you visit in its History folder; the default location is C:\WINNT\History. You can access these URLs in Internet Explorer with the View ➤ Explorer Bar ➤ History command or by clicking the History button on the toolbar. Your past history will be displayed in chronological order in the Explorer bar in the left-hand pane of the Internet Explorer window, where you can select one of the URLs to open that site in the right-hand pane.

Temporary Internet Files   It saves the files it downloads in a folder on your local drive, which serves as a cache. By default, this folder is C:\ WINNT\Temporary Internet Files. When you return to a site, any content that has not changed since the last time you visited that site will be opened directly from the cache on your drive. This saves a lot of time, compared with download-ing those files again (especially images). You can also open this folder and then open or otherwise use any of the files it contains. Choose View ➤ Internet Options, select the General tab, click the Settings button, and then click the View Files button.

NOTE

When multiple users share one computer, each may have their own History and Temporary Internet Files folders. By default, these folders reside within the C:\WINNT\Profiles folder.

SOME TIPS ON WEB SEARCHING

When you conduct a search from the Explorer bar, you'll see only an abbreviated version of the search engine you choose. Usually, you won't see all of the bells and whistles offered by the search engine's full Web page. If you want to do some more serious searching, you'll find it useful to actually go to the search engine's site. (Just enter the URL of the engine into the Address line and press Enter.)

As mentioned before, different search engines work differently. The infor-mation in this section will give you a very general understanding of how most of today's search engines work; for more information, read each search engine's full Web page. Most of them have a Help button or a Search Tips button that provides details about that engine's particular search methods.

Keywords

Most search engines work by providing a blank area where you can type in keywords that represent the information you want to find. For exam-ple, typing in **Hale-Bopp Comet** should find Web sites with information about that comet. Typing in **Comet** by itself would match every Web site with any information about comets.

A keyword is simply one word that represents information you want to find. A keyword is generally a noun, but it may also be a verb or some other part of speech. When you use a search engine, you are searching a database for documents that have words that match the keyword(s) you've entered.

NOTE

The most common words, such as conjunctions ("and," "but," etc.), pronouns ("I," "he," etc.), and prepositions ("of," "for," "into," etc.) are ignored by search engines. Most search engines also ignore the capitalization of your request.

Typically, you may enter as many keywords as you want. The engine will search for all the words and find any document that contains one or more of those words. Multiple keywords are treated as having an implicit Boolean OR operator. For example, if you entered the keywords **Chevy Impala**, the server would return documents that contain the word *Chevy* or the word *Impala*, and would therefore include pages containing mention of Chevy Impala, some pages containing mention of impala (probably natural wildlife pages, actually, since an impala is an animal), and pages that merely include mention of Chevy (without necessarily including Chevy Impala). Pages containing both words would be ranked higher and appear first in the resulting list.

For an OR search, you did not have to enter the word *OR*. To search only for pages that contain all your keywords, however, you need to insert the word *AND* between the two words. For example, to find documents that contain both Chevy and Impala, you would enter **Chevy and Impala**.

Even with the AND approach, you might still turn up pages that don't mention Chevy Impalas. It's possible you'll turn up pages describing somebody's trip across the country to photograph wild animals (lions, wildebeest, impala) from the back of his Chevy station wagon. If you only wanted to find pages that contain the words *Chevy* and *Impala* together as a phrase (okay, I admit I should have told you this up front—but, hey, I'm using this example as a teaching tool), then you should put the words together between quotation marks: "Chevy Impala". But see the discussion later in this section concerning exact matches, because there are some variations on this approach from one search engine to another.

Combining Criteria

Many engines let you combine criteria in complex ways. Here's a typical example. Suppose you wanted to find pages about child safety that do *not* discuss adolescents. Proper use of the words AND and OR will help you: **child and safety not adolescents**.

Wildcards

Most engines will let you enter partial keywords by means of wildcards. Here's an example. Suppose you were doing research about a car company and wanted to see any and all pages about it. You might want listings of any occurrences of *Chevy* or *Chevrolet*. You could do two separate searches, one for each. Or to be more expedient, you could use a wildcard in your search: **Chev***. The asterisk character (*) applied at the end of a partial keyword will match all documents that contain words that start with the partial word.

Exact Matches

Often, you'll want to search for an exact match of the words you enter. For example, you might want to find pages that contain the entire phrase *Hubble telescope repair*. Typically, you would specify that you want an exact match of this phrase by enclosing it within single (') or double quotation marks ("). Some engines, however, want you to use the + sign between the words instead. Thus, depending on the search engine you're using, you may have to use one of the following:

> **'Hubble telescope repair'**
>
> **"Hubble telescope repair"**
>
> **Hubble+telescope+repair**

One of these should find the pages that contain that exact phrase.

TIP

As a general game plan, when you're doing complex searches, start out with a *simple* search (it's faster and easier) and then check the first ten pages or so that result to see what they contain. In many cases, this will provide you with whatever you need, and you won't have spent your time concocting a complex set of search criteria. Of course, if too many pages are found and only a few of them are meeting your actual needs, you'll have to start to narrow the search. On the other hand, if no pages are resulting, ("no matches found"), you'll have to try again by widening the search.

Searching vs. Browsing

Some search engines, such as InfoSeek and Yahoo! offer a Browse option as well as a Search option. That means that in addition to being able to search for keywords, you can look through topics by category, such as *business, entertainment,* or *magazines,* just to see what is available. This is great if you are interested in seeing what's out there in a general category instead of searching for a specific topic.

ENDLESSLY INDEXING THE WEB

The ability to search the Web for specific sites or files relies on one tiny factor: the existence of searching and indexing sites that you can access to perform the search. These sites are often known as Web spiders, crawlers, or robots, because they endlessly and automatically search the Web and index the content they find.

Search sites literally create huge databases of all the words in all the pages they index, and you can search those databases simply by entering the keywords you want to find. Despite the size of this vast store of information, they can usually return the results to you in a second or two.

This is definitely a Herculean task, because the Web is huge and continues to grow with no end in sight. Plus, a search engine must regularly return to pages it has already indexed because those pages may have changed and will need to be indexed again. Don't forget that many pages are removed from the Web each day, and a search engine must remove those now invalid URLs from its database.

To give you an idea of just how big a job it is to search and index the Web, the popular AltaVista search site (www.altavista.digital.com) recently reported that its Web index as of that day covered 31 million pages from 1,158,000 host names on 627,000 servers. AltaVista also had indexed 4 million articles from 14,000 newsgroups. On top of that, this search site is accessed more than 30 million times each day.

Keeping track of what's on the Web is definitely a job for that infinite number of monkeys we've always heard about.

Searching in the Explorer Bar

Let's perform a keyword search in Internet Explorer. Although you could open one of the search sites, the easiest place to begin is with the Explorer bar. Select View ➤ Explorer Bar ➤ Search or click the Search button on the toolbar. Internet Explorer opens its Explorer bar, the separate pane on the left side of its window, while the page you had been viewing is displayed in the right pane. Figure 9.3 shows Internet Explorer with its window split into two panes.

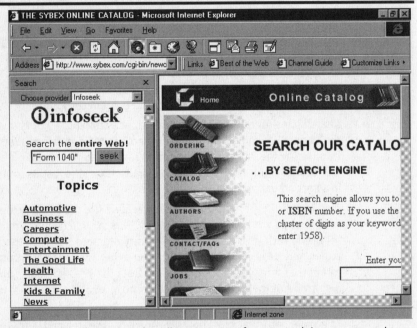

FIGURE 9.3: The Explorer bar allows you to perform a search in one pane and then sample its results while keeping those results on the screen.

TIP

You can close the search bar by choosing View ➤ Explorer Bar ➤ None, clicking the Search button on the toolbar, or clicking the Close button at the top of the Explorer bar. In this way, you can toggle the search bar open or closed while still retaining the results of the last search you performed.

Once the Explorer bar is open, performing the search is as easy as selecting a search site from the list and entering the keywords you want to search for. For example, in Figure 9.3, we selected the site named Infoseek and entered the search criteria **Form 1040** in the text-entry field. To perform the search, simply click the Seek button.

In a second or two (or more if the Internet or the search site you chose is having a busy day), the results of the search will appear in the Explorer bar, as shown in Figure 9.4.

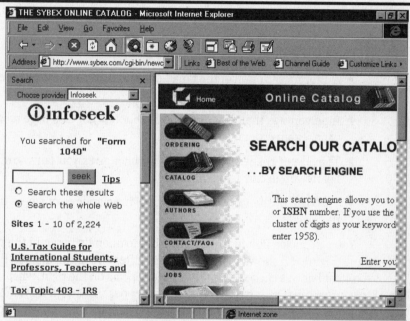

FIGURE 9.4: After you click the Seek button, the results of the search will appear as links in the search bar.

In this example, some 2,224 results were found, although only the first 10 are displayed in the search bar. You can click a link at the bottom of the results to view the next 10.

NOTE

If none of the results looks right, you can create an entirely new search by entering new keywords into the text-entry field and clicking the Seek button or by selecting a different search site and starting from that one.

Each result is a link to the page that was found to contain the keywords you entered. The Infoseek search site, like most others, arranges the resulting links in order of their likelihood of matching your query. If you point to one of the links with your mouse, a ToolTip displays information about it, as shown below.

Tax Topic 403 - IRS

Interest Received Topic 403. [Click for Text Only Version].
Generally, any interest that you receive or that is credited to
your account and can be withdrawn is taxable income. ...
73% [Size 8.4K]
http://www.irs.ustreas.gov/basic/tax_edu/teletax/tc403.html

The ToolTip includes the following information:

▶ A short description of the target page or the first few lines of text found on that page

▶ A percentage that describes the likelihood that this page meets your search criteria

▶ The size of the result's target file, which gives you fair warning before you decide to open it

▶ The URL of the target page, so you'll have an idea of where this file resides

You can click a link in the Explorer bar to open its target in the right pane. Figure 9.5 shows Internet Explorer after one of the links in the Explorer bar was clicked. The target page appears on the right, where you're free to work in it as you would with any other page. In fact, if this looks like a page you'll want to spend some time with, click the Search button to close the Explorer bar so you'll have the entire screen for the target page.

Common Search Engines

This section describes some of the most common search engines on the Web.

AltaVista www.altavista.com

Digital Equipment Corporation's AltaVista claims to be the largest search engine, searching 31 million pages on 627,000 servers, and 4 million articles from 14,000 Usenet newsgroups. It is accessed more than 29 million times per weekday.

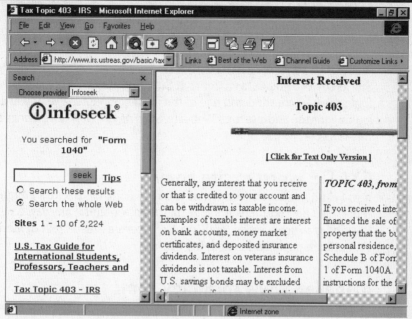

FIGURE 9.5:   When you click a link in the Explorer bar, its target is opened in the pane on the right.

Infoseek www.guide.infoseek.com/

Infoseek combines two powerful search systems, as well as a great news search engine that enables you to search wire services, publications, and more.

- ► Ultrasmart offers comprehensive query results. So you can narrow your results quickly, each new Ultrasmart query you perform searches within your previous results (unless you specify otherwise).

- ► Ultraseek offers the speed, accuracy and comprehensiveness of Ultrasmart, only in a streamlined form. It's aimed at power users who know what they want and want it fast.

- ► News Center offers the latest headlines listed by category. You can also "personalize" your news so you see only what interests you every time you return to Infoseek, including local weather, TV listings, and more. You may also search its "News Wires" (from Reuters, Business Wire, and PR News Wire) or "Premier News" (today's news from seven major national news organizations).

Lycos www.lycos.com/

Lycos searches not only text, but also graphics, sounds, and video!

Yahoo! www.yahoo.com

Started by two graduate students at Stanford, Yahoo! is considered the first search engine and still one of the most comprehensive. If you are looking for the address for a Web site, such as the New York Times site, this is a good way to find it.

EXCITE www.excite.com/

If you can't describe exactly what you're looking for, Excite's unique concept-based navigation technology may help you find it anyway. Excite's Web index is deep, broad, and current; it covers the full text of more than 11.5 million pages and is updated weekly.

Magellen www.mckinley.com/

Magellen offers a different concept in search engines. This one ranks the results using its own independent system in an effort to help you make more refined searches.

Search.com www.search.com/

The Search.com search engine lets you search up to eight search engines at one time. This is a fairly unique and powerful approach to searching. If nothing else, you'll probably get a lot of results from almost any search! It's also a good site for linking to other engines.

NetSearch home.netscape.com/home/internet-search.html

NetSearch is perhaps the most easily accessible search engine because it is available through a button in Netscape (if you happen to use Netscape).

Point www.pointcom.com

Point is another engine that rates Web site matches according to its own system.

Starting Point www.stpt.com/

Starting Point lets you select a subject area for your search.

Webcrawler www.webcrawler.com/

Webcrawler offers a speedy Web search engine and a "randomlinks" feature to find new and unusual sites. It also features a list of the 25 most visited sites on the Web.

Dejavu News www.dejanews.com/

Dejavu News enables you to search through millions of postings to Usenet newsgroups.

BigBook www.bigbook.com

BigBook is a national Yellow Pages listing of nearly every business in the U.S., with detailed maps of their locations.

WHO/WHERE? www.whowhere.com/

Who/Where? is a comprehensive White Pages service for locating people, e-mail addresses, and organizations. Who/Where? intuitively handles misspelled or incomplete names, and it lets you search by initials.

WWWomen www.wwwomen.com/

WWWomen is the premier search directory for women.

Environmental Organization Web Directory www.webdirectory.com/

The categories in the Environmental Organization Web directory cover topics such as animal rights, solar energy, and sustainable development.

CINET'S Shareware Directory www.shareware.com/

C|Net makes it simple to find trial and demo versions of software. More than 170,000 files are available for easy searching, browsing, and downloading from shareware and corporate archives on the Internet.

The Electric Library www.elibrary.com/

The Electric Library address searches across an extensive database of more than 1,000 full-text newspapers, magazines, and academic journals, images, reference books, literature, and art. (This is a pay-subscription site, but a free trial is offered.)

**Homework help tristate.pgh.net/~pinch13/

This Web site was put together by a nine-year-old boy (with the help of his dad) and provides a comprehensive collection of online information designed to help students with their homework. This excellent reference has won many awards.

TIP

An invaluable spot for comparing computer prices is www.computers.com.

WHAT'S NEXT?

This chapter explained the basics of using Internet Explorer and provided some tips on searching the Web. The next chapter discusses troubleshooting NT Workstation. You'll find information about common problems and suggestions for solving them.

Chapter 10

TROUBLESHOOTING

Troubleshooting is a daily occurrence for most NT MCSEs (Microsoft Certified Systems Engineers). This chapter will not prepare you for every problem you may encounter, but it does cover some of the more common problems you may see, as well as possible solutions to those problems.

Adapted from *MCSE Test Success™: NT® Workstation 4* by Todd Lammle and Lisa Donald

ISBN 0-7821-2149-7   384 pages $24.99

TROUBLESHOOTING A FAILED BOOT PROCESS

The NT boot process could fail for many reasons, but in most cases, it fails due to BOOT.INI file errors, missing or corrupted boot files, or hardware configuration errors. This section provides an overview of the NT boot process and discusses troubleshooting through:

- ▶ Examining the NT boot files
- ▶ Using the Emergency Repair Disk (ERD)
- ▶ Accessing the Last Known Good Option in the boot sequence

Overview of the NT Boot Process

When NT boots, the following steps occur:

1. The Power On Self Test (POST) runs on the computer.

2. The master boot record (MBR) is located and loaded. The MBR is scanned for the active partition, and the boot sector from the active partition is loaded.

3. The boot sector specifies that the NTLDR be loaded and initialized. The NTLDR file specifies that the processor use a flat 32-bit memory model.

4. NTLDR starts the mini-file system that will be used to boot NT from the system partition. Mini-file systems include FAT and NTFS.

5. NTLDR accesses the BOOT.INI file. The BOOT.INI file is used to specify the choices that are seen in the boot loader menu that is displayed during the NT boot sequence. This includes the option to boot NT Workstation, NT Workstation VGA mode, or any operating systems previously installed.

6. NTLDR calls NTDECTECT.COM, which scans for hardware installed on the computer. The information that is collected is passed on to the Registry.

7. NTLDR loads NTOSKERNEL.EXE. At this point, the Hardware Abstraction Layer (HAL) is loaded and the Registry is scanned for any drivers or services that should be loaded.

During this stage of the NT boot process, you see a blue screen. Across the top of the screen, you see the operating system build number, last service pack installed, processor type and number, and physical RAM.

8. The Kernel initialization phase begins, and drivers are initialized.

9. The services load phase begins, and the session manager is loaded. AUTOCHK.EXE is run to check each disk partition. The page file is set up, and any subsystems are loaded.

10. When the WIN32 subsystem is installed, the WINLOGON process starts, and the user sees the press Ctrl+Alt+Del message to start the logon process.

11. Any services that are still waiting to start are initialized at this point. The NT boot process is complete. The configuration is then copied to the Clone control set to update the Last Known Good option for subsequent system boots.

NT Boot Files

Corrupt or missing boot files can cause boot errors. In troubleshooting boot failures, you must first identify which file is causing the boot error, then correct the problem.

Boot File Descriptions

The primary files that are used to boot NT on an Intel platform are:

- ► NTLDR
- ► BOOT.INI
- ► BOOTSECT.DOS
- ► NTDETECT.COM
- ► NTOSKRNL.EXE

These files are described in the following subsections.

NTLDR This file is used to control the NT boot process.

BOOT.INI   This configuration file is responsible for building the menu choices that are displayed for the boot process. It is the only file that the end user can modify to directly control the boot process. If you select an NT option, it also provides the location on the boot partition on which NT is installed. The BOOT.INI file has two main sections:

▸ The boot loader section is used to specify which operating system is selected by default and how long the boot process waits before the default selection will be chosen.

▸ The operating system section lists the operating systems you select during the boot process. Each line in the operating system selection contains a description of the operating system and the Advanced RISC Computing (ARC) path to the location of the operating systems boot partition.

TIP

You can configure the boot loader section through the BOOT.INI file or through the Control Panel ➤ System ➤ Startup/Shutdown Configuration tab. Remember that BOOT.INI is stored as a read-only file.

BOOTSECT.DOS   This file is used to load any DOS-compliant operating system that was installed prior to NT (in a dual boot). BOOTSECT.DOS is loaded if you choose an alternate operating system that would expect to see a DOS environment during the boot process.

NTDETECT.COM   This file is used to detect installed hardware and add the hardware it detects to the Registry.

NTOSKRNL.EXE   This is the NT Kernel.

NOTE

If you are using a SCSI controller with the BIOS disabled, you also need the NTBOOTDD.SYS (the SCSI driver) file.

Boot File Error Messages

If any of the boot files are missing or corrupt, you will see the following error messages:

```
NTLDR
      Boot: Couldn't find NTLDR.
      Please insert another disk.
BOOT.INI
      Windows NT could not start because the following file is
      missing or corrupt:
      \winnt root\system32\ntoskrnl.exe
      Please re-install a copy of the above file.
BOOTSECT.DOS
      I\O Error accessing boot sector file
      multi(0)disk(0)rdisk(0) partition(1):\bootsect.dos
NTDETECT.COM
      NTDETECT v1.0 Checking Hardware...
      NTDETECT v1.0 Checking Hardware...
NTOSKRNL.EXE
      Windows NT could not start because the following file is
      missing or corrupt:
      winnt root\system32\ntoskrnl.exe
      Please re-install a copy of the above file.
```

If you use Disk Administrator and your system fails to boot, inspect the BOOT.INI file first. By adding logical partitions, you can cause the ARC name to change. When using Disk Administrator, pay careful attention to the exit messages, because you will be warned if the BOOT.INI needs to be edited, and if so, what the edits should be. If the BOOT.INI has the wrong ARC path name, you will see the following message:

```
Windows NT could not start because of a computer disk hard-
ware configuration problem. Could not read from the selected
boot disk. Check boot path and disk hardware.
```

If the NT boot files are missing or corrupt, you can restore them through the Emergency Repair Disk (ERD).

Emergency Repair Disk (ERD)

The ERD is used to create a snapshot of your system's configuration. To create an ERD, use the RDISK command.

The ERD is not bootable and is used in conjunction with three NT Setup disks.

▶ If you do not already have the Setup disks you can create them from the Windows NT Workstation CD by typing **WINNT /ox**.

▶ To create the ERD, type **RDISK** from a command prompt on the computer the ERD is being created for.

TIP

To force the entire Registry to be saved to the ERD, you should use the command RDISK /s. This assumes that the Registry is not so large that it is able to be compressed and still fit on the ERD.

When you use the Setup disks, you choose the repair option and insert the ERD when prompted.

You can then use the ERD to perform the following operations:

▶ Inspect the Registry files

▶ Inspect the startup environment

▶ Verify the NT system files

▶ Inspect the boot sector

NOTE

Whenever you make changes to your computer's configuration—for example, adding or deleting disk partitions through Disk Administrator—you should always update your ERD.

Recovery of NT Boot Files

If any of your boot files are missing or corrupt, you can repair the failure through the ERD. To repair your boot files, you need the three NT Setup disks and the ERD.

The steps to recover your boot files are as follows:

1. Boot with the NT Setup Boot disks. Insert Disk 1 and Disk 2 when prompted.

2. When prompted, choose R for Repair.

3. Insert Setup Disk 3 when prompted.

4. As requested, insert the ERD.

5. Select the Verify Windows NT system files option.

6. Select the components you wish to restore.

At this point, your NT boot files should be properly restored.

Contents of the ERD

The ERD contains the following:

▶ An information file that can be used to verify and recreate the NT boot files

▶ The security accounts manager (SAM)

▶ Portions of the Registry that relate to the computers configuration

▶ The CONFIG.NT and AUTOEXEC.NT configuration files

NOTE

The files on the ERD are compressed and can be expanded through the EXPAND command-line utility.

The Last Known Good Option

Each time a user successfully logs on, the system boot information is stored in the Registry. The purpose of Last Known Good is that it allows you to recover from system failures caused by incorrect system configuration changes or an incompatible driver.

To access the Last Known Good option, press the spacebar when prompted during the boot process. The system can also access the Last Known Good option if a serious or critical error keeps the computer from successfully booting.

TROUBLESHOOTING FAILED PRINT JOBS

Print errors have many causes. To troubleshoot a printing error, you should first try and isolate where the problem is occurring within the print process. The print process is composed of the following tasks:

1. A shared printer is created on a print server by the administrator.

2. A client makes a connection to the shared printer.

3. The client generates a print job and sends it to the shared printer.

4. The print server receives the job spools, and possibly renders (processes) the job.

5. The print server directs the job to the print device.

6. The print device prints the job.

NT installs printer drivers for NT 3.x and 4 and Windows 95. Additional operating system printer drivers must be added separately. Some common print errors that you might encounter are listed in Table 10.1 along with possible solutions.

TABLE 10.1: Common Print Problems and Solutions

Error	Possible Solution
The print job is printed as garbage or prints with strange characters or fonts.	Make sure the correct print driver is installed on the print server for the operating system on the client workstation.
Win16 applications report that they are out of memory or you are unable to select any fonts.	Make sure a default printer has been selected.
The hard disk is thrashing, and print jobs are not being sent to the print device.	Make sure that the disk has sufficient space to allow for spool file expansion; if not, move the spool file to another disk or partition .
Jobs are reaching the server and not printing or are not reaching the print server.	Stop and restart the spooler service.

You can also manage print jobs from the Printers window. For each printer, there is a list of the jobs that are waiting to be serviced by that printer. Users can remotely manage jobs from other NT computers or from Windows 95/98 systems, but they are limited to only those jobs that they have created or have access to. Through the Document menu in the Printers window, you can control print jobs:

Pause   Allows you to temporarily stop a print job from printing.

Resume   Starts the print job at the point where it left off.

Restart   Causes a print job to be resubmitted from the beginning.

Properties   Allows you to configure properties of the print job, such as notification, priority, and scheduling.

NOTE

See Chapter 5 for more information about printing and troubleshooting printing problems.

TROUBLESHOOTING FAILED INSTALLATIONS

Installation errors can have many causes. Some of the common causes are:

Media errors   You could have a bad floppy or the NT Server CD may be corrupt. If you suspect that you have media errors, try a different set of Setup disks or another NT Workstation CD. To recreate the NT Setup disks, use the NT Workstation CD and the command WINNT /ox.

Hardware that is not on the HCL (Hardware Compatibility List)   NT is picky about the hardware it uses. You should verify that all of the hardware you are using is on the HCL.

CD is not supported by NT   If your CD is supported under another operating system such as DOS or Windows 95/98, you can boot that operating system and copy the contents of the NT CD (on an Intel platform this would be the I386 folder) to the hard drive or to a shared network drive. The installation is then run from the local or network drive. The CD is still unavailable from the NT operating system until an NT driver can be installed.

Incorrect hardware configuration   Check hardware components such as the network card, video adapter, sound card, and modems for configuration settings. There must be no overlap in IRQ, base memory, base I/O addresses, or DMA. In addition, the software configurations must match the hardware configurations.

Blue screen or stop messages   Blue screen or stop messages during installation can be caused by incorrect or outdated drivers being initialized. One common problem is that NT cannot detect the mass-storage (disk) driver correctly. If this is a problem, don't let NT auto-detect your mass-storage device. Instead, manually identify the mass-storage device you are using and provide the correct driver. You should be able to get the correct driver from the manufacturer's Web site.

NOTE

NT 4 does not support Plug and Play. If your installation depends on Plug-and-Play hardware, you may have problems in this area.

TROUBLESHOOTING FAILED APPLICATIONS

NT ships with a utility called Dr. Watson, which is used to diagnose and log application errors. To access the Dr. Watson utility, you type **DRWTSN32** from the Run dialog box or in a command prompt window. You then see the window shown in Figure 10.1.

Through this utility, you can specify whether a crash dump file will be created upon an application failure and what the location of the crash file will be.

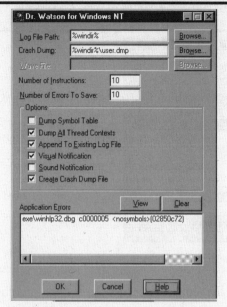

FIGURE 10.1:   The Dr. Watson window

TROUBLESHOOTING RESOURCE ACCESS PROBLEMS

If you are having trouble accessing a network resource, the most common problem is that the user account does not have the appropriate access permissions. The following subsections provide suggestions to help you troubleshoot access to local and network resources.

File and Directory Access

If you're accessing a resource locally, you should determine if the resource is on a FAT or an NTFS partition.

- ▶ If the partition is FAT, then you know the problem does not relate to access permissions.

- ▶ If the partition is NTFS, the problem may be related to access permissions.

Figure 10.2 is used to illustrate some common access problems.

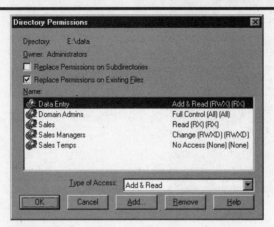

FIGURE 10.2:   NTFS permissions example

Here are some problems that could arise from the permissions shown in Figure 10.2:

▶ Brenda is a member of Sales and Sales Temps. Because Sales Temps has been assigned No Access, Brenda will have No Access regardless of the permissions she has been assigned through her membership in Sales.

▶ Dana is a member of Sales. She tries to access E:\DATA\SUBDIR but is denied access to that folder. When the administrator set up the permissions, the Replace Permissions on Subdirectories box was not checked. This is the default NTFS directory setting.

▶ Ron has been a member of the Sales group. He was recently promoted to a manager and added to the Sales Managers group. However, when he accesses the E:\DATA folder, he can only Read data. Ron needs to log out and log on again to have his access token updated with his new membership.

EDITING THE REGISTRY

The Registry is a hierarchical database used to store NT configuration information. It is made up of five main subtrees:

- ► HKEY_USERS

- ► HKEY_CURRENT_CONFIG

- ► HKEY_CLASSES_ROOT

- ► HKEY_CURRENT_USER

- ► HKEY_LOCAL_MACHINE

You can view and modify the information that is stored within the Registry through the Registry Editor. NT 4 ships with two utilities that can be used to edit the Registry: REGEDT32 and REGEDIT.

WARNING

You should always use the Registry Editors with caution. Incorrect settings can cause serious system malfunctions and can even cause NT to hang. Before editing the Registry, you should always back it up with the NT Backup program. If the system won't boot after editing the Registry, you should first try the Last Known Good option. If this does not correct the problem, you can then use the backup you previously created to restore a known good Registry.

REGEDT32

The REGEDT32 application is a 32-bit Registry Editor designed for NT. This utility provides better support for NT than does the REGEDIT utility, and it has more safeguards to prevent accidental or inadvertent changes. Unless you are using the search capabilities of REGEDIT, REGEDT32 is the preferred utility to use when editing the Registry.

REGEDIT

The REGEDIT program is from the Windows 95 operating system and is included with NT. REGEDIT has better search capabilities than REGEDT32. REGEDIT can search for keys and text. REGEDT32 can only search based on keys.

ADVANCED PROBLEM RESOLUTION

Advanced problem resolution techniques include creating a memory dump, using the Event Viewer, restoring the Administrator password, troubleshooting RAS errors, and troubleshooting display errors.

Creating a Memory Dump

You can configure NT to create a memory dump if a blue screen is generated. To create a memory dump, select Control Panel ➤ System ➤ Startup/Shutdown tab, as shown in Figure 10.3.

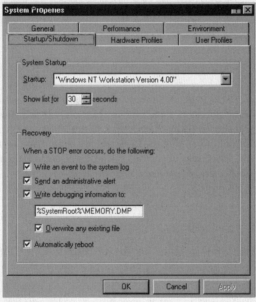

FIGURE 10.3: The Startup/Shutdown page of the System Properties box

To configure NT to create the dump file, check the Write Debugging Information To box. By default, the dump file is created in `%SystemRoot%\Memory.dmp`.

NOTE

To create a dump file, you must have a paging file on the boot partition that is at least 2MB larger than the amount of RAM installed on the NT Server.

The Event Viewer

The Event Viewer is used in NT to provide informational logs regarding your computer. Three different logs are kept:

- ▶ **System**   This log is used to provide information about the NT operating system. You can see information such as hardware failures, software configuration errors, and the general well-being of your computer.

- ▶ **Security**   This log contains information related to auditing. If you chose to enable auditing, you will see success or failure events related to auditing.

- ▶ **Application**   This log contains errors from applications that are running on your server. For example, SQL errors would be logged here.

Within each log, events are recorded into one of five event categories:

- ▶ Error
- ▶ Information
- ▶ Warning
- ▶ Success Audit
- ▶ Failure Audit

To access Event Viewer, select Start ➢ Programs ➢ Administrative Tools (Common) ➢ Event Viewer. Figure 10.4 shows an example of an Event View System log.

By default, the oldest events are at the bottom of the list and the newest events are recorded at the top of the list. In the example shown in Figure 10.4, the bottom Stop message is related to NE2000. If you click this entry, you will see more detailed information, as shown in Figure 10.5.

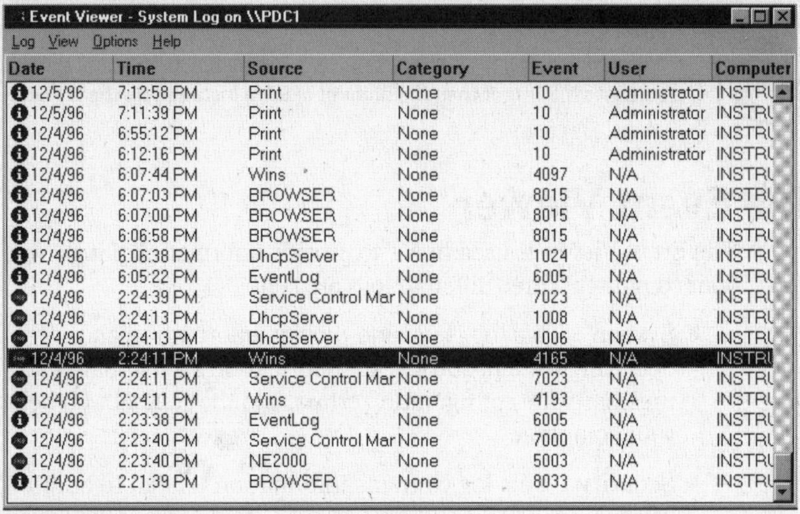

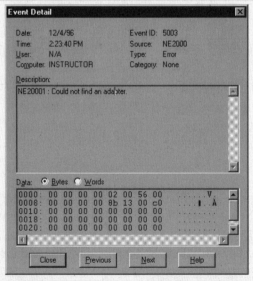

FIGURE 10.4: Event Viewer System Log

FIGURE 10.5: Event Detail within Event Viewer

In this case, the reported error specifies that the NE2000 adapter could not be found. It is important to identify the first error, because subsequent errors are often dependencies that are corrected when you correct the initial problem.

In this example, the NE2000 card has been configured incorrectly. To correct the problem, you would verify the NT settings with the actual configuration on your network card (though Control Panel ➤ Network ➤ Adapters ➤ Properties).

Restoring the Administrator Password

The best way to restore a forgotten Administrator password is to have a backup administrative account that you can log on with and change the Administrator password.

If this is not an option, you can restore the password by using the ERD or restoring a backup of the Registry. This assumes that you know the Administrator password in effect when the ERD or backup was made.

If you restore the Administrator password through the ERD or backup, then any changes that have been made to the SAM since the backup was made will be lost.

Troubleshooting RAS Problems

You can use the Remote Access Monitor and the DEVICE.LOG file to troubleshoot RAS problems.

Remote Access Monitor

You can use the Remote Access Monitor to view the status of your RAS ports, as well as to monitor incoming data, outgoing data, and any errors that have occurred.

DEVICE.LOG

The DEVICE.LOG file provides verbose information that you can use to diagnose RAS communication problems.

This file is enabled by editing the Registry so that the value of the following is set to 1:

```
HKEY_LOCAL_MACHINE\SYSTEM\CurrentControlSet\Services\RasMan\P
arameters\Logging
```

You can then view this file through the \WINNT root\System32\ RAS folder in a file called DEVICE.LOG.

Troubleshooting Display Errors

Display errors should be minimized because NT forces you to test the driver you select. When the driver is tested, you can verify the color palette, the Desktop area, and the refresh frequency. If any of these settings are incorrect, the display could be unreadable.

If this happens, you can select VGA mode from the NT boot screen. This will cause a standard VGA driver to be loaded.

WHAT'S NEXT?

This chapter concludes the NT Workstation part of this book. The next chapter begins Part II with an introduction to NT Server. You will learn where NT Server belongs in your network and the requirements for running it effectively.

PART ii

NT SERVER

Chapter 11

INTRODUCTION TO WINDOWS NT SERVER

I n this chapter, we explain what Windows NT Server is, where it came from, and where it is going. You will find out where NT Server belongs in your network and what kind of computer you need to run it effectively.

Adapted from *MCSE: NT® Server 4 Study Guide, Second Edition* by Matthew Strebe and Charles Perkins with James Chellis

ISBN 0-7821-2222-1   832 pages $49.99

WHAT IS NT SERVER?

Two identical beige computers are on a counter in front of you. They are both running Microsoft operating systems, and at first glance they look exactly the same (see Figure 11.1). They both have a Taskbar with a clock in one corner and a Start button in the other. Windows on the screen contain running programs, and buttons on the Taskbar switch between them. You notice the first difference when you click the Start button—one computer displays the text Windows 95 alongside the menu; the other displays Windows NT Server.

FIGURE 11.1:   Windows NT Server looks like Windows 95.

What are the differences between NT Server and Windows 95/98? Where does each belong in your network? What are the capabilities and hardware requirements of NT Server, and what are the alternatives? The following sections will help you answer these questions.

How Does NT Server Differ from Windows 95/98?

NT Server, as its name implies, is a server operating system. It is optimized to provide network services to client computers. Although NT Server could be used as a client operating system, NT Workstation is more suited to that task because it costs less. NT Server is at home as the center of your network, providing file and print services, routing mail and other network traffic, and supporting back-end software such as database servers and Internet host packages.

NOTE

You should use client operating systems such as Windows 95/98 or NT Workstation to run word processing and spreadsheet applications. You should use a server operating system such as NT Server to store files on the network.

NT Server may look like Windows 95/98, but it is completely different internally. Although Windows 95/98 can trace its genealogy all the way back to the first versions of MS-DOS, Microsoft wrote the NT operating system from scratch in the late 1980s. This fresh beginning allowed the developers of NT to take advantage of such advancements in operating systems and computer hardware as preemptive multitasking, multiprocessing, multiplatform support, secure file systems, and fault tolerance.

NOTE

NT Server and NT Workstation are essentially the same operating system with different features enabled.

Users do pay a small price for this new technology. Because NT is a completely new operating system, many programs that depend on the peculiarities of the original Windows or DOS operating systems will not operate under NT. However, the price is more than returned in the advanced features that NT provides.

NOTE

Windows 95/98 is actually much more complicated than NT because Windows 95/98 must be able to run all programs written for previous versions of Windows and DOS. And meeting that requirement is not easy. NT, on the other hand, has to run only programs written for NT and those programs for Windows and DOS that do not interfere with NT's security mechanisms.

NT maintains a degree of compatibility with older software running under MS-DOS, Windows 3.11, and OS/2 1.3 through the use of environment subsystems. *Environment subsystems* are services of NT that provide a simulated complete shell in which programs written for the above operating systems run. Inside this environment subsystem shell, the computer appears to be operating under DOS, Windows, or OS/2. The subsystem then translates commands from the applications running inside it to their NT equivalents and passes them on to the appropriate NT service.

Where Did NT Server Come From?

In the late 1980s, software developers created Windows as a graphical environment for programs running on Microsoft DOS. Microsoft and IBM collaborated on a replacement for DOS on Intel computers. Their new operating system had many advanced features and was called OS/2. At the same time, Microsoft recognized the need for another more advanced operating system that would have not only all the features of OS/2 (and more), but also the ability to run on other microprocessors, especially Reduced Instruction Set Computer (RISC) microprocessors, which at the time were much faster than Intel microprocessors. This visionary operating system would have to be written in a high-level language such as C that could be ported to other microprocessors, instead of in Intel assembly language, which was not portable.

Microsoft recruited operating system architects and programmers who had experience with advanced operating systems on minicomputers and mainframes. Microsoft hired Dave Cutler, who had led several operating system development projects for Digital Equipment Corporation, to lead the development program for the new operating system. The operating system at that time was called OS/2 NT. (*NT* stood for "new technology.")

In 1990, Microsoft released version 3.0 of its Windows operating system, which became very popular. Shortly thereafter, Microsoft and IBM disagreed on how their two operating systems—OS/2 and Windows— should be marketed. IBM wanted Windows to be viewed as a stepping stone to the more advanced OS/2, whereas Microsoft wanted to expand the capabilities and features of Windows to compete with OS/2. When cooperation broke down, IBM retained the OS/2 operating system, and Microsoft changed the name of the OS/2 NT project to Windows NT.

The first version of NT released to the public (in 1993, as Windows NT Advanced Server version 3.1) had the same user interface as the regular version of Windows. It was a true 32-bit operating system, and it provided a 32-bit environment for Windows programs to run in. This capability made the job of writing large, powerful programs easier because programmers did not have to work around memory boundaries and unprotected memory areas that plagued MS-DOS and Windows 3.0 software. Windows NT Advanced Server version 3.1 also provided a 16-bit environment in which programs written for earlier versions of Windows could run. In addition, it could run DOS and OS/2 version 1.3 programs (a legacy of its earlier incarnation as OS/2 NT). The NT development team also made it possible for developers to compile POSIX programs to run under NT, thereby making it more attractive to government organizations and more suited to Unix environments. (POSIX, which stands for Portable Open Systems Interface, is a government standard that promotes the standards for client/server software by providing an application environment similar to Unix.)

TIP

You can run programs written for OS/2 version 1.3 under Windows NT.

NT has since influenced the development of Microsoft's Windows client operating systems. In 1994, Microsoft released the Win32s software package, which allowed Windows 3.11 and earlier Windows computers to run a subset of 32-bit NT software. In late 1995, Microsoft released Windows 95, which includes most of the 32-bit software interfaces, including those supported by Win32s.

Windows 95 gave users a new interface that was much more flexible and easy to use than the interface in Windows 3.x. Users of NT had to wait until the release of version 4.0 in 1996 to experience the new interface. Version 4.0 also debuted services for support of the World Wide Web and the Internet.

In 1998, Microsoft released Windows 98, which resembles Windows 95 but has enhanced features. It is faster, supports a more efficient file system, integrates Internet Explorer into the operating system, and has a much better uninstall facility.

Part ii

Where Does NT Server Belong in Your Network?

As a server operating system, NT belongs at the heart of your network, providing services to client computers. You could use NT Server for other less demanding tasks, such as running word processor and spreadsheet applications, but other operating systems are more appropriate for that purpose.

The most common use for NT Server is as a file server. In this capacity, it provides a place for storing files for all the client computers on the network, and it enforces security on the network by ensuring that only individuals holding the proper permissions can access those files. One NT Server computer in a domain will also maintain a database of usernames and passwords, which is used by the servers on the network to log people on to the network. The server that maintains the database is called the Primary Domain Controller (PDC).

Computers running NT Server can also perform other server functions, such as hosting and controlling access to databases; routing e-mail, fax, and network traffic in and out of a local area network (LAN); and hosting Internet or intranet information. Figure 11.2 illustrates some server roles.

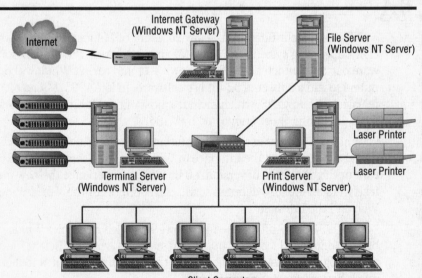

FIGURE 11.2:   NT Server can perform many roles in a local area network.

Where Is NT Server Going?

NT is Microsoft's path to the future of network computing. Microsoft is committed to extending NT technology into every aspect of computing, from handheld computers (the latest handheld computer specification from Microsoft provides a 32-bit application programming interface—or software environment—much like that first introduced by NT) to large multiple-processor enterprise servers at the center of corporate networks. NT currently supports multiple processors in the fastest RISC microcomputers available.

You can expect Microsoft to make NT Server technology even easier to manage in a large corporate network environment. Windows 2000 Server (scheduled for release in late 1999) will support 64-bit computing, Plug-and-Play technology, an Active Directory modeled on the X.500 Recommendation, advanced interdomain security, use of DNS rather than trusts, the inclusion of numerous new products such as Certificate Server, enhanced group management, and Dynamic DNS. As new microprocessor technologies become available and widely accepted, Windows 2000 Server will be ported to run on those microprocessors.

Part ii

NT Server Features and Capabilities

Although NT Server is a full-featured operating system capable of functioning as a client, supporting spreadsheets, word processing programs, World Wide Web browsers, database access programs, and any other type of application that you might find running under NT Workstation or Windows 95/98, running client applications is not its primary purpose. NT Server is intended to provide network services to other computers on a network, and for that reason, it has features and capabilities that client operating systems seldom have.

NT Server is a large and complex operating system with many modular components. However, three major constituents—the operating system kernel, the file system, and the networking services—interact to provide NT Server's features and capabilities as a network server. Figure 11.3 illustrates the components of NT Server.

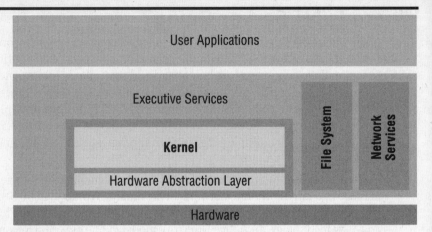

FIGURE 11.3:   The operating system's kernel, file system, and networking services provide the features of NT Server as a server on the network.

Operating System Kernel Features

The kernel, as its name implies, lies at the heart of the operating system. The kernel provides services to the programs running on the computer. Several features of the NT kernel make it an excellent choice for a network server.

Pervasive Security Mechanisms

Security is an integral part of the NT kernel. The system administrator establishes certain security privileges for every user of the operating system, and the kernel prevents users from performing any actions that would violate the security of the operating system. Normal users, for instance, are not allowed to install device drivers or to change the server's networking protocols, even if they are logged on directly to the server. These functions are reserved for users with system administrator's privileges.

Fault Tolerance

The NT kernel provides a fault-tolerant environment for the execution of programs and services by giving every program its own area in which to execute. No program may violate another program's access space or the access space of the server unless it has permission from the kernel to do so. This partitioning system keeps errant or malicious programs from causing damage to other executing programs or perhaps even to the kernel itself.

Preemptive Multitasking

NT has a preemptive multitasking kernel; that is, the kernel provides the illusion of many programs executing at once on the computer by dividing processor time among the programs and ensuring that no program can monopolize the time of the processor.

Symmetric Multiprocessing

The kernel also supports the use of up to 32 microprocessors in the computer. With this feature, as many programs as there are microprocessors in the computer can actually be executing at the same time. The kernel preemptively multitasks each microprocessor so that every program gets its proper share of executing time. Multiprocessing is *symmetric* in NT because NT does not associate particular types of programs with any particular microprocessor in the computer; instead, any task can execute on any microprocessor.

Platform Independence

NT was designed not only for Intel-based computers, but also for computers using RISC microprocessors such as the Digital Alpha. RISC microprocessors often deliver more processing power than do Intel-based microprocessors, but they do so at a price—computers using RISC chips cannot directly run programs or operating systems that have been written for Intel-based computers. Because NT was designed to be independent of any particular microprocessor platform, it can run on the most powerful microcomputers available.

File System and Disk Subsystem Features

The NT File System (NTFS) provides reliable and secure storage for files in a NT Server computer. Although NT supports the FAT file system used in MS-DOS and Windows, NTFS was designed specifically to meet the needs of storing information in a shared network environment.

File System Reliability

NTFS provides features for greater reliability than most other file systems do. NTFS can do so because it doesn't store files on the hard disk in the same manner that the FAT file system does. NTFS does not use a file allocation table (which is what gives the FAT system its name); instead, NTFS records changes to the stored data in a log on the hard disk. If a write operation is interrupted, NTFS (unlike FAT) can use the log to roll back any changes made to the data stored on the hard disk so that the data is not left in an inconsistent state. The FAT system does not have a log, and therefore operating systems that use it may not be able to tell that an operation has been interrupted and the data corrupted.

WARNING

Files stored in an NTFS drive from within NT will not be accessible from any other operating system because only NT supports NTFS.

NT Server supports one feature that is often used in conjunction with NTFS. That feature (although it is a feature of the NT disk subsystem rather than of NTFS itself) is RAID, which stands for Redundant Array of Inexpensive Disks. RAID allows NT to continue operating even if a physical hard disk drive fails. RAID can speed up disk access as well as provide fault tolerance because NT can request data from several drives simultaneously.

NOTE

Redundant Arrays of Inexpensive Disks are also referred to as Redundant Arrays of Independent Disks or disk arrays. All three terms are appropriate.

File System Security

A file system that provides file storage for many users on a network must have features that are not required for a stand-alone computer or a client operating system. Primary among these features is support for security. NTFS complements the security in the NT kernel, maintaining ownership information and providing file-and-directory level access control and auditing. This security system allows the network administrator to specify which users and groups have access to which files and directories, and it also allows the administrator to log successful or unsuccessful attempts to access those files or directories.

NOTE
Chapter 20 covers NTFS security features and shows you how to establish a secure networking environment on your server.

Networking Services Features

The third essential aspect of network server operating systems is network services. Most network server operating systems work best with one protocol or set of protocols, are designed to serve a certain kind of client, and expect to operate in a particular network environment. NT Server, however, arrived on the networking scene after many of the other network operating systems were already well-established and therefore had to adapt to those other networking environments rather than create its own. Therefore, the networking services on NT Server are among the most flexible of any network operating system.

Flexible Protocol Support

When you install NT Server, by default, you are given the choice of three protocols (IPX, NetBEUI, and TCP/IP) to use for networking; you can configure NT Server to provide network services over any one or all three. These protocols are not the only ones that NT Server supports, however. You can also configure NT Server to use AppleTalk or DLC, for example.

NT Server is flexible about the type of protocol it uses because it makes few assumptions about the protocol used to transport data over the network. For networking, NT Server can use any transport protocol that is written to the Transport Driver Interface (TDI) specification, which means that future protocols such as ATM will surely be supported.

Because NT Server is flexible about the protocols it uses, you can expect to find it in many different types of networks—NT Server is just as at home in a primarily Novell NetWare network as it is in a network of Unix workstations using TCP/IP or a Microsoft Windows/NetBEUI environment.

Support for Multiple Client Operating Systems

NT Server is meant to be a server operating system and comes with software to support most client operating systems such as DOS, Windows, NT Workstation, OS/2, and the Apple Macintosh. NT Server can also provide network file services for Unix computers, which are not often classified as clients.

Integration with Windows Clients and Other Windows Servers

Microsoft has paid special attention to providing network services for Windows client operating systems such as Windows 95/98. NT Server contains many features intended to make managing a large network of Windows computers easier and to make NT and Windows 95/98 interoperate seamlessly. NT Server also works well with other NT Server computers, and it is easy to manage the servers remotely using the graphical tools provided with the operating system.

NT Server computers can be organized into domains, which greatly simplifies administration of an NT network. One NT Server becomes the PDC, which maintains the security database and controls various aspects of the network's operation. In a domain-based network, the network users do not log on to each of the servers in the domain; rather, they log on once to the domain as a whole, and the information stored in the security database in the PDC determines which elements on the various servers the user can access. This method is much easier than maintaining account information and logging on to each server individually. Domains may contain Backup Domain Controllers (BDCs) that can take over logon authentication in the event that the PDC is busy or unreachable.

Enhanced Scalability

A network based on NT Server computers can easily grow into an enterprise network with many domains distributed throughout a building, across a campus, or even wider across wide area network (WAN) links. With NT Server, you can establish trust relationships between domains so that users on one network can access resources on another network or so that one network can allow users defined in another network to log on locally. You can use the pass-through nature of a trust in an NT network to develop sophisticated network environments that reduce the administrative burden and maximize the flexibility of your network.

NOTE

MCSE: NT Server 4 in the Enterprise Study Guide (Sybex, 1998) shows you how to implement large networks with NT Server computers.

OTHER SERVERS COMPARED TO NT

NT Server is one of many available server operating systems. Alternative server operating systems include:

- Novell NetWare
- Banyan Vines
- Unix
- Macintosh

Each operating system has its advantages and disadvantages, and no operating system is the best system for every environment.

Novell NetWare

Novell NetWare is the most widely installed network operating system. Novell was one of the earliest companies to provide a complete network operating system and network environment for IBM-compatible computers, and Novell NetWare file servers have always been among the fastest available. Two variants of NetWare are in widespread use today: NetWare 3.*x* and NetWare 4.*x*.

NetWare 3.*x*

The NetWare 3.*x* operating system is the product of years of evolution of the operating system and networking environment that Novell developed more than a decade ago. It is a fast and stable operating system optimized to serve files on a local area network. It is very conservative in its hardware requirements; NetWare 3.*x* will run comfortably on many computers that would strain to support NT Server.

Drawbacks to NetWare 3.*x* arise from its simplicity and age. Primary among them is that each NetWare 3.*x* server must be logged in to separately—you cannot log in to the network as a whole. In contrast, in NT domains, you log on to the domain once, and the resources of all of the servers in that domain become available to you. Logging in to a NetWare 3.*x* network can become cumbersome in a network with many servers. A related drawback is that NetWare 3.*x* does not have built-in facilities to manage a number of servers as a group (NT Server does). NetWare 3.*x* servers act as independent entities.

Part ii

The NetWare 3.x operating system is so specialized for serving files that you cannot execute programs on the server that were not specifically designed for NetWare. In contrast, NT Server can run any programs that NT Workstation can run, as well as most programs that Windows 95/98 and earlier operating systems can run. A further limitation to NetWare 3.x is that programs developed for this system are multitasked cooperatively within NetWare. Consequently, any one program can crash the operating system, which makes for a significantly less stable operating system when the programs are not well tested.

Because NetWare runs programs written only for NetWare, you cannot use programs written for a more widely adopted operating system (such as DOS, Windows 3.x, or Windows 95/98) to provide network services on the file server. This restriction obviously limits the range of software available to be run on the file server.

A minor irritant with NetWare 3.x is that the file server console is text based rather than graphical.

NetWare 4.x

With NetWare 4.x, as with NT Server, you can provide one network user-name and password and be allowed to access resources on many servers. In addition, NetWare 4.x provides sophisticated directory services and true multiple-server support. NT Server 4 provides limited support for NetWare Directory Services.

Nevertheless, NetWare 4.x is still limited to running only NetWare programs (although NetWare 4.x can run programs in a separate memory space, thereby protecting the operating system from program errors). Another drawback is that even though NetWare 4.x provides many more graphical tools for administering the network than does NetWare 3.x, the server console is still a command-line interface.

Banyan Vines

Banyan Vines is a network environment that runs on top of a host operating system such as SCO Unix. The host operating system performs the functions of controlling the hard disk drives, memory, and the network interface; Banyan Vines implements the protocol by which client computers are granted access to the file storage provided by the host operating system.

NT Server, in contrast, is a complete operating system that provides both the basic file and computing services as well as the networking services required by a network file server.

Banyan Vines was the first PC-based network operating environment to provide sophisticated directory services with true multiple-server support.

Banyan Vines, however, is not implemented widely beyond very large PC LAN networks, such as those used by the government. A StreetTalk directory services component (implementing directory services and support for multiple servers) has been implemented for NT Server, and this feature facilitates the migration of networks from Banyan Vines to NT.

Unix

Unix is not a single operating system, but rather a name for a family of related operating systems from various companies that have a common heritage and functionality. Like NT Server, the various versions of Unix are complete operating systems; they can run applications as well as network services. Unix does not differentiate between clients and servers. If a computer is used as a client, it is a client; if it is used as a server, it is a server. Unix computers can also be servers to other client operating systems such as Windows 95/98, DOS, the Macintosh operating system, or even NT.

Most versions of Unix, like NetWare, present a command-line interface for configuration and control of the operating system. However, with the X-Windows windowing system, which is similar to the Microsoft Windows graphical user interface, you can have as many command-line interfaces as you want.

Macintosh

The Apple Macintosh operating system with an AppleShare Server naturally provides file services for Macintosh computers over a network and is very easy to use and administer. Macintosh computers seldom provide file services for non-Macintosh computers. NT Server provides all the file and print services that the AppleShare Server provides, and it does so on a wider set of hardware platforms, including inexpensive Intel-based computers.

NT SERVER HARDWARE REQUIREMENTS

Specifying hardware requirements for operating systems is difficult because computer hardware improves at a rapid pace and the performance expectations of users grow with what hardware can produce. Table 11.1 shows the Microsoft-published minimum standards to run NT Server on Intel and RISC-based computers; however, the hardware listed here will not provide a very useful machine. We also present recommendations for the hardware required for acceptable performance of NT Server as a server operating system.

TABLE 11.1: Minimum Hardware Requirements for NT Server

COMPONENT	INTEL	RISC
Microprocessor	486/DX 33MHz or higher; or any Pentium, Pentium PRO, or Pentium II	233MHz Digital Alpha will provide acceptable performance
Disk storage	125MB	160MB
Memory	16MB (32MB is recommended; 64MB will reduce virtual memory usage and provide good performance; 128MB will increase performance)	16MB (48MB is recommended; 96MB will reduce virtual memory usage and provide good performance; 128MB will increase performance)
Display	VGA or higher-resolution video display adapter	VGA or higher-resolution video display adapter
Required additional drive	CD-ROM or access to files from a networked CD-ROM	SCSI CD-ROM drive or access to files from a networked CD-ROM

NT Server requirements for microprocessors, memory, disk space, and peripheral devices are explained in more detail in the following sections.

Microprocessor

NT Server will run on most microprocessors used in microcomputers today. Most NT Server computers are Intel-based because most microcomputers sold today are Intel-based computers. The minimum capacity

Intel-based microprocessor specified for use with NT Server is a 486DX running at 33MHz. This microprocessor would run the NT Server operating system, but it would be painfully slow for any real use. A more realistic minimum to meet today's networking requirements for a small network is a Pentium-class microprocessor running at 200MHz.

NT Server also supports the Digital Alpha. Microsoft has stopped development of NT for the formerly supported MIPS and PowerPC RISC microprocessors. All versions of these microprocessors provide sufficient computing power to comfortably run NT Server.

Memory

NT Server requires more memory to run than most other client operating systems. Whereas 16MB might be plenty for Windows 95/98, it is barely enough for NT Server. In order for NT Server to perform any useful function in that small amount of memory, it can swap memory out to disk to create more room and then bring that memory back when it's needed again.

On an Intel-based computer, NT Server needs 32MB to provide an "acceptable" level of performance; with 64MB, it will run well.

On a RISC-based computer, NT Server needs 48MB to provide an acceptable level of performance; with 96MB, it will run well. RISC-based computers require more memory than Intel-based computers require because the programs that run on them are larger (and an operating system is a computer program). The designers of RISC microprocessors chose to allow program instructions to take up more space so that they would execute more quickly—this is one of the reasons that RISC-based computers are often faster than Intel-based ones.

Disk Space

The disk files for NT Server occupy 120MB to 150MB of disk space, and the amount of disk space required does not vary much. A RISC-based computer requires a little more space than an Intel-based computer requires. You can select not to install parts of the operating system for modest savings in required disk space, but the amount of space saved would most likely not be worth the effort.

The primary consideration for configuring disk space in a computer for NT Server is the amount of program and user data that will be stored, rather than the space required for operating system files. The amount of

space required for programs and data vastly exceeds the storage requirements of NT Server.

Peripherals

A final consideration is the various computer peripherals that you will be
inserting in or attaching to your NT Server computer. Devices you attach
to your computer must have drivers for NT Server. Some devices are supported by NT Server itself (the keyboard and mouse, for instance); others
come with driver software that you can install from within NT Server.

The computer hardware market is characterized by an almost unlimited array of computers and hardware devices (network adapters, video
cards, etc.). NT Server supports most computers and hardware devices
available today. However, NT Server does not support every computer
and every hardware device ever manufactured. Some hardware devices
may appear to work with NT Server initially, but eventually they conflict
with other hardware devices or cause NT Server to become unstable.

The NT Hardware Compatibility List

The NT Hardware Compatibility List (HCL) lists the computers and other
hardware certified by Microsoft to run NT Server. Using a computer from
the HCL will considerably reduce incompatibility problems and will
assist the Microsoft help line staff in resolving any difficulties you may
have. You can use the NT Hardware Qualifier (NTHQ) to test any machine
for NT Server compatibility before trying to install the operating system.

NOTE

The Hardware Compatibility List ships as part of the NT Server documentation
package. Microsoft also maintains an electronic version of the HCL at its site
on the World Wide Web.

The HCL covers various types of hardware:

▶ Storage devices, including SCSI and RAID I/O subsystems

▶ Monitors, modems, network adapters, CD-ROMs, UPS systems,
keyboards, and pointing devices

▶ CPUs

The NT Server distribution CD-ROM contains many device drivers for NT Server. You are much more likely to find a device driver on the CD-ROM for your device if your device is on the HCL than if it isn't.

TIP

If your hardware is not listed on the HCL, you may have, or be able to obtain, drivers from the hardware manufacturer. When buying new hardware, make sure that, if the hardware is not on the HCL, the manufacturer includes an NT device driver with the hardware.

WHAT'S NEXT?

In this chapter, you learned that NT Server is a server operating system with the powerful architecture of earlier versions of Windows NT and the ease of use of Windows 95/98. The next chapter covers planning your network. You will learn about network design, security models, the roles your server may play, and types of software licensing.

Part ii

Chapter 12

PLANNING YOUR NETWORK

At the risk of stating the obvious, planning your NT network is by far the most important part of setting up your network. Nevertheless, the vast majority of networks are never planned at all—they are simply installed to meet current needs and evolve ad hoc to keep a minimum of services available to users. Networks installed in this manner tend to outgrow resources such as server capacities quickly; it soon becomes very difficult to tell why these networks run slowly and figure out how to improve their performance.

Adapted from *MCSE: NT® Server 4 Study Guide, Second Edition* by Matthew Strebe and Charles Perkins with James Chellis

ISBN 0-7821-2222-1   832 pages $49.99

Planning your network correctly from the start will prevent this chaos from happening to you. If your organization is growing at a steady and predictable pace (most established businesses follow this pattern), you should have no problem defining your network. If your organization is new or is growing rapidly, you can apply the same planning principles by designing the network for its maximum size in three to five years and then implementing the network plan as your organization grows into it. This approach will keep you from being overwhelmed by rapid growth or from investing in technologies that will not be sustainable as your organization grows.

The first section of this chapter walks you through designing a medium-sized network from the ground up. You will be able to apply the design principles used for this type of network to any smaller network. After designing the physical, data-link, and network layers of your network, you will be ready to concentrate on network operating system issues. The second section of this chapter discusses the security models that NT Server supports. The third section focuses on the different roles your server may play to support your chosen security model. The fourth section covers other special functions you may need your servers to perform. The fifth and final section introduces the different types of software licensing NT Server supports and shows you how to choose the type appropriate for your network.

PLANNING THE NETWORK FOUNDATION

Networks, like buildings, are constructed in many layers. Buildings rely upon a solid foundation to support their framework, which gives shape and structure to the building. Buildings are subdivided into floors to make efficient use of the available space. Floors are then further subdivided into rooms to create privacy and security and to prevent people from constantly interfering with one another. Imagine how unproductive a large organization would be if all its employees worked in one undivided space.

In the same way, networks rely upon sound cabling to transmit data among computers and networked devices. Data-link equipment requires properly designed cabling to communicate. Data-link equipment transmits information in units called *frames*, which address data to specific recipients and ensure the integrity of data transmissions.

Transport protocols allow data to move between different types of data-link equipment and guarantee the delivery of all data between any two nodes on the same internetwork. Transport protocols work by providing additional addressing embedded in units called *packets*, which are carried inside frames and tell routers and gateways how to switch the packet onto other data-link networks to which the gateway is attached. Network file systems and interprocess communication protocols rely upon transport protocols to provide seamless data streams by simulating the operation of local hard disks and message-passing systems. They hide the packet-based transmission of transport protocols so that software need not deal with or require any specific transport protocol.

Network operating systems rely upon network file systems and interprocess communication protocols to transfer data between servers and clients, to manage the logon and security processes, and to allow communications between clients and servers in client/server applications. Applications rely upon clients seamlessly connected to resource servers to perform their tasks. Finally, users rely upon networked applications to perform their work.

Each network layer requires thought and planning to ensure the proper operation of the entire network. But rather than starting at the foundation, the physical cable plant, you will start your planning at the top—with the needs of the end user. As you clarify the requirements for each level from the top down, your choices for the next lower level become clear.

The steps in creating a well-designed network are as follows:

- ▶ Conduct a survey of existing conditions.
- ▶ Plan network requirements.
- ▶ Plan the network operating system.
- ▶ Plan the network.
- ▶ Plan the physical plant.

The following sections explain each step in detail, and the exercises show you how to perform each step in your organization.

Conducting a Survey of Existing Conditions

The first step in planning a network is to record what you know about your organization's computing needs. Survey your organization to determine the following information:

▶ **How many computers are in use?** This answer will determine the size of your network, the number of servers you will need, and the quantity and type of data-link equipment you will require.

▶ **What types of computers are being used?** This answer will define the network operating system you should use, the transport protocols you can use, and some of the services you will need.

▶ **What special pieces of computing equipment, such as printers, are in use?** This step will identify additional special equipment, such as print servers, that might be required.

▶ **What services, such as Internet or private wide area network services, are in use?** This step will further isolate which network operating system you should use, as well as help you identify any third-party software that might be required.

▶ **What software is currently being used?** Some network-ready software will operate only under certain network operating systems. If your network is using this type of software, your choice of network operating systems may be limited.

▶ **Will you be integrating existing local area subnetworks into the new network?** These existing networks will have to be compatible with the network you install, or you will have to migrate them to other technologies.

Once you've surveyed your existing network, you can come up with a list of requirements for the network you are planning.

Planning Your Network Requirements

The next step in network planning is to define what you want to be able to do with your network. Common requirements include:

▶ **Supporting collaboration through groupware and e-mail.** How collaborative is your company? Some companies do not require teamwork because the tasks are individual in nature; other companies may depend on hundreds of carefully coordinated individuals to create a product.

▶ **Providing resource sharing for file storage and printing.** Nearly every network in existence must meet this requirement.

▶ **Providing easy access to the Internet or to private wide area networks.** This requirement is becoming more commonplace every day—but it is full of pitfalls and security risks.

▶ **Establishing a central point of network security and control.** For some organizations, the security of data is more important than networking; for others, security is of no concern at all. Find out what your security requirements are.

▶ **Centralizing administration and reducing training burden.** Networks do not have to grow into unmanageable beasts, and users can learn to assist with network administration. Putting together a set of procedures for common tasks such as adding new users, assigning passwords, and providing common training will help to keep your network running smoothly.

▶ **Supporting all existing computer hardware.** Few organizations can afford to throw away their existing computer and network equipment, so supporting legacy systems is an important priority when migrating to new technologies.

▶ **Implementing data archiving and disaster recovery.** This requirement is easy to implement in server-based networks because they provide central points of data storage.

▶ **Providing for the distribution of shared databases.** Servers support the replication of shared data among different servers to guarantee that a common set of information is available to everyone in the organization. Replication can keep the databases in different offices synchronized.

▶ **Increasing the speed at which information can be shared throughout the organization.** Years ago, before overnight delivery services and networks, sharing a document with colleagues in another city meant spending a week waiting for the mail. Even faxing did not really facilitate the sharing of complex information. But e-mail and groupware can transmit everything from blueprints to video presentations quickly and painlessly anywhere in the world.

Part ii

Your organization will have its own requirements. Use the list above to start thinking about the purpose of your network. Combine this list with the information generated from the existing-conditions survey of your organization's computing environment. These two sets of requirements constitute your networking goal and serve as your checklist for evaluating technologies and systems.

Planning the Network Operating System

After surveying your network, create a list of network operating systems you are considering using. This step comes before all others because it determines what sort of server hardware you can use, and it may determine which transport protocols you will support. These choices, in turn, can force your hand when you select data-link layer equipment, which in turn will determine what sort of cabling you will use. Notice that this sequence of decisions reinforces the top-down design structure.

Although you have many network operating systems from which to choose, NT Server is the most modern network operating system available. Its support for advanced features such as symmetric multiprocessing, deeply embedded security, preemptive multitasking, and software fault-tolerance systems (including disk mirroring and striping with parity) makes NT Server the most secure and reliable network operating system on the market. Outstanding security and reliability, coupled with strong support for TCP/IP and intra/Internet services and lower cost than most other network operating systems, make NT Server the obvious choice for new network installations.

Check each network operating system candidate to ensure that it can serve your existing conditions and your planned network requirements. Then select the operating system that comes closest to fulfilling your requirements.

Once you've selected a network operating system, make sure that it will not introduce any problems of its own. For instance, many older network operating systems require users to log in to each server separately. Although this process is of little consequence in small networks, it can become very intrusive in larger multiple-server networks.

You will also want to consider the administrative burden that network operating systems create. Some network operating systems are very easy to administer; others can be so difficult as to become a work hindrance to users in larger networks. If you intend to implement automated administration tools such as Simple Network Management Protocol (SNMP) or

Dynamic Host Configuration Protocol (DHCP), you will have to plan these now so you can ensure that the hardware and software you purchase will support them.

NT Server fills all these needs and is an excellent choice for both general network requirements, such as file and print sharing, and for special-purpose applications, such as application serving, Internet serving, and for use as a gateway or firewall.

NT Server supports all common network protocols, such as TCP/IP (used in Unix networks and the global Internet), IPX (used in Novell NetWare networks), NetBEUI (used by Microsoft and IBM networks), and AppleTalk (used by Apple Macintosh networks). Nearly every computer in existence supports these protocols, which makes NT Server an easy choice. Before you decide on a network operating system, answer the question at the end of Exercise 12.1. Then create your own list of requirements and make sure the network operating system you choose can satisfy them.

EXERCISE 12.1: CHOOSING A NETWORK OPERATING SYSTEM

You have a client who wants to integrate many small networks into a single organizational network. Current equipment includes:

▶ A Novell NetWare network used in accounting

▶ Apple Macintoshes networked in a peer environment in the marketing area

▶ OS/2 and NT Workstations for research and development

▶ UNIX computers in the software development department

Which network operating system(s) can support these existing conditions without loading new software on the client computers?

Planning the Logical Network

Planning the logical network involves selecting a transport protocol, selecting data-link technologies, and dividing the network into subnetworks and security domains.

Part ii

NETWORKING TERMINOLOGY

Network terminology is characterized by confusion and inconsistency. This brief glossary defines network terms as we use them in this book.

Subnetwork   Refers to a single, shared media network such as an Ethernet collision domain or a Token Ring.

Network   Refers to a group of similar subnetworks that are bridged or switched together.

Internetwork   Refers to networks that are connected via routers.

Internet   Refers to the global internetwork of TCP/IP hosts to which most major governments and businesses are now attached.

Intranet   Refers to TCP/IP internetworks that exist entirely inside an organization but use the software and methods made standard by the global Internet.

Domain   Refers to a shared security domain wherein a user can log on to one authentication server that will then introduce the user to all other secure shared resources. This type of domain is not the same as an *Internet domain*, which is a logical grouping of TCP/IP hosts, or an *Ethernet collision domain*, which is a single Ethernet subnetwork.

Planning the logical network is often the most difficult portion of network planning, because you won't have any obvious or easy ways to measure or determine network requirements or usage. Fortunately, we can spare you some trouble by passing on the experience of many network technicians.

If you were going to build a warehouse to store engines, you could simply measure the size of each engine, determine how high you can stack them, add floor space for access, and build a warehouse of the exact size you need. Most architects also add room for expansion and growth. Another method is to simply buy more space than you will ever need, but this approach obviously requires deep pockets.

Both techniques are used in networking, and unfortunately, the second is more common. Many organizations waste a tremendous amount of money on hardware to guarantee that they will not have a capacity problem. For very small networks, buying more hardware than you need can actually make financial sense, because network architects may charge more than the extra equipment will cost to design a network of the proper size. We will assume, however, that you intend to spend as little as you can to create a well-designed network. The steps in designing the logical network are as follows:

▶ Estimate the client load.

▶ Determine which data-link technologies will support that load.

▶ Determine which types of cable support that data-link layer technology.

▶ Decide whether you will centralize or distribute servers on the network.

▶ Lay out a network map.

Estimating Client Load

To estimate load capacities of networks, you need a way to compare very different network technologies and relate them to client computer requirements, often without the benefit of knowing exactly how those client computers will be used. Seasoned network integrators base their estimates on what they've done and seen work in the past.

Although no simple method will replace an experienced network integrator, experience can be distilled into methods that are useful for planning and estimating. A good working methodology will serve a number of roles:

▶ It will be useful for comparing data-link technologies.

▶ It will be useful for planning the network's physical layout.

▶ It will be able to predict the amount and type of hardware necessary to implement the network.

We have developed a simple method that will help you plan your network based upon the client load limit of various current data-link technologies. For instance, a single 10Mb/s Ethernet subnetwork can support a maximum of about 50 DOS clients. The same Ethernet subnetwork can reliably serve 20 or so NT Workstation computers.

Part ii

Of course, these estimations are not absolute—the way the client is used will affect its load on the network greatly, and as technology changes, so will the load estimates for various clients. The law of averages comes to our aid here by smoothing the usage characteristics of a single computer over the number of computers attached to the network. This method doesn't always work well, however. Consider the case of a diskless DOS workstation that must boot its operating system from a network server. This client will typically demand more from a network than a typical client because even its memory page file is being sent over the network.

You can use the method presented here if your operations conform to the common uses of computers. If you are doing something you know will require more bandwidth, consider revising the load values for clients upwards. We have presented worst-case capacities in this method, so resist the temptation to revise them downward.

Load Requirements of Typical Network Clients   We determined the client load requirements shown in Table 12.1 by dividing 100 by the maximum useful number of clients of that type that could operate on a single Ethernet segment. Make a map of all the computers in your organization based on their rough location in your facility, matching them to one of the types in Table 12.1. Sum the values to determine your organization's total client load.

TABLE 12.1: Load Requirements of Network Clients

CLIENT	METRIC	EXPLANATION
Macintosh	1	Macintoshes typically require very little from a network, so we used a typical Macintosh client as the basis for our network metric.
DOS	2	MS-DOS machines tend to run simpler application software that does not demand much from a network.
Diskless DOS client	6	Diskless MS-DOS clients are very demanding. These computers must use the network for every I/O command that would normally go to a local hard disk drive.
Windows	3	Windows is a more complex platform than MS-DOS is, and applications built to run on Windows are more complex and network-aware.

CONTINUED ➡

TABLE 12.1 continued: Load Requirements of Network Clients

CLIENT	METRIC	EXPLANATION
Power Macintosh	3	Macintosh computers based on the PowerPC micro-processor are very fast. Although Macintoshes demand less from a network than most PC file-sharing schemes demand, these computers can hit the network hard because of their speed.
Diskless Windows	9	Diskless Windows clients are extremely demanding of network bandwidth—more so than any other type of computer.
Windows 95/98	4	Windows 95/98 is a powerful multitasking operating system that typically runs on fast client computers.
OS/2	4	OS/2 is similar to Windows 95 in most respects. It runs on similar hardware and runs similar applications.
NT Workstation	5	NT Workstation is the most powerful operating system available for PCs. Its ability to multitask multiple network applications smoothly requires much from a network.
UNIX workstation	5	UNIX workstations are usually used by bandwidth-intensive users like programmers, graphic artists, and CAD operators.
UNIX X-terminal	3	X-terminals are diskless, but they operate as simple displays. Screen updates are sent from a server that actually performs the work requested by the user.
TCP/IP print server	10	Although print servers technically do not generate load of their own, printed documents do. Every document you print to a print server moves across the network twice—when it is sent from your computer to the Windows NT Server that processes it and again when it is sent to the print server attached to the printer. Because printed documents can also be quite large, they can create quite a load on your network.

Part ii

Load Capacities of Data-Link Technologies

Data-link technologies use various methods to arbitrate the sharing of media, which makes a comparison difficult. For example, although Token Ring uses a faster bit rate than Ethernet uses, a client must wait for the token before transmitting, which can make Ethernet seem more responsive. Adding clients to a Token Ring network will slow the network in a simple deterministic manner, whereas overloading an Ethernet network can cause it to suddenly cease operating all together. These differences mean that comparisons based on simple bit rate are meaningless.

We chose to use the worst-case number of clients we felt could be usefully attached to a single, shared media network rather than to use a comparison of raw throughput. We then applied this metric to the capacities of other types of networks that are not shared media, such as Asynchronous Transfer Mode (ATM), to show how these networks can be aggregated into large internetworks.

When creating internetworks, the capacity number used for a subnetwork becomes its load. For instance, a Fiber Distributed Data Interface (FDDI) ring with a capacity rating of 1,000 can handle up to ten Ethernet networks, each with a capacity rating of 100. Table 12.2 shows the load capacities of various network data-link technologies.

TABLE 12.2: Load Capacities of Network Technologies

NETWORK	CAPACITY	EXPLANATION
Ethernet	100	Ethernet was used as the basis for comparison because it is the most common network data-link technology. You can expect to attach 50 DOS clients to a single Ethernet subnetwork before it bogs down.
Token Ring	200	A single Token Ring subnetwork can support roughly twice as many computers as a single Ethernet subnetwork. Because Token Ring degrades gracefully, you can continue to load a Token Ring past this point, but your network will slow considerably.
Fast Ethernet	500	Although the bit rate for fast Ethernet is ten times the rate of Ethernet, it cannot handle ten times the traffic because of the delay involved in resolving collisions.
FDDI	1,000	You can reasonably connect ten Ethernet networks on a single FDDI ring. This arrangement depends greatly upon where you've chosen to place your servers—centralized servers demand more from the backbone.

CONTINUED ➡

TABLE 12.2 continued: Load Capacities of Network Technologies

NETWORK	CAPACITY	EXPLANATION
FiberChannel (1Gb/s)	10,000	Gigabit Ethernet will operate over FiberChannel at one gigabit per second. Although gigabit Ethernet retains the Ethernet name, it is full duplex point to point and does not have collisions. It is a perfect backbone technology in campus environments.
ATM-155		
OC-3	1000	ATM is a switched network technology. It is not shared. For this reason, you can count on being able to use about 80 percent of the bit rate for usable traffic, as long as you maintain constant connections between servers.
ATM		
OC-12	4000	ATM bandwidth increases linearly with speed. At 622Mb/s, ATM OC-12 is sufficient for the most demanding backbone applications.
ATM		
OC-48	16,000	ATM at OC-48 (2.2Gb/s) is typically used for metropolitan area networks. This capacity is appropriate for metropolitan area high-speed links.
ATM		
OC-192	48,000	ATM at OC-192 (8.8Gb/s) is used for major trunks between metropolitan areas by telephone companies. It is included here for completeness.

Part ii

When calculating load versus capacity, remember that these numbers are maximum capacity estimates. Erring on the side of excess capacity is preferable to being tied to a slow network. You should try to avoid coming within 25 percent of the maximum values presented here if you want your network to run smoothly.

Make a rough map of the computers in your organization based on location. Select a network technology and group clients into networks based upon location. Then sum the client load values of each group to make sure you are well within the load capacity for the network type you've selected.

NOTE

Backbones are high-speed links connecting shared media subnetworks. Back-bones may be shared media networks themselves, point-to-point links, or switched networks.

A Network Design Example   Figure 12.1 shows an organization's physical layout; the computers in use are represented as client loads. Using this map, the network administrator was able to segregate the network into Ethernet subnetworks, as shown in Figure 12.2. This network will operate properly under normal load conditions because the administrator stayed well below the worst-case capacity of Ethernet during the design. Exercise 12.2 will give you some practice in designing networks.

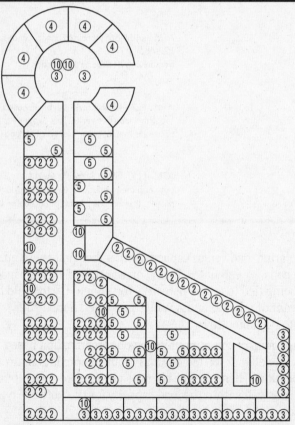

FIGURE 12.1:   Typical client loads for an organization

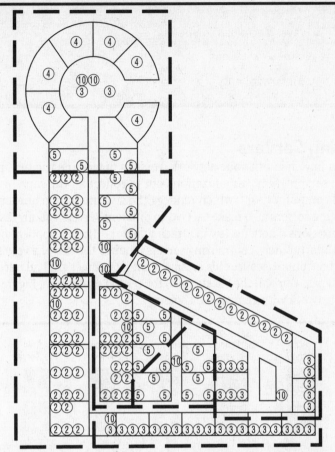

FIGURE 12.2: Creating subnetworks based upon estimated client load

EXERCISE 12.2: DESIGNING A NETWORK

Given the following information and using the method described above, determine how many Ethernet subnetworks you need to comfortably support these clients, allowing for 25 percent growth:

▶ 15 NT Workstation computers

▶ 250 MS-DOS clients

▶ 95 Macintosh computers

CONTINUED ➡

▶ 99 Power Macintosh computers

▶ 35 OS/2 workstations

▶ 155 Windows clients

Locating Servers

Once you have laid out your network, you can determine the best place to install servers. Many organizations opt to collect all the servers into a central computer room, which reduces the administrative burden. Centralizing servers also makes access to different servers equally fast for organizations where users will attach to many different application servers. Unfortunately, centralizing servers requires the use of a very fast network backbone because this arrangement guarantees that all network traffic will pass through the backbone to the central server farm. Figure 12.3 shows a network with centralized servers.

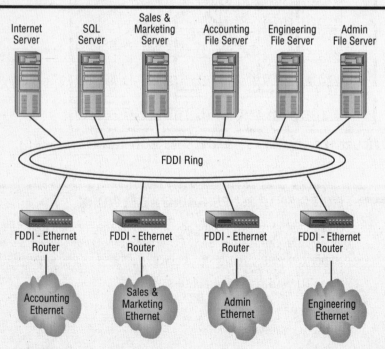

FIGURE 12.3:   Centralized servers

Other organizations distribute servers to the individual subnetworks and rely upon a slower backbone to connect users to resources outside their subnetwork. The backbone does not need to be high speed because (we hope) about 80 percent of all client traffic will be to the local server, which is on the subnetwork with the clients. Distributing servers physically throughout the organization reduces the cost of the network, but it tends to increase the administrative burden. Distributed serving can be very slow if users frequently need to access other servers on the network. If this situation exists in your organization, centralized servers (or a combination of centralized and local servers) may be more appropriate. Figure 12.4 shows a network with local servers.

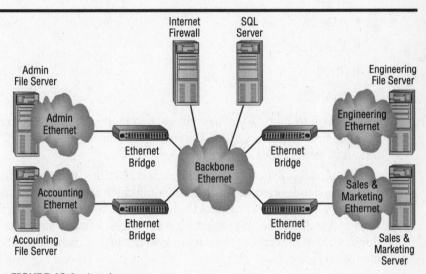

FIGURE 12.4: Local servers

Planning the Network Technology

Each type of shared media data-link technology can support only a limited number of clients. The actual number varies between networks depending on the load, but even the fastest shared media networks don't get very large. To create larger networks than those supported by a single, shared media network, you must use internetworking devices.

Once you've installed your physical plant, you will need to connect the various subnetworks. You create connections between subnetworks with devices called bridges, routers, and switches. *Bridges* connect two similar subnetworks. *Routers* connect subnetworks of different technologies. *Switches*, depending upon the type, can connect many subnetworks of similar or different technologies.

Choosing Network Technologies

Once you've determined what your client load will be, you can determine which network technologies are most appropriate to handle that load. Current popular network technologies include:

- ▸ Ethernet
- ▸ Token Ring
- ▸ ATM-25
- ▸ Fast Ethernet
- ▸ FDDI
- ▸ ATM-155

Although technically you have many choices, the inexpensive, easy-to-use data-link technology called Ethernet outdistances most network data-link technologies.

Now available in two flavors, 10Mbps and 100Mbps, Ethernet is fast enough to handle even the most demanding client loads. Another variant called gigabit Ethernet promises to eliminate the need for high-speed, high-cost technologies to connect even the largest campus networks. The dominance of Ethernet in the data-link technology market makes this choice very easy.

Ethernet supports all popular cable plant technologies. You can run Ethernet over coaxial cable, twisted-pair telephone cabling, and optical fiber. Most new installations will opt for twisted-pair wiring, because it solves many of the problems associated with coaxial wiring and is much less expensive than optical fiber. Optical fiber is usually used for internetwork connectivity in large buildings and campuses.

Choosing Backbone Technologies

Choosing a backbone technology is somewhat more complex than choosing a shared media network technology. Unlike subnetworks for which your choice should be obvious, no single backbone technology surpasses others in price, performance, or ease of use.

Most high-speed backbones in operation today run on 100Mbps FDDI, which is a ring technology that can support very large and distant networks. FDDI is expensive, however, and despite (and partly because of) its redundancy features, it can be difficult to work with. FDDI is also nearly obsolete as a backbone technology at a mere 100Mbps.

Many network integrators are using ATM as a backbone technology. ATM uses high-speed circuit switches to connect the various parts of a network in star hierarchies. ATM was designed primarily as a telephony, voice, and video service, however, and has some problems encapsulating the large packets typically used by transport protocols such as TCP/IP. Because ATM is fairly new and because many vendors are building devices that do not interoperate properly, ATM can be a risky choice. However, ATM will probably be installed worldwide as the telephony transport over the next 20 years, which will make it a more obvious choice as time goes by and incompatibilities are ironed out.

Gigabit Ethernet over FiberChannel may represent a simple and (relatively) inexpensive alternative to the two heavy-duty backbone technologies presented earlier. However, this new technology will carry a high price tag.

Full-duplex Fast Ethernet over fiber-optic cable is the least expensive high-speed backbone technology currently available, but it suffers from distance limitations that make it difficult to use in larger campuses or metropolitan area networks.

Planning the Physical Plant

Just as Ethernet is the easy choice for data-link technology, star-wired, category 5, unshielded twisted-pair (UTP) cable plants are the easy choice for physical plants. The combination of star wiring and UTP makes troubleshooting easy, since no cable fault affects more than one computer. There are no rules for termination, transceiver counts, or any of the myriad of problems that can occur with coaxial-based plants. UTP cabling operates at up to 100MHz, providing bit rates up to 155Mbps. If you anticipate a greater need, you will need to install optical fiber throughout your network.

NOTE

All modern networks operate over one of two types of cable: category 5 unshielded twisted-pair (UTP) or optical fiber. The distance limitations of UTP wiring restrict its use to connecting clients in a relatively small area (within 100 meters of a wiring closet) in a star architecture. Optical fiber connects these wiring closets to form the backbone of the network.

Although many other network cabling styles exist, they are all obsolete except in special circumstances. The advantages of the star-wired–UTP/optical fiber network far outweigh the minor cost advantages of coaxial wiring in all but the smallest peer-to-peer networks. If a network spans beyond a single room, it should use the architecture presented here. Figure 12.5 shows a typical star-wired network with an optical fiber backbone.

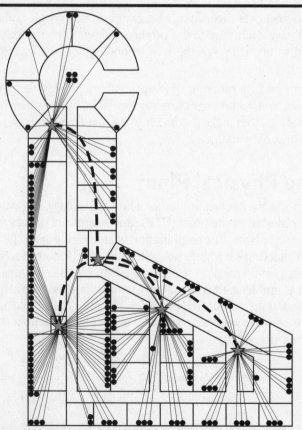

FIGURE 12.5: Star-wired—UTP/optical fiber hybrid network

The advantages of star-wired networks are many:

- ▶ They can emulate all other wiring topologies (ring or bus).

- ▶ They are inexpensive.

- ▶ You can add more stations simply by pulling a new cable.

- ▶ Cable faults typically affect only one computer and are easy to isolate.

Star-wired networks have only one disadvantage—they require more cable. But when you consider that UTP is typically one-tenth the cost of the coaxial cable required for bus networks, the difference in cost is inconsequential.

To plan your physical plant, simply lay out where you want UTP station locations, also called *drops*, on blueprints of your facility. You don't have to lay out cable paths, as you can count on the contractor who installs your network to make the shortest path to a wiring closet to save work.

Note that your physical plant should map somewhat to your subnetwork layout created in the client load section, but it does not have to match exactly. You can create more than one subnetwork in a single wiring closet, but it might be difficult (and unnecessary) for one subnetwork to span more than one wiring closet.

Each network device and computer attached to the network will require a drop. Note where you have space for wiring closets, also known as *intermediate distribution frames* (IDFs), which are generally required for the central point of each star. The *main distribution frame* (MDF) closet is where the backbone runs for each IDF end. If you have more than one floor, the MDF on each floor will terminate in the computer room.

NT SERVER SECURITY MODELS

You need to be aware of two security models when you network with NT Server: workgroup and domain. The first model, *workgroup*, governs the interactions of Windows and NT computers in a peer network; the second model, *domain*, governs the interactions of clients and servers in a server-based network with an NT Server computer (designated the PDC) coordinating the security of the network. The two models fulfill different security requirements.

The Workgroup Security Model

NT local area networks that are small and that do not need centralized network control or centralized data storage can be organized into workgroups. Workgroups are essentially peer-to-peer networks, which means that the users of each workstation select and manage the resources on that workstation. Workstation resources are made available to other users on the network. The user accounts and resources on the workstation are administered from that workstation, not from a network server.

A workgroup is a good choice for your networking model if your organization is small (ten users or fewer), the workstation users have the ability to administer their own workstations, and central file storage and central control of network security are not important.

The workgroup security model does not support user accounts in the same way that logging on to a domain does. Workgroup resources are simply protected by a password (or in the case of NT, by an account name and password). Anyone knowing the password to a shared resource on a workgroup has access to that resource.

NT allows servers to participate in workgroups as stand-alone servers. *Stand-alone servers* are servers that run NT Server but do not participate in any domain security. Stand-alone servers are discussed later in this chapter.

A workgroup is not a good choice for your networking model if you have many users, if you need to centralize user account management and network security, or if you cannot rely on the users of your network to administer their own workstations.

The Domain Security Model

Domains provide much more coherent security and network administration than the workgroup security model provides. In domains, accounts are managed on a single computer, called the PDC, which permits or denies access to all the shared resources in the domain. (BDCs keep a copy of the security accounts database and can log on users if the PDC is busy or unavailable.) Because accounts are managed centrally, users have to log on only once to gain access to all servers in the domain. The domain controller that logged them on will "introduce" the user to other servers in the domain by forwarding their account information in the form of a security access token.

The domain model of networking is a good choice if you have strict security requirements or multiple servers, or if you cannot rely on your users to administer their own computers.

Because this information is centrally controlled, the task of managing a large network is easier for the network administrator than it would be if the information had to be maintained individually on each computer in the network. Centralizing this information also means that users do not have to perform their own administrative tasks for their workstations.

In a domain, one or more servers store the shared network files for all workstations in the domain. The PDC controls workstation access to the files stored on the servers, using account and security information it stores in a central database. Storing the network files in servers helps the network administrator control access to information. A central location also helps to streamline the task of data backup.

Structuring Domains

A large network may have more than one domain. An organization that is divided into functional units—for instance, a business that is split into marketing, finance, manufacturing, and research departments—may divide its domain-based network along those same functional lines. Organizations that have offices in different parts of the country would probably choose to have a domain in each office.

NOTE

MSCE: NT Server 4 Study Guide focuses on single-domain networks. The companion book in this series, *MCSE: NT Server 4 in the Enterprise Study Guide* by Lisa Donald (Sybex, 1998), covers multiple-domain networks in detail.

Workgroup User Accounts and Domain User Accounts

The User Manager program that comes with NT Workstation cannot administer the domain user and administrator accounts. Instead, these accounts are administered by the User Manager for Domains program on the NT Server computer or by computers with remote server management software.

Local user and group accounts for individual workgroup resources are not added to the domain database. Local users and groups are still administered with the User Manager program. When you log on from the workstation that is part of a domain, you are given the choice of logging on to the domain (using an account in the domain user account database) or logging on to the workstation computer (using an account in the workstation's local user account database). If you log on using a user account that is local to the workstation, you may not have access to resources on the domain.

Trust Relationships

Trust relationships extend the domain logon process beyond the boundary of a single domain. You can establish trust relationships between NT domain controllers so that they can "introduce" clients from their domains to the domain controllers in the foreign trusted domain, thus allowing access to information in the foreign trusted domain without requiring another logon to that domain. The trust relationship then determines what access the foreign client is given.

Choosing a Security Model

Your choice of security models depends primarily upon two things: the level of security you require and the level of control you wish to exercise over your network.

The advantages of the domain model are numerous, and the disadvantages are few. For most server-based networks, the workgroup model has no advantages, since you must normally log on to a server anyway. The domain model supports a single logon to all shared resources in the domain, whereas the workgroup model requires a separate logon for each workstation shared resource. The domain model also supports centralized account management and user control.

The workgroup model is typically used only in networks where the users are computer experts and wish to retain a high level of control over resources that they share from their computers, as in peer-to-peer networks. Adding a server to an existing peer-to-peer network might be slightly easier if you choose the workgroup model. Exercise 12.3 will give you some practice in selecting a security model.

EXERCISE 12.3: SELECTING A SECURITY MODEL

You've just installed a ten-user Ethernet network for a group of real estate agents who intend to share e-mail, scheduling information, and a laser printer. Which security model is appropriate?

You've just installed a 400-user, six-server Fast Ethernet network for a consumer credit bureau. Which security model is appropriate in this case?

NT SERVER ROLES

NT defines the role of an NT server by its participation in the domain security model. You must choose from the four defined roles for an NT server during the initial installation of the NT Server software:

▶ The PDC (Primary Domain Controller) must be the first server operating in the domain because all other computers use this server to get permission to participate in the domain.

▶ BDCs (Backup Domain Controllers) assist the PDC in authenticating logons.

▶ Member servers are servers in the domain that do not participate as domain controllers.

▶ Stand-alone servers are not members of a domain, so they must provide their own local logon and security.

The PDC

In a security domain, one computer acts as the PDC. This computer authenticates logons for clients by validating the supplied username and password in the accounts database and returning a security token to the requesting client. The security token introduces that client to all other domain security participants on the network whenever the user requests a resource shared by that participant. The security-token scheme gives transparent access to the user and provides for a single logon to the domain without sacrificing security.

The first NT server in your network must be the PDC if you intend to use the domain security model. You indicate this decision during the installation of NT Server. This first server will be responsible for storing the security accounts database. It also names the domain. If you don't want the first server you install to remain the PDC, you can always promote a BDC later.

The BDCs

BDCs keep a copy of the entire security accounts database and can log on clients if the PDC is busy or cannot be reached.

BDCs keep copies of the security accounts database, and they cannot change their copies. You can use the Server Manager for Domains utility to promote any BDC to a PDC. (The current PDC then becomes a BDC.)

Servers

A server that is not configured as either a PDC or a BDC cannot create a security access token, so it cannot log clients on to the domain. Two types of servers are not domain controllers: member servers and stand-alone servers. Neither of these types of servers can be promoted to domain controller status. You must reinstall NT Server if you want to use these computers as domain controllers.

Member Servers

Member servers participate in domain security, but they cannot authenticate logons. Therefore, they cannot function alone. Users must log on to a PDC in order to gain access to member server resources.

Stand-Alone Servers

Stand-alone servers do not participate in domain security at all; they require their own specific logon. These servers are used in the workgroup security model.

SPECIAL-PURPOSE SERVERS

Special-purpose servers are computers configured to provide a network service other than file and print services. These servers are usually special cases of the basic application server. Your organization may not have any special-purpose servers, or you may have many, depending on your needs and your business model.

Application Servers

Application servers run powerful programs designed to serve the server portion of a client/server application. The server portion of a client/server application is often referred to as the *back end*, and the client portion is often referred to as the *front end*. Consequently, application servers are called *back-end servers*. All the Microsoft BackOffice applications are designed to be run on application servers. Figure 12.6 shows an application server in a local area network.

Part ii

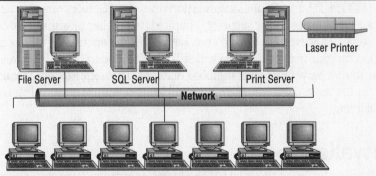

FILE SERVER   SQL SERVER   Print Server   Laser Printer

Network

Local Area Network Clients

FIGURE 12.6:   Local area network with an application server

Application servers are optimized for software execution speed. Typically, they have very fast processors, are likely to use symmetric multiprocessing, and generally have more RAM than any other type of server. Hard disk space for these servers varies widely depending on the type of application being served.

Application servers are most commonly implemented as back-end database servers using the Structured Query Language (SQL) protocol. SQL servers perform the compute-intensive task of tracking down data relations and returning a complete set of data based on a user's request. Microsoft SQL Server is an example of a SQL back end. Microsoft Access would typically be used as a front end to a SQL server.

Internet Servers

Internet servers are special application servers that answer (most commonly) HyperText Transfer Protocol (HTTP–the protocol of the World Wide Web), File Transfer Protocol (FTP), and Gopher requests from the Internet. Internet servers allow organizations to publish Web pages on the Internet, as well as post files and programs. Uniform Resource Locator (URL) addresses are the addresses to Internet servers.

The Internet Information Server (IIS) package that comes with NT Server 4 provides all the functionality necessary to use a NT Server computer as an Internet server. It provides secure storage and publication of HTTP, FTP, and Gopher information from a NT Server computer and keeps Internet traffic securely separated from other information on your server. However, IIS cannot keep hackers from penetrating other computers on your network, so you will still want to place a firewall between your Internet server and your in-house network. This requirement means that, for the most part, you will not be storing secure data on your Internet server.

Firewalls

The explosion of the Internet has forced companies to protect their computing resources from intrusion by unauthorized parties. The Internet protocols were not designed with security in mind; instead, they were optimized for ease of connectivity. Special security servers called *firewalls* patch the holes in Internet security.

Firewalls act as gatekeepers to the network and attempt to prevent unauthorized intrusion into the network through a number of complex security measures. Typically, firewalls can be configured to allow only computers from certain IP addresses to attach to your network. Firewalls also prevent external computers on the Internet from "seeing" IP addresses inside the network, thus preventing intruders from exploiting shared resources on interior servers. The only computer that can be seen is the firewall itself. Figure 12.7 shows an Internet server being isolated by a firewall in a local area network.

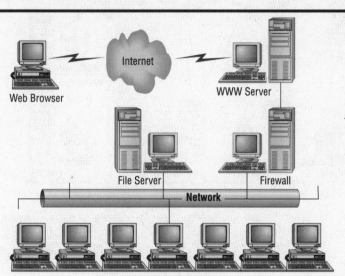

Web Browser

WWW Server

File Server

Firewall

Network

Local Area Network Clients

FIGURE 12.7: A firewall isolating an Internet server from a local area network

Messaging Servers

Messaging servers aggregate the many different types of messaging services that an organization requires. They typically run a LAN groupware package, such as Microsoft Exchange or Lotus Notes, and are usually configured as Internet e-mail gateways. Messaging servers may also be configured with modems to dial into paging services to contact personnel or forward high-priority messages to alphanumeric pagers. Message servers can also sort through Internet or private news services for articles that may be of interest to anyone on the network and forwarding them as e-mail. Figure 12.8 shows how a message gateway attaches to the various components of a network.

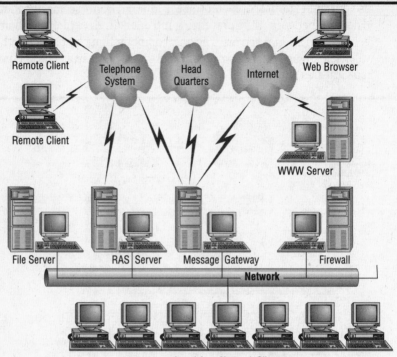

FIGURE 12.8:   A message gateway connecting network resources

Gateways

Gateways are servers configured to provide a link between two distinct networks, protocols, or services. Gateways may provide any sort of translation necessary to extend one network's service to another network. The Gateway Service for NetWare (GSNW) is built into NT Server. GSNW allows Microsoft network clients to attach to resources on a NetWare network. This configuration is a perfect example of a gateway.

Routers are a type of gateway optimized for connecting networks of dissimilar data-link technology that run the same transport protocol. Gateways might also be configured to translate an older mainframe interface to a local area network protocol or to periodically poll a private news, e-mail, or database server to allow clients not configured to attach to the service directly to access the information. Remote-access servers can be considered a serial-to-network gateway. Figure 12.9 shows a NT Server computer acting as a GSNW provider.

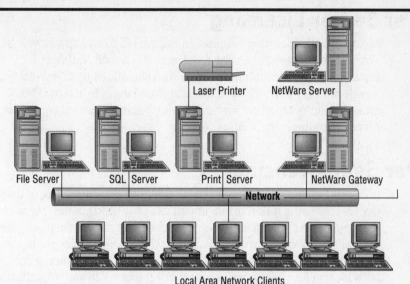

Laser Printer   NetWare Server

File Server   SQL Server   Print Server   NetWare Gateway

Network

Local Area Network Clients

FIGURE 12.9: NT Server can act as a gateway to NetWare servers

Remote-Access Servers

Remote-access servers answer incoming connections from remote clients. Typically, modems, ISDN interfaces, or Point-to-Point Tunneling Protocol (PPTP) connections from the Internet perform this function.

These servers have special security requirements because they are gateways to your network from public locations. For this reason, they may restrict access to confidential or sensitive information.

Because Remote Access Service (RAS) connections are very slow compared to LAN connections, RAS servers do not need to be located on high-bandwidth backbones. In Figure 12.8, a RAS server provides services to remote clients.

LICENSING

The final step in planning your network is satisfying the legal aspects of client licensing. Client licensing is the purchase of a license to attach to a network operating system, thus providing a way to scale the price of a network operating system by the number of people who will be using it, rather than simply charging all organizations, large or small, the same price.

Per Server Licensing

Most network operating systems, including NT Server and Novell Net-Ware, have stringent licensing requirements. Novell NetWare, for instance, limits the number of users who can attach to a NetWare server simultaneously and will not allow additional users to attach. This arrangement is called *per server licensing* because licenses are issued per server operating system sold.

Per Seat Licensing

NT Server allows per server licensing but gives you the choice of using per seat licensing if that arrangement fits your needs better. *Per seat licensing* means purchasing a separate client access license (CAL) for each computer on your network, which gives that computer license to attach to any number of NT Server computers. It is called per seat licensing because you purchase a license for every computer in your organization, thus freeing you from per server license limits.

How Purchased Licenses Are Applied

If you choose to use per server licensing, CALs are applied to the server. For instance, purchasing 50 CALs means you can have 50 users simultaneously logged on to a specific server.

If you choose to use per seat licensing, CALs are applied individually to computers in your organization. For instance, if you buy 50 CALs, you can allow 50 computers to log into any number of NT Server computers simultaneously.

Selecting a Licensing Method

Microsoft recommends choosing per server licensing for small, single-server organizations. Microsoft allows a one-time conversion of per server licenses into per seat licenses if your organization grows beyond one server. Choosing per server licensing will allow you to save on access costs if your computers are generally not all attached to the server at the same time. Microsoft recommends choosing per seat licensing for all networks larger than a single server.

We recommend using per seat licensing in all cases. The amount of money you may save using per server licensing is small, and the restrictions are simply not worth the savings. By adding the cost of a per seat license to every workstation purchase, you will have the administrative freedom to add servers as you please and will never have to worry about licensing issues. Practice choosing a licensing method with Exercise 12.4.

EXERCISE 12.4: CHOOSING A LICENSING METHOD

You have installed a network with four NT Server computers in an organization that will be using two of them as departmental servers and the other two as application servers. Which licensing method is appropriate?

WHAT'S NEXT?

This chapter described the steps for planning a network. After you've decided on the structure of your overall network, you can focus on the design of your NT Server computer. The next chapter covers the choices available for your server's software and hardware.

Part iii

Chapter 13
DESIGNING YOUR NT SERVER

In this chapter, you'll discover many of the design options available to you and get started on making the right choices. You probably want to jump right in, but the best thing to do at this point is to study up, make all the decisions in the comfort and quiet safety of your own cube, on paper, before entering the wild fray of server setup and installation. You'll be making decisions that will require you to reinstall from scratch if you change your mind. So it's better to change your mind on paper, where it's easy, rather than go through the hassle of stripping your server down for the fifth time in a row. And it's cheaper to make a simple mark with your pencil on the design review than it is to order some hardware, unpack it, and then have to send it back.

Don't get too worried. You'll be up to your armpits in computer guts in just a moment. Anticipation makes it all the better.

Adapted from Windows NT® Server 4: No experience required.™ by Robert Cowart and Boyd Waters

ISBN 0-7821-2081-4   512 pages $29.99

NT SERVER SOFTWARE DESIGN

What do you want to do with your server? Once you have an idea about what role your NT server is going to play on your network, you'll be able to determine the nature of the software that will be required. And once you know which software will be running on your system, you can provide for the computing resource requirements with an adequate hardware design.

In the following sections, we'll deal with these questions:

- ▶ Which client licensing option should I choose for my server software?
- ▶ What role should my server play on the NT network?
- ▶ What services will my server provide to my users?
- ▶ What components of NT Server software will be required?
- ▶ What other software will I need?

Once you finish designing your server software, designing your hardware will be a snap. And your NT installation will be that much easier.

WARNING

If you blow off the design of your server, you will die. Okay, maybe you won't die, but you will be sorry. Even if you're getting a server handed to you, ready to go, you'll have a chance to be the captain of your fate when it comes to the NT software setup. Server design is for everyone!

Which Client Licensing Option?

Every computer that connects to an NT server must have a license to do so from Microsoft. As explained in Chapter 12, you have two choices when determining the number of client licenses to purchase: per server and per seat.

If you can't decide which licensing mode is right for you, you should start with per server licensing. NT Server enables you to perform a one-time, one-way conversion from per server licensing to per seat licensing.

What Role Should My NT Server Play?

This is a very critical question; you must know the answer before installing NT.

As you learned in Chapter 12, NT servers can play four different roles in an NT network:

- ▶ Stand-alone server
- ▶ Member server
- ▶ Primary Domain Controller
- ▶ Backup Domain Controller

Which of these roles your NT server is playing on the network determines a great deal of that server's core system behavior. For this reason, changing the role of an NT server requires that you reinstall the software from scratch! Since setting up a server is a complex task, you really don't want to do this more than necessary. Make sure you understand the implications of your decision about your server's network role. For an in-depth discussion of NT Server network roles, refer to Chapter 12.

What Services Will My Server Provide?

Why are you purchasing your server? Is your server going to be a database server? Are you installing this server because your users need a central file server for their area? Or maybe you're installing the server to run that new order-entry system?

You can think of an NT server as a hard disk that happens to be in a remote location somewhere—a file server—or you can think of your server as a thing that can manipulate data in sophisticated ways in order to answer your questions—a computing or applications server.

What Server Software Components Will Be Required?

NT is a modular server system, allowing you to add software components to expand the functionality of your server. You will want to install some of these components when you set up your NT server for the first time. Most services can be easily installed after the system is up and running. Your installation plan should take into account the services that are available with NT.

Part ii

You might be surprised at the functionality that the NT Server package provides out of the box, with no further software purchase necessary. Here are some of the services that the standard NT Server 4 distribution provides:

Internet Information Server   Turns any NT Server computer into a Web server.

Services for Macintosh   Provides full interoperability with Macintosh networks, including AppleShare file services running on the NT Server computer and print queue services.

Gateway Services for NetWare   NT Server can integrate your Microsoft LAN Manager, Windows for Workgroups, and NT networks with your Novell LAN, by acting as a gateway between the Microsoft and NetWare LAN environments.

Network Protocols

The network protocols supported by NT Server are components that can be installed independently of the core server software. While some higher-level services might require a particular network protocol, there's nothing about NT that will absolutely die if you don't install the NetBEUI stack, for example. There is no "native" or privileged protocol. NT Server installs both the TCP/IP and NWLink protocols by default.

What Other Software Will I Need?

Although you get a great deal of functionality out of the box, some pieces must be added separately:

Database systems   If you are setting up your server to be a database server, you'll need to purchase one of the commercial database systems, such as Oracle, Sybase, or Microsoft SQL Server.

NetWare file and print services   Full integration with Novell NetWare networks might require the File and Print Services for NetWare package, which is an add-on package available from Microsoft that enables your NT Server to act like a NetWare 3.12 server on your network.

E-mail and groupware   NT Server is a good choice for a platform for a Notes server or for Microsoft Exchange Server.

While it's impossible to enumerate the requirements of every different possible software server platform in this book, in the following hardware design section, we'll indicate some requirements for components of the Microsoft BackOffice suite to give you a starting place. Consult your software system vendors to get some real numbers for your system.

Server Software Design Worksheet

The best way to capture all the information about the NT Server software choices is to document your choices in a worksheet. You'll find those choices in Worksheet 13.1.

WORKSHEET 13.1: Server Software Design

Software Design Decision	Choice
Server licensing (choose one)	Per Seat Per Server
Network role (choose one)	PDC (Primary Domain Controller) BDC (Backup Domain Controller) Stand-Alone Server
Are you installing optional components of NT Server?	Yes or No
Are you installing the Exchange Client?	Yes or No
Are you installing Internet Information Server?	Yes or No
Network protocols (circle all that apply)	NetBEUI IPX/SPX TCP/IP
Other applications to be installed on this server (list all, e.g., Notes, SQL Server, SMS, etc.)	

NT SERVER HARDWARE DESIGN

Consider the modern LAN server box. Believe it or not, even desktop PCs these days carry all the traits of the huge computers of just a few years ago. I mean, who thought they would be agonizing over how much level 2 cache to add to the motherboard? Strange to consider that one of my hard disks has four times the RAM on it—just on the disk controller card on the hard disk—than my most powerful computer of seven years ago had for system RAM. And so on.

These days, server systems designers are faced with choices about the various subsystems of their servers that were once only the realm of the mainframe acolytes. While the blaring magazine advertisements have made such terms as "Extended Data Out RAM" part of our vernacular, it's a good idea to take a look at the design of a modern server, to make sure we understand how the pieces fit together.

Servers are essentially a CPU, the computer chip, moving data along the system bus between the disk storage system and the network interface. To make things work well, the system needs a lot of fast local storage for data, the operating system, and the cache, so there's a lot of RAM in there, too. Other communications ports, for modems and the like, might be indicated. And of course, in order to make the system work, you'll need a video controller, monitor, keyboard, and mouse. Here are the questions we're going to answer in the following sections:

- What kind of CPU should I use for my server application?
- How many CPUs should be in my server?
- What kind of system bus should I use for a server these days?
- How much RAM do I need?
- What's the difference between SIMMs, DIMMs, EDO, and all that?
- What kind of disk controller should I use?
- What kind of hard disks should I use?
- How much hard disk storage should I have?
- How many hard disks should I have?
- Do I need a CD-ROM drive?

▸ What kind of network interface do I need?

▸ What kind of video system should I have on a server? Do I care?

▸ What about the keyboard and mouse?

▸ What kind of serial ports do I want on my server? How many?

▸ What other components should I have?

What Kind of CPU?

NT Server gives you a choice of CPU architectures. At the time of this writing, NT Server supports Intel *x*86, DEC Alpha AXP, MIPS RISC, and PowerPC-based systems. Apple has announced support for NT Server on its server hardware line. DEC Alpha minicomputer clusters are running NT alongside OpenVMS. NCR/AT&T will sell you an Intel-based box about twice the size of my (large) refrigerator that sports 16 processors, all screaming along in parallel. It's a wild world of CPUs out there.

The Case for Intel

For most folks, the question boils down to Intel or non-Intel CPUs. There's no denying that sticking with an Intel-based server is generally considered a safe bet; a quick scan of the NT Hardware Compatibility List shows most device drivers available for Intel platforms. And so far, Intel has shown a stubborn tenacity when it comes to performance; the high-end Intel Pentium Pro CPUs are still holding their own against the mainstream RISC systems. The newer Pentium II chips, especially the Xeon chips, are proving to have excellent performance for multiprocessor computers.

Intel 386   With the release of NT Server 4, the Intel 386 is no longer supported. Attempts to install NT Server 4 on an Intel 386 computer will fail.

Intel 486   The Intel 486 is showing its age, and it is probably too slow for your server. You can breathe more life into an aging 486 server in two ways: add another processor, if your server supports a dual-CPU design, or add an OverDrive Pentium upgrade. (You won't be able to do both, because timing issues preclude the possibility of multiprocessing with OverDrive processors.) Neither of these options is really satisfactory, but if I had to choose, I would probably opt for the dual 486 if possible. Since

NT Server is multitasking and multithreaded, you can see an almost-linear performance increase with the addition of a second processor.

But with Pentium systems so cheap these days, that nice 486 server is probably a good test machine, but it's not a great candidate for a production environment.

Pentium 60MHz and 66MHz   The 60MHz and 66MHz are the first-generation Pentiums. They are 5-volt chips, and they dissipate a respectable amount of heat during operation. What's more, the first few of these chips to be released included a bug in some floating-point division code, providing a public-relations free-for-all when this model first appeared. NT Server can detect this bug (using the PENTNT.EXE utility shown in Figure 13.1) and refuse to use the floating-point unit on the chip; but again, why settle for this when there are other cheap Pentiums out there?

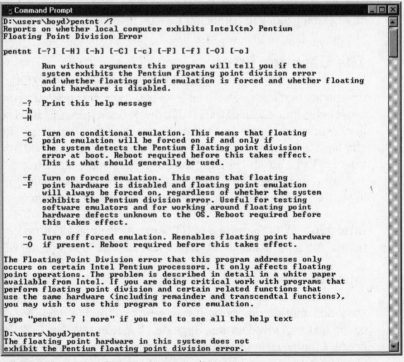

FIGURE 13.1:   The PENTNT utility for dealing with the Pentium floating-point division error

Contemporary Pentiums: 75MHz to 166MHz Systems built around
these second-generation Pentium CPUs are generally pretty solid. If you
have a choice of CPU speed, faster is better, of course. But beware—you
also want to maximize your system bus speed, which is the speed at which
the data moves through the computer. The system bus speeds of the Pentium chips are shown in Table 13.1.

TABLE 13.1: System Bus Speed of Pentium Processors

Bus Speed	CPU Chips
50MHz	75MHz
60MHz	90MHz, 120MHz, 150MHz
66MHz	100MHz, 133MHz, 166MHz, 200MHz, 233MHz

You can see that a 133MHz Pentium system should be faster than a
120MHz system, with everything else being equal. But you might not
notice much of a performance difference between a 133MHz and a
150MHz system, because the difference in processor speed is offset by
the slower system bus. As always, testing is the best way to make these
decisions.

Pentium Pro The next chip out from Intel, the Pentium Pro, is a nice
piece of work. Although criticized because of its lack of significant performance gain over the high-end Pentium when running Windows 95/98,
the Pentium Pro makes a great difference when running a real 32-bit
operating system like NT. In fact, the Pentium Pro is still being sold for
multiprocessor NT computers because it is optimized for this environment.

The thing to look out for here is the size of the on-chip, level 2 cache.
Chips with the more generous 512KB level 2 cache are available, and they
offer increased performance. For NT servers, the Pentium Pro makes a lot
of sense.

Pentium II The newest chip line from Intel is the Pentium II. Like the
Pentium Pro, this new chip is optimized for 32-bit operating systems.
Unlike the Pentium Pro, it offers greatly improved performance for Windows 95/98. One of the major complaints against the Pentium II chip is

Part ii

its limitation to 512MB of RAM. While that sounds like a huge amount of memory to you and me, a large production server might easily exceed that amount. To solve the memory limitation, Intel released the Pentium II Xeon chips, which allow memory configurations up to 4GB.

Xeon processors are available with cache memory ranging from 512KB to 2MB for large-scale applications. While the earlier Pentium II processors are limited to dual processing, the Xeon chips can be run in quad-processor computers easily.

The Case for Alpha

For the absolutely highest performance, the RISC systems may have something to offer over the Intel platforms. Microsoft's alliance with DEC shouldn't be ignored. If you can afford it, those Alpha systems sure are nice, especially for those of us used to servers that have the heritage of the scaled-up PC. At the high end, the RISC systems share the heritage of the scaled-down mainframe, and the difference in design philosophy shows. Unfortunately, the quality evidenced in this design philosophy comes hand-in-hand with the legacy of proprietary hardware culture. They're getting much better, but there it is: High-end hardware is likely to be more proprietary and more difficult to obtain skilled support for.

There are currently two choices of Alpha CPUs: the 21064 and the 21164.

Alpha 21064   The Alpha AXP 21064 chip was the first of the Alpha chips in wide distribution. You can get some of these systems cheap these days, and they still run faster than many Pentium-based servers. The early models of these chips dissipated an amazing amount of heat during operation, so be sure you get a server system that has been engineered from the ground up for reliability and accommodation of excess heat. Skimping on the case, power supply, or cooling fans won't do.

Alpha 21164   The Alpha 21164 is a significant step forward for Alpha chips, offering parallel, speculative execution, out-of-order execution, and all sorts of other modern chip tricks to squeeze the maximum performance possible out of the silicon. These chips are fast. The 21164 also sports the on-chip level 2 cache, much like the Pentium Pro. For these reasons, the 21164 is significantly more powerful than its 21064 predecessor, and it tends to command the price premium to match.

The Case for Other RISC Architectures

The other RISC architectures besides the Alpha, the MIPS, and the PowerPC might be interesting choices, if you already have server hardware based on these chips that matches the NT Hardware Compatibility List. But none of these types of systems have really taken off in the NT world as of yet.

The MIPS chip family was the first mainstream commercial RISC chip widely available. It showed tremendous promise when NT was first being developed, and it was the central CPU in an industry initiative called ACE (for Advanced Computing Environment). And then MIPS ran out of money and was bought by Silicon Graphics. The current crop of high-end MIPS chips are optimized for parallel processing of floating-point operations that most often occur in 3-D modeling. Their integer performance has not been as nifty. You might do well with a MIPS server, depending on your application, but most folks don't need lots of floating-point math in their servers. However, there are some beautiful computers being built based on MIPS, and the MIPS server story may be stronger by the time you read this.

Certainly, virtually all Apple computers being shipped right now are PowerPC-based, so there are millions of them out there. The problem here is that the PowerPC platform of NT only runs on a computer that conforms to the PowerPC Reference Platform (PReP) standard. The PowerMac does not comply with the PReP standard. Apple has started shipping PowerPC-based NT servers, based on a system that originally ran the AIX flavor of Unix. Apple's stellar reputation for brilliant industrial design is well-deserved, and these servers are really nice boxes. But price/performance versus a dual-processor Pentium Pro server? Hmm...

There are rumors that Microsoft will no longer support either the MIPS or the PowerPC platforms with future versions of NT Server, starting with Windows 2000. This alone might be reason to confine your choice of platform to either the Alpha or Intel processors.

A Word About RISC and Software Compatibility

NT Server 4 includes an Intel 486 emulator for the RISC architectures, so that when the server is executing software that has not yet been ported to the RISC platform in question, the software will still run, thinking that it's operating on an Intel 486 computer! Of course, software emulation is always slower than the real thing on silicon, but it does work.

Part ii

DEC is working on a more advanced Intel instruction execution scheme, which will examine Intel code and convert it to native code on-the-fly. The next time the code needs to be run, the converted, native code is run instead, so that the translation occurs only once. In effect, this new technology will recompile Intel code into native code and then store the native version on the hard disk, running it whenever it recognizes the need. This minimizes the amount of emulated code that needs to run.

With RISC chip performance being what it is, these emulation and translation schemes generally work out well. However, if for some reason you need to run a lot of old Intel code on your server, consider the Intel systems for best performance and compatibility. And now that Intel is closing the gap in performance with its newer chip offerings, you may actually see better performance from the Intel processors running native Intel-compatible code.

The take-home lesson from software 486 emulation and translation is that the RISC systems are not show stoppers, and they deserve consideration.

The Bottom Line: CPU Architecture

High-end Pentium II and Pentium Pro systems are a solid bet, with the DEC Alpha 21164 systems leading in the performance race. Alpha 21064 systems offer a price-to-performance ratio that can't be beat right now. But this may all change. If you are concerned about performance, your best bet is to read the trade magazines and see what the tests say. Things change very quickly in the computer world.

How Many CPUs?

Up to a point, you can realize great benefits by adding CPUs to servers that support multiprocessing. You won't get twice the performance out of two processors that you get out of one, but you should see a significant performance difference. However, don't spend all your money on a quad-processor server and then end up skimping on the memory and network interface—you'll have done yourself no good.

We recommend purchasing a server system that can hold at least two, and preferably four, processors up front. If you don't anticipate a real CPU crunch, and it makes economic sense, just get the server with one CPU installed. If you find a need for more CPUs, you'll have the option of adding them later. Adding CPUs should be a relatively simple task.

NOTE

You may choose to reinstall NT Server to take advantage of multiple CPUs after adding a CPU to a single-CPU system. NT Server uses a different HAL (hardware abstraction layer) for multiprocessing than for single-processor systems. There is a utility in the NT Server Resource Kit called UPTOMP.EXE that can perform the migration of affected files to the multiprocessor versions.

What Kind of System Bus?

The choices of system bus have gotten more and more diverse over the years. You now have a choice between ISA (Industry Standard Architecture), EISA (Extended Industry Standard Architecture), VLB (Video Local Bus), and PCI (Peripheral Component Interconnect). Oh, and don't forget IBM's MCA (Micro-Channel Architecture) used by IBM, NCR, and some other companies. These various bus architectures represent an evolution toward ever faster computer systems. See how they compare in Table 13.2.

TABLE 13.2: System Bus Bandwidth

Bus Type	Bandwidth (MB/sec)	Comments
ISA	2.5	Lowest-common denominator
MCA	40	Proprietary, limited hardware availability
EISA	32	More standard than MCA, faster than ISA, not as fast as PCI
VLB	132	Good for video, bad for anything else
PCI	132	Fastest available

For the cards that count—network and disk controllers—PCI makes a great deal of sense. But the number of PCI slots is typically limited to three or four, and PCI is overkill for a serial port. This is why motherboard manufacturers build hybrid systems, typically EISA/PCI, so that there are a number of EISA slots and a few PCI slots.

Get a system with as many PCI slots as possible, with the rest of the slots as EISA, and you'll not go far wrong.

Part ii

WARNING

Stay away from ISA-only systems in general, because you'll run into problems with them when you put more than 16MB of RAM in them. And you're going to put a lot more memory than that in them!

How Much RAM?

The answer to this question is lots and lots and lots. NT will love you for it. Get lots of RAM. We deployed systems with 80MB of RAM, and they could use more if we gave it to them. Getting as much RAM as possible will pay off, as you'll see after you fill out Worksheet 13.2.

WORKSHEET 13.2: RAM Worksheet

Line	What	RAM Needed
1	Starting Point	64 MB
	User Requirements	
2	Number of concurrent users	
3	Total User RAM (512 KB × line 2)	MB
	BackOffice Requirements	
4	Internet Information Server: 16 MB	
5	SNA Server: 8 MB	
6	SMS: 20 MB	
7	Exchange: 16 MB	
8	SQL Server: 8 MB	
9	Total BackOffice RAM	MB
	Other Application Requirements	
10	Average RAM needed per application	
11	Number of other applications running	
12	Total Other Application RAM (line 10 × line 11)	MB
13	Subtotal (add lines 1, 3, 9, and 12)	MB
14	If RISC add 20%	
15	ESTIMATED TOTAL RAM NEEDED	MB

As an example, I hooked up 250 people to one of my NT servers. I thought that I would get 250 people hitting my server all the time, but when I measured it, I found that I had a maximum of 80 concurrent users, and typically only 75. I still haven't figured that one out, but there it is. Now, I'm running a SQL Server database on this machine, which I connected to Microsoft's Web server, the Internet Information Server. This is a DEC Alpha computer. What's a good, healthy figure for the RAM on this server? Take a look at the worked example in Worksheet 13.3 to see the numbers I came up with.

TIP

Don't believe Microsoft's recommendations on sufficient NT Server RAM. Use at least 64MB as a starting point and work upward from there, using the RAM worksheet (Worksheet 13.2).

WORKSHEET 13.3: RAM Worksheet Example

Line	What	RAM Needed
1	Starting Point	64 MB
	User Requirements	
2	Number of concurrent users	75 users
3	Total User RAM (512 KB × line 2)	37.5 MB
	BackOffice Requirements	
4	Internet Information Server: 16 MB	16 MB
5	SNA Server: 8 MB	
6	SMS: 20 MB	
7	Exchange: 16 MB	
8	SQL Server: 8 MB	8 MB
9	Total BackOffice RAM	24 MB
	Other Application Requirements	
10	Average RAM needed per application	1 MB
11	Number of other applications running	3
12	Total Other Application RAM (line 10 × line 11)	3 MB
13	Subtotal (add lines 1, 3, 9, and 12)	128.5 MB
14	If RISC add 20%	25.7 MB
15	ESTIMATED TOTAL RAM NEEDED	154 MB

This worksheet shows that I should ideally have 154MB of RAM on the server! I would probably install ten 16MB SIMMs, for a 160MB total, keeping the numbers even.

The worksheet illustrates that you won't go wrong putting a lot of RAM in your server. At the other end of the scale, consider my test server, which typically has one or two concurrent users and 32MB of RAM, which is plenty enough—if you believe Microsoft. Don't! Using Performance Monitor, I see that my server often starts to thrash, especially when I start routing networks with the routing software built into NT Server. It often spends all of its time swapping memory pages, for hundreds of thousands of milliseconds at a time.

You don't want your server to swap too much. Your best bet is to measure your server, and keep an eye on memory utilization. Properly populated with sufficient RAM, your memory subsystem will account for about half the total system price of your server.

What Kind of RAM?

There was a time when you had plenty of choices in memory for your server—as long as you chose SIMMs (Single In-line Memory Modules) with DRAM (Dynamic RAM) on them. Recently, there has been a proliferation of different memory technologies, as manufacturers continually push the outside of the envelope. In some instances, the envelope that's being pushed is the performance one, which is a good thing. Some memory ideas haven't worked out so well, however, and sometimes the only increase you'll see is in the amount of marketing hype. Scan this section for a rundown on your memory choices and avoid the pitfalls!

30-pin SIMMs

This is the oldest type of SIMM, most common in pre-Pentium computer systems. 30-pin SIMMs each provide 16 data lines and 12 address lines, for a maximum of 4MB on a single SIMM. These SIMMs need to be installed in groups, or "banks," of four, which can cause confusion for the uninitiated. Every SIMM in a bank of four must be of the same size, and upgrading memory must be done a bank at a time. If you have a server with 16 SIMM slots on the motherboard, with all slots full of 2MB SIMMs (for a total of 32MB), you'll need to toss four of those (throwing away 8MB) when you upgrade a bank with 4MB SIMMs (adding 16MB), for a net increase of 8MB.

If someone gives you a server for free and it has 30-pin SIMMs, well and good. But these days, 30-pin SIMMs are obsolete. In general, you should steer clear of servers with this old memory technology.

72-pin SIMMs

This expanded SIMM is the successor to the first-generation 30-pin SIMMs. With 72 pins, the SIMM provides a full 32 address lines and 32 data lines to the RAM, so 72-pin SIMMs can be larger and faster than 30-pin SIMMs. 72-pin SIMMs are typical in Pentium computers, where the larger SIMMs provide a good match for the Pentium CPU 64-bit data bus.

Pentium-based servers typically have a 64-bit or 128-bit system data bus—check the documentation that came with your computer. For a 64-bit bus system, you install 72-pin SIMMs in same-size pairs. For 128-bit systems, you need to install the SIMMs four at a time, just like the SIMM banks on the 30-pin SIMM systems.

DIMMs

The word *Single* in the term *Single In-line Memory Module* implies that there's something bigger and better waiting around that next technology corner—and so it is: Dual In-line Memory Modules (DIMMs) are 168-pin packages that provide 64 address lines and 64 data lines. DIMMs currently provide the state of the art in convenient memory packaging.

WARNING

Be very certain to check the voltage of the memory your system requires. Many of today's current choices of memory are provided in different voltages for specific applications. Failure to comply with the design specification of your motherboard may result in burned out RAM and system damage.

Servers with a 64-bit system bus will let you install DIMMs one at a time, for maximum simplicity and flexibility. Servers with a 128-bit bus usually require DIMMs to be installed in pairs. Many systems allow the installation of single DIMMs but prefer DIMM pairs, because with two DIMMs they can perform memory interleaving (reading memory from one DIMM while the other is being strobed in its refresh cycle), which effectively doubles the speed of the RAM in the best case.

Servers with large system busses may greatly benefit from using DIMMs for their memory packaging. If you're looking to maximize your performance, DIMM is the memory configuration of choice.

TIP

Check with your server documentation to find out if your server requires memory modules to be installed in banks, pairs, or singles, or if memory modules can be interleaved.

Memory Speed

Memory modules come with a speed rating, which is the time that the memory requires for data access. Fast computers may well require memory with 60ns (nanosecond) times or faster. A RAM speed of 60ns is typical. Although 70ns RAM is still available, it is typically too slow for use in modern systems. DIMMs often come in speeds of 12ns or even 10ns, with faster memory soon to come.

WARNING

Avoid slow RAM (70ns or slower). Check your system specifications for the recommended RAM speed.

Memory Quality

The best memory modules have gold-plated connectors, which optimize the electrical connection between the pins and the socket. Go for the gold. It's actually worth the reliability.

If your modules have the more common tin-plated connectors, inspect the modules before installing them and remove any corrosion by firmly rubbing the pins on the SIMM with a pencil eraser (the tech tool of choice). Anything more abrasive, like a wire brush or sandpaper, will strip the tin off those pins, and boy, won't you look dumb holding a $300 DIMM with no pins? Oh, and be sure to wipe the rubber from the eraser off the pins with a clean cloth containing technical-grade Isopropyl alcohol or equivalent before inserting them.

Some memory manufacturers were making high-capacity SIMMs for a while by cramming a whole bunch of medium-density RAM chips on a single SIMM. Typically, a memory module might hold anywhere from two to nine memory chips. Anything over nine chips is considered a "composite" SIMM, and gangs the chips with on-SIMM electronics to simulate higher-density chips. In some installations, these composite SIMMs exhibit timing problems, since their electrical characteristics differ from normal SIMMs. Avoid composite SIMMs. I asked my vendor if the SIMMs he was selling me were composite, and he said "No," while handing me this thing that had 36 chips all over it. Just say "No" back.

WARNING

Avoid composite SIMMs or DIMMs. They might exhibit timing problems.

EDO RAM

EDO stands for Extended Data Out, and it is a fairly recent RAM innovation that aims to simplify system design by making the level 2 cache unnecessary. However, industry benchmarks have indicated that EDO systems without the level 2 cache are significantly slower than systems with "normal" DRAM and SRAM cache combinations. Adding a level 2 cache to a system with EDO RAM will boost performance to about five percent above a non-EDO system.

Even though EDO aims at replacing level 2 (L2) cache, you should always use a level 2 cache in your server.

Parity and Error Correction

For ever and ever, PCs shipped with parity-checking RAM systems, and required RAM to provide nine bits to the byte. The ninth bit was for the parity bit, which indicated whether the number of ones stored in that byte was even or odd. If the parity bit indicated an odd number of ones, but the number in the byte contained an even number of ones, a parity error was generated, because the system knew that one of the nine bits was messed up somehow.

Parity RAM is slowly fading from the scene. Many modern Intel systems will accept parity RAM but ignore the parity bit. This is because modern RAM is fairly reliable and tends to work when it's first installed. Chuckle, chuckle—of course, the grizzled veteran system administrators are saying, "Suuure, it does..." But PCs are a commodity market, and cutting out the parity-checking system reduces cost somewhat. RAM problems just aren't that common.

For servers, many vendors offer systems with Error Checking and Correction (ECC) RAM, which can not only detect single-bit errors, but can identify the error and correct it on-the-fly. If you're worried about maximum reliability, this is the way to go. All parity will get you is a halted system, which is preferable to corrupted data, but otherwise doesn't make your users very happy. ECC RAM systems provide that extra layer of robustness, at a price premium.

Part II

The Bottom Line: Memory Type

Properly populated with sufficient RAM, your memory subsystem is going to be at least half the total system price of your server. So you might not have all the money in the world to play with—where do you make the hard choices?

I would opt for DIMM systems, because this memory configuration is becoming common in servers and provides a good performance match for advanced systems. EDO is not worth the price.

Parity checking on the RAM is desired. ECC is better. Your best bet for maximum reliability and performance is ECC DIMMs. However, memory systems don't fail that often, relative to other system components, so this might be an area to do some cost-cutting. It depends on your installation, but I would at least go with parity checking.

System Cache RAM

RAM is very fast, but these days RAM can't keep up with a fast CPU without some help. Because you never want the CPU to be waiting around, system manufacturers buffer the system RAM with some special, more expensive, very fast cache RAM, which does a better job of keeping the CPU busy. This is the level 2 cache we've been talking about. It's called level 2 because the CPU chip has a bit of memory right on the chip, which is the level 1 cache.

Because the level 2 cache simply buffers the main system RAM, you don't need too much of it. Exactly how much you need is highly dependent upon the overall system design, so your server vendor will probably ship the system with an appropriate amount already installed. If you are installing the level 2 cache yourself, or upgrading an existing system, refer to Table 13.3 for a good rule of thumb. The guidelines in Table 13.3 tend to give you the right amount of cache RAM because the primary factor affecting the cache RAM requirement is the amount of system RAM.

TABLE 13.3: Cache RAM Requirements

Amount of System RAM	Cache RAM Size
Less than 32MB	256KB
32MB to 64MB	512KB
More than 64MB	1MB

What Kind of Disk Controller?

For Intel systems, you typically have two choices of disk subsystem type, but really you have just one: SCSI. Use a SCSI controller and SCSI disks for your server. Don't use IDE or its variations. Period. The new Ultra-DMA specification for IDE drives enables these drives to come very close to SCSI for single-disk performance, but SCSI is still the best for multiple disk servers.

From the NT Hardware Compatibility List, select a PCI bus SCSI controller that can handle RAID 0 and RAID 5 disk arrays in hardware, without server software intervention. Many of these controllers actually support combinations of RAID 1 and 5 for even more reliability.

Caching controllers can cause some problems with NT. SCSI controllers that support hardware RAID typically have some RAM on them to support the disk-array operations, but you don't want a whole lot of cache RAM, believe it or not.

What Kind of Hard Disks?

Use SCSI drives, as explained in the previous section. These days, it doesn't make much sense to purchase drives smaller than 4.3GB for servers. Get 4.3GB (or larger) drives. Get at least three of them.

Some disks are rated as AV, which stands for Audio-Visual and indicates that these drives perform well in digital media applications, where sustained, high-bandwidth input and output are critical over extended periods of time. These disks make great server drives.

You can really perceive a difference between a drive with a 12 ms (millisecond) access time rating and a drive with an 8 ms access time. Get fast drives, at least 10 ms access or faster.

How Much Hard Disk Storage?

Your hard disk storage is going to hold four types of data:

- NT system files
- NT virtual memory swap space
- Application files and storage
- User data

You'll need to count on enough storage for each of these. Fortunately, it's pretty easy these days to provide enough disk storage. Fill out Worksheet 13.4 to get a handle on how much storage you'll need.

WORKSHEET 13.4: Disk Storage Worksheet

Line	What	Disk Space
1	NT System Files	250 MB
	Virtual Memory Swap	
2	RAM installed	MB
3	Recommended Page File Size (line 2 × 1.5)	MB
	BackOffice Requirements	
4	Internet Information Server: 50 MB	
5	Total projected size of Web site files	
6	SNA Server: 30 MB	
7	SMS: 100 MB	
8	Exchange: 500 MB	
9	SQL Server: 60 MB	
10	Total size of SQL Server databases	
11	Total BackOffice Disk Storage (add lines 4–10)	MB
	Other Application Requirements	
12	Total required storage for other applications	MB
13	Total Application Disk Storage (line 11 + line 12)	MB
	User Storage Files	
14	Number of users on this server	users
15	Average storage required per user	MB
16	Total User Disk Storage (line 14 × line 15)	MB
17	Total Disk Storage (add lines 1, 3, 13, and 16)	MB
18	Fudge factor (add 15% to line 17)	MB
19	Subtotal (line 17 + line 18)	MB
20	RISC-based computers (add 25% to line 19)	MB
21	TOTAL DISK STORAGE NEEDED (line 19 + line 20)	MB

Let's take a look at my DEC Alpha server, which will run NT Server, Internet Information Server, and SQL Server. You can see my numbers for disk storage requirements in Worksheet 13.5.

WORKSHEET 13.5: Disk Storage Worksheet Example

Line	What	Disk Space
1	NT System Files	250 MB
	Virtual Memory Swap	
2	RAM installed	160 MB
3	Recommended Page File Size (line 2 × 1.5)	240 MB
	BackOffice Requirements	
4	Internet Information Server: 50 MB	50 MB
5	Total projected size of Web site files	50 MB
6	SNA Server: 30 MB	
7	SMS: 100 MB	
8	Exchange: 500 MB	
9	SQL Server: 60 MB	60 MB
10	Total size of SQL Server databases	1500 MB
11	Total BackOffice Disk Storage (add lines 4–10)	1660 MB
	Other Application Requirements	
12	Total required storage for other applications	-- MB
13	Total Application Disk Storage (line 11 + line 12)	1660 MB
	User Storage Files	
14	Number of users on this server	250 users
15	Average storage required per user	30 MB
16	Total User Disk Storage (line 14 × line 15)	7500 MB
17	Total Disk Storage (add lines 1, 3, 13, and 16)	9650 MB
18	Fudge factor (add 15% to line 17)	1448 MB
19	Subtotal (line 17 + line 18)	11098 MB
20	RISC-based computers (add 25% to line 19)	2775 MB
21	TOTAL DISK STORAGE NEEDED (line 19 + line 20)	13873 MB

Part ii

Per the Disk Storage worksheet, I will fill up at least 13,873MB—call it 13GB—of storage, just getting started. I feel like my estimate of the SQL Server databases is a bit high, and I've added in a fudge factor, so I think I'll be okay. And of course, my users won't start out with 30MB each of storage. All in all, I feel good about this number.

How Many Hard Disks?

After you've figured out how much storage you need, figuring out how many hard disks you'll need seems like a straightforward task. Decide on the hard disk sizes, get enough of them to accommodate your storage needs, and you're finished. But if you want to use fault-tolerant disk arrays, you'll need to figure for the storage overhead.

For disk mirroring, you'll need twice as much disk storage as your storage requirements indicate. So, according to my calculations in the previous section, I'll need 26GB of disk storage to do disk mirroring. If I used 9GB drives, I could use two disks for my storage, and mirror that—an 18GB mirrored volume, using a total of four disks. If a 9GB drive costs $1,000, my disk storage cost will be $4,000.

For RAID 5 arrays, the storage overhead goes down with the number of drives installed. I could use 4.3GB drives, and with five of them in a RAID 5 configuration, I would have a 17.2GB volume across the five disks (20 percent RAID overhead). If a 4.3GB drive costs $5,00, my disk storage cost will be $2,500.

NOTE

In RAID 5, striping with parity, the fault tolerance is provided by the parity information, which is distributed across all of the disks evenly. The total amount of parity information is always equal to one of the physical partitions in the RAID 5 set. The more disks in the set, the lower the percentage of space used for parity.

Note that the cost of my RAID 5 array is less than half that of the disk mirror array, but the disk mirror provides faster performance. Because I'm running a SQL Server database on my server, I'll need to think about that. Probably, I would want to go with the RAID 5 solution for now, and then eventually get another server with a mirror array, dedicated to the SQL Server application. It's a good idea to keep user file and print servers separate from application servers like my SQL/Web server. But I can't afford two servers right now, so the RAID 5 system will do—five disks it is!

Do I Need a CD-ROM Drive?

You'll need a CD-ROM for installation of NT Server 4. Floppy installation support was dropped in the step up from NT Server 3.51 to 4 (a good thing, too, with 60-plus floppy disks to fiddle with for an installation).

NT Server supports IDE (ATAPI), SCSI, and a handful of proprietary interface CD-ROM drives. Multiple CD-ROM drives are okay, but when installing NT Server for the first time, be sure to indicate the CD-ROM drive that contains the software distribution media.

WARNING
The NT Setup program might select the incorrect CD-ROM when you're installing.

What about CD-ROM changers? You may not notice many of them on the Hardware Compatibility List, but the CD-ROM changer that I've been using, and similar devices used by others, seem to work under NT Server 4. However, I would not recommend these mechanical changers in a production environment with NT Server 4, because the NT Explorer often "walks" the entire changer, shuffling in each of the CD-ROMs in turn, taking about two minutes to complete the process. Presumably, the Explorer needs to poll the CD-ROMs to get disk icon information and such. But the CDs often swap in and out for no obvious reason, and it takes a long time for such a swap to complete; this is a mechanical operation, similar to a jukebox. The adverse effect on system performance is difficult to predict or control. I love having all those CD-ROMs online, but I don't think that it's a good idea on a real server.

NOTE
A CD-ROM drive is required to use the Emergency Repair procedure in NT Server 4.

What Kind of Network Interface?

The fastest disk system in the world won't help very much if users can't get to your data through the network. Most installations are using Ethernet these days, but Fast Ethernet is a viable option, and stay tuned—ATM may soon be coming to a server near you.

To get started, choose a good network interface card that corresponds to your network (Ethernet? Token Ring?) and cabling type (10BaseT? coaxial cable?) from the Hardware Compatibility List.

Don't use 8-bit ISA controllers. The bus can't take the network bandwidth. Use a 32-bit bus-mastering controller.

You can't make a good decision about the kind of network interface without thinking about your network design.

What Kind of Video System?

You might not think that the video system on a server is very important. Relative to other things you could spend money on, I would provisionally agree with you. But don't ignore the need for a reasonable color display. If you're used to a UNIX or Banyan box, where a 12-inch amber monochrome monitor was the height of server fashion, think again. Discussed previously , the user interface is something that you can't run away from, and it pretty much requires a mid-size color monitor to get any work done.

Make sure that your video system can support SVGA—8-bit, 256 color at 800×600 resolution with a reasonable refresh rate (43MHz interlaced is unreasonable, for example); 72MHz and higher are comfortable refresh rates.

TIP

Where we have multiple servers in a data closet, we have one monitor, keyboard, and mouse, and we use a Cybex switch box to switch between the servers. In practice, this has worked out fine, but I can anticipate situations where you would want to see more than one server at a time. Our switch box works great, though, and I would recommend this alternative to those of you with constrained space and money. Just make sure that the video switch box can handle the SVGA bandwidth of 800x600, 256-color, at 72MHz or better.

What about the Keyboard and Mouse?

There's not much to say about the keyboard hardware. Your server probably already comes with one. You'll need a keyboard that's compatible with the IBM 101-key or 84-key standard, preferably the 101-key version.

NT supports various keyboard layouts, and you'll indicate the layout when you install NT Server.

As for the mouse, you need one. Because NT is a graphical environment, it's not realistic to do without the mouse. While Windows generally has a keyboard equivalent for just about everything, you'll find that certain operations with the new shell in NT Server 4 just scream for a mouse.

WARNING

Intel platforms generally won't boot without a keyboard attached. If you do so, you'll get a keyboard error at boot time, because the BIOS on the motherboard strobes the keyboard to make sure that one exists. Yeah, I think this is dumb, too. You might not want a keyboard or monitor on a server that you keep in the closet. But again, remember that with NT Server, there are things that you're going to have to do from the console. You'll need that monitor, keyboard, and mouse.

For Intel platforms, if you have a choice for the mouse, a Logitec-compatible bus mouse may be preferable to a serial mouse. That way, you won't need to sacrifice a serial port for the mouse. You'll need the serial ports to talk to the UPS (uninterruptible power supply) and the modem.

What Kind of Serial Ports?

You want at least two serial ports free on your server, after you hook up the serial mouse (if any). One of the serial ports will attach to the UPS, and one will attach to the El Cheapo 2400-baud modem that you dug out of the bottom of your desk.

Why is that? Well, you'll definitely want the UPS connection, so that your server will know about power failures and shut down gracefully when one occurs. You'll want the modem to be a phone dialer, so that you can get paged when the server has problems. Some server hardware platforms will handle this function in the hardware, or you can write a batch file to page you in the event of a terrible failure.

Here is a crude whack at a batch file that can send a page if you've got a modem hooked up to the COM2 serial port. This is for illustration purposes only; it doesn't really work that well. I'm sure you can come up with something better!

```
PAGER.BAT:
qbasic /run pager.bas

PAGER.BAS:
OPEN "COM2:2400,n,8,1" FOR RANDOM AS #1
  PRINT #1, "atdt 9,555-1234,,,,,,,,5551212#"
  ' wait for 20 seconds
  triggerTime = TIMER + 20
  WHILE (triggerTime > TIMER)
  WEND
CLOSE #1
```

WARNING

Because NT Server provides sophisticated remote network access capabilities with its Remote Access Service (RAS), you may not want a modem hooked up to your server if the line can be accessed from outside your company. Ideally, the line should be dial-out only, or you can disable RAS on the server. This is because you want to limit dial-in network services to only those systems that you carefully manage as your network entry points. Consider limiting modem devices to only the remote access servers.

You can also install multiport serial boards, such as those made by DigiBoard or ConSynsys, into your NT Server computer. These make a lot of sense if you're going to use the Remote Access Service (RAS) with NT Server to create a dial-in server system for remote access to your network.

What Other Components?

The other components you'll need are a UPS and a tape backup unit. You may also want to get a second SCSI controller.

UPS

You definitely want a UPS to protect your server from fluctuations in the line power. While the concept of a UPS is rather straightforward, actually getting one to work exactly right in practice can be a little tricky.

SCSI Tape Backup Unit

You'll want a tape drive on the server to perform routine server backups. You can go two routes:

- A tape drive on each server

- Centralized backup of NT servers to one dedicated tape backup system

In my experience, the more complex your backup system, the more likely it is to fail.

There are a few different types of SCSI tape backup systems: minicartridge tape, exabyte, 4 millimeter DAT, and DLT. You can just use whichever tape mechanism that you're already using on your other servers. If you don't have an existing system, consider DLT for large servers, and use DAT drives elsewhere. Check the SCSI tape backup units in the Hardware Compatibility List.

Second SCSI Controller?

It might make some sense for you to consider a SCSI controller dedicated to the CD-ROM and tape backup unit, independent of the hefty controller that may be running your RAID disk array. This may add some complexity to your server design, but it may streamline troubleshooting later. With this setup, you'll isolate the SCSI buses on the RAID system, so that it is relatively unaffected by whatever happens with your CD-ROM or tape drive.

Think of the RAID system, your hard disk storage, as your "production" side of the server storage equation. This is the part upon which the minute-by-minute operation of your server relies. You generally use the CD-ROM only for installation of software, and the tape drive for after-hours backup. You may want to treat your production storage system differently.

Many system designers will choose to add a low-cost 16-bit ISA SCSI controller to handle the CD-ROM and tape drives. This provides enough performance to handle these drives. The SCSI controller handling the hard disks should be the more expensive controller, typically a SCSI-3 Ultra-Wide controller.

The downsides to a second SCSI controller are the complexities of getting the two controllers to coexist and keeping straight which device is on which controller. Depending on your needs and your hardware configuration, this may or may not be a big deal, but you should know that you have the option.

Hardware Compatibility Issues

The Ugly Truth is that many LAN servers share hardware design legacy with the IBM PC. Almost all of the equipment on the NT Hardware Compatibility List requires you to set IRQ levels, DMA request channels, and I/O port settings. If you don't know what all this stuff is, now is the time to at least become passingly familiar with the concepts and vocabulary— at least until Plug and Pray (sorry, Plug and *Play*) is available for NT Server.

Interrupt Requests Explained

On a PC system, various hardware components grab the CPU's attention by means of an interrupt mechanism; a signal is applied to a control line on the system bus when the hardware component needs to do something. The system is responsible for coordinating the bus so that only one subunit can signal on the bus at a time. Each of the components gets to signal the bus, in turn, based on the level or its interrupt request (IRQ).

On the original IBM PC, the IRQ coordination was handled by an Intel 8259 chip, which could support up to eight different IRQ levels. By the advent of the IBM PC/AT, there were so many add-in cards and multifunction adapters that it was clear that the system needed more interrupt levels. IBM slipped in another 8259, but to maintain compatibility with the original PC, the designers added the unit by "piggybacking" it to the original interrupt controller, hard-wiring the original controller's IRQ 2 to the new controller's IRQ 9 (see Figure 13.2). When any of the second interrupt controller's interrupts are triggered, that triggers the original controller's IRQ 2 line. It's up to the system BIOS to figure out what's really going on.

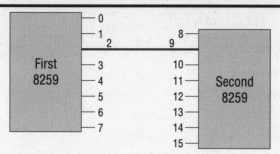

FIGURE 13.2: Cascaded interrupt controllers on the PC

Here are the cogent facts that come out of all this:

▶ The system services the interrupt requests based on the IRQ level. The lower the IRQ level, the more priority an interrupt has.

▶ Since the second controller's IRQs are wired in through the first one's IRQ 2, IRQs 8 through 15 have a higher priority than IRQs 3 through 7.

▶ Put faster devices on IRQs 8 through 15, and slower devices on IRQs 3 through 7.

▶ COM2 is slightly better-suited to high-speed serial connections (like a modem), and COM1 is better relegated to slower connections (like a UPS or a serial mouse), since COM2's IRQ is at a higher priority than COM1's.

▶ You can't use IRQ 2.

▶ In general, each device on your system should have its own IRQ level; otherwise, an interrupt conflict is likely to occur, and your system will act really, really weird.

▶ Eight-bit devices (some old sound cards, for example) can't use IRQs on the second IRQ controller and must be set to an IRQ between 3 and 7. (Don't use such old stuff on your cool server.)

Choosing a Card's IRQ Level

Some IRQ levels are defined by the core system hardware and cannot be changed. Over time it has become customary to use the remaining IRQs for specific tasks. Table 13.4 lists the IRQs in order of priority, noting their common use and whether they are available.

Part ii

TABLE 13.4: IRQs in Order of Priority

IRQ Level	Common Use	Comments
0	System timer	Don't use
1	Keyboard	Don't use—can't change
2	Hard-wired to IRQ 9	Don't use
9	Hard-wired to IRQ 2	Available
10	LAN interface	LAN/SCSI
11	SCSI controller	Adaptec SCSI controller default IRQ
12	Bus mouse	Also called PS/2 mouse or Logitec mouse
13	Math coprocessor	Don't use
14	IDE controller	Might be available if you don't use IDE disk drives
15		Secondary IDE controller. Available if you don't use IDE
3	COM2 or COM4	
4	COM1 or COM3	
5	LPT2	Possible LAN; few systems have two parallel ports, so this may be available
6	Floppy controller	Don't use
7	LPT1	Primary parallel port—NT doesn't use an IRQ for the printer port, so this may be available
8	Real-time clock	Don't use

Here are the steps for choosing a card's IRQ level:

1. In order to get the best performance and avoid interrupt conflicts, refer to Table 13.4 to find an available IRQ level. You can use any IRQ level except the ones already taken by the system, which are marked "Don't use" in the table.

2. Refer to the manufacturer's documentation that came with your card. Typically, there is a choice of two or three IRQs that you can use for that card.

3. Prioritize your cards. Place devices with the highest priority toward the top of the list, within the constraints set by the IRQ choices available for the card. Don't agonize over this, because there are other things that will affect system performance far more significantly. But be aware.

4. Once you've chosen the card's IRQ level, write it down in the IRQ System record (Worksheet 13.8, at the end of the chapter), and tattoo the worksheet on your forehead, backwards, so you see it every time you look in the mirror. Seriously, though, it's a fantastic idea to plaster a copy of the IRQ record to the side of the server's case, and keep a copy where every administrator can get to it.

5. Set the card's IRQ level using the procedures that came with the card. This will vary from card to card. Some cards have jumpers on the board that you set (ugh!), some have proprietary software that only works from DOS (ugh! ugh! ugh!), EISA boards will use the EISA Config utility that comes with your server (that usually only works from DOS), and PCI cards are generally self-configuring. Check your card's documentation.

DMA Channels Explained

DMA stands for Direct Memory Access. It's a way for a peripheral card to transfer data to and from system memory directly, without the intervention of the CPU. Cards that are capable of DMA are typically referred to as *bus-mastering* cards, which refers to the fact that a card initiating a direct memory access must first take control of the system's address and data bus.

Since DMA bypasses the central CPU when it moves data, memory transfers can happen even while the CPU is busy with other tasks, and overall system performance is enhanced. Good candidates for bus-mastering are those peripheral controllers that deal primarily with the movement of data into and out of the computer: SCSI disk controllers and network interface cards.

Like IRQs, DMAs take place through DMA *channels*, which must be uniquely assigned. In general, no two devices can share a DMA channel. So the procedure for allocating DMA channels to your cards is essentially the same as with IRQs. Refer to the device's documentation for the default and allowed DMA settings, and adjust the DMA settings for the device if necessary. You'll log the DMA settings for each device in the worksheet coming up in the next section.

I/O Ports Explained

The original PC used certain memory addresses for accessing input/output devices such as serial and parallel ports. Low-level software transfers data to these memory locations in order to move data out of the port, and reads these memory locations to read data from the port. To the software, the transfer of data looks exactly like a memory transfer, but it really has nothing to do with RAM at all; the hardware transfers the data to an I/O device instead. These magic memory locations are called *I/O ports*.

I/O ports are uniquely assigned one or two bytes at a time. Typically, I/O ports won't be something that you'll run into conflicts with, but when you do, you'll really want to be able to figure out what's going on. You'll log the I/O port settings for each device in the Hardware Design worksheet.

HARDWARE DESIGN: THE FINAL WORKSHEET

Now that you're ready to make some informed hardware design and purchasing decisions, it's time to bring all the information together in one place. You can use the worksheets included in this chapter as guides.

RAM System

Filling out the RAM worksheet in Worksheet 13.2 allows you to determine the amount of RAM you'll need for your system. We worked through an example in Worksheet 13.3. Once you've got an idea of the requirements for system RAM, you can estimate the amount of level 2 cache RAM your system will require by referring to Table 13.3. Note that some CPU chips (for example, most Pentium II, Pentium Pro, and Alpha 21164 chips) have level 2 caches on the chip, so you won't use Table 13.3 for these systems.

Disk Storage

The Disk Storage worksheet is Worksheet 13.4, and we worked through an example in Worksheet 13.5. Complete this worksheet and then enter the total storage requirements in line 18 of the worksheet in Worksheet 13.7, the Hardware Design worksheet.

System Device Record

The System Device record in Worksheet 13.6 is for recording the critical information about each system component installed in your server. You'll want to complete a copy of this table for each card that you install in your system.

WORKSHEET 13.6: System Device Record

Device Name:	
Expansion Slot Number:	
Manufacturer:	
Model:	
Version:	
Serial Number:	
Purchase Date:	
Replacement Part Number:	
Software Versions (if any):	
IRQ Level:	
DMA Channel:	
I/O Port Range(s):	

Part ii

WORKSHEET 13.7: Hardware Design Worksheet

Line	System	Requirements
	CPU	
1	Number of CPUs possible	
2	Number of CPUs installed	
3	CPU chip manufacturer	
4	CPU chip model	
5	CPU chip clock speed	
	System Bus	
6	CPU chip system bus speed	
7	Bus types (circle all that apply)	ISA EISA VLB PCI
	System RAM	
8	Amount of RAM installed (line 15 from the RAM worksheet, Worksheet 4.2)	
9	RAM configuration (circle one)	30-pin SIMM 2-pin SIMM DIMM
10	RAM type (circle all that apply)	Parity-checking ECC EDO
11	Amount of cache RAM installed	
	Disk System Controller	
12	Disk controller manufacturer	
13	Disk controller model	
14	Installed in server slot number	
15	*Fill out a System Device record for the disk controller.*	
16	Hardware RAID?	Yes No
17	Bus mastering?	

WORKSHEET 13.7 continued: Hardware Design Worksheet

Line	System	Requirements
	Disk Drives	
18	Total disk storage needed line 21 from the Disk Storage worksheet, Worksheet 4.4)	
19	Number of drives	
20	Drive size	
	CD-ROM Drives	
21	CD-ROM type	SCSI ATAPI Other
22	CD-ROM manufacturer	
23	CD-ROM model	
24	*Indicate the above information for each CD-ROM drive in your system.*	
	Network Interface (NIC)	
25	NIC manufacturer	
26	NIC model	
27	Installed in server slot number	
28	*Fill out a System Device record for the NIC.*	
	Video System	
29	Video card manufacturer	
30	Video card model	
31	Installed in server slot number	
32	*Fill out a System Device record for the video card.*	
33	Monitor manufacturer	
34	Monitor model	
	Input Devices	
35	Keyboard type (circle one)	101-key 84-key
36	Mouse type (circle one)	Serial Bus
37	For serial mouse: COM port	
38	*For bus mouse, fill out a System Device record.*	

WORKSHEET 13.7 continued: Hardware Design Worksheet

Line	System	Requirements
	I/O Devices (Serial Ports, etc.)	
39	*Fill out a System Device record for each installed I/O interface.*	
	UPS System	
40	UPS manufacturer	
41	UPS model	
42	UPS volt-amp rating	
43	Requires serial port signaling?	
44	Part number for the signaling cable	
	Tape Backup Unit	
45	Tape backup type	
46	Tape backup manufacturer	
47	Tape backup model	
48	Tape backup SCSI ID	

Completing the Hardware Design Worksheet

The Hardware Design worksheet, Worksheet 13.7, brings together all the information you need to build your server hardware system. Before you fill out this worksheet:

1. Complete the RAM worksheet in Worksheet 13.2.

2. Take a look at the Cache RAM numbers in Table 13.3.

3. Complete the Disk Storage worksheet in Worksheet 13.4.

4. Make sure you understand the System Device record in Worksheet 13.6.

System IRQ Record

Once you've filled out the Hardware Design worksheet, fill in the System IRQ record in Worksheet 13.8. Keep a copy of this information with the server, and make sure to keep it up to date!

WORKSHEET 13.8: System IRQ Record

IRQ Level	Common Use	Comments
0	System timer	Don't use
1	Keyboard	Don't use; can't change
2	"Hard-wired" to IRQ 9	Don't use
9	"Hard-wired" to IRQ 2	Don't use
10		
11		
12		
13	Math coprocessor	Don't use
14		
15		
3	COM2 or COM4	
4	COM1 or COM3	
5		
6	Floppy controller	Don't use
7	LPT1	Don't use; primary parallel port
8	Real-time clock	Don't use

Part ii

WHAT'S NEXT?

This chapter explained how to determine the software components you need for your NT Server computer, as well as how to choose its hardware components. After you've planned your network and the design of your server, you're ready to install NT Server. The next chapter shows you how to install the NT Server operating system software on a computer.

Chapter 14

INSTALLING WINDOWS NT SERVER

This chapter will show you how to install the NT Server operating system software on a computer. Topics covered here include:

- ▶ Installation media (from boot floppies, from a CD-ROM, from a network server)

- ▶ Installation roles (PDC, BDC, member server, and stand-alone server)

- ▶ Installing NT Server

- ▶ Uninstalling NT Server

Adapted from *MSCE: NT® Server 4 Study Guide, Second Edition* by Matthew Strebe and Charles Perkins with James Chellis

ISBN 0-7821-2222-1   832 pages $49.99

INSTALLING NT SERVER

Installing NT Server involves many decisions, quite a few tedious steps, and several rebootings of the server computer. The individual decisions are easy, and the steps are not difficult, but each one element must be correct to perform a successful installation.

The complexity of the installation process arises from the various installation media and server roles for NT Server. Before starting the actual installation process, we describe how to prepare the computer hardware for installation and explain the effect of each installation medium and installation role. The following topics are covered in the preliminary discussion:

- Hardware preparation
- Booting multiple operating systems
- Installation media
- Installation roles
- Installing versus upgrading
- Domain names

Hardware Preparation

This chapter assumes that your computer is capable of running NT Server. Make sure that your computer satisfies the operating system's hardware requirements. In addition, make sure that the components you intend to use appear on the Hardware Compatibility List or (if the components have not yet been evaluated by Microsoft) that the manufacturer *guarantees* that the components will work with Windows NT. Items that you should be particularly careful about include the CD-ROM, the SCSI controller card (for server computers with SCSI hard disk drives and peripherals), and the network adapter card or cards.

Before you install NT Server, you must be certain that none of the hardware components in the computer conflict. For example, if you have both a SCSI adapter and an Ethernet adapter in the computer, the Ethernet adapter cannot be configured to use the same interrupts as the SCSI adapter. You should be able to boot DOS from a floppy disk, ensuring that your computer hardware will at least boot, but the ability to boot DOS does not prove the absence of device conflicts. (DOS will run even when some of the devices in the computer are in conflict.) You should use the utilities that come with the devices to configure those devices to avoid memory and interrupt conflicts.

TIP

Being able to boot DOS is not proof that a computer can run NT Server. However, if Windows 95/98 can run, reports no errors in configuration, and can use each installed device, then you usually can be sure that the computer has no configuration problems.

When you use NT Server to host files on a network, you should make one or two partitions for the exclusive use of NT Server and format them for use with NTFS. (NT is the only operating system that can read and write NTFS.) You should format the first partition, which does not have to be very large, with the FAT file system for booting and for DOS and Windows.

You should make at least one partition NTFS because NT Server uses the security features of NTFS to provide file-level security for data shared over the network. You might make two partitions NTFS because you can then dedicate one partition to the NT Server system and administrative files and dedicate the other to user files. When you place user files and system files on separate partitions, you protect the file server from running out of disk space for system services when users fill all available user storage space.

TIP

You should keep one small partition formatted with the FAT file system for MS-DOS or a slightly larger one formatted with the FAT file system for DOS and Windows. This arrangement allows you to set up the server to multiboot DOS, Windows (if you leave enough space), and NT Server. You might wish to configure your server in this manner because many computer peripherals, such as some network adapters, SCSI adapters, and sound cards, come with DOS configuration programs. In many cases, these DOS programs will not perform correctly under NT Server because they violate the NT security mechanisms by writing directly to the hardware devices. Therefore, you may wish to keep these utilities in the FAT partition and boot to DOS or Windows when you need to configure them.

Booting Multiple Operating Systems

NT Server will coexist happily with other operating systems on your computer. NT Server can be installed in its own NTFS volume (the best choice as described in the previous section), or it can be installed alongside another operating system in a FAT volume. The NT boot loader allows you to choose from the operating systems installed in your computer.

When you install NT Server, the NT boot loader is installed in the boot partition of your computer. Initially, the boot loader's boot menu contains two entries for your NT Server operating system, as well as one for DOS or Windows if either operating system was installed on your computer before you installed NT Server. Each successive installation of NT adds to the boot loader menu, so you can, for example, install NT Server and NT Workstation along with Windows 95/98 on the same computer, each with its own boot menu option.

Installation Media

You can install NT Server from a number of different sources. This diversity reflects the many environments in which NT Server will be installed. In many cases, it will be installed on a computer using the boot floppies and a CD-ROM directly attached to the computer. However, if you do not wish to use the floppy disks or NT Server does not support your CD-ROM drive, then you can use the installation method that that does not require a floppy or a CD-ROM. In some larger networks, the installation files may be stored on a central server, and you will use a network share to install the operating system; you can use the Network Client Administrator to make installation disks for the new server.

NOTE

Since every NT Server installation should be customized to the requirements of the network in which it resides, the NT Server 4 installation process does not provide the installer with the express versus custom option (unlike the NT Workstation installation process, which does).

Most installation methods use the WINNT or the WINNT32 program. Their function is to adapt the NT installation process to the installation environment of your computer. These programs create floppy disks, copy installation files to your hard disk, or both, so that the NT Setup program can place NT Server on your computer.

The WINNT and WINNT32 Programs

The WINNT and the WINNT32 programs perform the same function and take almost the same command-line switches, but the WINNT32 program runs in the 32-bit NT environment. The command-line switches are as follows:

```
winnt /S:sourcepath /T:tempdrive /I:inffile /OX /X /F /C /B
/U:scriptfile /R:directory/E: command
```

/B   Install without installation boot floppies.

/C   Skip free space check on installation boot floppies. Not available in WINNT32.

/E   Specifies command to be executed at the end of GUI setup.

/F   Copy files from the boot floppies without verifying the copies. Not available in WINNT32.

/I   Specifies the filename (but not the path) of the setup information file. The default is dosnet.inf.

/OX   Create boot floppies for floppy-based installation from CD-ROM.

/R   Specifies optimal directory to be installed.

/RX   Specifies optimal directory to be copied. Not available in WINNT32.

/S   Specifies the source location of NT setup files. The source path must be fully qualified, of the form
        <driveletter>:\[<path>] or
        \\<servername>\<share>[\<path>].
        The default is the current directory.

/T   Specifies the drive to contain the temporary setup files.

/U   Specifies unattended operation and an optional script file.

/X   Specifies not to create the setup boot floppies.

TIP

If you are running from within NT, use WINNT32 rather than WINNT.

In the sections that follow, you will learn how to use these programs to install NT Server in various situations.

Installing with a Boot Floppy from the CD-ROM

The simplest method of installing the server software is to use the boot floppies to boot with the NT CD-ROM in a supported CD-ROM drive. You can use the boot floppies that come with the installation CD-ROM, or you can create new copies of the boot floppies using the WINNT or WINNT32 program on the CD-ROM. Later in this chapter, the section titled "Creating the Installation Boot Floppies from the CD-ROM" shows you how to re-create the boot floppies.

This method of installation does not require the hard disks in the computer to have any partitions or formatted file systems on them, not even DOS FAT. After booting from these installation disks, you have the option of creating partitions and formatting file systems on your server computer from within the installation program.

TIP

If your SCSI controller or BIOS supports booting from CD-ROM, you can skip booting floppies and simply boot from the NT Server CD-ROM.

Installing without a Floppy Disk from an Unsupported CD-ROM Drive or from the Network

This method of installation copies the installation files from the CD-ROM before continuing with the installation, but it also copies the files that would otherwise be copied to the boot disks to the hard disk so that the boot disks are not necessary. The drive must have enough free space to hold the installation temporary files.

▶ If you use this method to install from a CD-ROM drive, you must have DOS or Windows installed with drivers for using that CD-ROM drive.

▶ If you use this method to install from the network, you must have DOS or Windows installed with drivers that allow you to connect to the network share that holds the NT Server installation files. The /b option of WINNT and WINNT32 tells the installation program to perform an installation without a floppy disk.

Installing with a Floppy Disk from the Network

If you wish to install from the network and you do not have an operating system installed on the computer that can connect to the network share that holds the installation files, then you can use the NT Client Administrator to transform a bootable DOS floppy disk into a network boot disk. You can then use this network boot disk to connect to the network share and begin the installation.

If you use this method to install NT Server, you must have a partition on the hard disk of the computer large enough to contain installation files that will be stored temporarily during the installation. To facilitate this type of installation, you should make DOS tools such as FDISK and FORMAT available from a network share on the file server.

Exercise 14.1 shows you how to create a network boot floppy with the Client Administrator that will log on to an NT Server computer and allow you to use the WINNT program and installation files stored in a share on the server.

EXERCISE 14.1: CREATING A NETWORK BOOT DISK USING THE NT CLIENT ADMINISTRATOR

1. Log on to your NT Server computer as the administrator.

2. Select Start ➢ Programs ➢ Administrative Tools ➢ Network Client Administrator.

CONTINUED ➡

3. Select the Make Network Installation Startup Disk radio button and then click Continue.

4. Select the Share Files radio button, accept the default share name of Clients, and accept the default path of <CD-ROM Drive Letter>\Clients for the source of the client configuration files.

5. Click the OK button. The Network Client Administrator will inform you that it is making the client configuration files available on the network share.

6. Select the type of floppy drive you have in your server. Select Network Client version 3.0 for MS-DOS and Windows. From the Network Adapter Card list, select the type of network adapter card that you have in the computer and on which you will install NT Server. Click OK.

7. Enter a name for the computer on which you will install NT Server. This name does not have to be the name that the server will use after it is installed; this designation is a temporary name for use during the installation process.

8. Note that the Username field is filled with the account name of the account from which you ran the Network Client Administrator (in this case, the Administrator account). The computer for which you are making the floppy disk will use this account when it connects to the server.

9. Note that the domain name recorded in the next field is the same as the name of the server from which you are running Network Client Administrator. The computer will attach to this server when you boot the floppy disk.

10. Select a network protocol for the computer to use to attach to the server. The simplest network protocol is NetBEUI. If you choose TCP/IP, you may need to enter more information (the TCP/IP address, network mask, and so on) in the next set of fields. You must select a network protocol that your server supports. Click OK.

11. Insert a floppy disk formatted with DOS system files (format /s from a DOS, Windows, or Windows 95/98 command prompt) and then click OK.

CONTINUED ➡

12. Click OK when the Network Client Administrator tells you that files have been successfully copied to the floppy disk.

13. Click the Exit button in the Network Client Administrator. The program will inform you that certain defaults were used in creating the floppy disk and that you may have to modify some software settings. Click OK. Leave the floppy disk in the disk drive.

14. Open the floppy drive icon from the Desktop. (Double-click the My Computer icon and then double-click the 3½–inch floppy icon.)

15. Right-click the Autoexec.bat icon and then select the Edit menu. This step launches the Notepad program and allows you to edit the Autoexec.bat file.

16. Edit the line that includes the Net Use command to refer to the network share on your server that will hold the NT Server installation files instead of the share holding the client files. If you follow the exercise in the "Network Preparation for Network Installation" section below and you are installing to an Intel-based computer, the share name will be I386.

17. Delete the last two lines of the file (the line that says Echo running setup... and the line that runs the Setup program).

18. Select File ➢ Save from within Notepad and then select File ➢ Exit.

19. You may need to modify the network adapter settings in the Protocol.ini file in the Net subdirectory of the floppy disk. You will most likely need to do so if the interrupt, memory, or DMA settings are other than the default settings that NT Server expects.

Creating the Installation Boot Floppies from the CD-ROM

The NT Server software package contains three floppy disks and the NT Server installation CD-ROM. You do not need to have a previously installed operating system on your computer's hard disk drive if you install NT Server using these floppy disks. The WINNT and WINNT32 programs on the installation CD-ROM can re-create these floppy disks if they become damaged or lost. Figure 14.1 shows the MS-DOS WINNT program informing you about the floppy disk requirements.

```
Windows NT Server Setup

  Setup requires you to provide three formatted, blank high-density floppy
  disks. Setup will refer to these disks as "Windows NT Server Setup
  Boot Disk," "Windows NT Server Setup Disk #2," and "Windows NT
  Server Setup Disk #3."

  Please insert one of these three disks into drive A:.
  This disk will become "Windows NT Server Setup Disk #3."




 ENTER=Continue   F3=Exit
```

FIGURE 14.1:   Creating NT boot disks

To re-create the floppy disks from your installation CD-ROM, perform the steps described in Exercise 14.2.

EXERCISE 14.2: RE-CREATING NT BOOT FLOPPIES

1. Go to the command prompt. (In NT and Windows 95/98, select Start ➤ Programs ➤ MS-DOS Prompt; in earlier versions of Windows, exit Windows.)

2. Change drives to the CD-ROM drive. (At the command prompt, type the letter of the drive. For instance, if your CD-ROM is drive F:, type **F** and then press Enter.)

3. Type **CD \I386** (or the directory corresponding to your processor) to change to the I386 directory.

4. Do one of the following, depending on your current operating system:

   ▶ If you are at an NT command prompt, type **Winnt32 /OX** and then press Enter.

   ▶ If you are at a Windows, Windows 95/98, or DOS command prompt, type **Winnt /OX** and then press Enter.

CONTINUED ➜

5. Label a blank, formatted floppy disk as Windows NT Server 4 Setup Disk 3 and place it in the disk drive. Press Enter. The program will transfer files to the floppy disk and then ask for the second disk.

6. Label another disk as Windows NT Server 4 Setup Disk 2 and place it in the disk drive. Press Enter. The program will copy files to this second disk and then ask for the final disk.

7. Label a third disk as Windows NT Server 4 Boot Disk, insert it in the disk drive, and then press Enter.

8. Remove the boot disk from the drive after the program has finished transferring information to the boot disk.

Preparing the Network for a Network Installation

If you will be installing NT Server to many computers throughout a network, you may wish to put the NT Server installation files on a central file server and perform a network installation of the operating system at each of the computers on the network. If many of your computers are configured exactly the same, you can automate the process by using several of the installation program's software switches.

Another advantage of installing from the network is that when you reconfigure your NT Server (by adding an adapter card such as a new modem or video card, for instance), the operating system provides the network location as the default path for the operating system files it needs, instead of requiring you to insert the installation CD-ROM again.

Before you can install the NT Server operating system to your computer from the network, you must create a network share that contains the NT Server installation files. If you have many computers on your network, the best way to create the network share is to copy the installation files to a subdirectory on the central file server's hard disk and then share that directory.

On the installation CD-ROM, the basic installation files for a particular computer architecture reside in the subdirectory with the name of that architecture. The Intel files, for example, are in the I386 directory, and the PowerPC files are in the PPC directory. Additional files that are not a basic part of the operating system (new device driver software, demo programs, and so on) reside in other directories off the root directory of the CD-ROM.

If all the computers on your network use the same type of microprocessor (MIPS or Intel, for example), you may create shared network directories only for the installation files for those microprocessors. (In this case, you would copy only the files in the MIPS or the I386 subdirectories, respectively.)

Exercise 14.3 shows you how to create a shared installation subdirectory on your central NT 4 file server.

EXERCISE 14.3: CREATING A NETWORK SHARE OF THE NT SERVER 4 INSTALLATION FILES ON A CENTRAL NT 4 FILE SERVER

1. Log on as an administrator.

2. Place the NT Server 4 installation CD-ROM into the CD-ROM drive.

3. Click the Browse This CD button in the Windows NT CD-ROM window that will automatically start up when you insert the CD-ROM.

4. Open the My Computer icon on the Desktop.

5. Open the drive icon that will contain the directory for the installation files.

6. Drag the subdirectory that contains the installation files from the CD-ROM window to the drive window. For example, to copy the Intel installation files to your C drive, drag the I386 directory to the C window. The files will be copied to the hard disk drive from the CD-ROM. This process may take a while. When the file copies are done, a new subdirectory will be present on the disk drive. It will be selected (highlighted).

7. Select File ➤ Sharing in the drive window. Select Shared As in the Directory Properties window.

CONTINUED ➡

8. Click the Permissions button at the bottom of the screen. In the Access Through Share Permissions window, change the Type of Access from Everyone to Read. Click OK.

9. Click the OK button at the bottom of the Directory Properties window.

10. Close the CD-ROM window, close the drive window, and close the My Computer window.

Unattended Installation

You can configure the NT Server installation so that you do not have to respond to any prompts from the installation and Setup programs while NT Server is being installed. This installation method is called an *unattended install*. It takes a little more preparation to begin with, but if you have to install or upgrade many machines, the unattended install option can save you a lot of time and effort.

To perform the unattended install, you must customize unattended script files and answer files for your particular installation. These script and answer files must contain the information that you otherwise would type into prompts and dialog boxes during the installation process. The unattended install is useful because if you have many computers that are all configured mostly the same, you have to type the information only once—into the unattended install files.

The NT Server 4 CD-ROM includes a file called `Unattend.txt` that (once you customize it) allows you to install NT Server in a simple configuration or to upgrade NT versions 3.51 and earlier to NT Server 4. This `Unattend.txt` file is simple, because a basic installation requires very little information, and an upgrade from an earlier version of NT will use most of the earlier NT operating system's configuration information.

NOTE

If you wish to make unattended installation files for a more complex installation of NT Server, you need to use the Computer Profile Setup utility or the Setup Manager utility. The Computer Profile Setup utility comes with the Microsoft Windows NT Resource Kit, and you will need to refer to the documentation in the Resource Kit for instructions.

Creating Unattended Installation Answer Files

You can use the `Setupmgr.exe` program included on the NT Server installation CD-ROM to create unattended answer files. The Setup Manager program allows you to specify, before you install the operating system, the answers to questions that you would otherwise need to enter during the installation process. Figure 14.2 shows the Setup Manager's opening window.

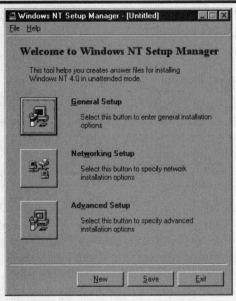

FIGURE 14.2: Setup Manager helps you create answer files

If you are using an Intel-based computer, you can find the Setup Manager program in the `\Support\Deptools\I386` subdirectory of the NT Server installation CD-ROM. Executing the `Setupmgr.exe` program allows you to configure the General Setup, Networking Setup, and Advanced Setup portions of the unattended installation text file. You access each portion (General, Networking, and Advanced) through its own button. Buttons for selecting a new unattended installation file, saving the file, and exiting the program appear at the bottom of the window.

The General Setup configuration choices are:

> **User Information**   You enter the user's name, the organization name, the name for the computer, and the product ID.

General   The Setup program can confirm the hardware settings, run a program during setup, and select the type of upgrade you are performing if you are upgrading rather than installing NT Server.

Computer Role   You can determine which NT operating system you are installing (Workstation or Server), the network architecture (workgroup or domain), and if the operating system is NT Server, if it will be a PDC or BDC. You will enter additional information here also, such as the domain or workgroup name and an (optional) computer account name.

Install Directory   You can tell the installation program to install to the default directory, ask the user for a directory, or install to a specified directory.

Display Settings   You can set the display configuration.

Time Zone   You can set the time zone settings for the computer's time clock.

License Mode   You can configure an NT Server computer to have a certain number of per seat or per server network connection licenses (applies only to NT Server installations).

The Networking Setup configuration choices are:

General   You can specify that networking will be configured during the installation process or that you will configure networking from the Setup Manager program. If you select Unattended Network Installation (which requires you to configure networking from the Setup Manager), you can specify that the Setup program will detect and install a network card using defaults, that the Setup program will detect the card from a list you provide, or that the Setup program will install the network driver for the card you specify.

Adapters   You can select adapter cards to be installed or detected and specify their communications parameters.

Protocols   You can specify the protocols to be installed and set their parameters.

Services   You can specify the services to be installed and set their parameters.

Internet   For NT Server computers, you can set which of the
Internet services will be installed and specify where the Internet services will store their information.

Modem   If RAS is installed and configured to use one or more
ports, you can use this tab to configure what type of modem is
connected to your computer and set the modem configuration.

The Advanced Setup options include a number of settings that you
will not want to change unless you have a good understanding of the
installation process and a need to perform an unorthodox installation.

NOTE

One setting that you may wish to change, however, is the Convert to NTFS
option found under the File System tab. This option will convert the NT installation partition to NTFS. You will want to check this option if you wish to use
the advanced features that NTFS provides.

After you specify how you want to install NT Server within the Setup
Manager program, select Save from the Setup Manager main screen. At
the prompt, select a directory and filename for the unattended installation file. If you have created a network share containing the NT setup
files, you should save the unattended installation file there.

The /u option for the WINNT and WINNT32 programs allows you to
specify an unattended answer file for an NT installation. The /u option
requires the /s option to also be selected, specifying the source directory
for NT installation files (including the unattended installation file). Type
the filename of the unattended installation file after the /u option.

Exercise 14.4 shows you how to create an unattended installation
answer file. This exercise assumes that you are installing a computer to
be part of a domain called DOMAIN and that the computer name will be
MY_SERVER. The username is Isaac Newton, and the organizational
name is Gravatic Technologies. The exercise assumes that you have an
NE2000-compatible Ethernet driver and that you are using an Intel-
compatible computer.

NOTE

The settings in this exercise will most likely not match those required for your
computer and your network.

EXERCISE 14.4: CREATING AN UNATTENDED INSTALLATION ANSWER FILE

1. Insert the NT Server 4 installation CD-ROM into the CD-ROM drive.

2. Double-click the My Computer icon.

3. Open the CD-ROM icon in the My Computer window. Select Browse This CD-ROM from the Autorun window that appears.

4. Select Support ➤ Deptools ➤ I386.

5. Open the Setupmgr program.

6. Click the New button at the bottom of the screen.

7. Click the General Setup button.

8. Click the User Information tab; type **Isaac Newton** into the User Name field, **Gravatic Technologies** into the Organization field, and **MY_SERVER** into the Computer Name field. Enter the product ID number for your server CD-ROM into the Product ID field.

9. Click the Computer Role tab. In the Select the Role of The Computer field, select Primary Domain Controller. Type **DOMAIN** into the Domain Name field.

10. Click the other tabs to observe the settings of each tab. You don't need to change any of them for this exercise.

11. Click the OK button at the bottom of the screen.

12. Click the Networking Setup button.

13. Click the General tab and select Unattended Network Installation. Then select Specify Adapters To Be Installed.

14. Click the Adapters tab. Click the Add button. In the Adding Adapters window, select Novell NE2000 Adapter. Click OK.

15. Click the Parameters button. Type **5** for the interrupt number and **320** for the I/O Base Address. Click OK.

16. Click the Protocols tab. Click the Add button. Select NetBEUI in the Adding Protocols window. Click the OK button. You do not have to set the parameters for NetBEUI.

CONTINUED ➡

17. Click OK at the bottom of the Networking Options window.

18. Click the Advanced Setup button. Click the File System tab. Select the Convert to NTFS option. Click OK at the bottom of the Advanced Options window.

19. Click the Save button at the bottom of the Setup Manager window. Type **C:\temp\test.txt** in the Name field. Click the Save button. This step saves the unattended installation file as test.txt in the temp directory of your C drive.

20. Click the Exit button.

Using a Text Editor to Create the Uniqueness Database File

If you have to install NT Workstation on a large number of similarly configured computers, you can use the unattended installation file (which you create just once; it contains the configuration information common to all the computers on which you will install NT) in conjunction with a uniqueness database file that identifies differences among installations, such as the computer name and the username for that installation. You can then use the /UDF option of WINNT and WINNT32 to specify a uniqueness database file (UDF) file that customizes the installation for a particular computer. An example of a UDF file for three computers follows.

```
; UDF file to customize the installation for three computers
;
[UniqueIds]
u1 = UserData
u2 = UserData
u3 = UserData
[u1:UserData]
FullName = "Charles Perkins"
OrgName = "Charles Perkins Elucidation"
ComputerName = YOYO
[u2:UserData]
FullName = "Matthew Strebe"
OrgName = "Netropolis"
ComputerName = BOOMERANG
[u3:UserData]
FullName = "Henry J Tillman"
OrgName = "Tillman World Enterprises Inc."
ComputerName = POGO
```

Each computer in the preceding example has a different full name, organization name, and computer name. The installation program merges the settings of the unattended text file and the UDF at the graphics portion of the installation process. An unattended installation answer file will supply all the other settings.

When you select the UDF option for WINNT or WINNT32, you can also specify the uniqueness ID for that installation. The sample UDF has three uniqueness IDs listed: u1, u2, and u3. When specifying u1 with the above UDF file, WINNT causes the Setup program to use the first set of sample information.

The format of the UDF file is simple, and it is very similar to the format of the unattended installation answer file. The [u1:UserData] section heading, for example, specifies that the data following it will add to or replace, for the u1 installation, information found in the [UserData] section of the unattended installation file. The FullName setting of Charles Perkins will replace, for the u1 installation, the full name information stored in the unattended installation file.

The UDF file is different from the unattended answer file in that it has a [UniqueIDs] section containing identifiers for unique installation; the unique ID prefixes each section of the answer file that contains information just for the unique ID.

You can create UDF files using a text editor such as Notepad. If you intend to use a UDF file to customize the installation process for several computers, you will need to provide unique settings for at least the computer name for each installation. Use the format outlined above to create UDF entries for each computer.

You use the UDF by specifying the UDF file and the uniqueness identifier for the installation on the WINNT or WINNT32 command line. The UDF file is used with the unattended answer file option (explained in the preceding section). You specify that setup will use a UDF file with the /UDF option shown here:

```
/UDF:ID[,database_filename]
```

The next example assumes the following:

▶ You have created an unattended answer file called unat1.txt using Setup Manager.

▶ You have created a UDF file called udf1.txt, which contains a unique ID of id1, with your text editor.

▶ The installation files (including the answer file and the UDF file) reside on a network share mapped to drive F.

Under these conditions, you can type this command from the DOS prompt:

```
winnt /s:f:\ /u:unat1.txt /UDF:id1,udf1.txt
```

Using the Sysdiff Utility

If you further wish to customize the installation of NT to one or more computers over a network, you can use the Sysdiff utility. This utility records the difference between a normal NT installation and an installation to which you have added other software, such as a standard application suite of files. The Sysdiff utility can perform in any of the following modes:

Snap   In this mode, Sysdiff takes a snapshot of the state of the NT operating system Registry and the state of the file system files and directories. The information it records is written out to a snapshot file.

Diff   This mode of operation records the differences between the state of a previous snapshot of an NT installation and the state of the installation at the time Sysdiff is run again. Sysdiff /Diff creates a difference file.

Apply   Executing Sysdiff with this option can apply the data in the difference file to an NT installation.

Inf   This mode creates an INF file containing information about your installation preferences and installation data from the difference file. You can apply this option to a server-based share of the NT installation files so that the differences captured with the Diff command are automatically applied to installations of NT made from that server-based share.

Dump   This command produces a file that lists the contents of the difference file.

The modes are set as follows:

```
sysdiff /snap [/log:log_file] snapshot_file
sysdiff /diff [/log:log_file] snapshot_file difference_file
sysdiff /apply [/log:log_file ] difference_file
sysdiff /inf [/u] sysdiff_file oem_root
sysdiff /dump difference_file dump_file
```

The command-line parameters are defined as follows:

`snapshot_file`   The file containing the state of the original installation.

`difference_file`   The file containing the differences between the original installation and your custom installation.

`log_file`   The file describing the operation of the Sysdiff utility.

`oem_root`   The directory containing the additional directories and files for your custom installation.

`dump_file`   The file containing a description of the data in the difference file.

The simplest way to use the Sysdiff utility is described in Exercise 14.5.

EXERCISE 14.5: USING THE SYSDIFF UTILITY TO CUSTOMIZE AN INSTALLATION

1. Perform an installation of the NT Server software to a typical computer.

2. Create a snapshot file with the Sysdiff /snap option.

3. Install to the typical computer the software that you wish to be distributed to each installation.

4. Create a difference file with the /diff option.

5. Install NT on each of the destination computers.

6. Run the Sysdiff utility with the /apply option after each installation is complete.

The Sysdiff utility is a powerful tool that can automate the distribution of both operating system and application software to a large number of computers. However, you must be very familiar with the installation process and the operation of the NT operating system and applications before you can use the Sysdiff utility to its fullest extent.

Installation Roles

As explained in the previous chapters, your NT Server can play several different roles in your network: PDC, BDC, member server, or stand-alone server.

NOTE

If you install a server without making it a domain controller (PDC or BDC), you cannot make it a PDC or a BDC later. You will have to reinstall the operating system software if you wish to change the role of the server.

If you are creating a new domain, you should designate the first server you install as the PDC. If the first computer you bring online is not the computer you want to be the PDC, install it as the PDC anyway. When you install NT Server on the computer you want to be the PDC, install it as a BDC and then promote it to the PDC.

You should configure the second server on your domain to be the BDC. If you plan to have a large number of servers in your domain, you should select several more servers to be BDCs.

NOTE

You do not have to promote a BDC if your PDC fails. BDCs will automatically provide logon services whenever a PDC is not available.

Not every server in your network must be a PDC or a BDC. The tasks that the PDC and BDCs perform exact a performance penalty from the server, and you may wish to dedicate some servers in your domain to a single purpose, such as serving files or hosting a database. If you already have a PDC and BDC and you require the best performance from a server computer, you may wish to designate it as a member server in your domain.

In some cases you will install a server that is not a part of a domain. In this case, you can make the computer a stand-alone server and configure it to use the workgroup networking model instead of the domain networking model. If the server will not be a part of a domain, you should designate it as a stand-alone server.

Installing versus Upgrading

If you have an earlier version of NT Server loaded on the computer, you will have the option of upgrading the earlier version of the operating system to version 4.

TIP

You should upgrade your server rather than perform a fresh installation when your computer is already running an earlier version of the software and you do not require a change in the server's role.

Upgrading the current installation is a much easier process than installing a new version of the operating system because, when the installation program upgrades from an earlier version, it can transfer many of the operating system settings to the new version.

You should be aware, however, that even if you upgrade a member server or stand-alone server, it will still be a member server or stand-alone server. If you wish to make a server that previously was not a PDC or BDC into a PDC or BDC, then you need to reinstall the operating system software.

Server and Domain Names

Before you begin installing servers and naming computers, you should devise a coherent plan to keep track of networked resources. Networks are often brought online chaotically, and servers are named as if they were pets. Although this free-form system is fun for the network administrator, it's not fun for new users who are trying to figure out where certain files reside.

The primary responsibility of a network administrator is to make network resources as easily available as possible. Part of this responsibility is to create a coherent naming scheme for all network resources.

To make a naming scheme, think about what is important in your organization. Are resources divided by department? Are they grouped by use? Should you use an obvious name?

For instance, if you dedicate a server to the accounting department, ACCOUNTING might be a good name for it. On the other hand, if the server stores x-ray files exclusively, XRAYS might be appropriate. Likewise, a printer loaded with invoices should probably be called INVOICE PRINTER.

The rule for naming conventions is consistency and uniqueness. If you name one server by department or location, name them all by department or location. If you find you can't follow through, then department or location naming probably isn't the right scheme for your situation.

You can also devise schemes based on major resource types. For example, you could name servers by department, such as MARKETING, and name printers by function, such as INVOICES or CHECKS, because most printers are used exclusively within departments, whereas servers are accessed throughout the organization. Names must be unique within domains, and they should be unique throughout your organization. If you have a CHECKS printer in the accounting domain and a CHECKS printer in finance domain, someone is certain to access one or both of them incorrectly. (Examples of how to resolve this kind of problem follow.)

Create a set of rules for naming shared resources. Give each department, location, purpose, and function a unique mnemonic and combine them to create unique names. For example, ACCSRV would be the accounting server, whereas MKTLPR would be the marketing laser printer, and ACCIPR would be the accounting invoices printer. When users are familiar with your naming scheme, they will know exactly what your named resources refer to when they see them in lists.

Small organizations should create naming schemes with an eye towards the future. Naming your server SERVER because it's the only one you have leaves you out in the cold when you add a second server. PRIMARY might be a bit better, but a name like your organization location or even HEADQUARTERS could easily support the addition of more servers down the line without changing your naming scheme.

If you have several domains in your network, you should choose a similar naming scheme for the each domain. You should at least select a domain name for your domain that will allow easy interoperation with other domains, such as one based on your physical location, like SANDIEGO. Leaving the domain name set to the default name of DOMAIN is not the best option. You can change your domain name later, but you'll have to go around to every computer in your facility to make the change.

Installation Process

Once you have decided which role the server will play on the network and have determined what media you will use to install the software, you can go on with the installation. The installation process requires four general steps:

1. Gathering information
2. Booting the floppies, starting WINNT or WINNT32
3. Using the text-based Setup program
4. Negotiating the graphical configuration program

The following sections move through these steps one at a time.

Gathering Information

The first step is to gather all of the information you will need during the installation process. The information you need includes the computer's name, the domain name, and the interrupt and memory settings of various components. (These settings are particularly hard to determine in the middle of an installation without aborting the installation and starting over.)

You should note at least the following information before you continue with an installation:

Computer name   This name will identify your server on the network. Computer names can be up to 15 characters long and must be unique.

Domain name   This is necessary if the computer is a member of a domain.

Workgroup name   This is necessary if the computer is a member of a workgroup.

Device settings   For each device in your computer with an interrupt, DMA, or memory setting, record the model and manufacturer of the device (this information is particularly important for network cards) and record each of the settings for the device.

Hard drive partitions   Record the purpose and format for each of the partitions in your computer. Specify which partition will contain the NT Server system files.

Windows NT directory   Record the directory that will contain the NT Server System files. (The default is \WINNT.)

Protocol selection Record which protocols you will configure this server to support. (Usual choices include TCP/IP, IPX/SPX, and NetBEUI.)

TCP/IP information If you will be installing the TCP/IP protocol, you need to record the TCP/IP address, subnet mask, gateway address, DNS address, WINS address, and TCP/IP domain name (which is not the same as the NT networking domain name listed above).

IPX information If you will be installing the IPX/SPX protocol, you should list the IPX network number for your network.

Ethernet information If you are installing an Ethernet card in your server (most NT servers have them), you should record the Ethernet frame type that you will be using on your network. You should also record which media type you will use if your card supports several media types (such as twisted-pair, fiber-optic, or Thinnet).

Licensing information Record the individual and organization name that this software is licensed to. You should also record the CD key that is printed on a label on the back of the CD-ROM case. Also record whether you will use per seat or per server licensing and the user limit.

Administrator password Record the administrator password. If at a later point you cannot recall the password, you may have to reinstall the software.

Because this list contains sensitive information such as the administrator password, you should keep the list in a safe place after you have installed the server software. You should not discard the list; however, it may be useful later when you need to reinstall, upgrade, or otherwise maintain the system.

Booting the Floppies, Starting WINNT or WINNT32

Just starting the installation process can be the most complicated part of installing NT Server, or it can be the easiest. If you use the installation boot floppies that come with the NT Server CD-ROM and you install from a CD-ROM drive that is compatible with NT, then this part of the installation process is very simple—you just insert the CD-ROM in the

CD-ROM drive, insert the first floppy disk in the floppy drive, and boot the computer. Figure 14.3 shows the MS-DOS based WINNT program copying installation files to the hard disk.

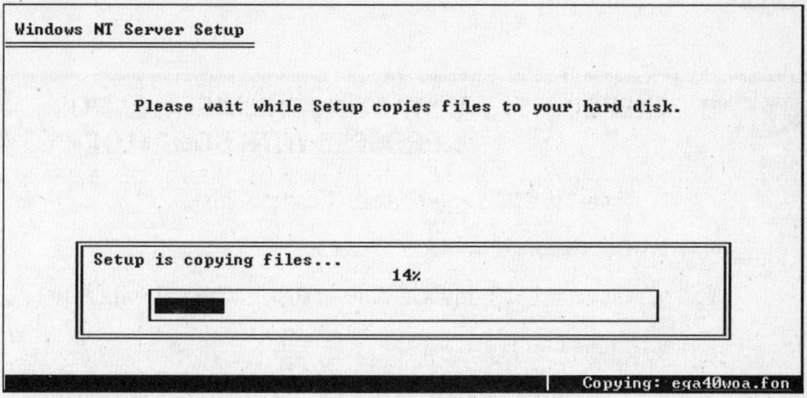

```
Windows NT Server Setup


            Please wait while Setup copies files to your hard disk.




     Setup is copying files...
                          14%
       ■■■■■■■■
```
```
                                              | Copying: eqa40woa.fon
```

FIGURE 14.3: Copying temporary files to the hard disk drive

The process becomes more complicated if you don't have the floppy disks or if you are booting from an unsupported CD-ROM drive. In these cases, you will use either the WINNT or WINNT32 program to make the floppy disks or start the installation without using the floppies.

▶ If you need to create floppy disks, refer to "Creating the Installation Boot Floppies from the CD-ROM" earlier in this chapter for instructions.

▶ If you will be installing from a network share and the installation files have not yet been made available over the network, refer to "Preparing the Network for a Network Installation" earlier in this chapter for instructions.

▶ If you will be installing from a network share and the computer does not have an operating system already installed that can connect to a network share, refer to "Installing with a Floppy Disk from the Network" for instructions on how to make a network boot disk.

The following exercises will get you started with the boot process. Follow Exercise 14.6a to use the installation boot floppies, Exercise 14.6b to perform a CD-ROM install without a floppy disk, and Exercise 14.6c to perform a network installation from a shared directory on a server.

TIP

If your computer supports a bootable CD-ROM, you can boot the NT Server Installation CD-ROM instead of the boot floppies.

EXERCISE 14.6A: STARTING THE INSTALLATION PROCESS WITH BOOT FLOPPIES

1. Insert the NT Server installation boot disk.

2. Boot your computer.

3. Insert the Windows NT Server Disk 2 when prompted.

4. Press Enter.

5. Proceed to Exercise 14.7.

EXERCISE 14.6B: STARTING A CD-ROM INSTALLATION PROCESS WITHOUT FLOPPY DISKS

1. Turn the computer on and boot to MS-DOS or Windows 95/98. Your current operating system must support your CD-ROM drive. You may boot from an MS-DOS floppy disk if you wish.

2. Go to the command prompt. If you have booted DOS, then you are already at the command prompt. From Windows for Workgroups and earlier versions of Windows, double-click the MS-DOS icon in the Main program group. From Windows 95/98 select Start ➤ Programs ➤ MS-DOS Prompt or Start ➤ Shut Down ➤ Restart in MS-DOS Mode.

3. Change drives to the CD-ROM drive (for instance, type **F:** if your CD-ROM is drive F).

4. Type **CD \I386** to change directories into the I386 subdirectory (for an installation on Intel-based computers).

5. Type **lock** at the command prompt to allow direct access to the hard drive if you are performing the installation from MS-DOS 7 or Windows 95/98.

CONTINUED ➞

6. Type **Winnt /b.**

7. Enter the location of the installation files. The default location will be the I386 directory of the CD-ROM or network share. You can simply accept the default location and press Enter to continue.

8. The Setup program will copy installation files to the hard disk drive of your computer. When the file transfer is complete, remove all floppy disks from the disk drives and then press Enter to reboot your computer. The computer will reboot and welcome you to Windows NT Server Setup. Go to the next section.

EXERCISE 14.6C: STARTING A NETWORK SHARE INSTALLATION PROCESS

1. If you are booting from a network boot floppy, insert the boot disk into the floppy disk drive. If you are performing an installation without floppy disks, leave the floppy disk drive empty.

2. Turn on the computer.

3. Go to the command prompt. If you have booted a network boot disk, then you are already at the command prompt. From Windows for Workgroups and earlier versions of Windows, double-click the MS-DOS icon in the Main program group. From Windows 95/98, select Start ➤ Programs ➤ MS-DOS Prompt.

4. Type **net use z: \\boomerang\I386** to map a drive to the network share that contains the NT Server installation files.

5. Type **Z:** to change drives to the network share.

6. Type **lock** if you are at a DOS 7 (Windows 95/98) or later command prompt to enable direct disk access for the NT Setup program.

7. Type **Winnt /b.**

CONTINUED ➡

Part ii

8. Enter the location of the installation files as **Z:\I386**. The default location will be the I386 directory of the CD-ROM or network share. You can simply accept the default location and press Enter to continue.

9. The Setup program will copy installation files to the hard disk drive of your computer. When the file transfer is complete, remove all floppy disks from disk drives and then press Enter to reboot your computer. If you are in Windows 95/98, you may have to exit the command prompt and shut down the computer manually. The computer will reboot and welcome you to Windows NT Server Setup. Go to the next section.

Using the Text-Based Setup Program

Once you have performed one of the beginning installation exercises (Exercises 14.6a through 14.6c), the NT Setup program executes. The process from here is the same regardless of the method of installation (network, CD-ROM, without a floppy, or with the installation boot disks).

In this portion of the installation process, you must respond to a sequence of text screens that examine your computer's hardware and allow you to select a partition to use with NT Server, the file system to use on the NT partition, and the directory for the NT files. Then the Setup program copies essential files (but not all the files) to their final location on your hard disk.

Exercise 14.7 shows you how to use the NT Setup program. Each step is explained in the text that follows the exercise.

EXERCISE 14.7: USING THE NT SETUP PROGRAM

1. Press Enter at the initial setup screen.

2. Insert the third floppy disk if necessary. At the hardware identification screen, press S if you need to specify additional adapters.

3. Press Enter to continue.

CONTINUED ➡

4. Scroll down through the Windows NT Licensing Agreement until you can press F8 to agree to the license. Press F8 to continue.

5. Select The Above List Matches My Computer and then press Enter. If Setup detects a previous version of NT, it will prompt for a fresh installation or an upgrade.

6. Select the primary partition on your hard drive. If you wish to install NT on another partition, create that partition now.

7. Press C to convert the partition to NTFS. Warning: The partition will no longer be available to MS-DOS or Windows 95/98. If you need to use these operating systems with this partition, skip this step.

8. Accept the default directory location of \WINNT.

9. Press Enter for an exhaustive examination of the hard disk.

10. Remove any floppy disks or CD-ROMs from your computer and press Enter to reboot.

The Initial Setup Screen   The initial setup screen displays four options:

▶ To learn more about NT Setup before continuing, press F1.

▶ To set up NT now, press Enter.

▶ To repair a damaged NT 4 installation, press R.

▶ To quit Setup without installing NT, press F3.

Press Enter to continue.

The License Agreement   You must view and agree to the license agreement before you can continue with the installation of NT Server. Press the Page Down key until you can press the F8 key to agree to the license.

Hardware Identification   The Setup program automatically detects many types of hard disk and CD-ROM controllers, but it cannot detect every type of controller. This screen allows you to select additional adapter drivers and, if necessary, to provide additional adapter drivers on floppy disk. This step is necessary because the Setup program must be able to access a hard disk drive before it can install NT Server, and you may have an unusual drive that NT does not automatically detect.

If you are installing from the installation boot floppies, you should insert the third floppy disk now.

At this point, you can press S to specify additional SCSI adapters, CD-ROM adapters, or special disk controllers. You can choose from the Setup program's list of supported devices or specify a manufacturer's floppy disk as the source for the adapter driver.

If NT is already installed on your computer, Setup skips to the "NT system directory location" step. Otherwise, the next screen shows the computer, display, keyboard, layout, and pointing device (mouse). You can select and change each item, or select The Above List Matches My Computer to continue.

In most cases, the Setup program provides a correct list.

File Systems and Partitions   The next screen displays a list of existing partitions and unpartitioned space. You can install NT Server on an existing partition or on the unpartitioned space. You can also create and delete partitions.

If the partition you choose is unformatted or is of type FAT, the installation program gives you the choice of converting the file system to NTFS or of leaving the file system as FAT. You can make the partition NTFS even if it is the system partition of the hard drive. However, if you do so, the partition will be unavailable to other operating systems. If you are following the recommended procedure and have created a second (large) partition for NT Server, you should choose the option to convert the file system to NTFS.

At this point, if you have created a partition for use with NT Server, you should choose NTFS as the format for the partition.

You will be asked to confirm that you wish to convert the partition to NTFS and warned that this step will make the partition unavailable to other operating systems such as DOS, Windows, and OS/2.

Press C to convert the partition, which will occur just before the graphical portion of the installation process, when you reboot to the actual NT operating system.

Windows NT System Directory Location   If an NT operating system is already installed on the partition, you must now decide whether you are going to upgrade the current operating system or install a new operating system.

If you have another version of Windows installed on the computer, NT will recognize it and ask if you want to install a new version of Windows or upgrade the current version. If you choose to install a new version and give the same file directory name as a version of Windows that is already installed, NT warns you that this installation will destroy the existing version of Windows.

Specify where you want to install the NT Server system files. The default location is \WINNT. You should keep this default unless you have a good reason to choose a different location. (One good reason is that you do not want to overwrite another version of Windows.)

Accept the default directory location of \WINNT.

Hard Disk Examination and Exhaustive Secondary Examination
The final screen of the second (text-based) part of the installation process allows you to select whether Setup will perform a cursory hard disk examination or an exhaustive examination before your computer reboots and the graphical portion of the installation begins.

The simple examination may take a few seconds if you had a freshly formatted or unformatted drive before you began the installation process, or it may take several minutes if you have many files stored on your hard drive. The exhaustive examination will test every location on your hard drive to find any bad locations and may take several minutes.

Press Enter to perform the exhaustive secondary examination (don't press it yet) or press Esc to skip the exhaustive examination. Now press Enter.

Once the examination is complete, the Setup program continues, copying more files to your hard disk drive. When it is finished copying files, you are prompted to remove any floppy disks or CD-ROMs from your computer and then press Enter to reboot. After the computer reboots, the graphical portion of the installation continues.

Part ii

Negotiating the Graphical Configuration Program

The third portion of the installation process is mostly graphical, and your computer is running NT while performing this part of the installation.

The first thing the computer will do after it reboots is to check the file systems on each of the hard disks. NT requires each file system to be in a consistent state (that is, the directory structure of the file system must be error free). At this time, NT converts the file system to NTFS if you selected the Convert option earlier in the installation process. After checking the file systems, NT reboots. This portion of the install process is still text-based, but the computer is now running NT instead of running the NT Setup program.

After converting the file system and then rebooting, you continue the installation in a graphical environment. Exercise 14.8 takes you through the graphical portion of the installation process.

EXERCISE 14.8: FOLLOWING THE GRAPHICAL PORTION OF THE INSTALLATION PROCESS

1. Click Next to begin the graphical portion of the installation.

2. Enter your name in the Name field.

3. Enter the name of your organization in the organization field.

4. Click Next.

5. Enter the CD key into the CD Key field.

6. Click Next.

7. Select Per Seat Licensing mode.

8. Click Next.

9. Enter a computer name in the Name field and then click Next.

10. Select the server type (PDC) and then click Next.

11. Enter the Administrator account password twice and then click Next.

CONTINUED ➡

12. Select Yes to create an Emergency Repair Disk and then click Next.

13. Accept the components listed and click Next.

14. Click Next to continue past the first Configure Network screen.

15. Check the Wired to the Network checkbox.

16. Make sure that the Remote Access to the Network checkbox is not checked.

17. Click Next.

18. Clear the Install Microsoft Internet Information Services checkbox and then click Next.

19. Select From List and then select the MS Loopback Adapter from the list of adapters. Click OK and then click Next.

20. Select the NetBEUI protocol and make sure that the other protocols are not selected. Click Next.

21. Accept the services listed by clicking Next to continue.

22. Click Next to install the components selected.

23. Respond to any requests for information required to configure the networking components. The only information required for the MS Loopback Adapter is the frame type—choose 802.3 and click Continue.

24. Click Next to continue past the screen that allows you to disable network bindings.

25. Click Next to start the network at the prompt.

26. Supply a domain name. (Type **MCSE_TEST** for the purposes of this exercise.)

27. Click Next.

28. Click Finish.

29. Select the correct time zone in the Time Zone tab of the Date/Time properties sheet. Click the Close button.

30. Click OK when the Detected Display window shows you what kind of display adapter it has detected.

CONTINUED ➡

Part ii

31. Click the Test button in the Display Properties window and click OK in the Testing mode window. Click Yes when the Testing mode window returns and asks if you saw the test screen properly.

32. Click OK in the Display Settings window and then click OK in the Display Properties window.

33. Insert a blank diskette on which to create the Emergency Repair Disk and click OK.

34. Remove any floppy disks from drives in the computer and click the Restart Computer button at the prompt.

Options   NT Server has several more setup options than NT Workstation has, but one option you won't see in NT Server is Typical, Portable, Compact, or Custom. Previous versions of NT Server allowed you to select between Express and Custom setups, but that option is not available in NT Server 4. Instead, the Setup program automatically selects all those features that it needs to provide network services and then lets you choose the other components you need.

The Registration Information and Key   You will then be asked to provide the name and an organization that this copy of NT Server is licensed to. You must provide this information or the installation process will not continue.

1. Enter your name in the Name field.

2. Enter the name of your organization in the organization field and then click Next.

3. Enter the CD key in the next screen. The key is recorded on a sticker on the back of the NT Server Installation CD-ROM case. You should also record this key in the installation information you gathered earlier in this chapter.

4. Select Per Seat and then click Next.

NOTE

The next screen allows you to select the licensing mode for this NT Server installation. Refer to Chapter 12 for information on how licensing modes impact the design of your network. For the purposes of this exercise, you should select per seat.

The Computer Name, Server Type, and Administrator Password

The computer name you select can be up to 15 characters long. You should make it simple and easy to type. Enter a name in the Name field and then click Next. Select PDC when prompted to select the role of your server in the domain and then click Next.

Next, you need to enter an Administrator account password. Although you can install NT Server without an Administrator account password by leaving both fields blank, some NT Server functions expect this password and will not operate correctly without it. Specifically, if the password is blank, you won't be able to join domains from the installation screens of other NT machines.

You should choose a password that is difficult to guess but that you will not forget. You should not write it down in a place that is easy for others to get to (such as on a yellow sticky note stuck to the computer's monitor), but if you are configuring this computer for use in an organization, you should make sure that at least one other (trusted) individual in the organization has the password or can get the password in case you are not available to administer the computer. (You could lock your sticky note in a safe.)

Enter the Administrator account password twice and then click Next to continue.

Emergency Repair Disk   The next screen asks if you wish to create an Emergency Repair Disk (ERD). The ERD can rescue your NT installation from system corruption that can happen when the power goes out unexpectedly or when a program or other operating system has disturbed the operating system's boot or system files.

Select Yes and then click Next to continue.

Common Components   You will then be asked which components you wish to install. Common components have already been selected for you, but you may wish to install some that are not installed by default (such as games or additional communications programs).

Accept the default selection of components and click Next to continue.

Network Configuration   Next, you will need to configure your network. Read the information screen and click Next.

Your first choice is to declare how you want the computer to participate in a network. Your choices are:

▶ Wired to the network

▶ Remote access to the network

Check the first box (Wired to the network) but not the second (Remote access). Click Next.

Then choose whether to install the Internet Information Server (IIS). Since you will be shown how to install and use IIS later in the book, you could skip installing it now.

Clear the Install Microsoft Internet Information Server checkbox and then click Next.

Before you can configure the network adapter for your NT computer, NT must know what type of adapter is installed in the computer. You can instruct NT to search for the adapter, or you can select the adapter from a list.

If NT finds an adapter, it will display the adapter and you can click Next to continue. If it does not find the adapter, you must select it from a list or provide drivers for the adapter from a floppy disk.

Even if you do not have a network adapter installed in your computer, you can still install the networking portions of the operating system. In that case, you will need to select the MS Loopback Adapter from the NT list of adapters. The MS Loopback Adapter is a software driver that pretends to be an adapter but doesn't really control a hardware device. You will not, of course, be able to connect to a network using the MS Loopback Adapter.

Click Select from List and then choose the MS Loopback Adapter. Click OK and then click Next.

Protocols   The next screen displays checkboxes for the three default networking protocols for NT networking. A checked protocol will be installed and configured during the installation process; an unchecked protocol may be installed later.

You can select from the additional protocols list to add other protocols (such as AppleTalk) to the list of protocols to install at this time.

NetBEUI is the simplest protocol and requires the least configuration during the installation process.

For this example, select NetBEUI and make sure that the other protocols are not selected. Then click Next.

The next screen displays networking services that will be installed in your NT Server computer. Accept the default configuration and click Next.

The next screen tells you that you will be configuring the protocols and components you selected earlier. Click Next.

At this point, you have to go through a configuration sequence for each of the networking components that you have just selected. For example, if you had selected TCP/IP or IPX/SPX at the protocol screen, you would now be required to enter TCP/IP and IPX/SPX information.

This example uses the simplest configurations, but if you have selected anything other than the MS Loopback Adapter, you might have to enter IRQ and DMA numbers and the base memory address of your network adapter card. Each card is different, and some require more information than others. Enter the information that you gathered about your hardware settings when you configured your hardware before installing NT Server. For the MS LoopBack Adapter, just enter the frame type (select 802.3) and click Continue.

The next screen allows you to disable network bindings. You should leave the bindings as they are and click Next.

Click Next to start the network and go to the next configuration step.

Workgroups and Domains   After the network components of NT Server have been started, you must enter the domain name of the domain your server will participate in. For the exercise in this section, type **MCSE_TEST** as the domain name. Click Next and then Finish.

Miscellaneous Settings   After setting up the network, you still need to configure some miscellaneous components. First, you need to configure the date and time and your time zone. The real-time clock on your computer will most likely have the correct date and time.

In the Time Zone tab of the Date/Time Properties window, select the correct time zone. Click the Close button.

The next part of the installation allows you to configure your video adapter and monitor settings. The default configuration is standard VGA with 16 colors. You can change the settings later; at this point, you should accept the default display settings.

The next screen shows you what kind of display adapter NT has detected. Click OK.

You must test the display before you go on, or NT will display a warning box. The display settings you are testing are the current settings, but you should test them anyway.

In the Display Properties window, click the Test button. Click OK in the Testing mode window and watch the test screen. Wait until the Testing mode window returns; if you saw the test screen properly, click Yes. Click OK to save the settings. Click OK in the Display Properties window.

Finishing the Installation

Finally, NT copies a few accessories, applications, and DLLs to the NT partition. It sets up the Start menu and shortcuts and then removes temporary installation files. If you have installed to an NTFS partition, it also sets security on system files.

NT saves the configuration of the operating system and then it creates the ERD. The last step is to remove any floppy disks and click the Restart Computer button.

Your computer restarts to an installed version of NT Server 4. Once you log on as an administrator, you can create a user account and configure your printers.

REMOVING NT SERVER

NT Server doesn't have a "uninstall" routine. If you decide to return to a previous operating system, you install that operating system over NT Server. However, you need to know a few tricks to make this process work, so follow these three steps:

- ▶ Remove the NTFS volume if necessary.
- ▶ Change the bootstrap routine.
- ▶ Delete the Windows NT directory.

Removing an NTFS Volume

If you have used the NTFS file system for your NT installation, you should remove the NTFS partition before installing another operating system. If you have data files that you want to keep on the NTFS partition, you must copy them onto another mass-storage device or back them up to a tape that can be read into the new operating system. Copying these files to a FAT volume is an effective and fast way to make them available to the operating system you move to.

After moving or archiving any data you wish to keep, you are ready to delete the NTFS partition. Removing an NTFS volume can be difficult because some versions of the MS-DOS FDISK program cannot delete an NTFS volume. No version of the MS-DOS FDISK program can remove an NTFS logical drive in an extended MS-DOS partition.

Perhaps the easiest way to remove an NTFS partition is with the NT Setup program used to create them, as shown in Exercise 14.9.

WARNING

Do not perform Exercise 14.9 unless you actually intend to remove an NTFS partition. This exercise can destroy information on your hard disk.

Removing the NTFS partition in which NT Server is installed automatically removes the NT files.

EXERCISE 14.9: DELETING AN NTFS PARTITION

1. Insert the Windows NT Setup Disk 1 and restart your computer.

2. Insert Setup Disk 2 when prompted.

3. Press Enter at the Welcome to Windows NT Setup screen.

4. Press Enter to automatically detect your mass-storage devices or press S if you need to specify them manually.

5. Insert Setup Disk 3 when prompted.

6. Press Enter when you have specified all necessary device drivers.

7. Press Page Down until you reach the end of the license agreement on the license page and then press F8.

8. Change your computer settings as necessary and press Enter.

9. Select the NTFS partition you wish to delete and press D.

10. Press L to confirm deletion. Note that the partition now shows up as free space in the partitions list.

11. Press F3 twice to exit NT Setup.

12. Press Enter to restart your computer.

Part ii

Changing the Boot Operating System

Changing the boot operating system involves simply replacing the boot record of the primary hard disk with the boot loader for the operating system you will be using. In MS-DOS, the SYS utility performs this task. Other operating systems use various methods. Exercise 14.10 shows you how to change the boot loader to MS-DOS in an existing FAT partition, and Exercise 14.11 shows how to create an MS-DOS boot partition.

This command replaces the bootstrap routine on the boot hard disk with the system files for MS-DOS. If you boot MS-DOS Setup Disk 1 to install MS-DOS, this step will be performed for you.

WARNING

Do not perform this exercise unless you intend to create an MS-DOS boot partition.

EXERCISE 14.10: CHANGING THE BOOT LOADER TO MS-DOS IN AN EXISTING FAT PARTITION

1. Boot an MS-DOS floppy disk containing the SYS utility or MS-DOS Setup disk 1.

2. Exit to the command prompt if necessary.

3. Type **SYS C:** at the A: prompt.

4. Restart the computer.

WARNING

The exact steps shown in Exercise 14.11 will not apply if you have other existing partitions on your disk.

EXERCISE 14.11: CREATING AN MS-DOS BOOT PARTITION

1. Boot an MS-DOS floppy disk containing the FDISK and format utilities or boot MS-DOS Setup Disk 1.

2. Exit to the command prompt if necessary.

3. Type **FDISK** at the A: prompt.

4. Select option 1—Create MS-DOS Primary Partition.

5. Select Y when asked if you wish to use the entire space available and make the partition active.

6. Press Esc to exit FDISK and reboot the computer.

7. Exit to the command prompt if necessary after the computer reboots the system floppy.

8. Type **FORMAT C: /S** at the A: prompt.

9. Remove the floppy disk and reboot the computer when the format finishes.

Part ii

WARNING
Use caution when partitioning a disk containing other partitions.

Other operating systems use other methods too numerous to cover. You usually have an option to replace your current bootstrap routine during the operating system installation. If you are installing another operating system, such as OS/2 or a version of Unix, select the boot option that will replace the NT boot loader.

Removing NT from a FAT Partition

If you have installed NT Server in a FAT partition, removing it is simple. You need only delete the contents of two directories and a few boot files. Exercise 14.12 shows how to remove an NT installation from a FAT volume in MS-DOS.

EXERCISE 14.12: REMOVING NT FROM A FAT PARTITION

1. Boot MS-DOS from a system disk containing the DELTREE utility.

2. Type **DELTREE WINNT** (or the name of your NT directory) at the C: prompt.

3. Type **CD PROGRA~1**.

4. Type **DELTREE WINDOW~1**.

5. Type **DEL NTLDR**.

6. Type **DEL NTDETECT.COM**.

7. Type **DEL BOOT.INI**.

8. Type **DEL PAGEFILE.SYS**.

9. Type **DEL BOOTSEC.DOS**.

WHAT'S NEXT?

This chapter covered installing NT Server 4, providing details about the various installation methods and running the NT Setup program. Now you're ready to use your new network operating system. In the next chapter, you will learn how to get around in the NT GUI, run Windows and DOS applications, work with files and folders, and use NT Server's administrative tools.

Chapter 15

WORKING FROM THE NT SERVER DESKTOP

Before going on to the more "high-end" skills related to performance tuning and administration, you need to master the basic skill of getting around in the NT interface. Even if you're an experienced NT 3.*x* or Windows 3.*x* user, NT 4's interface will be new to you. If you have used Windows 95/98, the GUI will be more familiar, but there are still some notable differences.

Here, you will learn how to run programs from the Desktop, switch between tasks, create shortcuts to applications, and work with files and folders. You'll also be introduced to NT Server's main system administration tools.

· ·

Adapted from *Windows NT® Server 4 : No experience required.* by Robert Cowart and Boyd Waters

ISBN 0-7821-2081-4   448 pages $29.99

RUNNING APPLICATIONS UNDER NT SERVER

When it comes to running applications, some significant differences exist between NT 4 and 3.*x*. However, NT's new approach is almost identical to that of Windows 95/98. The following sections explain the various ways that you can run applications under NT Server 4 and some things you should know about running DOS programs.

What Can and Can't Be Run

NT was designed to be *backward compatible* with Windows 3.*x* and DOS programs, and to be *forward compatible* with most 32-bit programs. Although Windows 95/98 may be the best of all worlds when it comes to running your existing programs due to its high compatibility with "legacy" software, NT is no slouch either. You can pretty much bet that much of your existing software arsenal will run under NT Server.

However, it is wiser not to run too many applications on a server in the first place, especially if your network traffic load is high. Why? An NT Server machine can be too busy dealing with resource sharing, authentication, remote-access services, and other high-end services to be bothered running typical "productivity" applications like word processors. Your NT Server station probably shouldn't be thought of as a "workstation." You'll need it to administer the network, so you'll be running a variety of NT network utilities, such as monitoring programs and user and disk administration programs. For some NT network administration tasks, you'll need to be running NT Server, *not* NT Workstation. We always recommend that NT network administrators have a fast desktop computer on their desk, running NT Server software.

One word of warning: Remember that certain older 16-bit programs (both DOS and Windows ones) can't be run under NT. NT will simply trap any calls that some wily old programs make directly to hardware or the hard disk. For example, some old disk utilities (such as Norton Utilities for DOS and Windows 3.*x*) were designed to read and write directly to the hard disk. NT's security subsystem doesn't allow this. As a rule, don't try to run utility programs that haven't been written for at least NT 3.*x* or Windows 95. They should preferably be written for NT 4.

Techniques for Running Programs

Launching an application in NT Server can be done in myriad ways. In fact, there are so many ways to run programs and open documents that it's a little mind-boggling. Microsoft developers outdid themselves making the new interface almost too flexible. Anyway, here's the basic list of ways to run programs:

▶ Choose the desired application from the Start menu. Just click Start, choose Programs, walk through the cascading menus until you see the program you want, and then click it. Gone too far in the menus? Press Esc to back up one level, or click somewhere outside the menu to close it and then click Start to try again from the beginning.

▶ Open My Computer, click the disk containing the program, and walk your way through directories until you find the application's icon. Then double-click it.

▶ Run the NT Explorer by clicking Start, choosing Programs, and then choosing Windows NT Explorer. Find the application's icon and double-click it. Another way to run Explorer is to right-click My Computer or a drive's icon in the My Computer window and choose Explore.

NOTE

If you're a diehard Windows 3.x user, you can use the good old File Manager, which is also included with NT Server. To run File Manager, choose Start ➤ Run, type **winfile,** and press Enter.

▶ Click Start, choose Find, and click File or Folders. Then enter the application's name (or portion thereof) and click Find Now. When the application is found, double-click its name in the Find box.

▶ Click Start, then Run, enter the name of the program, and press Enter. Note that you can use this method to start any type of program that NT is capable of running, such as DOS, POSIX, or Windows types. Entering Start alone will open a DOS window (actually called a command prompt window since it's not actually running DOS and isn't limited to DOS programs) from which you can enter Start commands. For help on the marvels of the Start command, check the NT Help file. But the catch is that Run requires the program to be in the DOS search path.

▶ Locate a document that was created with the application in question and double-click it. This will run the application and load the document into it. This works only if the document type has an associated application (for example, .DOC files are associated with WordPad or Word).

NOTE

In NT, there are five kinds of executable (applications) file types: Those with extensions of EXE, COM, BAT, CMD, and PIF. (CMD files are like DOS batch files, but written for NT.) If you double-click any other type, it either will not run or will run its associated program and load into it. For example, files with the extension BMP are graphics. Double-clicking such a file (for example, arches.bmp) will run the Paint program and load the graphic into the Paint window for editing.

▶ Right-click the Desktop or in a folder and choose New. (Right-click means to click the right mouse button on the item, not the usual left button.) Then choose a document type from the menu that appears. This creates a new document of that type, which you can double-click to run the application.

▶ Click Start, choose Documents, and choose the document from the list of recently edited documents. This will open the document in the appropriate application.

For many folks, the last three approaches in this list will make the most sense, because they deal with the document itself instead of the application that created it. Want to edit that letter to Aunt Jenny? Just find and open the folder it's stored in, then double-click the document. NT's document-centricity makes this approach straightforward. For more veteran users, the familiar approach of running an application first, then loading in a document will have more appeal. And for the old-timers who prefer to type in commands from the keyboard, well, that's possible too. Just use the Start menu's Run command and enter the name of the application manually. But even old-timers will soon discover that it really does make sense to organize your documents into folders, give them long names that you recognize, and simply double-click them when you want to edit, view, or print them.

When you aren't going directly to a document, running a program from the Start menu is the way to go. When you install a new program, the program's name is added to the Start menu's Program menu. Then you just find your way to the program's name and choose it.

NOTE

When you want to run a program or open a document by clicking it, don't double-click on its name slowly! If you do, this tells NT that you want to change the object's name. Just press Esc to get out of editing mode. This is a great feature when you want to rename a file or folder, but not when you're trying to run a program or open a folder. To be safe, it's better to click any item's little icon (the picture portion) when you want to run it. In short, stay away from clicking an object's name unless you want to change the name.

If you like using the My Computer approach to getting into your hard disk, fine. Many prefer to use the Explorer, which is basically the old File Manager on steroids. But My Computer can quickly lead you to some important items such as Printers, Dial-up Networking, and the Control Panel. And some folks like the windowing approach that it uses. A good way to minimize all open windows and see the Desktop (and thus the My Computer icon) is to right-click the clock in the Taskbar and choose Minimize All Windows. You can later choose Undo Minimize All to reverse the effect.

NOTE

If you don't like seeing a new window for each folder you explore from My Computer, Choose View, then Options, and then Browse Folders Using A Single Window. When you're browsing through the directory tree, you can use the Backspace key to back up a level to a folder's parent.

When you are working with folder windows, you may want to turn on the toolbar or alter the way files and folders are displayed. Check out the View menu for these options. Choose Small Icons, List, or Details. The Details view is helpful when you're looking for a specific file or folder. It shows the sizes of files, the dates they were created, their types, and other information about the files.

Normally, files with certain filename extensions (the last three letters of a file's name) are hidden from display in your folder windows. For example, files with DLL, SYS, VXD, 386, DRV, and CPL extensions will not be listed. This way, your display isn't cluttered with essentially useless files that perform duties for the operating system but not directly for users. If you want to see all the files in a folder, open the View menu in the folder's window, choose Options, and select the File Types tab. Then turn on the appropriate checkbox option.

Part ii

NOTE
If you've done a multi-boot install, remember that some programs require that you reinstall them under NT to get them to work correctly. You won't be able to just install them under, say Windows 95/98 in the Explorer or Find box, and then launch them by double-clicking from NT. You'll typically be told that some DLL files are missing and the program won't run. You must reinstall the program(s) in question, while running NT. The programs can actually be installed in the same directory they were in before (overwriting the old files), which will save you some disk space. The reinstallation process is necessary to get DLLs in the right directories and to update the NT Registry with details about the applications.

More about File Registration

As explained earlier, some documents will open when you double-click their icons—whether those icons are in the Find box, a folder, File Manager, Explorer, or wherever. Only special documents do this—ones that are *registered*. NT has an internal registry (basically just a list) of filename extensions that it knows about. Each registered file type is matched with a program that it works with. When you double-click any document, NT scans the list of registered file types to determine what it should do with it.

By default, filename extensions of registered files are not displayed on screen. This cuts down on visual clutter, letting you see simple names that make sense, such as 1995 Report instead of 1995 Report.wk3. You can change this by choosing Options from the View menu in Explorer or any folder window. If you choose to see filename extensions, it will be easier to change an extension. Sometimes, changing an extension can be useful, such as when you want to open a document with an application other than the normally registered one.

How Do File Types Become Registered?

You may be wondering how documents with certain extensions become registered so they will run an application when you double-click them. Some types are set up by NT when you install it. For example, HLP files (such as paint.hlp) are Help files and will open up in an appropriate window. Likewise, TXT files will open in Notepad, PCX files in Paint, DOC files in WordPad, and so on.

In addition to those extensions that are automatically established when you install NT, some others might have been imported into your system from an earlier version of Windows. If you upgraded to NT 4 from NT 3.x, any previous associations will be migrated to the new version.

Some programs register their file type when you install the program. So, for example, when you install Microsoft Word, NT changes the registration list so that DOC files will be opened by Word instead of by WordPad.

NOTE

With NT, you can type the path to a file in the Run dialog box or on a command line, and if that file type is registered, NT will launch the appropriate program and open the document. For example, if you type the path to a Word document, such as ups.doc, in the Run dialog box, Word will fire up with the document. With Windows 95/98, if you want to open a text file, you need to type notepad foo.txt in the Run dialog box. With NT, you simply type foo.txt, and the system will figure out which program to use to open it.

Running DOS Programs

DOS applications are by no means the preponderant genre of PC programs being sold today, but they were for many years. Consequently, thousands of useful and interesting programs exist for the IBM PC DOS environment. Many of these programs are not easily replaced with popular Windows programs, simply because they are specialized programs, custom designed for vertical market uses such as point-of-sale, transaction processing, inventory, scientific data gathering, and so on. As a result, much of the code that was written five to ten years ago that ran in DOS programs is still doing its job in companies and other institutions today.

For these reasons, NT runs DOS programs. You can run a DOS program these ways:

▶ Click Start, choose Programs, and look for the program on the submenus.

▶ Double-click the program's name in a folder, Explorer, File Manager, or Find box.

▶ Click Start, choose Run, enter the program's name into the Run box, and press Enter.

▶ Open a command prompt window (DOS session), type in the program's name at the DOS prompt, and press Enter.

▶ Double-click a document file with an extension that you've manually associated with the DOS program.

Part II

The command prompt window in NT is not DOS, but rather a full 32-bit program that understands almost all the DOS commands, plus many more. You can even launch POSIX and Windows programs from this window. For information about available commands, simply type **Help** at the prompt and press Enter. Note that both short and long filenames are shown in this new version of DOS. Long filenames are in the rightmost column, with corresponding short filenames over on the left.

You also get the line-editing capabilities of the DOSKEY command built right in; you can repeat previous commands by pressing the up arrow, and you can edit the current command line with the arrow, Insert, and Delete keys before pressing the Enter key.

Adjusting the Command Prompt Window

While running a DOS session, there are several easy adjustments you can make (more complex adjustments are described in the next section), which are either cosmetic or actually affect the performance of the program. You make these changes from the command prompt window's Control menu (click on the little icon in the upper-left corner of the window). Just open that menu and choose Properties. You'll see the dialog box shown in Figure 15.1.

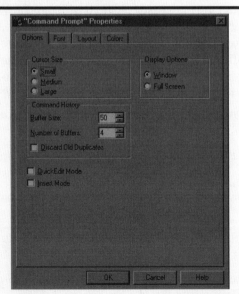

FIGURE 15.1: The "Command Prompt" Properties dialog box lets you control some aspects of your DOS session.

In the Properties dialog box, you can adjust these settings:

▸ Toggle the DOS session between full screen and windowed.

▸ Adjust the font and colors.

▸ Resize the DOS window.

▸ Set the number of command lines that will be buffered for later recall.

▸ Change the cursor size.

▸ Determine some details about cutting and pasting, and decide whether the DOS session should take over the computer's resources when in the foreground.

TIP

To quickly toggle a command prompt window between full screen and windowed, press Alt+Enter. Most DOS applications will run in a window. Some won't, however; you'll be advised if this is the case.

Advanced DOS Session Settings

NT offers additional advanced settings for optimizing DOS applications running in the NT environment. They may be necessary for MS-DOS programs of various types—whether a traditional program, a pop-up program, or another type of TSR (terminate-and-stay resident) program.

Unlike Windows applications, DOS programs were designed to run one at a time, and they are usually memory hogs. They often need at least 640KB of RAM, and some may require expanded or extended memory to perform well. Under Windows, when you switch from one running DOS program to another, intelligent memory reallocation is essential, or the DOS programs will hog precious system resources. Since DOS programs don't really "know" that other programs are running, they expect to have direct access to all the computer's resources, such as RAM, printer, communications ports, screen, and so on. In most cases, NT does pretty well at faking out the DOS program without your help, using various default settings and its own memory-management strategies. However, you may occasionally experience the ungracious shutting down of a program under NT with a message about attempts to corrupt "system integrity."

You may know that in previous versions of Windows, you could fine tune settings for a given DOS application by creating a PIF (Program Information File) for it. When you ran the PIF, the memory and other settings went into effect. In Windows 95/98 and NT 4, PIFs are replaced by Properties. The Properties dialog box for an MS-DOS program replaces PIFEdit (PIF Editor). If you are accustomed to using a PIF with your DOS programs, you can continue doing so with NT 4, but the new approach is easier. A PIF is now created anytime you create a shortcut or modify the default properties of an MS-DOS program. From then on, those settings go into effect whenever you run the program from within NT.

What Do PIFs Do?   First off, PIFs are used only with DOS programs. PIFs are short files, typically 1KB. They're stored on disk, usually in the same directory as the program or in the NT System directory (usually WINNT of the boot drive). The settings affect many aspects of the program's operation, such as the following:

▶ Filename and directory of the program

▶ File attributes

▶ Font and window size

▶ Directory that becomes active once a program starts

▶ Memory usage, including conventional, expanded, extended, and protected mode

▶ Multitasking priority levels

▶ Use of keyboard shortcut keys

▶ Foreground and background processing

▶ Toolbar display

▶ Program termination options

PIFs generally have the same first name as the program, but have PIF as the extension. Thus, the PIF for WordStar (WS.EXE) is typically named WS.PIF, although you can name it whatever you like.

Aside from the active directory, only directories listed in the search path (set up by your AUTOEXEC.BAT file) are examined for PIFs. If a PIF isn't found when a program is double-clicked, it won't be loaded. NT's default PIF settings are then used with the DOS program.

You can run a program directly from its PIF by clicking on the PIF file icon in a folder, Explorer, or a Find box. You can also add a PIF to the

Start menu, or type its full name into the Run dialog box (as you would to run any program). Running directly from a PIF is useful when the PIF isn't in the current search path or when you have more than one PIF for a program, each with its own settings.

TIP

PIFs are one of two types of shortcut files. Shortcuts for Windows applications and documents are given the .LNK extension. Only shortcuts for DOS applications are given the .PIF extension. Even if you select to display MS-DOS extensions of all files (through the Options command on the View menu in Explorer or a folder), you won't see the .PIF extension in listings. Use the Find utility to look for PIFs by extension, if you need to.

Making PIF Settings for a Program   Before you make PIF settings for a program, consider that there may be an easier approach: you can set some options on-the-fly from the command prompt window's Control menu, as explained earlier. Check there if the feature you want to change isn't among the advanced Properties settings.

To get to the more advanced settings, right-click the DOS program's icon (EXE or COM file) and choose Properties. You'll see the Properties dialog box, as shown in Figure 15.2.

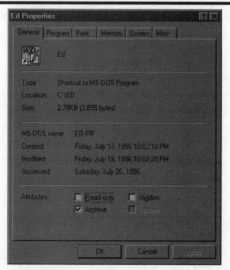

FIGURE 15.2:   The Properties dialog box for a DOS program. These tab pages replace the old NT 3.x PIF Editor. If you make changes to the default settings, a PIF for the program will be created.

Editing the CONFIG.NT and AUTOEXEC.NT Files You can also modify the configuration of the DOS environment by setting up two files that act much like CONFIG.SYS and AUTOEXEC.BAT do in normal DOS on a PC. These files are called CONFIG.NT and AUTOEXEC.NT. They're loaded when NT senses that you're running a DOS application.

When you run a DOS application, NT creates a DOS VDM (Virtual DOS Machine) by loading the DOS environment subsystem and sort of "booting up" DOS. In the process, it reads in settings from CONFIG.NT and AUTOEXEC.NT in the same way that real DOS does when it boots. The only differences are the filenames and the file locations. In this case, the files are in the System32 directory (usually \WINNT\System32 or \Windows\System32) instead of the root directory.

By editing these two files, you can set up the DOS environment used by every DOS application. The great thing about this is that you can change the settings, and when you rerun a program, the new settings are read and put into effect. It's like rebooting DOS after fine tuning CONFIG.SYS and AUTOEXEC.BAT, only faster.

TIP

Although it might sound strange at first, you can set the properties for batch files, too. (A batch file is a group of commands that executes DOS commands in sequence for you, without you typing them in.) When the batch file is run from its PIF, all the settings come into play, and they will affect all the programs in the batch file.

Closing a Command Prompt Window Enter the command **exit** when you're finished running non-NT programs or executing DOS or other (such as NT) commands from a command prompt window. This will close the DOS window and end the session. If no DOS program is actually running, clicking the DOS window's Close button will also end the DOS session. If a DOS program is running, you'll see a message prompting you to quit the DOS program first.

TASK SWITCHING

When you run a new program or open a folder, the Taskbar gets another button on it. Just click a Taskbar button to switch tasks. Simply clicking a button switches you to that program or folder.

For the first several programs, the buttons are long enough to read the names of the programs or folders. As you run more programs, the buttons automatically get shorter, so the names are truncated, like this:

You can resize the Taskbar to give it an extra line or two of buttons, if you want to see the full names. Just grab the upper edge of the Taskbar, as though it were a regular window you wanted to resize, and release. Position the cursor so that it turns into a double-headed arrow first, then drag it upwards. Here's a Taskbar with another line added:

Note that as you increase the size of the Taskbar, you decrease the effective size of your work area. To save space, you can set the Taskbar to disappear until you move the mouse pointer down to the bottom of the screen. This way, you sacrifice nothing in the way of screen real estate until you actually need the Taskbar. You do this via the Taskbar's Properties settings. Just right-click an empty part of the Taskbar and choose Properties. Then set Auto Hide on.

If you prefer, you can also position the Taskbar on the right, left, or top of the screen. Just click any part of the Taskbar other than a button and then drag it to the edge of your choice.

If you are a habituated Windows 3.*x* user, you may prefer using Alt+Tab to switch between tasks. Each press of the this key combination will advance to the next task. Shift+Alt+Tab moves in the opposite direction. Note that the name of the program or folder is displayed at the bottom of the box, which is especially useful when choosing folders, since all folders look the same.

NOTE

In Windows 3.*x*, pressing Ctrl+Esc brought up the Task List. It does not do this in NT 4. Ctrl+Esc simply opens the Start menu, as though you clicked the Start button. And don't try double-clicking the Desktop, because this won't bring up the Task List either. You may want to see the Task Manager (essentially the Task List on steroids) to deal with a runaway or dead application, or check which processes are running. Right-click the Taskbar and choose Task Manager to start it. The Task Manager is covered later in this chapter.

Part ii

SHORTCUT PRIMER

In addition to properties, a major feature in NT 4 is *shortcuts*. Shortcuts are alias icons (icons that represent other icons). You can have them almost anywhere, such as in folders or on the NT Desktop. Because a shortcut is really only a link or pointer to the real file or application it represents, you can create as many as you want without fear of duplicating your data or executable files unnecessarily. You just create aliases for them. So, for example, you can have shortcuts to all your favorite programs right on the Desktop while still keeping the programs' executables in their rightful folders. Then you can run them from there, without needing to click the Start button, walk through the Program menus, and so on.

The trick is knowing how to create shortcuts. Then you need to know how to cut, copy, and paste shortcuts, and how to place them so they are right there on the first menu you see when you click Start.

TIP

A quick way to modify the contents of the Start menu is to right-click the Start button and choose Explore.

Adding Shortcuts to the Start Button Menu

The first place you'll want to drop shortcuts is on the Start menu, so you can easily run the programs you use most. For example, as an administrator, you might run the same utilities day in and out. Cruising through all of the cascading menus from the Start menu is a hassle. So instead, you can drag documents and applications right to the Start menu's first level. (True, you can put your programs, folders, and documents right on the Desktop, and just double-click them to use them; but sometimes it's a hassle to get back to the Desktop, particularly when it's obscured by whatever windows you might have open.) The Start menu shown here is an example of one with added shortcuts.

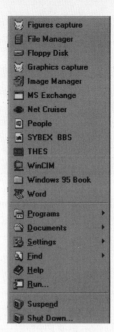

Part ii

As with most operations in Windows, there are several ways to add items to the Start menu. The easiest is to locate the document or executable file (EXE, COM, BAT, or CMD) and drag it to the Start button. When the file is positioned over the button, a little arrow appears under the icon to let you know that you're creating a shortcut.

Another way to manage the items on the Start menu—rearrange them, delete existing ones, and add new items—is through the Taskbar's Settings dialog box. From the Start menu, choose Settings, then Task Bar. Click the Start Menu tab, which includes options for adding and removing items from the Start menu.

Clicking Advanced brings up the whole hierarchy of programs in a two-paned "File Manageresque" arrangement. You can drag, drop, and select multiple items; right-click things; and cut, copy, or paste them at will.

Broken Shortcuts

Unlike on the Macintosh or in OS/2, NT shortcuts can be broken fairly easily. If you move the actual item to another drive or computer on the

LAN, the operating system doesn't update the alias. Double-clicking the shortcut results in a message like the one shown here.

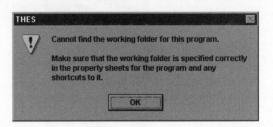

In some cases, NT will scan your computer looking for the item—a gracious gesture—and repair the pointer successfully. Other times, it won't succeed.

There will no doubt be times when you'll want to remove an item from one of your Start menus, such as when you've removed a program or no longer use it often enough to warrant its existence on the menu.

You can examine or repair a shortcut by displaying it with Explorer, right-clicking it, and choosing Properties. Or you can delete it and create a new one—perhaps a more efficient method.

NOTE

In case you're wondering where the Start menu shortcuts are and how the groupings are organized, here's how it works. This whole menu thing is based on directories, with LNK (link) files for the shortcuts. Check out the directory structure under this path: \winnt\profiles\administrator\start menu\. You'll find directories that correspond to each menu, with LNK files for each shortcut. Each user on the server will have a directory under Profiles, which contains that user's Start menu settings.

It's important for UNIX and Mac folks to understand that Windows shortcuts are *not* soft links (UNIX) or aliases (Mac). In many cases, the file system will *not* recognize a shortcut to a folder as a valid path. For example, consider a directory c:\users, which contains the directories default, alice, and bob. A shortcut to the folder c:\users\bob is created in Alice's directory as c:\users\alice\shortcut.lnk. The file c:\users\bob\text.doc *cannot* be opened by typing c:\users\alice\shortcut\text.doc. The shortcut to Bob's folder does not act like a folder, as a Unix soft link or Mac alias would; it's a file. Windows programs will see it as such and probably won't open it. And unlike Mac aliases, shortcuts to files on remote volumes don't work unless the remote server volume is already mounted.

WORKING WITH FILES AND FOLDERS

By now, you get the idea about the NT folder system. You know that folders are, technically speaking, disk directories, and that directories hold files (programs and documents are the main two types of files) and subdirectories.

Of course, being a system administrator type, you also know that you need to keep your files organized systematically, in folders. Now in addition to the normal folders, you have the Desktop to play with. Actually, the Desktop is a folder under the `\winnt\profiles` directory.

There are a few more things to know about how the folder system works. Here, we'll cover these topics:

- ▶ Making new folders
- ▶ Copying and moving items between folders
- ▶ Deleting items, including folders
- ▶ Putting items on the Desktop
- ▶ Copying files to and from floppy disks
- ▶ Setting viewing options for folders
- ▶ Checking the trashcan folder

WARNING

Be careful not to put a lot of important work in folders within Desktop folders. Why? Suppose you decide to erase the WINNT directory to do a fresh install. You'll lose everything on each user's Desktop. For this reason, you might consider keeping your work in directories below the user directory, rather than below the WINNT directory.

Organizing files was a bit difficult with the Windows 3.x interface. You really had to understand how to use the File Manager to create new directories, move files around, rename them, erase them, and so on. With NT, you have two file-management choices: the folder system and Explorer. The folder system is more Mac-like. Explorer is more File Manager-like. You choose. Either way works, and the techniques are much the same.

Once you have the basics of the folder system or Explorer under your belt, working with your files and folders is a piece of cake. As mentioned earlier, since everything in NT's new interface is object-oriented, you just drag, drop, cut, copy, and paste objects where you want them. It's very straightforward.

Making New Folders

If you need to create a new folder, first get the destination location in view. It may be the Desktop or it might be another folder, either on the local computer or on another computer. You can use Explorer, Network Neighborhood, or My Computer to browse to the destination. Once there, right-click in the destination location and choose New, then Folder. A new folder appears, called New Folder. Its name is highlighted and ready for editing. Whatever you type will replace the current name.

Moving and Copying Items

The techniques for moving and copying folders are important because they are the basis for managing all your NT objects—shortcuts, files, documents, executables, folders, and so on—within NT.

Let's say you want to pull several of your existing Desktop folders into a single new folder to reduce clutter. It's as simple as dragging and dropping. Begin by opening the destination folder's window. (Actually you don't even need to open the destination folder, but what you're about to do is more graphically understandable with that folder open.) Then size and position the destination folder's window so you can see the folder(s) you want to put in it. Now you can drag folders from the Desktop inside the perimeter of the destination folder's window. Figure 15.3 illustrates the process.

You can drag and drop most objects in NT using this same scheme. Every effort has gone into designing a uniform approach for manipulating objects on your screen. In general, if you want something placed somewhere else, you can drag it from the source to the destination.

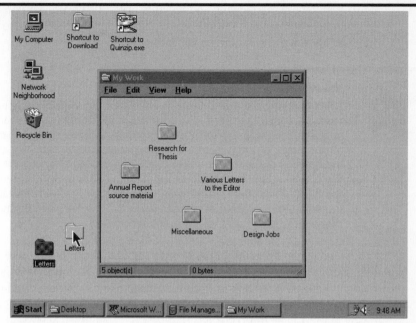

FIGURE 15.3:   Working with folder windows and objects is as simple as dragging and dropping. Rearranging your work is as simple as organizing your desk drawer.

About Moving versus Copying

When you drag an item from one location to another, NT does its best to figure out if you intend to copy it or move it. The general rule about moving versus copying is simple. When you move something by dragging, the mouse pointer keeps the shape of the moved object, as shown here.

When you copy an object by dragging, the cursor takes on a + sign, as in the example shown here.

To switch between copying and moving, press the Ctrl key as you drag. In general, holding down the Ctrl key causes a copy to be made. The + sign will show up in the icon, so you know you're making a copy.

WARNING

When dragging and dropping, be careful where you are aiming before you release the mouse button. If you drop an object too close to another object (or on top of it), it can be placed *inside* of that object. For example, when moving folders around, or even repositioning them on the Desktop, watch that a neighboring folder doesn't become highlighted. If something other than the object you're moving becomes highlighted, that means it has become the target for the object. If you release at that time, your object will go inside the target. If you accidentally do this, just open the target and drag the object out again, or click *any* folder window's Edit menu and choose Undo.

If you just can't remember whether to use Ctrl, Shift, or Alt, no problem. Here's a great little trick. The easiest way to fully control what's going to happen when you drag an item around—from folder to folder, to and from the Desktop, within the Explorer, from the Find box, and so on—is to right-click drag (just use the right mouse button when you drag). When you drop the object, you'll see a pop-up menu of choices, similar to the one shown here.

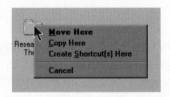

Selecting a number of objects can be useful when you want to move, copy, delete, or make shortcuts out of them in one fell swoop. Just draw a box around multiple items to select them (start in the upper left and drag down to the lower right). Once objects are selected as a group, you can then drag them or right-click and choose a command. All the selected items will be affected.

WARNING

Many "big time" programs, like those in Microsoft Office, Borland's office suite, database packages, and communications packages, are "installed" into NT. Almost any program that you actually install with an Install or Setup program will register itself with NT, indicating its location on the hard disk. Such files typically don't like to be moved around. Moving the program around after that (actually copying it rather than creating shortcuts that point to it) will bollix up something somewhere, unless the program actually comes with a utility program for relocating it. The bottom line? Use caution when relocating executable files.

Deleting Items

Of course, there will be times when you'll want to delete items, such as that old report from last year or all those old GIF or TIF files that take up so much space on your hard disk. Regular file deletion is very important if you don't want to become like everyone else—strapped for disk space. This is especially imperative on servers. You should know how to delete files and folders. As with moving and copying, the same deletion techniques apply to other objects (such as printers and fax machines) as well, because all objects are treated much the same way, regardless of their type or utility.

NT has a trashcan (much like the Mac) that lets you recover stuff you accidentally delete—until you empty the trash, that is. It's called the Recycle Bin. When you delete something (except from an external drive such as a floppy or on another computer), that's where it goes. Before deleting an item, you're prompted to confirm your action. There is no way around this other than by dragging something directly into the Recycle Bin.

If you realize you made a mistake after you've confirmed a deletion, just open the Recycle Bin, find the item you want to reclaim, and choose Restore. That's about it. You can find the Recycle Bin on the Desktop or in the Explorer, down at the bottom of the directory tree. The Recycle Bin is a hidden system resource (one for each hard disk on each computer). Good luck finding it in File Manager or as a folder. The only way I know to find it in NT is via the icon itself.

Part ii

NOTE

In Windows 95/98, the Recycle Bin is only one level deep. It doesn't store or display deleted folders. When you delete a folder in Windows 95/98, the folder's contents are dumped individually into the Recycle Bin, appearing as files. Trying to retrieve the folder is a hassle, because it doesn't appear as a single entity. In NT, this isn't the case. It's easy to restore a whole folder since you can see it.

Emptying the Recycle Bin

Once in a while, you will want to empty the Recycle Bin. You've probably already noticed the command that empties the Recycle Bin, since it's on the File menu. But the easiest way to empty the trash is to clear the Desktop (by right-clicking an empty portion of the Taskbar), then right-click the Recycle Bin and choose Empty Recycle Bin.

When you want to free some disk space and are sure that all the contents of the Recycle Bin can be dispensed with, go ahead and empty it. It's always a good idea to have plenty of free disk space for NT Server (in fact, you should have as much available disk space as possible!). Regularly emptying the trash, just like at home, is a good practice.

TIP

The Recycle Bin has a few properties worth noting by system administrators. Be sure to right-click it at some point and check them out. Most notable is the amount of the disk that is dedicated to trash.

Copying Files and Folders to and from Floppy Disks

As you might expect, there are a number of ways to copy files to and from floppies. You can use any of these paths:

- ▶ My Computer
- ▶ Explorer
- ▶ File Manager
- ▶ Command prompt window
- ▶ Right-click menu (choose Send To, then Floppy Disk)

Explorer is the choice of most experienced NT users. Unlike File Manager, Explorer shows the floppies on the same tree as the hard disks. Just scroll up to the top of the tree in the left pane and drag stuff to the floppy. If you prefer, open My Computer, double-click the floppy drive, and you have a window showing the contents of the floppy. You can drag stuff in and out of the floppy from there.

Of course, you can resort to the old File Manager if you want. You can even run a DOS session (from the command prompt window, described earlier in the chapter) and issue ye olde DOS commands, such as COPY, DIR, and DEL.

Note that when you drag a file to or from a floppy's window, NT assumes that you want to copy the file, not move it. (This is true of any external drive, such as a Syquest or a network drive, too.) For example, if you drag an item from the floppy's window to the Desktop, you'll be making a copy of the file and placing the copy on the Desktop. If you actually want to *move* the file rather than *copy* it, just hold down the Shift key while dragging, or use the right-click-drag approach.

When you replace one floppy diskette with another, the computer doesn't know about it automatically, as it does on the Mac. After you change the disk, the contents of an open floppy disk window will still be the same, even though the disk holds a completely different set of files. To update the contents of the floppy disk's window, press the F5 key. (This same technique is needed with File Manager and Explorer, incidentally, whenever you change a floppy.)

TIP

To see how much room is left on any disk drive, including a floppy, right-click the drive's icon in My Computer or Explorer and choose Properties. You'll see a display of your disk's free and used space.

Realizing that people frequently want an easy way to copy a file or folder to a floppy disk, Microsoft provides a cute little shortcut to the interface that does this from almost anywhere. Just right-click any file or folder icon that's on your Desktop—in a folder, networked shared folder, in the Find box, or wherever. Then choose the Send To option as shown here. Insert a floppy disk that has some free space on it, and choose the desired drive. The item will be copied to the drive you specify. Your choices

Part ii

on the Send To list depend on your computer's setup. You'll probably
have at least one floppy destination, and possibly two.

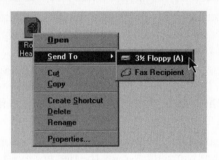

NOTE

As you know, disks must be formatted before you can write to them. You can
format a floppy disk by inserting the diskette, right-clicking the drive icon, and
choosing Format. You'll see options for the drive. You can only format floppies
as FAT drives, not NTFS.

The Send To option is very handy. Note that it can also send something to the Briefcase (a little program for helping you synchronize files
between multiple computers) or to a mail recipient. You can even customize the Send To list, adding other destinations, such as for sending a
file to a viewer program, to the Desktop, to a file compression program, to
a network destination, and so on. Look for the Send To directory under
\winnt\profiles. Put shortcuts into the directory, and they'll show
up in the Send To list.

Using the Cut, Copy, and Paste Commands with Files and Folders

An interesting NT feature is its inclusion of the Cut, Copy, and Paste commands when browsing folders, files, and other objects (such as printers,
fax machines, fonts, and so on). To a veteran Windows user, these commands don't make sense at first. You might wonder how *cutting* a file
would differ from *deleting* it. However, once you know how these commands work, you may find them very useful.

As we mentioned earlier, the Desktop is a useful temporary storage
medium when copying or moving objects between windows or folders.

Having the Desktop available means you don't need to arrange *both* the source and destination windows on screen at once to make the transfer. Well, the Cut, Copy, and Paste commands do the same thing, without needing the Desktop.

Here's how it works:

1. When you want to copy a file or directory, simply click it (or select multiple items by drawing a box around them). To select noncontiguous items, such as files in Details view in Explorer, hold down the Ctrl key and click each object you want to select. To select a range of items, click the first item you want to select, hold down the Shift key, and click the last item you want to select.

2. Right-click and choose the appropriate command: Copy if you want to make a duplicate, Cut if you plan to move the item, or Delete if you want to send it to the Recycle Bin.

3. Adjust your screen so you can see the destination window, folder, Desktop, or wherever. Now right-click the destination and choose Paste from the menu.

That's all there is to it. This is a powerful function. A great place to use it is in Explorer. Rather than first arranging your windows for a move by dragging (as you do in File Manager), just cut and paste.

NOTE

If when you go to paste, the Paste command is grayed out, this means you didn't properly cut or copy anything first. You must use the Cut or Copy commands on a file or other object *immediately* before using the Paste command, or it won't work. That is, if you go into, say, a word processor, and use the Cut or Copy commands there, then the Paste command as it applies to your files or other objects will be grayed out and won't work.

ADMINISTRATIVE TOOLS

The NT Server 4 Start menu organizes a complex array of tools, which is great news for the system administrator. You need a lot of tools to do your job, and organization is the key to finding the right tool for the right job. NT Server helps out; most of the key system administration tools are organized under the Programs submenu of the Start menu, in the Administrative Tools (Common) submenu, shown here.

Because this menu is common, it will show up for each person that logs into the NT Server console; that is, if you have physical access to the NT Server computer, and you log in right at that machine locally, you'll get the Administrative Tools list. Remote users won't be able to get to these tools from their Start menu. This works pretty well, because in practice, the people with physical access to your server should be trusted server operators and administrators.

Let's take a look at each of the commands on the Administrative Tools menu.

Administrative Wizards

The Administrative Wizards command opens up a "dashboard" for the server administrator, which lists many common tasks, such as adding new users. Figure 15.4 shows the main Administrative Wizards window. When you click one of the tasks, a scripted series of forms—a *wizard*, in Microsoft parlance—will guide you through the process.

As checklists, these wizards are great. You can use the wizards to perform the first couple of user installations or to add your first printer. Running through them can be a good way to get a feel for the kind of information that you'll need to have organized before starting a task. For example, the Add User Account Wizard, shown in Figure 15.5, lets you know that you need a full name, username, description, domain name, password, and other optional information for a new user.

FIGURE 15.4:   The Administrative Wizards window is the dashboard for administering your server.

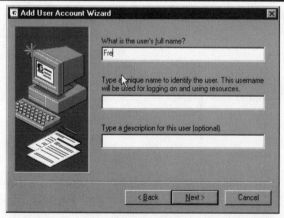

FIGURE 15.5:   The wizard for setting up new accounts on the server can help you remember to enter specific information about each user.

Part ii

However, once you're familiar with an administrative process, you will probably want to use the proper tool for the job, because you'll move more quickly and have more control over what you're doing. For example, you can use the User Manager for Domains tool to create and manage user accounts.

TIP

You may want to go ahead and take a look at all the Administrative Wizards now. Be careful, and don't do anything on a real server until you know what you're doing, but mouse around in there.

Backup

The Backup program lets you manage tape backups. You can select volumes for dumps to tape, or you can explore a tape to find files that you might want to restore. Figure 15.6 shows an example of the Drives and Tapes windows in this utility.

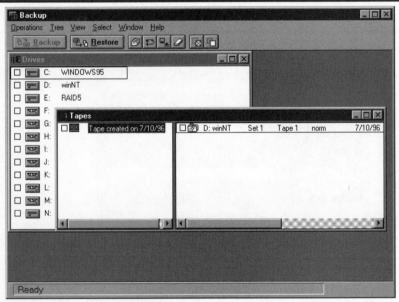

FIGURE 15.6:   The Backup program takes some pain out of tape backups.

Domain Name Service Manager

The Domain Naming Service (DNS) is the network service that you use to map TCP/IP addresses to host names. DNS is a standard Internet service, so it is in common use on computers that use the TCP/IP (Internet) networking protocol. NT Server 4 includes a DNS server service, so NT Server can provide names to any TCP/IP client that needs to look up TCP/IP hosts.

You can manage every NT-based DNS server in your enterprise with one easy-to-use graphical tool, the DNS Manager. For the uninitiated, this sure beats standard UNIX DNS administration! Even if you're experienced with UNIX, having a DNS server service on an NT Server computer (which can be managed remotely) gives you some interesting options. Figure 15.7 shows an example of a Server Statistics display in the Domain Name Service Manager window.

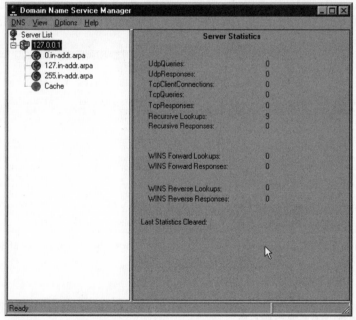

FIGURE 15.7:　The Domain Name Service Manager is important for TCP/IP work.

Event Viewer

As we've said, NT Server has support for auditing, and it logs system events as they occur. The Event Viewer allows you to look at the NT internal system logs. There are three main log areas:

System   For events relating to the NT system services.

Security   For events relating to access of system resources.

Application   For events relating to high-level services, such as network backup or printer spooling.

The Event Viewer can be one of your primary troubleshooting tools. It's great for those next-day postmortem analyses. Since the events are logged, the Event Viewer can tell you what happened after the fact. Figure 15.8 shows an example of an Event Viewer window with a Security Log listing.

Date	Time	Source	Category	Event	User	Computer
7/16/96	4:09:41 PM	Security	Detailed Tracking	592	boyd	FRANKENSTEIN
7/16/96	4:09:34 PM	Security	Detailed Tracking	593	boyd	FRANKENSTEIN
7/16/96	4:09:02 PM	Security	Detailed Tracking	593	boyd	FRANKENSTEIN
7/16/96	4:07:06 PM	Security	Detailed Tracking	593	boyd	FRANKENSTEIN
7/16/96	4:07:00 PM	Security	System Event	515	SYSTEM	FRANKENSTEIN
7/16/96	4:06:59 PM	Security	Detailed Tracking	592	boyd	FRANKENSTEIN
7/16/96	4:06:59 PM	Security	Logon/Logoff	529	SYSTEM	FRANKENSTEIN
7/16/96	4:06:57 PM	Security	System Event	515	SYSTEM	FRANKENSTEIN
7/16/96	4:06:36 PM	Security	Detailed Tracking	592	boyd	FRANKENSTEIN
7/16/96	4:06:33 PM	Security	Detailed Tracking	593	boyd	FRANKENSTEIN
7/16/96	4:05:35 PM	Security	Detailed Tracking	592	boyd	FRANKENSTEIN
7/16/96	4:04:48 PM	Security	Detailed Tracking	593	boyd	FRANKENSTEIN
7/16/96	4:04:36 PM	Security	Detailed Tracking	592	SYSTEM	FRANKENSTEIN
7/16/96	4:04:26 PM	Security	Detailed Tracking	593	SYSTEM	FRANKENSTEIN
7/16/96	4:04:05 PM	Security	Detailed Tracking	592	boyd	FRANKENSTEIN
7/16/96	4:00:57 PM	Security	Privilege Use	577	boyd	FRANKENSTEIN
7/16/96	4:00:34 PM	Security	Detailed Tracking	593	boyd	FRANKENSTEIN
7/16/96	3:49:18 PM	Security	Detailed Tracking	592	boyd	FRANKENSTEIN
7/16/96	3:48:28 PM	Security	Detailed Tracking	592	boyd	FRANKENSTEIN

FIGURE 15.8:   The Event Viewer lets you see NT logs. This is an example of Security Log information.

License Manager

With the License Manager, you'll be able to track the client licenses for NT Server and BackOffice programs, such as Microsoft's SQL Server database. Microsoft requires that you purchase a license for each client that you want to connect to an NT Server computer. This makes sense;

you pay more for the servers that are used by more people. In practice, tracking software licenses can get to be a big headache. The License Manager can track the client licenses that are actually being used on every server in your enterprise, enabling you to make informed decisions about the nature and number of licenses to purchase. Figure 15.9 shows an example of a Purchase History window in the License Manager.

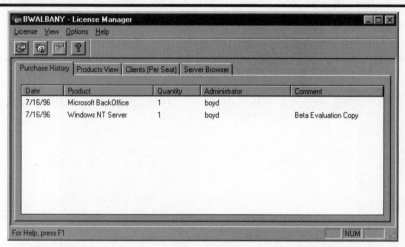

FIGURE 15.9:   The License Manager helps you keep track of software licenses.

You can also set up licensing on your server in the Licensing Control Panel.

NOTE

Microsoft has been working with other software vendors to standardize the tracking of software licenses on a network. This work comes out of Microsoft's Systems Management Server (SMS), which lets network administrators keep detailed tabs on their computer equipment inventory on the network ("Which programs are installed on the PCs in the Finance Department right now?"). The License Manager, now a standard part of NT Server, benefits from this work.

Migration Tools for NetWare

You tie one end of the Migration Tools for NetWare tool to a NetWare server, and you tie the other end to an NT Server computer. You pull the chain to fire it up, the sparks fly, and BAM! Your NT Server computer now has a bunch of user accounts, all filled in from the NetWare registry and ready to go.

There's at least a little NetWare LAN lurking in almost every company. It's no surprise that Microsoft wants to make it as easy as possible for you to purchase more NT servers, and fewer NetWare servers. But the reality is that Novell owns the market. Most NT servers will find themselves trying to live as good citizens within the context of a NetWare LAN. Migration Tools for NetWare makes it that much easier. Figure 15.10 shows an example of a Servers for Migration list in this tool.

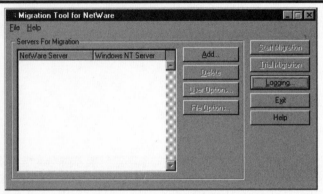

FIGURE 15.10: The Migration Tool for NetWare program is the key to integrating your server with a NetWare LAN.

Network Client Administrator

Windows for Workgroups and Windows 95/98 clients need some extra software enabled on them in order to be able to connect to your NT Server computer. Normally, when you start up Windows 95/98, your computer just starts up, or it asks you for a password so it knows which Desktop to display. With Client for Microsoft Networks software enabled on the computer, the username and password that you enter at your Windows 95/98 computer can be granted access to your entire NT enterprise.

Use the Network Client Administrator to create installer floppies for Client for Microsoft Networks software or to create installer floppies for a version of the Windows NT Server administration tools that can be run under Windows 95/98 (User Manager for Domains and Server Manager only). Figure 15.11 shows the Network Client Administrator window.

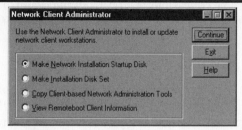

FIGURE 15.11: The Network Client Administrator lets you administer the Windows clients in an NT network.

Performance Monitor

Just as you use the Event Viewer the morning after the server crashed to review what went wrong, you use the Performance Monitor, to see what's happening with your server in real time, right as it occurs. Think of the Event Viewer as the doctor writing your case up for your file, late at night. The Performance Monitor is that same doctor, taking your pulse and sticking...well, you get the picture.

Because of the Performance Monitor's immediate, real-time nature, you can see the performance counters change in response to server activity; and after a while, you can get a feel for what to look for and what to monitor. If you prefer to be proactive in your troubleshooting, the Performance Monitor can show you stuff in that trajectory, on its way to hit the fan. Plus, all those squiggly lines look exactly like a computer monitor should, as you can see in Figure 15.12.

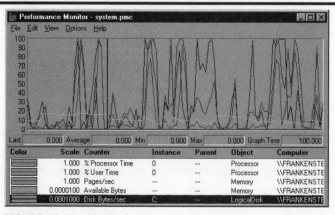

FIGURE 15.12: The Performance Monitor lets you see real-time activity on your server.

Seriously, you can get some critical information about the health of every server on your network right in one place: in the Performance Monitor.

Remote Access Admin

Your NT Server computer can be used as a dial-in server, enabling properly configured remote computers to dial up through a modem, ISDN, or X.25 connection and hop onto your network, just as if they were physically in the office. In this brave new world, where everybody's mom is starting a dial-up Internet access company, this concept should hold little mystery. It's just one more way that NT Server can be used to build flexible, useful networks.

The Remote Access Admin tool lets you manage the Remote Access Service on your server, keeping tabs on connections—who has dialed in, for how long, at what times, and at what speeds. Figure 15.13 shows an example of a Remote Access Admin dialog box for starting remote access to a server.

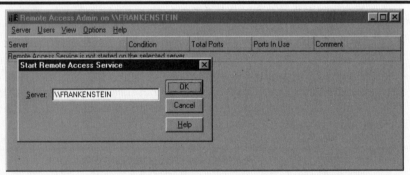

FIGURE 15.13: The Remote Access Admin tool lets you manage Remote Access Service on your computer.

Server Manager

By now, you're getting the idea that NT Server has a great system for administering a network. The Server Manager tool lets you manage every NT Server computer on your network (if you have the appropriate access privileges, of course).

The Server Manager displays a list of all the servers in your domain, as shown in Figure 15.14. When you double-click a server in the list, that server's Server Control Panel appears, letting you manage file sharing and users connected to the server. You can manage the server's services remotely, so that you can stop and restart that cranky printer spooler, for example. And if you're running the Server Manager from an NT Server computer that has the Services for Macintosh feature installed, you'll be able to administer all the NT-based Macintosh servers on your network, too.

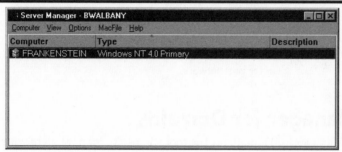

FIGURE 15.14: The Server Manager lets you manage every NT server on your network.

System Policy Editor

System Policies were introduced in Windows 95 as a way of managing complex, graphically rich network clients. Now that NT computers essentially share the same user interface, System Policies have found their way into NT.

Have you ever wished you could set a corporate standard for the contents of the Start menu? How would you like it if your network administrators' computers automatically configured themselves with a locking screen saver and distinctive background wallpaper? You could tell by glancing at the computer that the machine was a possible danger, and that danger would be minimized with the lock on the screen saver. You can set up all this kind of stuff and more with the System Policy Editor. Figure 15.15 shows an example of defaults set up in the System Policy Editor.

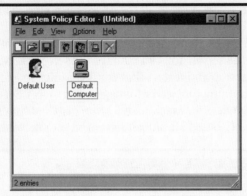

FIGURE 15.15: The System Policy Editor lets you manage standard configurations for your network.

User Manager for Domains

User Manager for Domains is the tool you use to manage all of your users and groups on your NT Server network. You can create new users, change passwords, set the profiles, audit security, and set up groups with this tool.

Figure 15.16 shows an example of a User Manager window that lists the username, full name, and description, as well as user group names and their descriptions.

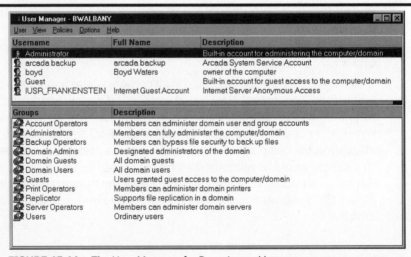

FIGURE 15.16: The User Manager for Domains tool lets you manage your network users and groups.

NOTE

Setting up user accounts with User Manager for Domains is covered in Chapter 17.

NT Server Diagnostics

The NT Diagnostics tool gives you a great deal of information about resource usage on your server. For example, you can get a listing of every DMA (Direct Memory Access) line and every I/O port being used on your server.

With this tool, you can go a long way toward resolving hardware conflicts on your server or another server on the network. You can also get quick-and-dirty counts of memory utilization and network statistics. Figure 15.17 shows an example of Resources information in an NT Diagnostics window.

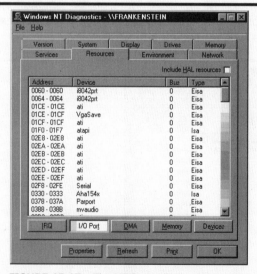

FIGURE 15.17: The NT Server Diagnostics program lets you see a lot of information about resource usage on your server.

THE TASK MANAGER

NT Server is a multitasking system, and a lot of stuff is happening all the time. If you're trying to use an NT Server computer, and it's acting really slow for no apparent reason, it might be helpful to get a quick snapshot of everything that the server is doing. NT provides a tool that does just that: the Task Manager.

The Task Manager was originally conceived for use with NT Workstation, where a user would be sitting at the computer for long periods of time, wondering why the computer is suddenly sluggish. But as a system administrator, you might find the Task Manager a great tool for getting a list of the active processes running on the server. In a pinch, you can even destroy processes that have gone berserk.

The Task Manager can't be used from the network; you can't kill a process on a remote server from your desktop computer using the Task Manager. But if you're at the console of an NT Server computer, and you want an immediate measurement of memory and CPU load, simply right-click the Taskbar and select Task Manager from the pop-up menu. You'll get answers, right away, without the need to resort to setting up counters in Performance Monitor.

You can see all the programs that are running on the computer by clicking the Applications tab in Task Manager. Figure 15.18 shows an example of this list.

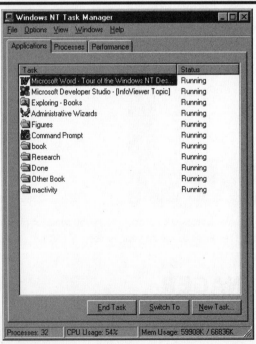

FIGURE 15.18: The Task Manager displays all the applications currently running.

TIP

Look for programs that have a status of "Not Responding." You'll probably need to kill these.

What's better, you can get an excruciatingly detailed listing of every process currently executing on the system. Click the Processes tab to see a window similar to the one shown in Figure 15.19.

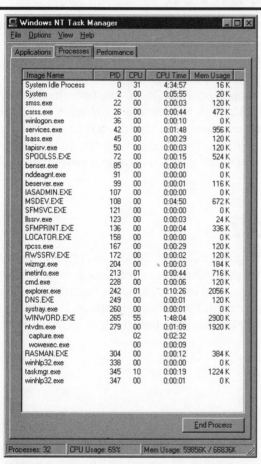

Image Name	PID	CPU	CPU Time	Mem Usage
System Idle Process	0	31	4:34:57	16 K
System	2	00	0:05:55	20 K
smss.exe	22	00	0:00:03	120 K
csrss.exe	26	00	0:00:44	472 K
winlogon.exe	36	00	0:00:10	0 K
services.exe	42	00	0:01:48	956 K
lsass.exe	45	00	0:00:29	120 K
tapisrv.exe	50	00	0:00:03	120 K
SPOOLSS.EXE	72	00	0:00:15	524 K
benser.exe	85	00	0:00:01	0 K
nddeagnt.exe	91	00	0:00:00	0 K
beserver.exe	99	00	0:00:01	116 K
IASADMIN.EXE	107	00	0:00:00	0 K
MSDEV.EXE	108	00	0:04:50	672 K
SFMSVC.EXE	121	00	0:00:00	0 K
llssrv.exe	123	00	0:00:03	24 K
SFMPRINT.EXE	136	00	0:00:04	336 K
LOCATOR.EXE	158	00	0:00:00	0 K
rpcss.exe	167	00	0:00:29	120 K
RWSSRV.EXE	172	00	0:00:02	120 K
wizmgr.exe	204	00	0:00:03	184 K
inetinfo.exe	213	01	0:00:44	716 K
cmd.exe	228	00	0:00:06	120 K
explorer.exe	242	01	0:10:26	2056 K
DNS.EXE	249	00	0:00:01	120 K
systray.exe	260	00	0:00:01	0 K
WINWORD.EXE	265	55	1:48:04	2900 K
ntvdm.exe	279	00	0:01:09	1920 K
capture.exe		02	0:02:32	
wowexec.exe		00	0:00:09	
RASMAN.EXE	304	00	0:00:12	384 K
winhlp32.exe	338	00	0:00:00	0 K
taskmgr.exe	345	10	0:00:19	1224 K
winhlp32.exe	347	00	0:00:01	0 K

FIGURE 15.19: The Task Manager can even display all the "processes" that are running in the machine, including elements of the NT Server operating system as well as programs.

TIP

Look for processes that are swallowing large chunks of memory and CPU time. You can click the CPU heading to sort by percentage of CPU time, and you can click the Mem Usage Heading to sort by process memory utilization.

EXITING NT SERVER

Exiting NT Server properly is very important. You can lose your work, lose the work of others who are logged in to your server, or otherwise foul up the NT Registry or other settings if you don't shut down NT Server correctly before turning off your computer.

To exit NT Server properly, choose Shut Down from the Start menu. Switch to the Program Manager window and double-click its Control box. You will be asked whether you want to shut down the computer, restart the computer, or log on as a different user. But before you do this, you should warn users who are using resources on your server that you are about to shut down.

WHAT'S NEXT?

This chapter covered the essentials of getting around the NT Server Desktop including running applications, organizing your files and folders, and finding all of NT Server's main tools for system administration. The next chapter provides details about the NT Server Registry. It describes the contents of the Registry keys and also provides some hints on working with the Registry.

Chapter 16

ANATOMY OF THE REGISTRY— THE BLOOD, GORE, AND GUTS

This chapter provides the details of what is actually in the Registry. If you're only interested in recovering from a disaster and not interested in *what* the Registry is, it might be possible to skip this chapter. However, if you're unsure about this, I'd recommend reading it anyway.

Now humor me for just a moment; I think I'm going to back up my Registry. In fact, it is a good time for *you* to do a backup as well, since it is entirely possible that, at any time, you might have some kind of problem (or disaster) with the Registry and really need that backup copy to restore it. Next, let some time pass by. Ah, that feels better—I've got a fresh backup copy of my Registry just in case I do something stupid, and so do you—not that we ever do anything stupid, right?

. . . .

Adapted from *Expert Guide™ to Windows NT® 4 Registry* by Peter D. Hipson

ISBN 0-7821-1983-2   816 pages $44.99

The Registry is subdivided into a number of clearly defined sections, called *subtrees*. Additionally, each subtree contains *keys* (represented as folders). Each key may contain *subkeys* (represented as subfolders), and keys or subkeys may contain *values*. Values are the actual settings, and are said to contain *data*. Another term you hear frequently when discussing the Registry is *hive*. A hive is a portion of the Registry contained within one discrete file on the hard drive.

Some portions of the Registry are less important than others. For example, if the Security Account Manager (SAM) hive is damaged, you can probably recover easily without serious permanent problems. You may possibly lose all of the user database, so no users would be able to log on to the server. However, as long as you can log on as administrator, the worst case is that you would have to reenter the other user information. The default SAM database will contain at least the initial administrator user ID and password, which you would have to know.

However, say you lose the System component of the Registry without adequate backup. In that case, it is unlikely that you'll be able to recover without reinstalling NT Server, and that would be a painful experience at best.

A REGISTRY OVERVIEW

The NT Registry (and the Registry for Windows 95/98) is arranged into logical units called subtrees. There are five subtrees that make up the Registry in NT. Each subtree is made up of keys, subkeys, values and data as discussed earlier. Here are a couple of important concepts:

▶ The Registry is arranged just like the folders and files contained on your hard drive. Keys are analogous to directories, and values are like files. In fact, this relationship is almost 100 percent parallel. Keys are usually shown separated by backslashes (just like directories on the drive), and values typically (but not always) have data. (Remember that a file may also be empty.)

▶ The Registry is a database of configuration information. All of the information that would have been stored in information files is now stored in this database. The Registry is arranged as a hierarchical database—nothing more, nothing less. If you are a database person, this view of the Registry might make more sense to you. In truth, this arrangement is more like the Registry's actual construction.

Specific data is assigned to a value. As I mentioned, some Registry values don't have any data set; this is also acceptable.

WARNING

Be careful not to delete empty keys or values just because they are empty. Even though they don't have a value, their presence in the Registry may be necessary for the health and well-being of NT Server. Never, ever, delete anything in the Registry unless you know that there will be no adverse side effects.

The Registry Subtrees

The Registry is divided into five subtrees and every one is named with the prefix HKEY_:

- ▶ HKEY_CLASSES_ROOT
- ▶ HKEY_CURRENT_USER
- ▶ HKEY_LOCAL_MACHINE
- ▶ HKEY_USERS
- ▶ HKEY_CURRENT_CONFIG

Each subtree embodies a major section contained in the Registry with a different functionality. These subtrees are discussed next.

Subtrees, Keys, and Values

In this chapter, I use a terminology similar to that used when referring to disk drives, directories, subdirectories, files, and the contents of files. Often Microsoft confuses the issue somewhat. I try to keep it clear:

Hive   A portion of the Registry that is stored in a single file on the hard disk. For example, the System key in HKEY_LOCAL_MACHINE is actually a hive, since it is stored as a single file in the %systemroot%\System32\Config folder. Hives typically do not represent subtrees, only a section of a subtree.

Subtree   Similar to a directory on a drive. Located inside a subtree may be keys (like folders) or values (like files). A hive need not be the highest level; a hive may actually be a key inside a subtree. An example of a subtree in the Registry is HKEY_LOCAL_MACHINE.

Key   Similar to a subdirectory on a drive. Located inside a key may be subkeys (like folders). A key may have one or more keys located above it and none or more subkeys contained within it. An example of a key in the Registry is HKEY_LOCAL_MACHINE \SAM.

Value   Similar to a file on a drive. A value may contain data, or a value may have no data set at all.

Data   Similar to a file's data. Each value will have one assigned data set (though the data set may consist of many parts), or a value may have no data set at all. There is also something called the default value, which is used when appropriate.

HKEY_CLASSES_ROOT

The HKEY_CLASSES_ROOT branch contains information about both OLE and various file associations. The purpose of HKEY_CLASSES_ROOT is to provide for compatibility with the existing Windows 3.x Registry.

The information contained in HKEY_CLASSES_ROOT is identical to information found in HKEY_LOCAL_MACHINE\SOFTWARE\CLASSES.

HKEY_CURRENT_USER

The HKEY_CURRENT_USER branch is used to manage specific information about the user who is currently logged on. This information includes:

▶ The user's Desktop and the appearance and behavior of NT 4 Server to the user.

▶ All connections to network devices, such as printers and shared disk resources.

▶ Desktop program items, application preferences, screen colors, and other personal preferences and security rights. They are stored for later retrieval by the system when the user logs on.

All other environment settings are retained for future use.

By accessing the roaming user profile, NT Server is able to make any workstation that the user logs on to appear the same to the user. Domain users need not worry about having to set up or customize each possible workstation that they will be using.

Information contained in HKEY_CURRENT_USER is updated as users make changes to their environments.

HKEY_LOCAL_MACHINE

The HKEY_LOCAL_MACHINE branch contains information about the computer that is running NT. This information includes applications, drivers, and hardware. There are five separate keys contained within HKEY_LOCAL_MACHINE:

HARDWARE   The key used to save information about the computer's detected hardware. NT doesn't detect much in the way of hardware, but it does track information such as type and number of processors, the keyboard and mouse, and the type of data buses in the computer. It is always re-created when the system is booted, and is stored in RAM rather than in a file. Changes to this key are not meaningful. Contained within the HARDWARE key are the following four subkeys:

DESCRIPTION   Contains information about the system, including the CPU, FPU (floating point unit), and the system bus. Under the system bus is information about I/O, storage, and other devices.

DEVICEMAP   Contains information about devices (keyboards, printer ports, pointers, and so on.)

OWNERMAP   Contains miscellaneous information about some of the PCI-based devices, such as SCSI, network interface, or video adapters. This key will not be present unless there is a multi-function bus such as a PCI bus.

RESOURCEMAP   Contains information about the HAL (Hardware Abstraction Layer). Also contained are I/O devices, drivers, SCSI adapters, system resources, and video resources.

SAM   The key used to store information about users and domains. The SAM is your user account database. On a domain controller, this is the user account database for the entire domain. This information is not accessible using any of the resource editors. Rather, this information is better managed using the administrator's User Manager program.

SECURITY   The key that contains information about local security and user rights. A copy of the SAM key is found in the SECURITY key. As with SAM, the SECURITY key is not accessible using the resource editors, and the information is best modified using the administrator's tools.

SOFTWARE The key that contains information about installed system and user software, including descriptions. There should be subkeys for each installed product where the product will store information, such as preferences, configurations, MRU (most recently used files) lists, and other application-modifiable items.

SYSTEM The key that contains information about the system startup, device drivers, services, and the NT 4 Server configuration.

HKEY_USERS

The HKEY_USERS key contains information about each active user who has a user profile. A minimum of two keys are in the HKEY_USERS key: .DEFAULT and the ID for the currently logged-on user. The purpose of the .DEFAULT key is to provide information for users who log on without a profile.

Personal profiles are contained in the %systemroot%\Profiles folder, unless roaming profiles are used. If there is a roaming profile, a copy will be stored there, but the original will reside on a server.

HKEY_CURRENT_CONFIG

The HKEY_CURRENT_CONFIG key is new to NT 4. It contains information about the system's current configuration. This information is typically derived from HKEY_LOCAL_MACHINE\SYSTEM\ and HKEY_LOCAL_MACHINE\SOFTWARE, though HKEY_CURRENT_CONFIG does not contain all the information that is contained in the source keys.

Registry Key Value Types

Values have different types:

REG_BINARY Used to represent binary values. They may be edited or entered as hexadecimal or binary numbers. Figure 16.1 shows the REGEDT32 Registry editor's Binary Editor window. REGEDIT has a similar edit window, though it is not as flexible in how data is entered.

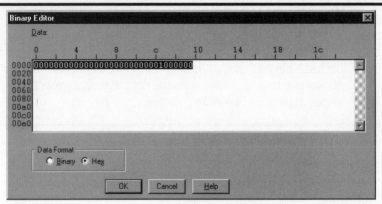

FIGURE 16.1:   The Binary Editor window for REGEDT32

REG_SZ   Used for Registry keys that contain strings. Editing is easy; just type in the new string. Case is preserved, but realize that the string is initially selected, so be careful not to inadvertently delete it. Strings are of fixed length and are defined when the key is created. Figure 16.2 shows a string being edited in the String Editor window. A string key may be made longer; it will be reallocated if this happens.

FIGURE 16.2:   The String Editor window for REGEDT32

REG_EXPAND_SZ   Used if the key is to contain a string that may be expanded. Some keys may need to contain values that reference environment variables, much like a batch file. For example, if a string contains the field %systemroot%\System32, and it is necessary for the %systemroot% part of the string to be expanded to the value that is assigned to it in the environment, this string must be a REG_EXPAND_SZ string. The result of the expansion would then be passed to the requestor. %systemroot% is a standard environment variable containing the location, drive, and directory where NT has been installed. The same window as is used for REG_SZ values is used to enter a REG_EXPAND_SZ key (see Figure 16.2).

REG_DWORD   Used to store a 32-bit value in the key, entered as decimal, hexadecimal, or binary. The DWORD Editor window allows entering only valid numeric data to help save us from sloppy typing, as Figure 16.3 shows.

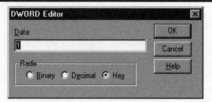

FIGURE 16.3: The DWORD Editor window for REGEDT32

REG_MULTI_SZ   Used to store multiple strings in a single Registry key. Normally, a string resource in the Registry may contain only one line. However, the multi-string type allows a string resource in the Registry to hold mutiple strings as needed. Figure 16.4 shows a multi-string value being edited. Only one line is present in this example. The REG_MULTI_SZ type is not supported by the Windows 95/98 Registry editor, REGEDIT. If a REG_MULTI_SZ item is edited with REGEDIT, it is possible to corrupt the data that is contained in it.

FIGURE 16.4: The Multi-String Editor window for REGEDT32

REG_FULL_RESOURCE_DESCRIPTOR   Used to manage information for hardware resources. No one should edit the items that appear in the Resource Editor fields. Figure 16.5 shows

REGEDT32 displaying a disk resource object. However, these objects are not normally changed manually with the resource editors.

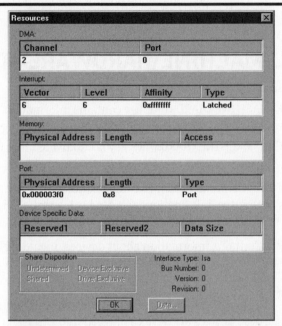

FIGURE 16.5: The Resources window for REGEDT32 (editing a disk resource)

REG_NONE   An identifier used when there is no data stored in the key. It doesn't take a rocket scientist to figure out that there is no editor for the none type.

REG_UNKNOWN   Used when the key's data type cannot be determined.

HKEY_LOCAL_MACHINE—The Machine's Configuration

The HKEY_LOCAL_MACHINE subtree contains information about the current hardware configuration of the local computer. The information stored in this subtree is updated using a variety of processes, including the Control Panel, hardware and software installation programs, administrative tools, and sometimes automatically by NT.

It is important not to make unintended changes to the HKEY_LOCAL_ MACHINE subtree. A change here could quite possibly render the entire system unstable.

HKEY_LOCAL_MACHINE\HARDWARE—The Installed Hardware Hive

The HKEY_LOCAL_MACHINE\HARDWARE key contains information about the hardware configuration of the local machine.

The HKEY_LOCAL_MACHINE\HARDWARE key is subdivided into four subkeys:

DESCRIPTION   Contains descriptive information about each device. This descriptive information includes both a verbal description and information, such as basic configurations.

DEVICEMAP   Contains information about devices, including locations in the Registry where the device's full configuration is saved.

OWNERMAP   Contains information about removable PCI bus type devices. These devices are devices plugged into the system's PCI bus, but generally not those permanently installed on the system's motherboard. However, not all PCI type devices will be listed in OWNERMAP.

RESOURCEMAP   Contains translation information about each major component that is installed in the system. Most consist of a set of entries called .Raw and .Translated.

DESCRIPTION

Within the HKEY_LOCAL_MACHINE\HARDWARE\DESCRIPTION key is a wealth of information about the installed hardware. Only the subkey, SYSTEM, describes the CPU and I/O fully. The following keys are contained in the SYSTEM subkey:

CentralProcessor   Contains information about the CPU. This includes speed, which is an identifier that contains the CPU's model, family, and stepping. Also included in this key is vendor information; for example, a "real" Intel CPU has the VendorIdentifier string "GenuineIntel."

FloatingPointProcessor   Describes the system's FPU in a set of entries similar to that of the CPU. The fact that the typical CPU has an integral FPU is not considered here; the FPU will be listed separately, regardless.

MultiFunctionAdapter   Describes the system's bus (PCI), any Plug-and-Play BIOS installed (regardless of the fact that NT 4 doesn't support Plug and Play), and other devices, including the controllers for disk drives, keyboards, parallel and serial ports, and the mouse. For a mouse that is connected to a serial port, the mouse will be found under the serial port; a mouse that is connected to a PS/2 mouse port will be shown connected to a pointer controller as a separate device.

Typically, the DESCRIPTION key can be used to determine what hardware is installed (and being used) and how the installed hardware is connected. However, some devices, such as storage devices (hard drives, SCSI, CD-ROM, video, and network interface cards), are not listed in HKEY_LOCAL_MACHINE\ HARDWARE\DESCRIPTION. Instead, they are listed in HKEY_LOCAL_ MACHINE\HARDWARE\DEVICEMAP. Why? Because these devices are not detected at bootup stage; instead, they are detected when they are installed.

DEVICEMAP

The HKEY_LOCAL_MACHINE\HARDWARE\DEVICEMAP key contains information about devices, arranged in a similar fashion to the HKEY_ LOCAL_ MACHINE\HARDWARE\DESCRIPTION key discussed earlier in this chapter. In the DEVICEMAP key are found the following keys:

KeyboardClass   Points to the key that manages information about the keyboard itself.

KeyboardPort   Points to the key that manages information about the keyboard interface unit, often called the 8042 after the original chip that served as the keyboard controller in the original PC.

PARALLEL PORTS   Points to the key that manages information about the parallel printer ports.

PointerClass   Points to the key that manages information about the system mouse.

PointerPort   Points to the key that manages information about the port that the system mouse is connected to.

Scsi   A complex key with information about each SCSI port found on the computer.

NOTE

NT Server pretends that IDE devices and many CD-ROM devices that are connected to special interface cards are SCSI devices. This is a management issue. NT Server is not converting these devices to be SCSI, nor is it using SCSI drivers; rather, NT is simply classing all these devices under a common heading.

SERIALCOMM   Points to the key that manages information about the available serial ports. If the system mouse is connected to a serial port, and not to a PS/2 mouse port, that port will not be listed in the SERIALCOMM key.

VIDEO   Points to the key that manages the video devices. There are typically two devices defined in VIDEO: One is the currently used adapter, and the second is a backup consisting of the previously installed, usually the generic VGA, adapter's settings to use as a backup in the event of a problem with the video system.

OWNERMAP

The HKEY_LOCAL_MACHINE\HARDWARE\OWNERMAP key (new to NT Server 4) is a simple key with descriptions for devices connected to an external PCI bus. These devices (often SCSI, video, and network interface cards) are listed with a key that NT Server uses and the internal device driver name.

RESOURCEMAP

The RESOURCEMAP subkey is used by all the various hardware device drivers to map resources that the driver will use. Each RESOURCEMAP entry will contain information about usage of:

▶ I/O ports

- ▶ I/O memory addresses
- ▶ Interrupts
- ▶ Direct Memory Access (DMA) channels

The organization of the RESOURCEMAP key is that there are entries for a class of device (such as VIDEO). Under these entries are found subkeys for a number of different video devices.

HKEY_LOCAL_MACHINE\SAM—The Security Accounts Manager

Contained in HKEY_LOCAL_MACHINE\SAM is information used by the NT Server security system. User information (accounts, passwords, and the like) is contained within this key.

This information is typically set using the User Manager or User Manager for Domains.

NOTE

The SAM keys (both in HKEY_LOCAL_MACHINE\SAM\SAM and HKEY_LOCAL_MACHINE\SECURITY\SAM) should be modified only by using the User Manager administrative programs. Attempts to modify information that is in the SAM keys typically results in disaster. For example, users will be unable to log on, wrong permissions will be assigned, and so on.

The two SAM keys (HKEY_LOCAL_MACHINE\SAM\SAM and HKEY_LOCAL_MACHINE\SECURITY\SAM) are mirrored. Changes made to one are automatically reflected in the other.

NOTE

Can't see the SAM or Security keys? Use REGEDT32 to select the key you cannot see and then select Security ➤ Permissions from the main menu. Next, change the Type of Access from Special Access to Full Control.

WARNING

Following the advice in the above note is dangerous. Once a user has full access to the SAM and Security keys, the user may make changes and modifications that could cause all sorts of problems. Don't do this unless you have a full backup of your Registry, including the SAM and Security keys.

Part ii

HKEY_LOCAL_MACHINE\Security—The Windows NT Security Key

Contained in the key HKEY_LOCAL_MACHINE\Security is information relevant to the security of the local machine. This information includes:

▶ User rights

▶ Password policy

▶ Membership of local groups

This information is typically set using the User Manager or User Manager for Domains program.

HKEY_LOCAL_MACHINE\Software—The Installed Software Information Key

The HKEY_LOCAL_MACHINE\Software key is the storage location for all software installed on the computer. The information contained in HKEY_LOCAL_MACHINE\Software is available to all users and consists of a number of standard subkeys as well as a few subkeys that may be unique to each computer.

The NT Server computer on my network has the following subkeys in HKEY_LOCAL_MACHINE\Software. These subkeys correspond to items that I have installed on my computer:

3Com   Contains information specific to the 3Com software that is installed. In the case of this computer, the installed devices are 3Com network interface cards.

Adobe   Contains information about the copy of Adobe's Acrobat program that was recently installed.

Dragon Systems   Contains information about a voice-recognition program called Naturally Speaking.

Federal Express   Contains information about the FedEx online access and support I have on my computer. All of my FedEx airbills are produced by computer, making shipments much easier.

INTEL   Contains information about the Intel 3D Scalability Toolkit that I installed at some point. I don't remember when or why, but it's there.

Intuit   Contains information specfic to the financial software that is Intuit's specialty. I've found Intuit products to be good performers. We all hope that Intuit will realize that it must support NT with its products in the future.

Qualcomm   Contains information specific to the Eudora e-mail program. The nice thing about Eudora is that there is a free version for private use.

The following are system subkeys probably installed on your computer; however, some of these subkeys, such as ODBC and Clients, may not be present on some minimal installations:

Classes   Contains two types of items. First are file type association items. For example, a typical association entry might have the name DIB, with a string that associates this name with the application PaintShopPro, a graphics editing program. Second are COM (Component Object Model) associations. For example, the name .DOC is associated with the WinWord application in Microsoft Word for Windows or with WordPad, the default viewer for DOC document files. Both WordPad and WinWord may be embedded in other applications. For instance, Outlook, Microsoft's upscale e-mail system, uses Word formatted documents and embeds either Word for Windows or WordPad to display and edit these documents.

Clients   Contains client-server relationships. For example, Microsoft Outlook is a multipurpose program with e-mail, a calendar, contact lists, news, and other features. Each of these parts of Outlook has a complex series of calling protocols that are defined in the Clients subkey.

Description   Contains names and version numbers for software installed on the local computer. Though any vendor may use this subkey, the author can only see one entry, which is entered during installation of NT. Microsoft RPC (Remote Procedure Call) has several entries in this subkey.

Microsoft   Stores a number of items that pertain to Microsoft products or parts of NT. There can be as few as 20 or as many as 100 entries in the Microsoft subkey.

Part ii

ODBC   Stores items that pertain to Open DataBase Connectivity (ODBC), which allows applications to retrieve data from a number of different data sources. ODBC may be installed directly or as a side effect of installing another product.

Program Groups   Contains one value, ConvertedTo-Links, which is used to indicate whether the program groups were converted. A value of one (0x1) shows that the conversion is complete. Even an NT 4 system installed on a new computer that didn't require conversion will have this value.

Secure   The location in which any application may store "secure" configuration information. Only an administrator may modify this subkey, so mere mortal users can't change secure configuration information. Not many, if any, applications use the Secure subkey.

Windows 3.1 Migration Status   Used to indicate if the computer was upgraded from Windows 3.x to NT 4. Though at one time there were many upgrades, more users today are likely to be doing clean installations, because virtually all existing Windows 3.x systems have already been upgraded. Two subkeys exist: IniFiles and REG.DAT. These values show whether the INI and REG.DAT files have been migrated successfully to NT 4 formats.

HKEY_LOCAL_MACHINE\System—The System Information Key

The HKEY_LOCAL_MACHINE\System subkey is used to hold startup information used by NT when booting. This subkey contains all the data that is stored and not recomputed at boot time.

NOTE
A full copy of the HKEY_LOCAL_MACHINE\System information is kept in the file SYSTEM.ALT, found in the %systemroot%\System32\config directory.

The HKEY_LOCAL_MACHINE\System key (aka, the System hive) is organized into control sets containing parameters for devices and services.

The main control sets are:

Clone   The volatile copy of the control set that was used to boot the system (usually `ControlSet001`). Created by the system Kernel during initialization, this key is not accessible from the Registry Editor. This subkey is used by the Service Controller system (SCREG.EXE).

ControlSet001   This may be the control set used to boot NT this time, or it may actually contain the `LastKnownGood` control set.

NOTE

At some point in the boot process, the current control set (contained in the subkey `Clone`) will be copied into the `LastKnownGood` control set. In NT 4, the process of replacing the `LastKnownGood` control set is done as soon as the user's logon is validated, either locally or by a domain controller.

ControlSet002   This may be the control set used to boot NT this time, or it may actually contain the `LastKnownGood` control set. Which set is contained here may be determined by checking the `Select` key.

ControlSet003   Control sets may be numbered other than 001 and 002 if for some reason NT needed to make a temporary copy of the control set being used to boot. The number of sets maintained is typically only two, but the numbers may vary.

CurrentControlSet   This is the control set that NT has booted from. It is mapped to either `ControlSet001` or `ControlSet002`, depending on which is the current set and which is the `LastKnownGood` set.

There are three other items in the HKEY_LOCAL_MACHINE\System key:

DISK   Contains information generated by Disk Administrator for the distribution of partitions and drive letters. This subkey is updated by the Disk Administrator tool. If Disk Administrator has never been run, this key will be missing.

Select   Contains four keys. It also has information on which control set was booted and which subkey is the `LastKnownGood` set. Also, if there is a "failed" control set, the failed control set's identity will be found in the `Select` subkey.

Setup Contains information used by setup to configure NT. This information includes locations of drives and directories; the setup command line; and a flag telling if setup is currently in progress.

The HKEY_LOCAL_MACHINE\System hive is critical to both the boot process and to the operation of the system. Microsoft has created a number of tools and processes that help protect the HKEY_LOCAL_MACHINE\System hive information. These include the LastKnownGood boot process, which allows mapping in a known (or so we hope) copy of the control set, allowing the system to boot if the original control set is too damaged to be booted.

When modifying the control sets, be aware of the process of booting and creating the control sets. Generally, modifying a backup control set won't affect the system.

WARNING

Do not, I repeat, *do not*, boot using the LastKnownGood control set unless it is necessary! Any changes made to the system during the previous session will be lost, gone, forever and forever!

HKEY_USERS—Settings for Users

Current user configurations are saved in HKEY_USERS. In HKEY_USERS, there are typically two keys. The first key, .DEFAULT, is the default user profile. This profile is used for any users who log on without having their own profile created. For users who have their own profile, their profile is loaded and stored as the second key found in HKEY_USERS.

NOTE

Actually, HKEY_USERS may contain more users. See the section, "NTUSER—The New User Profile," later in this chapter for information about how more users might be added, and why.

The second key is the key for a specific user's profile. The profile would be either the user's own profile or copied from the .DEFAULT profile if the user has not established his or her own profile. It appears as something like this:

```
S-1-5-21-45749729-16073390-2133884337-500
```

This long, magical Registry key needs some explanation. The number, as a whole, is called a SID (Security Identifier). There is a lot of information in a SID. For example, the ending three- or four-digit number is used to identify both the user, and for some users, the user type. Table 16.1 lists a number of general user types that might be assigned. The most commonly seen value is 500, which is assigned to the system administrator account.

TABLE 16.1: Common SID Values Used by NT

USER GROUP	SID
DomainName\Administrator	S-1-5-21-xxxxxxxxx-xxxxxxxxxx-xxxxxxxxxx-500
DomainName\Guest	S-1-5-21-xxxxxxxxx-xxxxxxxxxx-xxxxxxxxxx-501
DomainName\Domain Admins	S-1-5-21-xxxxxxxxx-xxxxxxxxxx-xxxxxxxxxx-512
DomainName\Domain Users	S-1-5-21-xxxxxxxxx-xxxxxxxxxx-xxxxxxxxxx-513

General users might be assigned SIDs ending in four-digit numbers starting at 1000. My domain has a user called Pixel, whose SID ends in 1003, and another user, Long, whose SID ends in 1006. Get the picture?

There are also a number of built-in and special groups of SIDs, as shown in Tables 16.2 and 16.3.

TABLE 16.2: The NT Built-In Local Groups

BUILT-IN LOCAL GROUP	SID
Built-in\Administrators	S-1-2-32-xxxxxxxxx-xxxxxxxxxx-xxxxxxxxxx-544
Built-in\Users	S-1-2-32-xxxxxxxxx-xxxxxxxxxx-xxxxxxxxxx-545
Built-in\Guests	S-1-2-32-xxxxxxxxx-xxxxxxxxxx-xxxxxxxxxx-546
Built-in\Power Users	S-1-2-32-xxxxxxxxx-xxxxxxxxxx-xxxxxxxxxx-547
Built-in\Account Operators	S-1-2-32-xxxxxxxxx-xxxxxxxxxx-xxxxxxxxxx-548
Built-in\Server Operators	S-1-2-32-xxxxxxxxx-xxxxxxxxxx-xxxxxxxxxx-549
Built-in\Print Operators	S-1-2-32-xxxxxxxxx-xxxxxxxxxx-xxxxxxxxxx-550
Built-in\Backup Operators	S-1-2-32-xxxxxxxxx-xxxxxxxxxx-xxxxxxxxxx-551

TABLE 16.3: The NT Special Groups

SPECIAL GROUP	SID
\Creator Owner	S-1-1-0x-xxxxxxxxx-xxxxxxxxxx-xxxxxxxxxx-xxx
\Everyone	S-1-1-0x-xxxxxxxxx-xxxxxxxxxx-xxxxxxxxxx-xxx
NT Authority\Network	S-1-1-2x-xxxxxxxxx-xxxxxxxxxx-xxxxxxxxxx-xxx
NT Authority\Interactive	S-1-1-4x-xxxxxxxxx-xxxxxxxxxx-xxxxxxxxxx-xxx

Naturally, there are many more SID codes and definitions. The above lists simply show a few of the more commonly used SIDs.

NOTE

Remember to differentiate between the HKEY_USERS subtree and the HKEY_CURRENT_ USER subtree. HKEY_CURRENT_USER contains a pointer that references the current user in HKEY_USERS.

The content of a user's profile, as it is found in the HKEY_USERS subtree, is interesting. For example, the following keys are present in a typical user's profile (Usually, there is nothing to guarantee that they will all be present, or that others might be added):

AppEvents   Contains information about events in a key called EventLabels. This information includes a text label for the event, such as the event close, which has the label "Close program." These labels are used for a number of purposes, but one that most of us see is in the Control Panel's Sounds applet. A second section in AppEvents is Schemes, which lists labels for each application that uses specific sounds for its own events.

Console   Contains the default command-prompt configuration. This configuration may be customized for each command prompt individually, or it is possible in this key to change the global default, which would be used for all new command prompts that are created. For an example of command-prompt customization, open a command window and select Properties from the System menu. There are more settings that may be configured in the Registry than are found in the Properties dialog box.

Control Panel   Contains information saved by many of the Control Panel's applets. Typically, these are default, or standard, values that are saved here, not user settings, which are stored elsewhere.

Environment   Contains the user environment variables for a user. Generally, the System Properties applet, in the Environment tab, is used to set user and system environment values.

Keyboard Layout   Contains the keyboard configuration. Most users, at least those in the U.S., will have few or no substitutions. However, users who are using special keyboards, or non-U.S. English, will have some substitutions for special characters found in their languages.

Network   Contains mappings for each network drive connected to the computer. Information about the connections includes the host (server), remote path, and username used for the connection. The `Network` key is not typically found in the `.DEFAULT` key because users with no user profile are not automatically connected to a remote drive.

Printers   Contains mappings for each remote (network) printer connected to the computer. Information about the printer connection includes the host (server) and the DLL file used to manage the connection. The `Printers` key is not typically found in the `.DEFAULT` key because users with no user profile are not automatically connected to a remote printer.

Software   Contains information about software installed, including components of NT, such as Schedule, Notepad, and so on. Also included in `Software` is NT itself, with configuration information specific to the currently logged-on user.

UNICODE Program Groups   Contains information about program groups that use Unicode. More commonly found on computers configured for languages other than English, Unicode is the scheme for displaying characters from other alphabets on computers.

Part ii

HKEY_CURRENT_CONFIG—THE CURRENT CONFIGURATION SETTINGS

The Registry key HKEY_CURRENT_CONFIG is created from two Registry keys, HKEY_LOCAL_MACHINE\SYSTEM and HKEY_LOCAL_MACHINE\ SOFTWARE. The HKEY_CURRENT_CONFIG key is created dynamically, so there is little value in modifying any of the objects found in this key.

The HKEY_CURRENT_CONFIG subtree is composed of two major subkeys:

Software   Contains current configurations for some software components. A typical configuration might have keys under Software for Microsoft Internet Explorer, for example.

System   Contains information about hardware. The most common device found in this key is the video display adapter (found in virtually all configurations) and sometimes information about the default video modes as well. The video mode settings contained here are typical for any video system: resolution, panning, refresh rates (didn't you wonder where refresh rates were saved?), and bits per pixel (color depth).

Generally, you would modify the source settings in HKEY_LOCAL_ MACHINE\ SYSTEM\ControlSet001\Hardware Profiles\ Current\System\CurrentControlSet\ Services\<device>\ Device0, where <device> is the device being modified. For example, my Matrox Millennium is listed under mga_mil. There is another device called mga, which is identical in configuration.

TIP

For more information about the source for HKEY_CURRENT_CONFIG, take a look at HKEY_LOCAL_MACHINE, described earlier in this chapter.

NTUSER—THE NEW USER PROFILE

With NT 4 networks, it is possible to modify the NTUSER.DAT file, which contains the new user profile, and have this change affect all new users created after the change is made.

It is possible to modify HKEY_CURRENT_USER in NTUSER to set settings such as internationalization, colors, schemes, and other items.

NT's installation process will create a default user profile. Whenever a new user logs on to a workstation or domain, this default user profile will then be copied to the user's profile. After that, the user may modify this default profile to his or her own requirements and needs.

As an example, NT's default language is typically U.S. English. (There are other language editions of NT; however, for this example, we'll assume you are using the U.S. English version.) Whenever a new user logs on, the user will have U.S. English as his or her language, even if the system administrator has selected a different, non-English locale.

The default user profile is saved in the disk directory at %system-root%\Profiles\Default User\ with the name NTUSER.DAT. There is an entire configuration for new users in this directory—check out the Start Menu, Desktop, and other directories, too. You will find that interesting modifications may be made to enable new users to become proficient quickly without spending too much time customizing their computers.

Before you modify the default new user's profile, you need to make this new user profile accessible to remote users (users other than those who log on locally). Copy the Default User directory to the share named Netlogon. This share is typically located in the directory at %system-root%\System32\Repl\Import\Scripts.

If there are BDCs, you would actually edit the file in the Export directory (same initial path) because this directory is locally replicated to the Import directory and to the other BDC Import directories, although it might be located elsewhere. The Netlogon share can be located quickly by typing the following command at a command prompt.

```
net share
```

The computer's shares will be displayed.

One way to copy these files is to create a new custom profile and copy the new custom profile using the Control Panel's System-User Profiles applet.

WARNING

Caution: This technique is an advanced use of the Registry Editor and you must exercise care not to inadvertently modify the wrong Registry or the wrong keys. Back up the Registry *before* doing the following.

Follow these steps to modify the default new user profile in your new default user directory (remember to create a new Default User directory, saving the current Default User directory as a backup):

1. Start REGEDT32 using either a command prompt or the Start menu's Run command. Don't use REGEDIT for this process.

2. Click the title bar of the HKEY_USERS on Local Machine window to make the window active.

3. Choose Registry ➤ Load Hive from the REGEDT32 menu.

4. Open the hive found in `%systemroot%\Profiles\ Default User`. (If your system is configured with different directory names, choose the correct name.) This hive has the filename `NTUSER.DAT`.

5. REGEDT32 will prompt for a new key name. Use the name NTUSER.

6. Change whatever keys in NTUSER need to be modified. There is a slew of changeable items in the new profile, including AppEvents, Console, Control Panel, Environment, Keyboard Layout, Software, and Unicode Program Groups. When adding new keys, do be careful to ensure that all users have at least read access to the new keys. No read access means that the key won't be accessible to the user.

TIP

To set the permissions for a key, select the key, and then select Security ➤ Permissions from the REGEDT32 menu. Ensure that the group Everyone has at least read access. Resist the urge to give everyone more than read access to this key, too. Too much power can be a dangerous thing!

7. After making all modifications to NTUSER, choose Registry ≻ Unload Hive from the REGEDT32 menu.

8. Exit REGEDT32.

Once this profile is saved in the Netlogon share location, each time a new user logs on, the user will get this new profile.

HINTS AND KINKS FROM THE EXPERTS

In your search for more information about NT, frequent www.microsoft.com on the Internet. You can for NT Server or NT Server 4 (or search for NT Workstation for information about that product).

The Resource Kits

From Microsoft, you can get the Microsoft Windows NT 4 Server Resource Kit. This is different from the Workstation Resource Kit 4. If you have both NT Server and NT Workstation systems installed, it might be a good idea to get both Resource Kits.

How Can I Tell What Changes Are Made to the Registry?

Using the REGEDIT program, it is possible to export portions of the Registry. This feature can be used as follows:

1. Start the REGEDIT program.

2. Select the key you want to monitor.

3. Select Registry ≻ Export Registry file.

4. Enter a filename (if you want to export the whole Registry, select Export Range All) and click OK.

5. Perform the change (install some software or change a system parameter).

6. Repeat steps 1 to 4 using a different filename.

7. Run the two files through a comparison utility, such as windiff.exe.

Part ii

8. If you are using windiff, select File ➣ Compare Files, and you will be prompted to select the two files to compare.

9. Once the files are compared, a summary will be displayed stating whether or not there are any differences. To view the changes, double-click the message.

10. Press F8 or select View ➣ Next Change to view the next change.

You have now found what changed.

(*Courtesy of* John Savill)

WHAT'S NEXT?

This chapter explained what's in the NT Registry. The next chapter describes how how to set up and manage user accounts. The topic of the Registry will come up again in that chapter. For one thing, when you use User Manager for Domains, your changes are stored in the PDC's Registry. Also, you will learn how you can achieve central control of users' Registries through user profiles and system policies.

Chapter 17

MANAGING AND CREATING USER ACCOUNTS

The previous chapters have introduced NT Server and some of its components. Now let's tackle the job of setting up user accounts. The tool you use to set up user accounts is called User Manager for Domains.

Adapted from *Mastering™ Windows® NT® Server 4 (Sixth Edition)* by Mark Minasi

ISBN 0-7821-2445-3   1616 pages $59.99

INTRODUCING USER MANAGER FOR DOMAINS

In NT Server, User Manager for Domains is the primary administrative tool for managing user accounts, groups, and security policies for Domains and computers on the network. User Manager for Domains only runs on NT Server machines, and even then by default only on domain controllers. Run User Manager on another machine, such as a regular old NT Workstation computer or an NT Server computer that is not a domain controller, and you get a cut-down version called simply User Manager rather than User Manager for Domains. You can run User Manager for Domains on those machines (heck, there are even versions for Windows for Workgroups and Windows 95/98), but you've got to load them from the NT CD-ROM in the \Clients\Srvtools directory.

User Manager for Domains versus User Manager

What does it mean to be User Manager *for Domains*? Well, recall that NT machines of all stripes flatly refuse to share data with anyone that they don't recognize; in a simple non-domain network, every single server would have to be introduced to every single user. NT workstations create and manage user accounts with a program called simply *User Manager*. The job of User Manager on machine XYZ is to create user accounts that are only relevant and useful on machine XYZ. If a user on machine ABC wanted to get access to data on machine XYZ, the owner of machine XYZ would have to create an account for the ABC owner on the XYZ machine with the User Manager on machine XYZ.

That would lead to a situation wherein a company with 20 servers (and therefore 20 copies of User Manager running) and 100 users would have to keep track of 2,000 accounts, making for an administrative nightmare. To simplify things, NT provides for a kind of "account sharing" called a *domain*. One NT machine, the PDC, holds a shared database of all users known to the machines that have all agreed to constitute a domain. That way, if user John needs access to all 20 servers in the domain, all you need to do is to build a single domain-wide account for John—and build that domain-wide account with User Manager for *Domains*. Put simply, User Manager is the program that manipulates a machine's SAM—the user database. The main difference is User Manager for *Domains* manipulates the SAM on the PDC. User Manager for Domains *always* points to the PDC; User Manager points to the local machine.

User Accounts Sit on the PDC

User accounts contain information like the username, the password, and a description. All of that data sits in a file called the SAM in the PDC's \WINNT\System32\Config directory. SAM, which is short for *Security Access Manager*, lives in the PDC's Registry, in an area that's grayed out if you try to peek into it.

NOTE

Backing up the Registry of your PDC is an important part of disaster prevention, because it contains all of your user accounts. If you ever have to rebuild a PDC from scratch, then you can restore your user accounts by restoring the Registry. The command RDISK /S backs up your Registry to \WINNT\Repair. While there are other Registry backup tools—and you should use them—a simple RDISK /S now and then is a good bit of insurance.

Whenever you run User Manager for Domains, you're directly manipulating that part of the Registry on the PDC. No matter which machine you run User Manager for Domains from, your changes are stored in the PDC's Registry. If your system cannot get a real-time connection to the PDC, you will be unable to modify user accounts. The connection must, again, be to a PDC—BDCs aren't good enough.

User Manager for Domains Functions

User Manager for Domains provides the network administrator with the means to:

► Create, modify, and delete user accounts in the domain.

► Define a user's Desktop environment and network connections.

► Assign logon scripts to user accounts.

► Manage groups and group membership within the accounts in a domain.

► Manage trust relationships between different domains in the network.

► Manage a domain's security policies.

If you are logged on as an administrator and you start up User Manager for Domains, all of its features are available to you. If you log on as a member of the Account Operators group, you won't be able to use some of User Manager for Domain's capabilities; you can manage most user accounts, but you cannot implement any of the security policies. If you log on as a mere mortal—"user," I believe, is the common term—you can only look at usernames with User Manager for Domains; User Manager for Domains won't let you make any changes to those accounts. Which reminds me...

NOTE

Most changes that you make to a user's account will not show up until the next time he or she logs on. That means, if he/she is in the middle of a network session, any changes you've made won't take effect until he/she logs off and then back on.

A Look around User Manager for Domains

When you open User Manager for Domains, you see a screen like Figure 17.1. In that screen, you can see a list of all of the accounts in the domain, followed by a list of the groups defined in the domain. The user and group information displayed initially is that for the domain where your user account is located (your home domain), and the name of the domain appears in the title bar; in this case, it's ORION.

Username	Full Name	Description
Administrator		Built-in account for administering the compute
Darcee	Darcee Minasi	My babe
Eric		Research Assistant
Guest		Built-in account for guest access to the comp
Holliday	Holliday Ridge	RA
maeve		
Mark	Mark Minasi	Mortal man account
MarkS	Mark Minasi	Mark's administrative account

Groups	Description
Account Operators	Members can administer domain user and group accounts
Administrators	Members can fully administer the computer/domain
Backup Operators	Members can bypass file security to back up files
Domain Admins	Designated administrators of the domain

FIGURE 17.1:   User Manager for Domains

To view users and groups from other trusted domains, use the Select Domain command under the User menu. In the resulting dialog box, seen in Figure 17.2, select or type in the name of the domain whose accounts you wish to view.

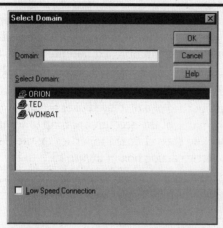

FIGURE 17.2:   Select Domain dialog box

You can also use this command to view the accounts on individual computers that maintain their own security databases (that is, workstations running NT). To do this, type in the computer name preceded by two backslashes (*computername*) in place of the domain name. At that point, User Manager for Domains looks more like the regular old User Manager that comes with NT Workstation. Oh, by the way, if the computer that you choose is a domain controller, the domain information is displayed instead. If you want to, you can open multiple instances of User Manager for Domains, each with a different domain's data.

If the domain or computer you choose happens to communicate with your computer through a connection that has relatively low transmission rates, select Low Speed Connection on the Options menu (or in the Select Domain dialog box). This option disables the producing and displaying of lists of user accounts and groups in the User Manager for Domains window (which can take a long time across a low-speed link). Although the option is disabled, you can still create or manage user accounts and local groups by using these commands: New User, New Local Group, Copy, Delete, Rename, or Properties. Under the Low Speed Connection option, global groups can't be created or copied, but global group membership can still be managed, somewhat indirectly, by managing the group memberships of individual users.

Lists of users and groups can be sorted by either username or by full name with the options on the View menu. Bear in mind that View menu commands are unavailable if the low-speed connection is selected. Any changes made to any account or group while in User Manager for Domains are automatically updated in the view. Other changes, such as an administrator adding an account in your domain from a different, trusted domain, are updated at fixed intervals. If necessary, use the Refresh command to get the latest information for the domain.

To view and manage the properties of a displayed user account or group, simply double-click the name of the account or group (alternatively, you can select the entry and then choose Properties on the User menu). You see the User Properties dialog box in Figure 17.3.

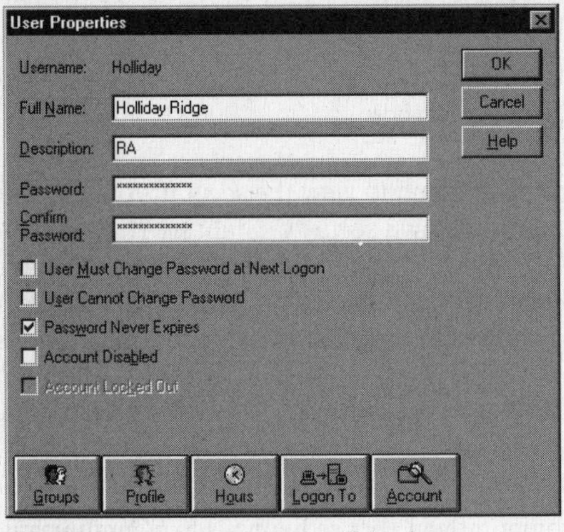

FIGURE 17.3:   User Properties dialog box

Sometimes you want to make a change to several user accounts at the same time—to change logon hours, for example. All you have to do in that case is choose a number of users (Ctrl+click the ones you want to work with) and then choose Users ➢ Properties.

In NT Server, a user account contains information such as the username, password, group membership, and rights and privileges the user has for accessing resources on the network. These details are explained in Table 17.1.

TABLE 17.1: Information in a User Account

PART OF USER ACCOUNT	DESCRIPTION
Account type	The particular type of user account; that is, a local or global account.
Expiration date	A future date when the user account automatically becomes disabled.
Full name	The user's full name.
Home directory	A directory on the server that is private to the user; the user controls access to this directory.
Logon hours	The hours during which the user is allowed to log on to and access network services.
Logon script	A batch or executable file that runs automatically when the user logs on.
Logon workstations	The computer names of the NT workstations that the user is allowed to work from (by default, the user can work from any workstation).
Password	The user's secret password for logging on to his or her account.
Profile	A file containing a record of the user's Desktop environment (program groups, network connections, screen colors, and settings that determine what aspects of the environment the user can change) on NT workstations.
Username	A unique name the user types when logging on. One suggestion is to use a combination of first and last names, such as JaneD for Jane Doherty.

Security Identifiers

User accounts, when first created, are automatically assigned a *security identifier* (SID). A SID is a unique number that identifies an account in the NT Server security system. SIDs are never reused; when an account is deleted, its SID is deleted with it. SIDs look like this:

S-1-5-21-D1-D2-D3-RID

where *S-1-5* is just a standard prefix (well, if you *must* know, the 1 is a version number, which hasn't changed since NT 3.1; the 5 means that the SID was assigned by NT); 21 is also an NT prefix; and D1, D2, and D3 are just 32-bit numbers that are specific to a domain. Once you create a domain, D1 through D3 are set, and all SIDs in that domain henceforth have the same three values. The *RID* stands for Relative ID. The RID is the unique part of any given SID.

Each new account always has a unique RID number, even if the username and other information is the same as an old account. This way, the new account will not have any of the previous rights and permissions of the old account, and security is preserved. (I know, you're wondering, "What if I run out of RIDs?" Well, there are 4 billion of them, so you're not likely to run out. If you *did* end up running so many people through your system that you ran out, would the system start reusing RIDs? I have no idea.)

Prebuilt Accounts: Administrator and Guest

If you're creating a new domain, you'll notice that two accounts called Administrator and Guest are built already. The Administrator account is, as you've guessed, an account with complete power over a domain. You can't delete it, but you can rename it.

WARNING

One of the first things to do after you've set up an NT machine is to rename the Administrator account. As you'll see later, it's dangerous and so it shouldn't be easy for people to figure out the new name of the Administrator account.

You assigned the password for the domain's Administrator account when you installed NT Server on the machine that became the PDC for the domain. Don't lose that password, because there's no way to get it back! (Well, you can always rebuild the domain from scratch with the installation disks, but it's no fun.)

The other account is the Guest account. *Guest* means "anyone that the domain doesn't recognize." By default, this account is disabled, and it should *stay* that way. If you've ever worked with a different network, like a UNIX or NetWare network, then you're probably familiar with the idea of a guest account—*but NT's works differently, so pay attention!* With most other operating systems, you can get access to the operating system by logging on with the username Guest and a blank password. That Guest account is usually pretty restricted in the things it can do. That's true with NT, as well, although remember that the Everyone group includes the guests.

Here's the part that *isn't* like other operating systems. Suppose someone tries to log on to an NT network that has the Guest account enabled. She logs on as melanie_wilson with the password "happy." Now, suppose further that this domain doesn't *have* a melanie_wilson account, so it rejects her logon. On a DOS, Windows for Workgroups, or Windows 95/98 workstation, Melanie can still do work, because none of those operating systems require you to log on to a domain in order to get access to the local workstation. On an NT workstation, she might log on to an account on the local machine. Now she's working at a computer and tries to access a domain resource. And guess what?

She gets in.

Even though an explicit domain login requires that you use a username of Guest, you needn't explicitly log on to a domain to use guest privileges. If your network is attached to my network and your Guest account is enabled, then I can browse through your network and attach to resources that the Guest can access. I needn't log on as Guest; the mere fact that there *is* an enabled Guest account pretty much says to NT, "Leave the back door open, okay?" So be careful when enabling the Guest account.

CREATING A NEW USER ACCOUNT

Creating new user accounts in NT Server is fairly easy. Under the User menu, choose the New User option. You'll see the dialog box shown in Figure 17.4.

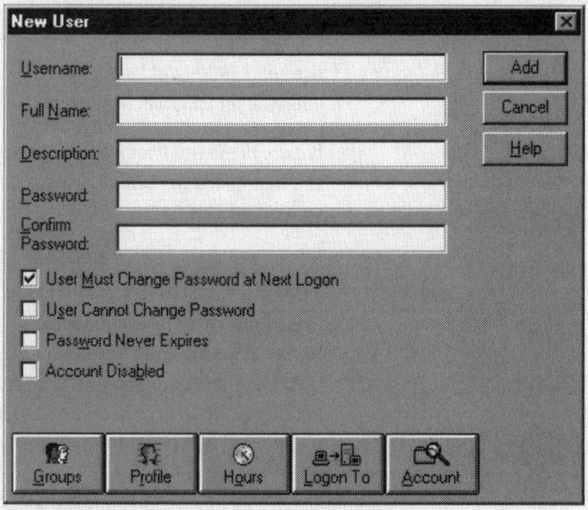

FIGURE 17.4: The New User dialog box

To begin, type in a unique username in the Username box (as suggested in Table 17.1, one option is a combination of the user's first and last name). The username can have up to 20 characters, either uppercase or lowercase, and can't include the following characters:

$$\le / \setminus [\ ] ; : | = , + * ? < >$$

Blanks are okay, but I'd avoid them, because they make it necessary to surround usernames with quotation marks when executing commands.

In the Full Name and Description boxes, type in the user's full name and a short description of the user or of the user account. Both of these entries are optional but recommended. Establish a standard for entering full names (last name first, for example), because the viewing options in User Manager for Domains allow you to sort user accounts by the user's full name instead of the username.

Next, type a password in both the Password and Confirm Password boxes. Passwords are case-sensitive, and their attributes are determined under the Account Policy, which I'll cover a bit later in the section about managing security. After you've entered and confirmed a password, select or clear the checkboxes that determine whether or not the user can or must change the password at the next logon. If you don't want anyone using the new account just yet, check the Account Disabled box. All of the options in this series of checkboxes are described in Table 17.2.

TABLE 17.2: Password and Account Options for Creating a New User Account

OPTION	DEFAULT	DESCRIPTION
Change Password at Next Logon?	Yes	Forces the user to change the password the next time that he or she logs on; this value is set to No afterwards.
Change Password at Next Logon?	No	If Yes, prevents the user from changing the account's password. This is useful for shared accounts.
Password Never Expires	No	If Yes, the user account ignores the password expiration policy, and the password for the account never expires. This is useful for accounts that represent services (such as the Replicator account) and accounts for which you want a permanent password (such as the Guest account).

CONTINUED →

TABLE 17.2 continued: Password and Account Options for Creating a New User Account

OPTION	DEFAULT	DESCRIPTION
Account Disabled	No	If Yes, the account is disabled and no one can log on to it until it is enabled (it is not, however, removed from the database). This is useful for accounts that are used as templates.

Assigning Groups

Selecting the Groups button at the bottom of the New User dialog box allows you to specify which groups the new user account will have membership in. NT Server has a number of useful predefined groups, and I'll explain them in more detail a bit later in this chapter in "Managing Groups." Group membership is shown in the Group Memberships dialog box, seen in Figure 17.5.

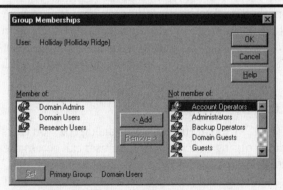

FIGURE 17.5: Group Memberships dialog box

You can click the Groups button to open this dialog box. The dialog box displays which groups the user is or isn't a member of. Note the icons next to the group names:

▸ An icon representing a white woman and a black man in front of a globe indicates a global group.

▸ A computer terminal behind the two faces indicates a local group.

I can't help but observe that the icon for single user accounts is neither white nor black, but *gray*. Perhaps these users are dead? Could this be a George Romero operating system—User Manager of the Living Dead? (Sorry, couldn't resist.)

Again, sorry to appear to be ducking the explanations of global and local groups, but the whole discussion of global and local groups is completely incomprehensible until you understand how to manage multiple domains under NT. To quickly summarize the differences, however, global groups are groups that can be made accessible to the entire network; local groups are local to the domain in which they are defined.

To give new group memberships to the user account, select those groups from the Not Member Of box, then choose the Add button or drag the group icon(s) to the Member Of box. To remove membership in any group from the user account, select the desired groups from the Member Of box and click the Remove button or drag the icon(s) to the Not Member Of box.

User accounts must be a member of at least one group, referred to as the *primary group*, which is used when the user logs on to NT Services for Macintosh or runs POSIX applications. Primary groups must be global groups, and you can't remove a user from that user's primary group. To remove a user from that user's primary group, you have to first move the user to a different primary group. To do this, select a global group from the Member Of box, then click the Set button beneath the Member Of frame. When you're finished configuring the group membership, click OK.

Permissible Logon Hours

By selecting the Hours button in the New User dialog box, you can specify the days and hours during which a particular user can access the network. Similarly, choosing the Logon To button lets you limit which workstations a user can log on from. Click the Hours button in the Properties dialog box of any user or group of users, and you see a dialog box like Figure 17.6.

By default, a user can connect to the network all hours of all days of the week. If for some reason you don't want a user to get access to the network all hours of the day, you can restrict logon hours with this dialog box.

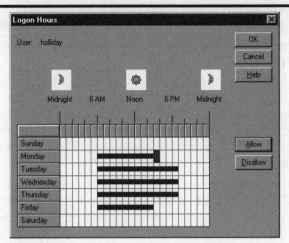

FIGURE 17.6: The Logon Hours dialog box

To administer the hours during which the user account is allowed to access the network, select the hours by dragging the cursor over a particular block of hours. Conversely, you can select all the hours of a certain day by clicking that day's button, or you can choose certain hours across all seven days by clicking the button on top of an hour's column. Then click either the Allow or Disallow button to grant or deny access to the network at those selected hours. Filled boxes indicate the hours when the user is authorized to connect to the network; empty ones indicate the time when access is denied. When you're finished, click OK.

As its title implies, you must understand that this dialog box controls *logon* hours. Suppose you've restricted someone so that she can only log on between 9 A.M. and 5 P.M. and she tries to log on at 8:59. She won't get on, and she will see a message like this (on an NT workstation):

```
Your account has time restrictions that prevent you from log-
ging on at this time. Please try again later.
```

Or, if she's at a Windows 95/98 workstation, she'll see this:

```
You are not allowed to log on at this time.
```

From a DOS workstation, the message is a bit more garrulous:

```
Error 2241: You do not have the necessary access rights to
log on at this time. To change access rights, contact your
network administrator about changing the logon hours listed
in your account.
```

Of course, if our imaginary user tries to log on a few minutes later, after 9 A.M., she gets in without a hitch. But what happens toward the *end* of the logon hours? What happens, for example, when 5:01 P.M. rolls around? Does the system dump her off?

No, not by default. A bit later in this chapter, you'll see a dialog box labeled Account Policy. (If you want to look ahead to it, turn to Figure 17.18 or select Policies ➤ Account in User Manager for Domains.) Account Policy is a big dialog box, and it would be easy to miss one small checkbox at the bottom labeled "Forcibly disconnect remote users from server when logon hours expire."

That's not a very clear statement in the Account Policies dialog box, is it? To me at least, a "remote user" is someone who's dialing into the network; but to NT, it just means anyone who is accessing the server via the network, rather than sitting right down at the server itself. By default, the box isn't checked. If you check it, the user gets this message five minutes before the end of the logon hours:

```
Your logon time at [domain name] ends at [end time]. Please
clean up and log off.
```

Three minutes after that, the message gets a bit more nasty:

```
WARNING: You have until [end time] to log off. If you have not
logged off at this time, your session will be disconnected,
and any open files or devices you have open may lose data.
```

Finally, at the appointed hour, you're history:

```
Your logon time at [domain name] has ended.
```

To get those messages, you must be running a message receiver like WinPopup (for Windows for Workgroups or Windows 95/98) or the Messenger service on an NT workstation. You get logged off even if you're not running a message receiver.

Once a user has been booted off, whatever network resources he or she was using just seem to vanish. Looking at a network drive named F:, for example, will likely generate this error message or one like it:

```
No files found on directory F:
```

Trying to browse in a domain server may lead to an error message like this:

```
[servername] is not accessible. You are not allowed to log on
at this time.
```

Remember that changes to a user's account don't take effect until the next time he or she logs on, so changing someone's logon hours today probably won't have any effect until tomorrow.

This talk of enforced logoff hours leads to a common question: "How can I boot everyone off the server at 2 A.M. so that the scheduled backup can occur?" That's simple. Just write a batch file with these commands:

```
Net pause server
Net send * The server is going down in 5 minutes for
maintenance.
Sleep 300
Net stop server
```

The pause command keeps anyone new from logging on. The send command sends a message to everyone running the messenger service and a network pop-up. The sleep command tells NT to just wait for 300 seconds (five minutes). SLEEP.EXE isn't shipped with NT, but it is on the CD-ROM that comes with the NT Resource Kit, and I highly recommend installing the SLEEP program. The stop command shuts down the server, disconnecting everyone.

Controlling Where Users Can Log On

When you select the Logon To button in the New User dialog box, you get the Logon Workstations dialog box shown in Figure 17.7. This dialog box allows you to restrict which workstations the user can log on from. Now, I know you're wondering, "Why does the button say 'Logon To' when it means 'Logon From?'" As to that question, all I can do is quote a Microsoft employee: "Well, yes, it should be 'Logon From,' but...well...a programmer built the dialog box, you know what I mean?" (For obvious reasons, the Microsoft employee asked to remain anonymous.) As with the logon times, the default is No Restrictions; a user is allowed to log on from any workstation on the network.

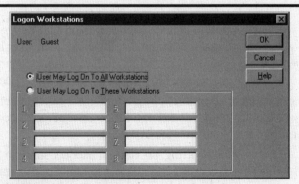

FIGURE 17.7: Logon Workstations dialog box

If you want to restrict the user's choice of workstations where he or she can log on to the network, select the User May Log On To These Workstations button and type in the computer names (without preceding backslashes) of the allowed workstations. Up to eight workstations can be specified. For example, if the machines that I regularly log on to are called SDG90 and LAPDOG, then I just punch in those names (again, without preceding backslashes).

This feature works for all workstation types.

Account Duration and Type

When creating or managing a user account, you can set the account to expire after a certain time period. If you have a summer intern or other temporary personnel, you don't want them to be able to log on to the network beyond the time that they're authorized. Setting an account to expire will avoid this problem. Click the Account button in the New User dialog box to display the Account Information dialog box shown in Figure 17.8.

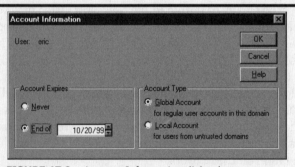

FIGURE 17.8:   Account Information dialog box

An account with an expiration date becomes disabled (not deleted) at the end of the day specified in the Account Expires box. If the user happens to be logged on, the session is not terminated, but no new connections can be made, and once the user logs off, he or she can't log back on.

In addition to setting an account expiration date, you can also set whether the user account in question is a *global account* or *local account* (don't confuse these with global and local *groups*).

Global accounts, the default setting, are normal user accounts in the user's home domain. These accounts can be used not only in the home domain, but also in any domain that has a trust relationship with the home domain. (More on trust relationships shortly.)

Local user accounts, on the other hand, are accounts provided in a particular domain for a user whose global user account is not in a trusted domain (that is, an untrusted NT Server domain or a LAN Manager 2.*x* domain). A local account can't be used to log on interactively at an NT workstation or an NT Server server. Like other accounts, however, a local account can access NT and NT Server computers over the network, can be placed in local and global groups, and can be assigned rights and permissions. If a user from an untrusted domain (either NT Server or LAN Manager 2.*x*) needs access to other NT Server domains, that user needs to have a local account on each of those other domains, since local accounts from one domain (the user's home domain) can't be used in other trusting domains.

Now, by default, all user accounts are global—you've got to click a radio button, as you can see in the dialog box in Figure 17.8, to make a user account a local account. The main difference between a local account and a global account is that you can never get an external domain to recognize a local account. When would you use a local user account, then? "I wouldn't," replied a Microsoft employee, when I asked. "It really doesn't have much use right now," he continued, implying, I suppose, that it had some meaning once but no longer does.

When you've finished selecting the desired account options, choose Add, choose Close, and then choose OK. Then, choose OK in the New User dialog box to create the new user account with the properties you've just specified. The new account will now appear in the list of users on the current domain shown in the User Manager for Domains window.

HOW DO I CREATE A USER ACCOUNT IN A DOMAIN?

Open User Manager for Domains and select User ➤ New User. In the New User dialog box, do the following:

1. Type in a username and the user's full name.

2. Type in a description of the user or account (optional).

3. Type in a password in the Password and Confirm Password boxes. Select the password's characteristics from the options presented. Choose whether or not the account will be disabled.

CONTINUED ➡

4. Using the Groups, Profile, Hours, Logon To, and Account buttons, do the following: set the user's group membership; user profile, logon script, and/or home directory; hours that the network will be available to the user; from which workstations the user is allowed to log on; and account characteristics (expiration date and account type).

5. When you're finished configuring the account using the options in step 4, choose Add.

MANAGING USER ACCOUNTS

Once a user account has been created, you can look at and modify its properties either by double-clicking that account or by highlighting the account and choosing User ≻ Properties. You'll see the User Properties dialog box, as shown in Figure 17.9.

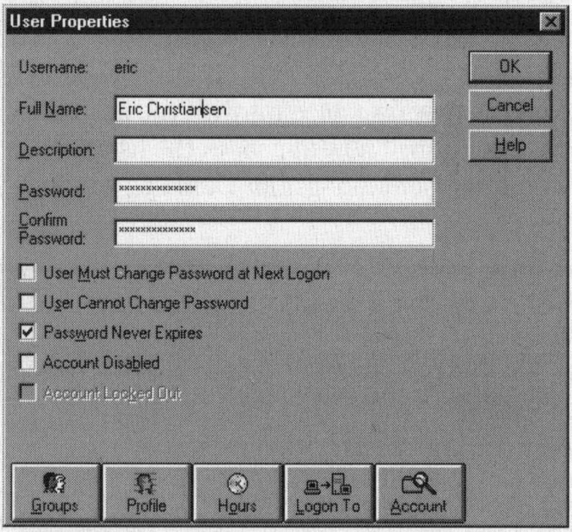

FIGURE 17.9:   User Properties dialog box

Anyone logged on as an administrator or as a member of the Account Operators local group (more on groups shortly) can reconfigure the account's properties, following the same procedure used for creating a new user account.

Copying Accounts

Instead of creating each user account on your network individually, you can also copy existing user accounts. The primary advantage of creating user accounts this way is that all of the original user account's properties (including group memberships) are copied over to the new user account, thus speeding up administrative chores. If you have a large network, you might want to create one or more template accounts that contain specific properties shared by groups of users. For greater security, keep the template accounts disabled so that no one can actually log on to them.

To copy an existing user account, select the account from the list of user accounts in the User Manager for Domains window, then choose User ➤ Copy. You see the Copy dialog box shown in Figure 17.10.

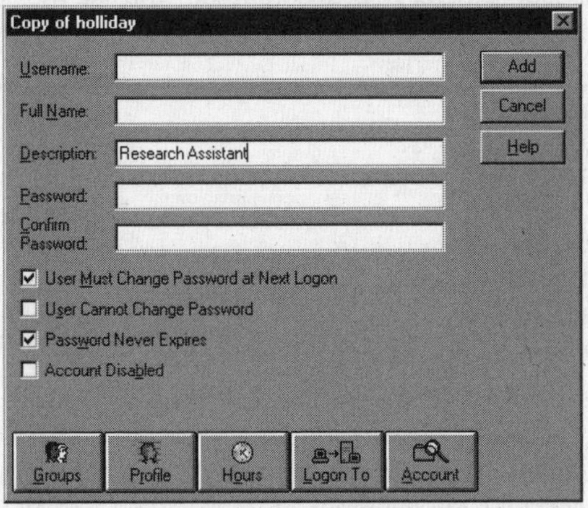

Part ii

FIGURE 17.10:   Copying an existing user account

The copy retains all of the information from the original, except for the username, full name, and password, which you must provide. Configure the new account, making changes to names and properties as needed, and then choose Add. When you're finished, select Close.

Note that the original user's rights, as defined by the User Rights command under the Policy menu, are not copied from one user account to another. If the newly copied accounts must have certain rights, you must grant them separately. Granting rights to a group and putting accounts in that group is the best way to manage rights for multiple users.

All user accounts, including the built-in ones, can be renamed by choosing User ➤ Rename. Renamed accounts retain their original security identifier (SID), and thereby keep all of their original properties, rights, and permissions.

Managing Properties for More Than One Account

You can manage several user account properties for more than one account at once. To do this, first select two or more user accounts. You can select a number of accounts either individually with the mouse from the currently displayed list of users, or (if there are a significant number of user accounts) you can select all members of a particular group within the domain with the User ➤ Select Users command. You see the Select Users dialog box shown in Figure 17.11.

FIGURE 17.11:   Select Users dialog box

You'll notice that the Select Users command is actually more of a "Select Group" command; by choosing a group on the domain, you are selecting all of the users who are members of that group. The Select Users option is cumulative; if you first select Administrators and then select Backup Operators, all members who are either in the Administrators group or the Backup Operators group are selected (the Deselect button lets you take groups off of the selected list). Note that when you choose a group using the Select Users command, only members from the local domain are chosen. For example, if you select a local group (which can contain both users from the home domain as well as users from other, trusted domains), any changes that are made won't affect members from the trusted domains.

After you've selected the user accounts, choose User ➤ Properties. Figure 17.12 is the screen you see next.

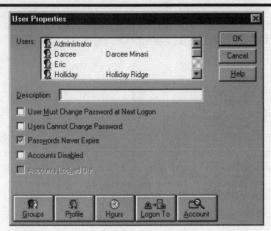

FIGURE 17.12: Modifying the properties of a group of user accounts

As with a single user account, you can select any of the buttons at the bottom of the dialog box to make certain modifications to all of the selected accounts.

For example, let's say you want to modify the group membership for the selected user accounts. By choosing the Groups button, you can see the group memberships that each of the selected accounts have in common in the All Are Members Of box. You can see this box in Figure 17.13.

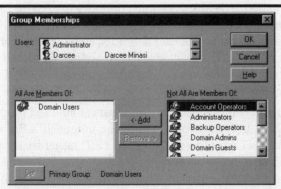

FIGURE 17.13: Modifying the group membership of selected users

You can then add or remove group membership from the selection of users by highlighting the groups and choosing the Add or Remove button.

Part ii

HOW DO I MAKE SURE THAT SELECTED USERS ARE *Not* MEMBERS OF A PARTICULAR GROUP IN A DOMAIN?

To make sure, do the following:

1. Select the users in the User Manager for Domains window.

2. Choose User ➤ Properties.

3. In the User Properties dialog box, choose Groups. Add the particular group from the Not All Are Members Of box to the Members Of box.

4. Choose OK to save the change.

5. In the User Properties dialog box, choose Groups again.

6. Select the group in the All Are Members Of box and choose Remove.

Deleting User Accounts

There are three ways to rescind a user's ability to log on to the network with his or her account: by disabling the account, by restricting the access hours, and by deleting the account.

As mentioned earlier, a disabled account continues to exist on the server, but no one can access it. Even so, it (and with it, its properties) can be copied, it appears on lists of user accounts, and it can be restored to enabled status at any time. A deleted account, on the other hand, is completely removed from the system, vanishes from user account lists, and cannot be recovered or restored.

A new user account can be created with the same name and properties as a deleted account, but it will receive a different, unique SID. Because internal processes in NT refer to a user account's SID rather than its username, none of the rights or permissions granted to the deleted user account will transfer to any new account that has the same name as the old.

As a measure against inadvertent, hasty, and perhaps regretted deletions of user accounts, you might choose to first disable unused accounts, then periodically remove those disabled accounts. Incidentally, NT Server prevents the deletion of the built-in Administrator and Guest accounts.

To delete one or more user accounts, select the account or accounts from the list in the opening window of User Manager for Domains. Then choose User ➤ Delete. Confirmation boxes appear to remind you of your choice and ask if you want to continue. Select OK to proceed.

MANAGING GROUPS

In NT Server, a user group is a set of users who have identical network rights. Placing your domain's user accounts in groups not only simplifies general (as well as security) management, but also makes it easier and faster to grant multiple users access to a network resource. Additionally, to give a right or permission to all of the users in a single group, all you have to do is grant that permission or right to the group.

NT uses two kinds of groups: local groups and global groups.

Local groups are the basic kind of user group in NT. Every NT machine, whether workstation or server, contains a local group called Users and another called Administrators. (There are others also, but these two are fundamental and simple to understand.) Any person with an account in the Users group is, well, a user. He or she can do anything that users can do on this machine. Any person with an account in Administrators has full administrative powers.

Local groups are called *local* because they are local to a given NT machine. One machine's Administrators group cannot be connected to another machine's Administrators group. A given user might be included in machine X's Administrators group but might only be in machine Y's Users group; in that case, when that user sits down and logs in to machine X, then X will treat him as an administrator—but if he sits down and logs in to machine Y, then Y will only treat him as a regular old user.

This arrangement makes managing a large number of machines difficult. Suppose you had 200 NT Workstation machines to administer in your department, and you just hired Lynn, a new administrator. From what I've said, you'd have to walk around to all 200 machines, log in as an administrator on that machine, create a Lynn account, and put it in each machine's local Administrators group. Not much fun—and that's why there are *global* groups.

Global groups can be created only on a domain controller; workstations and member servers can't contain them. But global groups are different from local groups in that they can be essentially "seen" from one machine to another—it's possible for a local group of machine X to contain global groups from machine Y.

Where that becomes useful is in managing domains. You can create a global group on your domain controller and fill it with accounts of users who should have administrative rights all over the domain. Then you can put that global group in the *local* Administrators group on each NT workstation and server machine. Result: when you hire Lynn, all you need to do is put her in the global Administrators group. Because that group is a member of every local Administrators group, she is instantly recognized as an administrator on every machine in the domain.

By the way, that's done automatically in the NT world. Remember that every machine has local groups named Users and Administrators? Well, each domain controller *also* has pre-built *global* groups named Domain Users and Domain Admins. By default, when an NT machine joins a domain, that NT machine's local Users group gets the domain's Domain Users group inserted into it, and that NT machine's Administrators group gets the domain's Domain Admins group inserted into it.

For now, understand that there are two kinds of groups: local and global. Every machine has local groups; only domain controllers can have global groups. And it's possible to include a global group inside a local group.

Creating and Deleting Groups

To create a new local group, select User ➢ New Local Group. You see the dialog box shown in Figure 17.14.

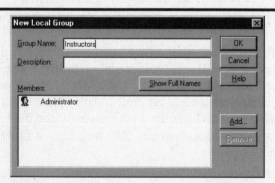

FIGURE 17.14: New Local Group dialog box

Type in the name of the local group you wish to create (in this example, I'm creating a group called Instructors). Include a description of the group, if you want.

Select the Add button to add members to the group. You will see the Add Users and Groups dialog box in Figure 17.15.

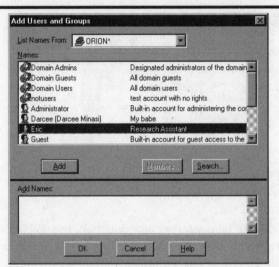

FIGURE 17.15:   Adding accounts to the new local group

In the Add Users and Groups dialog box, select a name or global group from the desired domain list and click the Add button to place the group in the Add Names list (remember, a local group can contain both users and global groups from trusted domains as well as from the local domain). Alternatively, you can type the usernames into the Add Names list; make sure you separate the names with a semicolon. When you've collected all of the names in the Add Names list, click OK.

The names you've chosen will appear in the Members box of the New Local Group dialog box. (To see their full names, click the Show Full Names button.) To remove a name from the list, just highlight it and click the Remove button. When your new local group's membership is to your satisfaction, click OK. The new group will now appear in the User Manager for Domains list of groups.

Creating a Global Group

Creating a new global group is just as easy. Choose User ➢ New Global Group. In the New Global Group dialog box, as seen in Figure 17.16, type in a name and description for the new group. In this example, the new global group is called Research Assistants.

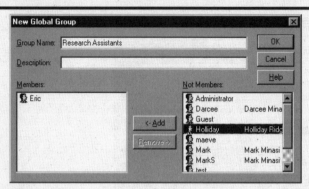

FIGURE 17.16:   New Global Group dialog box

A global group can contain only user accounts from the domain where it is created, so the Not Members box will contain only those accounts on the current domain. To give any user on the list group membership, select one of the entries in the Not Members list and click the Add button. When finished, choose OK; the new global group will be visible in the User Manager for Domains group list.

You can change any user's or group's membership in another group by displaying that group's Properties (in the User Manager for Domains window, either select the group and choose User ➢ Properties or double-click that group). The dialog boxes for Group Properties are identical to those for New Groups, and you can add and remove members using the same procedures described above.

Deleting groups is accomplished by selecting the group in the User Manager for Domains window and choosing User ➢ Delete. The same cautions about deleting user accounts also apply to deleting groups, since groups also have their own unique SIDs. Before allowing you to delete a group, NT Server prompts you with a reminder message, as in Figure 17.17. Deleting a group removes only that group from NT Server; all user accounts and groups within the deleted group are unaffected.

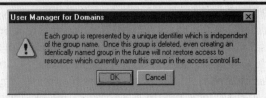

FIGURE 17.17:   Warning message for deleting a group

Examining the Predefined Groups

A number of predefined groups, both local and global, are built into NT Server to aid in network administration and management. The local groups are described in the following pages.

Administrators

Not surprisingly, Administrators is the most powerful group. Members of the Administrators local group have more control over the domain than any other users, and they are granted all of the rights necessary to manage the overall configuration of the domain and the domain's servers. Incidentally, users in the Administrators group do not automatically have access to every file in the domain. If the file's permissions do not grant access to Administrators, then the members of the Administrator's group cannot access the file. If it becomes necessary, however, an administrator can take ownership of such a file and thus have access to it. If he or she does, the event is recorded in the security log (provided that auditing of files has been activated), and the administrator does not have the ability to give ownership back to the original owner (or to anyone else for that matter).

Within the Administrators group is a built-in Administrator user account that cannot be deleted. By default, the Domain Admins global group is also a member of the Administrators group, but it can be removed.

Given that it's possible for the Administrator account to be disabled, it might be wise to create a backup administrator account to be used in case of emergency.

Server Operators

The Server Operators local group has all of the rights needed to manage the domain's servers. Members of the Server Operations group can create, manage, and delete printer shares at servers; create, manage, and delete network shares at servers; back up and restore files on servers; format a server's fixed disk; lock and unlock servers; unlock files; and change the system time. In addition, Server Operators can log on to the network from the domain's servers as well as shut down the servers.

Account Operators

Members of the Account Operators local group are allowed to use User Manager for Domains to create user accounts and groups for the domain, and to modify or delete most of the domain's user accounts and groups.

An Account Operator cannot modify or delete the following groups: Administrators, Domain Admins, Account Operators, Backup Operators, Print Operators, and Server Operators. Likewise, members of this group cannot modify or delete user accounts of administrators. They cannot administer the security policies, but they can use Server Manager to add computers to a domain, log on at servers, and shut down servers.

Print Operators

Members of this group can create, manage, and delete printer shares for an NT Server. Additionally, they can log on at and shut down servers.

Backup Operators

The Backup Operators local group provides its members the rights necessary to back up directories and files from a server and to restore directories and files to a server. Like the Print Operators, they can also log on at and shut down servers.

Everyone

Everyone is not actually a group, and it doesn't appear in the User Management list, but you can assign rights and permissions to it. Anyone who has a user account in the domain, including all local and remote users, is automatically a member of the Everyone local group. Not only are members of this group allowed to connect over the network to a domain's servers, but they are also granted the advanced right to change directories and travel through a directory tree that they may not have permissions on. Members of the Everyone group also have the right to lock the server, but they won't be able to unless they've been granted the right to log on locally at the server.

Users

Members of the group simply called Users have minimal rights at servers running NT Server. They are granted the right to create and manage local groups, but unless they have access to the User Manager for Domains tool (such as by being allowed to log on locally at the server), they can't perform this task. Members of the Users group do possess certain rights at their local NT workstations.

Guests

This is NT Server's built-in local group for occasional or one-time users to log on. Members of this group are granted very limited abilities. Guests have no rights at NT Server servers, but they do possess certain rights at their own individual workstations. The built-in Guest user account is automatically a member of the Guests group.

Replicator

This local group, different from the others, supports directory replication functions. The only member of a domain's Replicator local group should be a single domain user account, which is used to log on to the Replicator services of the domain controller and to the other servers in the domain. User accounts of actual users should *not* be added to this group at all.

Table 17.3 summarizes the user rights (more on user rights in the next section) and special abilities granted to NT Server's predefined local groups.

TABLE 17.3: Rights/Special Abilities Granted to Predefined Local Groups

USER RIGHTS	MEMBERS CAN ALSO
GROUP: ADMINISTRATORS	
Log on locally	Create and manage user accounts
Access this computer from the network	Create and manage global groups
Take ownership of files	Assign user rights

CONTINUED ➡

TABLE 17.3 continued: Rights/Special Abilities Granted to Predefined Local Groups

User Rights	Members Can Also
Group: Administrators	
Manage auditing and security log	Lock the server
Change the system time	Override the server's lock
Shut down the system	Format the server's hard disk
Force shutdown from a remote system	Create common groups
Back up files and directories	Keep a local profile
	Share and stop sharing directories
	Share and stop sharing printers
Group: Server Operators	
Log on locally	Lock the server
Change the system time	Override server's lock
Shut down the system	Format the server's hard disk
Force shutdown from a remote system	Create common groups
Back up files and directories	Keep a local profile
Restore files and directories	Share and stop sharing directories
	Share and stop sharing printers
Group: Account Operators	
Log on locally	Create and manage user accounts, global
groups, and local groups	
Shut down the system	Keep a local profile
Group: Print Operators	
Log on locally	Keep a local profile
Shut down the system	Share and stop sharing printers
Group: Backup Operators	
Log on locally	Keep a local profile
Shut down the system	
Back up files and directories	
Restore files and directories	

TABLE 17.3 continued: Rights/Special Abilities Granted to Predefined Local Groups

User Rights	Members Can Also
Group: Everyone	
Access this computer from the network locally at the server)	Lock the server (must have the right to log on
Group: Users	
(None)	Create and manage local groups (must have the right to log on locally at the server or have access to the User Manager for Domains tool)
Group: Guests	
(None)	(None)

NT Server has only three built-in global groups: Domain Admins, Domain Users, and Domain Guests. These will only appear on NT Server computers that are acting as domain controllers. In fact, it's *only* possible to create global groups on domain controllers. Each group does the following:

Domain Admins By placing a user account into this global group, you provide administrative-level abilities to that user. Members of Domain Admins can administer the home domain, the workstations of the domain, and any other trusted domains that have added the Domain Admins global group to their own Administrators local group. By default, the built-in Domain Admins global group is a member of both the domain's Administrators local group and the Administrators local groups for every NT workstation in the domain. The built-in Administrator user account for the domain is automatically a member of the Domain Admins global group.

Domain Users Members of the Domain Users global group have normal user access to, and abilities for, both the domain itself and for any NT workstation in the domain. This group contains all domain user accounts and is, by default, a member of the Users local groups for both the domain and for every NT workstation on the domain.

Part ii

Domain Guests   This group allows guest accounts to access resources across domain boundaries, if they've been allowed to by the domain administrators.

Built-In Special Groups

In addition to the built-in local and global groups, a few special groups appear now and again when viewing certain lists of groups:

Interactive   Anyone using the computer locally.

Network   All users connected over the network to a computer.

System   The operating system.

Creator Owner   The creator and/or owner of subdirectories, files, and print jobs.

Incidentally, the Interactive and Network groups combined form the Everyone local group.

SYSTEM POLICIES: CENTRAL REGISTRY CONTROL

Over the years, Microsoft has accomplished many things in some areas but hasn't been too successful in others. NT has superbly implemented multitasking, a large memory model (when was the last time you worried about whether or not something would fit into 640KB?), and a vastly improved user interface. Put simply, users have just *got* to love many of the things that NT offers.

Support people, on the other hand, haven't got so much to like. In the typical modern corporation, each corporate support person must ride herd on hundreds or sometimes thousands of PC desktops, solving problems, installing upgrades, and giving advice. But modern PC operating systems don't offer much help to those support folks. Want to remotely control a PC over a network? Remotely install a new piece of software? Can't do any of that with the tools that come in the box with NT. What happens when you've got NT half-installed and the Setup program goes into the weeds? You have a completely useless computer—half installed is no better than newborn as far as NT (or just about any other PC operating system, for that matter) goes.

All that's supposed to change with Windows 2000 Server and its associated Zero Administration Windows. But you don't have to wait until Windows 2000 Server for support relief—there are two tools built into NT Server 4 that make it a bit easier to support and control hundreds of workstations from a single point. The first is *user profiles*, which you read about earlier in this chapter. The other tool is *system policies*.

So what's a system policy and why do you care? That's the topic of the next few dozen pages, but first let's look at the overview. System policies are essentially *central control of users' Registries*.

Why Would You Want to Control Registries?

As you know, virtually *everything* that has anything to do with controlling an NT machine (and a Windows 95/98 machine, for that matter) is in the Registry. But I'll bet you didn't know all of the things that you can control with the Registry; certainly some of these surprised *me*. Here are a few examples:

- ▶ The contents of the folders that a user sees when she clicks the Start button

- ▶ Which icons and controls appear on the Desktop

- ▶ Whether or not a user can directly access the drives on her computer

- ▶ Which programs she can use on her computer

The basic idea is this: You can use Registry entries to lock down an NT workstation or Windows 95/98 Desktop, thereby offering users a consistent and simplified user interface and making the support task simpler. Cool!

Using System Policies

Well, cool except for the fact that to change these important Registry entries on a bunch of machines, it seems like you'd have to walk around to each computer in the building, sit down at the computer, and run REGEDT32 or REGEDIT to modify that machine's Registry. Don't worry: There's an answer to that. There's an automatic feature built right into

NT and Windows 95/98 machines that can make remote Registry modification much easier. Whenever a user logs onto a domain from an NT or Windows 95/98 machine, the machine looks on the domain's PDC for a file called a *system policy* file. The system policy file basically consists of a bunch of instructions, like "Make sure that HKEY_LOCAL_MACHINE\ System\CurrentControlSet\Services\Browser\Parameters has a key named MaintainServerList, and be sure to set it to No." This system policy can centrally control *any* Registry entry except for those of type REG_MULTI_SZ, and this isn't a big restriction, because there aren't that many REG_MULTI_SZ entries.

Central Registry control through system policies is a neat feature, but there are a few problems with it:

- ▶ A user must be logging in to a domain for the user's system to look for the system policy file.

- ▶ You can't have one common system policy file for both the NT and Windows 95/98 machines; you have to build one set of policies for NT desktops and another for Windows 95/98 desktops.

- ▶ The policy file is automatically read from only the PDC, not the BDC, which may pose problems for some large networks. You *can* change that, but it involves some machine-by-machine modifications, and that's what we're trying to avoid in the first place.

- ▶ Because these system policies are just changes to the Registry and because different Registry entries get read at different times, it can be a little confusing to try to figure out whether a system policy actually took effect—it may take an extra reboot to see the change in action.

The system policy files are created for NT and Windows 95/98 with programs named the System Policy Editor for NT and the System Policy Editor for Windows 95/98. Both System Policy Editors are actually user-configurable Registry editors. But unlike REGEDT32 and REGEDIT, they do not show all of the Registry: you essentially "program" them to work with the small subset of Registry entries that you care about, using files called *templates*. Fortunately, you don't usually need to do any of that "programming," because Microsoft includes some pre-built templates that will serve most people's needs.

Using the Registry to Restrict a Desktop: A Basic Example

But before I get into the specifics of system policies, and in particular the administrative tool that you use to create system policies, let's try out one of those Registry changes that I mentioned.

Two important things to understand about system policies are that first, they're just remote-controlled Registry changes, and second, a lot of the Registry changes that we'll find useful for central control of desktops are Registry entries that restrict the user shell program EXPLORER.EXE. EXPLORER.EXE—what's that? Well, you probably know that all of the programs that you run on a PC are just specially designed files with the extension .EXE or, on some older programs, .COM. (There are no NT programs that use .COM, but there are some old DOS programs that do.) You probably also know that the Registry just contains program-specific settings; for example, the Word for Windows section of the Registry contains settings that are only obeyed by Word—put a Registry parameter intended for the Computer Browser service into the Word section, and it'll be ignored.

If I asked you what Windows program you ran most often, you might tell me Word, your Web browser, or perhaps your e-mail program. But there's a Windows program that you use much more—the *shell program* EXPLORER.EXE. Explorer is the program that puts the Desktop on your screen; it starts automatically when you log on to an NT computer. Explorer is the program that knows, when you double-click an icon, to start the program associated with that icon. Explorer puts the Start button on the Desktop and controls what possible actions you can take when you click Start. It's also the program that displays the time in the system tray area of the Taskbar.

So, again, what's the value of controlling Explorer? Well, as you'll see, Explorer is normally the program that you use to start *other* programs— Word, Internet Explorer, Solitaire, or whatever. Being able to control which programs a user can run adds up to some real power.

One of the things that Explorer shows you is the Network Neighborhood folder. Let's see how to modify Explorer's Registry settings to make Network Neighborhood disappear.

The Network Neighborhood icon that appears on Windows 95/98 and NT Desktops can be more trouble than it's worth. As you know, NetHood (as it's known internally to NT) is the user interface for the network browser, which allows someone to view the servers and shares on a network. It's nice, but in many cases it's also superfluous, since the network's administrators probably create pre-mapped drives for users. Network Neighborhood can, then, end up being an invitation to waste time browsing the local network. You can keep NetHood from appearing on a Desktop by adding an entry to *USER*\Software\Microsoft\ Windows\CurrentVersion\Policies\Explorer, where *USER* is the user-specific part of a Registry. The new value (the entry is almost certainly not there by default) is NoNetHood, of type REG_DWORD. Set it to 1, and the next time that user logs on. she won't see the Network Neighborhood icon. You can demonstrate it on your own account (I'll show you how to undo it, don't worry) like so:

1. Open up REGEDIT.

2. Open up HKEY_CURRENT_USER\Software\Microsoft\ Windows\CurrentVersion\Policies\Explorer.

3. With the cursor on the Explorer folder, right-click and choose New ➢ DWORD Value. The screen will look the one shown in Figure 17.18.

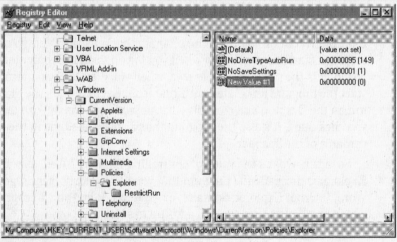

FIGURE 17.18: Setting a new value in Registry Editor

4. Click Edit ➢ Rename, change New Value #1 to NoNet-Hood, double-click NoNetHood, and then change the value from 0 to 1.

5. Exit REGEDIT.

6. Log off and log back on using the same username.

You'll see that the Network Neighborhood icon isn't present any more.

NOTE

To make NetHood appear again, return to REGEDIT and change the 1 value to 0, exit REGEDIT, and again log off and log back on.

Following the steps above imposed the restriction on *your* account. But suppose several people share a particular NT machine, either workstation or server; can you modify how the machine treats them? Sure; it's just a bit more work.

By default, REGEDT32 and REGEDIT only load the Registry for the user who's currently logged on and the Registry for the "System Default" user, the settings that are in effect when no one's logged in. (For example, if you set the Desktop background color to red for the "default" user, then the screen background will be red when no one is logged in at the computer.) But if you have a number of people who use a given computer, then that computer will retain Registry settings for those people; you just need to grab those settings in order to modify them.

Unfortunately, you can't tell REGEDIT to load the Registry settings for another user. However, you *can* tell REGEDT32 to load another user's Registry settings. I sometimes use a user account called TESTUSER on my machine; as a result, there are Registry settings for TESTUSER, and I'll demonstrate how to load them.

NOTE

You'll need to be working on a computer with an account named TESTUSER in order to follow along. TESTUSER must have logged on to and off of this computer at least once for TESTUSER's Registry entries to be sitting on the computer.

1. Run REGEDT32; again, REGEDIT won't work here.

2. Open the HKEY_USERS subtree and click the HKEY_USERS key.

3. Click Registry ➢ Load Hive, and you'll get a dialog box labeled Load Hive, which looks like a normal File ➢ Open dialog box.

4. Navigate over to whichever directory and drive holds your operating system. In my case, it's E:\WINNT, but it'll be different for you. Within that directory is a directory named PROFILES. You'll see a dialog box like the one shown in Figure 17.19.

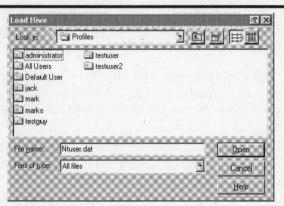

FIGURE 17.19: Viewing user profiles using the Load Hive dialog box

There's a directory for every person who has ever logged on to this computer—administrator, jack, mark, marks, testguy, and TESTUSER—as well as a couple of extra directories labeled All Users and Default User.

5. Open the TESTUSER folder; you'll see the dialog box shown in Figure 17.20.

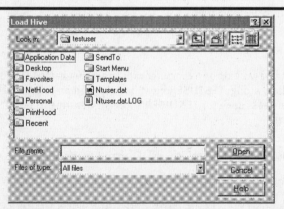

FIGURE 17.20: Viewing user Registry entries in the Load Hive dialog box

6. Choose the file NTUSER.DAT because it contains the user-specific Registry entries for this user. REGEDT32 then needs to know what to call this new hive, as shown in Figure 17.21.

FIGURE 17.21: Naming a user's hive

7. Name it **TESTUSER**. Click OK, and REGEDT32 will look like Figure 17.22.

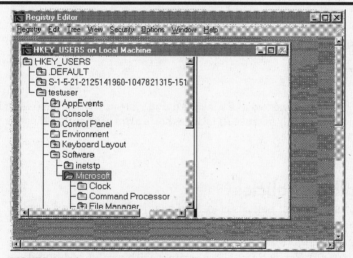

FIGURE 17.22: Registering user entries

8. Now you can edit the Registry entries for TESTUSER just as I did for my own entries—just navigate down to HKEY_USERS\TESTUSER\Software\Microsoft\Windows\CurrentVersion\Policies\Explorer and add No-NetHood as before.

Part ii

9. Once you're finished modifying TESTUSER's settings, click the TESTUSER key and choose Registry ➤ Unload Hive.

The next time TESTUSER logs on, he won't see a Network Neighborhood folder.

Desktop Control Policy Entries

There are about two dozen settings like NoNetHood that you can use to restrict the NT (or Windows 95/98) Desktop located in various places in the Registry. I'll discuss them according to their location. But before going any further, this important warning:

WARNING

My experiments show that many of these Registry entries have no effect whatsoever unless you're running Service Pack 2 or later on your NT Workstation machine.

And this note:

NOTE

If you have worked with Windows 95/98 systems policies, then read this section carefully because NT includes some *extra* policies that Windows 95/98 doesn't have.

Explorer Policies

The first bunch of policies is located near NoNetHood, in a user's HKEY_CURRENT_USER\Software\Microsoft\Windows\ CurrentVersion\Policies\Explorer. Each entry is of type REG_DWORD. You activate these settings with a value of 1 and deactivate them with a value of 0 unless otherwise stated.

NoClose   Removes the Shut Down option from the Start menu if set to 1. The user can still shut down using the Security dialog box (Ctrl+Alt+Del).

NoCommonGroups   Removes the common groups from the Start ➤ Programs menu if set to 1. Recall that "common groups" are the program icons that everyone who logs onto this computer sees. If you've never noticed them before, click Start ➤

Programs, and you'll see one or more lines separating some of the program groups; the bottom bunch shows the common groups. If you don't want particular users seeing those common groups, use this Registry entry.

NoFileMenu   Removes the File menu from NT Explorer. Removing it largely defangs NT Explorer—it becomes one less tool a user can employ to create, move, copy, or delete files.

NoTrayContextMenu   Removes the little pop-up menu (the official term is the *context menu*) that you get when you right-click the Taskbar.

NoViewContextMenu   Removes *all* the pop-up (oops, I mean *context*) menus that appear in the Explorer user interface. This keeps menus from appearing if you right-click the Desktop, My Computer, the Taskbar, or any other object on the Desktop.

NoNetConnectDisconnect   Removes the option to connect and disconnect to/from network resources using Network Neighborhood and My Computer. You might not have even known that you can do this, but if you right-click My Computer or Network Neighborhood, two of the options you'll get on the context menu (hey, that "context menu" stuff kind of slips off the tongue after a while, doesn't it?) will raise dialog boxes to control network connections; forget that possibility, and you're leaving a hole in your Desktop.

DisableLinkTracking   Does *something*—it's in the Registry—but I can't figure out quite what, and of course it's not documented like the other user interface-oriented Registry entries.

ApprovedShellEx   If set to 1, tells the shell to show items on the Desktop or in program menus only if they have recognized file extensions, like .EXE, .LNK, .TXT, and the like. As far as I can see, it's of no use; after all, if you put an object in one of those places that *doesn't* have an extension that NT recognizes, then you can't do anything with it anyway.

NoDesktop   Removes everything from the Desktop when set to 1. You don't see Internet Explorer, Briefcase, or any user-supplied icons. This can be very useful if you're just going to pare a user's options down to just a couple of applications. So far as I know, it's the only way to get rid of the My Computer folder, which is pretty useless anyway when you've removed all the drives from it (see the NoDrives setting, covered a bit later).

NoFind   If enabled (set to 1), removes, the Find option from the Start menu.

NoNetHood   Keeps Network Neighborhood (NetHood) from appearing on the Desktop. There are two related settings that you might find useful if you *are* using the Network Neighborhood: NoEntireNetwork and NoWorkgroupContents, both of which are in a different Registry key, HKEY_LOCAL_USER\ Software\Microsoft\Windows\CurrentVersion\ Policies\Network. NoEntireNetwork removes the Entire Network entry from the Network Neighborhood, and NoWork- groupContents hides machines, just like the Entire Network entry. To see the machines in your workgroup, you'd actually have to click Entire Network, then Microsoft Windows Network, then your workgroup's name. It's not clear to me why this is useful, but it's available.

NoRun   Removes the Run option from the Start menu.

NoSaveSettings   Will, in theory, ignore any user changes to the Desktop—colors, icons, open windows, and the like—and on Windows 95/98 machines, it works fine. Unfortunately, under NT, it doesn't work at all, and a call to Microsoft support got an official acknowledgment of that fact. Maybe Service Pack 23?

NoSetFolders   Has a name that doesn't offer much of a clue about what it does. If set to 1, the Settings folder (the one that normally contains the Control Panel and the Printers folder) does not appear on the Start menu.

NoSetTaskbar   Removes the ability to set options for the Taskbar if set to 1. That's the dialog box that lets you set Auto-Hide and the like for the Taskbar.

NoStartMenuSubFolders   Is associated with custom program folders. You'll read in a page or two how you can control exactly what the user sees when she clicks Start ➤ Programs. But if you *do* use a custom program folder, you must set No- StartMenuSubFolders to 1, or NT will not only display your nice hand-crafted program folders, it'll *also* show the standard ones, which you probably didn't want to happen if you created your own program folders.

NoDrives   Allows you to hide one or more drives from the My Computer folder. How it works is a bit esoteric, so don't worry if you need to read this a couple of times. The REG_DWORD value is a 32-bit number that isn't just 0 or 1. Rather, this uses the rightmost 26 bits of the 32-bit number (see, I told you it was esoteric) to describe whether or not to show a given drive. The rightmost bit in the number controls whether or not you see drive A:. Set it to 0 and you see A:, set it to 1 and you don't. The next bit to the left controls B: in the same way. Here are a few examples:

▶ Suppose you want to hide only the C: drive. The C: drive is the third drive, so you set the third bit over from the right to 1, and the others to 0. The correct value for NoDrives is 00000000000000000000000000000100 in binary, which is 4 in decimal. (Use the Calculator if you hate converting between binary and decimal.)

▶ Suppose you want to hide the floppy drives from My Computer. They're drives A: and B:, first and second, so set only the two rightmost bits to 1, a value of 00000000000000000000000000000011, or 3 in decimal.

▶ If you want to hide *all* drives, the value for NoDrives should be 00000011111111111111111111111111 to hide all 26 drive letters. That's 03FFFFFF in hex, or 67,108,863 in decimal. This removes all drives from My Computer and the Explorer, but not the old Windows 3.*x* File Manager, which still ships with NT as WINFILE.EXE.

Now that you know how you can set Explorer policies to lock down what a user sees when running Explorer, let's look at how you can set them to restrict the programs the user runs.

Restricting What Programs a User Can Run with Explorer Policies

RestrictRun is another mildly complex Registry setting; it's incredibly powerful. You can use it to say to the Windows interface, "Do not run any programs unless they are on the following list." For example, you could say, "The only programs that this user can run are Word and Internet Explorer." RestrictRun is another 1 or 0 Registry setting: 0 says, "Don't restrict which programs this user can run," and 1 says, "Only allow this user to run the programs listed in HKEY_CURRENT_USER\ Software\Microsoft\CurrentVersion\Windows\Policies\ Explorer\RestrictRun." *That* key is just a list of applications that can run, and it consists of as many value entries as you like, all of type REG_SZ, and one application to a value. The name of the first entry must be, simply, 1, and again should contain the filename of the acceptable program. The second would be named 2, and so on. It's probably easiest to see an example, as in Figure 17.23. In that example, I've allowed this user to run (respectively) the Calculator, Internet Explorer, Word, and the command Prompt.

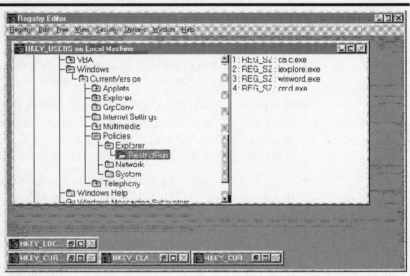

FIGURE 17.23: Using RestrictRun to limit user applications

I've said RestrictRun is a powerful way to control what runs on a Desktop, but it's not perfect.

As you read a few pages back, one of the main reasons to control Explorer, the Windows user interface, is so you can control which programs run on a given computer. Whether you start a program by clicking an icon on the Desktop, by clicking Start ➣ Programs, or by opening My Computer and clicking an icon from one of the drives, the program is launched by Explorer. Suppose you use RestrictRun to tell Explorer,

"Allow user Max to run only WINWORD.EXE, EXCEL.EXE, CMD.EXE (the command prompt), and IEXPLORE.EXE (Internet Explorer). Reject attempts to run any other programs." Suppose then that Max decides that he wants to run FreeCell. He opens My Computer and looks around for FREECELL.EXE, the actual FreeCell program. He double-clicks it and gets a message, "This operation has been canceled because of restrictions in effect on this computer. Please contact your system administrator." He sees the same message when he tries to run FreeCell from Start ➤ Programs ➤ Accessories ➤ Games ➤ Freecell. If he tries to run it from the NT Explorer, he won't even get started; the NT Explorer isn't on the approved list, so it won't run either. Is Max FreeCell-less?

No, and that's one of the weaknesses of the policies approach. It only controls the behavior of the Explorer. Max *could* open up a command prompt, type **freecell**, and FreeCell would start up! Why? Because Explorer didn't start FreeCell; CMD.EXE, the command prompt, did. In most cases, the launching pad for applications is Explorer; but in this case, CMD.EXE started FreeCell. So to really lock down a Desktop—to control absolutely what applications can be run on a given computer—you'd need restrictions on CMD.EXE. Unfortunately, that's not an option. As a result, it's probably not a good idea to include CMD.EXE on the "approved" programs list, if you intend to restrict what programs can run on a user's Desktop.

Are there any other program loopholes? Other ways to launch programs? Yes, unfortunately: someone who knows what she's doing can write a three-line Word macro that will launch a program from inside Word; and, again, there are no ways to restrict what programs launch from inside Word. I'm sure other programs have macro languages that are as powerful.

How about browsing the hard disks? Any ways to do that on a locked-down Desktop? Believe it or not, Internet Explorer is a lockdown hole big enough to drive a truck through. Go to the URL line, type **C:**, and you'll get an entire view of your C: drive, complete with icons for your viewing and clicking pleasure. You won't be able to run any restricted executable files from Internet Explorer, but you can certainly view, copy, and delete files. So, in the final analysis, be aware that RestrictRun is a *nice* feature, but it's not an airtight one.

Keeping People from Getting to the Display Applet in the Control Panel

In HKEY_CURRENT_USER\Software\Microsoft\Windows\Current-Version\Policies\System, there's a setting, NoDispCPL, that will keep NT from allowing a user to access the Display part of the Control Panel. When set to 1, this setting prevents a user from changing the screen by either right-clicking the Desktop or opening Control Panel.

This could be particularly useful in a classroom setting, where you don't want users wasting time playing with colors and background bitmaps.

Keeping People from Using the Registry-Editing Tools

After restricting the Explorer, you don't want people using the Registry editors to undo your work. You can prevent that by adding an entry in HKEY_CURRENT_USER\Software\Microsoft\Windows\Current-Version\Policies\System for a particular user. The entry's name is DisableRegistryTools. If this is set to 1, it will keep the user from running either REGEDIT or REGEDT32. Be aware though, that it will *not* keep that user from running POLEDIT, the System Policy Editor that we'll work with in a few pages. POLEDIT can modify the Registry, so either keep it off the approved list of programs (assuming you're using RestrictRun) or just make sure that it's not anywhere that a user can easily get to.

Getting Rid of the "Welcome" Tips

I know this is a matter of taste, but I find that Welcome screen with the helpful tip *really* annoying. Yes, you can check the box that says, "Don't show me these any more," but I create and use a lot of accounts for testing purposes, and so I'm forever clicking the darn box. Instead, however, you can use a Registry entry to keep the silly box from appearing in the first place. In HKEY_CURRENT_USER\Software\Microsoft\Windows\CurrentVersion\Explorer\Tips, just create a key named Show of type REG_DWORD and set it to 0. Set it to 1, and the dumb tips appear.

On the other hand, you might want to be *sure* that people read the tips. You might do that because you can redefine the tips, as they live in the Registry in HKEY_LOCAL_MACHINE\Software\Microsoft\Windows\CurrentVersion\Explorer\Tips. There is a value entry for each tip; they're all of type REG_SZ, and the value entry names are just numbers: 1, 2, and so on. You *could* use the central Registry control that we're leading up to in order to essentially "download" a bunch of tips to everyone's machine. Users would see those tips whenever they logged on to their system.

Controlling the Start Programs Folders

Part of creating a custom Desktop for a user includes controlling the programs that he can run. Once you've gone to all the trouble of keeping him from running all but a few programs, you'll have to give him a way to *get* to those few programs.

Most of the items that you see on the Start menu are just folders pointed to by various Registry entries. Look in any user's Software\ Microsoft\Windows\CurrentVersion\Explorer\User Shell Folders, and you'll see the values AppData, Desktop, Favorites, Fonts, NetHood, Personal, PrintHood, Programs, Recent, SendTo, Start Menu, Startup, and Templates. They contain the locations of directories that contain user-specific information. For instance, Startup contains the location of a folder that contains shortcuts to the programs that you want that user to automatically run when he logs in.

Where the Menus Come From

The folder that we're most interested in at the moment is Programs. How can a disk directory correspond to menu items? Take a look at Figure 17.24, a full screen shot of an NT Desktop with some menus and submenus opened.

Note that the Programs menu has four submenus: Accessories, Startup, Administrative Tools (Common), and another Startup. You can tell from the folder-and-PC icons for the Administrative Tools (Common) and lower Startup folders that they are common folders. In a fully controlled Desktop, they probably wouldn't appear, as you'd use the No-CommonGroups Registry entry to keep them out of the picture anyway, so let's just focus on the Programs menu without the common folders. In addition to the Accessories and upper Startup submenus, there are icons for Books Online, Command Prompt, Microsoft Access, Microsoft Binder, Microsoft Excel, Microsoft PowerPoint, Microsoft Schedule+, Microsoft

Word, and Windows NT Explorer. I've also opened the Accessories sub-menu, which contains a number of items and two of what might be called sub-submenus, Hyperterminal and Multimedia.

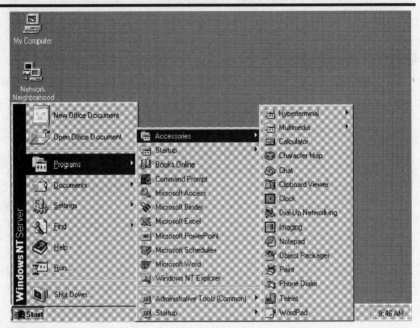

FIGURE 17.24: An NT Desktop with opened menus and submenus

To look under the hood and see how this is actually accomplished, I go to the Profiles directory of my NT installation. I'm currently logged on as MarkS, and I've installed NT Server in a directory called \TORUSMM; so if I look in \TORUSMM\PROFILES\MARKS, I will see a number of folders, and one of them will be named Start Menu. Looking in that, I find a folder named Programs, which has shortcuts for each icon that appears on the menu. There is also a folder named Accessories in the Programs folder, and opening that shows me, again, shortcuts corresponding to each icon in the Accessories menu. You can see the Programs and Accessories folders in Figure 17.25. In this figure, you see two open directories. The top one shows the shortcuts that appear when user MarkS clicks Start and Programs; the bottom one shows the shortcuts when that user clicks Start ➤ Programs ➤ Accessories.

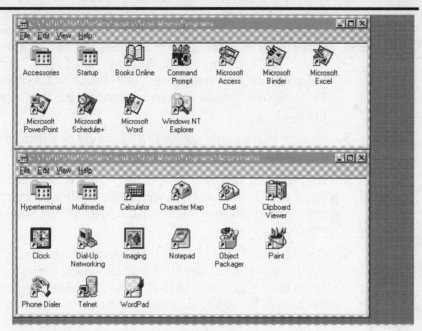

FIGURE 17.25: Two open applications directories

How can all of this help *you*? Well, again, suppose you've got a set of approved applications that you want to restrict users to. Just create a folder on the network that contains shortcuts to those applications. Then modify each user's Registry so that `Software\Microsoft\Windows\CurrentVersion\Explorer\User Shell Folders\Programs` points to the UNC of that folder. When the user logs in, his only program icons will then be the ones that you've placed in this centrally located folder.

A Sample Custom Programs Folder

You can try this out by creating a "throw-away" user account and giving it a very limited menu of programs. I'm going to tell you to place all of the relevant files on the local system so you don't even need a network to try this out; even a copy of NT Workstation would work fine. I'll assume for the example that you've installed NT in the default location, `C:\WINNT`.

1.   Create a folder named PROGS on the root of C:, `C:\PROGS`.

2. In C:\PROGS, create shortcuts for Internet Explorer, the Calculator, and Notepad. (You can do this either by right-clicking in the folder, choosing New ➤ Shortcut and following the wizard, or locating `IEXPLORE.EXE`, `CALC.EXE`, and `NOTEPAD.EXE` and dragging them into the C:\PROGS folder. The shell will automatically create shortcuts rather than copy the files.)

3. Create a bogus user account; BOGUS would be a perfectly good name.

4. Log on and off once as BOGUS so that NT will create a directory for the BOGUS user account in the Profiles directory. Log back on with an account with the administrator level of privilege.

5. Start up REGEDT32 and load the Registry for user BOGUS. Put the cursor on the top of `HKEY_USERS`, select Registry ➤ Load Hive, navigate to `C:\WINNT\Profiles\Bogus`, select the file `NTUSER.DAT`, and give it a name when prompted— again, "bogus" works just fine.

6. In BOGUS, open `Software\Microsoft\Windows\CurrentVersion\Explorer\User Shell Folders` and look at the current contents of the Programs entry. It's probably `C:\WINNT\Profiles\Bogus\Programs`. Change it to `C:\PROGS`.

7. While you're there, go to `Bogus\Software\Microsoft\Windows\CurrentVersion\Policies\Explorer` and add a new value, `NoStartMenuSubFolders`, type `REG_DWORD`, and set it to 1. In the same key, add `NoCommonGroups`, again `REG_DWORD`, set to 1.

8. Click the top of the Bogus tree and unload it with Registry ➤ Unload Hive.

9. Confirm unloading the hive and exit REGEDT32.

10. Log on as BOGUS. Click Start ➤ Programs. See the difference? On my computer, when I click Start ➤ Programs, my screen looks like Figure 17.26.

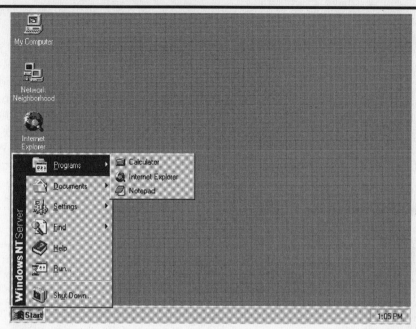

FIGURE 17.26:   Limiting the Programs folder

If you're interested, let's take this a bit further and *really* lock down this Desktop. In addition to the NoCommonGroups and NoStartMenuSub-Folders settings, add NoDesktop, NoFind, NoRun, NoSetFolders, NoTrayContextMenu, and NoViewContextMenu (remember that they all go in Software\Microsoft\Windows\CurrentVersion\ Policies\Explorer) and set them all to 1. The result is a *very* simplified Desktop perfect for someone who just needs to run a few programs and doesn't want to be bothered with the other Desktop clutter.

Again, this simple example was fairly labor-intensive, and I'll show you very soon how to set up this kind of control through the network. But there's an important point to be made here: eventually, I'll have to put the folder that I called PROGS on the network, so that I can deliver the same set of program icons to everyone. But NT shortcuts refer to particular locations, so how can one set of program shortcuts serve an entire network? For example, my Calculator icon has embedded in it the fact that the Calculator program's full path is C:\TORUSMM\SYSTEM32\CALC .EXE, because that's where I have the Calculator on my system. If I networked the PROGS folder and distributed it to a user whose Calculator wasn't in C:\TORUSMM\SYSTEM32, she wouldn't be able to access the

Calculator. How, then, do you create a set of common program folders that are networkable?

One way is to network the applications; point the shortcuts not to drive letters like C:\TORUSMM\SYSTEM32 but to UNCs like \\APPSERVER\ ENGINEERING\. This won't work for complex applications like Office 95, because Office 95 *must* install some files to the local hard disk before running. (Office 97 is a bit better behaved but still poses some problems.) The other possible approach is to standardize the locations of applications on each workstation's hard disk. If one machine loads Word in C:\MSOFFICE, make sure that they *all* do. It's a bit of a pain, but it's necessary to make networked program groups work.

NOTE

Remember that if you intend to distribute program menu folders to multiple users, you *must* be sure that all of the users have the applications that are in those folders in the same directories: if Word is in C:\MSOFFICE\WINWORD on one computer, make sure it's in C:\MSOFFICE\WINWORD in *all* of those users' computers. Otherwise, Word will show up as an option on the Program menu, but clicking it won't do anything.

You can also control what a user sees in the *common* program folders, if you allow those folders. There is a key in HKEY_LOCAL_MACHINE that lets you designate a location for common folders. Look in any of the "machine" icons in the System Policy Editor.

Distributing Registry Changes over a Network with NTCONFIG.POL

Just that little demonstration of controlling a program menu illustrated how powerful a few Registry changes can be. Imagine if you were to take what we did a step further and use RestrictRun to let that computer run only Internet Explorer, Calculator, and Notepad. Then, not only would the user see only those three, but they also would be the only things that would run. I'm simplifying the matter a trifle, of course, if you recall the discussion of all the loopholes in the user interface. But with a few more changes, you could pretty quickly bolt down a user's Desktop. (As I mentioned a page or two back, in addition to RestrictRun, I'd use NoDesktop, NoFind, NoRun, NoSetFolders, NoTrayContextMenu, and NoViewContextMenu.)

This sounds like a lot of work, and indeed it would be if you had to go out to every user's machine and hand-edit his Registry. So, as I mentioned in the beginning of this section, NT has this cool built-in way to order changes to Registries automatically over the network. (It'll actually also allow you to control Windows 95/98 Registries as well with a little extra work, as you'll see.)

The trick is this: when an NT workstation (or a Windows 95/98 computer, for that matter) logs on to an NT domain, the networking client software is designed to look on the PDC's NETLOGON share—the place where you normally keep login batch scripts—for the system policy file that I mentioned earlier. More specifically, the system policy file is a binary file called either NTCONFIG.POL (the file that NT machines look for) or CONFIG.POL (the file that Windows 95/98 machines look for).

It's logical at this point to wonder why there are different files for NT policies versus Windows 95/98 policies. It's because Windows 95/98 stores character data using ASCII (the American Standard Code for Information Interchange, a 35-year-old, English-centric method for storing characters), while NT, surprisingly, does *not* use ASCII; rather, it uses a more flexible character set called Unicode. NT's use of Unicode is one reason that it works so well in international environments. Microsoft's decision to *not* use Unicode in Windows 95/98 was unfortunate, but it's one of the dozens of reasons to use NT instead. (One Microsoft person— an *NT* developer, mind you, not a 95 developer—wryly commented to me that it was a sad example of what he called "MESE thinking." MESE is pronounced *meezie*, and he explained that it stood for "Make 'Em Speak English.")

The bottom line is this: You'll have to build all your policies twice— once for the Windows 95/98 machines and once for the NT machines. And when I say the files use ASCII or Unicode, I don't mean that these are simple text files—they're not—but that the portion of the file that *is* text is either stored as ASCII or Unicode. The other reason you end up with two different policy files is that NT and Windows 95/98 Registry entries are *similar* but not identical; Windows 95/98 has some Registry entries that NT doesn't, and vice versa.

Again, the POL file is largely binary, neither ASCII nor Unicode, so you can't just create one with Notepad. As you'll see in a minute, you need to use a particular tool called the System Policy Editor to create a POL file.

Again, this notion of modifying Registries remotely with the POL files is called *system policies*. Thus, if you created a central POL file that removed Network Neighborhood from a user's Desktop, then it's just a Registry change. But because it was effected via the POL files, you'd say that you'd imposed a system policy.

These POL files essentially contain commands that your system uses to modify its Registry. So, before going any further, let me summarize some specifics of how the POL files work:

- ▶ The files must be created by one of the System Policy Editors.

- ▶ POL files will affect only the behavior of Windows 95/98, NT Workstation 4, or NT Server 4 machines. They won't work with NT 3.x or Windows 3.x machines.

- ▶ They must reside on the NETLOGON share of the PDC. BDCs are of no help here. (Recall that NETLOGON is in \WINNT\SYS-TEM32\REPL\IMPORT\SCRIPTS, although you may alternatively keep yours in \WINNT\SYSTEM32\EXPORT\SCRIPTS.)

This is a "pull" technology in the sense that the PDC never forces the POL files, or their effects, on the workstations. Rather, a workstation *requests* a file as a side effect to a domain logon, which brings me to the next point:

- ▶ This approach works *only* if you're doing a domain logon. You need to specifically configure a Windows 95/98 workstation to do a domain logon (Control Panel ➤ Networking ➤ Client for Microsoft Networks ➤ Properties). In the same way, you need to be logging on to a domain account from an NT machine for the NT system policies to take effect.

- ▶ These changes are Registry changes, so they won't always take effect until after the user's rebooted.

Using NTCONFIG.POL to Modify a User's Registry

The first example I gave of a Registry change was to eliminate the Network Neighborhood from TESTUSER's Desktop. Let's do that again, but this time let's do it with the System Policy Editor.

Before, I walked over to the computer that I usually use, fired up a Registry editor, and directly edited HKEY_CURRENT_USER\Software\ Microsoft\Windows\CurrentVersion\Policies\Explorer, logged off, and then logged back on. *Now*, I'm going to use the System

Policy Editor to create a CONFIG.POL with instructions to remove Network Neighborhood, and I'll save that CONFIG.POL on my domain's PDC. If you want to follow along, you'll need a user account named TESTUSER.

First, I'll need the NT System Policy Editor. The NT System Policy Editor ships with NT Server, and it appears in Start ➢ Administrative Tools (Common). If you're using NT Workstation, then you'll get the System Policy Editor with the other administration tools in the \CLIENTS\SRV-TOOLS directory of the NT CD-ROM. Start up System Policy Editor, and you'll see a blank screen. Select File ➢ New Policy, and you'll see something like Figure 17.27.

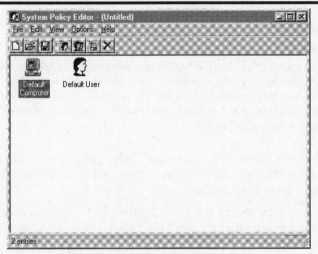

FIGURE 17.27: Creating policies in Systems Policy Editor

There's an icon of a PC and an icon of a gray-colored guy (there's that dead user again) with a dopey-looking haircut or, come to think of it, that might be a gray-colored icon of a *woman* with a dopey-looking haircut; hmmm, many's the time I wish for insider information at Microsoft. In any case, why the two icons? Well, recall that Registry entries tend to be either machine-specific, like the things in HKEY_LOCAL_MACHINE (SAM, Security, System, Software), or user-specific, like the things in \WINNT\PROFILES directory (NTUSER.DAT.LOG). You modify machine Registry entries through PC icons, and you modify user-specific Registry entries through user icons.

WARNING

The icons that appear automatically, the Default Computer and Default User icons, are *extremely powerful* and *extremely dangerous*.

Any policies that you impose through Default Computer or Default User apply to every machine or every person, even domain controllers and administrators. Do something like hide the Desktop of the Default User and set Default User to a very restricted set of program folders, and *no one* will be able to undo that from an NT workstation; it's very possible that poorly set policies on Default User or Computer would make you have to rebuild your entire domain.

WARNING

Any changes that you make to Default User will automatically be copied to *all specific user policies*. (Ditto machines.) This makes it extremely difficult to create a diverse set of policies, as the dumb Default User keeps overwriting what you've done. My advice: Don't do anything with Default User or Machine unless you have a really good reason.

In fact, you can delete Default User and Default Machine, and I usually do. If you ever want them back, just re-create a user named Default User or a machine named Default Machine.

So, because I want to affect only *my* Desktop, I'll tell System Policy Editor to create a policy for just user TESTUSER. I know that I'm modifying a user icon rather than a machine icon because I know that the entry that I want to modify is in the user part of the Registry rather than the machine part.

Choose Edit ≻ Add User, and you'll see a dialog box allowing you to either type in a username (like ORION\TESTUSER in my case, as that's the name of my master domain) or to browse a list of users. I browse over to my ORION domain, where TESTUSER lives, and choose TESTUSER. My screen now looks like the one shown in Figure 17.28.

Now double-click TESTUSER, and you'll see a Properties dialog box, as shown in Figure 17.29.

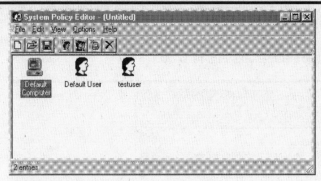

FIGURE 17.28: Adding a new user

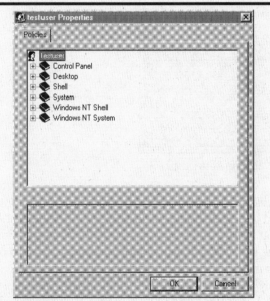

FIGURE 17.29: The User Properties dialog box

Hey, *this* looks quite a bit different from the Registry editing tools! System Policy Editor is organized completely differently than REGEDT32 and REGEDIT are. As I mentioned earlier, System Policy Editor doesn't contain all of the thousands of Registry entries—just a small subset that it has been directed to offer to you. (I will explain later how you can control which Registry entries show up.) Open up the Shell book (click the plus sign), and you'll see another book, labeled Restrictions. Open that, and you'll see a screen like Figure 17.30.

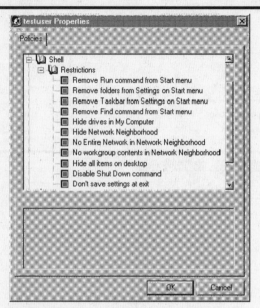

FIGURE 17.30: User Properties Restrictions

See the entry labeled Hide Network Neighborhood? Click it, and it'll show up as a checked box. A checked box means, "Set the value to 1." Click it again, and you'll see that it is now a cleared box. A cleared box means, "Set the value to 0." Click it again, and it becomes gray, as it originally was. A gray box means, "There's no system policy about this, so leave it alone." Finally, click it yet again, and it will appear checked: recall that we want the value of NoNetHood to be 1 so that Network Neighborhood will not appear. Then click OK to clear the TESTUSER Properties dialog box.

Next, tell System Policy Editor to save the policy file so that it'll take effect. Click File ➢ Save As and navigate over to the NETLOGON share of your domain's PDC. If you are sitting at the PDC, then recall that it is in \WINNT\SYSTEM32\REPL\IMPORT\SCRIPTS. If you're going to access the PDC's NETLOGON share over the network, then remember beforehand to give yourself the share permissions to save files in NET-LOGON—by default, NETLOGON only has share permissions of Everyone/Read. Save it as file `NTCONFIG.POL`.

Next, I log off and log onto the domain using the TESTUSER account. (Again, TESTUSER must log onto an *NT* machine to see the effect of the policy change; there's no Windows 95/98 policy file, and so if I logged onto the domain with a Windows 95/98 computer as TESTUSER, I'd still see Network Neighborhood.) The result: no Network Neighborhood. (How did checking Hide Network Neighborhood cause a change in the Policies key of the Registry? Through template files, which I'll explain later.) But first, let's see how to undo a policy.

Undoing the System Policy

Now suppose I want to restore the Network Neighborhood to TESTUSER, or, better, what if TESTUSER tries to *take* it back. Can he just edit his Registry to restore NetHood? Actually, TESTUSER can't change the `NoNetHood` entry; by default, regular old user accounts only have Read permission on entries in the `HKEY_CURRENT_USERS\Software\Microsoft\CurrentVersion\Windows\Policies` key. But suppose he *could* change his Registry? Would that let him get NetHood back? No. The next time he logged on, his system would read `NTCONFIG.POL`, see the order to remove NetHood, and he would be back where he started.

Suppose, however, that while he can't modify his own local Registry, he talks some administrator into erasing `NTCONFIG.POL`. Then what happens? As it turns out, nothing. In the same way, what if an administrator decides to change the Hide Network Neighborhood policy from checked to gray—what happens? Again, nothing; our user still doesn't have a Network Neighborhood.

The sequence of events for central Registry control goes like this: assume there's an `NTCONFIG.POL` on the PDC, and the file has a no-NetHood policy in it. Over on TESTUSER's desk, TESTUSER turns on his computer. The computer powers up and reads its local Registry, the part relevant to the machine only. The PC doesn't know who is going to log on to it. Next, TESTUSER logs onto the domain using his account. When TESTUSER's workstation PC contacts the domain's PDC, the PDC's `NTCONFIG.POL` file essentially tells TESTUSER's workstation,

"Change the value of
HKEY_CURRENT_USERS\Software\Microsoft\
CurrentVersion\Windows\Policies\Explorer NoNetHood to
1 and then log this TESTUSER guy in." The local user-specific Registry
information for TESTUSER is changed accordingly, and so as Explorer
starts up, it leaves out NetHood.

Now suppose someone erases NTCONFIG.POL on the PDC. TEST-
USER logs off and then back on. Will that get NetHood back?

No. Remember that the NoNetHood=1 setting is in his *local Registry
on the workstation's hard disk*. He must either modify that Registry
(which he can't do, because he has only Read access to the Policies
key) or ask an administrator to use a system policy to return Network
Neighborhood to his Desktop. (If it sounds like I'm beating a dead horse,
trust me, I'm not; many people find system policies confusing if they
don't take the time to think through what NT is doing on the Desktop.)

So TESTUSER comes to you, his friendly administrator, and asks that
NetHood be returned to him. How do you do it? Start up the System Policy
Editor, load the policy file—it's conveniently located on the Most Recently
Used list at the bottom of the File menu—and open TESTUSER back to
the Shell/Restrictions screen.

Recall that the checkbox had not two, but three states: checked, which
meant, "Force TESTUSER not to have NetHood"; unchecked, which meant,
"Force TESTUSER to *have* NetHood"; and gray, which meant, "Do not
modify this part of TESTUSER's Registry." If you were to simply say, "We
don't care anymore what users do with their NetHoods" and gray the
box, where would that leave TESTUSER? He still wouldn't have a Network Neighborhood, because gray means, "Don't change anything," and
the current state of his Registry says to not show NetHood. To restore
NetHood would require a three-step process:

1. Clear the box. Don't check it or leave it gray.

2. Ask TESTUSER to log on. He should now have NetHood back.

3. The current system policies now *force* TESTUSER to have
   NetHood, but you want the policy to be silent. Once TEST-
   USER's logged off, go back and edit NTCONFIG.POL to make
   the box gray.

NetHood is now restored.

NOTE

It's not intuitive (until someone explains it), but it's important to understand the above steps. Remember that to release people from a policy, it's not sufficient to simply gray the policy's box. You must first re-enable whatever the policy disabled, *then* gray the box.

Changing a Policy about a Machine

In most cases, you'll use the System Policy Editor and the POL files to control user settings. But what about machine settings? Are they ever useful? Personally, I can think of two things I'd like to set about a machine, both of which are discussed later: HKEY_LOCAL_MACHINE\ System\CurrentControlSet\Services\Browser\Parameters\ MaintainServerList=No, which removes a machine from contention to be the master browser; and HKEY_LOCAL_MACHINE\System\ CurrentControlSet\Services\NetBT\Parameters\Enable-Proxy=1, which allows a machine to be a WINS proxy agent. Without going into detail here, you can reduce your network's chatter by telling 99 percent of your machines to stay out of the race to be browser (hence the first Registry change), and you can assist your computers to find one another by designating one computer on each network segment to be a WINS proxy agent (hence the second Registry change), but *don't* make more than one computer per segment into a proxy agent, or you'll be making things worse.

Neither of those useful possibilities is handled by the System Policy Editor by default, however, so let's look at a couple of less useful ones that are built in: the logon legal notice caption and whether or not to update the "access time" information in the file system. You can set your systems up so that they will display a legal notice banner when someone tries to log on to them, a message along the lines of "You'll be prosecuted if you try to hack this computer." It's a Registry entry, HKEY_LOCAL_ MACHINE\System\CurrentControlSet\Software\Microsoft\ Windows NT\CurrentVersion\Winlogon, and two REG_SZ entries: LegalNoticeCaption and LegalNoticeText. The caption is the text that goes on the title bar of the warning dialog box, and the text is the text inside the dialog box.

Open a machine icon in the System Policy Editor, open the NT System book, and open the Logon book. You'll see a dialog box like the one shown in Figure 17.31.

Part ii

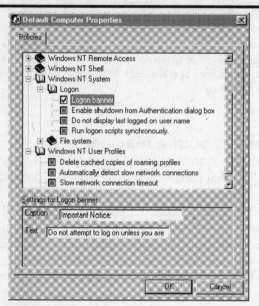

FIGURE 17.31:   The Default Computer Properties dialog box

This option isn't enabled by default, so I checked it to allow you to see the caption and text fields. You can put any text that you like into the fields. If you want to try it out, check the box and type in the text of your choice.

The other possible change effected in System Policy Editor is whether or not to update a field in NTFS called "access time." Not only does NTFS keep track of when you created a file, it also remembers when you last modified it and when you last accessed it. That's useful, but constantly recording when a file was last looked at can slow the computer down a bit. So there's a Registry entry that says, "Don't bother keeping track of when the file was last accessed."

While neither the legal caption setting nor the "Don't keep track of the last access time" setting is earth-shattering, they're good, simple examples of when you make a change in NTCONFIG.POL versus when the change takes effect.

Suppose you make this policy change for some specific machine, say a machine named PPRO200, the name of one of my NT machines. When does the change take effect? Well, the policy file is read only when a user logs in. Suppose I log in at PPRO200. In the process of logging me onto the domain, PPRO200 reads NTCONFIG.POL and receives the commands to incorporate the legal caption and not to record access times. The relevant questions here are:

- When will I first see the legal notice?
- When will the system stop logging access times?

The legal notice change is a modification to a Registry entry for Winlogon, the program that runs whenever you press Ctrl+Alt+Del to log on to a system. How often, then, does Winlogon check its Registry for changes? Every time someone logs on. As a result, you'll see the legal notice caption the next time you log onto that machine.

The access-time information is part of the Registry entries for NTFS, however. When do *they* get examined by NTFS? Only at system boot time. You could log on 50 times and not see the "Don't keep track of access times" change take place. The reason is that you must reboot the computer for these changes to take effect. Moral of the story: System policies can drive you crazy because when you make a bunch of changes (like the two I just made), some of them take effect almost immediately and some may take a day or two. That is, you may not have the occasion to reboot for that long, and so you won't see your changes until then. So before you start tearing your hair out, stop and analyze the matter: What change *did* the System Policy Editor make to the Registry? Should I reboot before the change will take effect? And, here's one of my favorite dumb things to do when playing with system policies—did you remember to *save* the updated NTCONFIG.POL?

Which Domain to Save the Policy To?

We won't take up the question of managing multiple-domain NT networks until later, but let's consider the following question. I log in as MarkA, my administrative account, which is a member of a domain named ORION. But my workstation, PPRO200, is a member of domain TAURUS. Now, I want to save a policy that affects my *machine*, which again is a member of domain TAURUS, not me. So the $64,000 question is: Should I create (or modify) the NTCONFIG.POL on the ORION PDC, or the one on the TAURUS PDC?

My analysis says to put it on the user's domain, not the machine's domain. Examining the power-up and logon sequences with a network monitor, I see that the machine upon power-up certainly communicates with a domain controller so that the NT machine can essentially "log on to" its domain, but it never looks for NTCONFIG.POL. It's only when a user logs in that NTCONFIG.POL is read. Therefore, oddly enough, even though your machines may be members of one domain (often called the *resource domain*) and your user accounts are members of another domain (often called the *master domain*), *all* policies, user and machine, should go on the PDC of the user's ("master") domain.

Battling Policies: Default User versus Groups, Groups versus Users

You may have noticed when browsing to add a new username that not only can you create policies for particular users, you can also create policies for particular domain-wide groups (global groups).

How can you use group-based policies to your advantage? My colleague Clayton Johnson, another contributor to *Windows NT Magazine*, has suggested that you could create new global groups—Beginning Users, Intermediate Users, and Advanced Users—and then you could create different program folders for them. When someone starts working for your firm, you make her a Beginning User, perhaps with access to nothing more than simple e-mail and some online tutorials. Intermediate and Advanced Users would then have access to appropriately more functions. The power of this is, again, the centralizing power of system policies. Just put a user into the Beginning Users group, and upon her next reboot, she'll see whatever policies and program menus you've assigned to beginners.

That's a cool idea—thanks, Clayton, for thinking of it, and thanks, Microsoft, for system policies—but what about a conflict in policies? For example, let's return to user TESTUSER. Suppose also that I've put him into both the group Domain Admins and the group Domain Users. Further, I decide that I want to create policies that are group-wide for the Domain Admins and Domain Users groups. Adding the groups is easy—just select Edit ➤ Add Group and browse to find the group or groups that you want to add. I now have a System Policy Editor that looks Figure 17.32.

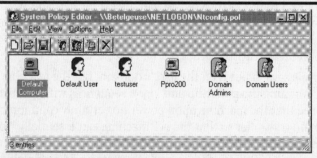

FIGURE 17.32: Adding groups using System Policy Editor

It's now possible for me to say, "Everyone in Default User's Desktop background color will be *red,* everyone in the Domain Users group will have a green background, everyone in Domain Admins will have blue backgrounds, and TESTUSER in particular will have a yellow background." TESTUSER logs on. Who wins?

The hierarchy of policies is as follows:

▶ If there's a policy that is specific to a particular user account, it predominates any group or Default User settings.

▶ If there *aren't* any policies specific to the user who is logging on, then any relevant group policies predominate any Default User settings.

▶ If there are no user-specific settings and no group settings relevant to the user who is logging on, but there are Default User settings, then the Default User settings will take effect.

Because TESTUSER has a specific policy, his background will be yellow.

Summarizing, then, user-specific settings beat group settings, which beat Default User settings. Sounds good, *except* for group-versus-group conflicts! Suppose that I've added a policy that specifically removes Network Neighborhood from the Desktops of all Domain Users and specifically *adds* it to the Desktops of all Domain Admins. (Suppose also that I had never created a user-specific policy for TESTUSER.) So TESTUSER's a member of Domain Admins, which gets NetHood, but TESTUSER's also a member of Domain Users, which *doesn't* get NetHood. Who wins?

I guessed Domain Admins, but I was wrong. As it turns out, System Policy Editor just remembers which groups it heard of *first* and gives them priority. You can control that, however, by clicking a group and choosing Options ➣ Group Priority; you'll see a dialog box like Figure 17.33.

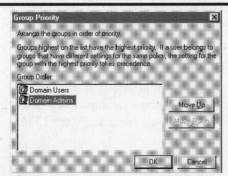

FIGURE 17.33: Group Priority dialog box

I just choose Domain Admins and click Move Up, and Domain Admins takes its rightful place in the grand scheme of things or, rather, in the grand scheme of policies.

Using Templates to Create New Policies

Let's return to a question I posed a few pages back: Why does clicking Remove Network Neighborhood from the Desktop cause a change in HKEY_CURRENT_USERS\Software\Microsoft\CurrentVersion\ Windows\Policies\Explorer? Because of *policy templates*. Rather than simply presenting a somewhat raw and sometimes cryptic set of Registry entries, the System Policy Editor uses a simple kind of programming language that allows the System Policy Editor's user to see a somewhat more friendly, explanatory interface. The files containing the programming commands are called *templates*.

Introducing the Template Language

As I said, templates are intended to make the System Policy Editor look friendlier, but "friendly" isn't the word I'd use for the programming language itself. Here's the code that you'd use to tell the System Policy Editor to produce a checkbox for Remove Network Neighborhood from the Desktop that will create an entry in HKEY_CURRENT_USERS\Software\Microsoft\CurrentVersion\Windows\Policies\Explorer. The System Policy Editor will call the entry NoNetHood and will set it to either 0 or 1:

```
CLASS USER
CATEGORY "Shell"
 CATEGORY "Restrictions"
  KEYNAME
Software\Microsoft\Windows\CurrentVersion\Policies\Explorer
    POLICY "Hide Network Neighborhood"
     VALUENAME "NoNetHood"
    END POLICY
 END CATEGORY    ; End of Restrictions category
END CATEGORY    ; End of Shell category
```

See, I *told* you it was ugly. Put these lines into an ASCII file and load them into the System Policy Editor (I'll show you how in a moment), and you'll see *just* the NetHood adjustment, as shown in Figure 17.34.

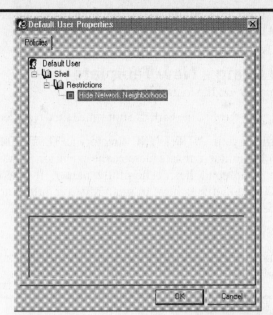

FIGURE 17.34: Changing User Properties in the System Policy Editor

Here's how the template program works. First, recall that policies are either relevant to a machine or to a user; the first line, CLASS USER, defines which it is—the alternative is CLASS MACHINE. The next two commands are CATEGORY; they define the books that you see. You can have books inside books, so each CATEGORY command is paired with an END CATEGORY command. Anything that appears on a line after a semicolon is ignored—it's a comment for *your* use, not the System Policy Editor's—and so I've added comments to clarify which END CATEGORY goes with which CATEGORY command. Note that CATEGORY really doesn't have anything to do with which Registry entries you're modifying; it's just there to allow you to define the user interface. As you've probably guessed, the labels in quotation marks after the CATEGORY command ("Shell" and "Restrictions" in the two examples you see here) are the labels that should appear in the System Policy Editor.

The next four lines, KEYNAME, POLICY, VALUENAME, and END POLICY, go together. KEYNAME and VALUENAME together define the actual Registry entry to work with. KEYNAME, as you'd guess, defines the particular Registry key that we're working with. VALUENAME is the name of the particular Registry entry. The POLICY/END POLICY pair just does some more System Policy Editor user-interface stuff, defining the Hide Network Neighborhood label.

Creating and Using a New Template

If you want to try this out, do the following steps:

1. Using Notepad, create a file with the nine lines shown earlier.

2. Save the file in your \WINNT\INF directory as TEST.ADM. (System Policy Editor template files use the extension ADM.) Check that Notepad hasn't helpfully named it TEST .ADM.TXT; I sometimes have to open My Computer and rename the file myself.

3. Start the System Policy Editor.

4. Select Options ➤ Policy Template, and you'll see a dialog box like Figure 17.35.

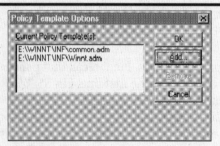

FIGURE 17.35: Adding a policy template

5. For all the files listed in the Current Policy Template(s), click the template file and then click Remove.

6. Once you've cleared out all of the existing template files, click Add and choose TEST.ADM.

7. Click OK.

8. Click File ➤ New Policy and open Default User.

You'll see the System Policy Editor showing just the Network Neighborhood policy, as in the screen shown a couple of pages back. To restore your System Policy Editor back to where it was, close the policy (File ≻ Close), open the Templates dialog box (Options ≻ Policy Template), and add WINNT.ADM and COMMON.ADM back; again, you'll find them in \WINNT\INF.

The Existing Template Files

You probably noticed that there are three ADM files: WINNT.ADM, WINDOWS.ADM, and COMMON.ADM. Why three files? Because you'll probably want to create POL files for both NT and Windows 95/98 Desktops, but the NT and Windows 95/98 Registries aren't exactly the same. Microsoft thought about what Registry entries an administrator would find useful to control as policies, and so they built these three templates to save you the trouble of having to build a template. Both the NT and Windows 95/98 System Policy Editors use the same format for their templates, however, so you can load COMMON.ADM into either System Policy Editor.

COMMON.ADM contains the Registry entries that are common to both NT and Windows 95/98. WINNT.ADM contains Registry entries that don't exist in Windows 95/98, and WINDOWS.ADM contains Registry entries that exist in Windows 95/98 but not in NT. Remember, however, that you *cannot* use the NT System Policy Editor to create a policy file that Windows 95/98 machines can understand or respond to. So, then, to summarize how you'd use the System Policy Editors and the templates to control Registries on machines in a domain:

▸ NT computers respond to a file that is named NTCONFIG.POL.

▸ Windows 95/98 computers respond to a file called CONFIG.POL.

▸ You must create NTCONFIG.POL using the NT version System Policy Editor, which ships with NT Server. Load the WINNT.ADM and COMMON.ADM templates, as well as any templates you've defined, to help you create an NTCONFIG.POL. NTCONFIG.POL must be stored on the NETLOGON share on the PDC of your users' domain.

▸ You must create CONFIG.POL using the Windows 95/98 version System Policy Editor, which you can install from the Windows 95/98 CD-ROM; you'll find it in ADMIN\APPTOOLS\POLEDIT. (Not all Windows 95/98 CDs contain this file, but most do. If yours doesn't have it, then you'll definitely find it in the Windows 95/98 Resource Kit.) Load the WINDOWS.ADM and COMMON

.ADM templates, as well as any templates you've defined, to help you create a CONFIG.POL. CONFIG.POL must also be stored on the NETLOGON share on the PDC of your users' domain. Windows 95/98 will ignore policies unless the user explicitly logs on to the domain.

▶ Remember that policy files are read when *users* log on, not when machines start up, so put the policy files into the NETLOGON share of the *users'* domain's PDC.

Building a Template to Enable a WINS Proxy

I've demonstrated how the template language allows us to control the NoNetHood Registry parameter, but in truth that's not all that useful, as Microsoft has already *done* that work for us. How about a more useful example?

If your network is based on the TCP/IP protocol (and if it's not, start using TCP/IP—Windows Server 2000 will require it), and if you have a mix of computer types, then some of the computers on your network may have trouble finding others on the network. You can help them out by installing a *WINS proxy server* on each network segment. First, it's a good idea to designate one machine per segment as a WINS proxy server. It doesn't take much CPU power, so virtually any machine can serve in the role. Second, under Windows 3.*x* and NT 3.*x*, it was easy to make a machine a WINS proxy server through the Control Panel, but this is no longer the case. Windows 95/98 and NT 4 machines can act as proxy servers if instructed to via their Registries, but there's no way through the user interface to adjust the Registry entry that controls it, the EnableProxy entry in HKEY_LOCAL_MACHINE\System\Current-ControlSet\Services\NetBT\Parameters. It's of type REG_DWORD; if its value is 0, which is the default, then the machine isn't a proxy server; if it's 1, then it's a proxy server.

Anyway, suppose I want PPRO200 to be my WINS proxy server for its segment. Again, I could walk over to the machine and modify its Registry, but let's create a system policy. The template would look like the following:

```
CLASS MACHINE
CATEGORY "WINS proxy"
KEYNAME System\CurrentControlSet\Services\NetBT\Parameters
    POLICY "Make this computer a WINS proxy server"
    VALUENAME "EnableProxy"
    END POLICY
END CATEGORY
```

All I did there was basically copy what I did before for NoNetHood, and then change these items:

► It's a machine entry, so it goes under CLASS MACHINE rather than CLASS USER.

► I didn't use a category inside a category; I just created a single-level category called "WINS proxy".

► The name of the key that I wanted to control is HKEY_LOCAL_MACHINE\System\CurrentControlSet\Services\NetBT\Parameters, but as I've already said it's a machine entry, I didn't need the HKEY_LOCAL_MACHINE; the result is on the KEYNAME line.

I then loaded this template and applied the policy to a machine on my network called PPRO200. The next time someone logged on and the machine had been rebooted, the machine became a WINS proxy agent.

Programming More Complex Entries

Thus far, we've seen REG_DWORD entries whose values are only 0 or 1. But how do you set up the System Policy Editor to offer you one of several options? For example, you'll read later that you can reduce network chatter by introducing a setting to all of your NT Workstation machines: Just modify the entry MaintainServerList in HKLM\System\Current-ControlSet\Services\Browser\Parameters, setting it to No. The result is that when your domain is holding network elections to determine who will be the master browser, the workstations won't take part in the election, reducing the number of candidates and thus reducing network chatter. (Again, don't worry so much about the details; I'm just using this as an example.)

Setting up a MaintainServerList policy will be a bit more complex than the policies we've looked at so far, so we'll have to delve further into the template programming language. I can't document every possible command in the template language here, but if you need to do something fancy with the System Policy Editor, look to the existing ADM files for examples. As far as I know, the only time that Microsoft has documented this was in the Windows 95 Resource Kit; I can't find it in the NT Workstation or NT Server Resource Kit.

In addition to No, `MaintainServerList` can also accept values of Auto or Yes. Auto, the default value for NT workstations, means, "I'm willing to be the master browser if necessary." Yes means, "Not only am I willing to be a browser, but I'd like my machine to be a preferred candidate to be a browser." Yes gives a small edge to that machine during the election. As you've probably guessed, `MaintainServerList` is of type REG_SZ. Previously, I set up a checkbox with the System Policy Editor, which the System Policy Editor translates into (1) use REG_DWORD and (2) if checked, store a value of 1 and if unchecked, store a value of 0. `MaintainServerList` is a bit different—first, it uses REG_SZ values; and, second, it should respond to only a few particular values (Yes, No, and Auto). How do you get the System Policy Editor to offer only three options?

If you want the System Policy Editor to offer anything but the most basic checkboxes, you need to create what it calls a *part*. A part allows you to define in some detail what kinds of values a user can give to a System Policy Editor item. Here's how you'd set up `MaintainServerList`:

```
CLASS MACHINE
CATEGORY "Browser Elections"
 KEYNAME System\CurrentControlSet\Services\Browser\Parameters
 POLICY "Can this machine act as the master browser?"
  PART "Possible options:" DROPDOWNLIST REQUIRED
   VALUENAME "MaintainServerList"
   ITEMLIST
    NAME "Do not ever act as a browser" VALUE NO
    NAME "Prefer PC selected as a browser" VALUE YES
    NAME "Willing to be a browser if necessary" VALUE AUTO
   END ITEMLIST
  END PART
 END POLICY
END CATEGORY
```

Much of this looks familiar: the CLASS, CATEGORY, KEYNAME, POLICY, and VALUENAME commands. But notice that between POLICY and VALUENAME comes PART. PART defines the user-interface component that the System Policy Editor should use to offer options to a user: CHECKBOX for a simple checkbox, NUMERIC for a single value that should be a number, EDITTEXT for a single value that should be textual information, COMBOBOX for a single value with suggested possible values, or DROPDOWNLIST for a single value with only a few possible legal values. The REQUIRED keyword means, "Don't accept this policy unless the user picks a value, and don't take null or blank as an option."

Once you've chosen DROPDOWNLIST, you must specify the list of possible legal values; that's what the ITEMLIST/END ITEMLIST group does. Each NAME line lets you specify labels that the user will see, like "Do not ever act as a browser," along with the corresponding value to store in the Registry. Create a template like that, and the System Policy Editor will look like the one shown in Figure 17.36.

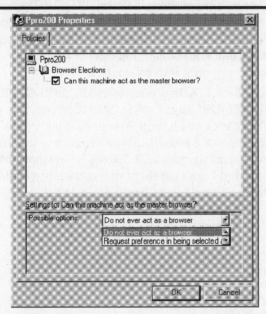

FIGURE 17.36: Using parts to offer a limited number of values

What if those labels need to correspond to numeric values? Suppose the possible legal values of MaintainServerList were ̄1, 0, and 1 rather than No, Yes, and Auto. How would you tell the System Policy Editor to save those values? With just one extra parameter on VALUE, VALUE NUMERIC. The ITEMLIST would then look like this:

```
ITEMLIST
  NAME "Do not ever act as a browser" VALUE NUMERIC -1
  NAME "Prefer PC selected as a browser" VALUE NUMERIC 0
  NAME "Willing to be a browser if necessary" VALUE NUMERIC 1
END ITEMLIST
```

Part ii

Allowing Numeric Inputs   Sometimes you'll need to create a policy that affects a numeric Registry entry that ranges from some minimum to some maximum. Use a NUMERIC part for that; they look like:

```
PART label NUMERIC DEFAULT value MIN value MAX value SPIN
value REQUIRED
```

Here, DEFAULT, MIN, and MAX specify the default value, the minimum allowable value, and the maximum allowable value. REQUIRED again means that the user must specify a value, or the System Policy Editor should not store the policy. SPIN tells the System Policy Editor what increments to use for the numeric spinner; you can use the default value of 1, or you can disable the spinner with a value of 0.

For example, you can tell a PDC how often to update its BDCs with an entry in HKEY_LOCAL_MACHINE\System\CurrentControlSet\ System\Netlogon\Parameters named Pulse. Pulse says how often in seconds to communicate with BDCs; the minimum allowed value is 60 (one minute) and the maximum is 172,800 (48 hours; that's what the documentation says, but I can't say that I've tested it). You could create a policy to allow administrators to easily modify Pulse, like so:

```
CLASS MACHINE
CATEGORY "PDC-BDC updates"
 KEYNAME
System\CurrentControlSet\Services\Netlogon\Parameters
 POLICY "Frequency of user data updates"
  PART "Time interval in seconds:" NUMERIC
  MIN 60 MAX 172800 DEFAULT 600
   VALUENAME "Pulse"
  END PART
 END POLICY
END CATEGORY
```

This *ought* to work, but it doesn't, due to a bug in the System Policy Editor: it can't handle an integer larger than 32767. If that number looks odd, it shouldn't: it's the largest integer (well, okay, the largest *signed* integer, an integer that can take either a positive or negative value) that can fit into 16 bits. Unfortunately, most Registry numeric values have *32* bits to play with, so whoever programmed the System Policy Editor to only handle 16 bits in Windows 95 was seriously derelict in his or her job. The bottom line is that if you want to create a policy with a numeric value, it'll work best if you keep the value under 32767. So if you want to do the above example, change 172800 to 32767, and it'll work. Once you do that, the System Policy Editor looks like Figure 17.37.

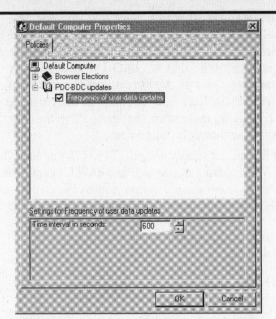

FIGURE 17.37: Using parts to allow numeric inputs

One other bug you'll run into is that the System Policy Editor won't let you punch in a value larger than 9999. In the `Pulse` example above, you could specify `MIN 60 MAX 32767 DEFAULT 600`, but you'd actually have to lean on the spinner buttons (those are the little buttons with the upward-facing and downward-facing triangles) to get to 32767. By my calculations, on a Pentium Pro 200 that takes about 35 minutes. Hmmm, perhaps a `DROPDOWNLISTBOX` would be a better answer here...

Sometimes you'll just want your users to punch in a numeric value, and don't want to show them the spinners; in that case, add the parameter `SPIN 0`, which makes the spinners disappear. Alternatively, you may want to keep the spinners but have them increment by, say, 100 with each click; you can do that with the parameter `SPIN 100`. That would modify the PART statement above to look like:

```
PART "Time interval in seconds:" NUMERIC MIN 60 MAX 32767
DEFAULT 600 SPIN 100
```

Allowing Free-Form Text Input   We've seen checkboxes, text input restricted to a few options, and numeric input, but how can you create a policy that allows the user to type in any old text that she likes? For example, you've probably noticed that if you click Help ➢ About on any

Part ii

screen, you get the name and organization name that someone typed in when he or she installed NT on the computer. Can you change that? Can you force the organization name to be consistent across all computers? Sure. It's in the Registry key HKEY_LOCAL_MACHINE \Software\ Microsoft\Windows NT\CurrentVersion, with the entry name RegisteredOrganization. It's a REG_SZ, and you can type in any old thing. Let's build a policy that makes sure that every PC in the company uses Acme Technologies as the organization name.

The part type we'll need is a simple one, EDITTEXT. It can have the REQUIRED and DEFAULT parameters, as well as a MAXLEN parameter. So, for example, if we wanted to set the maximum length of Registered-Organization to 80 characters, we'd build a template like the following:

```
CLASS MACHINE
CATEGORY "General Information"
 KEYNAME "Software\Microsoft\Windows NT\CurrentVersion"
 POLICY "Setup info"
  PART "Organization name:" EDITTEXT MAXLEN 80
   VALUENAME "RegisteredOrganization"
  END PART
 END POLICY
END CATEGORY
```

Notice that we had to use quotation marks in the KEYNAME line. That's because there was a space in the key's name. You can see what it looks like in Figure 17.38.

I hope you've learned three things here:

▶ You can create a wide array of templates to allow you to control the Registry entries of systems throughout your network.

▶ The language is a bit obtuse, but not impossible to master.

▶ You'll have to be ready to do a fair amount of experimentation, because the System Policy Editor and templates are a bit buggy.

But before you get *too* heady a rush at the prospect of controlling everything from your desktop, recall that system policies *cannot* modify any Registry entries of type REG_MULTI_SZ.

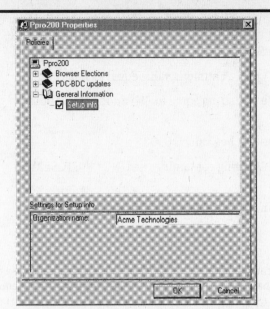

FIGURE 17.38: Using parts to allow free-form text input

Another Example: Assigning Mapped Drives with Policies

Here's another great application of system policies, and it illustrates how you can start from a Registry entry and use system policies to propagate user configurations.

Suppose you want a given user upon logon to see a drive V: connected to \\BIGSERVE\COOLDATA—how would you accomplish this? You can use logon batch scripts to assign this drive; just add this line to the logon batch script:

```
Net use v: \\bigserve\cooldata
```

But a little poking around in the Registry shows that once you've mapped a drive, it appears in your user profile. Under HKEY_CURRENT_USER, you'll find a key called Network, which contains a key for each drive letter. The keys are named F for the mapped F: drive, V for the mapped

V: drive, and so on. Thus, if I'd mapped my V: drive to \\BIGSERVE\ COOLDATA, I'd find (after logging off and then on) a key HKEY_CUR-RENT_USER\Network\V. It contains these value entries:

ConnectionType   A numeric value equal to 1.

ProviderName   A string equal to "Microsoft Windows Network".

ProviderType   A hex value 20000.

RemotePath   A string containing the UNC (\\BIGSERVE\ COOLDATA).

UserName   Another string with my name (ORION\MarkM).

NOTE

A bit of experimentation shows that UserName works just as well with a blank value. That's probably because when the user tries to use the V: drive and NT's security system asks, "Who are you?" the user's workstation simply replies with the user's name. One could imagine a case when you'd want to attach under another name, but not often.

Let's see how to make this a policy. The first question is, does this go in USER or MACHINE? Simple—we found the Registry entry in HKEY_ CURRENT_USER, so it's CLASS USER. We'll have a key Network\V, because that's the name of the key with the drive mapping information.

This template item will have five value entries in it, four of which we don't want to have to fill in—ConnectionType, ProviderName, ProviderType, and UserName—because we already know what values they're supposed to take. Rather than hard-wiring RemotePath to \\BIGSERVE\COOLDATA, let's allow an administrator to tailor this to her needs. So it would be neat if we could build a template that essentially says, "If you enter a UNC for the V: drive, then I'll automatically also fill in these four other value entries." You can, with a thing called ACTIONLISTON. It's best explained in the template itself, which follows.

```
CLASS USER
CATEGORY "Map Drive V:"
   POLICY "Map drives"
   KEYNAME "Network\V"
     ACTIONLISTON
        VALUENAME ConnectionType   VALUE NUMERIC 1
        VALUENAME ProviderName     VALUE "Microsoft Windows
Network"
```

```
        VALUENAME ProviderType    VALUE NUMERIC 131072
        VALUENAME UserName        VALUE ""
     END ACTIONLISTON
     PART "Drive V:" EDITTEXT
        VALUENAME RemotePath
     END PART
    PART "Enter the UNC path." TEXT END PART
    END POLICY
  END CATEGORY
```

The one thing here that may be a bit odd-looking is the numeric value 131072; where did that come from? Again, recall that the original value for ProviderType was 20000, but that was a hex value, and policies want decimal. A few mouse clicks in Calculator convert 20000 hex to 131072 decimal.

Notice how the ACTIONLISTON part works. Between ACTIONLISTON and END ACTIONLISTON, I just specify some value entries and their desired values. When the associated part—the EDITTEXT part—is used, the items in the ACTIONLISTON group just "wake up."

Home-Grown Zero Admin Windows: Locking Down a Desktop

Let me just wrap up this section on locking down a Desktop with Registry entries and system policies with a set of policies that you can use today to greatly simplify both the user interface that your users see and your support task. Microsoft has been working on some very powerful tools that will allow you to centrally control Windows Desktops, a project the developers call Zero Administration Windows (ZAW), but you needn't wait for that. You can do some pretty amazing things right now.

Open up the System Policy Editor using the standard WINNT.ADM and COMMON.ADM templates; you don't need to build any custom templates. Then enact the following policies, all of which are user policies rather than machine policies.

In Shell/Restrictions   Remove Run command from Start menu, remove folders from Settings on Start menu, remove Taskbar from Settings on Start menu, remove Find command from Start menu, hide drives in My Computer, hide Network Neighborhood, and hide all items on Desktop.

Part ii

`System/Restrictions`   Run only allowed Windows applications (and name them, of course).

`Windows NT Shell/Custom Folders`   Create a folder, as you learned earlier in this section, containing shortcuts to the programs that you want the users to be able to access.

`Windows NT Shell/Restrictions`   Remove File menu from Explorer (if you've allowed Explorer in the first place), remove common program groups from Start menu, disable context menus for the Taskbar, and disable Explorer's default context menu.

`Windows NT System`   It's just personal taste, but I disable the "Show welcome tips at logon" setting.

Remember that you've got to come up with a completely standard set of locations for program files across the enterprise, or your users won't be able to get to their applications. And a final piece of advice: make these policies specific to a group, not to Default User, or you'll have a domain that you can't do any administration from!

WHAT'S NEXT?

This chapter showed you how to set up and manage users through User Manager for Domains and how to control users' Desktops with Registry entries and system policies. The next chapter introduces Microsoft Exchange Server, which lets users work together in a variety of productivity-enhancing ways.

Chapter 18

INTRODUCING EXCHANGE

Microsoft's Exchange client/server electronic messaging system is a major player in what I call the "e-messaging decade." It lets people work together in a variety of productivity-enhancing ways. The Exchange system is one of the most exciting, innovative, and promising software products I've ever seen. I can't wait to get started, so let's go to it.

EXCHANGE AND THE E-MESSAGING DECADE

Electronic messaging is more than e-mail. It is the use of an underlying messaging infrastructure (addresses, routing, and so on) to build applications that are based on cooperative tasking, whether by humans or computers. We can expect the years 1996 to 2005 to be the decade of electronic messaging *(e-messaging)*, store-and-forward-based messaging systems and real-time interactive

Adapted from *Mastering™ Microsoft® Exchange Server 5.5* by Barry Gerber

ISBN 0-7821-2237-X   912 pages $44.99

technologies will complement each other to produce wildly imaginative business, entertainment, and educational applications with high payoff potential.

Microsoft's Exchange Server will play a key role in e-messaging. Exchange Server is one of the most powerful, extensible, scalable, easy-to-use, and manageable e-messaging back ends currently on the market. Combined with Microsoft's excellent Exchange clients, Internet-based clients from other vendors, and third-party or home-grown applications, Exchange Server can help your organization move smoothly and productively into the e-messaging decade.

This chapter introduces you to the Exchange client/server system. We start with a quick look at several of the neat ways you can use Exchange for e-mail and more, then focus on some of Exchange's key characteristics and capabilities.

By the way, when I use the word *Exchange* or the words *Exchange system* from here on, I'm talking about the whole Exchange client/server system. *Exchange Server* means just the server product, and an *Exchange server* is any computer running the Exchange Server product. *Exchange client* refers to any client that lets you access all or some of the features of Exchange Server, for example, Microsoft's stable of Exchange clients. *Exchange client* does not refer to general-purpose clients like IMAP4 or POP3 clients or Internet browser–based clients that provide limited access to Exchange Server's features. When I talk about these, I'll use their commercial or generic names or both, for example, *the Eudora POP3 client*. Got that? Okay, explain it to me.

Exchange Applications

I dare you not to get excited about e-messaging and Exchange as you read this section. Just look at what's possible and imagine what you could do with all of this potential.

E-Mail Is Only the Beginning

Together, Exchange Server and its clients perform a variety of messaging-based functions. These include e-mail, message routing, scheduling, and supporting several types of custom applications. E-mail is certainly a key feature of any messaging system. And the Schedule+ 7.5 or Outlook Calendar client that comes with Exchange Server is far and away better than previous versions of Microsoft's appointment and meeting–scheduling software. (Figure 18.1 shows the Exchange and Schedule+ clients for Windows in action.) Take a look at Figures 18.2, 18.3, 18.4, and 18.5 for a glimpse of the new Internet-based POP3, IMAP4, Web browser, and full Exchange client–Microsoft Outlook. Outlook is the recommended e-mail client to use with Exchange 5.0 and Exchange 5.5 Servers. Finally, take a look at Figure 18.6 to see how Outlook's Calendar handles your schedule.

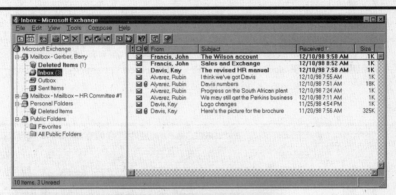

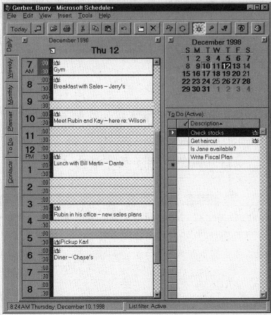

FIGURE 18.1: The Exchange and Schedule+ clients for Windows

FIGURE 18.2: Qualcomm's Eudora Pro 3.0 POP3-compliant client accesses mail stored on an Exchange server.

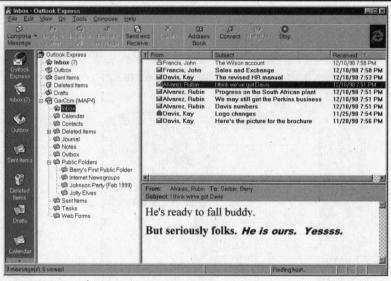

FIGURE 18.3: Microsoft's Outlook Express IMAP4 client function accesses messages and folders on an Exchange server.

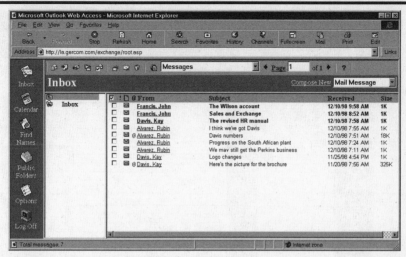

FIGURE 18.4:   Microsoft's Internet Explorer 4.0 Web browser accesses mail
stored on an Exchange server.

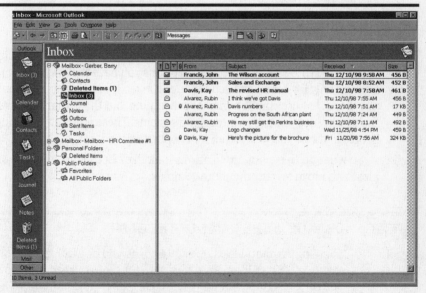

FIGURE 18.5:   Microsoft's Outlook client for Exchange Server accesses mail
stored on an Exchange server.

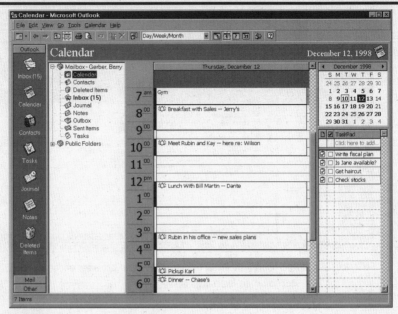

FIGURE 18.6: Microsoft's Outlook client for Exchange Server accesses a schedule stored on an Exchange server.

E-mail clients are exciting and sexy, but to get the most out of Exchange, you need to throw away any preconceptions you have that messaging packages are only for e-mail and scheduling. The really exciting applications are not those that use simple e-mail or scheduling, but those that are based on the routing capabilities of messaging systems. These applications bring people and computers together for cooperative work.

So what do these hot applications look like? Let's start with the simplest and move toward the more complex.

CHANGE IS THE NAME OF THE GAME

Some of the marvelous user interfaces you see in Figures 18.1 through 18.6 may look very different by the time you read this book. Software development and marketing, especially in the world of electronic communications, is running at hyperspeed. Updates and even major revisions hit the market at a breakneck pace. The Internet makes it even easier for vendors to market and deliver their

CONTINUED ➞

wares. New pieces and parts of applications appear almost daily for manual or totally automatic download and installation.

The basic architecture of Exchange Server and its clients are unlikely to change much over the next couple of years. The outward appearance of user interfaces is likely to change dramatically. As far as Exchange goes, plan for change as a way of life. Keep an open mind and at least one eye on Microsoft's Internet pages.

In the long run, all of this hyperactivity will prove a good thing. Our requirements will find their way into, and bugs will find their way out of, products faster. I will admit, however, that I sometimes long for the days of yearly or less-frequent updates on low-density $5^1/_4$-inch floppies.

Just a Step beyond Mail

You're probably familiar with e-mail *attachments*—those word processor, spreadsheet, and other work files you can drop into messages. Attachments are a simple way to move work files to the people who need to see them.

Sure, you could send your files on floppy disk or tell people where on the network they can find and download the files. But e-mail attachments let you make the files available to others with a click of their mouse buttons: They just double-click an icon, and the attachment opens in the original application that produced it (if your correspondent has access to the application, of course).

Using attachments has the added advantage of putting the files and accompanying messages right in the faces of those who need to see them. This leaves less room for excuses like "Oh, I forgot" or "The dog ate the floppy disk."

As great as attachments can be, they have one real weakness: The minute an attachment leaves your Outbox, it's out of date. If you do further work on the original file, that work is not reflected in the copy you sent to others. If someone then edits a copy of the attached file, it's totally out of sync with the original and all other copies. Getting everything synchronized again can involve tedious hours or days of manually comparing different versions and cutting and pasting them to create one master document.

Exchange offers several ways to avoid this problem. One of the simplest is the *attachment link:* Instead of putting the actual file into a message, you put in a link to the file (see Figure 18.7), which can be stored anywhere on the network. The real kicker is that the file can also be stored in Exchange public folders. (More about these later.) When someone double-clicks an attachment link icon, the linked file opens. Everyone who receives the message works with the same linked attachment. Everyone reads and can modify the same file.

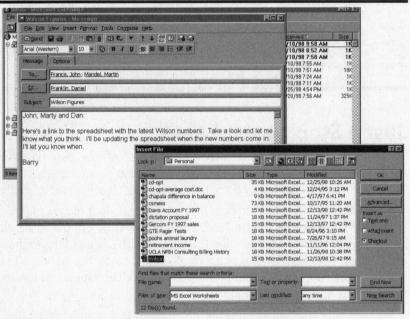

FIGURE 18.7:   Exchange links keep attachments alive.

Off-the-Shelf Messaging-Enabled Applications

Here's another way to guard against dead work files: Microsoft Windows enables messaging in many word processor and spreadsheet applications. For example, when you install the Exchange client on your computer, Microsoft's Office products like Word and Excel are e-messaging enabled. You can select Send or Route options from the applications' File menu;

this pops up a routing slip. You then add addresses to the slip from your Exchange client's address book, select the routing method you want to use, and assign a right-to-modify level for the route. Finally, you ship your work off to others with just a click of the Route button.

Figure 18.8 shows how all of this works. Though it's simple, application-based messaging can significantly improve user productivity and speed up a range of business processes.

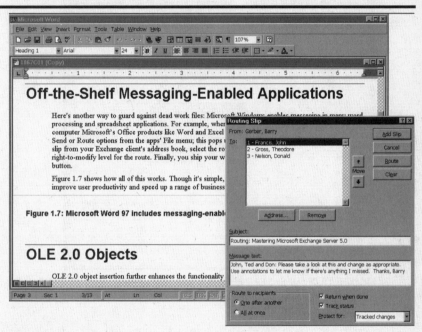

FIGURE 18.8:   Microsoft Word 97 includes messaging-enabled Send and Route functions.

OLE 2 Objects

OLE 2 object insertion further enhances the functionality of the Exchange messaging system. Take a close look at Figure 18.9. Yes, the message includes an Excel spreadsheet and chart. The person who sent the message simply selected Object from the Insert menu that appears on every Exchange message. The Exchange client then inserted a blank Excel spreadsheet into the message as an OLE 2 object. Having received the message, we can see the spreadsheet as an item in the message, as shown in Figure 18.9.

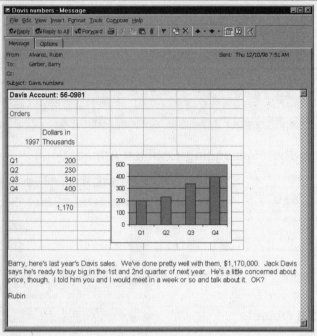

FIGURE 18.9:   With OLE 2 objects, sophisticated messaging-enabled applications are easy to build.

When we double-click the spreadsheet, Excel is launched, and Excel's menus and toolbars replace those of the message (Figure 18.10). In essence, the message becomes Excel.

The Excel spreadsheet is fully editable. Though Excel must be available to your recipients, they don't have to launch it to read and work on the spreadsheet. Even if your recipients don't have Excel, they can still view the contents of the spreadsheet, though they won't be able to work on it. (That is, even if they don't have the application, they can still view the object when they open the message.)

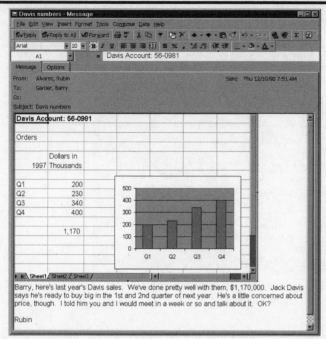

FIGURE 18.10: Double-clicking an OLE 2-embedded Excel spreadsheet in a message enables Excel menus and toolbars.

Electronic Forms

Exchange Server 4.0, 5.0, and 5.5 come with the Exchange Forms Designer that is based on Microsoft Visual Basic. You can use the Forms Designer to build information-gathering forms containing a number of the bells and whistles you're used to in Windows applications. These include dropdown list boxes, checkboxes, fill-in text forms, tab dialog controls, and radio buttons.

The Forms Designer, which is easy enough for nontechnical types to use, includes a variety of messaging-oriented fields and actions. For example, you can choose to include a preaddressed To field in a form, as shown in Figure 18.11, so users of the form can easily mail it off to the appropriate recipient. Once you've designed a form, it can be made available to all or selected users, who can access the completed form by simply selecting it while in an Exchange client or Outlook. Forms designed in

Outlook (32-bit client) will not work in the Exchange client (16-bit client), but forms designed in the Exchange client will work in Outlook.

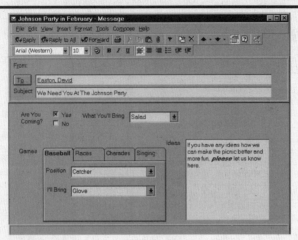

FIGURE 18.11:   Electronic forms turn messages into structured information-gathering tools.

Exchange 5.0/5.5 is compatible with the Outlook Forms Designer. This Visual Basic script–capable application opens many new doors, especially when linked with Exchange 5.0/5.5's groupware-enabling server scripting features.

Applications Built on APIs

If all of this functionality isn't enough, you can go to the heart of Exchange Server and use its Application Program Interface (API). Exchange Server supports both the Simple and Extended versions of Microsoft's Windows-based Mail Application Program Interface (MAPI). It also supports the X.400-oriented, platform-independent Common Mail Call (CMC) APIs, which have functions similar to those of Simple MAPI (an Exchange client). Using Simple MAPI or CMC, you can build applications that use e-messaging addresses behind the scenes to route data between users and programs. Extended MAPI (an Outlook client) lets you get more deeply into Exchange's storage and e-messaging address books to create virtually any messaging-enabled application you can imagine.

These custom-built applications may involve some level of automation, such as regular updates of your company's price lists for trading partners or sending a weekly multimedia message from the president to employees at your organization. Building applications based on MAPI or CMC requires someone with programming skills in languages like Visual Basic or C++.

Applications Using Exchange Public Folders

Exchange Server supports both private and public folders. When a user creates a public folder, it is actually a private folder; to make it public, the Exchange Server administrator must "unhide" it. Both kinds of folders can hold messages and any kind of computer application or data file. Private folders are the place where Exchange users store and manage their messages and files. Public folders are for common access to messages and files. Files can be dragged from file access interfaces, like Explorer in Windows 95/98 and NT 4, and dropped into private or public folders. If you begin thinking of private and public folders as a messaging-enabled extension of Explorer, you'll have a fairly clear picture of Microsoft's vision of the future in regard to how an operating system organizes and displays stored information.

You can set up sorting rules for a private or public folder so that items in the folder are organized by a range of attributes, such as the name of the sender or creator of the item or the date the item arrived or was placed in the folder. Items in a private or public folder can be sorted by conversation threads. Private and public folders can contain applications built on existing products, such as Word or Excel, or created with Exchange or Outlook Forms Designer, server scripting, or the API set. In public folders, where they are accessed by many people, items can replace the tons of maddening paper-based processes that abound in every organization.

If all of this isn't already enough, Exchange is very much Internet-aware. With Exchange 5.x, you can publish all or selected public folders on the Internet, where they become accessible with a simple Web browser. You can limit Internet access to public folders to only those who have access under Exchange's security system, or you can open public folders to anyone on the Internet. Just think about it: Internet-enabled public folders let you put information on the Internet without the fuss and bother of Web site design and development. Any item can be placed on the Internet by simply adding a message to a public folder. Figure 18.12 shows a public folder–enabled price list for the one product produced by my favorite fictitious company, GerCom.

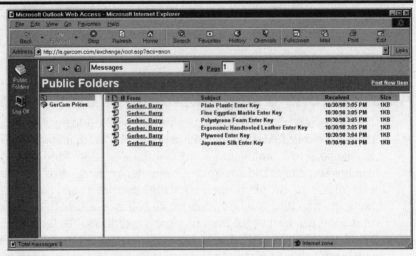

FIGURE 18.12:   Using Exchange public folders to publish a price list on the Internet

Before we leave public folder applications, I want to mention one more option. Exchange Server 5.0 and later lets you bring any or all of those devilishly delightful Usenet Internet newsgroups to your public folder environment. With their Exchange clients, users then can read and reply to newsgroup items, just as though they were using a standard newsgroup reader application. Exchange Server comes with all the tools you need to make it so. All you need is an Internet connection, access to a newsfeed provider, and a set of rules about which groups to exclude. Remember, this is where some infamous newsgroups live.

SOME EXCHANGE BASICS

It's important to get a handle on some of Exchange's key characteristics and capabilities. Once you do, you'll better appreciate the depth and breadth of Microsoft's efforts in developing Exchange. In this section, we'll take a look at:

- ▶ Exchange as a client/server system

- ▶ The Exchange client

- ▶ Exchange Server's dependency on NT Server

- ▶ Exchange Server's object orientation

▶ Exchange Server scalability

▶ Exchange Server security

▶ Exchange Server and other e-messaging systems

Exchange as a Client/Server System

The term *client/server* has been overused and overworked. To put it simply, there are two kinds of networked applications: shared-file and client/server.

Shared-File Applications

Early networked applications were all based on *shared-file* systems. The network shell that let you load your word processor from a network server also allowed you to read from and write to files stored on a server. At the time, it was the easiest and most natural way to grow networked applications.

Microsoft Mail for PC Networks is a shared-file application. You run Windows, OS/2, DOS, or Macintosh front ends, which send and receive messages by accessing files on a Microsoft Mail for PC Networks "post office" (a post office is the share) that resides on a network file server. The front end and your PC do all the work; the server is passive. Figure 18.13 shows a typical Microsoft Mail for PC Networks setup.

Easy as it was to develop, this architecture leads to some serious problems in today's networked computing world:

▶ Changing the underlying structure of the server file system is difficult, because you have to change both the server and the client.

▶ System security is always compromised, because users must have read and write permissions for the whole server file system, which includes all other users' message files. Things are so bad that a naive or malicious user can actually destroy shared-file system databases in some cases.

▶ Network traffic is high, because the client must constantly poll the server's file system for user messages.

▶ Because the user workstation acts directly on shared files, these can be destroyed if workstation hardware or software stop functioning for some unexpected reason.

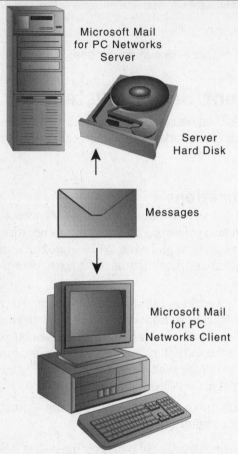

FIGURE 18.13: Microsoft Mail for PC Networks is a typical shared-file e-messaging system.

Shared-file applications are in decline. Sure, plenty of "legacy" (that is, out-of-date) applications will probably live on for the data-processing equivalent of eternity, but client/server systems have quickly supplanted the shared-file model. This is especially true in the world of e-messaging.

Client/Server Applications

Today, more and more networked applications are based on the client/server model. The server is an active partner in client/server applications. Clients tell servers what they want done, and if security requirements are met, servers do what they are asked.

Processes running on a server find and ship data off to processes running on a client. When a client process sends data, a server receives it and writes it to a database. Server processes can do more than simply interact with client processes. For example, they can compact data files on the server or—as they do on Exchange Server—automatically reply to incoming messages to let people know, for instance, that you're going to be out of the office for a period of time. Figure 18.14 shows how Exchange implements the client/server model.

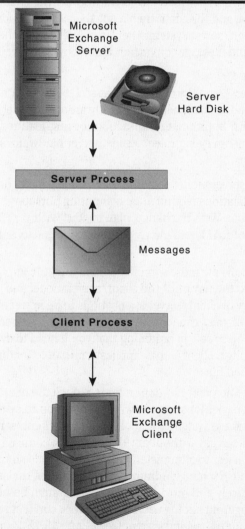

FIGURE 18.14: Microsoft Exchange is based on the client/server model.

Client/server applications are strong in all of the areas in which shared-file applications are weak:

▶ Changing the underlying structure of the server file system is easier than with shared-file systems, because only the server processes access the file system.

▶ System security can be much tighter, again because only the server processes access the file system.

▶ Network traffic is lighter, because the server informs the client that mail has arrived, and the client then reads the message from the database; in client/server systems there is no polling. All the work of file access and message conversion is done by the server, on the server.

▶ Because server processes are the only ones that access server data, breakdowns of user workstation hardware or software are less likely to destroy data. With appropriate transaction logging features, client/server systems can even protect against server hardware or software malfunctions.

As good as the client/server model is, it does have some general drawbacks. Client/server applications require more computing horsepower, especially on the server side. With Exchange, plan to start with very fast Pentium machines, a lot of RAM, and plenty of hard disk capacity—and expect to grow from there.

Client/server applications are more complex than shared-file applications. This is partly due to the nature of the client/server model and partly due to the tendency of client/server applications to be newer and thus filled with all kinds of great capabilities you won't find in shared-file applications. Generally, you're safe in assuming that you'll need to devote more resources to managing a client/server application than to tending a similar one based on shared files.

The good news is that Microsoft has done a lot to reduce the management load and to make it easier for someone who isn't a computer scientist to administer an Exchange system. I've looked at many client/server messaging systems, and I can say without any doubt that Exchange Server is absolutely the easiest to administer. Exchange Server's administrative front end, called the Exchange Administrator, organizes the management processes very nicely and provides an excellent system based on a GUI for doing everything from adding users and network connections to assessing the health of your messaging system (see Figure 18.15).

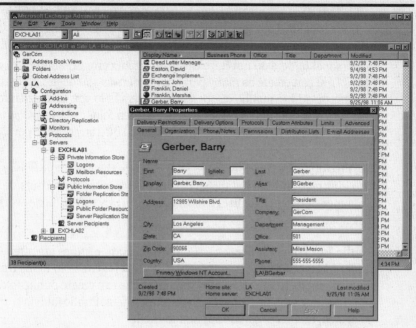

FIGURE 18.15: The Exchange Administrator makes management easier.

A Quick Take on the Exchange Client

As should be clear from our look at some of its applications earlier in this chapter, the Exchange client is the sexy part of Exchange. It's where the action is—the view screen for the backroom bits and bytes of Exchange Server. You can't implement an Exchange system without the clients, so let's discuss some client basics.

Information Storage

The client stores information in one of two places: private or public information stores. Each has a different purpose and function.

Private Information Stores   Though you can share them with others, private information stores generally hold items that you and you alone have access to. There are two basic kinds of private information stores: mailboxes and personal folders. You access mailboxes and personal folders using an Exchange client.

Mailboxes can send and receive messages. You can add folders to a mailbox to help you organize your messages. If you have the rights to other mailboxes, you can open them in your Exchange client as well.

Personal folders do not have the send and receive capabilities of mailboxes. You can create as many personal folders as you desire. Like the folders you add to mailboxes, personal folders help you organize information. You can drag and drop messages between folders. Using *rules* (discussed shortly), you can direct incoming mail into any of your personal folders.

The contents of mailboxes are stored inside the Exchange Server private information store database. Personal folders are stored outside Exchange Server on the user's local machine (private) or on networked disk space.

Public Information Stores   Public information stores are often called *public folders*. Let's use that term here. Public folders hold items that you want others to see. Users whom you authorize can create public folders and drag and drop anything they wish into them. Public folders can also be nested, and rules can be applied to them.

Public folders are stored inside the Exchange Server public information store database. They are key to the organization-wide implementation of Exchange. Some, all, or none of an Exchange server's public folders can be automatically replicated to other Exchange servers. This lets you post items to public folders on one Exchange server and have them quickly and painlessly appear on any combination of the Exchange servers in your system. Even without replication, users throughout your organization can access public folders.

Sharing Information

You can share information with others by sending it to them or placing it in public folders for them to retrieve on their own. You can drop messages, word processor documents, and other work files—even whole applications—into public folders. You can use public folders to implement many of the kinds of applications I talked about at the beginning of this chapter.

For example, instead of electronically routing a draft word processor document to a bunch of colleagues, you can just drop it into a public folder. Then you can send e-mail to your colleagues asking them to look at the document and even to edit it right there in the public folder.

Organizing Information

Creating a set of personal and public folders and dropping messages in them is a simple way to organize information. More sophisticated approaches include the use of rules, views, and the Exchange client's Finder.

Rules As a user, you can set up a range of *rules* to move mail from your Inbox into personal or public folders. For example, you might want to move all the messages from your boss into a folder marked URGENT. Rules can be based on anything from the sender of a message to its contents. Because Exchange is a client/server system, rules run on the Exchange server, so the Exchange client doesn't need to be running for your rules to execute (unless the rules involve personal folders).

Views Exchange messages can have numerous attributes. These include the obvious, such as sender, subject, and date received, as well as less common information, including sender's company, last author, and number of words. You can build views of messages using any combination of attributes and any sorting scheme. Then you can apply a particular view to a folder to specially organize the messages it contains.

The Finder You can use the Exchange Finder to search all folders or a single folder for messages from or to specific correspondents, messages with specific information in the subject field or message body, and even messages received between specific dates or of a specific size.

Exchange Server's Dependency on NT Server

Exchange Server is a component of the Microsoft BackOffice suite. Like Microsoft's SQL Server and Systems Management Server, Exchange Server runs only with NT Server. It won't run on top of NT Workstation or Windows 95/98; even though both are 32-bit operating systems, they can't host Exchange Server.

Figure 18.16 shows one of my NT Server/Exchange server desktops with some NT Server and Exchange management applications running.

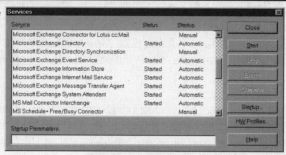

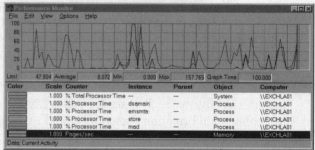

FIGURE 18.16:   NT Server and Exchange

NT Server is chock-full of features that make it an especially attractive operating system. One of these is its very usable and functional implementation of Microsoft's domain-based security system. Domains have names—one of mine is called LA for my hometown, Los Angeles—and include NT servers, NT workstations, and all flavors of Windows- and DOS-based machines. Though there are a number of domain security models, the general rule is that the members of a domain can use any resource they have been given permission to use—disk files, printers, and so on—in the domain without having to enter a password for each. Exchange Server depends on NT Server domain security for a good deal of its security.

Exchange Server's Object Orientation

Exchange is a classic example of an *object-oriented* system. Take another look at Figure 18.15. See all those items on the tree on the left-hand side of the Exchange Administrator menu, such as GerCom, LA, EXCHLA01, EXCHLA02, and Recipients? Each of these is an *object*. Each object has attributes and can interact with other objects in specific ways. Exchange objects can hold other objects, serving as what Microsoft calls *containers*.

GerCom is the name of the fictitious organization I created; it is the equivalent of a company name like IBM or TRW. (People often ask if I'm related to the baby-food Gerbers. I'm not, but GerCom at least lets me dream. Want to buy some stock?) Microsoft refers to this object as *the organization*. The GerCom organization contains all of the objects below it.

LA is the name of a physical site in the GerCom corporate hierarchy, Los Angeles. It is also a home for Exchange servers. The GerCom/LA hierarchy has two servers, named EXCHLA01 and EXCHLA02.

The Recipients object way down at the bottom of the hierarchy is a container for Exchange Server recipients. *Recipients* are objects that can send or receive messages. Among other things, recipients include user mailboxes and distribution lists (a distribution list allows a user to e-mail one name and have that message copied to many people). Each recipient object can contain a large number of attributes. The tabbed Properties dialog box in Figure 18.15 should give you some idea of the breadth of attributes that can be assigned to a mailbox.

Notice that the Recipients container is a part of the LA site hierarchy. *Sites* are the most important containers in Exchange. They hold configuration information about recipients and how to reach them, as well as information about servers and other Exchange objects. This information is stored in what Microsoft calls the *Exchange Server directory*. Though specific instances of the directory are stored on the servers in a site, any instance of the directory actually contains information about all of the servers in an organization.

Object orientation makes it easy for Microsoft to distribute Exchange Server's functionality and management, and it makes it easy for you to administer an Exchange Server environment. For example, based on my security clearances, I can manage any set of recipients—from those in only a single site to all of the recipients in my organization.

Exchange Server Scalability

Exchange Server scales very well both vertically and horizontally. NT Server runs on top of computers based on single and multiple Intel and DEC Alpha processors, so it's very easy to scale an Exchange server upward to more powerful hardware when increased user loads make additional computing power necessary. Since you'll be taking both Exchange Server and NT with you, you really won't have to learn much more about your new machine than the location of its power switch.

If vertical scalability isn't what you need, horizontal scaling is also a breeze with Exchange Server. You can set up a new Exchange server and quickly get its directory and public folders in sync with all or some of your other servers. You can even move mailboxes between Exchange servers in a site with a few clicks of your mouse.

How do you know if it's time to scale up or out? Microsoft has an answer for this, too: You can use the LoadSim application included with Exchange Server to simulate a range of different user loads on your server hardware. By analyzing the results of your LoadSim tests, you'll get some idea of the messaging loads you can expect a server to handle in a production environment.

Exchange Server Security

Exchange Server security starts with NT Server's security system. Several different NT security models are available; the one that's right for you depends mostly on the size and structure of your organization and the department that supports Exchange Server. In all cases, the idea is to select a security model that puts the lightest burden on users and system administrators while still appropriately barring unauthorized users from messaging and accessing other system resources.

NT Server also audits security. It can let you know when a user tries to add, delete, or access system resources.

The security of Exchange Server is enhanced in several ways beyond the NT operating system's security. Access to Exchange Server objects such as public folders can be limited by the creator of the folder. Data encryption on the server and client protects messages and other Exchange resources from eavesdropping by those with server, workstation, or Internet access. Digital signatures prove the authenticity of a message. Even traffic between servers can be encrypted.

Exchange Server and Other E-Messaging Systems

The world of e-messaging is far from a single-standard nirvana. A good e-messaging system must connect to and communicate with a variety of other messaging systems. Microsoft has done a nice job of providing Exchange Server with key links, called *connectors,* to other systems. The company has also built some cross-system message-content translators into Exchange Server that work automatically and are very effective. With these translators, you're less likely to send a message containing, say, a beautiful embedded image that can't be viewed by some or all of the message's recipients.

In the case of Microsoft's legacy messaging systems—Microsoft Mail for PC Networks and Microsoft Mail for AppleTalk Networks—you have an option beyond connectivity. You can choose to migrate users to Exchange. Migration utilities for other messaging systems like Lotus cc:Mail are also provided with Exchange.

X.400

A fully standards-compatible X.400 connector is built into Exchange Server and can be used to link Exchange sites. The 1984 and 1988 standards for X.400 are supported. The connector also supports attachment to foreign X.400 messaging systems.

SMTP

As with the X.400 connector, a Simple Message Transport Protocol (SMTP) connector is built into Exchange Server; unlike the old Microsoft Mail for PC Networks SMTP gateway, it is a full-fledged system capable of relaying messages and resolving addresses, while supporting several Enhanced SMTP (ESMTP) commands. UUencode/UUdecode and MIME (Multipurpose Internet Mail Extensions) message-content standards are also supported. So, once you've moved your users from Microsoft Mail for PC Networks to Exchange, you won't hear any more of those vexing complaints about the meaningless MIME-source attachments that users get because the SMTP gateway was unable to convert them back to their original binary format.

Microsoft Mail for PC Networks

A built-in connector makes Microsoft Mail for PC Networks 3.x (Microsoft Mail 3.x) post offices look like Exchange servers to Exchange clients and vice versa. If connectivity isn't enough, you can transfer Microsoft Mail 3.x users to Exchange with a supplied migration tool. If all of this is too much, Exchange clients can directly access Microsoft Mail 3.x post offices. So you can keep your Microsoft Mail 3.x post offices, at least until you have Exchange Server running the way you want and have moved everyone off of the legacy mail system.

Part ii

Microsoft Mail for AppleTalk Networks

Connectivity for Microsoft Mail for AppleTalk Networks systems is also provided by a connector built into Exchange. When connectivity isn't enough, Mail for AppleTalk users can be migrated to Exchange Server.

cc:Mail

If Lotus cc:Mail is running in your shop, you'll be happy to hear that Exchange 5.x comes with tools to connect and migrate users to Exchange. Never let it be said that Microsoft doesn't care about users of IBM/Lotus products. At least there's a way to pull them into the Microsoft camp.

Lotus Notes

Exchange 5.5 adds a connector for Lotus Notes. With this connector, Exchange and Notes clients can see each other's address directories and exchange mail.

Other Messaging Systems

Gateways are or will be available for links to other messaging systems such as PROFS, SNADS, fax, and MCI Mail. Both Microsoft and third parties will build and support these networks. You can even extend the benefit of these gateways to your Microsoft Mail users.

WHAT'S NEXT?

In this chapter, you learned about some of the things you can do with Exchange and had a look at some key aspects and characteristics of the system. NT Server's security features have been mentioned in this and previous chapters. The next two chapters focus on security. Chapter 19 provides an overview of security basics and approaches to security.

Chapter 19

SECURITY CONCEPTS AND TERMINOLOGY

S ecurity is one of the most critical areas of networking and yet one of the most commonly overlooked. Many companies build huge networks and use them for years before they start worrying about security, and they are usually prompted to do so only after a devastating security breach has taken place.

In this chapter, security basics and some common security approaches are examined, as are the policies your company should establish for dealing with security. Finally, the security features of NT Server and other common operating systems are compared.

Adapted from *NT 4® Network Security, Second Edition* by Matthew Strebe, Charles Perkins, and Michael J. Moncur

ISBN 0-7821-2425-9   976 pages $49.99

SECURITY DEFINED

When you hear the term *security*, you probably think of two basic ideas: protection and peace of mind. Network security is the sum of all measures taken to prevent loss of any kind, and when correctly implemented, it ensures both protection and peace of mind. Securing your network requires coordination of a wide variety of security measures—from creating user accounts, to hiring loyal employees, to keeping the server in a locked room.

Security is a continual process. You cannot apply only the security measures known at the time you install your Web server, lock it in a secure room, and assume that no one will ever find a bug in the operating system or server software that can be exploited. You must stay aware of new security issues that come up with the operating system and application software you use and then apply new security measures constantly. The following sections describe some basic categories of network security.

NOTE

The security categories described in this chapter aren't necessarily the only components of network security. On the contrary, there are some extremely specific types of security that are complex enough to fill a book of their own. The following sections describe the basic types of security that apply to most networks.

Logon Security

In a secure network, the first thing a user encounters is a prompt for a username and password. This is the network's first defense against security problems. To use a secure building as an analogy, this is like having a security guard or electronic lock at the building's door. While these measures don't prevent problems entirely, they do ensure that you'll know who was in the building (or the network) and when and that unauthorized users can't enter.

Unfortunately, no logon security system is flawless. Users can choose easy-to-guess passwords, write their passwords down in obvious places, or share passwords. NT provides various methods you can use to avoid these problems.

TERMINOLOGY

Account   A record containing (at least) a username and password you create to give a user access to the network (or to a single machine). Along with the name and password, an account includes other information about the user, such as groups the user belongs to and directories and files the user can access.

Hackers   People who makes it their business to break into networks they have no right to access. Hackers range from teenagers looking for a challenge to foreign operatives looking for information. The word *hacker* originally referred to someone who was simply good with computers, but it is now much more widely used with this negative connotation.

Intruders   A general term for people who attempt to log into a system without proper authorization. Intruders can be hackers, corporate spies, disgruntled former employees, or simply ordinary employees who've forgotten their passwords.

File System Security

Users log in to a network for one main reason: to access files and directories on the server. *File system security* controls which files each user is able to access. Users can have rights to any number of files and directories, and each has a specific list of rights. For example, a user may have full rights in one directory (read files, create files, erase files, and so on) and read-only access in another directory.

In securing the files on the network, you should be sure to account for both files on the server and files on the local workstation. This is more difficult than it sounds. Many client operating systems, such as DOS and Windows 95/98, have few security features. The best solution is to encourage (and require) users to save their files on a server.

NOTE

Windows 95 and Windows 98 are no different from the point of view of security. Windows 98 is the same operating system as Windows 95 with a few updates and features added—few of which relate to security and none of which actually manage to improve Windows 95's serious security flaws. FAT32, the version of the FAT file system included in Windows 95 OS revision 2 and Windows 98, does not have additional security features.

DOS, Windows 3.*x*, Windows 95/98, and NT can all use the FAT file system. This system hasn't changed much since the early versions of DOS (except for improvements to storage capacity and efficiency) and, as you might expect, it isn't very secure. While there are ways of increasing the security of FAT files, the best approach is to use a more secure file system. NT supports the NTFS (NT File System) system, which fully supports security.

Data Communication Security

Another aspect of security has to do with data communication. Data traveling through the network includes sensitive information, such as confidential files. File system security isn't useful unless the network traffic between the workstation and the server is also secure.

It's possible to gain unauthorized access to information by monitoring the traffic through the network, unless care has been taken to secure the data. In addition to preventing unauthorized access to the wires and devices that make up the network, securing data also includes the use of encryption (encoding the data at one end and decoding it at the other to make it useless to anyone who intercepts it). Figure 19.1 illustrates how a secure communication system might work.

FIGURE 19.1:   Secure data communication is accomplished by using encryption.

While communication security is a relatively minor issue on local area networks, it is more of a concern with larger networks. When a network is connected to the Internet, this type of security becomes critical.

Administration

Another aspect of security is the administration of your network. If your network is small (one building and 50 or fewer users), chances are there's a single administrator. In this case, that one administrator will handle all aspects of security. In a larger network, which may include hundreds of users and span multiple locations, it's necessary to divide the workload.

In addition to giving users access to files and network services, you can also give them the ability to act as administrators.

There are many ways to distribute the administrative duties for a network. As a simple example, you could assign an administrator for each company location. More complex arrangements can include naming specialized administrators, such as a file system administrator or Internet gateway administrator.

A large and complex network can have an entire hierarchy of administrators. You may even allow branch administrators to further subdivide administration by granting administration abilities to other users.

TIP

By default, NT includes a user account called Administrator, which is given full administrative privileges. You can use this account to create other administrators.

Auditing

Returning to the building analogy, note that many companies use videotaped security cameras. While these can't prevent a problem when it happens, they are valuable after the fact: They give you a record of what happened, who did it, and when. In network security, *auditing* performs a similar monitoring function.

NT's auditing feature can automatically log certain events when they happen. For example, you might want to know which users access a certain file. You can examine the log file later to determine if there is unauthorized access.

You can turn on auditing for various features with the User Manager for Domains utility's Audit Policy option. This dialog box is shown in Figure 19.2.

Depending on the level of security (and risk) in your network, you may wish to leave auditing turned on all of the time, or you may want to depend on it only for certain files, certain directories, or certain users. You can also turn on auditing after a security problem has occurred, in the hope of obtaining more information when the problem occurs again.

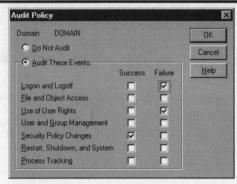

FIGURE 19.2: The Audit Policy dialog box in the User Manager for Domains utility allows you to control auditing.

Physical Security

Of course, even the most secure server is only as safe as the building—and the room—it's in. The term *physical security* means the security of the machines themselves. Your network's security can easily be compromised by a workstation or server left logged in and unattended, or even by someone physically stealing a machine.

WARNING

There is one general rule when it comes to physical security: If someone can physically access your server, they can cause trouble.

REALITY CHECK: OUT IN THE OPEN

When I worked as a network consultant, I visited a company to train their IS department in managing and securing their NetWare server. I arrived to find that the server was stored inconspicuously next to the copier and coffee machine.

The server console required a password to access, but that wouldn't stop a determined intruder. (Not to mention the potential consequences of spilled coffee!)

Human Security

Another important aspect of security deals with the most chaotic element in the network: the users. Human security encompasses many issues, from unauthorized break-ins, to training users, to avoiding security breaches.

Since users are the heart of the network, human security overlaps with many other types of security, and a network with a human security problem is not likely to be secure in other areas.

PLANNING A SECURITY APPROACH

When you plan the security of your network, you can take one of two basic approaches:

- ▶ In the *optimistic approach*, you initially give all users access to everything, then explicitly deny access to critical information.

- ▶ In the *pessimistic approach*, you initially restrict access to everything, then explicitly enable access to needed information.

Each of these approaches has its advantages, as you'll see in the following sections. Of course, you may use an approach that falls somewhere between these two, or use different approaches for different parts of the network. Following the discussion of the optimistic and pessimistic approaches, we'll look at security policies you should create to document your security approach.

The Optimistic Approach

The optimistic approach is the easiest way to go, at least from an administrative standpoint. At an extreme, you could use the ultimate optimistic approach: All users get access to everything. This requires very little administration; as a matter of fact, NT defaults to this approach.

The disadvantages of too much optimism are obvious. In all but the smallest networks, it's hard to think of every conceivable problem when you set up a user. Therefore, this approach tends to result in *corrective security*; that is, each new security improvement is made to address a security breach that has already happened.

Network administrators who use the optimistic approach often fall into the trap of relying on *security through obscurity*. In other words, they assume that if a directory is buried a few levels deep in the file system, or if you need to know complex DOS or UNIX commands to access the information, the data is reasonably safe. Needless to say, it usually isn't. When a network's administration is that casual, there's a good chance that one of the users knows more than the administrator.

WARNING

Another trap of the optimistic approach is to assume that users won't harm data unless they have a motive. Unfortunately, well-meaning users are just as capable of causing trouble as hackers and corporate spies.

Of course, it's possible to use the optimistic approach without going to extremes. If you have relatively few items that are confidential, this can be the best choice. For example, users in a small company wear many hats—the same secretary might need to access accounts payable, accounts receivable, and general ledger data. In this situation, the optimistic approach works well. Most users need to access most areas, and critical areas—such as payroll data—can be secured.

The Pessimistic Approach

By contrast, the pessimistic approach requires a great deal of time and effort to administer. Each user starts out with no access, and you carefully add access for each specific need. Every time a user gains new responsibility or changes jobs, you'll find yourself making changes to the account.

Obviously, this approach requires a commitment to administration; and since many IS departments are understaffed, this is not a popular choice. However, it is widely used in situations where security is critical, such as in government offices and in banking, healthcare, and other highly regulated industries.

There is a distinct advantage to the pessimistic approach: It allows you to avoid most security problems, including problems you haven't thought of yet. This makes it a very appealing choice for anyone concerned with security. While a strict pessimistic approach may not be practical in your organization, you should consider using some elements of this approach, or using it for areas of your network that require high security.

NOTE

One situation where you'll definitely want to use the pessimistic approach is in any system that is accessible through the Internet. While users in your company may not be obsessed with breaking your security, you can be assured that someone on the Net is.

Security Policies

Keeping a secure network requires organization—a sloppy approach will inevitably result in security holes. To ensure that the security on your network is effective, you should create a document that specifies the exact security features in use and their configuration. Ideally, you should plan and create a policy when you're planning and installing the network in the first place.

Your security policy should be clearly documented, and it should be agreed upon by management and the IS department. You may even want to post it or distribute it to employees (perhaps on a company intranet) so everyone knows their role in the security of the company and its data.

A security policy should clearly state the following:

- ► Your organization's basic security approach (optimistic or pessimistic) and the portions of the network that are exceptions to the rule

- ► Details of all aspects of security, including physical and human security

- ► What access is required for each employee or group of employees

A network security policy should be part of a bigger plan that includes security for the building itself, the telephone system, and other aspects of the company.

Along with the policies you create to manage your company's security, there is another type of policy. NT includes several options called *policies* that allow you to configure the basic rules for securing your network. For example, the Account Policy dialog box (see Figure 19.3) includes options for password requirements, minimum password length, and other items related to user accounts. Your policy documentation should include values for each of NT's policy options.

Part ii

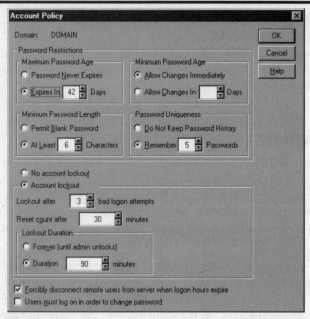

FIGURE 19.3:   NT's Account Policy dialog box includes options related to user accounts and passwords.

NOTE

See Chapter 17 for more information about creating policies to control user accounts.

OPERATING SYSTEMS AND SECURITY

Of course, many of the security capabilities of your network depend on the operating system you're running it on. The operating systems available today for network servers and workstations have vastly different approaches to security and vastly different features.

Because you're reading an NT book, you're probably most concerned with the security features of NT. However, unless your network is very well planned (or very small), there's a good chance you're also running one or more other operating systems. To give you an idea of how they compare, the following sections briefly describe the security approaches of today's common operating systems.

NT

Although NT was originally intended to replace Windows (and it still may someday), it has evolved into a platform for reliable network servers.

There are many similarities between NT Workstation and NT Server. The main difference is in what the software license allows you to do (and the price). NT Server is usually the platform of choice for servers, so users expect more from it in terms of security.

Although NT was designed with security in mind, it wasn't widely used for networking at first, and it was plagued with security problems. Microsoft has improved its security significantly, but there are still security holes. Nevertheless, it is possible to run a very secure system using NT; all it takes are the latest security fixes from Microsoft and some well-planned strategies.

REALITY CHECK: AN UNEXPECTED BENEFIT FROM HACKERS

At the time of this writing, Microsoft is getting some unwanted help in finding security flaws in NT. It seems that several groups of hackers have devoted themselves to finding security holes in NT and demonstrating them by attacking a rather popular NT server: Microsoft's own Web server.

I can't really say that this is a good thing—but then again, I've never seen Microsoft release security fixes so quickly in the past. Microsoft calls these updates "hot fixes," and they're available on the Web at: http://support.microsoft.com/support/.

Windows 95/98

You may have noticed that there are no books on Windows 95/98 security. There's a simple reason for this: Any such book would consist of a few pages describing Windows 95/98's security features and a few pages listing all of the reasons why you should use NT instead.

Windows 95/98's operation is limited to the FAT file system, which does not include any security features to speak of. When Windows 95/98 files are shared across the network, they use a simple password scheme with limited security.

Because of these and other limitations, you should not use Windows 95/98 for applications that require security. Of course, Windows 95/98 can be used for client workstations in an NT network with little security risk—provided your users save their files on the server rather than a local hard drive, log out whenever they leave the console, and don't log in as a member of the Administrators group over the network.

Unix

Like NT, Unix was plagued with security problems in its early days. Unix wasn't really developed with security in mind. As a matter of fact, the creators of Unix initially developed it so that they would have a platform to play games on. Despite its origins, Unix is now the most widely used system for Internet servers, and it is widely considered secure.

The reason Unix is considered more secure than NT is simple: It's been around longer. Unix was created in 1969 and since then has been the preferred victim for hackers everywhere. Because of this, developers of the various Unix systems have rushed to keep up, plugging security holes as the hackers found them.

Despite its maturity, Unix still has security problems. Although it's possible to make an extremely secure Unix system by carefully configuring features and installing security fixes, many administrators don't have the time or budget to maintain a completely secure system.

Unix systems are still the most commonly broken into systems on the Internet. While these incidents occasionally involve a newly discovered security flaw, the vast majority exploit the old security holes. Information on exploiting these holes is widespread in the hacker community, and it's common for hackers to attack machine after machine until they find one with an unplugged security hole.

NetWare

NetWare, from Novell Inc., was the original dedicated network operating system. Novell's operating system products are based on the pessimistic approach. Although it's losing ground to NT, NetWare remains a widely used network operating system. The latest version, NetWare 5 and Novell's Directory Services, uses TCP/IP and other industry standards such as DNS and DHCP.

Unlike NT, NetWare uses a vastly different operating system on the server than the one it uses on workstations. The NetWare server is a dedicated machine with a simple text-based user interface. Most of the administration can be performed from a DOS or Windows workstation.

NetWare has included security features from the beginning, and it has been around for nearly 20 years. So as you might expect, it's one of the more secure systems. The latest version's security is comparable to NT's level of security. Nevertheless, it does have its vulnerabilities.

One major security advantage of NetWare had been its use of the Internetwork Packet Exchange (IPX) protocol, which is not compatible with TCP/IP. The protocol incompatibility made it difficult to accidentally expose your server to the Internet without having your security set up correctly. The new version of NetWare fully supports TCP/IP and is now much easier to subvert from the Internet.

DOS and Windows 3.x

The first version of DOS was developed by Microsoft engineers working with only one goal: to finish an operating system before IBM came up with one of its own. DOS has evolved through the years, with version 6.22 the last official release. Microsoft has ceased further development of DOS as a distinct operating system, although Windows 95/98 is still based on a version of DOS.

DOS was never intended as a network operating system, of course, and security wasn't much of a concern. DOS uses the non-secure FAT file system, and isn't really equipped to deal with multiple users.

Windows 3.x is a shell that runs on top of DOS, and doesn't really improve security. Although basic networking features are included (notably in the network-specialized version, Windows for Workgroups), these are fundamentally intended as client operating systems and don't even attempt to be secure.

What's Next?

This chapter provided an introduction to security. The next chapter provides more details about NT Server's security features, including file system security, logging and auditing, and Microsoft TCP/IP security. It also discusses some security-related items to consider when installing NT Server and IIS (Internet Information Server).

Chapter 20

NT Server Operating System Security

This chapter covers the internal security features of the NT operating system. You'll learn about the NT security model, the role of domains, and security for users and groups. You'll also learn how to set user permissions and resource-sharing permissions, as well as how to establish security audit trails and how to review the NT event logs.

Implementing and maintaining user and group accounts and other security elements are some of the most overlooked aspects in managing a network computing system. Begin with the premise that any user of your Web site is a potential intruder, and design your checks and balances accordingly.

Adapted from *Mastering™ Microsoft® Internet Information Server™, Second Edition* by Peter Dyson

ISBN 0-7821-2080-6   848 pages $39.99

A LITTLE HISTORICAL BACKGROUND

Maintaining the security of a computer system has long been a priority. Initially, that control was required for inter-department billing for computer services in a company. Today, security from intruders requires serious attention, especially if you are connecting to the Internet.

System security on Microsoft networks has evolved proportionately, and Microsoft has had the advantage of being a relatively new player in the network operating system market. There were literally hundreds of proposals, trials, errors, modifications, and enhancements over the years that Microsoft developers could analyze carefully as they designed the foundations for the security systems built into NT Server. As a result, NT is one of the most secure and robust operating system platforms on the market today.

Microsoft's first major operating system, MS-DOS, contained absolutely no security features. In fact, no version of MS-DOS has ever had any significant security features. The first security mechanisms for Windows systems were actually not provided by Microsoft but by the manufacturers that made network operating systems to connect computers running Windows.

Not until the development of Windows for Workgroups did Microsoft begin to include even the slightest security, and it was implemented when you installed Microsoft's NetBEUI networking software. In this situation, a user received a logon name and password combination and a workgroup name, and those computers in the same workgroup could share disk drives and printers—really not much security at all compared with the security features found on other network operating systems.

Real security became a major design focus for NT 3.1, and NT 4 has even more advanced security features. If you are installing NT and Internet Information Server (IIS), read this chapter carefully, and take the necessary steps to secure your Web site and server. Without security, your server can become a playground for malicious intruders.

AN OVERVIEW OF NT SECURITY

Although the NT security model involves several components, it is an integral subsystem that affects the entire operating system and makes it easy to control security on a number of servers. The security subsystem controls access to resources, known as *objects*. Within this subsystem is the NT version of a domain. An NT domain is a collection or association of servers and has nothing to do with Internet domains.

A domain is a workgroup with centralized security control; a server is designated as the PDC or, in some cases, as a BDC, and these servers act as security administrators for all the objects within the domain.

Security in NT also extends to the user and the file level; you can say that user A can only read file B, whereas user C can both read and write file B. The users belong to user groups. Each user or group of users can have varying rights to objects and to the operation of the network. NT security provides event auditing and detailed logging and allows you to monitor the access and use of objects on your network.

The NT security model includes these components: Local Security Authority, the Security Account Manager, and the Security Reference Monitor. Each component is an integral part of the overall security model, and here is what each one does.

▶ The Local Security Authority (LSA) ensures that users requesting access to resources do in fact have the correct permissions.

▶ The Security Account Manager, commonly referred to as the SAM, maintains the actual user account database, which contains all the permissions and rights for users and groups belonging to a domain. The SAM provides user validation services to the LSA.

▶ The Security Reference Monitor (SRM) ensures that a user or a process has permission to access an object and determines that whatever action the user is attempting to perform is actually allowed in that user's security profile. The SRM enforces access validation and any audit generation policies that the LSA has defined.

NT DOMAINS EXPLAINED

An NT domain is a group of one or more controllers, servers, and workstations, along with the associated users and objects. A domain is a purely logical grouping of computers and has nothing to do with their physical arrangement; members of a domain can be connected on the same local area network or can be scattered to the four corners of the earth, connected by high-speed communication links. An *object* is any information made available for use on the network. You can also think of an object as a resource. When you share an object, it becomes a shared resource.

A domain is controlled by an NT server that is installed and configured as a PDC or BDC. You must designate an NT server as a domain controller when you install and configure NT Server.

WARNING

If you install NT as a stand-alone server, and not as a domain controller, you must reinstall NT if you change your mind later and want that server to be a domain controller.

Domain controllers provide security for access to objects, including objects in other NT domains. Domain controllers in the same domain share security policies information and user account databases and can be configured to allow access to other NT domains and their resources through *trust relationships*. Other NT servers on the network can join the domain and share their objects with the domain. Within a domain, the network administrator creates one user account for each user; this account specifies user information, group memberships, and security policy information. The user can then log on to the domain once, using one password, rather than logging on to each server in the domain in turn.

Several NT domain models are available when you design your network. Selecting the right model for your network depends on your requirements and how you need to secure access; so plan carefully.

TIP

The Windows NT Resource Kit has a nice little tool called the Domain Planner that can assist you in designing your network's domains.

When you load TCP/IP on NT, you define a TCP/IP domain name, also called an Internet domain name. Do not confuse this domain name with the NT domain name. They are two separate names; one is for TCP/IP, and one is for NT. This also holds true for the host name and the server name. The NT server name is completely different from the TCP/IP host name.

Overall, the NT domain structure allows a network to be designed so that users and resource objects can be created, grouped, and controlled in a reasonable fashion.

To complete this discussion of NT domains, we need to introduce another Microsoft concept: the *workgroup*. A workgroup is a collection of computers (not a collection of users) that do not belong to a domain. Within a workgroup, each computer tracks its own user and group account information and does not share this information with other workgroup computers, which is in sharp contrast to domain controllers.

THE ADVANTAGES OF USING DOMAINS

Using domains has several important advantages, including the following:

▶ A domain has a single password, and that password grants access to all the resources in the domain that you have authorization to use.

▶ This password is user-specific and can be administered by an individual user. Thus, network administrators can assign particular file or printer access permissions to individual users.

This idea of the domain is the fundamental building block upon which NT networks are constructed.

LOOKING AT USER SECURITY

The NT domain—including users, groups, and resources—is administered by a user who has the authority to do so, usually the system administrator. Generally, the first step after setting up a NT server is to rename the Administrator account (anyone who is familiar with NT knows the default username for the system administrator is Administrator) and then to add another user account for yourself and/or the network administrator. After you add the basic user account, add the user ID to the NT Administrators group.

Adding an Administrator

Adding a user to the Administrators group gives the user the authority of an Administrator—the user can configure all aspects of NT security. An important reason for adding a user to the Administrators group is that it creates an *audit trail*, a mechanism for tracking all the security settings the user changes. If you simply use the Administrator logon ID and share the password with numerous users, you have no way of telling who actually made changes.

Guest User Accounts

Now that you understand the importance and use of the Administrator account and the Administrators group, I'll mention one other important aspect of security—the Guest user account. When NT Server is initially installed, it adds two user accounts by default. One is the Administrator account, and the other is the Guest account. You cannot delete, disable, or remove the Administrator account; thus, it is impossible to lock yourself out of the network by accidentally deleting or disabling all the administrative accounts.

During the installation procedures, you are asked to define a password for the Administrator account; however, you are not asked to define a password for the Guest account. The installation process establishes this account with a predefined password, and the account is disabled by default. Thus, no one can log on with this user account.

WARNING

It is usually best to leave the Guest account disabled until you have a genuine need to enable it. Be sure to verify that it is in fact disabled.

User security is important when installing IIS because anonymous access to the services actually uses the authority of a user account, which by default is called IUSR_*MACHINE_NAME* (*MACHINE_NAME* is the computer's name). For example, if the computer name is MARKETING, the anonymous user account is IUSR_MARKETING.

User security is managed by a network administrator, who creates an account for each user of the domain that needs network resources. NT generates a unique security ID for each user account, and that unique ID is stored with the user's permissions and rights as part of that user's profile. When a user attempts to log on, the SAM checks the logon information against the user information in the user accounts database and attempts to authenticate the logon.

Global and Local User Accounts

The NT security model has two types of user accounts: global and local. This arrangement is similar to that of global and local user groups; however, the parameters of user groups are somewhat different from the parameters of user accounts.

On computers running NT Server, user accounts that are not domain controllers are global user accounts. Global users are authenticated by the PDC or BDCs or through the trust relationships established with other NT domains.

Local user accounts fully participate in a domain through a remote logon. Don't be confused here by the phrase "remote logon." Remote doesn't always mean logging on through a dial-up or other distant communications link. In this instance, a user with a remote logon is "remote" from the domain. In other words, the workstation and user do not belong to any domain other than the domain to which the user account is being added. Thus, any user that is a local user and not a global user must be authenticated by the NT server on which that account is being created. Such a user cannot be authenticated through a trust relationship with another domain.

For example, in a network composed of one or more NT domains, one or more Windows workgroups, perhaps a UNIX system, and maybe even a Novell NetWare network, member users are considered local users and are subject to local user limitations.

New User Accounts

In NT Server, the User Manager for Domains is the administrative tool used to control user accounts, groups, and security policies for domains and computers on the network. The network administrator uses it to do the following:

- ▶ Create, modify, or delete user accounts in the domain
- ▶ Define a user's desktop environment and network connection
- ▶ Manage the domain's security policies
- ▶ Manage the relationships among domains on the network
- ▶ Add logon scripts to user accounts

Part ii

NOTE

See Chapter 17 for details about adding new users through User Manager for Domains.

Along with many other options for new users, you can define their environment profile and dial-in connections. In the New User dialog box (displayed in User Manager for Domains by selecting User ➤ New User), click on the Profile button to bring up the User Environment Profile dialog box, as shown in Figure 20.1.

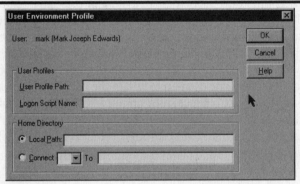

FIGURE 20.1: The User Environment Profile dialog box

In this dialog box, you define the following settings that can be very useful in managing users:

User Profile Path   Fill in this text box to define a user profile for the user account by typing its full path and filename. A user profile is a file that contains all the user-specific desktop and program settings needed to define a user's environment. The system loads these settings, which are identified by username, as the user logs on. Local user profiles are created the first time that a user logs on and are always available for that user in the future. Roaming user profiles, specified here by a complete path and filename, are downloaded each time the user logs on and are updated with changes when the user logs off. Mandatory user profiles are created by the administrator and cannot be changed by the user. When the user logs off, the user profile is not saved, and the local profile is not copied to the server.

Logon Script Name   Fill in this text box with the name of a command file or a batch file that runs on the client machine when this user logs on if a logon script is being used.

Local Path   Click this radio button, and then in the text box, to define a modified path for the files and programs for this user. This path to the user's home directory becomes the default path for File Open and Save As dialog boxes.

Connect To   Click this radio button to select a network drive and path from the drop-down list box as the local path instead of using the Local Path setting.

NT Server provides domain-based security for RAS users. To allow mobile users to connect from a remote system, click the Dialin button in the New Users dialog box. When you click this button, NT displays the Dialin Information dialog box, shown in Figure 20.2.

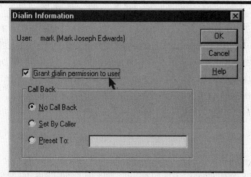

FIGURE 20.2:   The Dialin Information dialog box

In this dialog box, you specify whether and how a user can dial in to the network. The options are as follows:

Grant Dialin Permission to User   Check this checkbox to give the user access to the network via a dial-in connection.

Call Back   Use the three selections in this part of the dialog box to specify how a user can connect to the server.

▶ Click the No Call Back radio button to ensure that the user is connected immediately with no call back. This option offers no additional security and is a poor choice for most installations.

▶ Click the Set by Caller radio button, and the dialin server calls the user back at a number the user has defined once the user's account has been validated. This option also offers little in the way of security, but it is one way for mobile users to avoid running up large telephone bills.

▶ Click the Preset To radio button and enter a phone number in the text box. This is the only secure option of the three available. It is useful for mobile users who always call in from the same number. After the user calls in and the account is validated, the RAS server breaks the connection and then calls the user back at the preset number. If a user tries to call in from a different number, he or she won't be able to make the connection.

UNDERSTANDING GROUP SECURITY

NT user groups categorize users according to privileges and rights; a *user group* is a set of users who all have identical network rights. NT predefines several groups, a feature you will find beneficial. The most important group is the Administrators group. Users in this group have complete control over the domain security and certain hosts on the network; so be careful which users you assign to it.

NOTE

In a nutshell, using groups eases the management of assigning access to the various resources on the network. User groups can be a powerful tool in administering user security and control over your NT domains.

You can also define your own groups and assign them the privileges and rights you choose. For example, you have installed some accounting software on your server, and you want only certain users to have access to that shared directory. You can create an Accounting group and then add the users you want to it. Now, instead of manually giving each user permission to access the share, you simply give the accounting group the permission(s).

The two types of NT user groups are global and local. *Global groups* can contain only individual user accounts from the domain in which the group was created, collected together under one group account name, and cannot contain other global or local groups. Global groups are useful in granting permissions and rights to groups of users, either for local resource access or for resource access in another trusted NT domain.

NOTE

See Chapter 17 for details about global and local groups, predefined groups, and adding new groups through User Manager for Domains.

NT FILE SYSTEM SECURITY

In this section, I'll review the file system types and features and discuss managing file system security and shared directories.

Two basic types of file systems are supported under NT Server 4:

▶ The FAT file system

▶ The NTFS file system

NOTE

NT 3.51 supported an additional file system called HPFS (High Performance File System); however, that file system is no longer supported by Microsoft. HPFS was developed for use on OS/2 version 1.2, which was released in 1989. It has been phased out of NT in favor of Microsoft's own NTFS.

FAT versus NTFS

FAT stands for File Allocation Table and was originally developed by Microsoft for use under MS-DOS. The FAT file system has no real security features other than the ability to set the attributes of a file to hidden, system, or read only, which simply makes it harder to accidentally delete a file. The only real advantage of the FAT file system today is that it is supported by MS-DOS.

WARNING

For a secure network connected to the Internet, FAT is a very poor choice. I don't recommend using it at all on NT servers; you should use NTFS instead.

Part ii

NTFS stands for NT File System and is certainly the correct choice for your intranet or your Internet connection. NTFS offers a robust mechanism to control access to hard drives and their contents. It also offers performance features over MS-DOS file systems. Some of the main features of NTFS include the following:

- It allows permissions to be set on files and directories.

- It gives faster access to larger sequential access files.

- It gives faster access to random-access files.

- File and directory names can be a maximum of 256 characters.

- It automatically converts long filenames to the MS-DOS standard of 8.3 when accessed by MS-DOS workstations on the network. (The 8.3 standard dictates an eight-character filename with a three-character extension.)

- It allows file- and directory-sharing with Macintosh systems.

- It uses drive space more efficiently.

- It automatically sorts directories.

- It supports uppercase and lowercase letters in filenames and supports Unicode characters.

CONVERTING FILE SYSTEMS

NT includes a utility called CONVERT.EXE that you can use to convert a FAT or an HPFS hard disk to NTFS format. This conversion is a one-way process; there is no way to go from NTFS back to either FAT or HPFS formats. Use this utility from a command prompt with the following general syntax:

CONVERT *drive* /fs:ntfs

The *drive* variable is the letter of the drive you want to convert to NTFS. If CONVERT cannot get exclusive access to the drive you have specified, perhaps because files on the drive are open, you will see an error message to that effect. You can elect to convert the drive when the system restarts after the next shutdown. As soon as the conversion is complete, run NTBACKUP *immediately* to create the first backup of the new file system.

CONTINUED ➞

A few words of caution are in order here. If you convert a FAT file system to NTFS, you will not be able to boot your server with MS-DOS using a floppy disk and access the NTFS partition. MS-DOS doesn't understand NTFS and simply cannot read it. Additionally, if you are converting a Novell NetWare server to NT Server, as so many administrators are, you cannot simply convert the file system to NTFS; doing so destroys all the data on the NetWare volume. First, back up your NetWare server. Now, install NT Server, and then restore your data to the hard drive after it is converted to NTFS. After you have finished the conversion, make a complete backup of your entire system immediately so that you have an up-to-date backup in the new format.

Sharing Directories

Now that we have reviewed the file systems themselves, let's talk about file system security. Most servers on a network act as repositories for data files of various types and for software programs that network users can access and run. Before users can access files and programs across the network, they must be shared. Sharing a directory allows users to connect to the share and use it as if it were a local drive on the user's workstation.

Once a directory is shared, all its contents (files, subdirectories, and files in those subdirectories) are accessible to the users that have permission to access the share. Some restrictions can be applied to the contents of a directory, which allows a bit more control over access to its contents. I'll go over that later in this section.

File system security under NT has four basic parts: share permissions, directory permissions, file access, and ownership. I'll cover each of these in this section.

Sharing directories is really straightforward. Under NT Server 4, you begin this process by opening Explorer (choose Start ➤ Programs ➤ Windows NT Explorer). Explorer (see Figure 20.3) is a welcome replacement for the old File Manager found in all previous versions of the NT operating system.

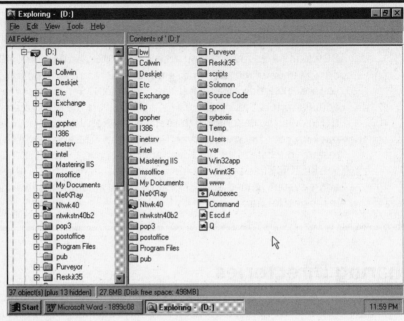

FIGURE 20.3: Windows NT Explorer

On the left side of the Explorer window, you will see a directory tree listing all the directories (also called folders) on the chosen hard disk; on the right side of the window, you will see a list of all the files and folders that the selected directory contains.

NOTE

See Chapter 3 for details on using Explorer to organize your programs and documents.

Follow these steps to create a shared directory:

1. On the left of the Explorer, locate the name of the directory you want and right-click it.

2. In the pop-up menu that Explorer displays, select the Sharing option. NT displays the Properties dialog box, with the Sharing tab selected by default (see Figure 20.4).

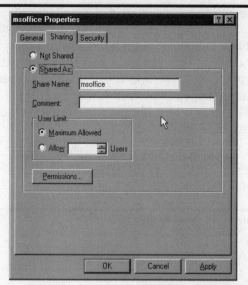

FIGURE 20.4: The Properties dialog box, with the Sharing tab selected by default

3. Click the Shared As radio button. The name of the directory
    appears in the Share Name text box, and the other fields in
    the dialog box are now enabled. The name in the Share Name
    text box is the one that users will see across the network
    when they access a shared resource.

In some cases, using a descriptive Share Name such as MSOffice
might be beneficial; in others, you might want to disguise the share's
true contents by giving it a nondescriptive share name. The Comment
field also appears to users accessing shares across the network, and you
can use this field for information that you want users to read. The Comment text box need not be filled in; however, you must fill in the Share
Name text box to share a resource such as a directory.

4. You can use the other options in this dialog box to help con-
    trol server loads, as follows:

    Maximum Allowed   Click this radio button, which is
    selected by default, if you want the maximum number of
    users that the server can handle to connect to the share.

Allow   To manually limit the number of simultaneous connections to the share, click the Allow radio button and select or enter the number in the drop-down list box. You might want to do this to ensure that the server doesn't get overloaded or to prevent more than the prescribed number of users from accessing a licensed software package that is installed in a shared directory. Normally, you can leave the default of Maximum Allowed.

Permissions   Click this button to establish the permissions for the share. NT displays the Access Through Share Permissions dialog box, as shown in Figure 20.5.

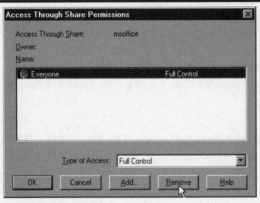

FIGURE 20.5:   The Access Through Share Permissions dialog box

5. NT Server gives global access to a new share as the default, and because that is not usually what you want, be sure to remove it. The Everyone group for NT encompasses every user in the domain. Since, in this case, we don't want everyone to have access, select Everyone and click the Remove button.

6. To add permission for a group of users to access the share, click the Add button. NT displays the Add Users and Groups dialog box, shown in Figure 20.6.

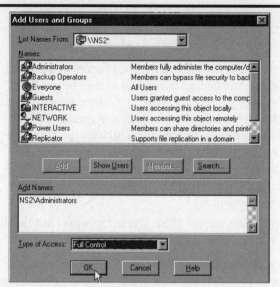

FIGURE 20.6: The Add Users and Groups dialog box

7. The upper part of this dialog box lists all the defined groups in your domain. To see a list of the users in each group, click the Show Users button. In this example, we want to give permission to access the share to a user group called Administrators. Select Administrators in the list and click the Add button.

8. The name of the Administrators group appears in the Add Names list. To define the group's type of shared access, select the Type of Access drop-down list. Click the downward-pointing arrow, and you'll see the four basic types of access that can be assigned:

    No Access   If you select this access type, users in the groups in the Add Names list do not have access to the shared directory, its subdirectories, or any files in these subdirectories.

    Read   If you select this access type, users in the groups in the Add Names list have read-only access. They cannot change, delete, or modify the contents of the share in any way; they can change to the shared directory's subdirectories and then run application programs stored there.

Part ii

Change If you select this type of access, users in the groups in the Add Names list can read and write to the shared resource, but they cannot delete it.

Full Control If you select this type of access, users in the groups in the Add Names list can do as they please with the share. They can read it, write to it, execute programs in it, add files and programs to it, change permissions, and even delete it entirely. Be careful about who has this type of access to your shares; it makes sense to restrict Full Control to the network administrator. Full Control can be self-defeating when you are attempting to secure your network server's resources.

Keep in mind that these are the share access types and not the directory access types. More on directory access types in a moment.

9. Because we want the Administrators to have full control over the share to do with it what they may, select the Full Control access type. Now, click the OK button to establish the permissions and close the dialog box. Click OK again to close the Access Through Share Permissions dialog box.

10. In the Properties dialog box, click the Security tab. NT displays the Security tab, as shown in Figure 20.7.

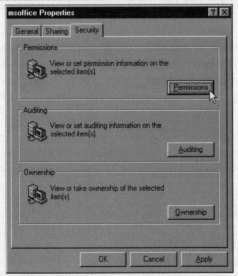

FIGURE 20.7: The Properties dialog box, with the Security tab selected

This dialog box has three areas of interest: Permissions, Auditing, and Ownership. We'll cover each of these in a fair amount of detail in the following sections.

By placing permissions on a directory, you can specify the type of access that a group or an individual has to that directory and the files it contains, but this doesn't necessarily grant the same permissions to the subdirectories that it contains.

11. To look at or change the permissions on a directory, click the Permissions button. NT displays the Directory Permissions dialog box, shown in Figure 20.8.

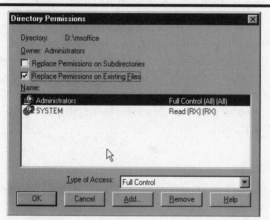

FIGURE 20.8:   The Directory Permissions dialog box

12. To select an access type for the Administrators group, click the downward-pointing arrow in the Type of Access dropdown list box. You'll see the following options:

No Access   Select this access type to prohibit any type of access by any user in the group, even if he or she belongs to another group that has access to this directory.

List   Select this access type to allow users in this group to view this directory, its subdirectories, and its files.

Read   Select this access type to allow users in this group to view this directory, its subdirectories, and its files and to run programs in this directory and its subdirectories.

Add   Select this access type to allow users in this group to add files to this directory and its subdirectories but not allow access to the files in the directory unless allowed by other directory or file permission settings.

Add & Read   Select this access type to give users in this group all the permissions of the Add access type as well as permission to run programs from the directory and its subdirectories.

Change   Select this access type to give users in this group all the permissions of the Add & Read access type as well as permission to delete the directory, its subdirectories, and its files.

Full Control   Select this access type to give users in this group all the permissions of the Change access type as well as the permission to change permissions on the directory, its subdirectories, and its files and to take ownership of the directory and its files. (More on ownership later in this section.)

WARNING

Assign the Full Control type of access with care; you don't want to compromise the security of your network server resources.

Special Directory Access   Select this access type if you want to customize the permission settings for this directory. When you select Special Directory Access, NT displays the Special Directory Access dialog box, as shown in Figure 20.9.

Special File Access   Select this access type if you want to customize the permission settings for files. When you choose this option, NT displays the Special File Access dialog box shown in Figure 20.10. The options in the Special File Access dialog box are listed in Table 20.1.

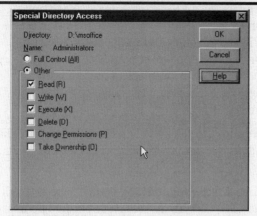

FIGURE 20.9: The Special Directory Access dialog box, with Read and Execute permissions selected

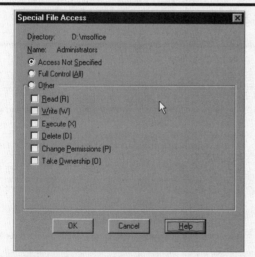

FIGURE 20.10: The Special File Access dialog box, with which you specify permissions for an individual file

13. When you have completed your settings, click OK. Windows NT displays the Directory Permissions dialog box, which has the following options:

Replace Permissions on Subdirectories Check this checkbox to set the same permissions on all files and subdirectories of this share.

Part ii

Replace Permissions on Existing Files   Check this
checkbox, which is the default, to apply permission settings to files in the directory and to the directory itself.
Clear this checkbox to apply your permission settings
to this directory only. If the Replace Permissions on
Subdirectories box is checked, permissions are also set
on all subdirectories.

14. Click the OK button to close the Directory Permissions dia-
    log box. Windows NT displays the Properties dialog box once
    again.

By default, all files in a directory inherit the permissions of the directory in which they reside. If a user has Access Not Specified permission,
he or she can prevent this inheritance and can customize the permissions
on a per file basis. When you select Access Not Specified, NT displays the
Special File Access dialog box (shown in Figure 20.10) with which you
specify permissions for an individual file. These permissions are the same
as those listed in Table 20.1.

TABLE 20.1: NT Server Individual Permissions

PERMISSION	DESCRIPTION
Read (R)	Allows users in this group to view the names of files and subdi-rectories in this directory
Write (W)	Allows users in this group to add files and subdirectories to this directory
Execute (X)	Allows users in this group to change to subdirectories in this directory
Delete (D)	Allows users in this group to delete this directory
Change Permissions (P)	Allows users in this group to change the permissions for this directory
Take Ownership (O)	Allows users in this group to change ownership of this directory

Generally speaking, you should use the settings shown in Table 20.2
for your IIS directories.

TABLE 20.2: Settings for IIS Directories

DIRECTORY TYPE	SUGGESTED ACCESS TYPE
Content	Read
Programs and scripts	Read and Execute
Databases	Read and Write

Directory Auditing

At times, you will want to monitor different kinds of user activity, both to assess network performance and for security reasons. NT Server gives the network administrator several important tools to audit network events and stores this information in one of three logs:

- ▶ The Applications Log
- ▶ The Systems Log
- ▶ The Security Log

In NT Server, you can specify which groups or users, as well as which network actions, should be audited for any file or directory. You set audit policy using User Manager for Domains. To do this, in User Manager, choose Policies ➤ Audit to open the Audit Policy dialog box. We'll return to this dialog box and cover all its options in detail later in this chapter.

One of the options in this dialog box is File and Object Access; be sure to check this box, and notice that you can audit both successful and unsuccessful accesses. Once this is done, the next step is to return to Explorer and choose the files and/or directories and groups of users that you want to audit. Continuing with the example we started earlier, here are the steps to follow:

1. In the Properties dialog box, be sure that the Security tab is selected and then click the Auditing button. Explorer displays the Directory Auditing dialog box, as shown in Figure 20.11.

Part ii

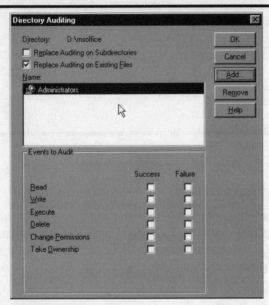

FIGURE 20.11: The Directory Auditing dialog box, with the Administrators group selected

2. In the Name list box, select the Administrators group (since that is the group for which we are establishing permission) and click the Add button. In the bottom half of this dialog box, select the events to audit. (All audit trails are written to the Event Log, which is covered later in this chapter.) The options are as follows:

Read Audits the display of filenames, attributes, permissions, and owners.

Write Audits the creation of subdirectories and files, the changes to attributes, and the display of permissions and owners.

Execute Audits the display of attributes, permissions, and owners and the changes to subdirectories.

Delete Audits the deletion of the directory.

Change Permissions Audits the changes to directory permissions.

Take Ownership   Audits the changes to directory ownership.

3. Above the Name list box are the following checkboxes:

Replace Auditing on Subdirectories   This option applies auditing to the directory and subdirectory only, but not to existing files in either.

Replace Auditing on Existing Files   This is the default setting. When you select it, you allow the auditing to apply to the directory and to the files within that directory only, not to any subdirectories.

Check both boxes to apply auditing to the directory and its files as well as to any existing subdirectories and files it contains.

Clear both boxes to apply auditing to the directory only, and not to any of the files or directories it contains.

WARNING

Remember, the more items you audit, the larger the audit file will become.

4. Click OK to set the audit trails and close the Directory Auditing dialog box. Explorer returns to the Properties dialog box.

Ownership Properties

Every file and directory on an NTFS hard disk under NT has an owner. When you create a file or a directory, you become its owner. Owners can grant permissions, controlling how the file or directory is used. The owner of a file or a directory and members of the Administrators group can grant permission to other users to take ownership of a file or directory.

Although any administrator can take ownership of a directory or a file, an administrator cannot transfer ownership to others. This preserves the security mechanism. For example, only an administrator who takes ownership and changes permissions can gain access to a file on which you have set the No Access permission. By checking the ownership of a file, you see that the ownership has changed and find out who violated the permission you set on the file.

Part ii

TIP

To ensure that your files are secure, check their ownership regularly. Furthermore, always establish a degree of auditing and routinely check the Event Log for security-related events. We'll cover both auditing and the Event Log in a fair amount of detail later in this chapter.

To check ownership, follow these steps:

1. In the Properties dialog box, be sure that the Security tab is selected and click the Ownership button. NT displays the Owner dialog box, as shown in Figure 20.12. This dialog box shows the directory name and the current owner of the directory.

FIGURE 20.12:   The Owner dialog box, showing the directory name and owner

2. If you are logged on as an administrator and you don't have permission to view the owner, you will be given the option of taking ownership of the file. Taking ownership lets you look at all the security information for the file. Once transferred, ownership cannot be transferred back to the file's original owner.

3. Click Close. NT displays the Properties dialog box once again.

NOTE

If you have to take control of a directory, to delete it, for example, don't be surprised if you can't seem to access it for a few minutes. The change in ownership may not be immediately reflected across the domain in all the security databases.

General Properties of Files and Folders

Finally, let's take a look at the information contained in the General tab of the Properties dialog box, shown in Figure 20.13.

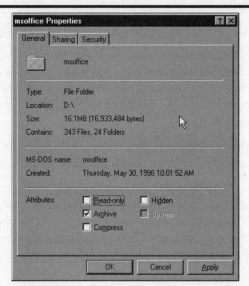

FIGURE 20.13: The General tab of the Properties dialog box

The first part of the General tab shows you the name of the file or directory for which you are establishing parameters and its associated icon; in this case, MSOFFICE. It also contains the following information:

Type   MSOFFICE is a file folder, or directory.

Location   The hard disk on which the file or directory is located.

Size   The number of bytes.

Contents   If the file type is file folder (or directory), the number of files and folders it contains.

MS-DOS Name   The MS-DOS filename, the 8.3 form of the filename, which is used by MS-DOS operating systems that have access to the directory. In this case, the file type is directory and so has no filename extension.

Created   The day, date, and time the file or directory was created.

At the bottom of the General tab of the Properties dialog box are five checkboxes that correspond to the five attributes that any NT file or directory can have. File attributes allow low-level control over the directory. They are established by NT when the file or directory is initially created and are defined as follows:

▶ Read Only ensures that the file or directory can't be accidentally rewritten or deleted.

▶ Archive indicates that this file has changed since it was last backed up, and so the archive copy of this file is now out of date. Some software programs use this setting to determine whether to back up a file or a directory.

▶ Compress shows whether this file or directory is compressed. NT can compress files and directories on-the-fly, saving precious hard disk space.

▶ Hidden indicates that this file or directory is hidden and not normally visible in Explorer or when you issue the NT dir command. You cannot use a hidden directory or a hidden file unless you know its name and location.

WARNING

Hiding a file can sometimes be useful, following the basic principle that "if you can't see it, you can't fool around with it." Be aware, however, that there are ways of seeking and finding all hidden files on a hard disk.

▶ System indicates that the file or directory is typically part of the operating system and is required for the operating system to run properly. By default, system files appear in the Explorer folder listings. Do not delete files with this attribute unless you know exactly what the file is for and you are absolutely certain that you can do without it.

In review, you can see that establishing file system security consists of setting two types of parameters: file system and shared resource. You can think of the file system security parameters as being underneath the shared resource security parameters. The two are complementary and provide a great deal of control over who has permission to access the file systems.

TIP

For more information on Windows NT Server security, see Mark Minasi's excellent book, *Mastering Windows NT Server 4*, available from Sybex.

USING THE ADMINISTRATIVE WIZARDS

If you are using NT Server 4, you can use one of the Administrative Wizards located in the Administrative Tools menu to create a new user account, to manage aspects of file and folder access, and to set up a printer.

The following Wizards are available to make some aspects of system administration easier and faster:

- ► Add User Accounts
- ► Group Management
- ► Managing File and Folder Access
- ► Add Printer
- ► Add/Remove Programs
- ► Install New Modem
- ► Network Client Administrator
- ► License Compliance

Each Wizard is designed to take you through a specific process, step by step, prompting you with possible choices at each decision point.

NOTE

These Wizards are not available in Windows NT Server 3.5 or 3.51; so if you are using one of these systems, you have no choice but to use User Manager for Domains to accomplish these tasks.

Part ii

NT Logging and Auditing

The three types of logging in NT are System, Security, and Application. Each type keeps its own log records, and each is viewed with the Event Log, which is in the Administrative Tools folder.

Each log tracks the same basic parameters in and around an event: the date and time of a log entry, the source of the event, the event subcategory, the event ID, the user-related event entry if any, and the machine name of the system on which the event occurred.

The Event Log

The Event Log uses a few standard icons to represent the urgency of a log entry. The Information icon is a blue circle with the letter *i* in the center. Informational entries are usually just that and normally require no immediate action on your part. The Warning icon is a yellow circle with an exclamation point inside. Warning log entries are items that NT wants you to know about and that may require some action. The Error icon is a red stop sign with the word *Stop* in the center. Error log entries are serious, and you should handle them as soon as possible.

Basic logging is always enabled on NT. You can, however, enhance the logging levels of an NT server by turning on the audit trails in User Manager for Domains. To do so, follow these steps:

1. Choose Start ➢ Programs ➢ Administrative Tools ➢ User Manager for Domains.

2. In User Manager for Domains, choose Policies ➢ Audit. NT displays the Audit Policy dialog box, as shown in Figure 20.14.

The default is Do Not Audit; when this option is selected, all the Audit These Events checkboxes are grayed and unavailable. When you activate auditing, information about the selected event type is stored in NT's Security Log when the event takes place. You can look at the contents of the Security Log, along with the Application and Systems logs, with the Event Viewer, as you'll see in a moment.

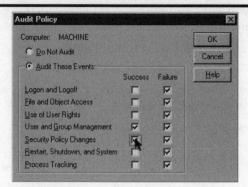

FIGURE 20.14: The Audit Policy dialog box

Check the appropriate checkboxes to audit the following events for either success or failure:

- ▶ Logon and Logoff tracks each logon and logoff event that occurs and tracks all connections to the network.

- ▶ File and Object Access tracks the use of files and resource objects in the domain if they were set for auditing; also tracks print spooling if the printer resource is set for auditing.

- ▶ Use of User Rights tracks any exercise of a user's rights, except for logon and logoff events, which are tracked by Logon and Logoff.

- ▶ User and Group Management tracks when a user account or group is successfully created, changed, or deleted; when a user account is renamed, enabled, or disabled; and when a password is changed.

- ▶ Security Policy Changes tracks changes to user rights, audit policies, and trust relationships of the domain.

- ▶ Restart, Shutdown, and System tracks startup and shutdown of the server and events that affect the entire security system.

- ▶ Process Tracking tracks events such as program activation, indirect object access, and process exits.

Part ii

You should make system auditing a normal part of day-to-day operations on your network, and you should review the logs regularly.

WARNING

If you suspect an intruder is attempting to gain access to your system, you and your staff should review these logs every day.

The System Log

Let's take a look at some log entries that you may encounter. First, let's look at a System event. To do so, choose Start ➤ Programs ➤ Administrative Tools ➤ Event Viewer. In the Event Viewer, choose Log ➤ System. You'll see a list of logged events; to view any of them, simply double-click its entry.

TIP

To change the size of the logs on your system, use the Log Settings option from the Log menu in the Event Viewer.

The System Log tracks all system-level events, including successful and failed events that take place during system startup, such as services starting, drivers being loaded, disk capacity checks, and many other items that may be of interest or concern to the administrator.

Take a look at Figure 20.15 for an idea of what a System Log entry might look like when displayed in the Event Detail dialog box. This particular event was logged because an Ethernet driver failed to load properly, and you can see information such as the time and date the event occurred, the name of the computer the event occurred on, the event ID number, and the NT Server element that created the event. In this case, the event was created by the NT Service Control Manager.

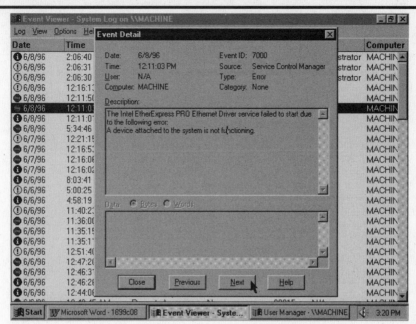

FIGURE 20.15:   The Event Detail dialog box, displaying a System Log event

The Security Log

Now let's take a look at a Security Log entry (see Figure 20.16). The Security Log tracks all security-related events, including changes in security policy, attempts to log on to the system, and attempts to access a file or directory based on the policy you established when using the Audit Policy dialog box in User Manager for Domains, described in an earlier section in this chapter. This example entry shows that someone attempted to log on with the Administrator account at 3:36 PM on June 8, 1996, and failed. The entry also tells us that the machine used to attempt the logon was called MACHINE and that the reason for the event being logged is an unknown username or a bad password.

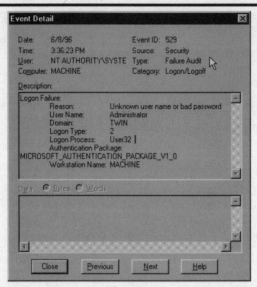

FIGURE 20.16:   The Event Detail dialog box, displaying a Security Log event

Application Logs

Application Logs are generated by application programs that execute on the network. Technically, an application is software other than the NT operating system. The log entry in Figure 20.17 shows that NT `chkdsk` command ran and displayed the results. In this instance, `chkdsk` found the following:

> 527138816 bytes of total disk space
>
> 2203648 bytes in 58 hidden files
>
> 2383872 bytes in 281 directories
>
> 443916288 bytes in 5325 user files
>
> 78635008 total bytes available on drive D

Auditing and the Event Logs are necessary and useful tools in the administration of your network and its related services. Logs can help you find out why certain aspects of the system or network are not functioning properly, and they can give you distinct information that may assist you in identifying and preventing intrusion. Learn to use them accurately, and make a habit of checking them thoroughly and routinely.

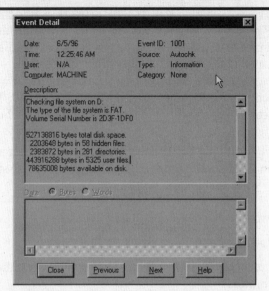

FIGURE 20.17:   The Event Detail dialog box, displaying an event in the Application Log

MICROSOFT TCP/IP SECURITY

With the release of NT 4, Microsoft added the ability to filter out packets from certain types of protocols destined for the TCP/IP network. This feature is commonplace in the world of TCP/IP and is commonly referred to as *packet filtering*.

You can limit three types of network traffic with the new TCP/IP configuration:

▶ TCP

▶ UDP

▶ IP

The process for limiting these traffic types is based on a port address for which the traffic is destined. Thus, if you want to stop any traffic from arriving at your DNS port, which is a UDP port, you do so by configuring the security aspects of the Microsoft TCP/IP protocol settings as well as those of UDP and IP.

Part ii

This is a powerful way of securing your TCP/IP network; traffic that can't get to a TCP/IP port on your server can't break in. To learn which types of services and protocols use which ports, take a look at the file called Services located in the \%system_root%\ System32\ Drivers\Etc directory. Replace the %system_root% parameter with the name of the directory in which you installed NT, such as NT40. This file lists most of the common protocols and their associated ports, but certainly not all of them.

Let's take a quick look at the TCP/IP security settings, as shown in Figure 20.18. To open the TCP/IP Security dialog box, follow these steps:

1. Choose Start ➤ Settings ➤ Control Panel ➤ Network.

2. In the Network dialog box, select the Protocols tab.

3. In the Protocols section, double-click TCP/IP Protocol.

4. In the Microsoft TCP/IP Properties dialog box, click the Advanced button.

5. In the Advanced IP Addressing dialog box, check the Enable Security checkbox, and click the Configure button. NT displays the TCP/IP Security dialog box.

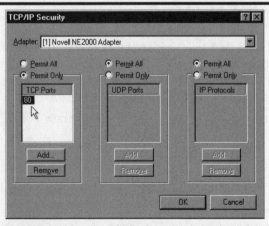

FIGURE 20.18:   The TCP/IP Security dialog box, showing TCP Port access restricted to port 80

In this dialog box are three groups of settings: TCP, UDP, and IP. Each has a Permit All radio button to allow access on all ports and has a Permit Only radio button to restrict access to certain specific ports. Let's assume that we want to allow access only to the Web server port, which is normally port 80 and uses the TCP protocol.

NOTE

With IIS, you cannot configure the Web server port address manually; so you must run your IIS Web server on port 80, which is the standard default port for any Web server.

To restrict access to all TCP ports except port 80 for the Web server, follow these steps:

1. In the TCP Ports tab, click the Permit Only radio button.

2. Click the Add button. Enter **80** for the port number.

3. Click OK.

That's it. You've just eliminated all TCP traffic other than Web traffic from your server!

NOTE

You can permit access to any ports you wish; you simply need to know the protocol type and its actual port number. Packet filtering is a basic and powerful way to control access to your server; so don't be afraid to use it.

NT INSTALLATION CONSIDERATIONS

This section reviews some considerations you may want to take into account when initially installing NT Server or NT Workstation.

First, when installing NT Server or NT Workstation, be sure that all NT domain controllers are turned on and live on the network before you begin. For NT machines to be able to join a domain, a domain controller must be available on the network during installation. This avoids the possibility of accidentally installing two PDCs in the same domain and also ensures that the machine is authorized to join the domain.

You will want to use the NTFS file system rather than the FAT file system, since when using the FAT, a large portion of the security features built into NT are simply unavailable.

Think carefully about how your domain should be structured, about who will administer it, and about how users will be allowed to access it.

When installing NT, be careful to record the Administrator's password and keep it in a safe place. Once the server is up and running, immediately add at least one user account to the Administrators group.

IIS Installation Considerations

Before we get into this brief section, I'll remind you that the IIS relies almost entirely on Windows NT for most of its security functionality. Windows NT provides IIS the tools it needs to work: features for user and file system security.

NOTE
See Chapter 22 for details on requirements for and installing IIS.

When planning your IIS installation, you don't have many considerations; IIS takes care of most settings for you by default. Do pay attention, though, to the username that IIS sets up for anonymous logons and to the starting directory for your Web site files, which is commonly referred to as the *home directory*.

Your home directory can actually reside on any server available to the IIS server itself across the network. When choosing the location of your Web site's files, consider that locating them on another server could, in some cases, degrade performance. Be sure that the host for your files isn't already overburdened. As a rule, you'll find that locating them and the IIS server on the same machine provides the best overall performance. This may not be possible if you plan to use databases or information that resides on other systems, but keep it in mind.

TIP
IIS uses a normal NT user account to facilitate anonymous logons to your Web server. Are anonymous logons important? Absolutely. In general, most public Web sites use only anonymous logons—the user is not required to enter a username and password. If you're establishing a Web site for the general public, leave anonymous logons enabled.

When the IIS installation is complete, open User Manager for Domains and review the security settings for the IIS user account. This account has a name that is easy to locate: IUSR_*MACHINE_NAME*. In this name,

MACHINE_NAME is the NetBIOS name of your computer. Be sure that all the security settings are in line with the policies for your site.

Most of the time, you will have a good idea of the purpose of your Web site before it's actually installed. Granted, the purpose may change over time, but you should at least know the initial purpose. If it involves delivering Web pages that contain sensitive information, you'll have to establish a security policy for the directories that will contain the sensitive information. Doing so is a direct function of who you want to access the information. You can establish usernames and passwords to control access to certain parts of your Web site, and IIS provides three methods of user authentication:

▶ Anonymous

▶ Clear text

▶ NT Challenge/Response (NTCR also referred to as NTLM)

IIS, in conjunction with the Internet Service Manager, allows you to do two things that I find rather powerful for a Web server: control the amount of total bandwidth and restrict or grant access by IP address. You actually control the amount of total bandwidth that your Microsoft Internet services use as a whole—the FTP and Web servers combined—using the Internet Service Manager.

Part ii

FTP AND FILE PERMISSIONS

Under NT, FTP is entirely controlled by file permissions. For users to be able to FTP to your server, they must have access permissions to the FTP service's home directory. Without these permissions, even users with valid IDs and passwords will be denied logon access. This is one of the most frustrating aspects when you are first learning about FTP on NT.

If a valid user cannot log on successfully, double-check the file permissions for the FTP service's home directory. They should at least allow Read and Execute access for the directory, and they should allow Read access for the files. If they do not, logons will fail every time.

A Note about Passwords

Choosing or specifying a password is a subject I have touched on several times in this chapter, and now it is time to suggest some guidelines you can follow to make your password choices as effective as possible:

▶ Passwords should be a mixture of uppercase and lowercase letters and numbers.

▶ Passwords should be a minimum of six characters.

▶ Keep passwords secret and change them frequently. The worst passwords are the obvious ones: your name, your initials, your telephone number, the name of your city, names of your pets or children, names of TV characters or anyone associated with *Star Trek*, birth dates, groups of the same letter or sequences such as *qwerty*, or complete English words. The English language has a finite number of words, and a computer can run through them quickly.

▶ Don't display any company information or help screens until *after* a user has successfully logged on.

▶ Add expiration dates to user accounts to force password changes and the termination of short-term user accounts, such as those assigned to vendors, contractors, and temporary employees.

▶ Change all passwords at least every 90 days, and change those associated with high-security privileges more often.

▶ Be sure that all default passwords are removed from the system. If a service company set up your server, be on the lookout for passwords such as GUEST, MANAGER, SERVICE, and the like. Remove these passwords immediately.

▶ Do not allow more than two invalid password attempts before disconnecting.

▶ Promptly remove the accounts of transferred or terminated employees, as well as all unused accounts.

TIP

You should also remember to review the log files covered earlier in this chapter on a regular basis and turn off any operating system services that you don't need.

TESTING YOUR SECURITY

Administrators in the Unix world have been using a set of programs collectively known as SATAN to test the effectiveness of the security established at their site. Users of NT Server can now use Kane Security Analyst (KSA) from Intrusion Detection Inc. or Internet Security Systems' SAFE-suite for this same purpose.

NOTE

SATAN, or Security Administrator Tool for Analyzing Networks, is available free on the Internet, and for this reason, many critics have argued that SATAN lets potential intruders take advantage of the information it contains on how to infiltrate systems. So far, at least, the program seems to have acted as a wake-up call to network administrators.

KSA is a complete commercial package, and is also available for Novell's NetWare versions 3.*x* and 4.*x*. Future versions will be available for Unix systems and networks using Lotus Notes. Check out the Web site at www.intrusion.com for more details.

KSA examines your NT Server system and then presents three-dimensional bar charts of the following six major categories:

Account Restrictions   Assesses password controls, use of logon scripts, and password expiration dates.

Password Strength   Rates your password policies. A future version will include a password-cracking dictionary to show you how easily your passwords can be guessed.

Access Control   Checks user rights and removable drive allocations.

System Monitoring   Collects together a miscellaneous set of security-related concerns.

Data Integrity   Checks the UPS installation and configuration.

The KSA Report Manager is easy to use and offers almost 30 reports; data can be exported in the usual database formats. KSA creates no accounts or services. To use it, you must be logged in as the administrator, although once the analysis is complete, the results can be shared with all users with access to the system. KSA takes an instant snapshot of the state of your system; as you follow its recommendations and make improvements in your security policies, you will need to rerun the program to see how you are doing.

Internet Security Systems' SAFEsuite package combines the company's Web Security Scanner, Intranet Scanner, Firewall Scanner, and System Security Scanner. The Web Security Scanner looks at the underlying operating system, the Web server, and your CGI scripts. The Intranet Scanner probes your network and learns about it using a custom discovery process. The Firewall Scanner checks the security of your firewall, the firewall application, and the services enabled through the firewall; it also checks packet-filtering and application proxy-based firewalls. The System Security Scanner continuously checks for file ownership and permissions, operating system configurations, and any signs of an intruder—all in real time. See Internet Security Systems' Web site at `www.iss.net` for more details.

These products can do little to actually catch intruders; that's up to you. What they can do is present the security weaknesses in your system to you in a very powerful form that is just about impossible to ignore.

GET YOURSELF CERTIFIED

The ICSA, formerly the NCSA (National Computer Security Association), is an independent organization composed of vendors, technology consultants, and ICSA staffers and is well known for its technical standards and certification of products that meet these standards.

Now the ICSA has turned its attention to Web sites with its rigorous Web Certification Program. This program covers the spectrum of security issues, including everything from a physical inspection of your location to testing your firewall. As a part of the certification, ICSA also verifies that the company sponsoring the Web site actually exists and has appropriate backup plans in place. In addition, they conduct spot checks from time to time to ensure that your company is maintaining its security policy.

The benefits of the ICSA certificate on your Web site are huge and go a long way to reassure visitors that you are who you say you are and that you have a comprehensive security scheme in place.

To apply for certification or to get details, visit the ICSA Web site at `www.icsa.net`.

TAKING THE INTRUDER'S POINT OF VIEW

Like it or not, your network and its systems are an open invitation to intruders. They are a motivational challenge to the would-be intruder, and you should always keep this in mind. If you do not guard the access to your network and its resources carefully, they can be compromised.

The best information I can give a network administrator is this: Intruders love simple passwords and old passwords that never change. Make passwords difficult, unrelated to an individual, and cryptic, and change them often. Remember that intruders may use a dictionary and a robot program in attempting to guess your passwords!

WHAT'S NEXT?

This chapter covered a broad range of topics related to NT system security, including setting up permissions, auditing, logging, TCP/IP security, and testing your security. This chapter also described some security considerations for IIS (Internet Information Server). In the next chapter, you'll learn how to use IIS to link SQL Server databases with Web clients on your company's intranet. This way, you can develop intranet applications that use a Web browser as the front end.

Chapter 21

DEVELOPING INTRANET SYSTEMS

Many companies have multiple networks, with multiple computer platforms; their networks resemble the worldwide Internet. These diverse corporate networks and the Internet have similar problems, and tools that were developed to solve Internet problems can be of considerable value in corporate environments. When you use Internet technologies to implement or replace a traditional client/server system, you have an *intranet*—an internet that's internal to an organization.

With the explosion of technology that the Internet has brought to business computing, we can overcome many of these limitations by abandoning the proprietary Visual Basic front end and using a Web browser as the front-end application instead.

Microsoft's Internet Information Server (IIS) provides an easy way to link SQL Server databases with any Web client on your intranet. IIS is now an integral part of the NT Server 4 installation process, and it is supported by NT's security and MIME file type file-system information. Coupled with SQL Server and ODBC connectors, IIS becomes a powerful, easy-to-use, client/server intranet system.

Adapted from *Windows NT® Server 4 : No experience required.™* by Robert Cowart and Boyd Waters

ISBN 0-7821-2081-4   512 pages $29.99

LIMITATIONS OF TRADITIONAL CLIENT/SERVER SYSTEMS

The development of client/server applications enable you to consolidate information into centralized databases while preserving the end-user interaction advantages of graphical desktop systems.

SQL Server, which runs under NT, makes it easy for us to scale up a simple database from a desktop-based system to one that could handle multiple users on the network. It is easy to set up and maintain a SQL Server system, which provides graphical tools with enterprise-wide management capabilities. SQL Server on an NT machine can interact with existing desktop programs such as Microsoft Access. With limited knowledge of SQL (Structured Query Language), we can create SQL databases on the server.

A method we use for implementing the front end, Visual Basic, has some serious limitations. In order to deploy a Visual Basic application, we need to distribute the application—the application's executable file as well as the libraries that implement the application's controls—to every desktop in the enterprise. Even if you use an installer program, the "installation event" must occur. Visual Basic programs with the requisite controls do not run (at the time of this writing) on DOS, Macintosh, or UNIX workstations, limiting our "company-wide" database system to those who use Windows-based PCs.

A client/server development system, such as PowerBuilder, won't completely insulate you from the complexities of cross-platform development. The way in which Macintosh and Windows computers typically connect to back-end databases is different for each platform. Although the systems are getting better, the Macintosh implementations typically lag behind the Windows ones, and setting up such a system requires a degree of sophistication on both Windows and Macintosh platforms. You need to translate the documentation into something that makes sense, and this can be a challenge.

In my experience, cross-platform client/server tools add a great deal of complexity to a project, in terms of development, training, and deployment. For most systems, there is now a better alternative, based on Internet technology: an intranet.

INTRANETS EXPLAINED

With the proliferation of the Internet, and most particularly the World Wide Web, rich tools have become available. These tools provide the functionality of traditional client/server systems while avoiding many of their limitations. The main advantages of using Internet tools are:

- ▶ Universal implementations

- ▶ Easy deployment

It is now possible to provide the functionality of the Visual Basic program, including a graphic interface, using standard Web browsers. These browsers are available from a number of vendors and run on every platform. The "Windows-only" rule no longer applies.

Once you have set up a Web browser infrastructure, with a TCP/IP network and Web browsers installed on the client computers, deploying a new Web-based application is almost trivial. You simply add a link to your company's home page, and let people know about the new service. All they need to do is click the link to "launch" the new program. You don't need to touch the client computers at all.

Internet Basics

The Internet is a large collection of computer networks that are all interconnected. If you have a multisite, corporate WAN (wide-area network), you have your own "internet."

The worldwide Internet is comprised of computer networks that speak the TCP/IP protocol and follow conventions regarding the assignment of computer names and network addresses. We could fill up a book talking about these conventions. Suffice to say that when you're using the Internet network, you're relying upon a whole bunch of networks to get your data from point A to point B, using the best route available at the time. Using this connection is like skateboarding from Los Angeles to San Francisco: You start at your office building in L.A., cut across a couple of parking lots to avoid the one-way streets and busy intersections, get on the highway for a while, and eventually make your way to your destination. In order to get where you're going, you might take a really complex route.

These days, you lease Internet connectivity from your Internet service provider (ISP), who in turn leases transit bandwidth from a big carrier such as Sprint or MCI. It's best if your service provider is not "downstream" from a smaller bandwidth reseller, because you don't want too many hops between you and the big backbones, the superhighways.

You can find out how your data is getting from point A to point B on the Internet with the `Traceroute` function. On a UNIX system, type **traceroute** and give an IP address or hostname. (On NT, you can use the `Tracert` command, but its output is limited.) You'll see the Internet routes your data used to establish the connection. You can get a program for NT that includes the `Traceroute` function, WSPING32. Figure 21.1 shows an example of the result of using the `Traceroute` function of the WSPING32 tool.

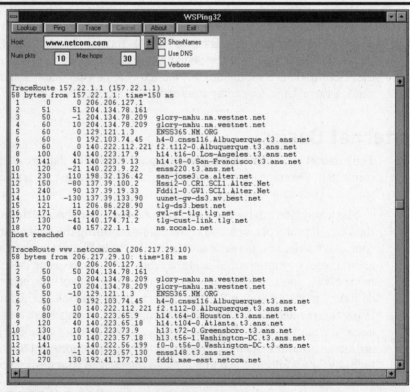

FIGURE 21.1: Using a common Traceroute tool, we can see that the Internet is comprised of a cooperative tangle of multiple networks.

Understanding Web Technology

The Internet, when used in the context of intranet application development, typically signifies the interaction between Web browsers and servers. Understanding World Wide Web technology is crucial to successful implementation of intranet systems.

The World Wide Web (WWW) is the product of a number of key standards:

- ▶ HTML (HyperText Markup Language)
- ▶ HTTP (HyperText Transfer Protocol)
- ▶ URLs (Universal Resource Locators)
- ▶ MIME (Multimedia Internet Mail Extension) file types
- ▶ GIF and JPEG (standard graphics file formats)

HTML (Hypertext Markup Language)

HTML is a way of adding properties to lines of text, such as "major heading" or "underlined" or "this text is a link to another page" or "put a picture here." HTML also describes various elements of the document, such as pictures, text, and sounds, and tells the Web browser where to find each element. The Web browser is a program on the client computer that interprets these notations—these text mark-ups—and renders the page appropriately. Figure 21.2 shows how a Web browser interprets HTML.

The best way to gain an understanding of HTML is to compare HTML code to the page that it describes. Some Web browsers allow you to see the underlying HTML codes with a View Source command. See Table 21.1 for the meanings of some of the most common HTML tags.

TABLE 21.1: Some Common HTML Tags

HTML CODE	MEANING
<H1>	Heading 1
<H2>	Heading 2
<p>	New paragraph (typically, with space in between)
 	Line break (typically, with no space in between)

CONTINUED ➡

TABLE 21.1 continued: Some Common HTML Tags

HTML CODE	MEANING
<EM>	Emphasized text (typically bold)
<IMG>	Insert picture
<A HREF=source>	Hyperlink to source

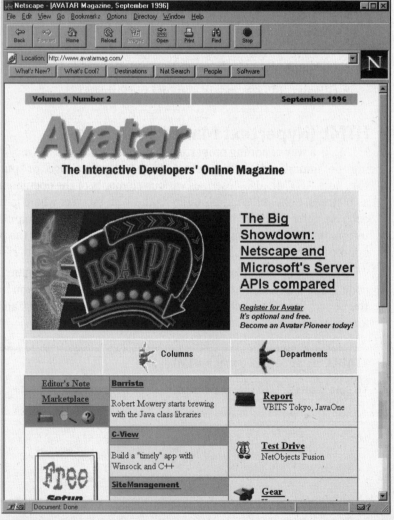

FIGURE 21.2: Web browsers interpret HTML code and render sophisticated pages.

NOTE

Table 21.1 is by no means a complete list! Take a look at Web pages in your browser and choose the View Source command to see what is really happening with HTML.

It's important to understand the distinction between this method of text annotation and page-description languages such as PostScript, which completely determine the appearance of a page. Initially, HTML was designed with the idea that the Web browser would make decisions about the appearance of the page on the screen. A tag like "Heading 1" doesn't say anything about the size or style of the type; it's up to the Web browsers to decide how to represent these styles. Presumably, a heading 1 style will have a larger text face than a heading 2 style, but that's not part of the specification.

Recent extensions to HTML give a page's designer more control over the ultimate appearance of the document. Microsoft and Netscape have proposed HTML tags to specify text color and font size, and Microsoft has been promoting the use of TrueType fonts in HTML pages. The HTML 3 specification defines the use of style sheets, which are referenced at the beginning of an HTML document. A style sheet explicitly describes the font, size, style, and alignment of particular tags. If your browser understands style sheets, you can design pages with HTML tags and specify the appearance of the text. For example, you could say that the H1 tag means right-aligned, 30-point Arial Bold underlined.

HTTP (Hypertext Transfer Protocol)

HTTP defines the interaction between the Web browser on the client computer and any number of servers out there on the Internet. HTTP is the language that the Web browser uses to ask for the HTML documents and any included elements (like pictures). A program that responds appropriately to HTTP requests can act as a server to any Web browser.

The most basic HTTP interactions are a series of HTTP requests made by the client computer, which are answered by HTTP responses from the server. For example, a client might ask the server to send a particular document, and the server might respond with the document itself, an indication that the user lacks file permissions to receive the document, or an error indicating that the document cannot be found.

HTTP specifies important information about documents. Last modification times are used by the Web browser to determine if the document is the same document that has been visited before. The Web browser might choose to retrieve the document from a local cache, rather than request the entire document from the server again. For this reason, it's possible for the Web browser to ask the server for a document *header* only. The header contains the document's attribute information, rather that the entire document body.

HTTP also specifies the document's type, so that the browser can handle the document appropriately. The type specification uses the MIME standard, discussed shortly.

Recent extensions to HTTP allow for the secure transfer of data utilizing encrypted connections.

URLs (Universal Resource Locators)

HTTP clients would not be able to find anything if they could not request specific documents from the servers. URLs provide a standardized way to refer to a local file, a file on an HTTP server, or a file on an FTP server. Here are some examples of URLs that specify HTTP, FTP, Telnet, and Gopher servers:

```
http://www.w3.org/pub/WWW/Protocols/HTTP-NG/Overview.html
ftp://ftp.cdrom.com/
telnet://starwars.arcade.com:4442
gopher://gopher.dartmouth.edu
```

UNCS OR URLS?

If you're familiar with Windows networking UNC (Universal Naming Convention) notation, you'll see a remarkable similarity between the purpose of URLs and UNCs. Indeed, in a future revision of NT, you'll be able to use URLs most anywhere you can currently use UNCs.

Here's a UNC that specifies a program on my computer:

```
\\FRANKENSTEIN\C$\WINNT\SYSTEM32\notepad.exe
```

And here's a UNC to read an executable file on a remote computer, have that program load onto the local computer, and get the program to display a text file on a third computer:

```
\\POOH\LanTeam\programs\wordpad.exe
\\EMV02\pub\showplan.txt
```

CONTINUED ➡

Because Microsoft's Internet Explorer understands UNCs, if you have peer file sharing enabled in Windows 95/98, you can create pages with links to files specifying the UNC, and have any Windows 95/98 computer (or NT workstation or server, for that matter) act as a Web server.

MIME (Multimedia Internet Mail Extension) File Types

MIME permits the association of file types and applications on the Internet. A MIME type is simply a text tag with a major and minor category. For example, the MIME type for a Microsoft Word file is `application/msword`.

To tag a file with the MIME type, the first line should contain the text "Content-type:" and the MIME type. The second line should be a blank line, and then the rest of the document is the file itself. For example, a Microsoft Word document would begin with the line:

```
Content-type: application/msword
```

followed by a blank line, followed by the Word document.

This method of encoding the file type in the first few characters of the file itself is common in the UNIX world, but is not so common for PCs running Microsoft software. Such computers use the filename extension to specify the file type. The Netscape Web browser lets you maintain a mapping of file extensions to MIME file types in the Helpers tab of the Preferences dialog box. Figure 21.3 shows an example.

NT 4 maintains the association of file extensions and MIME types in the file system. Internet Explorer and other applications can use this system-wide data to obtain the appropriate MIME file type information. Figure 21.4 shows the list of file type associations in NT.

Part ii

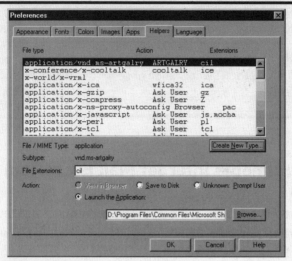

FIGURE 21.3: A mapping of file extensions to MIME types in the Helpers tab of Netscape's Preferences dialog box

FIGURE 21.4: NT 4 keeps a list of file extensions and MIME types.

GIF and JPEG Graphics File Formats

Just as HTML gives the standard for normal text files, GIF (Graphics Interchange Format) and JPEG (Joint Photography Engineering Group) are standards that define picture file formats on the Internet.

GIF is a file format developed by CompuServe. It's appropriate for computer-generated bitmaps with limited color palettes (say, less than 1,000 colors). The GIF format compresses the data using a run-length encoding scheme. For example, if the bitmap has large regions of blue in it, instead of storing a thousand blue pixels, the GIF format stores a single tag which means, "the next 1,000 pixels are blue." Virtually all Web browsers capable of displaying graphics can render GIF images.

JPEG is a graphics standard developed for high-level compression of photographic images, and it generally does a better job than GIF at storing digitized photos. Most modern graphics-capable Web browsers can render JPEG images. You care about the image compression specified in these graphics file formats if you're downloading an image across a slow data link (like a modem). Most slow connections use compression on the data stream. PPP specifies this automatically, and modems or ISDN adapters typically use compression to increase apparent data-transfer rates. But since the GIF file is made up of compressed data, the data compression used on your connection won't make much difference; that 130KB GIF file is going to come across your 28,800kbps connection in 7 to 10 seconds (on a really good day, taking into account the protocol overhead), whether or not your connection is using data compression.

WEB BROWSERS AND GRAPHICS

With Netscape as the corporate standard, and Internet Explorer capturing some of the market, you might think that you don't need to worry about the graphics capabilities of browsers. However, at some of the companies that I've helped to deploy intranet services, many of the people were using text-only browsers on terminals connected to mainframe computers. Because a major motivation for developing an intranet system is the universal distribution of (usually textual) corporate data, you should design your pages so that they make sense when viewed on these types of browsers.

CONTINUED ➡

Even if you know that only Netscape or other graphical browsers are going to be used with your intranet system, unless graphics are essential to the system (for example, in a chemical structure database), you should design the pages for text first. This is because the user may choose to turn off the picture downloads (which a graphical browser allows), in order to render the pages more quickly.

Use graphics to emphasize the data, as navigational aids, and to make the use of your system more pleasant. But unless you have to, don't require graphics displays in order to use your system.

Web Server Scripting

Web technology would not be interesting if it were not for the ability to add program logic to the server with the addition of server programs, or *scripts*. Instead of specifying an HTML document, a URL might point to a program that can generate the data on the fly. Scripts that can be called by an HTTP server conform to a specification called the Common Gateway Interface, and they are referred to as CGI scripts.

Here is an example of a very simple CGI script, written for a UNIX C-shell:

```
cat << EOF
Content-type: text/html

<html>
 <head><title>This is a test</title></head>
 <body>
 <h1>This is a test of the emergency CGI scripting
system.</h1>
 <hr>
 Uh, this is only a test...
 </body>
 </html>
EOF
```

When this file is invoked, it simply sends the HTML text to the standard output. (Of course, this CGI script is not particularly useful, since you could simply use a static HTML document instead.)

Here is another CGI script, which returns the date and time of the script's invocation:

```
#!/bin/sh

DATE=/bin/date
echo Content-type: text/plain
echo

if [ -x $DATE ]; then
    $DATE
else
    echo Cannot find date command on this system.
fi
```

Now we can start to consider useful applications. How about a CGI script that returns the formatted result of a SQL query?

INTEGRATING IIS WITH SQL SERVER

Now that we've discussed how you can take advantage of Web technology in conjunction with SQL Server and Internet Information Server, it's time to see how all this actually works. After a quick rundown of the components, we'll develop an intranet application.

NOTE

If you didn't install IIS when you installed NT Server, see Chapter 22 for instructions on installing IIS.

The Cast of Players

The connection between IIS and SQL Server is managed by the following pieces:

The IIS Database Connector   A filter program that ships with IIS, and is installed with it, is able to interpret special Internet Database Connector (IDC) files.

An IDC file   The Internet Database Connector program is driven by an IDC file, which specifies the data source (the name of an ODBC data source), the username passed to the data source, the HTML template file used to format the results of the query, and the SQL query itself.

An ODBC Data Source   Since you installed SQL Server, there should already be a System DSN defined for the SQL Server. If not, you'll need to create a System DSN in the ODBC Control Panel of the Web server.

An HTML template file   The Internet Database Connector will format the results of the SQL query according to the HTML template provided. Such template files have a file extension of .HTX. Template files are similar to HTML files, with a number of additional special directives that indicate where the SQL query results are to be inserted in the file.

NOTE

System DSNs allow the system processes to connect to databases via ODBC without an active user session. This is very desirable for a Web server, since you'll want the server to be making connections to the database, but you really don't want to leave a user logged in at the console of the NT server in order for everything to work.

Note that the SQL server and the Web server can be two different computers. A single Web server can query a different SQL server for each IDC file defined. Each IDC file would specify a separate ODBC connection for each of the desired SQL Server systems. However, for performance reasons, it's usually desirable to have the SQL server running on the same machine as the Web server. You don't want the (potentially large) set of results moving across the network to the Web server, only to have to make another trip from the Web server to the client. Don't move the data any more than you have to—keep the SQL server local to the Web server.

An Intranet Application

Ride-share applications are intended to help employees of a company find a car-pool buddy. Employees sign up for the ride-share program, giving permission to have their home address and phone number made available to other people in the program. Using the ride-share application, employees are able to search by city and find the employees who live close by.

Implementation Structure

A Visual Basic program can be used to essentially wrap a canned SQL query in a nice graphical browser. We have three tables in our sample employee database. The Core Employee table holds the name, office location, and office extension of the employees. This is the central table of the relational system—an arbitrary design decision. The Employee Address table holds the home street address and phone number information for the employees, keyed to the Core Employee table on an employee ID. The Employee Tax table was included in this discussion as an example of some very restricted information regarding the employees. It contains their salaries and tax ID information.

To make this implementation better meet the system's goals, I've added another table, Riders, which lists the employees who have signed up for the ride-share program. The improved ride-share system will check against the Riders table to verify that an employee wants to share a ride before listing that employee as a candidate.

In these sample IDC files, the System DSN, "Web SQL," is used as the ODBC data source, and the master SQL Server account, "sa," is used as the data source user. In a real production environment, you would want to create a robot user on the SQL server, specifically for this system. The Web SQL ODBC system DSN was created using the ODBC Control Panel.

NOTE

For more information about SQL Server and ODBC connectors, see the SQL Server documentation.

The City Query Screen

The first screen that the user will see is a pretty barren query screen, which asks the user to specify a city to search. You could do this a number of ways, such as by getting the name of the user, and then presenting the user with a list of employees in the same city. I decided to simply query on the city name.

A Visual Basic application can use a drop-down list box that lists all the possible cities. This drop-down box is a Visual Basic data-aware bound control. We specify a data source for the drop-down box, which returns the list of cities in the database, which we use to populate the list. All this stuff happens behind the screens for us via the magic of Visual Basic data-aware controls.

To accomplish the same feature with a Web-based implementation, we'll use an IDC file to specify the data source for the Web page. An IDC file specifies the ODBC data source, the HTML template used to format the query results, and the SQL query itself. To create a drop-down list that's populated with the list of city names in the database, we'll write an IDC file that has a SQL query of SELECT CITY FROM ADDRESS... for all of the employees who have signed up for the ride-share program:

```
Datasource: Web SQL
Username: sa
Template: form1.htx
SQLStatement:
+SELECT distinct city
+FROM  sybex.boyd.address a, sybex.boyd.rideshare r
+WHERE r.rider = 1
+AND   r.emp_id = a.emp_id
+ORDER BY city
```

The IDC file's query will return a list of all the cities. The HTX (HTML format template) file that we use to format this list of cities will create an HTML form, the action of which is to fire off our primary query (which ride-share employees live in the specified city?). The HTML page will display some explanatory information and the list of possible cities that results from the query in the IDC file. Note how we display each city name with a hyperlink to the buddies.idc database query:

```
<HTML>
<HEAD><TITLE>Find a RideShare Buddy</TITLE></HEAD>
<BODY>
<H1>Find a RideShare Buddy</H1>
This is a form that gets data from the database in order to
build a list of choices.
<p>
<p>
<%begindetail%>
<%if CurrentRecord EQ 0 %>
<b>Find RideShare Employees from:</b>
<p>
<%endif%>
<A
HREF="buddies.idc?selected_city='<%city%>'"><%city%></A><br>
<%enddetail%>
<p>
<hr>
</body>
</HTML>
```

When the user clicks a city name, the name of the city is passed to the "find a ride-share buddy" query as determined by the hyperlink:

```
<A HREF="buddies.idc?selected_city='<%city%>'"><%city%></A>
```

The IDC lets you express the value of variables with the `<%variablename%>` syntax. Note how the hyperlink for each city is set to the successive values of the list of cities with the `<%begindetail%>`... `<%enddetail%>` loop.

NOTE

For more information about the syntax and use of the HTML templates in the IDC file, see Chapter 8 of the IIS documentation.

See Figure 21.5 for a shot of our City Query page in action.

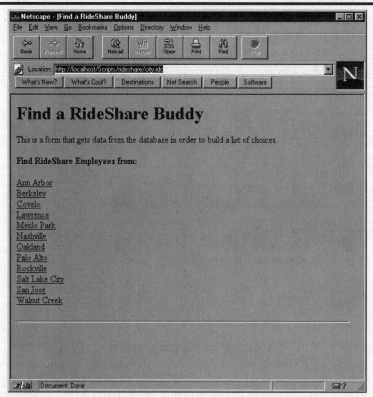

FIGURE 21.5: Users specify the desired city for the ride-share application by choosing the city from a list. The list is populated by the results of a SQL query, which returns all the cities inhabited by program participants.

Ride-Share Buddies Results Screen

After the user has specified the desired city, the city name is passed to the second IDC file, which queries the SQL database again, asking for all ride-share employees who live in the specified city.

```
Datasource: Web SQL
Username: sa
Template: buddies.htx
SQLStatement:
+SELECT fname, lname, e.phone extension, address, a.phone
hphone, areac
+FROM  sybex.boyd.phone e, sybex.boyd.rideshare r,
sybex.boyd.address a
+WHERE        r.rider = 1
+AND r.emp_id = e.emp_id
+AND e.emp_id = a.emp_id
+AND a.city  = '%selected_city%'
+ORDER BY e.lname
```

After the data is returned, the HTML template file simply displays the data as an HTML table. There is nothing fancy here:

```
<HTML>
<HEAD><TITLE>Rideshare Buddies in
<%idc.selected_city%></TITLE></HEAD>
<BODY>
<h1>Rideshare Buddies in <%idc.selected_city%></h1>
<hr>
<TABLE>
<%begindetail%>
<%if CurrentRecord EQ 0 %>
<TR BGCOLOR="#DDDDDD" FONT="Arial" SIZE=+1>
    <TH>Name</TH>
    <TH>Extension</TH>
    <TH>Home Phone</TH>
    <TH>Street Address</TH>
</TR>
<%endif%>
<TR>
    <TD><%fname%> <%lname%></TD>
    <TD><%extension%></TD>
    <TD>(<%areac%>) <%hphone%></TD>
    <TD><%address%></TD>
```

```
</TR>
<%enddetail%>
</TABLE>
<hr>
<A HREF="city.idc">Choose another city</A>
</body>
</HTML>
```

Note the way in which we check the record number. If we have not yet displayed any of the returned records, then the CurrentRecord is zero, and we'll display the table heading row. For each of the returned records, we write out the data, one row per returned record. See Figure 21.6 for an example of the query results.

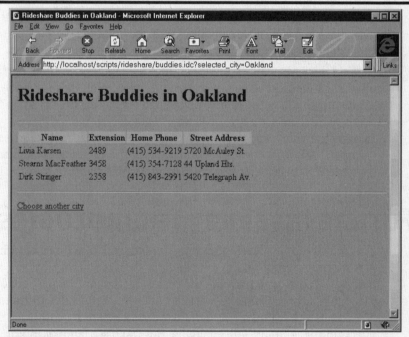

FIGURE 21.6: The ride-share program employees who live in the selected city are displayed in an HTML table.

Summary: The Ride-Share Application

In this example, we were able to integrate SQL Server and Web server systems on an NT Server 4 system to produce a simple application that allows anyone in the company to query the employee database in a well-defined fashion. You may have noticed from the screen shots that the application is equally accessible to PC and Macintosh users, running any of the standard Web browsers.

Aside from the TCP/IP protocol and the Web browser software, there is no configuration necessary on the client computers. We saw how simple it is to set up the server as well, because the ODBC connector makes it easy to get the data from the SQL Server database.

The example given here can be fleshed out in a number of ways. One feature that could be easily implemented within the framework of the current system is to have employees indicate preferred working hours, so that people would know which schedules could be accommodated.

It's dubious to restrict queries on the city name, since cities can border on one another, and someone just up the street might have an address in a different city. A better query would be to display a map, based on the user's name. The system would know the street address of the user performing the query, and could center the map on that street address, indicating ride-share partners on the map. With the ability to dynamically generate Web pages that may contain graphical data, the sky is the limit!

FUTURE INTERNET TECHNOLOGIES

This is a wild time to be in the computer industry. The Internet technologies spewing forth from the software industry are whizzing by very, very quickly. Internet standards are the best thing that ever happened to Microsoft, a company that's masterful at co-opting technology trends. The company has undergone a dramatic realignment recently, and the effects of that shift are still emerging. But you'll see familiar Internet-inspired standards pervading the newest pieces of Microsoft technology.

On the Server

The IDC file that we played with is but one example of a standard IIS extension. These extensions are implemented in a programming language like C++, and are written to a specification called the Internet Server Application Programming Interface (ISAPI).

Earlier, I implied that the IDC file was a CGI script, a program that IIS called in response to an HTTP request. I lied. The IDC file is an ISAPI extension to IIS, and ISAPI extensions are qualitatively different from the CGI scripts. Instead of running as a completely separate process, ISAPI extensions are loaded into the server's process memory space and are invoked like a simple binary function call. It's as if you were able to rewrite and recompile the Web server program; the extended functionality can be just as fast as the "core" Web server binary program. (You Apache-server programmers should feel right at home with this.)

Obviously, ISAPI extensions are not limited to SQL Server integration. With ISAPI, you are able to extend the Web server so it can look more and more like a standard application and file server, if you wish.

On the Desktop

The most dramatic changes effected by Internet technologies are occurring on the client PC desktops.

Document Objects

The most widely significant of the Microsoft Internet technologies on the desktop is the ability of Internet Explorer to act as a full Office application when displaying files that conform to the Document Object specification. DocObjects are files that know how to render themselves; they maintain a reference back to the application that created them. When a DocObject is displayed in a DocObject-compatible viewer, the viewer launches enough of the creating application to allow users to display and edit the document.

The end result is that when Internet Explorer opens a Word document, the Word application fires up, right in the Internet Explorer window. As far as the user is concerned, there is only the super-application, Internet Explorer, which knows how to display all the toolbars and menus appropriate to the current document. Figure 21.7 shows an example of Microsoft Word running inside the Internet Explorer window (note the Internet Explorer navigation buttons at the top).

Using DocObjects, you could use the Web server as a file server, as a document-management system. The user queries the system for the appropriate document, which is retrieved from the SQL database and then forwarded to Internet Explorer. When Internet Explorer receives the document, it's immediately displayed for editing in the Internet Explorer window.

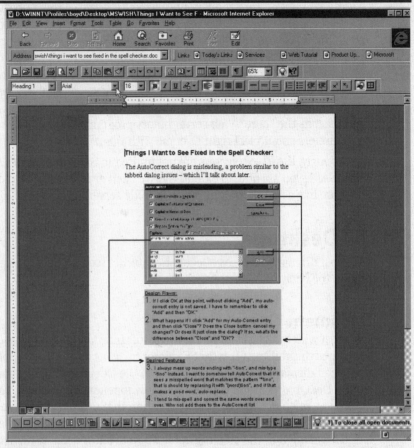

FIGURE 21.7: Internet Explorer is a Document Object container, so the Web browser can host standard desktop documents without switching to a separate application. Here, Microsoft Word is running inside the Internet Explorer frame.

The reference that the document maintains back to the creator application is *not* a file association; it's an OLE signature. Future versions of the NT file system will use OLE to maintain relationships between files and the applications that created them. This will clean up a lot of problems that currently exist with file types (maintained by filename extension associations) and file creators (which are not maintained at all in current versions of Microsoft operating systems).

The Document Object idea is one of the most far-reaching because Microsoft folks claim that they're committed to delivering this technology to the Macintosh platform as well as the PCs. If a Mac has Microsoft Office and Internet Explorer installed, it will be able to participate in the document-management system described here.

Ubiquitous Web Explorer

The Windows Explorer and Internet Explorer are being folded together to yield one program: Explorer. You will be able to "surf" your computer, or your Network Neighborhood, in precisely the same fashion as you currently surf the Web.

We've already used HTML template files to format the display of SQL query results. The next release of Windows will use an optional HTML template file in each directory of the computer to format the display of that directory's contents. A directory window could have any and all of the characteristics of an HTML page, including hyperlinks to other files or directories, embedded graphics, and even ActiveX Controls.

Note that HTML can create multiple-frame displays. You could set the Desktop to have many panes. For example, a long, narrow pane at the bottom might point to an "actual" Web site on the Internet, which could display stock price information. A pane in the upper-right corner might render an HTML file of your favorite places, or point to the corporate home page on the LAN, with links to important messages of the day (good-bye to junk e-mail and phone messages!).

For the Developer

And of course, the emerging Internet technologies give application developers a whole new set of tools.

ActiveX Controls

Currently, all you can display on an HTML page is some formatted text, graphics and simple animations, and the few user-interface goodies that are necessary for the creation of Web forms: radio buttons, checkboxes, pop-up menus, and text-entry fields. If you want users to enter a number within a specified range by using a slider control, you're out of luck.

And there are more limitations. Three-tier client/server applications need to be able to validate data entry according to business rules. Currently, people using a Web form must submit data to the Web server and have it parsed out before they're rewarded with the error message that indicates an inappropriate entry. This is very bad—there's no way to check the data as it's being entered, and the lack of feedback frustrates people.

Microsoft wants you to be able to create HTML pages and forms that contain any custom control that can be contained by a Visual Basic form. So with ActiveX technology, we could take all the pop-up menus and data grids from our application, plop them onto a Web page, and have that page served up from the server. This gives you all the benefits of Visual Basic program development, with freedom from the deployment issues that keelhauled our Visual Basic implementation.

Microsoft is committed to delivering ActiveX technology to the Macintosh clients. We'll need to see if any ActiveX control vendors are willing to jump into Mac development. The Java programming language may make that easier.

Integrated Java Development

All of the cool emerging Microsoft technologies are based on Microsoft's object-oriented software component model, the Common Object Model, or COM. Programmers who wish to take full advantage of all this technology have had to get comfortable with COM programming, and this can be an onerous task for the C++ developer.

Java to the rescue! The design of the Java programming language is apparently ideally suited to the development of COM objects. Microsoft has integrated COM support into its implementation of Java, so that you'll be able to create ActiveX controls and other Windows applications in Java.

To that end, the Microsoft implementation of Java is completely integrated into the Developer Studio programming environment, as you can see in Figure 21.8.

FIGURE 21.8: The Microsoft Developer Studio screen

WHAT'S NEXT?

This chapter explained how to develop intranet applications using IIS and SQL Server and introduced some other Internet technologies for developing intranet applications. The next chapter explains how to install IIS.

Part ii

Chapter 22

INSTALLING IIS

Microsoft Internet Information Server 4 (IIS 4) is included as a part of the NT 4 Option Pack CD (IIS 2 is included on the NT Server 4 CD and is upgraded to IIS 3 when Service Pack 3 is installed). IIS 4 is also available for download from Microsoft's Web site. In this short chapter, I'll go through the steps to install the IIS family of programs onto NT Server 4.

Adapted from *Mastering™ Microsoft® Internet Information Server™, Second Edition* by Peter Dyson

ISBN 0-7821-2080-6   848 pages $39.99

BEFORE YOU START

Installing IIS 4 is an easy, straightforward process, but you must do a few things before you start:

- ▶ If you are already running other versions of an FTP, a Web, or a news server from another vendor, you must disable these services or uninstall them from your system before you start the installation of IIS. Check the documentation provided with the original application for information on how to do this.

- ▶ If you are running previous versions of IIS, such as version 2 or 3, they must be uninstalled prior to installing IIS 4.

- ▶ You must be logged on to the server with Administrator permissions before you can install IIS.

- ▶ Be sure that Internet Explorer is not running on your server.

- ▶ Close any applications that use ODBC until after the installation is complete.

Once these operational requirements are met, you need to consider the hardware requirements.

Hardware Requirements for Your Web Server

Before you start the installation process, you must make sure that your computer meets the hardware requirements of NT Server running as a Web server. As usual, you should plan to spend as much as your budget will allow, especially on the critical areas of processor, memory, hard-disk space, and the communications link to your ISP (Internet service provider).

In the Intel world, use a Pentium processor running at 100MHz or faster, with at least 32MB of memory—more if you can get it. The amount of hard disk space you need depends on how large your Web content files turn out to be, but you will need at least 200MB of free space to begin with. On a busy Internet site, you may find that you are managing a large number of HTML files, graphics, scripts, and audio and video files, and so you will need a lot more hard disk space.

You will need a VGA video card to load NT Server. Many of the administration programs you will be using certainly look much better on SVGA, but you certainly don't need the latest, all-turbo video accelerator board installed on the server. A CD-ROM drive and a fast tape drive are also essential elements, along with a UPS system and appropriate modems for dial-up RAS (Remote Access Service) users.

In the Alpha world, the requirements are similar. A 200MHz processor is recommended, along with at least 200MB of free hard disk space and 64MB of memory. And once again, a CD-ROM drive, tape drive, and UPS complete the picture.

You will also need the appropriate communications equipment to support your link to the Internet. This can be as small and compact as the terminal adapter needed to hook into an ISDN link, or it can be a whole room full of equipment for some of the larger data communications connections. In some instances, most of the communications equipment may be at the phone company's facility rather than at yours.

The larger the communications requirement, the more equipment you will need, and the more crucial proper air-conditioning becomes, even in northern climates and in Europe—areas that don't normally use air-conditioners at any time. And depending on the final configuration you choose for your Web server, you may well find yourself looking for a location for a firewall computer, as well as a router or two.

Completing the Preinstallation Checklist

To install Microsoft IIS 4, you must have the following:

- ▶ A server computer with at least sufficient hardware to support NT Server 4 and IIS 4.

- ▶ An installed copy of NT Server 4.

- ▶ An installed copy of the NT Server Service Pack 3.

- ▶ The TCP/IP networking protocol installed on the server. You can use the Network applet in the Control Panel to install and configure the TCP/IP protocol and several other related items.

- ▶ Sufficient hard disk space to load the parts of the IIS package that you want to use, as well as space for all the Web content files your site will host.

To publish on the Internet, you will also need the following:

▶ A suitable link to the Internet, provided by your ISP or InterNIC

▶ The appropriate device drivers to connect your server to that communications circuit

▶ An IP address, also provided by your ISP or InterNIC

▶ A DNS-registered name for that IP address from InterNIC or one of the other name-registration organizations such as an ISP

If you plan to publish Web content using an intranet instead, the requirements are a little different. You will need the following:

▶ An appropriate network interface card and a suitable connection to your local area network.

▶ WINS or DNS installed on a computer connected to your intranet. This is optional, but it means that users of your intranet can use a friendly name rather than the dotted-decimal IP address when they want to access the server and your Web content.

Adding IIS to a Busy Network Server

The hardware we looked at earlier describes the main components for your Web server, but what should you do if you are adding a Web service to your existing NT Server network, which already has certain hardware installed and an existing population of users?

Do not underestimate the impact that the additional Web traffic will have on the performance of your server, and be ready to upgrade your hardware if the existing installation proves inadequate.

If you have to run IIS within your existing system, you may not only alienate new visitors to your Web site as they wait for an overburdened server to respond, but also aggravate existing corporate users as they watch their previously speedy applications grind to a halt.

INSTALLING IIS 4 ON NT SERVER 4

Installing IIS 4 is straightforward—all you have to do is run the Setup program from the CD. If you already have your connection to the Internet via your ISP or if you are publishing content on an intranet, you can simply accept many of the default values during installation, and your Web site will be up and running in no time. Your ISP will tell you the IP address to use with your Web server, as well as the subnet mask and the IP address of the default gateway system through which your server will route all traffic to the Internet.

IIS 4 includes the following components:

Internet Information Server   The Web and FTP server

Microsoft Transaction Server   A transaction-processing server for distributed server applications

Active Server Pages   A server mechanism that provides dynamic content accessible by all browsers

Data Access Components   A set of database-access components

Posting Acceptor   An application used when posting Web site content to your own server or to an ISP's server

FrontPage and FrontPage Extensions   An HTML authoring tool and a set of server extensions

Microsoft Management Console (MMC)   A new administrative tool that provides a basic set of tools; additional functions are provided by specific snap-ins

Internet Service Manager Snap-in for MMC   An MMC snap-in application used to configure all aspects of your Web and FTP services

Index Server   A search engine capable of indexing a variety of document types

Internet Service Manager (HTML Version)   An HTML-based version of Internet Service Manager used to administer IIS 4 using a browser

Script Debugger   A tool used to debug server and client scripts

Java Virtual Machine   A Java environment used to run Java applications on the server

Documentation   Online documentation in HTML format accessible with a browser

Usage Import   A tool used to provide Web site statistical information derived from IIS 4 log files

Part ii

Report Writer   A tool used to create reports of Web site activity

Content Analyzer   A Web management tool used to look at and explore your Web site

Web Publishing Wizard   An application used to publish Web content to a server

News Server   A news server you can use to host local discussion groups

Certificate Server   A server capable of issuing client and server digital certificates

NOTE

If you are upgrading from IIS version 3, you may already have the Crystal Reports and NetShow packages installed and running on your system.

The dialog boxes you will see during the installation of IIS depend on which of the components described in this section you choose to install. A basic intranet Web site will need IIS, along with perhaps Posting Acceptor and the Web Publishing Wizard. As your site grows larger and more complex, you will probably add the Site Server Express components Content Analyzer, Usage Import, and Report Writer to track your Web site statistics. If you work with a large number of simple text and Microsoft BackOffice documents, add Index Server so that you can search and index these documents.

As your site continues to grow and connects to the Internet, you might add Active Server Pages to provide dynamic content to your users, as well as Certificate Server as your need for security increases. And as your Web site begins to attract many visitors, add Transaction Server to smooth out the problems caused by a large number of simultaneous ASP requests. If you initially installed an IIS component, only to find that you are not using it, remove it as soon as convenient, and use the system resources for other, more important purposes.

WARNING

A full installation of all the IIS component parts can take an hour or so, and you will need to shut down the server a time or two so that your new settings can take effect. Yes, it looks like another long night or a weekend session is required for the installation to avoid inconveniencing your day-time users too much. If you are setting up a dedicated Web server, you're in luck; this warning obviously does not apply.

Adding or Removing IIS 4 Options

You can always add (or remove) IIS components once your initial installation is complete by following these steps:

1. Choose Start ➤ Programs ➤ Windows NT 4.0 Option Pack ➤ Windows NT 4.0 Option Pack Setup.

2. In the Options dialog box, click the Add/Remove button.

3. Select the checkboxes for the options you want to install, and clear the boxes for any components you want to remove.

4. Follow the directions on the screen. These directions depend on the options you chose to install or remove.

Once your installation is complete, you are ready to use the Internet Service Manager to configure your system.

TESTING YOUR IIS INSTALLATION

When you complete the installation, you can test your IIS very quickly indeed to make sure that everything is working properly. If you have prepared files in HTML, simply copy them into the default home directory; if you are using the Web server, copy them into the `\Inetpub\wwwroot` directory. Be sure your home page HTML file is called `default.htm`. What you do next depends on whether you are creating an Internet or an intranet site.

Testing a Server Connected to Your Intranet

To test a server attached to your internal corporate intranet, follow these steps:

1. Be sure the server is physically connected into the network and that the WINS server service or another name-resolution service is running.

2. Start Internet Explorer or your favorite browser on one of the workstations attached to your network.

Part ii

3. Choose File ➤ Open to enter the URL for the default home directory of the newly installed server and press Enter. If the name of your server is registered with WINS as `Wallaby` and if the home page you want to view has the filename `default.htm`, this URL becomes:

    `http://Wallaby/default.htm`

The home page will be displayed on your screen in the browser.

Testing a Server Connected to the Internet

The steps used to test a server connected to the Internet are quite similar:

1. Start Internet Explorer on a workstation or on the server; it doesn't matter which, but the computer must have an active connection to the Internet.

2. Choose File ➤ Open to enter the URL for the default home directory of the server. If your server is registered as `www.company.com` and if the name of the file you want to view is `default.htm`, this URL becomes:

    `http://www.company.com/default.htm`

The home page will be displayed on your screen in the browser.

WHAT'S NEXT?

This chapter described how to install IIS 4 on your NT Server computer. Now that we've covered getting NT Server up and running, managing users and security, and integrating electronic messaging systems (Exchange Server) and Internet/intranet systems (IIS), the final topic in this part is disaster. In Chapter 23, you'll learn about how to prevent data loss due to disaster, as well as how to recover from a disaster.

Chapter 23

NETWORK PROTECTION AND DISASTER RECOVERY

N o matter how fault-tolerant your system is, there's always *some* fault it can't tolerate. It could be something as simple as an incorrectly configured NT server, or something as dramatic as your server falling down a crack in an earthquake. RAID is nice, but disk mirroring or disk striping is not going to help you here. What you need now is a way to rebuild your server's operating system and data, from the bottom up if need be.

Adapted from *Mastering™ Windows® NT® Server 4 (Sixth Edition)* by Mark Minasi

ISBN 0-7821-2445-3   1616 pages $59.99

DEFEATING DISASTERS: AN OVERVIEW

I'll get to the particular tools that you can use to examine and recover from disasters in a bit. But first, let's look at how to avoid the disasters in the first place. You do this with several approaches:

▶ Create and maintain physical security on your network. If the bad guys (and the good guys who just happen to be careless) can't get to your network hardware, it's a lot harder for them to damage it.

▶ Protect your data with a good backup strategy. You have to back up both user data and system areas. There are two different tools for this, named NTBACKUP and RDISK. (RDISK requires an undocumented option to make it really useful, but I'll explain that later in this chapter.)

▶ When the worst happens, you must be ready for it with a specific, written-down disaster recovery plan. Everybody must know what they're expected to do in the case of a massive network failure.

▶ When things go wrong, it's useful to have some knowledge about how the system starts up, when it crashes, and *why* it crashes. Two NT tools called the Kernel Debugger and DUMPEXAM can give you some insight into that.

NETWORK PHYSICAL SECURITY

An ounce of prevention is worth a pound of cure, right? One of the main concerns of computer security, and the one that this chapter addresses, is *physical security*. Physical security is a blanket term for the ways in which you *physically* protect your server and network from harm— stupid accidents, environmental incidents, espionage, and theft.

Preventing Environmental Problems

It would be terrible if you went to all the trouble of protecting your server from theft or tampering and then lost it to a cup of coffee spilled into its air-intake vents.

Provide Electrical Protection

The first source of environmental problems that should never be ignored is the wall socket.

▶ Use a UPS/power conditioner on your servers to protect them from dirty power and power surges. If you don't want to buy a UPS for every workstation (and I don't blame you if you don't—that can get expensive), buy a *power conditioner*. This (roughly) $150 device cleans up noisy power and compensates for low voltage.

▶ While nothing will guarantee 100 percent protection from lightning damage, you can reduce lightning damage with an odd trick: tie five knots in each workstation's power cord, as close to the wall as you can get them. That way, if lightning strikes the wiring, it will kill the cord rather than travel through the cord and kill the computer.

NOTE

Does this really work? Well, Washington, DC, where I live, was hit by a terrible lightning storm in 1990. I tied knots in the cords of all the computers in my house beforehand, but hadn't thought to do it to the television set cord. During the storm, one of my neighbors took a direct lightning hit and a huge power surge hit my wiring. The cords of all the computers were warmed up a bit, but the power surge never touched the computers themselves. The television set was another matter—the surge traveled straight through the cord to the television's innards and rendered the television DOA. I couldn't have asked for a better test, though at the time I wasn't in a mood to appreciate the benefits of having had an unknotted control group to compare the knotted cords with.

▶ Don't plug any computer into the same plug as a power hog like a refrigerator, copier, or laser printer. Laser printers periodically draw as much power as an entire kitchen full of appliances.

▶ If your computers are all in one room and you want to ground the room, don't just ground that room; ground the entire office. Otherwise, it's kind of like putting a giant "KICK ME" sign on your computers, because they will be the easiest thing around for lightning to reach.

If you're looking for a one-stop-shopping answer to your server's power needs, I like the American Power Conversion Smart-UPS series quite a bit. These UPSs are a combination of a power conditioner and a standby power supply.

Part ii

There is more to know about power and PCs, but so ends the quick overview.

Know Your Building

When you're positioning servers and workstations, know what's in the building that could affect them. For example, are there old (or new) leaks in the building? Putting a server or workstation underneath a suspicious brown stain in the ceiling is a bad idea, even if the leak was "fixed" years ago and the building manager claims that "it can't possibly be a problem."

Excessive heat and moisture are bad for equipment. Is heat-producing equipment mounted in the ceiling? How about equipment that produces water condensation? One company moved into a new building and discovered that the air-conditioning equipment was mounted in the ceiling over the server room. Not only did the air-conditioning generate copious amounts of heat in exactly the place where it was least wanted, but the water condensation that the units generated began raining down onto the servers one morning. Luckily, the servers recovered nicely, but it could have been an ugly scene.

If the servers are locked in their own room, is that room staying cool enough for safety? The regular air-conditioning that the rest of the office uses might not be enough, due to the restricted ventilation in a closed room and all the heat that computers generate.

Obviously, you shouldn't position *any* computer—whether it's a workstation or a server—in direct sunlight.

Keep Contaminants Away from the Servers

It is hard to keep people from eating or drinking near their workstations, but this should not be true in the server room. A strict no-food-or-beverage policy is necessary in that room to keep someone from pouring a cola into the file server. The proliferation of nonsmoking offices makes the next comment almost unnecessary, but even if employees can smoke in the office, the one place they should *not* smoke is around the servers or workstations. Smoke particles in the hard disk are a *very* bad idea.

Preventing Theft and Tampering

Although the lion's share of physical security problems stem from accidents, theft and tampering are also things to watch out for if the information on your system might be valuable to someone else. You need to keep unauthorized people from gaining access to the network's information.

Keep the Server Room Locked

Most people who use the network don't have a valid reason for going into the server room, so you can keep it locked. If people can't get into the server room, they can't:

- ▶ Reboot the server. If you are using the FAT file system, an intruder could reboot the server from a floppy (assuming that there are floppy drives on your server) and copy or delete valuable data. This, by the way, is one of the main reasons for using the NTFS file system—NTFS files and directories are invisible to users of the FAT file system.

- ▶ Steal the hard drive(s). This might sound improbable, but someone who has the tools and experience can simply remove the hard drive and take it elsewhere to crack into it at leisure, rather than try to work with it on-site. Stealing a hard drive is less awkward than stealing an entire server, but locking the file server room can also prevent server theft.

- ▶ Reinstall NT Server. While this sounds like a lot of trouble to go through, it's perfectly possible. Reinstalling the operating system doesn't harm the data already on the drive (unless you repartition it), so someone with the knowledge and the time could reinstall NT Server and change all the passwords to get access to your data.

Limit Access to the Server

Even if you can't lock up the server for space or administrative reasons, you can still limit people's physical access to it with the following tactics:

- ▶ Disable the server's A: drive. Without an A: drive, no one can reboot the system from a floppy unless they reconnect the A: drive first. Admittedly, this means you can't reboot either, but this could buy you some time if someone broke in intending to reboot the server. Use the floplock service that comes with the Windows NT Resource Kit. When the floplock service is running, only members of the Administrators group can access the floppy drives.

Part ii

▶ Disable the reset button and the on/off switch. Most of the time, if you need to reboot the server, you do it with the Shutdown option on the Start menu. Without a big red switch or reset button, no one can boot the server unless they use the Shutdown option.

These are somewhat extreme measures, and truthfully I don't have enough need for security to use them on my network. Some of my clients, however (hint: I live in Washington DC, remember?), have found these suggestions quite implementable.

Use Passwords Well

Well-chosen passwords are an important part of the security process. When selecting them, strike a balance between passwords that are too easy to guess and in service too long, and passwords that are so complicated and changed so frequently that users must write them down to remember them. An eight-letter minimum and a 30-day change policy (with the user unable to use the same password more than once every three changes) are probably about right. Experimentation and experience will help you choose a combination that fits your needs.

NT Server passwords are case-sensitive, so you can make them more difficult to guess by capitalizing them in unexpected places (like pAssword). Don't get too creative with this, however, or your users will never be able to type them in right.

There are programs that can guess passwords. These programs feed a dictionary to the system until the system accepts a word. To eliminate this path into your system, use words not found in the dictionary: names (picard), misspelled words (phantum), foreign words (*chamaca*), or made-up words (aooga). At password-changing time in one government installation, the users are presented with a two-column list of four-letter words (not obscenities, just words with four letters in them). The users pick one word from column A and one from column B, and then they combine them to form a new password, leading to such combinations as PINKFEET or BOATHEAD. These passwords are easy to remember and can't be found in the dictionary. Better yet, take the two words and string them together with a punctuation mark, like stars.geronimo.

Most names are not found in the dictionary, but don't let your users use the names of their spouses, children, pets, or anything else as passwords. One branch security manager at the Pentagon tells me that he had to go in and change all of his users' passwords when he discovered that a number of them had chosen the names of Japanese World War II battleships—a subject related to their mission and therefore not impossible to guess.

While the password-generating programs that randomly select a number-letter combination create nearly invulnerable passwords, these passwords may not be the most effective protection. They're too hard for most people to remember and often end up being written down.

Remove old user accounts from the system if the person using the account no longer needs it. If the user may need the account again (a summer intern, for example, could return the following summer), disable the account rather than wiping it out altogether, but don't keep accounts active on the system unless someone is using them.

Finally, even if someone figures out a password and breaks into the system, you can reduce the possible damage by giving users only the minimum access to the system and to files that they need.

 NOTE
See Chapter 20 for information about account and file permissions.

Control Access to the Printer

The printer might seem like a harmless part of your network, but think again: if you have company secrets, those secrets could leave your network via your printer even if you've adopted diskless workstations. To try to avoid this, take these steps:

▶ Restrict printer access to those who need it. (You can also restrict access to keep people from playing with an expensive color printer.)

▶ Audit printer use in the Printers folder so that you know who is printing what. If you discover someone who prints more output to the printer than his work would justify, he may not be stealing company secrets—but he might be wasting company time and resources on personal projects. Be aware, however, that auditing server activity slows down the server.

▶ Restrict printer access time to normal working hours.

▶ Don't give out Power User rights to just anyone. Power users can create and connect to network devices, thereby negating all that you've done to control access to the devices.

Part II

Prevent Portable Penetration

Say that you have an Ethernet bus network. What happens if someone comes in with a portable and plugs in? What rights does this person have on the network?

Potentially disastrous as this may sound, if you've set up the network as a domain and the person with the portable does not know the administrator's password, plugging the portable into the network won't get that person anywhere. This is because the administrator is the only one who can add a computer to the domain, and a non-member is shut out of the domain.

If, however, your network is set up on a peer-to-peer basis, a plugged-in portable can do a lot more damage, due to the Guest account on all the machines. Many people never bother to change the Guest account password from the default, and one of the easiest ways of accessing a network is through the Guest account. While Guest account access is not as powerful as that of the Administrator account, Guest account users can still view, copy, and delete files to which they have not been expressly refused access.

Therefore, to protect your network best, institute a domain controller so that no one can log on to the system from a new computer. If you *must* have a peer-to-peer setup, eliminate the Guest account on all the network's workstations or, at the very least, change the password on a regular basis.

How Much Protection Is Too Much?

Protecting your system is a never-ending process; for every safeguard you use, there is always a means to get past it. Therefore, when protecting your network, come up with a balance between how much the data is worth and how much the protection costs. If protecting your data costs more than the data is worth, it's time to relax a little. The cost of perfect protection is infinite amounts of money and eternal vigilance. If you hope to ever get anything done or to have money to spend on anything else, weigh your protection costs against what you're protecting and plan accordingly. There's little point in spending the money for more drives so that you can have RAID fault tolerance, for example, if all that you're protecting are applications for which you have the original disks and backups.

When something goes wrong with your system, think *non-invasive*. Three of your most valuable troubleshooting implements are:

▶ An NT-bootable disk

- ▸ The Emergency Repair Disk for the machine in trouble (don't forget, these disks are specific to the machine on which they were made)

- ▸ Your notebook, in which you record every change you make to the servers and workstations, so that when something goes wrong, you can figure out what changed since the last time it worked

BACKUP STRATEGIES

Physical security keeps people and the outside environment from getting to your equipment. Now let's consider how to protect your data. The first line of defense against data loss is backups. Backups are like exercise—they're necessary but they often don't get done unless they're easy to do. NT Server does a lot toward making sure that backups get done by providing a tape backup program that is fast and easy to use.

Performing Backups

You can find the Backup icon in the Start menu under the Administrative Tools program group. When you highlight the icon, you see a screen that looks like Figure 23.1.

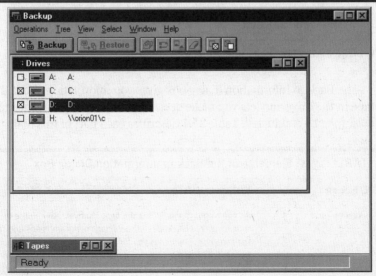

FIGURE 23.1: The opening screen for Backup

When you want to back up a drive, you first need to select the drive, even if you have only one on your server. To do so, click in the checkbox next to the drive until it has an *X* in it. If for some reason you open the Backup screen and the drives window is only an icon similar to the Tapes icon at the bottom of Figure 23.1, just double-click it to open it.

Once you've selected the drive that you want to back up and a tape is in the drive, you're ready to go. Click the Backup button in the upper-left corner or select the Backup option from the Operations drop-down menu. You see a screen that looks like Figure 23.2.

FIGURE 23.2:   The Backup Information dialog box

The Backup Information dialog box gives you information about the tape in the drive and lets you make decisions about how you want the backup to be conducted. Table 23.1 describes each part of this dialog box.

TABLE 23.1: Elements of the Backup Information Dialog Box

OPTION	WHAT IT DOES
Current Tape	As you might guess, this is the tape that you have in the drive. I'm reusing an old backup, so the Backup program reads and gives me the tape name, which is the tape's creation date. This is good, because if I use this tape for my backup, I'll lose the data from the 5/30 backup, and this reminder of when the tape was made could save me from mistakenly overwriting my data.

TABLE 23.1 continued: Elements of the Backup Information Dialog Box

Option	What It Does
Creation Date	If you named the tape something other than the date it was created, this tells you when the current tape was created.
Owner	This is the domain and username of the person who made the backup.
Tape Name	This is the name that you give the new information on this tape. You can use the default name of "Tape created on [*date*]" if you like, or you can call it something like "Backup before installing OS/2 do not erase" to give your memory a little extra jog. The tape name can be up to 50 characters long, including spaces, but if it's longer than 32 characters, you won't be able to see the entire name without scrolling down the line.
Verify After Backup	If you select this option, the Backup program checks to make sure that, after it's done, the backup matches the original data on the disk. Verification takes a little longer, but it's a good way to double-check that your backups are actually complete and accurate when you need them.
Backup Local Registry	Check this box to include a copy of the local Registry files in the backup set. The local Registry files are your disk configuration information, and in the case of disaster, having this information might not be a bad idea.
Operation	Selecting Append or Replace makes a decision about what happens to the data already on the tape, if there is any. Select Append to add the new backup to the backup already on the tape and not lose anything. Make sure that you have enough room on the tape for both the old data and the new. Select Replace to have the new backup overwrite the old one. Be sure that you no longer need an old backup before selecting Replace, because you can't get back the data once you overwrite it.
Restrict Access to Owner or Administrator	Restricting access is probably a good idea for a number of reasons. First, no one but the owner or administrator should have any need to access backed-up files. If someone else needs an old copy of a file, they can ask the people authorized to give it to them. Second, making everyone responsible for their own backups helps avoid recrimination when a backup is missing or corrupted. If no one can use a backup other than its owner, then, if something happens to it, it's clear who did it.
Drive Name	The drive name is the name of the drive you selected for the backup before you got to this dialog box. You can't change it here, so if you selected the wrong drive, cancel out of this box and change your selection.

CONTINUED ➡

TABLE 23.1 continued: Elements of the Backup Information Dialog Box

OPTION	WHAT IT DOES
Description	You can fill in a description of the backup in addition to its name. Therefore, if you wanted to record both the date and the contents of the drive, you could name the tape "Backup from 03/09/97" and *describe* it as "Pre-OS/2 installation backup—keep," or some such thing.
Backup Type	If you click on the down-arrow on the right side of this box, you see a number of different backup types to choose from:

	Normal	A full backup—everything selected gets backed up, whether or not the archive bit is set. (The archive bit is attached to a file when it's changed and removed during backup, allowing selective backups of the files that have changed since the last backup.) This is the default option. Even if you normally do incremental backups (described below), periodically doing a normal backup to make sure that everything on the disk is backed up is a good idea.
	Copy	A full backup of all the selected files on the disk. In this case, however, the archive bit is not reset after the files have been backed up—from looking at Explorer, you can't tell that anything was backed up.
	Differential	Backs up only those files with the archive bit set, but doesn't reset it afterwards. This is useful for interim backups between full backups, because restoring the data only requires restoring the last full backup and the most recent differential.
	Incremental	Like a differential backup, this option backs up only those files with the archive bit set, but the incremental backup then resets the bit.
	Daily	Backs up only those files that have been modified *that day* (as opposed to since the last backup), and does not reset the archive bit. If you want to take home the files that you've worked on during a given day, this can be a good way of getting them all.

Log Information	Backup log records how the backup went: how many files were backed up, how many skipped (if any), how many errors there were (if any), and how long the backup took. You might as well keep the backup logs in the default directory unless you have a good reason to move them elsewhere, just so you don't forget where they are.

TABLE 23.1 continued: Elements of the Backup Information Dialog Box

OPTION	WHAT IT DOES
Full Detail, Summary Only	On the bottom of the dialog box you can see that you have a choice of two kinds of backup log records: Full Detail and Summary Only (or no log). A full log records the name of every file backed up in addition to the other information about major events that are described above. A summary merely records major events. For most purposes, a summary log is fine. The only time that you might need a full log is if you were doing a differential backup and wanted to have some record of what files you backed up.

Now that you've filled out the Backup Information dialog box, you're ready to do the backup. Click OK, and, if you're using an old backup tape and you selected the Replace option, you see a screen that looks like Figure 23.3. Once again, if you're sure that you want to overwrite the data, click Yes.

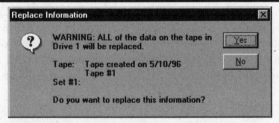

FIGURE 23.3: Warning that data will be overwritten

You move now to the dialog box in Figure 23.4, which keeps you informed of the backup's progress. Normally, when you see this screen, Abort will not be grayed out unless you had to abort the backup, and OK won't be a viable choice from the time you begin the backup until it's finished. As the backup progresses, you can keep track of it by looking at this screen.

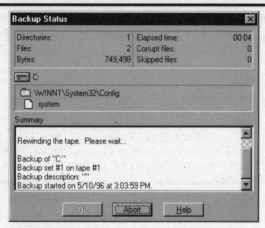

FIGURE 23.4: The Backup Status screen

Performing Automatic Backups

To be safe, you should back up your drive every day, since that way you never lose more than one day's worth of work. Unfortunately, running even an easy-to-use backup program like NT Server's takes time away from your day—the task-switching involved causes you to take time from your real work, and you might forget altogether if you get caught up in something else.

Fortunately, you don't have to depend on your memory or your schedule to run daily backups. NT Server provides two ways to run backups on a regular schedule: the command prompt and the WINAT.EXE GUI program.

HOW DO I BACK UP DATA?

With a tape in the drive, start the Backup program by selecting Start ➤ Programs ➤ Administrative Tools ➤ Backup. Select the drive that you want to back up, then click the Backup button in the upper-left area of the screen. Fill in the Backup Information dialog box as appropriate and click OK.

The backup should proceed normally.

Important note: You cannot read or restore tapes backed up in NT Server 4 on a server running a previous version of NT Server.

Backing Up from the Command Prompt

Alternate methods of backing up include using net schedule and at commands, to schedule batch commands to run at a certain time. Among the other programs that you can run with the at command is the DOS version of NT Server's Backup program, called NTBACKUP. The parameters this command uses provide you with almost the same flexibility that the GUI backup program does—it's just a little trickier to use.

To run NTBACKUP, type the following:

```
ntbackup backup path options
```

where *path* is the drive (and directory, if you're only backing up part of a drive) that you want to back up and *options* is one of the switches shown in Table 23.2. You can select more than one drive at a time—just type the drive letters with colons after them. In the path, you can also specify individual files to back up, or specify all the files of a certain type with the asterisk wildcard (*).

TABLE 23.2: Switches for Use with NTBACKUP

SWITCH	DESCRIPTION
/a	Makes the mode of backup append, so that the backed up files will be added to those already on the tape. If this switch is omitted, the new files will overwrite any files now on the tape.
/b	Backs up the local registry.
/d	Lets you describe the backup. Enclose your text in quotation marks after the /d switch.
/l	Writes a log of the backup. You must specify a location for the log to be written, like this: /l "c:\log\log.txt". As shown, you enclose the log's destination in quotation marks.
/r	Restricts access to the tape's owner and the network administrator.
/t	Lets you select the backup type. You can choose to do a Normal, Copy, Incremental, Differential, or Daily backup; /t incremental gives you an incremental backup. If you don't use this switch, you perform a normal backup.
/v	Verifies that the backup was done correctly by comparing the data on the tape with the original data on the drive after the backup is done. Backups take a little longer with verification, but this lets you know that the data was written correctly.

Part ii

Let's start with a simple example. To obtain a full backup of all the files on a C:\WPFILES directory that end with the extension DOC, you would type this:

```
ntbackup backup c:\wpfiles\*.doc
```

Finally, to perform a differential backup of all the files in both drives C: and D:, verify the backup, describe the backup as the monster drives on the server, perform a backup of the local Registry, restrict access to the owner and network administrator, and record a backup log under the name C:\LOG\LOG.TXT, you would type the following on one line:

```
ntbackup backup c: d: /v/r/b/d "The monster drives on the
server" /l "c:\log\log.txt"
```

Now that you're familiar with the DOS parameters for the Backup program, you can use it to do timed backups. Start the scheduler service using the command net start schedule, and then use the at command to set up the automatic backup. For instance, to do an incremental backup every day at 3 A.M. of the \WPFILES directory on drive C, verify the backup, append the files to the ones already on the disk, describe the backup as "My word-processing files," and record the log in C:\LOG\LOG.TXT, you would type this on one line:

```
at 3:00 /every:M,Tu,W,Th,F,Sa,Su ntbackup backup c:\wpfiles
/t incremental /v/a/d "My wordprocessing files" /l
"c:\log\log.txt"
```

For another example, to back up your C: drive at 11:00 every Wednesday, start the scheduling service by typing net start schedule, and then type:

```
at 11:00 /every:wednesday ntbackup backup c:
```

These commands would then be entered on the job list, which you can view by typing at from the command prompt. You don't have to set up the command as you see it in the example; you can use the switches to configure your backup procedure as you see fit. No matter what combination of switches you use to customize your automatic backups, however, using the /a switch to append the new backups to the ones already on your tape is probably a good idea. You're using this daily incremental backup to keep your backups current between weekly full backups, so you want to keep a complete record of all changes made between those full backups.

Using the Scheduler (Winat) Program

Unless you're really fond of working from the command prompt, the WINAT GUI program is probably easier to use, even though you still need to know the MS-DOS syntax. WINAT is one of a number of handy applications that come with the NT Resource Kit. Once you load the Resource Kit, you need to use the Program Manager's New option to add it manually to one of the program groups. You can put the program item wherever you like; I put mine in the Administrative Tools program group.

When you've added WINAT to a program group, you're ready to go. Double-click the program icon, pull down the File menu, choose Select Computer, type in your computer name if it is not already there, click OK, and then choose the Add button. You see a screen that looks like Figure 23.5.

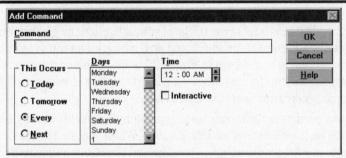

FIGURE 23.5:   The Add Command dialog box

In the Command text box, type in the command syntax, following the rules in the previous section on using the command prompt. Once you've typed in the command, use the radio buttons to select how often you want the event to occur (since we're configuring a daily incremental backup, choose Every). Next, Ctrl+click all the days of the week on which you want the backup to run. For our installation, we selected every day, for those times when someone's working over the weekend, but you may want to choose different days. Finally, choose the time when you want the backup to run. It's best to choose a time very late at night or early in the morning when there is little network activity. Once you've set up the command and the times, click OK to return to the original screen. It should look like Figure 23.6.

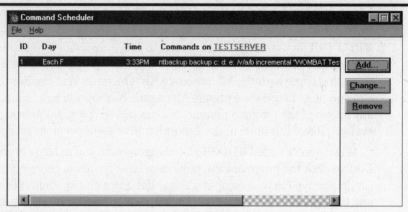

FIGURE 23.6: The Command Scheduler dialog box

If you need to adjust the settings of your job, click the Change button. You see the Change Command dialog box, which looks much like the Add Command dialog box shown in Figure 23.5. From this screen, you can adjust your backup (or any other scheduled service) as necessary by using the same procedures that you used to add it.

If you need to remove your backup command, select it in the Command Scheduler screen and click Remove. When you do, the system prompts you for confirmation. Click Yes and the command is removed. Don't remove an event unless you're sure that you want to, however, because no Cancel function is on that screen. Every time you add a job to this list, it will be assigned a job identification number. When you remove a job, the numbers assigned to the other jobs in the list do not change, and future jobs take the next highest number available. If you erase job 0, leaving job 1 intact, and then add job 0 back, it will become job 2.

What about the Scheduler service? Yes, it still needs to be running for WINAT to work, just as it does for the at command in the command prompt. You can start it from the Services icon in the Control Panel, or you can just go ahead and start WINAT. A message box will tell you that the Scheduler is not running and ask you if you want to start running it. When you say Yes, the service will begin.

Special Backup Operations

We've just discussed how to do a normal, vanilla-flavored backup that hits every file on your hard disk, only requires one tape, backs up a local disk, and doesn't need to be aborted. However, special circumstances may require you to do the job a bit differently, and that's what the following sections cover.

Backing Up Only Selected Files

At some point, you may want to back up only certain directories or files on your hard disk, not necessarily the ones with the archive bit set, but an assortment. To do this, you must select the directories or files to be copied, and deselect everything else.

The process begins as though you were backing up the entire disk. Go to the initial Backup screen and select the drive that you want to back up. Rather than clicking the Backup button, however, double-click the gray drive icon. You see a screen that looks like Figure 23.7.

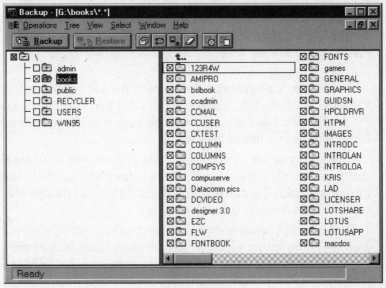

FIGURE 23.7: Selection of directories to back up

When I opened this screen, every directory had a filled checkbox next to it. Since I wanted to back up files from only some of the directories, I clicked the checkbox next to the C: drive to deselect it so that I could select the individual directory that I wanted. From here, I chose as many directories as I liked. When I double-clicked NTCLASS, I got a list of its files and subdirectories, as shown in Figure 23.8.

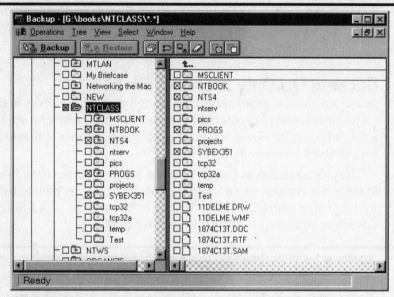

FIGURE 23.8: Selection of files and subdirectories to back up

Once again, to keep from selecting every file and subdirectory in the NTCLASS directory, I clicked the checkbox for that directory to deselect it. Only the files that I selected would be backed up. As you can see in the figure, I chose four files to back up.

Now we're ready to complete the backup. From here, click the Backup button, as you did earlier to back up the entire drive. You are returned to the initial Backup Information dialog box. The rest of the operation is exactly like backing up an entire directory.

By the way, please note that, although I selected only one directory to draw files from for this example, you can choose files from as many directories and subdirectories as you like. Just make sure that you deselect everything before you select anything, or else you end up backing up more files than you intended.

Using More Than One Tape

Using more than one tape isn't difficult to do. If you choose Append from the Backup Information dialog box or have an absolutely huge hard drive, you may run out of space on your tape before the backup is done. If this happens, the Backup program prompts for a new tape. Just insert the new tape and click OK.

Aborting a Backup

If you realize that you don't want to back up your data once you've started, you can click the Abort button to make the process stop. If the program was in the middle of backing up a file and there was less than 1MB to go, the file will be completed; otherwise a message box appears and asks if you really want to stop now and have the file corrupted on the tape.

Clicking Abort does not cancel the backup; it only stops it at the point at which you aborted. Whatever files were backed up before you aborted the process will be on the tape.

Backing Up to Floppy Disks

If you don't have a tape drive, you can still back up your most important files to floppy disks. To do so, go to the command prompt and use either the xcopy or the backup command. The backup command is perhaps a little simpler.

When using the backup command, you can specify drives (although that's not likely if you're backing up to floppies), directories, or individual files. The syntax looks like this:

```
backup source destination drive: options
```

where *source* specifies the source files, directories, or drive. You can use wildcards to specify all the files of a certain type, or you can spell out all the filenames. For example, to back up all of directory C:\WPFILES, you would type **c:\wpfiles**. To back up all the files in that directory with the DOC suffix, you would type **c:\ wpfiles*.doc**. For *destination drive*, substitute the name of the drive (such as A) where you want the backups to be stored. For *options*, include one or more of the switches shown in Table 23.3.

TABLE 23.3: Switches for Use in Backing Up to Floppy Disks with Backup

Switch	What it Does
/a	Appends the current backup to the files already on the destination disk. Omitting this switch causes the destination disk to be overwritten.
/d: [date]	Backs up only the files that have changed after the date you place after the colon, whether or not they have the archive bit set.

CONTINUED ➡

TABLE 23.3 continued: Switches for Use in Backing Up to Floppy Disks with Backup

SWITCH	WHAT IT DOES
/f:[size]	Specifies the size of the disk to be formatted, if you want the destination disk to be formatted before you write to it. Put the size of the disk (1.44MB, for example) after the colon.
/l[drive:path]	Creates a log file in the drive and path you specify.
/m	Backs up only the files with the archive bit set—the ones that have changed since the last backup.
/s	Tells the Backup program to search all subdirectories for files. If you don't select this option, the Backup program backs up only the files in the directory that you're actually in—if you specify C:*.DOC for the source directory and don't use the /s switch, only DOC files in the root directory will be backed up.
/t:[time]	Backs up only those files that have changed after the time you specify, whether or not they have the archive bit set.

Alternatively, you can use xcopy to back up your files or put files on disk to take them on a trip. Use xcopy rather than copy, because copy doesn't use the archive bit and is not as easy to customize. While xcopy has many switches, Table 23.4 lists those that are the most relevant to backing up NTFS files.

TABLE 23.4: Switches for Use in Backing Up to Floppy Disks with Xcopy

SWITCH	WHAT IT DOES
/a	Copies files with the archive attribute set, but doesn't change the attribute (good for when you're copying the files that you've worked with on a given day but don't want them to get skipped by the daily incremental backup).
/d:date	Copies only the files changed on or after the date you specify.
/h	Copies hidden and system files, as well as normal ones.
/m	Copies with the archive bit set and then removes the bit.
/n	Copies NTFS files, using shorter names created for use with the FAT file system. Only works on NTFS files.
/u	Updates the files in the destination.

If you want more help with xcopy, type the following command from the command prompt (there's more than one screen of options):

```
xcopy /? |more
```

Backing Up Removable Media

If you want to back up the data in a removable media drive (such as a Bernoulli or a Floptical), it may seem impossible at first because NT Server's Backup program doesn't recognize removable drives as available for backup. You can, however, get around this fairly easily.

To back up a removable drive:

1. Go to the File Manager or the command prompt and share the drive that you want to back up.

2. Connect to the shared drive from the File Manager or command prompt.

The Backup program will now be able to see the drive under the letter assigned to it, as long as you have a disk in the drive.

You're set. Back up your removable drives as you would any other drive.

Backing Up a Network Drive

Even if you're using an internal tape drive on your server, you can still use that drive to back up other hard disks on your system. The process is quite straightforward:

1. Go to the computer that you want to back up and share the drive or directory for backup with the network.

2. From the server's Explorer, map a network drive to the shared directory.

Now, when you start the Backup program, you notice a new icon for a network drive in the list of available drives for backup. From here, the backup process is identical to that of backing up a local drive.

Backing Up Open Files

NT's Backup program has one distinct failure: it can't back up open files. If you normally schedule backups for 2 A.M. when no one is working, this wouldn't seem to be a problem. However, if you're connecting to the

Internet or running TCP/IP protocol with DHCP with or without WINS-DNS, some files will be open at 2 A.M. and *must* stay open: the files that control the internal naming services, and, if you're using DHCP, the files that allocate IP addresses.

Luckily, there's an easy way around this. To make sure that the WINS and DHCP files get backed up, make this simple batch file part of your regularly scheduled backup:

```
C:
CD \USERS
CACLS DHCP /T /E /G EVERYONE:F
CACLS WINS /T /E /G EVERYONE:F
net stop "Microsoft DHCP Server"
net stop "Windows internet name service"
xcopy c:\winnt35\system32\dhcp c:\users\sysjunk\dhcp
   >>C:\USERS\DBAK.LOG
xcopy c:\winnt35\system32\wins c:\users\sysjunk\wins
   >>C:\USERS\DBAK.LOG
net start "Windows internet name service"
net start "Microsoft DHCP Server"
```

It's not hard to tell what's going on here: The files that run the DHCP server and WINS are getting copied from the \System32 directory to an (unopened) log file in the \Users directory so that they can be backed up. This batch file stops the DHCP Service and the Windows Internet Name Service before it copies the files and restarts the services after the files are copied. However, because the whole batch file takes only a few seconds to execute, the services are not shut down long enough to present a problem.

If you don't recognize the CACLS command, that's because it's not documented except in Microsoft's TechNet. CACLS is a useful NT command that allows you to change the ownership and control of a file or directory from the command line. In our version of the batch file, we had to include a command giving the Everyone group full control of the WINS and DHCP directories because these directories were owned by the System and thus even Administrators could not copy them. You could give only Administrators or Backup Operators full control if you liked; in our case, it didn't matter if Everyone could control the directories.

If you're using the at command to schedule backups, you can make this batch file part of your weekly backup: just add it to the Scheduler to run a few minutes before the backup job.

Protecting Backups

Backing up your system is a vital part of any decent security program. However, it's quite easy for an intruder to access your confidential files on the tapes that you back up to. If you don't keep an eye on the tapes, they can be rendered useless when you need to restore them. Any user can back up files that he or she has access to, and any Administrator or Backup Operator can back up the entire drive (even if, for example, your Backup Operator cannot normally access the files that she is backing up). Be very careful about who you assign backup rights to.

Once you have your backup tapes, you need to protect them from damage, as well as from theft. To this end, here are some things to consider when storing tapes:

▶ Tapes are comfortable under approximately the same conditions that you are. Excessive heat and dampness do your backups no good. *Never* store tapes on a window sill.

▶ While you want your backups to be fairly convenient, so that you can restore information if you blast your hard drive, it doesn't do you any good to have backups if your office burns down and takes the originals and the backups of all your data with it. For the best protection, store all of your backups but the most recent at a safe location (locked, fireproof, waterproof), off-site.

▶ Enable the Restrict Access to Owner or Administrator option when backing up files. For extra protection, keep server backups locked up and only allow the network administrator or the security manager access to them. If workstations get backed up, the tapes and their usability should be the responsibility of the workstation's user.

▶ Label your tapes clearly and completely (on both their paper labels and their electronic volume labels), so that you don't erase a vital tape by thinking that it's something else. In NT Server, you can be very explicit about the volume label on a tape, so use this capability to identify tapes that you don't want to reuse.

Restoring Files

Your backups are useless unless you can restore them to your machine in good order. Restoring files is much like backing them up. First, open the Backup program in the Administrative Tools program group. You see the Backup screen that you saw when you backed up originally. But this time, select the Tapes window instead of a drive. You see a screen that looks like Figure 23.9.

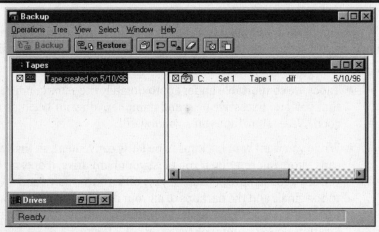

FIGURE 23.9:   The opening screen for Restore

To begin the restoration process, select the tape by clicking in the checkbox next to it. If you want to restore an entire tape, the selection process is done. However, you probably want to restore only selected files from a tape, not the whole thing, so we'll go through the selection process now.

Double-click the tape icon, and the Restore program loads the tape's catalog, so that it can find files on the tape. This process takes a couple of minutes, and while it's doing this, you will see a screen that looks like Figure 23.10.

When the cataloging process is finished, you can click the yellow file icon on the other side of the initial screen. When you do, you see a screen like the one in Figure 23.11 that shows all the available directories on the tape. Any corrupt files (that is, files that contain errors) and their corresponding directories are marked by an icon with a red *X*.

FIGURE 23.10: The Catalog Status message

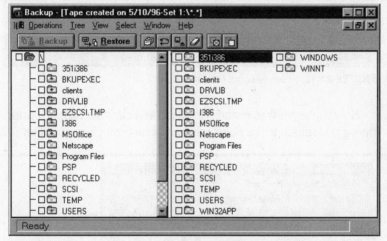

FIGURE 23.11: Available directories for restoration

As you can see, everything is currently deselected. I didn't want to restore every file, so I unchecked the drive's checkbox. Subdirectories can then be selected by double-clicking their yellow file icons. You don't have to check the checkboxes to select a drive or a directory before expanding it, and it's safer not to if you're doing a selective restore as I am in this example. If you select a drive or directory, everything in it will be restored.

Once you've progressed to the directory that you want, click on the file or files that you want to restore, just as you did when you were backing up. Your screen should look something like Figure 23.12.

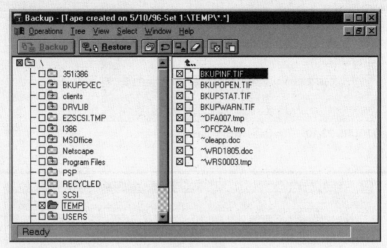

FIGURE 23.12:   Files selected for restoration

Now you're ready to restore. Go ahead and click the Restore button. A dialog box similar to the Backup Information box opens, as in Figure 23.13.

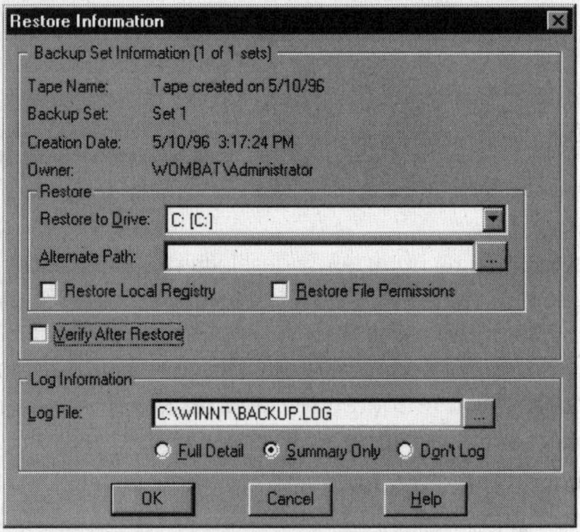

FIGURE 23.13:   The Restore Information dialog box

The Restore Information dialog box is much simpler than the Backup Information dialog box. Essentially, all that you must do here is decide whether or not to verify that the information was written correctly (a good idea, even though it adds time to the restoration process), restore the local Registry if you backed it up, and restore the file permissions that were in place for the file when you backed it up. If you like, you can choose to restore the data to a different drive than the one you backed it up from, although you cannot restore Registry information to a drive other than the one from which you backed it up. You can also choose what kind of log file you want and where you would like to store it.

When you're done, click OK, and the restoration progress begins. You can watch the process on the screen, as in Figure 23.14.

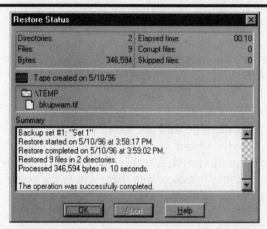

FIGURE 23.14: The file restoration progress screen

If you're restoring individual files to your drive because the originals were corrupted somehow, the Restore program asks you if you're sure that you want to replace the file on disk with the file on the tape. You see a dialog box like the one in Figure 23.15. Your files are now restored to your hard disk.

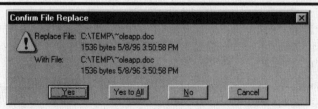

FIGURE 23.15: The Confirm File Replace dialog box

Part ii

Side Note: Restoring Data After Reinstalling NT Server

When writing this book, there were some things that I could not experiment with unless I reinstalled NT Server. Given that the operating system really isn't too difficult to install (although it's time-consuming), this wasn't much of a problem, but one instance of reinstalling the operating system and trying to restore my data nearly gave me heart failure.

I was experimenting with Disk Administrator and needed to repartition the drive with the NT Server installation on it, so I prepared to back up my data and reinstall the server. I did everything by the book: backed up the hard disk to tape, verified the backup, and restored a couple of files from the backup (just to make sure that the files could be read). Now I was ready to go. I installed NT Server, blowing away my old disk partition in the process so that *none* of the data was left, and then, two hours later when the installation was done, prepared to restore the data.

When I tried to catalog the tape, all I got was a cryptic Dr. Watson message advising me that the system had generated an application error, and then the Backup program closed. When I reopened it, I could see the icon for the tape catalog tantalizingly sitting there, but when I tried to double-click it to open it, I got the same Dr. Watson message.

In desperation, I selected the catalog and attempted to restore without being able to access it, but all that got me was the data thrown back on the hard disk any which way, not in its original directories but in strange directories with names that the system seemed to have made up from truncated filenames. I checked a couple of the files after this strange restoration and they seemed okay, but I knew that I couldn't count on the data's integrity, and I'd never be able to find anything anyway. Restoring the data without the catalog was useless.

If the situation I was in isn't quite clear, let me just explain that the tape that I couldn't read contained all the data on the hard drive: all my books, all the company's manuals, all of *everything* except the mailing list. I had the backup—I was clutching it, white-knuckled, in my hand—but I couldn't read it.

I reinstalled NT Server, just to see if there was a problem with the installation that prevented me from reading my tape. Then I did it again... and again. I scoured the documentation, looking for clues. Finally, I got desperate (well, more desperate), decided that it was time to call in the Marines, and called Microsoft's $150-per-question Tech Support line with my problem. Even at $150 per question, however, they didn't know the answer. (That didn't keep them from charging me, however, and now the price has risen to $195.)

Finally, many hours and several installations later, I decided to try installing all the system software and *then* restoring the data. I reinstalled everything that I had on the system before, including the Service Pack 2 patches (this was under NT 3.1) that had been on the system before, on the theory that it might affect how the backup worked. *This* time, I could restore the data.

The moral of this story? Before trying to restore data after a complete reinstallation of NT Server, install all your system software first. It seems obvious now, but it wasn't at the time, and that mistake nearly killed me. (End of digression.)

HOW DO I RESTORE DATA FROM BACKUPS?

1. With the tape from which you wish to restore in the drive, select Start ➤ Programs ➤ Administrative Tools ➤ Backup.

2. Double-click the tape icon to catalog it.

3. Select the item(s) that you wish to restore or select the entire catalog, and then click the Restore button. A dialog box appears; fill it in as appropriate.

The restoration process should take place normally. If you don't have a tape drive, the programs REGBACK and REGREST, available with the NT Resource Kit, will save and restore Registries to and from floppies.

Special Restoration Operations

Sometimes, you can't restore files in the traditional way described above because a backup set is spread over more than one tape or you've blasted the disk Registry and you need to restore it. In cases like these, you need special restoration techniques.

Restoring from a Tape Set with a Missing Tape   To restore data from a backup set that extends over more than one tape, you need to insert the last tape in the set and load the backup catalog from there.

If that tape has been lost or destroyed, you can still load the backup catalogs from the tapes that you have, but it's a more arduous process. In this case, you must build a partial tape catalog by inserting the available tapes and loading their individual catalogs. Once you've done that, you can restore the data. If you're restoring the data from the command prompt, run NTBACKUP with the /missingtape switch.

Restoring Data to a Networked Drive   The process of restoring data to a networked drive is pretty much what you expect. Connect to the drive or directory through Explorer, and then choose to restore to that drive letter when you're setting up the Restore program options. From here, the process is identical to restoring locally.

NTBACKUP Test Trivia

In general, I find that most people don't use NTBACKUP because its tape library facilities are limited, it can't handle tape auto-loaders, and it doesn't do software compression. Don't misunderstand me, it's great that Microsoft included NTBACKUP for free in the box, and for many small businesses (like mine), it's an adequate backup solution.

But when taking the NT 4 core technologies test (exam number 70-067), I was startled by the number of questions about the NTBACKUP program: *four* out of about 54 questions! I *use* the program, as I said, and so I knew about its idiosyncrasies, but it occurred to me that anyone working in a medium-sized or large firm might not know these things. Here's a brief compendium of factoids that you might need to know if you take the NT 4 Server test.

Backing Up the Registry

In order to back up the Registry, you must do two things. Remember that the Registry lives in the \WINNT\System32\Configs directory on some drive; Microsoft calls the drive that you've got the \WINNT directory on the "system drive." So, first, you've got to be backing up at least one file on the system drive in order to back up the Registry. Second, either use the /b option from the command line, or check the Backup Registry box from the GUI.

Restoring the Registry

Again, you must be restoring at least one file, or you can't raise the Restore Files dialog box. You must be restoring a file to the same volume that the Registry resides on: the system drive. Then, just check the Restore Local Registry box, and you'll get your old Registry back. You must be running NTBACKUP physically on the machine that you want to do the Registry backup or restore on in order for this to work.

You Can't Restore to Another Name

If you have a file named MYSTUFF.TXT that you want to restore, but you want it restored under the name (for example) MYSTUFF2.TXT, you can't. You can restore a file to a different directory or drive from the one that it came from (that capability first appeared in NT 3.51), but you can't rename it. There *is* a workaround, of course—just restore it under its original name and then rename it.

Restoring a Configuration

Sometimes, no matter how vigilant you've been, mistakes happen or something just goes wrong, and you need to fix your system. These fixes range from easy to horrific.

We'll start with a relatively easy one. What happens if you successfully install NT Server, try to adjust your system configuration, and render your server unusable—or even unbootable? Something as simple as changing the video driver to something that your system can't handle will do that, and it's hard to restore the original driver if you can't read what's on your screen. If you've messed up your system's configuration, what do you do?

One approach to fixing a diseased server would be to simply reinstall it from scratch—wipe the system drive and reinstall. That sounds like a lot of work, and it can be—reconfiguring all those services and reinstalling applications can be time-consuming and error-prone if you don't have a good disaster-recovery document—but you can make it simpler if you take the time to build an automated install script for each important server. It's my experience that once you've got an installation script working, a full reinstall, complete with all settings and such, can take as little as 15 minutes. The servers are expensive, yes, but their cost is nothing compared to downtime's cost (and your labor's cost), so a fresh install may well be the strategy that gets a server back up and running. Another great approach is to use a disk-copier program like Ghost. Get the system the way you want it and then Ghost the entire system drive to a JAZ drive or some other safe place. Rebuilding the server then takes the 20 or so minutes that Ghost will take to copy back a gigabyte or so.

Of course, many problems don't require anything that drastic, and sometimes you just plain don't have an install script or a Ghost image lying around. In that case, you need to dig in and do some kind of system repair. The remainder of this section talks about some tools you can use to accomplish that.

The Last Known Good Menu

If you've changed your system so that it can't boot NT Server, one of the better solutions to this problem can be seen while you're rebooting. If you watch while your machine's boot up, you see a message on a black screen that says:

    Press spacebar NOW to use the Last Known Good Configuration.

If you press the spacebar, you see a menu asking you whether you want to

- ▶ Use the current configuration

- ▶ Use the *Last Known Good Configuration*—the configuration that was used the last time the machine booted successfully

- ▶ Restart the computer

- ▶ Use another hardware configuration, if you have more than one

The idea with Last Known Good Configuration is that NT's Registry contains a key, HKEY_ LOCAL_MACHINE\System\CurrentControlSet, which is basically a "CONFIG .SYS" for your NT system. A control set's main job is to list all possible drivers and services that NT knows of, to list the exact filenames and options for those drivers, and to tell NT whether or not to *load* those drivers. For example, if you poke around in a control set, you'll see a key called Services, and inside that you'll see a key named Spock. That's the driver for an old PS/2 SCSI host adapter. Now, the chances are *extremely good* that you're not running NT on a PS/2 with a Micro Channel Architecture SCSI host adapter, but NT knows:

- ▶ There is at least a possibility, however incredibly small, that you *do* have such a thing, and so NT should be ready in case that happens

▶ What the filename of the driver is, provided that you tell NT to actually use this driver

▶ Most important, whether or not to actually load the driver

So, for example, if you buy a brand-new SCSI host adapter or video card and load the drivers for it, NT may end up learning about an altogether new piece of hardware. There would be a new key in the control set with information about using that driver. If you wanted NT to *forget* that information, reverting to an old control set (Last Known Good) would be helpful.

If, on the other hand, you haven't changed your hardware but have updated a driver, then invoking Last Known Good may do nothing for you at all. If you've got an Adaptec 2940 SCSI host adapter in your system, then all the control set knows is that you should load a driver called AIC78XX.SYS. That's important because when you update your Adaptec driver, the name doesn't change (usually); you just use a new AIC78XX.SYS that overrides the old one. The control set *used* to say, "Load AIC78XX .SYS," before you installed the new driver, and now it *still* says, "Load AIC78XX.SYS." The control set would not know about different versions of AIC78XX.SYS, and so if you updated a driver and then decided that you didn't like the driver, Last Known Good couldn't help you.

Where *is* Last Known Good useful? Well, if your machine won't boot, you probably don't want to use the current configuration, so instead go to the Last Known Good Configuration. It should make your machine bootable.

How did Last Known Good get to be considered "good" by the system? To qualify, a configuration must not have produced any system critical errors involving a driver or a system file, and a user must have been able to log on to the system at least once.

A change in drivers isn't the only time that a Last Known Good Configuration can't help you. (Consider how often restoring an old CONFIG .SYS under DOS solves problems—sometimes, but not always—and you'll have an idea about roughly how often Last Known Good is helpful.) If any of the following things is true, you have to use another solution to restore things as you want them:

▶ You made a change more than one successful boot ago and want to restore things as they were before the change.

▶ The information that you want to change is not related to control set information—user profiles and file permissions fall into the category of information that can't be changed with the Last Known Good menu.

▶ The system boots, a user logs on, and then the system hangs.

▶ You change your video driver to an incompatible driver, restart the system, and log on with the bad driver (you can still type, even if you can't see).

Running an NT Repair

If you've screwed up your operating system setup such that using the Last Known Good Configuration can't help you, you still have another option before (groan) reinstalling the operating system. Every time you make a successful change to your system's configuration, you should back it up with a combination of Disk Administrator, a program called RDISK (you'll see how to do that in just a minute), and whatever your favorite NT backup program is. The information from RDISK and Disk Administrator will often fit on a single floppy, a floppy whose name you may recognize from Setup—the Emergency Repair Disk (ERD). As a matter of fact, you can use NT Repair for a number of useful tasks even if you *don't* have an ERD; I'll get to those tasks in a minute.

Starting NT Repair   You kick off an NT repair in a way that you probably wouldn't expect—by running Setup. Either boot from the three Setup floppies, run WINNT, or run WINNT32 just as though you planned to reinstall NT entirely. When you see the "Welcome to Setup" screen, however, you'll notice that you have a number of options besides the one you normally choose to commence NT Setup.

One of those options is:

```
To repair a damaged Windows NT 4.0 installation, press R.
```

Press R, and you'll see a screen that says:

```
As part of the repair process, Setup will perform each
    optional task shown below with an 'X' in its checkbox.
To perform the selected tasks, press ENTER to indicate
    "Continue." If you want to select or deselect any item in
    the list, press the UP or DOWN ARROW key to move the
    highlight to the item you want to change. Then press
ENTER.
[ ] Inspect registry files
```

```
[ ] Inspect startup environment
[ ] Verify Windows NT system files
[ ] Inspect boot sector
     Continue (perform selected tasks)
```

By default, all of these options are checked.

Understanding Repair Options   Before continuing with Repair, however, let's take a short side trip to see what each option does.

Inspect Registry Files   Doesn't actually inspect the files. Instead, it lets you restore a Registry hive file from a backup.

Inspect Startup Environment   Tells NT to rebuild an erased or damaged BOOT.INI. Repair will search your computer's disks attempting to find any NT installations on the disk. Its performance is, in my experience, not great, but it can't hurt to try, right?

Verify Windows NT System Files   Checks that all of the hundreds of files that NT installs are still there and that they're in the same shape as they were when first installed. Unfortunately, if you've installed a Service Pack, this option is pretty useless; Repair's not bright enough to understand that the reason that all of those files are "corrupt" is because they're new-and-improved versions. Give this option a miss.

Inspect Boot Sector   Fixes the boot sector on drive C: so that it starts up NT, loading and executing the NTLDR file. This is useful if NT no longer boots, either because of inadvertent damage to C:'s boot sector—power surges or viruses—or because someone installed DOS or Windows on top of NT. (Even Windows 98 isn't smart enough to understand that when it's installed on top of an NT installation, it should respect the NT boot loader and just insert itself in BOOT.INI.) This happens most often when some dodo sees there's a problem booting an NT machine and decides that the best answer is to boot the server with a bootable DOS disk and then type SYS C:.

Running NT Repair   Anyway, back to Repair. Choose the option or options that you want, then highlight "Continue (perform selected tasks)" and press Enter. Just as it did with the initial Setup, NT must figure out what kind of hard disk host adapter you have. (If you've started Repair with the NT floppies, you'll then have to insert Disk 3.) As with

Part ii

Setup, NT Repair auto-detects mass-storage devices, and, again as with Setup, if you've got an oddball disk controller, you'll have to tell Repair about it here. The process is exactly the same as with Setup, so I'll assume you have already figured this part of Repair out.

Emergency Repair Disk Options   The next screen asks for the ERD:

```
Setup needs to know if you have the Emergency Repair Disk for
   the Windows NT version 4.0 installation which you want to
   repair. NOTE: Setup can only repair Windows NT 4.0
   installations.
If you have the Emergency Repair Disk, press ENTER.
If you do not have the Emergency Repair Disk, press ESC.
   Setup will attempt to locate Windows NT version 4.0
   for you.
```

Now here's some good news. If you were lazy and didn't create an ERD, NT made one anyway, creating a backup of your ERD information in a directory named \Repair inside your NT system root. So, for example, if you installed NT in a directory named D:\WINNTS, then you'll find a directory named D:\WINNTS\Repair on your disk. Either choose Enter or Esc, and NT will search the disk to find as many NT installations as it can. It then reports any installed copies of NT. The screen looks a bit different when it finds one copy than when it finds multiple copies; with multiple copies the screen looks like this:

```
The list below shows the Windows NT installation on your
   computer that may be repaired.
Use the UP and DOWN ARROW keys to move the highlight to an
   item in the list.
To repair the highlighted Windows NT installation, press
   ENTER.
To return to the previous screen, press ESC.
To exit Setup, press F3.
```

You'll then see a list of the locations for the installations that Repair found. On the system I'm looking at now, it looks like this:

```
E:\WINNT.0 "Windows NT Server Version 4.00"
C:\WTSRV "Windows NT Terminal Server Version 4.00"
```

The one problem with this tool is that sometimes NT *can't* find an installation. In that case, it would be nice to see a browse window or to just plain be able to punch in a drive letter and subdirectory name—but you can't, unfortunately.

Following that screen, you see the "Setup will now examine your drive(s) for corruption" message, same as in regular Setup. As with regular Setup, press Esc to skip it or Enter to let Repair do the disk test. What happens next depends on what you asked Repair to do.

"Inspect Registry Files" Actions   If you choose Inspect Registry Files, you'll next see a screen that says:

```
Setup will restore each registry file shown below with an 'X'
    in its checkbox.
To restore the selected files, press ENTER to indicate
    "Continue." If you want to select or deselect any item
    in the list, press the UP or DOWN arrow to move the
    highlight to the item you want to change. Then press
    ENTER.
WARNING: Restore a registry file only as a last resort.
    Existing configuration may be lost. Press F1 for more
    information.
```

Repair then offers to restore five Registry files:

▶ System

▶ Software

▶ Default (the default user profile, the one that runs when no one's logged on)

▶ NTUSER.DAT (the profile that new users get)

▶ A combination of SAM and Security (the two files that contain user accounts; whether a server is a member server, BDC, or PDC; and other domain and local security information)

You can't restore Security without SAM or vice versa—they're a matched set. You get a checkbox for each one, and once you've checked the ones that you want to restore, you choose "Continue (perform selected tasks)." That tells Repair to copy the selected Registry hive files from either an ERD or the \WINNT\Repair directory. Repair then copies the files and reports:

```
Setup has completed repairs.
If there is a floppy disk inserted in drive A:, remove it.
Also remove any compact disks from your CD-ROM drive(s).
Press ENTER to restart your computer.
```

"Inspect Startup Environment" Actions   Choose this if there's an NT installation on your system but the installation is not in your BOOT .INI. As noted earlier, Repair's not that great at finding those old installations, but it has a better chance if the installations are in system roots

Part ii

with names of WINNT or WINNT with a period and digit, as in WINNT.0, WINNT.1, and so on.

If you choose Inspect Startup Environment, then Repair will work as described before, except it will *not* run through the Registry questions. It just runs the disk for a few seconds and ends with this message:

```
Setup has completed repairs.
If there is a floppy disk inserted in drive A:, remove it.
Also remove any compact disks from your CD-ROM drive(s).
Press ENTER to restart your computer.
```

"Inspect Boot Sector" Actions   This option doesn't produce much interaction, either. You use it, again, if there's a copy of NT on your system but you never even see the "OS Loader" message. It'll run for a second or two after you tell it which instance of NT to repair, then you'll see the "Setup has completed repairs" message and have the opportunity to reboot. The only other way in which this option is different is that for some reason Repair does not offer to test the drive.

Running a System Repair without a CD-ROM Drive

For a couple of years, my main laptop was a Digital Ultra Hinote II, a pretty good, light, power-stretching laptop for its time (96MB of RAM, a 133MHz processor, and an 800×600 screen were pretty sexy not too long ago). It had one fatal flaw, however: its CD-ROM. The drive wasn't a standard EIDE interface, but instead an oddball PCMCIA interface that, needless to say, required a few oddball drivers to make it work.

Running a system repair caused me trouble, therefore, Repair could not see the CD-ROM. How to run a repair without a CD-ROM? Well, there wasn't a way until Service Pack 2 came around. Got a server or a laptop that doesn't always have a CD-ROM available? Then use this technique.

First, you'll need at least one drive formatted as FAT so that you can get to the drive from a bootable DOS floppy—DOS doesn't read NTFS very well, as you know. (Yes, I know about the drivers that let DOS read NTFS, but in a repair situation, I'm not exactly thrilled about the idea of relying on even more third-party software.) On that drive, place a copy of the I386 directory with your version of NT: Workstation, Server, Enterprise Edition, or Terminal Server. You are then going to make four modifications in order to make this system able to do a repair from the I386 on the disk, rather than insisting on accessing an I386 on a CD-ROM.

1. Create a file inside I386 called CDROM_S.40 if it's Server, Enterprise Edition, or Terminal Server code, or CDROM_W.40 if it's Workstation code. Give the file the appropriate name *exactly*. The file can be empty and this'll work fine. (Right-click I386 folder, click New ➤ Text Document, then rename it to **CDROM_W.40** or **CDROM_S.40**.)

2. Edit a file named TXTSETUP.SIF, a big text file in I386. (Perhaps it's a good idea to back it up first.) Search for the string ;SetupSourceDevice=. Remove the semicolon from the beginning of the line—this converts the line from a comment to be ignored to a command to be followed. Then indicate which hard disk the I386 directory is on. Of course, you can't use simple labels like C:, E:, or whatever. Instead, use **\device\harddisk*N**partition*M**, where *N* is the physical drive number (starting with 0 for the first) and *M* is the partition number (starting with 1 for the first). If I386 is on drive C:, then, as C: is usually the first partition on the first hard disk, the line would look like this:

```
SetupSourceDevice=\device\harddisk0\partition1
```

If you've got I386 on drive D:, E:, or some other drive letter, then I can't tell you exactly what values to use because I don't know how your disks are set up. Sometimes people have two hard disks on their system; the first partition of the first drive is C: and the first partition of the second drive is D:. In that case, the device name would be:

```
\device\harddisk1\partition1
```

In other cases, the computer has only one hard disk that's been chopped up and D: is the second partition; in that case, the device name would be:

```
device\harddisk0\partition2
```

Look in Disk Administrator to see exactly which hard disk and partition number your drive is.

Part ii

3. Just a line or two below where you found `SetupSource-Device`, you'll find a line saying `SetupSourcePath=\`. Change the `\` to the name of the directory where you put the files. I've been using the example `I386`, as that's what I name the directory where I keep my NT distribution files, so in my case the revised line would look like this: `SetupSource-Path=\I386`. Notice that you don't include a drive letter, as you already indicated that with `SetupSourceDevice`.

4. In `I386`, you'll find a file named `SETUPDD.SYS`. The one that shipped with the original version of NT 4 isn't smart enough to look elsewhere than a CD-ROM, so you need a newer one.

   But where to find one? That turned out to be a fairly interesting story. The `SETUPDD.SYS` from Service Pack 2, 3, or 4 will do. Service Pack 2 shipped as a whole bunch of files, so if you've got Service Pack 2 then go ahead and steal the `SETUPDD.SYS` from that and copy it into your `I386`. Service Packs 3 and 4 were available in two formats. Most people who pulled the Service Packs off the Web got a single, large executable file with a name like `NT4SP3_I.EXE` or `SP4I386.EXE`—you ran it and it unpacked all of its files to a temporary directory, installed the Service Pack, and then erased the temporary files. Alternatively, you could order the entire service pack on a CD-ROM. On the CD-ROM, the files were already extracted. If you have the CD-ROM, you'll find `SETUPDD.SYS` right there with the other files. If you have the executable, then the story's a bit different.

   First, you've got to get the Service Pack executable to unpack all of the files and *keep* them unpacked. That's easy; just run the executable with the `-x` option, either `nt4sp3_i -x` or `sp4i386 -x`. The executable will ask you where to put the files, and it'll unpack them to that directory.

   Here's the weird part, however: Service Pack 3's unpacked directory includes `SETUPDD.SYS`. Service Pack 4's unpacked directory *does not*. As a result, if you need a copy of `SETUPDD.SYS` so that you can do a no-CD repair, you either need Service Pack 2, Service Pack 3 (in either CD or executable format), or Service Pack 4 in a CD format.

5. Once you've finished making your four changes—created the CDROM_S.40 file, modified SetupSourceDevice, modified SetupSourcePath, and copied over the revised SETUPDD.SYS—then you're ready to do a repair. Again, you need not even use floppies, as you can start a repair with WINNT /b or WINNT32 /b. So you brave souls running NT on a Toshiba Libretto without a CD or a floppy—the floppy is PCMCIA and you might need to put another card in the one slot—you can still do NT repairs!

Updating the Repair Disk and/or Directory

It's a good idea now and then to tuck away an updated backup of the Registry. All that repair stuff is of no value if you've never updated the ERD or the \WINNT\Repair directory, because they only contain a Registry based on your initial setup. For example, there are no users save for the Administrator and the Guest unless you've updated the Repair files. Additionally, none of the permissions that you've established is on the ERD.

How to update this information? You can update your ERD (or create a completely new disk) with a program called RDISK in the System32 directory. Just run it (Start ➤ Run ➤ RDISK) and follow the instructions.

Unfortunately, however, RDISK doesn't back up *all* of the Registry: it overlooks the SAM and Security files. You can overcome that oversight with the undocumented /s option—click Start, then Run, then type **RDISK /S** and press Enter.

Backing Up Your Disk Configuration

In addition to the ERD, you can save your partition information so that you can replace it if you do something that you regret doing. Here's how:

1. Go to Disk Administrator.

2. Select Partition ➤ Configuration ➤ Save. You'll see a screen that looks like Figure 23.16.

3. Insert the disk and click OK. The system saves the information, and shows the message in Figure 23.17. This message confirms that the configuration was saved.

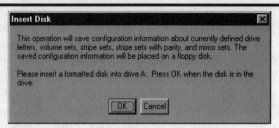

FIGURE 23.16:   The Insert Disk dialog box

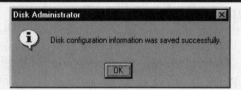

FIGURE 23.17:   Disk Administrator confirmation of your configuration change

4.   Click OK and you're finished. Remove the disk from the drive, label it with the date, and put it somewhere safe. You now have a backup of your disk configuration on your ERD.

WARNING

If you blast a partition and your data, restoring the partition won't restore the data.

Recovering from Bad Video Drivers

You may recall from the earlier discussion of the Last Known Good Configuration that if you change the video drivers to something that your system can't handle and you reboot and log on with the bad drivers (you can still type a password even if the screen is messed up), the Last Known Good solution can no longer help you. You have, after all, successfully rebooted and logged onto the system; the fact that you can't *see* anything is immaterial.

Under NT 3.1, this was something of a rigmarole. But NT 4 builds into BOOT.INI the option NT Server 4 (VGA drivers). All you have to do then is to shut down the server, restart it, and choose the setup with VGA drivers. Then, once the system is back up, just select Display from the Control Panel and take a second shot at choosing a video driver. Even better, there is a Test button in the display screen that NT forces you to use, to find out *before* you commit yourself whether or not the video drivers work.

Backing Up the Registry (and the SAM)

You'll recall that backing up open files is a bit of a pain, impossible sometimes. Few files on an NT machine are more important than the Registry hives. Registry hives are the files named SAM, Security, Software, and System, all of which live in \WINNT\System32\Config.

Alternatives for Backing Up the Registry

Unfortunately, Registry hives are constantly open. You can't use a simple copy or xcopy command, but there are several tools that you can use to back up these hives.

First, there's NTBACKUP. You'll recall that there is a checkbox or a command-line option (/b) that instructs NTBACKUP to back up the Registry. You can restore it by using NTBACKUP, as well.

The NT Resource Kit includes two programs named REGBACK and REGREST that back up and restore the Registry to a floppy.

You may recall that the ERD contains a copy of the Registry as it looked when you first installed your server. If you run NT Setup and choose the Repair option, then one of the things that you can do is restore the Registry to the state found on the ERD.

Now, that may not sound like an especially attractive option, since a lot of water has no doubt gone under the bridge between the time that you installed the server and now, but it *is* one way to restore a damaged Registry to a "known good" state. Of course, it would be more desirable to simply keep the copy of the Registry on the ERD up to date—and you can do that.

As you read a page or two back, NT includes a program called RDISK. RDISK will not only write a brand-new ERD, it will update \WINNT\ Repair. But why doesn't RDISK back up SAM and Security without the extra /s option? The problem with putting the Registry on the ERD is that part of the Registry—SAM—may be too big. Remember that SAM may be megabytes and megabytes on a domain controller. *That's* why

RDISK doesn't back up SAM or Security unless asked. It makes sense; I just wish Microsoft had documented how to do it.

TIP

It's a good idea to put RDISK on the Administrative Tools menu to remind yourself to keep it constantly updated over time, as your machine's configuration changes.

Restoring a Registry

If you backed up the Registry with RDISK, restore it by starting up NT Setup and choosing Repair rather than Install NT. If you backed up the Registry with REGBACK, then use REGREST to restore it.

But what if you can't run an NT system repair? How do you restore the RDISK-created Registry files? You'll need to do two operations:

1. Uncompress the files.

2. Copy them to \WINNT\System32\Configs.

Take a look in your \WINNT\Repair directory or on your ERD, and you'll see files with names like SAM_, Security._, System._, and so on. These are compressed versions of the original Registry hive files SAM, Security, System, and the others. You can uncompress them with the Expand program that comes with NT. Just open up a command prompt, change to \WINNT\Repair, and type **expand** *compressedname expandedname*. For example, if you uncompress SAM, you'll see something like the next few lines:

```
E:\WINNT\repair>expand sam._ sam
Microsoft (R) File Expansion Utility Version 2.50
Copyright (C) Microsoft Corp 1990-1994. All rights reserved.
Expanding sam._ to sam.
sam._: 6289 bytes expanded to 20480 bytes, 225% increase.
```

The next thing to do is copy it over to \WINNT\System32\Configs, but you can't just do that—the current SAM file is locked, and you can't overwrite it. You've got two options here:

▶ Put your system files (\WINNT and the bunch) on a FAT partition, in which case all you need to do is boot to DOS and copy the files.

▶ If the system is on an NTFS partition, put a *second* copy of NT in a different directory, then boot from the second copy of NT (cumbersome, but it works). Because the first copy is not active, the files in \WINNT\System32\Configs files on the first configuration aren't locked, and you can copy SAM to your heart's content.

If your Registry backup is on NTBACKUP, you must restore it from the NTBACKUP program. To restore it from the GUI interface, click the Restore Registry checkbox.

You cannot restore a disk Registry to any disk except the one from which you backed it up. In other words, you can't apply the disk Registry from drive C: to drive E:. That way, you can't sneak around NT's security system.

PLANNING FOR DISASTER RECOVERY

Sometimes using the Last Known Good Configuration or the ERD doesn't fix your problems. Hard disk failures or natural disasters require a bit more in the way of hard-core disaster recovery.

What does *disaster recovery* mean? Essentially, it's exactly what it sounds like: a way of recovering from a disaster—at best, turning a potential disaster into a minor inconvenience. Disaster can mean anything: theft, flood, an earthquake, a virus, or anything else that keeps you from being able to access your data. After all, it's not really the server that's important. While a server may be expensive, it is replaceable. Your data, on the other hand, is either difficult or impossible to recover. Could you reproduce your client mailing list from memory? What about the corporate accounts?

Creating a Disaster Recovery Plan

The most important part of a disaster recovery plan lies in identifying what "disaster" means to you and your company. Obviously, permanently losing all of your company's data would be a disaster, but what else would? How about your installation becoming inaccessible for a week or longer? When planning for disaster, think about all the conditions that could render your data or your workplace unreachable and plan accordingly.

Part ii

Implementing Disaster Recovery

Okay, it's 2:00 P.M. on Thursday, and you get a report that the network has died. What do you do?

Write Things Down   Immediately write down everything that everyone tells you: what happened, when it happened, who gave you the information, and anything else that happened at the same time that might possibly be related.

Check the Event Logs   If you can get to them, look at the security and event logs on the server to see if you can tell what happened right before the server crashed. If you're using directory replication to maintain a physically identical file server (also known as a *hot start* server because it's ready to go whenever you need it), the log information may be on the replicated server even if you can't get to the original.

Ascertain the Cause of the Failure and Fix It   "Easy for you to say," I hear someone muttering. It can be done, however. Once you know what events happened, it becomes easier to find out what they happened to.

Find Out If It's a Software Problem   Is it a software problem? If it is, have you changed the configuration? If you've changed something, rebooted, and been unable to boot, it's time to use the Last Known Good Configuration discussed earlier. If you can boot but the operating system won't function properly, use the ERD to restore the hardware configuration.

If you have another server with NT Server already installed identically to the server that failed, switch servers and see if the backup server works before you reinstall the operating system. If the hot start server doesn't work, you could be facing a network problem.

Find Out If It's a Hardware Problem   Is it a hardware problem? If you have a hot start server around the office, put it in place of the failed server and see if you can bring the network back up. If so, the problem lies with the dead server and you can fix or replace it while you have the other one in place. If not, check the network's cabling.

If one drive from a stripe set or mirror set has died, the system should still be fine (if the drive that died is not the one with the system partition on it), but you should still fix the set anyway. Striping and mirroring give you access to your data while the missing data is being regenerated, but if something else happens to the set before you regenerate the missing data, you're sunk because the set can only deal with one error at a time.

If necessary, reload the backups.

Make a Recovery "Coloring Book"

No matter how much you know about reformatting SCSI drives or rebuilding boot sectors byte by byte, I guarantee you that the fastest way to recover from a disaster will often turn out to be a three-step process: replace the bad hard disk and attendant hardware, install a fresh copy of NT Server on the new hard disk, and restore the data on the disk.

That sounds simple, but it's amazing how complex it can be in the heat of battle. Let's see, I'm reinstalling NT Server, but what was the name of the domain? What IP address does the domain controller get? What's the WINS server address? Which services went on this server? What was the administrator's password set to?

At my shop, we decided to sit down and write a step-by-step, click-by-click instruction manual. It tells a future network administrator which buttons to click and what text to type in the unlikely event that he or she ever needs to take a brand-new machine and rebuild our PDC on it.

Just for an example, we have a PDC on one of our domains that (as the logon traffic is relatively light) is also our DHCP, WINS, and DNS server. So, suppose the machine goes up in smoke, leaving us nothing but backup tapes—how do we rebuild that machine? We sat down and wrote out exactly what to do in order to:

- ▶ Install NT Server on a new machine
- ▶ Restore the SAM and Security databases
- ▶ Install DHCP on the machine
- ▶ Restore the old DHCP database to the machine
- ▶ Install WINS on the machine
- ▶ Restore the WINS database
- ▶ Install the DNS server on the machine
- ▶ Restore our DNS zones and records

Assume that the person who will be doing this knows nothing more than how to click a mouse and shove CDs into drives—someone with oatmeal for brains. Sound insulting? It's not; I like to think of myself as of at least basic intelligence, but under pressure, I sometimes just don't think as well as I need to. If you're good under pressure, then great—but making the disaster recovery guide an easy read is also a big help to your co-workers.

Don't underestimate how long this will take: putting the whole document together took two research assistants a couple of weeks, and it ended up as a 100+ page Word document! (Part of the reason why it was so large is that it made lavish use of screen shots wherever possible, and yours should, too. Just click on the window you want to include in your document, press Alt+Prtsc, choose Edit ➤ Paste Special in Word, choose Bitmap, and uncheck Float Over Text.)

NOTE

Once you finish the document, be careful where you keep it. The document will contain the keys to your network: usernames of domain administrator accounts, the passwords of those accounts, and the like.

Making Sure the Plan Works

The first casualty of war isn't always the truth—it's often the battle plan itself.

The most crucial part of any disaster recovery plan lies in making sure that it works down to the last detail. Don't just check the hardware; check everything. When a server crashes, backups do no good at all if they are locked in a cabinet to which only the business manager has the keys and the business manager is on vacation in Tahiti.

In the interest of having your plan actually work, make sure you know the answers to the following questions.

Who Has the Keys? Who has the keys to the backups and/or the file server case? The example mentioned above of the business manager having the only set of keys is not an acceptable situation, for reasons that should be painfully obvious. At any given time, someone *must* have access to the backups.

You could set up a rotating schedule of duty, wherein one person who has the keys is always on call, and the keys are passed on to the next person when a shift is up. However, that solution is not foolproof. If there's an emergency, the person on call could forget to hand the keys off to the next person, or the person on call could be rendered inaccessible through a dead beeper battery or downed telephone line. Better to trust two people with the keys to the backups and server, so that if the person on call can't be reached, you have a backup key person.

Is Special Software Required for the Backups?   Must any special software be loaded for the backups to work? I nearly gave myself heart failure when, after repartitioning a hard disk and reinstalling the operating system, I attempted to restore the backups that I'd made before wiping out all the data on the file server's hard disk. The backups wouldn't work. After much frustration, I figured out that Service Pack 2 was installed on the server before. I reinstalled the Service Pack from my copy on another computer and the backups worked. I just wish I had figured that out several hours earlier....

Do the Backups Work and Can You Restore Them?   Do the backups work and do you know how to restore them? Verifying backups takes a little longer than just backing them up, but if you verify, you know that what's on the tape matches what's on the drive. So, as far as restoring goes, practice restoring files *before* you have a problem. Learning to do it right is a lot easier if you don't have to learn under pressure, and if you restore files periodically, you know that the files backed up okay.

Have Users Backed Up Their Own Work?   In the interest of preventing your operation from coming to a complete halt while you're fixing the downed network, it might not be a bad idea to have people store a copy of whatever they're working on, and the application needed to run it, on their workstation. People who work on only one or two things at a time could still work while you're getting the server back online.

WHAT'S NEXT?

This chapter completes the section on NT Server. The next part of this books deals with the topic of certification for Microsoft network professionals, beginning with a chapter that answers the question, "Why become certified?"

PART iii
CERTIFICATION

Chapter 24

WHY BECOME CERTIFIED?

Computer and networking professionals are in demand across the employment spectrum, from business and industry to government and education. And the current high level of demand for information technology professionals—whether highly experienced or newly certified—is expected to continue and even accelerate in the years to come. This chapter outlines some of the many benefits that certification can offer you as a computer or networking professional, including jobs, promotions, professional credibility, and financial rewards. A number of these benefits offer advantages for employers and customers as well.

Adapted from *Computer and Network Professional's Certification Guide* by J. Scott Christianson and Ava Fajen

ISBN 0-7821-2260-4   560 pages $19.99

OPEN JOB MARKET FOR INFORMATION TECHNOLOGY PROFESSIONALS

The present shortage of information technology workers in the United States has been well documented. What's more, estimates of the extent of this shortage are quickly being revised upward. As recently as February 1997, the Information Technology Association of America (ITAA) estimated that 190,000 such positions were unfilled; by January 1998, ITAA's second annual study reported a shortage of 346,000 individuals—including programmers, systems analysts, and computer engineers—in the United States information technology work force ("Help Wanted: The IT Workforce Gap at the Dawn of a New Century," ITAA report, February 1997; and "Help Wanted: A Call for Collaborative Action for the New Millenium," report by ITAA and Virginia Polytechnic Institute, January 1998).

Similarly, estimates of the number of information technology personnel that will be needed in the future have recently been revised upward. In October 1997, the Office of Technology Policy (OTP) warned that the United States was not keeping up with the demand for new information technology workers and predicted that an average of 95,000 new jobs would open in the field annually; by January 1998, an updated report already had been issued, projecting a need for almost 140,000 information technology workers each year until the year 2006 ("America's New Deficit: The Shortage of Information Technology Workers," October 1997, OTP, US Department of Commerce; Update Report, OTP, January 1998).

Meanwhile, the number of college students graduating with bachelor's degrees in computer science dropped from a peak of 41,889 per year in 1986 to 24,200 per year in 1994, a decrease of 42 percent (*Digest of Education Statistics*, Department of Education, 1996). Universities are clearly not training the numbers of information technology workers that will be needed to meet the demands of the marketplace.

It is anticipated that the shortage of information technology workers will have broad-ranging effects, not just in the computer industry, but in business and industry in general, as well as in education and the government. The ITAA and OTP reports suggest that a competent skilled work force in information technology is crucial to the nation's economy. The ITAA urges industry, education, government, and professional associations to undertake a collaborative effort to head off this shortage. More and more, the information industry is turning to certification programs to fill the gap.

NEW AVENUES TO HIGH-SKILLED JOBS

To address the shortage of information technology professionals, some companies — Microsoft and Novell, for example — are actively taking their certification programs to higher education partners and even to high schools. Jackson Hole High School in Wyoming was the first high school to offer its students the opportunity to become Microsoft Certified Professionals. Other businesses are reaching out to train new workers as well. In 1997, 23 seniors at Ballou High School in Washington, DC took special courses on network administration. The students were trained on computers donated by technology companies in the area, and those who passed standard certification exams were guaranteed jobs at starting salaries of $25,000 to $30,000 (Peter Behr, "Hire Education at Ballou," *Washington Post*, March 7, 1997).

Through its Skills 2000 program, Microsoft has additional strategies in place to encourage new entrants in the information technology field, including a new loan program that lets people pay off training and related costs over time; a partnership with the Green Thumb organization to train adults 55 and over to be software developers, support specialists, and network administrators; reduced-cost programs to help practicing technical professionals keep their skills updated; and a number of new strategies for linking up qualified applicants with available jobs. According to Microsoft's Web page, the company provided training for 1,230,000 information technology workers in 1997 and certified 118,000. Microsoft indicates that its certification programs are growing by 100 percent annually.

BENEFITS FOR INDIVIDUALS

Many people pursue computer and networking certifications because they expect to receive increased salaries, promotions, or job offers. Evidence does indicate that having the right certification at the right time can have excellent salary and promotion potential. Magazines are full of stories about newly certified individuals with little or no experience who have snagged high-paying jobs.

But certification offers other benefits as well. It provides a portable credential that validates your knowledge and abilities, and it shows others that you are willing to do what it takes to keep your knowledge and skills current. As a result, certification improves your marketability and increases your options, whether you seek regular employment or want to promote your skills and abilities as an independent contractor.

Although the effort and cost involved in attaining some certifications is considerable, it is generally much less than the time and expense involved in obtaining a college degree. And, in many situations, an employer will carry the financial burden for certification training and testing. A 1995 study by Dataquest, Inc., a research unit of Dun & Bradstreet, reported that computer companies were paying for more than 80 percent of certification training for their employees (Bob Filipczak, "Certifiable!" *Training* magazine, August 1995). In addition, a number of certification programs can help you accumulate college credit at the same time as you are earning a certification.

Increased Salary

A number of surveys have documented the financial benefits of certification. Salaries of Microsoft certified professionals have been tracked for several years now, and these figures offer persuasive evidence of the impact of certification on salaries. Between February 1997 and February 1998, salaries for individuals with the entry-level Microsoft Certified Professional (MCP) credential went up by $3,900 to $61,200 annually, while average 1998 salaries were $77,700 for Microsoft Certified Trainers (MCTs) and $67,600 for Microsoft Certified Systems Engineers (MCSEs), according to Linda Briggs's third annual salary survey in *Microsoft Certified Professional* magazine (February 1998). These salaries were for persons with an average total of five-and-a-half years of experience in information technology. Survey results also indicated that 58 percent believed that their certifications had resulted in salary increases. Briggs estimates that earning an MCSE credential can add approximately $11,000 per year to a previously uncertified individual's salary.

NOTE

Chapters 25 through 28 provide more information about the MCP, MCSE, and MCT certification programs.

Jobs and Promotions

Certification provides employers with objective evidence that you have a defined set of skills and abilities. Job-seekers and independent contractors alike find that having the right certification can get them preference in the hiring process. Certification can open doors for individuals who have the initiative to seek out new knowledge and skills but have limited on-the-job experience. Certification can also help experienced computer and networking professionals move up within their current organizations or get good job offers elsewhere. In Linda Briggs's survey, 42 percent of Microsoft-certified respondents received a promotion as a result of attaining certification. Some businesses have actually incorporated vendor certification programs into their internal company certification programs.

Improved Professional Credibility

Potential employers or clients respond well when a computing or networking professional can offer clear evidence of having the skills needed to get the job done. Having relevant, current certifications on your resume gives you an important advantage in this regard; college degrees or years of experience on the resume may not tell employers whether you have the specific abilities they seek.

A 1995 evaluation of the MCSE credential found that more than 90 percent of the 89 MCSEs surveyed felt that obtaining certification was useful in improving their professional credibility, and 70 percent rated certification as "very useful" in that regard ("Evaluation of the Microsoft Systems Engineer Certification," report by the Applied Experimental Psychology Group at SIU-Carbondale in conjunction with Applied Research Consultants, July 1995).

Part iii

Education

The recent surge of interest in certification programs coincides with a trend toward performance-based assessment that can be seen across the educational spectrum. From kindergarten through college, an emphasis on competency-based assessment of knowledge and skills is beginning to replace the traditional focus on seat-time and rote memorization. For example, the new Western Governor's University—a nonprofit, independent corporation being developed by the Western Governor's Association—will provide distance-learning courses and programs to people in 15 western states and Guam. These courses and programs will be provided by both traditional providers and corporations and will feature competency-based assessment of knowledge and experience.

Certification programs have increasingly incorporated more sophisticated assessment methods to measure and certify learning and competency. A number of certification programs have established a level of quality and reliability that has made them eligible to provide college credit to their participants. For example, it is possible to obtain college credit for Learning Tree International certifications or courses. The American Council of Education (ACE) in Washington, DC has determined college course equivalencies for Learning Tree International's courses and certifications. As a general rule, ACE will recommend two college credit hours for each four-day Learning Tree course. The ICCP Certified Computing Professional exams also have been approved by ACE for college credit. Approximately 1,500 colleges and universities in the United States will accept ACE recommendations for college credit.

Other opportunities for getting college credit exist as well. A number of community and technical colleges in the United States offer college credit for courses that are part of the Microsoft curriculum. Vendors have partnered with colleges and universities in some interesting ways. For example, at North Carolina's High Point University, computer information system majors can graduate with both a degree and certification in Visual Basic, Windows NT, and Microsoft Office. Lord Fairfax Community College in Virginia offers a popular 15-credit Network Engineer Certificate Program that gives students hands-on experience in installing and configuring servers and workstations, implementing network security, and planning for disaster recovery. At Seattle Pacific University in Washington, the Microsoft Certified Engineer curriculum, implemented in 1996, attempts to ensure the quality of its graduates by incorporating an experience requirement—students must have either a degree or industry experience to be admitted to the program. If you are interested in college credit, look for similar opportunities in your area.

BENEFITS FOR EMPLOYERS

In the world of computers and networking, both hardware and software change quickly. Technologies and programs that are cutting edge this year may be considered outdated by next year. In this environment of fast-paced change, traditional resume credentials may not provide an employer much information about whether an individual has up-to-date knowledge and skills. How can an employer know whether a prospective employee will be competent to use, implement, or support the most current technologies and programs? For many employers today, certification is the answer.

Hiring

Many employers and human resources managers don't have the information technology background they would need in order to be able to quickly assess an individual's abilities, by reading a resume. In addition, many hiring managers find that a person's years of computer-related experience are not always an indication that an individual has the specific technical knowledge that is needed. For these reasons, employers may view certification as an objective measure for evaluating the abilities of applicants. If an employer needs someone to set up a system for secure, online commerce, for example, he or she needs to know that a potential hire or independent consultant has some pretty specific skills.

While certification may not guarantee that an individual knows all there is to know about a certain piece of hardware or software, it does provide information that employers value. It indicates that a person has at least a basic knowledge of a product—a core level of knowledge that can be the foundation for additional learning. It indicates that an individual is interested in learning about new technologies or products and maintaining up-to-date skills. And it can—depending on the comprehensiveness and rigor of the certification program—indicate an advanced level of knowledge and skill with a particular system or even the ability to manage complex, heterogeneous company networks.

Employers admit that they sometimes use the presence of relevant certifications as a screening device when reviewing job applications. When interviewed for the August 1996 issue of *Training* magazine, Candace Sutherland of Digital Storagework put it like this: "Yes, I would take someone who has been certified more seriously than someone who hasn't. It's not official policy, but I'll pull that resume out of the stack."

Certified Employees Get the Job Done

Certifications help employers identify individuals with proven knowledge and skill levels. As we have noted, this is certainly important in hiring. But certification has other benefits and uses for employers. Many employers are encouraging their current employees to get certified. Companies need to have individuals with specific skills on staff, and many have found that certification programs offer the verifiable skills and knowledge their employees need.

Employers who send staff for training want concrete results. Certifications that use performance-based exams measure a candidate's ability to perform specific tasks on the job. Since such exams are designed with the help of computer and networking professionals, they measure skills that are directly applicable to the workplace. As a result, certification programs that involve performance-based testing give employers independently verified results that demonstrate the value of their training investments.

Research indicates that certification increases employee productivity and effectiveness. A 1995 study by Dataquest, Inc., a research unit of Dun & Bradstreet, reported that "...managers feel that certified employees provide higher levels of service, learn new technologies faster, and are generally more productive." (Bob Filipczak, "Certification!" *Training* magazine, August 1995). Other studies confirm these results. A 1996 survey of managers who supervise individuals with the Microsoft Certified Solution Developer (MCSD) credential found that managers considered their certified employees to have a significantly higher level of competence on those tasks that were key to their job effectiveness than did non-certified employees under their supervision ("The Value of Certification for Solution Developers," report by the Applied Experimental Psychology Group at SIU-Carbondale, August 1996).

In 1995, IDC Consulting, a Massachusetts research firm, surveyed managers on the benefits of certification. They found that managers felt certification gave their employees a reliable level of skill and expertise. Managers said that with certified information technology professionals on staff, a company could operate a more complex and decentralized information technology environment without hiring additional employees. Further, the IDC survey reported that managers found the average payback time for certification costs was only nine months. Having certified employees resulted in increased network availability and more effective technical support. These improvements were judged to be worth approximately $14,000 per year to the company per trained employee ("Benefits and Productivity Gains Realized Through IT Certification," IDC report, 1995).

Benefits to Customers and Clients

Hiring and supporting certified employees gives resellers and service firms a competitive advantage. In the current market, having a staff that has earned respected certifications in a variety of relevant computing and networking technologies can be crucial to getting clients. When companies outsource their information technology management needs, they expect a service provider to have employees with in-depth knowledge and proven competency with a variety of systems. Service firms with certified employees can provide clients with high-quality, consistent services; many organizations know this and hire only contractors who offer certified staff.

Even companies that are not specifically in the business of providing information technology services to others are likely to find that they can provide higher quality service to their customers by having certified employees on staff. Certification improves user support, whether for internal or external purposes. Employees with certified technical skills can provide effective support for other employees and facilitate quick resolution of problems that impede customer service.

Employees Value Career Growth Opportunities

In today's volatile business environment, companies are unable to guarantee their employees lifetime job security and generous pension plans. Some companies that want to keep their employees happy have begun offering them meaningful career development opportunities instead. Some employers are fearful that paying for training and certification will help employees find better jobs outside their company. Such employers, however, may find themselves losing out anyway, as their employees move to different companies that support their employees in maintaining up-to-date, marketable credentials.

At the same time that career growth increases employees' job capabilities and enhances their marketability, it can also lead to higher morale and job commitment. Employees appreciate the opportunity to maintain current job skills. As a result, employers that support their employees in obtaining certification may see improved employee morale and job satisfaction at the same time as the company benefits from improved productivity and customer service.

CRITICISMS OF CERTIFICATION

Certification is not without its detractors. Some critics assert that a single multiple-choice test can't tell you whether a person can handle real-world problems using a particular product. It is true that not all certification programs involve hands-on, performance-based testing. Many programs do, however, and the general trend is to move certification programs in that direction. Furthermore, the multiple-choice tests that vendors use are typically designed—by teams of practicing information technology professionals and skilled prometricians (professionals in testing and measurement)—to assess knowledge and abilities as they will be needed in real-world applications.

In addition, some critics have observed that there are certification programs available that do not actually require either any experience or any testing. Such programs are not covered in this book. It is true that certification programs vary widely in their level of difficulty. Some programs don't offer much challenge, while others—such as Cisco's CCIE program or Sun's Java Developer certification—have gained notoriety for their difficulty. In addition, some of the more rigorous certification programs require documentation of a specified number of months or years of relevant on-the-job experience as a prerequisite to even entering the program.

Other critics of vendor-based certification assert that the vendors are the primary beneficiaries of certification programs because they generate vendor income, create product loyalty, and improve customer satisfaction (because the availability of certified personnel gives customers improved access to qualified product support). While some of this skepticism is undoubtedly justified, those who reject certification outright because it benefits vendors will miss out on the many benefits that certification offers to individuals, employers, and customers. Furthermore, many of the criticisms leveled against vendor-based certification programs are not applicable to organization- or association-based programs, which tend to offer substantive, comprehensive, standards-based training at a reasonable cost.

Other detractors remind us that good customer service requires more than technical skill. There is an important lesson here as well. Without a doubt, the individuals who reap the most success in the information technology field are those who combine high levels of product-related skill and knowledge with strong interpersonal skills.

Importance of Recertification

An issue that will take on increasing importance over time is the need for recertification. Many certification programs are brand new, or less than a year or two old, while others have been revamped recently. But any certification will have a limited useful life.

Many certification programs are tied to specific versions of certain products. Certification programs that are tied to specific versions of products typically do not offer recertification on that product version. An individual who wants to have current credentials will need to obtain certification on new versions as they are released. Programs that do offer recertification options vary widely in the effort required for maintaining certification. Some require testing or extensive continuing education coursework; in other programs, the effort needed to maintain certification is relatively trivial. Alternatively, the issuance of a new software version may be a time when an individual reassesses which certifications to maintain; it will be important to periodically decide whether you want to adhere to the same certification path you have been following or whether it's time to target different technologies or product lines instead.

It is important to keep in mind the fact that, in the field of information technology, your need to seek new education opportunities will be ongoing. Because skills and knowledge can become outdated more quickly today than ever before, the most successful computer and networking professionals are those who commit themselves to lifelong learning. An eagerness to learn new technologies and products as they emerge will keep you highly employable for many years to come.

What's Next?

Now that you know why you might want to become certified, you need to decide which certification is right for you. The next chapter discusses how to select a certification program and how to plan your steps to attain that certification.

Part iii

Chapter 25

CHOOSING THE RIGHT CERTIFICATION FOR YOU

The decision to pursue a certification should be made with forethought. It can take months or years, and a good amount of money, to reach your goal. You want to be certain that the certification(s) you obtain will help you meet your career goals. There may be advantages to obtaining almost any certification related to your career, but taking the time to define your goals and outline a career development plan will allow you to maximize your return on the certification investment.

This chapter offers suggestions on how to go about selecting a certification program, a set of questions that will help you plan specific steps, and a timeline for attaining your certification.

Adapted from *Computer and Network Professional's Certification Guide* by J. Scott Christianson and Ava Fajen

ISBN 0-7821-2260-4   560 pages $19.99

Selecting a Certification Program

Matching your career goals with a specific certification program can be challenging. One of the main reasons that certification is so popular is because it attempts to keep pace with the rapid changes in the computer and networking industry; certification programs are rapidly being developed and changed to accommodate the latest technology. This can make a certification goal into a moving target for the candidate. At the same time, as new technologies emerge and evolve, your own career goals may change rapidly as well.

There are a number of things you may want to consider in choosing your certification path. Relevant questions include: Do you need to establish a new set of skills or do you have evidence of your core skills and just want something recent to add to your resume? Will you have to pay for all tests and required courses or will your employer pay? Are you looking for a comprehensive knowledge base in a certain area or do you need vendor-specific product knowledge?

This chapter offers you an introduction to all the certification programs available (that we know of). As you consider which certification programs may be of most interest to you, use the tables in this chapter to get a feel for the options that are available within certain general categories.

If you are just beginning your career, we suggest that you try to obtain a respected entry-level certification that covers a wide variety of skills. For example, if you are not yet in the computer networking field and you want certification in order to get a networking job at a company that uses Novell NetWare, you might choose to obtain the Certified Novell Administrator (CNA) certification. The CNA program requires only one test, which covers general knowledge of Novell's network operating system. This might be a more logical starting point than the Certified Novell Engineer (CNE) certification, which, while more impressive, involves six tests that require a very detailed working knowledge of the product.

In addition, you may want to consider selecting a certification program that has multiple levels (see the tables later in this chapter for examples). Once you attain the entry-level certification, you have the option of building on that certification by taking it to the next higher level or pursuing a different product certification in order to diversify your credentials.

For some, the choice of which certification program to pursue will be easier. If you have set your sights on a job or a promotion that requires a specific certification, your goal is very clear. But it never hurts to think ahead as well. See if you can meet the certification requirement in a way that will help you add on other certifications later. For example, if you decide to get the Microsoft Certified Professional (MCP) credential, make sure that the test you take can also be applied to a more advanced certification, such as the Microsoft Certified Systems Engineer (MCSE) or Microsoft Certified Solutions Developer (MCSD), whichever would be more appropriate for you.

We also recommend that you take time to study the job market. Even if you are not ready to make an immediate move, following developments in the market can be extremely valuable. It will be worth your while to notice the directions the computer and networking industry is taking and to track current salary ranges, duties, and requirements for jobs that are of interest. A surefire way to make your certification efforts pay off is to notice what technology or product is just getting hot and make sure that you are one of the first people to get credentials in that area.

REACHING YOUR CERTIFICATION GOALS

Once you have selected a certification goal, it's important to make a definite plan for achieving your goal. A lot of folks never develop a concrete plan for attaining their goals, and, as a result, never reach them. For example, we have a friend who passed one Novell test three years ago and is not officially certified, but always claims to be "working on my CNE." Don't let yourself get caught in certification limbo. First, write down your goals. Next, outline specific steps that will help you accomplish them. Then develop a strategy for taking those steps within a reasonable time frame.

The questions that follow will help you to chart a plan for meeting your goals. Use Figure 25.1 to answer the questions. To get a bigger form with more space for completing each section, check out the online version of this form at the Certification Update Web site (http://www .certification-update.com). If you are working toward more than one certification, complete a separate form for each one.

Part iii

Certification goal   What is the title of the certification program you have selected?

Purpose of certification   How will attaining this certification help you meet your job or career goals?

Deadline for attaining certification When will you be certified? This can be a self-imposed deadline, or there may be a time limitation imposed by your employer or the certification program itself. For example, some programs demand that you meet all the requirements for a certification within one year of taking your first certification test.

What I need to know Take a look at the exam objectives. Are you already proficient in any of the content areas? Take any available sample tests to check your knowledge. Determine what areas you need to focus on, what topics you will need to review, and what hands-on experience you will need.

Hands-on time How will you gain hands-on experience with the product or technology? Are you currently using it every day? If not, can you make special arrangements with a friend who has it, or will you need take a course?

Self-study opportunities What opportunities exist for self-study? Are books, CD-ROMs, or Internet courses available that are specifically designed for this certification? What study guides and resources are available from the certifying entity? Will you will able to learn all that you need to know from these resources? If not, how will you address these areas?

Courses and other opportunities What formal courses are available that would help you? Be sure to check with area community colleges and high schools for any continuing education courses that might address the topics you need to learn. Is there a friend or colleague that you can go to for help or mentoring? Can you form a study group with others who are pursuing this certification?

Study plan timeline After you have collected the information above, construct a detailed timeline for completing your certification. List the specific steps you plan to take to get the education and training you need. We suggest that you mark your timeline in terms of weeks, noting what you will be studying, courses or tests you will be taking, and topics that you will be reviewing each week. Some certification programs may require longer time frames; in this case, months or quarters would be appropriate markers.

TIP

The purpose of a timeline is not to make you feel bad if you miss a deadline, but to allow you to chart your progress toward your goal and to keep moving forward. If you find that you need extra time, simply revise your timeline as you go along.

Mapping Your Certification Goals

Certification Goal:

Purpose of Certification:

Deadline:

What I Need to Know:

Hands-On Time:

Self-Study Opportunities:

Courses and Other Opportunities:

Study Plan Timeline (add more rows as needed):

Step	Start Date	End Date	Learning Objective or Task	Resources Needed
1				
2				
3				
4				
5				

FIGURE 25.1: Mapping your goals

Part iii

After you have selected the certification track that meets your professional development and career goals, you may also want to contact the organization or vendor that awards the certification you seek. In this way, you can find out more about the company that will be providing the certification that you are counting on to make a difference in your career. By talking to the certification staff, you may gain additional insight into the long-term value of attaining this particular certification, and learn about any imminent changes to the program.

CERTIFICATIONS

The sections that follow describe what certifications are available by category and present tables to help you compare the number of required tests, the test format, the approximate costs of taking the test(s), number of required courses, costs of any required courses, and the relative difficulty of the certification program. Use the cost information as a general guideline; since things change rapidly in the world of certification programs, once you have selected a specific course of action, you may want to double-check the costs.

NOTE

Before you start pursuing a certification, check with the Certification Update Web site (http://www.certification-update.com) or the certifying entity to make sure that the ID numbers and costs for the required tests and/or courses have not changed.

We rated the difficulty of attaining particular certifications by sorting them into three categories—Moderate, Challenging, and Extremely Challenging—based on the number of required tests and courses, and the relative difficulty of those tests or lab exams. These ratings are approximate and are offered simply as a general guide to help the reader distinguish between entry-level programs and those that require more advanced skill and knowledge. This rating scale assumes that one has experience with the product or technology and has studied the appropriate subject content before attempting the exams.

Hardware Certifications

These are certification programs that validate an individual's ability to set up, maintain, and troubleshoot computer hardware. Compaq and IBM have programs to certify professionals who have knowledge and experience with their product lines. Learning Tree International, a training organization, has developed its own vendor-independent hardware certification program. The other certification program listed in this chapter—offered by the Disaster Recovery Institute International—involves training to ensure that a company can survive a disaster or natural catastrophe.

TABLE 25.1: Hardware Certifications

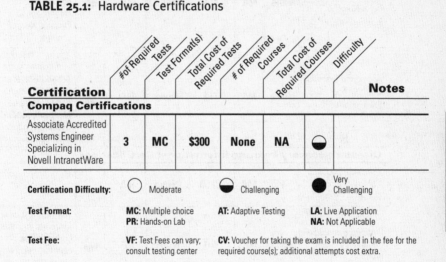

Certification	#of Required Tests	Test Format(s)	Total Cost of Required Tests	# of Required Courses	Total Cost of Required Courses	Difficulty	Notes
Compaq Certifications							
Associate Accredited Systems Engineer Specializing in Novell IntranetWare	3	MC	$300	None	NA	◖	

Certification Difficulty: ○ Moderate ◖ Challenging ● Very Challenging

Test Format: **MC:** Multiple choice **AT:** Adaptive Testing **LA:** Live Application
PR: Hands-on Lab **NA:** Not Applicable

Test Fee: **VF:** Test Fees can vary; consult testing center **CV:** Voucher for taking the exam is included in the fee for the required course(s); additional attempts cost extra.

Part iii

TABLE 25.1 continued: Hardware Certifications

Certification	# of Required Tests	Test Format(s)	Total Cost of Required Tests	# of Required Courses	Total Cost of Required Courses	Difficulty	Notes
Compaq Certifications (continued)							
Associate Accredited Systems Engineer Specializing in Microsoft Windows NT	3	MC	$300	None	NA	◐	
Accredited Systems Engineer Specializing in Novell IntranetWare	None	NA	NA	None	NA	●	You must first obtain certification at the Associate level and must hold current certification as a Certified Novell Engineer (CNE).
Accredited Systems Engineer Specializing in Microsoft Windows NT	None	NA	NA	None	NA	●	You must first obtain certification at the Associate level and must hold current certification as a Microsoft Certified Systems Engineer (MCSE).
Disaster Recovery Institute International Certifications							
Associate Business Continuity Planner (ABCP)	1	MC	$250	None	NA	○	
Certified Business Continuity Planner (CBCP)	None	NA	NA	None	NA	◐	You must first be an Associate Business Continuity Planner and have two years of experience in the field. $100 application fee.

Certification Difficulty: ○ Moderate   ◐ Challenging   ● Very Challenging

Test Format: **MC:** Multiple choice   **AT:** Adaptive Testing   **LA:** Live Application
                    PR: Hands-on Lab   **NA:** Not Applicable

Test Fee: **VF:** Test Fees can vary; consult testing center   **CV:** Voucher for taking the exam is included in the fee for the required course(s); additional attempts cost extra.

TABLE 25.1 continued: Hardware Certifications

Certification	# of Required Tests	Test Format(s)	Total Cost of Required Tests	# of Required Courses	Total Cost of Required Courses	Difficulty	Notes
Disaster Recovery Institute International Certifications (continued)							
Master Business Continuity Planner (MBCP)	None	NA	NA	None	NA	●	You must first be a Certified Business Continuity Planner, have five years of experience and complete a case study or independent research project. $200 application fee.
IBM Certifications							
Professional Server Specialist (PSS)	1	MC	CV	1	$750	○	
Professional Server Expert (PSE): Novell NetWare	1	MC	CV	1	$600	●	You must first obtain PSS certification and hold current certification as a Certified Novell Engineer (CNE).
Professional Server Expert (PSE): OS/2 Warp Server	1	MC	CV	1	$600	●	You must first obtain PSS certification and hold current certification as an OS/2 Warp Server Engineer.
Professional Server Expert (PSE): Windows NT Server	1	MC	CV	1	$600	●	You must first obtain PSS certification and hold current certification as a Microsoft Certified Systems Engineer (MCSE).

Certification Difficulty: ○ Moderate   ◒ Challenging   ● Very Challenging

Test Format: **MC:** Multiple choice   **AT:** Adaptive Testing   **LA:** Live Application
PR: Hands-on Lab   **NA:** Not Applicable

Test Fee: **VF:** Test Fees can vary; consult testing center   **CV:** Voucher for taking the exam is included in the fee for the required course(s); additional attempts cost extra.

Part iii

TABLE 25.1 continued: Hardware Certifications

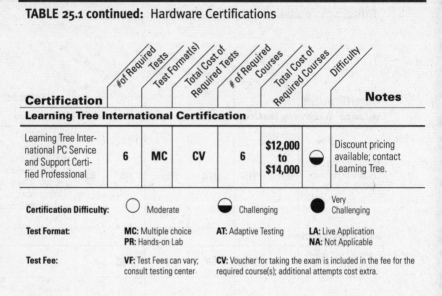

Certification	#of Required Tests	Test Format(s)	Total Cost of Required Tests	# of Required Courses	Total Cost of Required Courses	Difficulty	Notes
Learning Tree International Certification							
Learning Tree International PC Service and Support Certified Professional	6	MC	CV	6	$12,000 to $14,000	◐	Discount pricing available; contact Learning Tree.

Certification Difficulty:	○ Moderate	◐ Challenging	● Very Challenging	
Test Format:	**MC:** Multiple choice **PR:** Hands-on Lab	**AT:** Adaptive Testing	**LA:** Live Application **NA:** Not Applicable	
Test Fee:	**VF:** Test Fees can vary; consult testing center	**CV:** Voucher for taking the exam is included in the fee for the required course(s); additional attempts cost extra.		

Operating System Certifications

Operating system certifications are offered by several makers of UNIX-based operating systems—IBM, Santa Cruz Organization, Silicon Graphics, and Sun—as well as Learning Tree International's vendor-independent UNIX certification. In addition, IBM offers certifications related to its AS/400 systems and two certification programs on OS/2, IBM's PC-based operating system. Finally, Microsoft offers the Microsoft Certified Professional (MCP) credential for technical professionals who are proficient in either Windows 95/98 or Windows NT.

TABLE 25.2 : Operating System Certifications

Certification	# of Required Tests	Test Format(s)	Total Cost of Required Tests	# of Required Courses	Total Cost of Required Courses	Difficulty	Notes
IBM AIX Certifications							
IBM Certified AIX User	1	MC	VF	None	NA	◯	Designed for AIX users rather than technical specialists.
IBM Certified Specialist: AIX System Administration	1	MC	VF	None	NA	◯	
IBM Certified Specialist: AIX Support	1	MC	VF	None	NA	◯	
IBM Certified Advanced Technical Expert: RS/6000 AIX	3	MC	VF	None	NA	●	You must first be an IBM Certified Specialist in AIX System Administration or Support.
IBM AS/400 Certifications							
IBM Certified Specialist: AS/400 Associate System Operator	1	MC	VF	None	NA	◯	
IBM Certified Specialist: AS/400 Professional System Operator	1	MC	VF	None	NA	◯	
IBM Certified Specialist: AS/400 Associate System Administrator	1	MC	VF	None	NA	◯	

Certification Difficulty: ◯ Moderate   ◖ Challenging   ● Very Challenging

Test Format: **MC:** Multiple choice   **AT:** Adaptive Testing   **LA:** Live Application
PR: Hands-on Lab   **NA:** Not Applicable

Test Fee: **VF:** Test Fees can vary; consult testing center   **CV:** Voucher for taking the exam is included in the fee for the required course(s); additional attempts cost extra.

Part iii

TABLE 25.2 continued: Operating System Certifications

Certification	# of Required Tests	Test Format(s)	Total Cost of Required Tests	# of Required Courses	Total Cost of Required Courses	Difficulty	Notes
IBM AS/400 Certifications (continued)							
IBM Certified Specialist: AS/400 Professional System Administrator	1	MC	VF	None	NA	◒	
IBM OS/2 Certifications							
IBM Certified Systems Expert: OS/2 Warp	4	MC	VF	None	NA	◒	Covers OS/2 Warp version 3.
IBM Certified Systems Expert: OS/2 Warp 4	3	MC	VF	None	NA	◒	
Learning Tree International Certification							
Learning Tree International Unix Systems Certified Professional	6	MC	CV	6	$12,000-$14,000	◒	Discount pricing available; contact Learning Tree.
Microsoft Certification							
Microsoft Certified Professional	1	MC	$100	None	NA	○	
Santa Cruz Organization (SCO) Certifications							
Santa Cruz Organization Advanced Certified Engineer (SCO ACE): Server Track	4	MC	VF ($500-$640)	None	NA	◒	
SCO ACE: Open Server Release 5 Track	3	MC	VF ($375-$540)	None	NA	◒	

Certification Difficulty: ○ Moderate   ◒ Challenging   ● Very Challenging

Test Format: **MC:** Multiple choice   **AT:** Adaptive Testing   **LA:** Live Application
PR: Hands-on Lab   **NA:** Not Applicable

Test Fee: **VF:** Test Fees can vary; consult testing center   **CV:** Voucher for taking the exam is included in the fee for the required course(s); additional attempts cost extra.

TABLE 25.2 continued: Operating System Certifications

Certification	# of Required Tests	Test Format(s)	Total Cost of Required Tests	# of Required Courses	Total Cost of Required Courses	Difficulty	Notes
Santa Cruz Organization (SCO) Certifications (continued)							
SCO ACE UnixWare 2.1 Track	3	MC	VF ($375–$540)	None	NA	◐	
Silicon Graphics Certifications							
Silicon Graphics Certified IRIX 6.*x* System Administrator	2	MC	VF	None	NA	◐	
Silicon Graphics Certified IRIX Network Administrator	1	MC	VF	None	NA	●	You must first be a Silicon Graphics Certified IRIX 6.*x* Systems Administrator.
Sun Certifications							
Sun Certified Solaris Administrator	2	MC	$300	None	NA	◐	
Sun Certified Solaris 2.5 Network Administrator	1	MC	$150	None	NA	●	You must first be a Sun Certified Solaris Administrator.

Certification Difficulty: ○ Moderate   ◐ Challenging   ● Very Challenging

Test Format: **MC:** Multiple choice   **AT:** Adaptive Testing   **LA:** Live Application
PR: Hands-on Lab   **NA:** Not Applicable

Test Fee: **VF:** Test Fees can vary; consult testing center   **CV:** Voucher for taking the exam is included in the fee for the required course(s); additional attempts cost extra.

Part iii

Software Certifications

There are a number of software certifications that are of interest to all computer users. Adobe offers the Adobe Certified Expert certification for a number of its products. Baan, a maker of business intelligence software, offers both basic and advanced certifications. Corel's certification program includes two levels of certification on its WordPerfect, Quattro Pro, and Presentations programs. Lotus offers a wide variety of certifications on its software. In addition, Microsoft offers several levels of certification on its Microsoft Office and related software products.

TABLE 25.3: Software Certifications

Certification	# of Required Tests	Test Format(s)	Total Cost of Required Tests	# of Required Courses	Total Cost of Required Courses	Difficulty	Notes
Adobe Certification							
Adobe Certified Expert	1	MC	$150	None	NA	○	Available on: Illustrator 7.0, Acrobat 3.0, After-Effects 3.1, Framemaker 5.5, Pagemaker 6.5, PageMill 2.0, Photoshop 4.0
Baan Certifications							
Baan Basic Certification	1	MC	$300	None	NA	○	
Baan Advanced Certification in Enterprise Logistics	1	MC	$300	None	NA	◖	You must first obtain the Baan Basic Certification.

Certification Difficulty:	○ Moderate	◖ Challenging	● Very Challenging
Test Format:	**MC:** Multiple choice **PR:** Hands-on Lab	**AT:** Adaptive Testing	**LA:** Live Application **NA:** Not Applicable
Test Fee:	**VF:** Test Fees can vary; consult testing center	**CV:** Voucher for taking the exam is included in the fee for the required course(s); additional attempts cost extra.	

TABLE 25.3 continued: Software Certifications

Certification	#of Required Tests	Test Format(s)	Total Cost of Required Tests	# of Required Courses	Total Cost of Required Courses	Difficulty	Notes
Baan Certifications (continued)							
Baan Advanced Certification in Enterprise Finance	1	MC	$300	None	NA	◒	You must first obtain the Baan Basic Certification.
Baan Advanced Certification in Enterprise Tools	1	MC	$300	None	NA	◒	You must first obtain the Baan Basic Certification.
Baan Advanced Certification in Enterprise Modeler	1	MC	$300	None	NA	◒	You must first obtain the Baan Basic Certification.
Corel Certifications							
Corel WordPerfect 7 Certified Resource	1	MC	$55	None	NA	○	
Corel Quattro Pro 7 Certified Resource	1	MC	$55	None	NA	○	
Corel Presentations 7 Certified Resource	1	MC	$55	None	NA	○	
Corel WordPerfect 7 Certified Expert	1	MC	$80	None	NA	◒	$55 application fee (currently waived).
Corel Quattro Pro 7 Certified Expert	1	MC	$80	None	NA	◒	$55 application fee (currently waived).
Corel Presentations 7 Certified Expert	1	MC	$80	None	NA	◒	$55 application fee (currently waived).

Certification Difficulty:	○ Moderate	◒ Challenging	● Very Challenging
Test Format:	**MC:** Multiple choice **PR:** Hands-on Lab	**AT:** Adaptive Testing	**LA:** Live Application **NA:** Not Applicable
Test Fee:	**VF:** Test Fees can vary; consult testing center	**CV:** Voucher for taking the exam is included in the fee for the required course(s); additional attempts cost extra.	

Part iii

TABLE 25.3 continued: Software Certifications

Certification	# of Required Tests	Test Format(s)	Total Cost of Required Tests	# of Required Courses	Total Cost of Required Courses	Difficulty	Notes
Lotus Certifications							
Certified Lotus Specialist (CLS)	1	MC	$90	None	NA	○	
Certified Lotus Professional (CLP): Application Developer	3	MC or LA	$270	None	NA	◐	
Certified Lotus Professional (CLP): Principal Application Developer	1	MC or LA	$90	None	NA	●	You must first be a CLP Application Developer.
Certified Lotus Professional (CLP): System Administrator	3	MC or LA	$270	None	NA	◐	
Certified Lotus Professional (CLP): Principal System Administrator	1	MC or LA	$90	None	NA	●	You must first be a CLP System Administrator.
Certified Lotus Professional (CLP): cc:Mail System Administrator	2	MC	$90	None	NA	◐	
Microsoft Certifications							
Microsoft Office Proficient Specialist	1	LA	VF (suggested fee is $50)	None	NA	○	Available for Word 95, Word 97, Excel 95, and Excel 97.

Certification Difficulty:	○ Moderate	◐ Challenging	● Very Challenging
Test Format:	**MC:** Multiple choice **PR:** Hands-on Lab	**AT:** Adaptive Testing	**LA:** Live Application **NA:** Not Applicable
Test Fee:	**VF:** Test Fees can vary; consult testing center	**CV:** Voucher for taking the exam is included in the fee for the required course(s); additional attempts cost extra.	

TABLE 25.3 continued: Software Certifications

Certification	#of Required Tests	Test Format(s)	Total Cost of Required Tests	# of Required Courses	Total Cost of Required Courses	Difficulty	Notes
Microsoft Certifications (continued)							
Microsoft Office Expert Specialist	1	LA	VF (suggested fee is $50)	None	NA	◒	Available for Access 97, Excel 95, Excel 97, FrontPage 97, Outlook 97, PowerPoint 95, PowerPoint 97, Word 95, and Word 97.
Microsoft Office Expert	1	LA	VF (suggested fee is $50)	None	NA	●	You must first be a Microsoft Office Expert Specialist in five core Office 97 applications (Word, Excel, Access, PowerPoint, and Outlook).

Certification Difficulty: ○ Moderate   ◒ Challenging   ● Very Challenging

Test Format: **MC:** Multiple choice   **AT:** Adaptive Testing   **LA:** Live Application
PR: Hands-on Lab   **NA:** Not Applicable

Test Fee: **VF:** Test Fees can vary; consult testing center   **CV:** Voucher for taking the exam is included in the fee for the required course(s); additional attempts cost extra.

Part iii

Networking Hardware Certifications

Networking hardware certifications are from the major manufacturers of networking equipment. Ascend offers a certification for its product line, which includes remote-access and switching equipment. Bay Networks and Cisco are both well-known for their routers, but are also big players in remote-access and switching technology. Bay Networks offers two levels of certification in a number of different types of technology. Cisco's Certified Internetworking Expert (CCIE) program has recently expanded to include Cisco Certified Network Associate (CCNA), Cisco Certified Network Professional (CCNP), Cisco Certified Design Associate (CCDA), and Cisco Certified Design Professional (CCDP).

Learning Tree International offers vendor-independent certification programs in local area networking, wide area networking, and internetworking. Finally, Xylan offers two new certifications in its switching technology product line: the Xylan Switch Specialist and the Xylan Switch Expert.

TABLE 25.4: Networking Hardware Certifications

Certification	# of Required Tests	Test Format(s)	Total Cost of Required Tests	# of Required Courses	Total Cost of Required Courses	Difficulty	Notes
Ascend Certification							
Ascend Certified Technical Expert	3	MC, PR	$1250	None	NA	●	
Bay Networks Certifications							
Bay Networks Certified Specialist: Hub Technology	1	MC	$125	None	NA	○	
Bay Networks Certified Expert: Hub Technology	2	MC, PR	$550	None	NA	●	You must first be a Certified Specialist in Hub Technology.
Bay Networks Certified Specialist: Router Technology	1	MC	$125	None	NA	○	
Bay Networks Certified Expert: Router Technology	2	MC, PR	$650	None	NA	●	You must first be a Certified Specialist in Router Technology.
Bay Networks Certified Specialist: Network Management Technology	1	MC	$125	None	NA	○	

Certification Difficulty: ○ Moderate   ◐ Challenging   ● Very Challenging

Test Format: **MC:** Multiple choice   **AT:** Adaptive Testing   **LA:** Live Application
                   PR: Hands-on Lab   **NA:** Not Applicable

Test Fee: **VF:** Test Fees can vary;   **CV:** Voucher for taking the exam is included in the fee for the
                consult testing center   required course(s); additional attempts cost extra.

TABLE 25.4 continued: Networking Hardware Certifications

Certification	# of Required Tests	Test Format(s)	Total Cost of Required Tests	# of Required Courses	Total Cost of Required Courses	Difficulty	Notes
Bay Networks Certifications (continued)							
Bay Networks Certified Expert: Network Management Technology	2	MC, PR	$800	None	NA	●	You must first be a Certified Specialist in Network Management Technology.
Bay Networks Certified Specialist: Switching Technology	1	MC	$125	None	NA	○	
Bay Networks Certified Expert: Remote Access Technology	1	MC	$125	None	NA	○	
Cisco Certifications							
Cisco Certified Internetworking Expert (CCIE): WAN Switching Expert	2	MC, PR	$1200	None	NA	●	
Cisco Certified Internetworking Expert (CCIE): Internet Service Provider Dial Expert	2	MC, PR	$1200	None	NA	●	
Cisco Certified Internetworking Expert (CCIE): Routing and Switching Expert	2	MC, PR	$1200	None	NA	●	

Certification Difficulty: ○ Moderate   ◐ Challenging   ● Very Challenging

Test Format: **MC:** Multiple choice   **AT:** Adaptive Testing   **LA:** Live Application
PR: Hands-on Lab   **NA:** Not Applicable

Test Fee: **VF:** Test Fees can vary; consult testing center   **CV:** Voucher for taking the exam is included in the fee for the required course(s); additional attempts cost extra.

Part iii

TABLE 25.4 continued: Networking Hardware Certifications

Certification	#of Required Tests	Test Format(s)	Total Cost of Required Tests	# of Required Courses	Total Cost of Required Courses	Difficulty	Notes
Learning Tree International Certifications							
Learning Tree International Local Area Networks Certified Professional	5	MC	CV	5	$12,000-$14,000	◖	Discount pricing available; contact Learning Tree.
Learning Tree International Wide Area Networks Certified Professional	5	MC	CV	5	$12,000-$14,000	◖	Discount pricing available; contact Learning Tree.
Learning Tree International Internetworking Certified Professional	5	MC	CV	5	$12,000-$14,000	◖	Discount pricing available; contact Learning Tree.
Xylan Certifications							
Xylan Certified Switching Specialist (XCSS)	1	MC	$100	None	NA	○	
Xylan Certified Switching Expert (XCSE)	1	MC	$200	None	NA	◖	You must first be a Certified Switching Specialist.

Certification Difficulty: ○ Moderate   ◖ Challenging   ● Very Challenging

Test Format:	**MC:** Multiple choice	**AT:** Adaptive Testing	**LA:** Live Application
	PR: Hands-on Lab		**NA:** Not Applicable

Test Fee: **VF:** Test Fees can vary; consult testing center   **CV:** Voucher for taking the exam is included in the fee for the required course(s); additional attempts cost extra.

Networking Operating System Certifications

There are currently four certification programs related to network operating systems. Banyan's certification program concentrates on the Vines network operating system, which is used primarily to link UNIX servers with a variety of clients. IBM offers certifications on its PC-based network operating systems—OS/2 Warp Server and OS/2 LAN server. Novell's certification program, initiated in 1987, offers four levels of certification on Novell NetWare, IntranetWare, and GroupWare products. The Microsoft Certified Systems Engineer (MSCE) credential certifies individuals on Microsoft's network operating system, Windows NT Server.

TABLE 25.5: Networking Operating Systems Certifications

Certification	# of Required Tests	Test Format(s)	Total Cost of Required Tests	# of Required Courses	Total Cost of Required Courses	Difficulty	Notes
Banyan Certifications							
Certified Banyan Specialist (CBS)	3	MC	$360	None	NA	○	
Certified Banyan Specialist (CBS): Windows NT	3	MC	$340	2	$3,300	◑	
Certified Banyan Engineer (CBE)	2	MC	$240	2	$4,500	●	You must first be a Certified Banyan Specialist.
IBM Certifications							
IBM Certified Specialist: OS/2 Warp Server Administration	1	MC	VF	None	NA	○	

Certification Difficulty: ○ Moderate ◑ Challenging ● Very Challenging

Test Format: **MC:** Multiple choice **PR:** Hands-on Lab **AT:** Adaptive Testing **LA:** Live Application **NA:** Not Applicable

Test Fee: **VF:** Test Fees can vary; consult testing center **CV:** Voucher for taking the exam is included in the fee for the required course(s); additional attempts cost extra.

Part iii

TABLE 25.5 continued: Networking Operating Systems Certifications

Certification	# of Required Tests	Test Format(s)	Total Cost of Required Tests	# of Required Courses	Total Cost of Required Courses	Difficulty	Notes
IBM Certifications (continued)							
IBM Certified Expert: OS/2 Warp Server	3	MC	VF	None	NA	◑	
IBM Certified Specialist: OS/2 LAN Server 4.0 Administration	1	MC	VF	None	NA	○	
IBM Certified Expert: OS/2 LAN Server 4.0	6	MC	VF	None	NA	●	
Microsoft Certification							
Microsoft Certified Systems Engineer (MCSE)	6	MC	$600	None	NA	●	Pick your elective test carefully and you can obtain MCP + Internet at the same time.
Novell Certifications							
Certified Novell Administrator (CNA)	1	AT, MC	$85	None	NA	○	Available in either NetWare 3, Intranet-Ware, GroupWise 4, GroupWise 5.
Certified Novell Engineer (CNE)	7	AT, MC	VF	None	NA	●	Available in either NetWare 3, Intranet-Ware, GroupWise 4, GroupWise 5.
Master Certified Novell Engineer (MCNE)	4 to 6	AT, MC	VF	None	NA	●	Available to current CNEs. MCNE specialties are Management, Connectivity, Messaging, Internet/Intranet Solutions, AS/400 Integration, Unix Integration, or Windows NT Integration.

Certification Difficulty:	○ Moderate	◑ Challenging	● Very Challenging
Test Format:	**MC:** Multiple choice **PR:** Hands-on Lab	**AT:** Adaptive Testing	**LA:** Live Application **NA:** Not Applicable
Test Fee:	**VF:** Test Fees can vary; consult testing center	**CV:** Voucher for taking the exam is included in the fee for the required course(s); additional attempts cost extra.	

Client/Server and Database System Certifications

Several highly specialized certification programs were designed by vendors that make database and client/server products. Borland, Centura, Informix, Oracle, and Sybase all offer certifications on their database products. These certifications focus on the tasks involved in administering and managing large databases for a variety of purposes.

TABLE 25.6: Client/Server Certifications

Certification	#of Required Tests	Test Format(s)	Total Cost of Required Tests	# of Required Courses	Total Cost of Required Courses	Difficulty	Notes
Borland Certification							
Delphi 3 Certified Developer	1	MC	$150	None	NA	◯	
Centura Certifications							
Centura Database Developer	1	MC	$120	None	NA	◯	
Centura Database Administrator	1	MC	$120	None	NA	◯	
Informix Certifications							
Database Specialist: Informix Dynamic Server	2	MC	$500	None	NA	◑	

Certification Difficulty: ◯ Moderate   ◑ Challenging   ● Very Challenging

Test Format: **MC:** Multiple choice   **AT:** Adaptive Testing   **LA:** Live Application
PR: Hands-on Lab   **NA:** Not Applicable

Test Fee: **VF:** Test Fees can vary; consult testing center   **CV:** Voucher for taking the exam is included in the fee for the required course(s); additional attempts cost extra.

Part iii

TABLE 25.6 continued: Client/Server Certifications

Certification	# of Required Tests	Test Format(s)	Total Cost of Required Tests	# of Required Courses	Total Cost of Required Courses	Difficulty	Notes
Informix Certifications (continued)							
System Administration: Informix Dynamic Server	2	MC	$500	None	NA	◒	
INFORMIX-4GL Certified Professional	2	MC	$500	None	NA	◒	
Oracle Certifications							
Certified Database Administrator	4	MC	$500	None	NA	●	
Certified Application Developer for Developer/2000	5	MC	$625	None	NA	●	
Sybase Certifications							
Certified Power-Builder Developer Associate	2	MC	VF	None	NA	◒	
Certified Power-Builder Developer Professional	1	LA	VF	None	NA	●	You must first be a PowerBuilder Developer Associate.
Certified Database Administrator	2	MC	VF	None	NA	◒	
Certified Performance and Tuning Specialist	1	MC	VF	None	NA	●	You must first be a Certified Database Administrator.

Certification Difficulty: ◯ Moderate   ◒ Challenging   ● Very Challenging

Test Format: **MC:** Multiple choice   **AT:** Adaptive Testing   **LA:** Live Application
PR: Hands-on Lab   **NA:** Not Applicable

Test Fee: **VF:** Test Fees can vary; consult testing center   **CV:** Voucher for taking the exam is included in the fee for the required course(s); additional attempts cost extra.

Internet Certifications

Internet certifications are both vendor-based and vendor-independent certification programs that address Internet strategies, procedures, and protocols. The IBM Certified Solutions Expert: Net.Commerce addresses security for financial transactions on the Internet; the IBM Certified Solution Expert: Firewall targets technical professionals who install secure links between company networks and the Internet. The vendor-independent Learning Tree International certification program covers TCP/IP protocols for setting up and administering intranets and Internet connections.

The Microsoft certifications—Microsoft Certified Professional + Internet and Microsoft Certified Systems Engineer + Internet—are focused on the implementation of intranet and Internet solutions using Microsoft products. Novell offers a number of certifications for Internet professionals. Prosoft/Net Guru Technologies offers certification programs in all aspects of the Internet, from Web site design and business strategies to server administration and TCP/IP security. Finally, USWeb Learning offers two vendor-neutral certifications that focus on broadly applicable fundamentals and principles of Web development.

TABLE 25.7: Internet Certifications

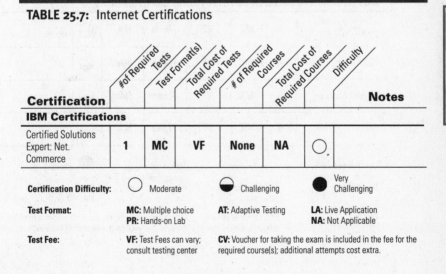

Certification	# of Required Tests	Test Format(s)	Total Cost of Required Tests	# of Required Courses	Total Cost of Required Courses	Difficulty	Notes
IBM Certifications							
Certified Solutions Expert: Net. Commerce	1	MC	VF	None	NA	○	

Certification Difficulty: ○ Moderate   ◓ Challenging   ● Very Challenging

Test Format: **MC:** Multiple choice   **AT:** Adaptive Testing   **LA:** Live Application
PR: Hands-on Lab   **NA:** Not Applicable

Test Fee: **VF:** Test Fees can vary; consult testing center   **CV:** Voucher for taking the exam is included in the fee for the required course(s); additional attempts cost extra.

Part iii

TABLE 25.7 continued: Internet Certifications

Certification	# of Required Tests	Test Format(s)	Total Cost of Required Tests	# of Required Courses	Total Cost of Required Courses	Difficulty	Notes
IBM Certifications (continued)							
Certified Solutions Expert: Firewall Resources	1	MC	VF	None	NA	○	
Learning Tree International Certification							
Learning Tree International Internet/ Intranet Certified Professional	5	MC	CV	5	$12,000-$14,000	◐	Discount pricing available; contact Learning Tree.
Microsoft Certifications							
Microsoft Certified Professional + Internet	3	MC	$300	None	NA	◐	
Microsoft Certified Systems Engineer + Internet	9	MC	$900	None	NA	●	
Novell Certified Internet Professional Certifications							
Internet Business Strategist	1	MC	VF	None	NA	○	
Web Designer	4	MC	VF	None	NA	◐	
Intranet Manager	5	MC	VF	None	NA	◐	
Internet Architect	5	MC	VF	None	NA	◐	

Certification Difficulty: ○ Moderate   ◐ Challenging   ● Very Challenging

Test Format: **MC:** Multiple choice   **AT:** Adaptive Testing   **LA:** Live Application
PR: Hands-on Lab   **NA:** Not Applicable

Test Fee: **VF:** Test Fees can vary; consult testing center   **CV:** Voucher for taking the exam is included in the fee for the required course(s); additional attempts cost extra.

TABLE 25.7 continued: Internet Certifications

Certification	#of Required Tests	Test Format(s)	Total Cost of Required Tests	# of Required Courses	Total Cost of Required Courses	Difficulty	Notes
Prosoft/Net Guru Technologies Certified Internet Webmaster Certifications							
Designer	1	MC	CV	3	$995	◐	
Developer I	1	MC	CV	2	$2275	◐	
Developer II	1	MC	CV	2	$2275	◐	
Administrator	1	MC	CV	2	$2440	◐	
Network Professional	1	MC	CV	2	$2275	◐	
Security Professional	1	MC	CV	4	$4400	●	
ECommerce Professional	2	MC	CV	1	$1445	◐	
USWeb Learning Certifications							
Certified Specialist	2	MC	VF	3-4	VF	◐	
Certified Architect	3	MC	VF	5	VF	●	

Certification Difficulty:	◯ Moderate ◐ Challenging	● Very Challenging
Test Format:	**MC:** Multiple choice **PR:** Hands-on Lab	**AT:** Adaptive Testing **LA:** Live Application **NA:** Not Applicable
Test Fee:	**VF:** Test Fees can vary; consult testing center	**CV:** Voucher for taking the exam is included in the fee for the required course(s); additional attempts cost extra.

Part iii

Instructor and Trainer Certifications

There are a number of certification programs for instructors and trainers who want to provide "authorized training" for specific vendors, including Adobe, Banyan, Borland, Corel, IBM, Lotus, Microsoft, Novell, and Prosoft/ Net Guru Technologies. The vendor-independent Certified Technical Trainer credential offered by the Chauncey Group is a widely respected certification program and a required component of several of the vendor-based training certifications.

TABLE 25.8: Instructor/Trainer Certifications

Certification	# of Required Tests	Test Format(s)	Total Cost of Required Tests	# of Required Courses	Total Cost of Required Courses	Difficulty	Notes
Adobe Certification							
Adobe Certified Instructor	None	NA	NA	None	NA	◒	Your must be a Certified Technical Trainer and be an Adobe Certified Expert on the product you will teach.
Banyan Certifications							
Certified Banyan Instructor (CBI)	None	NA	NA	1	VF	●	Must be a CBE. Must also be a CTT, have vendor instructor certification, or take an approved instructional skills course.
CBI: Problem Solving for Vines Networks Authorization	None	NA	NA	1	VF	●	Obtain CBI status first.

Certification Difficulty: ◯ Moderate   ◒ Challenging   ● Very Challenging

Test Format: **MC:** Multiple choice   **AT:** Adaptive Testing   **LA:** Live Application
PR: Hands-on Lab   **NA:** Not Applicable

Test Fee: **VF:** Test Fees can vary; consult testing center   **CV:** Voucher for taking the exam is included in the fee for the required course(s); additional attempts cost extra.

TABLE 25.8 continued: Instructor/Trainer Certifications

Certification	# of Required Tests	Test Format(s)	Total Cost of Required Tests	# of Required Courses	Total Cost of Required Courses	Difficulty	Notes
Borland Certification							
Borland Delphi 3 Certified Trainer	None	NA	NA	1	$1000	◑	You must first be a Delphi 3 Certified Developer.
Chauncey Group International Certification							
Certified Technical Trainer (CTT)	1	MC	$150	None	NA	◑	Also requires a performance video ($135 fee for processing).
Corel Certifications							
Corel WordPerfect Suite 7 Certified Instructor	None	NA	NA	None	NA	◑	You must first be a WordPerfect Certified Expert and a CTT. $200 application fee.
CorelDRAW 5 Certified Instructor	1	MC	VF	None	NA	◑	
IBM Certifications							
IBM Certified Instructor: OS/2 Warp	None	NA	NA	None	NA	◑	Must be a Certified Systems Expert: OS/2 Warp and provide proof of teaching experience.
IBM Certified Instructor: OS/2 LAN Server	None	NA	NA	None	NA	◑	Must be a Certified Systems Expert: OS/2 Warp and provide proof of teaching experience.
IBM Certified Instructor: OS/2 Warp Server	None	NA	NA	None	NA	◑	Must be a Certified Systems Expert: OS/2 Warp and provide proof of teaching experience.

Certification Difficulty: ○ Moderate   ◑ Challenging   ● Very Challenging

Test Format: **MC:** Multiple choice   **AT:** Adaptive Testing   **LA:** Live Application
PR: Hands-on Lab   **NA:** Not Applicable

Test Fee: **VF:** Test Fees can vary; consult testing center   **CV:** Voucher for taking the exam is included in the fee for the required course(s); additional attempts cost extra.

Part III

TABLE 25.8 continued:　Instructor/Trainer Certifications

Certification	# of Required Tests	Test Format(s)	Total Cost of Required Tests	# of Required Courses	Total Cost of Required Courses	Difficulty	Notes
Lotus Certifications							
Certified Lotus Instructor (CLI): Level One	2	MC	$180	3	VF ($1500-2000)	◯	Must provide proof of instructional experience.
Certified Lotus Instructor (CLI): Level Two	2	MC	$180	3	VF ($1500-2000)	◒	Must also have experience teaching Level One courses.
Certified Lotus Instructor (CLI): Advanced Course	None	NA	C	None	NA	●	Must have experience teaching Level Two courses; take courses, and pass tests on what you will teach.
Microsoft Certification							
Microsoft Certified Trainer	None	NA	NA	None	NA	◒	Must prove instructional skills (CTT, instructional course, or other vendor trainer certification).
Novell Certifications							
Certified InfiLearning Instructor	None	NA	NA	None	NA	◒	Must prove instructional skills (CTT or course); attend course and pass test for the course you will teach.
Certified Novell Instructor	None	NA	NA	None	NA	●	Obtain CNE, prove instructional skills (CTT or course); take course and pass test for course you will teach.

Certification Difficulty: ◯ Moderate　　◒ Challenging　　● Very Challenging

Test Format:　　**MC:** Multiple choice　　**AT:** Adaptive Testing　　**LA:** Live Application
　　　　　　　　PR: Hands-on Lab　　　　　　　　　　　　　　　**NA:** Not Applicable

Test Fee:　　**VF:** Test Fees can vary; consult testing center　　**CV:** Voucher for taking the exam is included in the fee for the required course(s); additional attempts cost extra.

TABLE 25.8 continued: Instructor/Trainer Certifications

Certification	#of Required Tests	Test Format(s)	Total Cost of Required Tests	# of Required Courses	Total Cost of Required Courses	Difficulty	Notes
Novell Certifications (continued)							
Master Certified Novell Instructor	None	NA	NA	None	NA	●	Obtain Master CNE, prove instructional skills (CTT or course); take course and pass test for course you will teach.
Prosoft/Net Guru Technology Certifications							
Prosoft/NGT Certified Windows NT Instructor	1	MC	CV	2	$3425	◐	
Prosoft/NGT Certified Network Professional Instructor	1	MC	CV	4	$5700	◐	
Prosoft/NGT Certified Security Professional Instructor	3	MC	CV	4	$7775	●	
Prosoft/NGT Certified Internet Web Developer Instructor	3	MC	CV	3	$6645	●	

Certification Difficulty: ○ Moderate   ◐ Challenging   ● Very Challenging

Test Format: **MC:** Multiple choice   **AT:** Adaptive Testing   **LA:** Live Application
PR: Hands-on Lab   **NA:** Not Applicable

Test Fee: **VF:** Test Fees can vary; consult testing center   **CV:** Voucher for taking the exam is included in the fee for the required course(s); additional attempts cost extra.

Part iii

Other Vendor-Based Certifications

Additional vendor-based certification programs cover aspects of computing and networking that did not fit neatly into the previous categories. Two certification programs concentrate on computer security: the Certified Information Systems Security Professional designation, offered by the International Information Systems Security Certification Consortium, and the Certified Information Systems Auditor credential, offered by Information Systems Audit and Control Association.

Two certifications focus on programming. The Microsoft Certified Solution Developer certification program is designed for computer professionals who develop custom applications using Microsoft products and/or programming languages. The Sun Certified Java Programmer and Developer are two popular certifications offered by the inventors of the Java programming language.

The final two certifications in this category concentrate on network management software. This type of software is used for large-scale monitoring and troubleshooting of networks that are comprised of equipment and software from multiple vendors. The two network management certifications are Computer Associates' Certified Unicenter Engineer credential and Hewlett-Packard's OpenView Certified Consultant designation.

TABLE 25.9: Other Vendor Certifications

Certification	# of Required Tests	Test Format(s)	Total Cost of Required Tests	# of Required Courses	Total Cost of Required Courses	Difficulty	Notes
International Information Systems Security Certification Consortium							
(ISC)²Certified Information Systems Security Professional	1	MC	$395	None	NA	◒	Three years field experience required
Information Systems Audit and Control Association Certification							
Certified Information Systems Auditor (CISA)	2	MC	$295-$385	None	NA	●	Five years field experience required
Microsoft Certification							
Microsoft Certified Solutions Developer	4	MC	$400	None	NA	●	
Sun Certifications							
Certified Java Programmer: JDK 1.0.2	1	MC	$150	None	NA	◒	
Certified Java Programmer: JDK 1.1	1	MC	$150	None	NA	◒	
Certified Java Developer: JDK 1.0.2	1	MC	$150	None	NA	●	Must complete a programming assignment ($250 fee).
Certified Java Developer: JDK 1.1	1	MC	$150	None	NA	●	Must complete a programming assignment ($250 fee).

Certification Difficulty: ○ Moderate   ◒ Challenging   ● Very Challenging

Test Format: **MC:** Multiple choice   **AT:** Adaptive Testing   **LA:** Live Application
PR: Hands-on Lab   **NA:** Not Applicable

Test Fee: **VF:** Test Fees can vary; consult testing center   **CV:** Voucher for taking the exam is included in the fee for the required course(s); additional attempts cost extra.

Part iii

TABLE 25.9 continued: Other Vendor Certifications

Certification	# of Required Tests	Test Format(s)	Total Cost of Required Tests	# of Required Courses	Total Cost of Required Courses	Difficulty	Notes
Computer Associates Certification							
Certified Unicenter Engineer	2	MC	VF	2	VF	◑	
Hewlett-Packard Certifications							
HP OpenView Certified Consultant: UNIX	2	MC	VF	None	NA	◑	
HP OpenView Certified Consultant: Windows NT	2	MC	VF	None	NA	◑	
HP OpenView Certified Consultant: UNIX and Windows NT	2	MC	VF	None	NA	◑	

Certification Difficulty: ○ Moderate   ◑ Challenging   ● Very Challenging

Test Format: **MC:** Multiple choice   **AT:** Adaptive Testing   **LA:** Live Application
PR: Hands-on Lab   **NA:** Not Applicable

Test Fee: **VF:** Test Fees can vary; consult testing center   **CV:** Voucher for taking the exam is included in the fee for the required course(s); additional attempts cost extra.

Organization-Based Certifications

These certifications are offered by organizations or associations, rather than by vendors. These certification programs are well respected in the computer and networking fields because they tend to be comprehensive and standards-based.

BICSI offers the Registered Communications Distribution Designer program, which certifies experts who design and install cabling and networking for new and existing buildings. The Computer Technology Industry Association, or CompTIA, offers two important certifications: the A+ certification for computer service technicians, and the Certified Document Architect for imaging specialists. The Certified Network Professional credential—developed by the Network Professional Association—certifies networking expertise, as does the Certified Network Expert credential, which is offered by a consortium of industry representatives. The Institute for Certification of Computing Professionals (ICCP) was founded in 1973 and offers the Certified Computing Professional credential, which covers many different aspects of computing and networking.

TABLE 25.10: Organization-Based Certifications

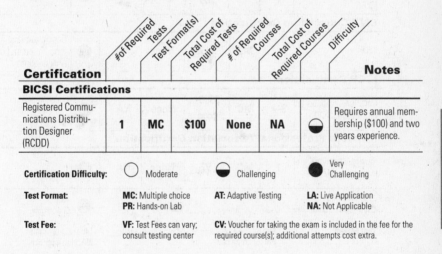

Certification	# of Required Tests	Test Format(s)	Total Cost of Required Tests	# of Required Courses	Total Cost of Required Courses	Difficulty	Notes
BICSI Certifications							
Registered Communications Distribution Designer (RCDD)	1	MC	$100	None	NA	◒	Requires annual membership ($100) and two years experience.

Certification Difficulty:	○ Moderate	◒ Challenging	● Very Challenging
Test Format:	**MC:** Multiple choice **PR:** Hands-on Lab	**AT:** Adaptive Testing	**LA:** Live Application **NA:** Not Applicable
Test Fee:	**VF:** Test Fees can vary; consult testing center	**CV:** Voucher for taking the exam is included in the fee for the required course(s); additional attempts cost extra.	

TABLE 25.10 continued: Organization-Based Certifications

Certification	# of Required Tests	Test Format(s)	Total Cost of Required Tests	# of Required Courses	Total Cost of Required Courses	Difficulty	Notes
BICSI Certifications (continued)							
RCDD: Local Area Network Specialty	1	MC	$100	None	NA	◒	Must obtain an RCDD.
CompTIA Certifications							
A+ Certification	2	MC	$190-220	None	NA	●	
Certified Document Image Architect (CDIA)	1	MC	$150-165	None	NA	◒	
CNX Consortium Certification							
CNX	1	MC	$250	None	NA	●	Specializations: Token Ring, Ethernet, FDDI, or LAN Cabling
ICCP Certification							
Certified Computer Professional (CCP)	3-4	MC	$350-$400	None	NA	●	
Network Professional Association Certification							
Certified Network Professional (CNP)	1	MC	VF	None	NA	●	

Certification Difficulty: ◯ Moderate   ◒ Challenging   ● Very Challenging

Test Format: MC: Multiple choice   AT: Adaptive Testing   LA: Live Application
PR: Hands-on Lab   NA: Not Applicable

Test Fee: VF: Test Fees can vary; consult testing center   CV: Voucher for taking the exam is included in the fee for the required course(s); additional attempts cost extra.

WHAT'S NEXT?

This chapter provided an overview of the many certification programs that are available. The next chapter focuses on Microsoft Certified Systems Engineer (MCSE) certification.

Chapter 26

INTRODUCTION TO THE NT WORKSTATION AND SERVER STUDY GUIDES

The Microsoft Certified Systems Engineer (MCSE) certification is *the* hottest ticket to career advancement in the computer industry today. Hundreds of thousands of corporations and organizations worldwide are choosing Windows NT for their networks. This has created a tremendous need for qualified personnel and consultants to help implement and support NT. The MCSE certification is your way to show these corporations and organizations that you have the professional abilities they need.

• •

Adapted from *MCSE: NT® Workstation 4 Study Guide, Second Edition* by Charles Perkins and Matthew Strebe with James Chellis

ISBN 0-7821-2223-X   752 pages $49.99

and from *MCSE: NT® Server 4 Study Guide* by Matthew Strebe and Charles Perkins with James Chellis

ISBN 0-7821-2222-1   832 pages $49.99

Today, personal computers are more powerful than even mainframes and supercomputers were a few years ago. Personal computer users often have gigabytes of hard disk space, megabytes of memory, and even hundreds of megahertz of processing power at their disposal. Personal computers are being used for much more than their original purposes of editing text and calculating spreadsheet values. The incredible computing capacity of today's computers is being used to combine audio, video, and textual information in multimedia software, to edit and present three-dimensional graphics and animation, and to communicate with other computers around the world via the Internet—just to name a few of the tasks of personal computers today.

Windows NT is the operating system that Microsoft developed to support today's computing requirements. The "NT" stands for New Technology. The new technology in Windows NT enables software writers to create sophisticated software and makes it easier for users to use that software.

Whether you are just getting started or are ready to move ahead in the computer industry, the knowledge and skills you have are your most valuable assets. Microsoft, recognizing these assets, has developed its Microsoft Certified Professional (MCP) program to give you credentials that verify your ability to work with Microsoft products effectively and professionally. The MCP credential, designed for professionals who work with Microsoft networks, is the MCSE certification.

MSCE: NT Workstation Study Guide covers the Microsoft Windows NT Workstation operating system. It provides the information you need to acquire a solid foundation in the field of computer networks and study for the Windows NT Workstation exam.

MSCE: NT Server 4 Study Guide gives you the knowledge and skills you need to prepare for one of the core requirements of the MCSE certification program—Windows NT Server. Certified by Microsoft, this book presents the information you need to acquire a solid understanding of the fundamentals of Windows NT Server and to study for the NT Server exam. Both books help you take a big step toward MCSE certification.

NOTE

Microsoft Certified Professional Magazine recently completed a survey that revealed the average MCSE is earning well over $70,000 (US) per year, while the average MCSE consultant is earning more than $95,000 per year. You can read the entire *Microsoft Certified Professional Magazine* annual salary survey at http://www.mcpmag.com.

How Do You Become an MCSE?

Attaining MCSE status is a serious challenge. The exams cover a wide range of topics and require dedicated study and expertise. Many people who have achieved other computer industry credentials have had trouble with the MCSE. This challenge is, however, why the MCSE certificate is so valuable. If achieving MCSE status were easy, the market would be quickly flooded by MCSEs and the certification would quickly become meaningless. Microsoft, keenly aware of this fact, has taken steps to ensure that the certification means its holder is truly knowledgeable and skilled.

To become an MCSE, you must pass four core requirements and two electives. Most people select the following exam combination for the MCSE core requirements for the 4.0 track:

Client Requirement

70-073: Implementing and Supporting Windows NT Workstation 4.0

Networking Requirement

70-058: Networking Essentials

Windows NT Server 4.0 Requirement

70-067: Implementing and Supporting Windows NT Server 4.0

Windows NT Server 4.0 in the Enterprise Requirement

70-068: Implementing and Supporting Windows NT Server 4.0 in the Enterprise

Part iii

For the electives, you have about ten choices. The two most popular electives at present are:

70-059: Internetworking Microsoft TCP/IP on Microsoft Windows NT 4.0

70-081: Implementing and Supporting Microsoft Exchange Server 5.5

The Windows NT Workstation exam is the most popular of the client requirement exams. For those people that will specialize in NT 4, studying for this exam is the best way to get started. Studying for and passing this exam reduces the amount of studying required for the Implementing and Supporting Windows NT Server 4.0 exam, because it allows the candidate to concentrate on just the differences between NT Workstation and NT Server. For a Microsoft Certified Trainer to be "Certified to Instruct" the course Supporting Microsoft Windows NT 4.0 Core Technologies, he or she must pass both the Workstation exam (70-073) and the Server exam (70-067).

NOTE

For a more detailed description of the MCSE program, go to http://www.cyberstateu.com/text/mcp.

WHERE DO YOU TAKE THE EXAMS?

You may take the exams at any of more than 800 Authorized Prometric Testing Centers (APTCs) around the world. For the location of an APTC near you, call 800-755-EXAM (755-3926). Outside the United States and Canada, contact your local Sylvan Prometric Registration Center.

To register for a Microsoft Certified Professional exam:

1. Determine the number of the exam you want to take.

2. Register with the Sylvan Prometric Registration Center that is nearest to you. At this point, you will be asked for advance payment for the exam. Exams must be taken within one year of payment. You can schedule exams up to six weeks in advance or as late as one working day prior to the date of the exam. You can cancel or reschedule your exam if you contact Sylvan Prometric at least two working days prior to the exam.

Same-day registration is available in some locations, subject to space availability. Where same-day registration is available, you must register a minimum of two hours before test time.

You will receive a registration and payment confirmation letter from Sylvan Prometric.

3. Call a nearby Authorized Prometric Testing Center (APTC) to schedule your exam.

When you schedule the exam, you'll be provided with instructions regarding appointment and cancellation procedures, ID requirements, and information about the testing center location.

What the Windows NT Exams Measure

The Windows NT Workstation exam covers concepts and skills required for the support of NT Workstation computers. The Windows NT Server exam covers concepts and skills required for the support of NT Server computers. Both emphasize the following areas of support:

- ▶ Standards and terminology
- ▶ Planning
- ▶ Implementation
- ▶ Troubleshooting

This exam can be quite specific regarding NT requirements and operational settings, and it can be particularly detailed about how administrative tasks are performed in the operating system. It also focuses on fundamental concepts relating to NT's operation.

NOTE

Microsoft provides exam objectives to give you a very general overview of possible areas of coverage of the Microsoft exams. The actual Microsoft exams, however, tend to emphasize certain of these exam objectives, while ignoring others. Exam objectives are subject to change at any time without prior notice and at Microsoft's sole discretion. Please visit Microsoft's Training & Certification Web site (www.microsoft.com/Train_Cert) for the most current exam objectives listing.

Part iii

How Microsoft Develops the Exam Questions

Microsoft follows an exam development process consisting of eight mandatory phases. The process takes an average of seven months and contains more than 150 specific steps. The phases of MCP exam development are:

1. Job analysis
2. Objective domain definition
3. Blueprint survey
4. Item development
5. Alpha review and item revision
6. Beta exam
7. Item selection and cut-score setting
8. Exam live

Microsoft describes each phase as described in the following sections.

Phase 1: Job Analysis

Phase 1 is an analysis of all the tasks that make up the specific job function, based on tasks performed by people who are currently performing the job function. This phase also identifies the knowledge, skills, and abilities that relate specifically to the performance area to be certified.

Phase 2: Objective Domain Definition

The results of the job analysis provide the framework used to develop objectives. The development of objectives involves translating the job function tasks into a comprehensive set of more specific and measurable knowledge, skills, and abilities. The resulting list of objectives, or the objective domain, is the basis for the development of both the certification exams and the training materials.

Phase 3: Blueprint Survey

The final objective domain is transformed into a blueprint survey in which contributors—technology professionals who are performing the applicable job function—are asked to rate each objective. Contributors may be selected from lists of past Certified Professional candidates, from appropriately skilled exam development volunteers, and from within Microsoft. Based on the contributors' input, the objectives are prioritized and weighted. The actual exam items are written according to the prioritized objectives. Contributors are queried about how they spend their time on the job, and if a contributor doesn't spend an adequate amount of time actually performing the specified job function, his or her data is eliminated from the analysis.

The blueprint survey phase helps determine which objectives to measure, as well as the appropriate number and types of items to include on the exam.

Phase 4: Item Development

A pool of items is developed to measure the blueprinted objective domain. The number and types of items to be written are based on the results of the blueprint survey. During this phase, items are reviewed and revised to ensure that they are:

- ▶ Technically accurate

- ▶ Clear, unambiguous, and plausible

- ▶ Not biased for any population subgroup or culture

- ▶ Not misleading or tricky

- ▶ Testing at the correct level of Bloom's Taxonomy

- ▶ Testing for useful knowledge, not obscure or trivial facts

Items that meet these criteria are included in the initial item pool.

Phase 5: Alpha Review and Item Revision

During this phase, a panel of technical and job function experts review each item for technical accuracy, then answers to each item, reaching a consensus on all technical issues. Once the items have been verified as technically accurate, they are edited to ensure that they are expressed in the clearest language possible.

Phase 6: Beta Exam

The reviewed and edited items are collected into a beta exam pool. During the beta exam, each participant has the opportunity to respond to all the items in this beta exam pool. Based on the responses of all beta participants, Microsoft performs a statistical analysis to verify the validity of the exam items and to determine which items will be used in the certification exam. Once the analysis has been completed, the items are distributed into multiple parallel forms, or versions, of the final certification exam.

Phase 7: Item Selection and Cut-Score Setting

The results of the beta exam are analyzed to determine which items should be included in the certification exam based on many factors, including item difficulty and relevance. Generally, the desired items are those that were answered correctly by anywhere from 25 percent to 90 percent of the beta exam candidates. This helps ensure that the exam consists of a variety of difficulty levels, from somewhat easy to extremely difficult.

Also during this phase, a panel of job function experts determines the cut score (minimum passing score) for the exam. The cut score differs from exam to exam because it is based on an item-by-item determination of the percentage of candidates who answered the item correctly and who would be expected to answer the item correctly. The cut score is determined in a group session to increase the reliability among the experts.

Phase 8: Exam Live

MCP exams are administered by Sylvan Prometric.

TIPS FOR TAKING THE NT EXAMS

Here are some general tips for taking the exams successfully:

- ► Arrive early at the exam center so you can relax and take one last review of your study materials, particularly tables and lists of exam-related information.

▶ Read the questions carefully. Don't be tempted to jump to an early conclusion. Make sure you know *exactly* what the question is asking.

▶ Don't leave any unanswered questions. They count against you.

▶ Many examinees find that it is helpful to mark and then skip all multiple-choice scenario questions until all other questions have been answered. Then you can gauge how much time is remaining and the number of scenario questions to be answered.

▶ Use a process of elimination to get rid of the obviously incorrect answers first on multiple-choice questions that you're not sure about. This method will improve your odds of selecting the correct answer if you need to make an educated guess.

▶ Save the hard questions for last because they will eat up the most time. You can move forward and back through the exam.

NOTE

The new exams are adaptive. If you get a question wrong, the test can add additional questions focusing on that particular area. Adaptive exams are usually about 25 questions long but can increase to 35, due to their adaptive quality.

WHAT'S NEXT?

Using the *MSCE: NT Workstation Study Guide* and *MSCE: NT Server Study Guide*, you can prepare yourself for the Windows NT Workstation and Windows NT Server exams, moving toward the goal of MSCE certification. Both of those books include many sample questions to test your knowledge as you complete each section. The next chapter presents 40 sample questions from *MSCE: NT Workstation Study Guide*.

Part iii

Chapter 27

SAMPLE STUDY QUESTIONS: WINDOWS NT WORKSTATION EXAM

The following are sample study questions to help prepare you for the Windows NT 4 Workstation Exam. Answers to these questions can be found in the appendix.

Adapted from *MCSE: NT® Workstation 4 Study Guide, Second Edition* by Charles Perkins and Matthew Strebe with James Chellis

ISBN 0-7821-2223-X   752 pages $49.99

The following are sample study questions to help prepare you for the Windows NT 4 Workstation Exam. Answers to these questions can be found in the appendix.

1. Multiprocessing is

   A. running more than one process at a time on one microprocessor.

   B. having multiple processors on the network.

   C. using more than one microprocessor in the same computer.

   D. running more than one process at a time on one microcomputer.

2. Windows NT divides memory into _____.

   A. user and protected

   B. conventional and expanded

   C. conventional and extended

   D. Windows NT does not segment memory

3. What is the Sysdiff utility used for?

   A. It creates a mirror image of a hard drive onto another hard drive across the network.

   B. It creates difference files used to automate the installation of third-party applications onto NT Workstation.

   C. It creates users and groups, plus it established the low-level security for resource access.

   D. It is used to convert Windows NT 3.51 and Windows 95 Program Groups to Start Menu shortcuts.

4. You currently have a computer with only a single hard drive that is already configured with a single partition. You want to install Windows 95 and Windows NT Workstation in a dual-boot configuration. You do not share this computer with anyone else, thus security is not important. Plus, you want to be able to access your data files from either operating system. Which of the following is your best option?

A. Back up any files currently on the computer. Reconfigure the drive with two partitions. Install Windows 95 onto one partition and restore your backed-up files to that partition. Format the other partition with NTFS and install NT Workstation on it.

B. Format the partition as FAT and install Windows 95. Then install NT Workstation into a different directory on the same partition.

C. Install Windows 95. Upgrade the Windows 95 installation to NT Workstation by installing into the same directory. Leave the partition formatted as FAT.

D. It is not possible to have both Windows 95 and NT Workstation on the same computer.

5. You are the administrator for a client-server network comprised of 28 Windows NT Workstation computers and three Windows NT Servers (one is the PDC). Some of your users use different clients each day. The users claim that when they change their password on one of the client machines, it is not automatically changed on any of the other computers. You have roaming profiles enabled. What is the problem and how can you resolve it?

A. The client machines are set to join a workgroup instead of a domain. Properly configure all of the computers to participate in the domain.

B. The previous passwords assigned to the user accounts have not expired. Deselect the Password Never Expires checkbox for these user accounts.

C. The user accounts are only local user accounts on the individual workstations. Create domain user accounts for everyone.

D. The User Cannot Change Password field has been checked for these users. Deselect this item on these accounts.

6. Your organization's security policy requires that notification be given at the time of logon to all potential intruders that unauthorized attempted access will be prosecuted to the full

extent of the law. You must edit the LegalNoticeCaption and LegalNoticeText Registry keys to create such a message. What tools can you use to perform this task? Choose all that apply.

A. Performance Monitor

B. REGEDIT.EXE

C. Server Manager

D. REGEDT32.EXE

7. After installing a new hard drive in your Windows NT Workstation computer, you create a single FAT-formatted partition on it. Who has access to this drive and what permission level do they have by default?

A. Read for Everyone, Full Control for Administrators and the owner/creator

B. No Access for Everyone, Change for PowerUsers

C. FAT does not support any security restrictions, thus it has the equivalent of Full Control for Everyone

D. Full Control to Administrators, Change for PowerUsers, Read for Guests

8. When using the NT Backup utility that accompanies Windows NT Workstation, you can make backups of files stored on partitions formatted with which file system types?

A. FAT

B. NTFS

C. HPFS

D. CDFS

9. NWLink is the protocol most commonly used by Windows NT Workstation clients to connect to or communicate with what types of servers or computer systems?

A. MacOS

B. NetWare

    C. Linux

    D. UNIX

10. If your DNS Server address in your TCP/IP settings for your Windows NT Workstation client is defined incorrectly (in other words, you typed in the wrong IP address), then which of the following activities will be affected?

    A. Accessing NT-hosted directory shares and network printers

    B. Use of domain names for Internet-hosted Web resources

    C. Accessing an FTP server via IP address

    D. Saving files in your home directory

11. Your network hosts a NetWare server in addition to the three NT Servers. You install CSNW on your Windows NT Workstation so you can gain access to the NetWare hosted resources. However, when you try to access those resources, your client is unable to locate the server. What is most likely the cause of this problem?

    A. NetWare and NT are incompatible.

    B. The NWLink frame type used by the NetWare server and NT are different.

    C. The client is using a different subnet mask from the NetWare server.

    D. A trust relationship has not been created between NetWare and NT.

12. You attempt to move a client from the SALES workgroup to the MARKETING domain. You log in to the Windows NT Workstation client. You open the Network applet and select the Identification tab. You select the Domain radio button and type in MARKETING in the blank field. After rebooting, you discover that the client cannot communicate with the domain. Why?

    A. You must reinstall NT Workstation to change from a workgroup to a domain.

    B. A computer account was not established in the domain for the NT client.

Part iii

C. The browse list on the NT Workstation client has not been updated with the new resource list from the domain.

D. You did not select Domain from the Network Type menu in Server Manager.

13. The New Phonebook Entry Wizard is used to create what?

A. An entry containing contact information for your closest friends

B. A new dial-up connection definition for an outbound RAS session

C. Dialing property settings, such as area code, credit card, and call waiting, for a modem

D. A new user account to be used exclusively for RAS

14. You have been contracted by a publishing firm to author a multi-page article on the hobbies of dead presidents. You are required to submit the completed article on a floppy. However, they stipulated that the file should be a capture of printer output instead of a standard word processing document file. Since you are using Windows NT Workstation, you know you can accomplish this without any difficulty. Which tab of the printer's Properties dialog box is used to redirect a print job to a file?

A. General

B. Ports

C. Sharing

D. Device Settings

15. You have several utilities on your Windows NT Workstation computer that analyze data and perform complex calculations. The data from these utilities is saved in a text file. While the results of the utilities are important, they can take hours to complete. You notice that if you attempt to perform other normal activities such as check e-mail, type a document, and download files while these utilities are executing, the system is very slow. You need to be around while the calculations are performed, just in case the utilities encounter errors or require user interaction, but you also need to perform other work. You really can't afford to sit around and wait, so what can you do to improve your situation?

A. Increase the foreground priority boost on the Performance tab of the System applet.

B. Launch the utilities in a separate memory space.

C. Launch the utilities at a lower execution priority: start /low <application>.

D. Decrease the size of the paging file.

16. What methods can you use to launch Win16 applications so that if one fails the others are not affected?

A. From Start ➤ Run, check the Run in Separate Memory Space option.

B. Right-click the application's main icon (in Explorer, My Computer, or on the Desktop) and select Launch in Separate Memory Space from the pop-up menu.

C. Edit a shortcut to the application, check the Run in Separate Memory Space box on the General tab.

D. From a command prompt: start/separate <application>.

17. You currently have Windows 95 installed on your computer. You install a second hard drive and install Windows NT Workstation in a dual-boot configuration. When your computer is first booted, the boot menu displays MS-DOS instead of Windows 95 as the selection to access Windows 95. What can you do to correct this?

A. Use the System applet's Startup/Shutdown tab to edit the names listed in the boot menu.

B. Reinstall Windows 95.

C. Edit the BOOT.INI file, under the [operating systems] section so the line reads "Windows 95" instead of "MS-DOS".

D. Use REGEDT32 to search for the string "BootMenuList" and edit the Value# item corresponding to "MS-DOS".

18. Your Windows NT Workstation has a multimedia sound card installed. You download new drivers and install them through the Multimedia applet. To complete the installation, you need to reboot your computer. However, after the OS Loader displays the blue screen that lists the OS name and version, nothing else happens. What is the simplest method to restore the system so it will boot normally?

A. When prompted, press the spacebar to access the Last Known Good configuration.

B. Reinstall NT Workstation.

C. Boot to DOS, execute the SETUPMGR.EXE program and remove the new multimedia driver.

D. Create three new installation floppies using the WINNT /OX command, use these with the ERD to perform a repair of the boot areas.

19. You currently have Windows 95 installed on your computer. You install a second hard drive and install Windows NT Workstation in a dual-boot configuration. Currently, Windows NT Workstation is the default OS and it takes 30 seconds for the boot menu to use the default selection. How can you change this?

A. On the Startup/Shutdown tab of the System applet

B. By using REGEDT32 to search and edit BootMenuList and BootMenuTimer

C. By editing the BOOT.INI file

D. By changing the PIF for WIN.COM

20. Your Windows NT Workstation–based computer has two hard drives. One is an IDE drive formatted with FAT, the other a SCSI drive formatted with NTFS. NT Workstation is hosted on the SCSI drive. You replace your old no-frills non-BIOS SCSI controller with a new fast-wide, BIOS-enabled

SCSI controller. When you attempt to boot your machine, you see the following error:

```
Windows NT could not start because the following file
    is missing or corrupt:
\<winnt root>\system32\ntoskrnl.exe
```

You try to boot again, but this time select to boot to DOS, which does succeed. What is the problem and how can you correct it?

A. The ARC name listed in the BOOT.INI file points to the wrong partition. Edit the BOOT.INI file to change partition(1) to partition(0).

B. The ARC name listed in the BOOT.INI file for the NT Workstation boot partition is using a 'scsi' prefix instead of a 'multi' prefix. Edit the BOOT.INI file to use 'multi.'

C. You accidentally attached the IDE hard drive to the SCSI controller and the SCSI drive to the IDE controller. Switch the drive connectors back to the correct controllers.

D. NTDETECT is missing or corrupted.

21. Windows NT is not available for which of the following computers:

A. Intel 386 class machines

B. Digital Alpha–based computers

C. MIPS-based computers

D. PowerPC-based computers

E. VAX minicomputers

22. All of the following operating systems can be used in a peer-to-peer network (in other words, a network without a dedicated server), except for which one?

A. Windows NT Server

B. Windows NT Workstation

C. Windows 95

D. MS-DOS

23. Which process implements the security user interface when the computer is booted?

A. Account policy dialog box

B. WinLogon

C. Access token

D. Boot interface

24. You have attempted to remove NT Workstation from your computer, but each time you boot, the boot menu still appears. What step must you take to remove this?

A. Before removing NT Workstation, you need to set the Display Menu time to 0 (zero) on the Boot Options tab of the System applet and select Windows 95 as the default boot option.

B. Use the three NT Workstation setup floppies and select D from the menu to remove the boot loader.

C. Back up your system, reformat the hard disk, and then reinstall your operating system and restore your files.

D. At a command prompt from DOS or Windows 95, execute SYS C:.

25. At the end of each financial year, your organization spends the remainder of your equipment budget on purchasing large quantities of identically configured computers. You need to install NT Workstation on 100 identical Pentium computers, 80 identical 486DX100 computers, and 35 identical notebook computers. Instead of performing each install one at a time manually, how can you automate or simplify the installation procedure?

A. Create an unattended answer file for each computer type and a single uniqueness database file. Use these files as parameters of the Winnt setup utility launched from a network share.

B. Move the NT Workstation CD-ROM from one machine to the next as you complete each install.

C. Create one unattended answer file and a uniqueness database file for each computer type. Use these files as parameters of the Winnt setup utility launched from a network share.

D. NT Workstation cannot be installed onto notebook computers.

E. Create a single unattended answer file and a single uniqueness database file. Use these files as parameters of the Winnt setup utility launched from a network share.

26. To improve security, your organization has a security policy that states users can select their own passwords and should not share them with anyone, including the administrators. What setting on a user account will force users to change the temporary password an administrator provides when initially creating the account?

A. Check User Must Change Password at Next Logon in the New User window.

B. Check Account Disabled in the New User window.

C. Set Maximum Password Age to zero in the Account Policy window.

D. Check Users Must Log On in Order to Change Password in the Account Policy window.

27. On a Windows NT Workstation computer, what is the process for creating new user accounts?

A. Use the NET USER command line utility with the following parameters: NET USER /NEW /N:<username> /P:<password>.

B. Launch User Manager, Select User ≻ New User from the menu bar. Provide the requested information, then click OK.

C. Use the Users tab of the Environment applet.

D. Enter a new username and password at the logon prompt, NT Workstation will automatically create a new account for the unknown N/P pair.

28. You want to store all user profiles on a single computer within your network. However, your network is just a workgroup of 10 Windows NT Workstations. What can you do to store all profiles on just one of these machines?

   A. Change the home directory path for each user to the UNC path to the destination directory on the specified Windows NT Workstation computer.

   B. Change the User Profile path for each user to the UNC path to the destination directory on the specified Windows NT Workstation computer.

   C. Profiles cannot be redirected within a workgroup; this can be performed only on a client-server network.

   D. Enable roaming profiles for all accounts on the PDC.

29. A system administrator, named Elvis, left your organization. This user account was deleted by another SysAdmin. The president of your organization was able to convince Elvis to return and assume his previous responsibilities. Elvis' user account is re-created by the SysAdmin that deleted it. When Elvis tries to access certain files and resources that he had access to previously, he is unable to access them. Why?

   A. Elvis' new account has a new SID, thus he is not the same user as he was previously.

   B. The new account is not using a roaming profile.

   C. Obviously, if Elvis cannot access a file or a resource, it was deleted when his account was deleted.

   D. Elvis has forgotten his password.

30. What user accounts are created by default when Windows NT Workstation is installed? Choose all that apply.

   A. Administrator

   B. Supervisor

   C. Guest

   D. Superuser

   E. Everyone

31. After installing a new high-performance video card in your Windows NT Workstation computer, the machine boots but the screen remains blank. What can you do to enable NT Workstation to properly use this new video card?

A. Use the VGA Mode selection from the boot menu, and then install the correct driver through the Display applet.

B. Boot into Safe Mode using the F8 Startup menu, and then install the correct driver through the Video applet.

C. Boot using the Last Known Good configuration option (accessed by pressing the spacebar when prompted during bootup), and then install the correct driver through the Display applet.

D. Use the VGA Mode selection from the boot menu, and then install the correct driver through the Video applet.

32. You purchased a UPS to provide power protection for your Windows NT Workstation computer. What Control Panel applet is used to configure NT to communicate properly with the UPS?

A. UPS

B. System

C. Devices

D. Power

33. Windows NT Workstation system services can be started, paused, and stopped through which Control Panel applet?

A. System

B. Network

C. Devices

D. Services

34. You have deployed a Windows NT Workstation machine to be used as the central repository for your company's financial data. To provide the most reliable storage possible on this computer, you want to implement a fault-tolerant drive configuration. How can you accomplish this?

A. Install three hard drives and use disk striping with parity.

B. Windows NT Workstation does not support fault-tolerant drive configurations.

C. Create a disk duplex with two drives, each on a separate drive controller.

D. Use partitions on four or more drives to create an expandable volume.

35. You performed a system-wide complete backup yesterday. Today, you have made changes to several new files, copied files from other machines to your local drive, and downloaded many new archives from a Web site. If you only want to back up the files that have changed or are new on your system since yesterday's backup, what type of a backup operation should you perform?

A. Normal

B. Copy

C. Incremental

D. Differential

36. After installing a new hard drive in your Windows NT Workstation computer, you create a single NTFS formatted partition on it. Who has access to this drive and what permission level do they have by default?

A. The owner/creator has Read.

B. The Everyone group has Full Control.

C. The Administrators group has Full Control.

D. The PowerUsers group has Change.

37. You have been hired to improve the operation of an existing network. The primary activity on the network is users accessing an NT Workstation–hosted database over NWLink. Unfortunately, three protocols are in use: TCP/IP (primary), NWLink, and NetBEUI. The NT Workstation hosting the database has a single 4GB SCSI drive that is almost full and whose performance is degrading fast.

Required result: Improve network access to the database.

Optional results: Improve the performance of the NT Workstation machine.

Solve the low storage space problem.

Implement fault protection for the database.

Solution: Bind NWLink as the primary protocol on the NT Workstation machine. Install an 8GB SCSI drive. Move the database to the new drive.

Which of the following is true?

A. The solution gives you the required result and all optional results.

B. The solution gives you the required result and two optional result.

C. The solution gives you the required result only.

D. The solution does not give you the required result.

38. PPTP or Point-to-Point Tunneling Protocol can be used by Windows NT Workstation to establish what?

A. A communication link via a hollow pipe

B. A remote-control connection with a server on another network

C. A secure network connection over the Internet

D. A community link where multiple users can interact directly over telephone lines

39. The design department of your organization creates complex graphical architectural drawings. These drawings often take 15 minutes or more to print, even on your high-speed laser printer. You want to allow members of the DESIGN group to print, but don't want their print jobs to supercede the smaller print jobs of the rest of the company. Which of the following describes the proper steps you can take to establish such a system?

A. Create two logical printers for the same printer—DESIGN-PRNT and ALLPRNT. Set DESIGNPRNT so it prints only after the entire print job is spooled and grant the DESIGN group Print access to this printer. Set ALLPRNT with a priority of 2 (one more than DESIGNPRINT) and set the DESIGN group permission to No Access.

B. Grant the DESIGN group Print access to the existing printer. Grant the Everyone group Full Control.

C. Create two logical printers for the same printer—DESIGN-PRNT and ALLPRNT. Set ALLPRNT so it prints only after the entire print job is spooled and set the DESIGN group permission to No Access. Set DESIGNPRNT with a priority of 2 (one more than ALLPRNT) and grant the DESIGN group Print access to this printer.

D. Create two logical printers for the same printer—DESIGN-PRNT and ALLPRNT. Set DESIGNPRNT so it prints directly to the printer, and grant the DESIGN group Print access to this printer. Set ALLPRNT with a priority of 2 (one more than DESIGNPRINT), and set the DESIGN group permission to No Access.

40. After returning from vacation, you boot your Windows NT Workstation computer. You allow the default boot menu item of NT Workstation to be activated. However, the following error message appears and continues to repeat:

```
I/O Error accessing boot sector file
multi(0)disk(0)rdisk(0)partition(1):\bootsect.dos
```

What could cause this error to appear?

A. The BOOT.INI file points to the wrong partition.

B. NTDETECT.COM is missing or corrupted.

C. NTLDR is missing or corrupted.

D. BOOTSECT.DOS is missing or corrupted.

WHAT'S NEXT?

The questions presented in this chapter give you an idea of what you'll find on the Windows NT Workstation exam. Check the appendix to see how you did. Continue on to the next chapter for sample questions from *MSCE: NT Server Study Guide* to get an idea of what you need to know to pass the Windows NT Server exam.

Part iii

Chapter 28

SAMPLE STUDY QUESTIONS: WINDOWS NT SERVER EXAM

T his chapter contains sample study questions to help prepare you for the Windows NT 4 Server exam. Answers to these questions can be found in the appendix.

Adapted from *MCSE: NT® Server 4 Study Guide* by
Matthew Strebe and Charles Perkins with James Chellis

ISBN 0-7821-2222-1   832 pages $49.99

1. You have a Pentium 100 computer with 8MB of memory and a 1.2GB hard drive that you would like to turn into the server for your small network.

    Required Result: The operating system you install must provide file system security for data stored on the server's hard drive.

    Optional Result 1: You want your server to be able to provide print services.

    Optional Result 2: You want your server to be able to provide file services.

    Suggested Solution: Install Windows NT Server, implement NTFS and RAID on the hard disk drives, and create domain user accounts for network users. Share the printers attached to the server computer.

    Which of the following is correct?

    A. The suggested solution provides the required result and both of the optional results.

    B. The suggested solution provides the required result and only one of the optional results.

    C. The suggested solution provides only the required result.

    D. The suggested solution does not provide the required result.

2. You are considering the purchase of a new computer for a server. You need to determine whether or not the hardware is compatible with Windows NT. The salesperson shows you Windows 95 running on the computer, but he doesn't have Windows NT. Which tools will help you determine whether or not this computer is capable of running Windows NT?

    A. If it runs Windows 95, it will run Windows NT.

    B. Run the HAL utility and check the HCL.

    C. Run the NTHQ utility and check the HCL.

    D. Run the HCL and check the HAL.

3. You have been tasked with establishing a multiple-domain Windows NT-based network for a company with a central office and five outlying branch offices. The branch offices are linked to the central office via leased lines. You must structure the network for centralized administration of user accounts and distributed administration of network resources.

   Required Result: User accounts must be established and managed from one central location.

   Optional Result 1: Resources must be controlled from the domains in which they reside.

   Optional Result 2: Users must still be able to log on to the network even when the network link to the main office is down.

   Proposed Solution: Create one domain for the central office and a separate domain for each of the branch offices. Configure each branch office domain to trust the central office domain. Create all user accounts on the central office domain. Configure the resources (file storage, printers, etc.) in the domains in which they reside.

   Which of the following is correct?

   A. The proposed solution satisfies the required result and both optional results.

   B. The proposed solution satisfies the required result and one optional result.

   C. The proposed solution satisfies the required result only.

   D. The proposed solution does not satisfy the required result.

4. You have been asked to install computers and network software for an architectural firm with nine employees. They want a computer dedicated to storing files so that they have one place to back files up, but they are not interested in security (each user will have full control of their own computer). Which security role should the Windows NT Server computer play in this network?

   A. Primary Domain Controller

   B. Backup Domain Controller

   C. Member Server

   D. Stand Alone Server

5. Your company uses Microsoft SQL Server on a 180MHz Pentium Windows NT Server computer with 96MB of RAM. This server also runs several network software packages that are only available for the Intel platform. As your network has grown and new database clients have begun querying the central database, database performance has deteriorated. You have received funds to replace the SQL Server computer.

Required Result: The new server must provide more than twice the computing power of the existing server in order to speed up the Microsoft SQL Server software.

Optional Result 1: The server should support multiple processors to take advantage of Windows NT's multiprocessor architecture.

Optional Result 2: The server should support server-based applications compiled for the Intel microprocessor.

Proposed Solution: Purchase a four processor 600MHz Digital Alpha workstation with Windows NT and the FX!32 software installed. Install SQL Server for the Alpha architecture.

Which of the following is correct?

   A. The proposed solution satisfies the required result and both optional results.

   B. The proposed solution satisfies the required result and one optional result.

   C. The proposed solution satisfies the required result only.

   D. The proposed solution does not satisfy the required result.

6. You must install the Windows NT operating system on 35 identically configured 266 MHz Pentium-II computers connected to your LAN. It is important that the software be installed quickly and without a lot of user intervention at the target computers during the install process.

Required Result: Centralize the installation files so that the distribution media does not have to be physically present at each of the target computers and so that multiple installations can occur simultaneously.

Optional Result 1: Automate the installation process so that hardware-specific installation choices (video card settings, etc.) are not required at the target computers.

Optional Result 2: Automate the installation process so that installation-specific choices (computer name, etc.) are not required at the target computers.

Proposed Solution: Copy the Windows NT operating system installation files (the I386 directory) to a share on a file server. Create an unattended answer file for the computers. Create a boot disk for the target computers that maps a drive to the I386 server share and starts the Winnt program with the /u: option specifying the unattended answer file.

Which of the following is correct?

A. The proposed solution satisfies the required result and both optional results.

B. The proposed solution satisfies the required result and one optional result.

C. The proposed solution satisfies the required result only.

D. The proposed solution does not satisfy the required result.

7. You have purchased a 266MHz dual Pentium-II computer for use as the file server on your network. You installed four 9GB hard drives for the operating system and user file storage. It is important that user data not be lost in the event that a hard drive fails. The server should also provide file and directory security and respond as quickly as possible to file requests from network clients. You must configure the server computer appropriately.

Required Result: A single hard drive failure should not result in the loss of user data.

Optional Result 1: Disk access speed should be optimized.

Optional Result 2: The system administrator should be able to grant or revoke access to data on a file-by-file basis.

Suggested Solution: Divide each drive into a 512MB partition and a 8.5GB partition. Create a stripe set (RAID level 0) with the 8.5GB partitions and format it with NTFS. Store user data on this volume. Create a mirror set with two of the 512MB partitions, format it with Windows NT, and install the operating system to the resulting 1GB volume.

Which of the following is correct?

A. The proposed solution satisfies the required result and both optional results.

B. The proposed solution satisfies the required result and one optional result.

C. The proposed solution satisfies the required result only.

D. The proposed solution does not satisfy the required result.

8. You are installing a Windows NT Server computer in an IPX–based NetWare network. What transport protocol should you select for maximum interoperability between the NT and NetWare servers?

A. TCP/IP

B. AppleTalk

C. NWLink

D. NetBEUI

9. What tool do you use to add a network adapter driver to your Windows NT Server computer?

A. The Server Control Panel

B. The Services Control Panel

C. The Network Control Panel

D. A screwdriver

10. You have been tasked with establishing a multiple-domain Windows NT–based network for a company with a central office and five outlying branch offices. The branch offices are linked to the central office via leased lines. You must structure the network for centralized administration of user accounts and distributed administration of network resources.

Required Result: User accounts must be established and managed from one central location.

Optional Result 1: Resources must be controlled from the domains in which they reside.

Optional Result 2: Users must still be able to log on to the network even when the network link to the main office is down.

Suggested Solution: Create one domain for the central office and a separate domain for each of the branch offices. Configure each branch office domain to trust the central office domain. Create all user accounts at each branch office domain. Configure the resources (file storage, printers, etc.) in the domains in which they reside.

Which of the following is correct?

A. The suggested solution satisfies the required result and both of the optional results.

B. The suggested solution satisfies the required result and just one of the optional results.

C. The suggested solution satisfies the required result only.

D. The suggested solution does not satisfy the required result.

11. Rather than using cryptic usernames like hjtillman on your network you would like to create more readable usernames like Tillman, Henry J. Why won't User Manager for Domains let you create a user account name like this?

A. Spaces are not allowed in usernames.

B. That kind of name is too inconvenient to type every time you log on.

C. Usernames must be eight characters or less.

D. Usernames may not contain a comma.

12. What tool should you use to configure directory replication?

A. Server Manager

B. Event Viewer

C. User Manager for Domains

D. DHCP Manager

13. You are configuring RAS for your network. You have employees that work at home and that use Windows NT, Windows 95, Unix, and Macintosh computers. You would like to protect your network from intrusion and you want to provide the most bandwidth you can to dial-in users.

Required Result: All remote clients must be able to dial in to your network.

Optional Result 1: The dial-in connection should be secure.

Optional Result 2: The connecting user should be able to combine several dial-up lines.

Suggested Solution: Configure RAS to Require Microsoft Encrypted Authentication. Also select Require Data Encryption. Use the RAS callback feature. Allow dial-in clients to use the Multilink feature.

Which of the following is correct?

A. The suggested solution satisfies the required result and both of the optional results.

B. The suggested solution satisfies the required result and just one of the optional results.

C. The suggested solution satisfies the required result only.

D. The suggested solution does not satisfy the required result.

14. Internet Information Server provides which of the following Internet services? Select all that apply.

A. FTP

B. WAIS

C. HTTP

D. Gopher

15. You have configured your Windows NT Server computer to share a NetWare print queue as an NT printer. A user with sufficient privileges to administer printing on the Windows NT domain tried to stop printing to the printer but documents from NetWare clients continued to print. What is the problem?

A. You have the wrong printer driver installed on the Windows NT Server computer.

B. You have the wrong printer driver installed on the user's client computer.

C. The user's client software only has the ability to manage the software print share on the NT Server, not the actual NetWare print queue.

D. NetWare print queues cannot be stopped.

16. How do you limit the hours of operation of a specific printer?

A. Enter the hours of operation from the Hours button of the user's entry in the User Manager for Domains program.

B. Enter the hours of operation in the Hours tab of the Printer entry in the Services Control Panel.

C. Start and stop the printer service at regular intervals using the AT command.

D. Enter the hours of operation in the Scheduling tab of the Properties window of the printer.

Part iii

17. What service would you install on your Windows NT Server computer to automatically configure the IP addresses of Microsoft networking clients on a TCP/IP network?

    A. SNMP

    B. DHCP

    C. DNS

    D. WINS

18. You have a single Windows NT Server computer on your 10BaseT Ethernet network as both a file and print server as well as an application server. You have doubled the number of client computers on your network in the last year and server performance has diminished. Using Performance Monitor, you determine that the file server is disk bound for file requests and memory bound for client access to the server-based application. Your top priority is to speed up access to files, but you would also like to speed up access to the server application.

    Required Result: Significantly improve file access from network clients.

    Optional Result: Significantly improve server-based application performance.

    Suggested Solution: Install additional hard disk drives and create a RAID level 0 stripe set. Place files accessed by network clients on the RAID volume. Upgrade the network from 10Mbps Ethernet to 100Mbps Ethernet.

    Which of the following is correct?

    A. The suggested solution satisfies the required result and the optional result.

    B. The suggested solution satisfies the required result only.

    C. The suggested solution does not satisfy the required result.

19. You are evaluating a computer for use as a Windows NT Server on your network. You have just upgraded the memory, added a new hard drive, and installed a faster micro-processor. You want to make sure that these components work together. You would also like to be sure that the computer's other components (networking adapter, sound card, video adapter, etc.) are installed properly, without conflicts, and are compatible with Windows NT.

Required Result: Verify that the memory, microprocessor, and hard drive work.

Optional Result 1: Verify that the computer's components are installed correctly and without conflicts.

Optional Result 2: Verify that the components work with Windows NT.

Suggested Solution: Install DOS on the computer's hard drive and boot DOS.

Which of the following is correct?

A. The suggested solution satisfies the required result and both of the optional results.

B. The suggested solution satisfies the required result and just one of the optional results.

C. The suggested solution satisfies the required result only.

D. The suggested solution does not satisfy the required result.

20. Your Windows NT Server has reported several errors on startup. How do you view additional information about the errors?

A. Review the /etc/sys.log file in a text editor.

B. Click the System Events tab in Performance Monitor.

C. Select System from the Log menu of the Event Viewer.

D. Select Security from the Log menu of the Event Viewer.

Part iii

21. Your boss tells you that he wants to convert the company's Sun Microsystems Sparc Ultra RISC-based server into a Windows NT Server. The machine has 10GB of disk space, 256MB RAM, and runs at 300MHz. This machine:

A. Won't work because the Sparc Ultra is not on the Hardware Compatibility List

B. Will work because it has adequate disk space, RAM, and processor speed

C. Won't work because Windows NT doesn't support the Sparc microprocessor

D. Will work because Sun is closely allied with Microsoft

22. Which of the following network client operating systems will Windows NT Server support? Choose all that apply.

A. MS-DOS

B. Windows 95

C. Macintosh

D. Windows NT Workstation

23. You are moving from a Windows 95–based workgroup to a Windows NT–based domain. You are upgrading a Windows 95 computer to Windows NT. Which of the following can you still use from Windows NT Server? Choose all that apply.

A. 32-bit Windows (Win32) application software

B. Simple DOS programs that do not communicate directly with the computer hardware

C. Windows 95 device drivers

D. OS/2 version 1.3 programs

24. You are designing a network for a company that is concerned about the security and reliability of their network. The company will use a SQL database to track parts, production, and sales contacts. The budget will support two server computers and 37 client computers (as well as miscellaneous printers and network devices).

Required Result: The network must provide centrally managed security, centrally stored user files, and SQL Server database support.

Optional Result 1: Users should still be authenticated by the network even if the Primary Domain Controller goes down.

Optional Result 2: Users should still have access to their files even if the Primary Domain Controller goes down.

Proposed Solution: Install one Windows NT Server computer as a Primary Domain Controller for the domain and store all user files to this server computer. Install another Windows NT Server as a Backup Domain Controller and then install SQL Server on that computer.

Which of the following is correct?

A. The proposed solution satisfies the required result and both optional results.

B. The proposed solution satisfies the required result and one optional result.

C. The proposed solution satisfies the required result only.

D. The proposed solution does not satisfy the required result.

25. Your medium-sized network has grown. You now have 2 Windows NT Server computers and 75 Windows 95 client computers. You have purchased another computer to store network data and to host server-based software. You do not want this computer to authenticate logon requests or maintain a copy of the domain security database. Which security role should the Windows NT Server computer play in this network?

A. Primary Domain Controller

B. Backup Domain Controller

C. Member Server

D. Stand Alone Server

26. You have a Member Server computer that you would like to promote to a Backup Domain Controller for your network. What must you do to enact this role change for this server?

A. Use the Server Manager program to promote the server from Member Server to Backup Domain Controller.

B. Use the Server Manager program to demote the Backup Domain Controller to Member Server. The Member Server computer will be promoted in the absence of a Backup Domain Controller.

C. Use the Service tab of the Network Control Panel to enable the Backup Domain Controller option.

D. Reinstall the operating system software.

27. Your file server uses a dual-Pentium motherboard but has only one Pentium microprocessor installed. As the network has grown, file server responsiveness to file requests has become sluggish. You must improve file request responsiveness. Also, file server applications could use more compute power, and a more responsive user interface on the file server would be appreciated.

Required Result: The server must be twice as quick in responding to network client's file access requests.

Optional Result 1: The server should be more responsive to a user at the file server console.

Optional Result 2: The server should provide more computing power to server-based applications.

Proposed Solution: Install a second 200MHz processor in the server computer.

Which of the following is correct?

A. The proposed solution satisfies the required result and both optional results.

B. The proposed solution satisfies the required result and one optional result.

C. The proposed solution satisfies the required result only.

D. The proposed solution does not satisfy the required result.

28. Which hardware component has the least impact on file server performance as observed from a network client?

A. Microprocessor

B. Hard drive

C. Video adapter

D. Networking adapter

29. You have a Windows NT Server 3.51 computer that you want to upgrade to Windows NT Server 4. You would like to keep the current configuration settings (networking protocols, computer name, etc.), and you do not intend to dual-boot between versions of the operating system. You would like version 4 of the operating system to replace version 3.51. How should you install version 4?

A. Install Windows NT Server to the same directory and select Upgrade.

B. Install Windows NT Server to a different directory in the same volume.

C. Install Windows NT Server to the same directory and select Replace.

D. Install Windows NT Server to a different volume.

30. You have created a uniqueness database file (UDF) containing unique information for each of the Windows NT computers you will install operating system software for on your network. What Winnt command line switch instructs the Winnt program to use the UDF file?

A. /O:

B. /U:

C. /UDF:

D. /OX

31. The file server on your network is the repository for large graphic files generated by computer animation software. It is important that the file server respond as quickly as possible to client file requests; fault tolerance for the data is less important (the images can always be recomputed). Fault tolerance is important for the operating system files, however, and users should not be able to access other user's files without the other user's permission. You are configuring a new computer to be the file server, and you have installed four 9GB hard drives to store operating system and user data. How should you configure this file storage?

    Required Result: Disk access for user data must be as fast as possible.

    Optional Result 1: Failure of a single hard drive should not cause the loss of operating system files or data.

    Optional Result 2: Users should be able to set permissions on files and directories that they own.

    Suggested Solution: Divide each drive into a 512MB partition and a 8.5GB partition. Create a stripe set (RAID level 0) with the 8.5GB partitions and format it with NTFS. Store user data on this volume. Create a mirror set with two of the 512MB partitions, format it with Windows NT, and install the operating system to the resulting 1GB volume.

    Which of the following is correct?

    A. The proposed solution satisfies the required result and both optional results.

    B. The proposed solution satisfies the required result and one optional result.

    C. The proposed solution satisfies the required result only.

    D. The proposed solution does not satisfy the required result.

32. You are planning the disk configuration for your Windows NT Server computer. Which of the following file storage configurations provide fault tolerance?

    A. Volume set

    B. Stripe set

    C. Mirror set

    D. Stripe set with parity

33. You have installed a new 9GB hard drive in your Windows NT Server computer. You want to make the additional file space available to network users. You want users to be able to restrict who may have access to the files they place on this drive. What file system should you format the volume with?

    A. DOS FAT

    B. NTFS

    C. HPFS

    D. HFS

34. You are configuring a new network for a medium-sized company that has a traveling sales force equipped with laptops as well as several work-at-home professionals. The company has three branch offices linked to the main office by leased lines and routers. The main office and each branch office will have a server computer, but account information will be maintained on the central main office server computer. You must select a protocol for Windows NT and Windows 95 computers to use to connect to your Windows NT Server computers.

Required Result: All of the client computers must be able to connect to all of the server computers, regardless of which network the client computer is on or if the client computer is connected via dial-up networking.

Optional Result 1: The protocol should be efficient so that users connected to the network over dial-up lines or connecting to a server through a router and over a leased line are not penalized.

Optional Result 2: The protocol should be easy to configure.

Suggested Solution: Configure the servers and all of the client computers to use the NetBEUI transport protocol.

Which of the following is correct?

    A. The suggested solution satisfies the required result and both of the optional results.

B. The suggested solution satisfies the required result and just one of the optional results.

C. The suggested solution satisfies the required result only.

D. The suggested solution does not satisfy the required result.

35. A router's primary function is at which layer of the OSI stack?

A. The physical layer

B. The logical link layer

C. The network layer

D. The session layer

36. Which Control Panel do you use to configure the screen saver?

A. Console

B. Display

C. Screen

D. Multimedia

37. Which of the following operations can you perform from the Display Control Panel? Select all that apply.

A. Set the resolution and color depth of the display.

B. Install a display adapter driver.

C. Select the mouse pointer icons.

D. Select screen fonts and window border colors.

38. What tool do you use to configure trust relationships in Windows NT Server?

A. Syscon

B. Server Manager

C. User Manager for Domains

D. Network Control Panel

39. You have two domains: CorpCentral and Subsidiary. You want users in the Subsidiary domain to be able to log on using accounts created in the CorpCentral domain, but not vice versa. How should you configure the two domains?

    A. Configure CorpCentral as the trusting domain and Subsidiary as the trusted domain.

    B. Configure both domains as trusting and trusted.

    C. Configure Subsidiary as the trusting domain and CorpCentral as the trusted domain.

    D. You cannot establish a one-way trusting/trusted relationship.

40. You want to connect your network to the Internet. What transport protocol must you use?

    A. NWLink

    B. OSI

    C. TCP/IP

    D. NetBEUI

What's Next?

The questions presented in this chapter give you an idea of what you'll find on the Windows NT Server exam. See the appendix for the answers.

This completes the part of the book about certification. The next part provides reference information, beginning with a summary of essential NT tasks.

Part iii

PART iV
REFERENCE

Chapter 29
ESSENTIAL NT OPERATIONS

I n this chapter, we will look at the most common and important functions you will need to master in NT. We will begin with installing NT and move on to partitioning and formatting disks. Next, we will cover administering users, including how to set permissions. The last portions of the chapter will address NT networking, including how to install network adapters, protocols, and services. We will finish by discussing printing and extending NT with new features.

Some of these operations have been covered in depth in earlier chapters. This chapter is intended as a central reference to essential NT operations.

NT INSTALLATION

In this section, we will discuss how to get started with NT from the very beginning—the installation process. Toward that end, we will look at the basic installation methods; from disk and from a network server.

NOTE

For details on installing NT Workstation, see Chapter 2. For details on installing NT Server, see Chapter 14.

Installing from Disk

If your computer meets the basic hardware requirements needed to run NT, you can use the CD-ROM to install the product. The hardware requirements for both NT Workstation and Server are listed in Table 29.1.

TABLE 29.1: Hardware Requirements for NT 4

HARDWARE RESOURCE	NT WORKSTATION	NT SERVER
Processor	486-33 DX or compatible Alpha, MIPS, and PowerPC	486-33 DX or compatible Alpha, MIPS, and PowerPC
Memory	12MB required; 16MB recommended	16MB required; 32MB recommended
Disk space	110MB	125MB
Display	VGA or higher	VGA or higher
Other drives	CD-ROM recommended	CD-ROM recommended
Pointing device	Mouse or compatible	Mouse or compatible

It's always a good idea to refer to the Hardware Compatibility List (HCL) provided with NT to see if your hardware is supported by NT 4. The HCL is also found on Microsoft's Web site at www.microsoft.com/windows/compatible. The HCL lists computer hardware that has been tested by Microsoft and guaranteed to work with NT.

Starting Setup

The most common way to install NT is to begin the installation by booting the computer with the three Setup floppies that are provided in the package. This method works for the Intel and compatible platforms only. To begin the Setup program with this method, simply insert Setup Disk 1 into your floppy drive and turn on the computer. Setup will prompt you for each disk in turn as it loads a miniature version of NT to perform the installation.

An alternative is to install NT by booting directly from the CD-ROM. If your computer BIOS supports the El Torito standard for bootable CD-ROMs, NT 4 can be set up in this fashion. Simply insert the Windows NT CD-ROM into the drive and turn on the computer.

On an RISC platform such as the Alpha, MIPS, or PowerPC, you will be starting the installation directly from the CD-ROM, but the method will be different from the one on the Intel platform. All RISC computers boot from a hardware-supplied menu. On this menu will be the option to run a program. In some cases, there will even be an option to install Windows NT. Select the option to run a program, and direct it to the appropriate directory on the Windows NT CD-ROM to run the `setupldr` program.

After Setup has been initiated, it will run exactly the same on all supported hardware platforms.

Setup Phases

NT Setup has four distinct phases. Table 29.2 list the phases and describes what they entail.

TABLE 29.2: The Four Phases of NT Setup

SETUP PHASE	DESCRIPTION
Initializing Setup	This phase is text-based and includes options to upgrade existing versions of NT, detect hardware, select the partition and file system for Setup, and confirm the location of the Setup source files. At the end of this phase, the computer must be rebooted.
Gathering information	This phase gathers the basic information necessary to configure NT. You will be asked to provide the Installation Type (Workstation), Name and Organization of Licensee, Licensing Mode (Server), Computer Name, Type of Server (Server), Password for the Administrator account, Emergency Repair Disk, and Optional Components (depending on the type of setup selected).

Part iv

CONTINUED →

TABLE 29.2 continued: The Four Phases of NT Setup

SETUP PHASE	DESCRIPTION
Installing NT networking	In this phase of Setup, your network card is detected and installed. The network services and transport protocols are selected, and you have the option to install Internet Information Server.
Finishing Setup	Here you configure the display, set the time and date, and possibly set up your Windows Messaging Inbox (if you chose to install it).

Installing Over the Network

There are many situations where you might choose not to use the Setup floppy disks or even the CD-ROM. The most obvious is when you are installing NT over the network from a shared folder on a server. Many people prefer to perform a "floppy-less" installation to avoid the slow performance of a floppy drive while beginning Setup.

One of the things you'll discover when trying to set up NT is that there is no setup.exe program to run. The program used to initiate Setup is winnt.exe or winnt32.exe, depending on the operating system you are running when you start the process. The winnt program is used when you are starting Setup from an operating system other than NT, and winnt32 is used when starting Setup from within NT.

OF DISKS AND FILE SYSTEMS

Whenever you add a hard disk to a computer system, you must complete certain tasks before it can be used to store data. First, let's review some terminology. A *file system* is a set of rules for storing the data you work with on your computer. It defines the *how* of placing the bits of data into meaningful forms of storage so they can be retrieved later. A *partition* is the boundaries on the physical disk within which the file system is created.

Partitioning Disks

Microsoft uses two terms to describe where NT is installed on your computer. The *system partition* is the drive you boot the computer from, typically the C: drive. The *boot partition* is the drive where NT is installed. These may be the same partition, or they may be different partitions.

Extended versus Primary Partitions

There are two types of partitions available on most computers today: *primary* and *extended*. A primary partition is the most common type, and as a matter of fact, every computer must have at least one primary partition. A primary partition may contain all of the space on the physical disk or a smaller portion. It will be assigned only one drive letter by NT. There can be as many as four primary partitions per disk under NT.

Extended partitions may include the entire disk or just a portion of it. Unlike primary partitions, extended partitions usually contain multiple volumes, each of which is assigned a drive letter. There can be only one extended partition per physical disk. The total number of partitions per disk can be only four. That means you can have a maximum of four primary partitions, or three primaries and one extended.

Stripe Sets

A *stripe set* is a combination of equal-sized partitions from multiple physical disks into one logical volume. In simpler terms, there are many pieces, but NT sees them as one drive. Stripe sets store their data in small pieces spread across all of the physical drives, essentially a thin "stripe" of information going across all of the disks.

The benefit of striping is *speed*. Striping is the fastest partitioning scheme available in NT. It is particularly useful for applications that require very fast access to larger files.

The downside of stripe sets is that they do not provide any kind of protection for the data. If one physical disk in a stripe set fails, you will lose *all* of the data in the stripe set. Needless to say, this would be a bad thing. If you choose to implement striping, be very sure to perform tape backups on a regular basis.

Part iv

Volume Sets

Another method of combining multiple pieces of disks into one logical drive is to create a *volume set*. Volume sets combine unused portions of hard disks into one logical drive. This means that if you have multiple disks in your computer with unused space, you can combine those portions into one larger drive that NT and your applications see as one drive letter.

In NT, volume sets can be made up of 2 to 32 discrete partitions, but they cannot contain the system or boot partitions. They are available in both NT Server and Workstation. Volume sets can be formatted as either FAT or NTFS and can contain multiple partitions from the same physical disk. Volume sets are not fault tolerant. If you lose one disk, you will lose all that data.

Managing Fault Tolerance

Servers are the storage space for critical information in most networks. This data defines the business, or perhaps even *is* the business. This data must be protected if the business is to survive and grow. Fault tolerance describes a storage method that allows for failure of a portion of the storage without losing data. A storage mechanism is said to be fault tolerant if it can tolerate the loss of one or more parts of the whole system without losing any information.

Fault tolerance can be implemented in software or hardware. In the case of hardware implementations, the disk controller provides all of the support necessary to create a fault-tolerant storage system. In software implementations, the operating system is responsible for providing the support. NT Server provides fault-tolerance capabilities implemented in software. NT Workstation does not support fault tolerance.

The most prevalent type of fault tolerance for today's servers is to include a RAID set. RAID is actually a set of standards that define different methods of storing data on multiple hard disks. These standards provide varying levels of fault tolerance. Table 29.3 lists the current RAID standards.

TABLE 29.3: RAID Standards

RAID Type	Description
Level 1	Disk mirroring. Mirroring uses two disks to store the data of one disk. Everything written to the first disk is also written to the second disk, creating a mirror image. NT Server provides support for mirroring both the system and boot partitions.
Level 2	Disk striping with error correction code (ECC). This system is similar to disk striping in terms of how the data is stored, but for each stripe of data there is some information stored to aid in recovery from errors.
Level 3	Disk striping with ECC stored as parity. Here the ECC is stored as a mathematical expression that can be used to regenerate the data.
Level 4	Disk striping with large blocks, parity stored on one disk. In this system, data is distributed across the disks in large stripes, and the parity code is stored entirely on one disk.
Level 5	Disk striping with parity distributed across all disks. This is perhaps the best RAID system, certainly the most common. Here the data is spread across multiple disks in small stripes (64KB in NT) and the parity is distributed across all of the disks evenly. NT Server provides RAID 5 support for data partitions.

The number of disks that you can add to a RAID set depends on a variety of factors, such as type of controller, number of controllers, physical space for disks, and power supply.

Software versus Hardware RAID

NT Server provides software implementations of RAID levels 1 and 5. This is great for small networks with a small budget for server hardware. However, software RAID requires system resources to operate and the attention of the operating system to manage the data storage. RAID 1 is not very intensive on system resources because it only requires that the operating system write two copies of everything. When NT reads from a mirrored drive, it is only reading from the primary image, which is no different from reading from any single hard disk.

RAID 5, on the other hand, is very resource-intensive in that it requires more memory and CPU time to compute the parity information when data is written to the stripe set. But when NT is reading data from a stripe set with parity, the performance is outstanding, very much like disk striping.

When RAID sets are implemented in hardware, the disk controller is responsible for computing all parity information and for the management of the data. Typically, these disk controllers have a CPU chip of their own and some memory to handle the work of running a RAID system. It's almost like having a computer within a computer. Hardware RAID is fast and requires nothing from the operating system. If you have a RAID 5 set with ten hard disks in it, NT has no way of knowing how many disks are there. It sees only one logical drive.

Striping with Parity

NT Server supports RAID 5 sets with a minimum of 3 and a maximum of 32 hard disks. You can add only equal-sized partitions from each physical disk into the set, but there can be more than one stripe set using space on a physical disk. Figure 29.1 shows the distribution of two stripe sets with parity across four physical disks. Notice that the C: drive is not part of either set. The C: drive is where you would install NT, since it cannot be installed on a stripe set with parity.

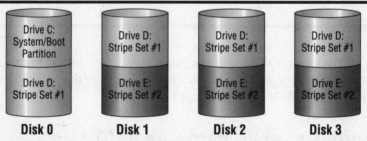

FIGURE 29.1: Striping with parity (RAID 5)

The amount of storage provided by a stripe set with parity will equal the total of all the partitions minus one partition. If you have ten 2GB hard disks in a stripe set with parity, you would have 20GB minus one 2GB partition, for a total of 18GB of storage and 2GB of parity information. RAID 5 benefits greatly from adding a large number of smaller physical disks, rather than a small number of large disks.

NOTE

The parity information in a RAID 5 stripe set with parity always equals one of the individual partitions in the set.

The fault tolerance of striping with parity allows for the failure of one physical disk in the set. If one disk fails, the remaining data can be combined with the parity information to re-create the missing data. This is done on-the-fly; there is no downtime when a disk fails. To recover from a disk failure, the bad disk is replaced, and the set is regenerated.

Refer to the "Using Disk Administrator" section later in the chapter for specific instructions for setting up striping with parity in NT.

Disk Mirroring

RAID 1, disk mirroring, provides an exact copy of all data stored on a drive. This is a very good form of fault tolerance, since if one disk fails, you still have the mirror image. In this system, one disk is considered the primary image and one is the mirror image, as illustrated in Figure 29.2.

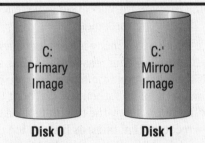

Disk 0   **Disk 1**

FIGURE 29.2: Disk mirroring (RAID 1)

Disk mirroring is the only form of fault tolerance provided by NT Server that can protect the partition where NT is installed. The software implementation of mirroring in NT Server can be used for both the system and boot partitions.

Understanding File Systems

Disk partitions define the boundaries of a drive, and a file system defines how data will be store within those limits. NT supports both the FAT and NTFS file systems.

NOTE

See Chapter 20 for details on NT file system security.

Using FAT

The FAT file system is probably the most widely supported file system for personal computers. This is the file system used by MS-DOS and Windows. Windows 95 OEM Service Release 2 (OSR2) introduced a 32-bit version of the FAT file system called FAT32 for large drive support. Windows 95 OSR2 and Windows 98 are currently the only operating systems that support the FAT32 file system. NT 4 does not support or even see FAT32, but the next version of NT, called Windows 2000, will support FAT32.

FAT works by storing information about where files are located in a table, like a database. That allocation table is what gives the file system its name. The FAT file system works best for partitions that are less than 512MB in size. On these small drives, FAT can be the fastest file system available for NT. The only exception to this statement is when the drive is full of many small files (perhaps several thousand files). If this is the case, FAT will have trouble reading through the allocation table quickly, and you will notice a severe slow down in performance.

Fast performance is one of the reasons that many NT experts suggest that you install NT on a FAT partition. The other reason is that it is easier to repair the system. If your NT Workstation won't boot because of corrupted files, and you have it installed on FAT, then you can boot the computer with an MS-DOS boot floppy and copy the files to replace the corrupted files. This can lead to a recovery that takes as little as ten minutes instead of the several hours required for other methods.

The drawbacks of using FAT are security and inefficiency. The FAT file system has no security capability. If someone can log on to your NT Workstation locally, that person can access all of your data. FAT is also a somewhat inefficient file system in the way that it stores files. A FAT partition can only have 1,024 areas called *cylinders*. The total number of sectors (the smallest unit of storage on a hard disk) is divided by 1,024 to produce the number of *clusters*. In the FAT file system, a cluster is the smallest unit of storage that can be written to. On a 500MB partition, the size of a cluster is 8KB. This means that if you want to store a one-byte file, it will consume eight kilobytes of disk space.

The larger the partition, the more this becomes an issue. The 8KB clusters hold true up to a partition size of 512MB. From 513MB to 1024MB, the cluster size is 16KB. Over a gigabyte, the cluster size goes to 32KB. The bigger the partition, the more space is wasted by clustering.

Using NTFS

The preferred file system for NT is NTFS. Unlike FAT, NTFS provides native file security to protect your files and folders across the network or even when someone logs on to your computer locally. NTFS is a fast, reliable file system. It provides excellent performance even on extremely large volumes. It does use clustering like FAT, but the cluster sizes are much smaller.

The smallest unit of storage on a hard disk, if you recall the previous section, is the sector. A sector is 512 bytes in size. NTFS uses a default cluster size of 512 bytes, or one sector for most drives. The default cluster size will increase when the volumes grow in size.

NTFS is capable of formatting extremely large volumes. In theory, a single file on NTFS, or a single NTFS volume, can be up to 16 *exabytes* in size. The current practical limit for NTFS is 2 terabytes, but that should be extended to the full size very soon.

NOTE

An exabyte is a very large number indeed. If you were to assume that five billion people each had two thousand pages of text, they could store their pages in a single exabyte. NTFS will handle 16 times that amount. A single exabyte equals 1,152,921,504,606,846,976 bytes!

Using Disk Administrator

NT provides a graphical tool to create and maintain disk partitions called Disk Administrator, which is located in the Administrative Tools group on the Start menu's Programs submenu. This program gives you all the functionality of the old MS-DOS utility FDISK.EXE, and more. In addition to creating primary and extended partitions, Disk Administrator can set up volume sets and stripe sets. Using Disk Administrator on NT Server, you can also create fault-tolerant sets such as mirrors and stripe sets with parity.

Figure 29.3 shows the default appearance of Disk Administrator, except that the color for the active partition was changed to allow you to see the asterisk in the color stripe on that partition. The active partition is the one that will actually boot the computer.

Part iv

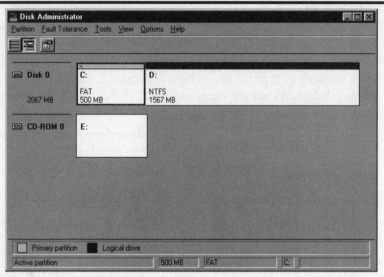

FIGURE 29.3: The main window of Disk Administrator

CUSTOMIZING COLOR SCHEMES

In Disk Administrator, having that little asterisk in the color stripe on the active partition can be very helpful if you are using the old method of dual-booting between NT and UNIX—switching the active partition flag when you want to boot to the other operating system. But the default color chosen by Microsoft is a dark blue that makes it difficult (if not impossible) to see the asterisk. The good news is that you can easily customize the color schemes. To change the colors and patterns used for the display, follow these steps:

1. Select Start ➤ Programs ➤ Administrative Tools ➤ Disk Administrator to start Disk Administrator.

2. Select Options ➤ Colors and Patterns to open the Colors and Patterns dialog box.

3. Select the item you want to change from the Color and Pattern for drop-down list box.

4. Choose the color and pattern you wish to use.

5. Click OK to close the dialog box and apply the change.

CONTINUED ➡

You can also choose how you want to display the partitions in the Disk Administrator's graphs. Under the Options menu, the Disk Display Options give you the choice of sizing disks based on actual size or sizing all disks equally. (This applies only to the display of the disk regions on the graphs, not to the actual partitions.)

Creating Partitions

Creating new partitions in Disk Administrator is easy. Assuming you have NT already installed, and there is free space on at least one of your hard disks, you can follow these steps to create a partition using Disk Administrator:

1. Start Disk Administrator. In its display, locate an area of free space on the hard disk you wish to partition. Free space can be either unpartitioned space or available space within an extended partition. You can tell the difference by examining the crosshatch pattern. Unpartitioned space will be cross-hatched from right to left, and free space in an extended partition will be crosshatched from left to right.

2. Click the free space area to highlight it.

3. Select Partition ➢ Create to create a primary partition, or select Partition ➢ Create Extended to create an extended partition.

4. Select Partition ➢ Commit Changes Now to apply the changes.

5. Once the changes have been committed, click the new partition to highlight it.

6. Select Tools ➢ Format to open the Format dialog box.

7. Choose the file system to use and the allocation unit size (NTFS only). Click OK to begin the format operation.

After the formatting has been completed, the new partition is ready for use.

Part iv

Creating Stripe Sets and Volumes

To create a stripe set or a volume set, follow these steps:

1. In Disk Administrator, select one area of free space to be included in the stripe or volume set and click to highlight it.

2. Press and hold down the Ctrl key, then click the other areas of free space to include in the set. For a stripe set, these should be of equal size, though Disk Administrator will automatically size them. Free space for a volume set may be on the same physical disk, but stripe sets cannot contain pieces from the same physical disk.

3. Once all sections are highlighted, select the set you wish to create from the Partition menu. Only appropriate selections will be available on the Partition menu. If you have selected two sections of free space from the same physical disk, you will not have the option to create a stripe set.

4. Select Partition ➢ Commit Changes Now to apply the change.

5. Select Tools ➢ Format to open the Format dialog box.

6. Choose the file system to use and the allocation unit size (NTFS only), then click OK.

Changing Drive Letters

Another useful function of Disk Administrator is to assign drive letters to disks, including removable drives and CD-ROM drives. NT doesn't really care about drive letters, since it uses Advanced RISC Computing (ARC) paths to boot the operating system, but your applications may care very much which drive letter they are installed on. Follow these steps to change a drive letter:

1. In Disk Administrator, highlight the drive you want you assign.

2. Select Tools ➢ Assign Drive Letter to open the Assign Drive Letter dialog box.

3. Choose the drive letter you want to assign to this drive. Click OK to apply the change.

Initially, you may not be able to set the letter you want if it is already assigned. If the letter you want to use is already in use by a network connection, disconnect the network drive first. If the drive letter is in use by another disk in your computer, you can assign that drive a letter first, then assign the desired drive letter to the new partition. (This is kind of like playing with a sliding puzzle where you have to move one piece out of the way before you can move the piece you want.)

ADMINISTERING USERS

NT was designed to be a secure operating system. One of the consequences of that design goal is that you must have a user account in order to use NT. In Windows 95/98 systems, you can simply press the Esc key to bypass the logon prompt and get into the operating system. With NT, however, you cannot bypass this logon. Even without a network, NT requires a user account and password.

One of the reasons that NT takes this attitude about logons is to provide a way to determine which user is accessing which resource. NT also offers the ability to grant or deny permissions to use those precious resources on your system. NT does this through *user security*, which means that every user has an account to which permissions can be applied.

Understanding User Accounts

User accounts are the essential building blocks for NT security. They provide the capability to allow access to resources, maintain individual settings, and provide a trail of activity for administrators to monitor. With NT Workstation, you can create local user accounts that exist only on your computer, or you can access user accounts stored on a domain. NT Server enables you to create user accounts on the local computer, to access accounts from a domain, and even to create a domain to store those accounts. The tool for creating and managing user accounts in NT Workstation is User Manager. In NT Server, the tool is User Manager for Domains.

Every user must have a unique account name. The names can be up to 20 characters in length, but they must be unique in the database where they are created. It is possible to have the same username on your local computer that you have on the domain. Usernames are not case-sensitive. Passwords are case-sensitive.

User accounts give you the capability to define where a user's home folder will be. You can define the location of the user's profile, either on the local computer or centrally stored on a server. You can determine users' logon scripts, logon hours, even the computers they are allowed to logon from. All in all, user accounts are very important to NT.

NOTE

See Chapter 17 for details on using User Manager for Domains to set up user accounts, as well as information about user profiles and system policies.

Planning for User Accounts

Because usernames must be unique, it is a good idea to do some planning before you start creating them. If you are in a domain environment, it makes sense to consider that you might have duplicate names among your users and perhaps even several people with the same or very similar names. You should consider a naming convention that allows for this.

There are many types of jobs in the typical company today, and the use of temporary or contract workers is growing. You might want to plan a naming convention that easily depicts the type of job by adding a letter to the beginning of the name. Many companies use something like v-*username* or t-*username* to signify that this user is a vendor or a temporary worker. Another benefit is that these names will sort together when the list of usernames is generated alphabetically.

If there will be many user accounts that have the same properties added to the domain, consider the use of account templates. A template account is one that you create with all the properties common to this job or user type. Give the account a name that begins with an underscore and describes the users the template applies to. For example, the template that will be used for any user added to the sales department could be named _Sales. The leading underscore causes the template accounts to sort at the top of an alphabetic listing, where they can be easily located.

Understanding SIDs

Every object in NT has a unique property called a Security Identifier, or SID. A SID is a long number that uniquely represents each and every item that NT works with. This includes things like files, folders, printers, and even users. NT cares more about the SID of an object than it does about the name.

You can delete a user account, realize you made a mistake, and re-create the account with exactly the same name and properties, but NT still sees it as a different account. That's because the SID will be different for the new account. The moral of this story is don't delete accounts unless you know what you're doing.

Deleting and Renaming Accounts

People come and go from your network. It's a fact of life nowadays. Most administrators like to clean up after someone has left the company, but that may not always be a good idea. Consider the situation where a person, let's say Tom, leaves the company for another job, then decides to return because he didn't like the new company. You could find yourself in the position of having to create the user account and all of its properties from scratch. If you don't delete the account when Tom leaves, you will have it when he returns.

"Wait a minute," you say, "I don't want all those accounts hanging around." That's true. You don't want a bunch of user accounts left around when no one is supposed to be using them. But instead of deleting the account, you can disable it, and no one will be able to use it. That way, if the person comes back, you can simply re-enable his account, and he or she can get right to work.

Understanding Group Accounts

Group accounts are the fundamental containers for organizing your users. You can think of group accounts being the baskets that you carry all of your eggs in.

Global Groups versus Local Groups

There are two kinds of group accounts in NT: local and global. Global groups are only available in NT domains. They cannot be created on NT Workstation computers. Local groups are only valid in the database where they were created, whether that database was a domain or a NT Workstation computer. Table 29.4 summarizes the properties of and differences between NT global and local groups.

TABLE 29.4: Global and Local Group Account Features

FEATURE	GLOBAL GROUP	LOCAL GROUP
Usage	Organizing domain user accounts.	Granting permissions and rights to users.
Members	Can contain *only* user accounts from the domain where the group is created.	May contain local user accounts, domain user accounts, and global groups from the local domain or from trusted domains.
Scope	Can be used anywhere in the domain. Can also be assigned to local groups in trusting domains.	Can be used only in the database where created. If a local group is created on the PDC, it can be used on any domain controller in that domain. If the group is created on an NT Workstation computer, it can be used only on that computer.
Location	Always created on the PDC.	Can be created on any NT computer. If the local group is created on a domain controller, it can be used on any domain controller in the domain.
Rights and permissions	Typically inherits rights and permissions by being added to local groups.	Normally receives rights and permissions directly.

Administering Groups

While it is possible to use only user accounts for assigning rights and permissions in NT, local and global groups make the job easier. Good, practical administration includes using both user and group accounts to manage security in a network environment. When you assign permissions to local groups and add global groups to those local groups, the members of the groups inherit the permissions assigned to the local group.

The best way to use groups and user accounts for assigning permissions is illustrated in Figure 29.4. In this strategy, user accounts are organized by placing them into global groups. The global groups are then added to the local group, and the local group is assigned permission to use a resource. Yes, there are other ways to administer your users, but this way offers many benefits over the long term.

| User Accounts | Added to | Global Groups | Added to | Local Groups | Permissions | Assigned Permissions |

FIGURE 29.4: A recommended group strategy

One advantage is that members, including the global groups contained within the local group, inherit any permissions assigned to the local group. This also means that the permissions are inherited by all of the user accounts contained in the global group. The permissions, in effect, ripple down through the layers to affect each and every user account in the groups. So why is that so cool? Think about a real business situation where someone is hired on at your company. It's your job to give this new user permissions to the resources located on the 400 servers in your network. Would you rather add the new user to a few groups or touch each one of those 400 servers individually?

Setting Permissions

There are two levels of permissions in NT: share-level permissions, applied to shared network folders, and file permissions, assigned to individual files and folders on the hard drive. We will explore each one of these levels separately, and then we will show you how to combine these different permissions to provide maximum security for server resources.

Share-Level Permissions

Share permissions are assigned to shared folders on either an NT Server or Workstation computer. They are effective only when the folder is accessed across the network. Share permissions will not prevent a user who is logged on locally from accessing your data files, but they will control the user who connects remotely. (See the "Sharing Folders" section later in this chapter for instructions on how to share folders.)

Part iv

There are four levels of share permissions: Full Control, Change, Read, and No Access. These permissions are comprised of six individual permissions:

Read   Allows you to view the contents of a file.

Write   Permits you to create a file in the folder and to save changes made to an existing file.

Execute   Allows you to run an executable program file.

Delete   Lets you erase the file.

Take Ownership   Allows you to take ownership. The owner of a file has all permissions for that file.

Change   Gives you the ability to set permissions for other users or to change your own level of permission.

When these permissions are combined, they form the four default permissions.

Share permissions are said to be *cumulative* because you need to evaluate every permission assigned to a user and every group that user belongs to, then add them together to determine the effective permission. For example, suppose that you have a user on your network named Mary and a folder on your server called Data. If Mary has been assigned Change permission to the Data shared folder, she will be able to read, write, execute, and delete anything in the Data folder. But what if Mary (like most users) is a member of several groups, for instance Group1, Group2, and Group3. The following list shows the permissions assigned to these accounts.

User or Group Account	Permission for Data Folder
Mary	Change
Group1	Read
Group2	<Not specified>
Group3	Full Control

The first thing to notice is that Group2 has no assigned permission granted. This means that if you were a member of Group2 and no other group in the list, you would not be able to access the Data folder because you have not been specifically granted permission. But Mary has permission and is a member of all these groups. Because share permissions are cumulative, we simply add all of these permissions together and say that Mary has the effective permissions of Read, Change, *and* Full Control, or just Full Control, since that permission contains all of the other permissions.

The single exception to this rule is the No Access permission. No Access overrides every other permission, without exception. If you assign No Access to any of the accounts in our example, the effective permission becomes No Access, and Mary will receive an Access Denied message when she tries to connect to the Data folder.

Share permissions are effective when a network user accesses anything stored in a shared folder or in folders within the shared folder. Share permissions trickle down through all of the folders contained within the shared folder. Whatever effective permission you have for the shared folder is what you have for the subfolders and all of their files. This can create a problem with security. The default permission when you share a folder is for the Everyone group to have Full Control permission. Remember that share permissions flow downward through the folder structure.

Figure 29.5 illustrates the potential problem that can arise with share permissions. In this example, the Apps folder was shared correctly with Read permission assigned to the Users group. This means that anyone in the Users group can access the share and the Excel program folder below it, to read and execute files. They can run the Excel program. But the problem here comes from the Public share that still has the default share permission of Everyone, which is the Full Control permission. When users connect to the Public share, they can do anything they want to the files in that folder *and every subfolder*. This means they can browse down through the folder structure and delete files in the Excel folder if they choose to do so. If a user does delete files in the Excel folder, the program may not run for anyone.

To prevent this problem, be careful when sharing folders and different points in the same folder hierarchy. You need to ensure that you will not inadvertently give higher permissions when someone connects through a higher-level share. In this example, only those users responsible for updating the files in the Apps folder should have Full Control or Change permission for the share above the Apps folder.

Part iv

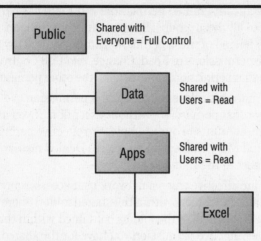

FIGURE 29.5: Shares at different levels can open security issues.

NTFS Permissions

Assigning permissions to shared folders is fine to protect your data when accessed across the network, but what about protecting the data from local users? For that level of protection, you need permissions that are built directly into the file system itself—permissions like those provided by NTFS. NTFS permissions are stored in the file system, directly with the files and folders, so they are effective when accessed through a share across the network or when a user logs on locally.

Permissions in NTFS can be assigned to either an individual file or to a folder. You can even mix and match your permissions, giving a user one permission to the folder and a different permission to the file contained in the folder. You can assign four permissions to a file:

Read Includes only Read and Execute permissions.

Change Includes Read, Write, Execute, and Delete permissions. This is usually what we mean when we think of full access.

Full Control Includes all permissions: Read, Write, Execute, Delete, Take Ownership, and Change.

No Access Has no individual permissions at all. This permission overrides all other permissions to an object.

Most users in an NT network belong to more than one user group. When evaluating a user's permissions for a file located on an NTFS partition, you must look at every permission assigned to that user and any group the user belongs to. List all of the permissions and add them up. NTFS permissions are cumulative. They add up to form an effective permission, except for the No Access permission, which overrides everything else.

For example, if you are assigned the Read permission for the file `sample` `.txt`, and you belong to the group Sales that has been assigned the Change permission for the file, your effective permission is both Change *and* Read. But if you belonged to a group that had been assigned the No Access permission, then it wouldn't matter what any of your other permissions were, because the effective permission would always be No Access.

WARNING

Don't make the mistake of thinking that you are assigning No Access to everyone *but* the group or user that you give a specific permission to. Always remember that the No Access permission overrides every other assigned permission.

NTFS also provides permissions for folders that work in very much the same way as file permissions, but include a few more possible combinations. With folder permissions, the individual permissions are the same: Read, Write, Execute, Delete, Take Ownership, and Change. The difference is that you are assigning permissions to the folder itself *and* to the contents. These are the NTFS permissions for folders:

No Access   Means there is absolutely no permission to either the folder or its contents.

List   Gives the user Read and Execute permissions for the folder, but permissions are not specified for the contents of the folder. With List permission, you can display a listing of the folder's contents but not much more than that.

Read   Enables a user to read and execute the folder and everything in the folder.

Add   Gives a user Write and Execute permissions for the folder, but permissions are not specified for the contents of the folder. This means you can save a file to this folder, but you can't view the file after you've written it.

Add & Read   Allows a user Read, Write, and Execute permissions for the folder, but only Read and Execute for the contents of the folder. You can save a file to the folder, and you can read it afterward, but you can't modify it.

Change   Allows a user Read, Write, Execute, and Delete permissions both at the folder level and for the contents of the folder.

Full Control   Gives all permissions; a user has Read, Write, Execute, Delete, Take Ownership, and Change permissions.

Special Directory Access   Allows you to mix and match the individual permissions for your own special combination. Applies at the folder level only.

Special File Access   Gives you the ability to custom define the permissions for the contents of a folder or for a particular file.

WARNING

Never assign the No Access permission to the Everyone group on the root of the C: drive or to the folders where NT is installed. The operating system itself is a part of the Everyone group. If you assign No Access to these folders, your computer will not boot.

So what do you do if you do not want to give someone access to a file or folder? Simple—just don't give them permission. Many people use the No Access permission to deny access to files and folders when all they need to do is simply not give a specific user or group any permission. In NT, if you have not been granted a specific permission that allows access to a resource, you do not have any access. The effect is the same as granting the No Access permission, but without the unpleasant side effects that can result from No Access.

Combining Permissions

For the best security available in NT, you should consider combining both share permissions and NTFS permissions by applying both types. This enables you to protect the folders, files, and all subfolders appropriately.

Always remember that share permissions are cumulative and NTFS permissions are cumulative. To determine a user's effective permissions with either set of permissions, add together all of that user's permissions with the exception of No Access, which overrides all other permissions.

When you are combining both share and NTFS permissions, first evaluate share permissions separately. Then determine the effective NTFS permissions separately. Once you have each of the effective permissions, compare them to determine which effective permission is most restrictive. The most restrictive permission will be the effective permission for the user. Consider the following example:

User or Group Account	Share Permission	NTFS Permission
Mary	Change	Change
Group1	Full Control	Read
Group2	Read	Change
Group3	Full Control	<Not specified>

In this example, if Mary is a member of each of the groups, what are her effective permissions? Start with the share permissions. Mary would have the effective share permission of Read, Change, and Full Control, or just Full Control (since Full Control contains both Read and Change). Mary's effective NTFS permission would be both Read and Change, or just Change (since Change contains the Read permission). So we are then evaluating the two effective permissions to determine which is more restrictive. Both permissions have Read, Write, Execute, and Delete permissions, but Full Control also has Take Ownership and Change Permissions. Thus, Change is the most restrictive permission of the two effective permissions. Change becomes the effective permission for Mary when she accesses the shared folder across the network.

Combining share and NTFS permissions takes practice. They can easily become *very* complicated when there are many groups to evaluate, but the procedure is still the same. Simply add up all of the share permissions for a user and the user's groups to find the effective share permission. Then do the same with the NTFS permissions to find the user's effective NTFS permission. Finally, compare the two effective permissions to determine which is most restrictive. This final result is always the user's effective permission when used across the network.

NETWORKING WITH NT

Adding networking support to NT involves installing a network adapter, the transport protocols, and the network services. You can install the network when you install the NT operating system, or you can add new network components later. After you've installed network support, you can share resources across the network, including folders and printers.

Installing Network Adapters

To install a new network interface card (NIC) in NT, first install the hardware according to the manufacturer's instructions. Be very careful to turn off the computer before doing this. To install the driver for the NIC, you need to open the Network applet in Control Panel. You can do this either by opening the Control Panel, then double-clicking the Network icon, or by right-clicking Network Neighborhood on the Desktop, then choosing Properties from the context menu. Select the Adapters tab of the Network applet, as shown in Figure 29.6.

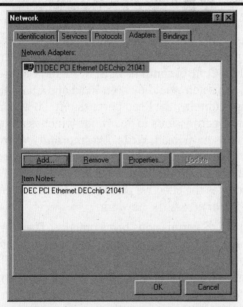

FIGURE 29.6:   The Adapters tab of the Network Control Panel applet

Click the Add button to install the new driver. You will need to locate the manufacturer and model of your NIC on the list, or click the Have Disk button, to give NT the path to the drivers. As the drivers are installed, you may be prompted for information such as the hardware resources to use for the card and any addressing information for installed protocols.

Once the drivers are installed, click OK to finalize the settings. NT will go through a series of network bindings and process the settings to be added to the Registry. Once this has completed, you will be prompted to shut down and restart the computer. After the computer has fully rebooted, your NIC is installed.

Installing Transport Protocols

Transport protocols are the basic language your computer will use to communicate with a remote computer on the network. The fundamental ingredients for a conversation are at least two parties involved and a common language. In network communications, the end points for the conversation are two computers. The common language is your transport protocol. A network protocol is simply the rules that the two computers will use when they communicate.

Deciding on a Protocol

The default protocol installed during NT Setup is TCP/IP, since nearly every network using NT is running TCP/IP. However, if you are installing network support after installing NT, you need to make the protocol choice on your own. You may also need to select other protocols to suit the requirements of your network. NT provides support for the following protocols:

TCP/IP   The standard for most networks today because it is just that—standard. TCP/IP is an industry-standard suite of protocols and the most widely used protocol on today's networks. It is also the protocol used for the Internet.

NWLink   The IPX/SPX-compatible protocol provided to communicate with NetWare networks that use IPX/SPX. NWLink provides NetBIOS support, as well as named pipes and windows sockets.

NetBEUI   Also called the NetBIOS Frames protocol in NT, a legacy protocol in Microsoft networks. NetBEUI is useful for small networks since it is fast and self-tuning. Its major drawback is that it cannot be routed from one network to another.

AppleTalk   Provided to give Macintosh clients access to NT Server for file and print services.

DLC   Provided to facilitate communication between an NT computer and a mainframe. It is also useful for communicating with old print servers like the original JetDirect cards from Hewlett Packard, which only used DLC in their original versions.

The number one question to ask for today's networks is: Will you connect to the Internet? If so, then you must install TCP/IP for your network protocol. If you need to communicate with Novell NetWare networks that run IPX/SPX, you will want to install NWLink.

When choosing a protocol you also need to consider the size and growth of your network. If your network is growing, sooner or later you will need to segment it using a router. You then need to consider which of the protocols can be routed. Both TCP/IP and NWLink can be used in a routed environment. NetBEUI cannot be routed since it has no way of carrying network address information. But if your network is small and likely to stay small, then NetBEUI is a very good choice because of its speed and simplicity.

Protocols are installed, like other network components, in the Network Control Panel applet, as follows:

1. Open the Control Panel and double-click the Network icon.

2. Click the Protocols tab.

3. Click the Add button to add a new protocol.

4. Select the protocol from the list of provided protocols or click the Have Disk button to provide the path to the protocol files you wish to install.

5. Click OK. Depending on the protocol, you may be prompted for more information at this point.

6. Click OK to close the Network applet. NT will reconfigure the network settings in the Registry at this point, and you may be prompted to restart the computer.

You can also use the Protocols tab in the Network applet to remove or configure installed protocols. To configure a protocol, highlight the desired protocol and click the Properties button. To remove an installed protocol, highlight the desired protocol and click the Remove button.

Fine-Tuning Protocols

When we talk about optimizing performance in network protocols, we usually discuss configuring the *bindings*. A network binding is a path from a file system driver like the Server service to an NIC. Every possible path is represented by default when the network is installed in NT. Figure 29.7 shows the bindings for a typical NT Server running TCP/IP, with an NIC and a modem installed.

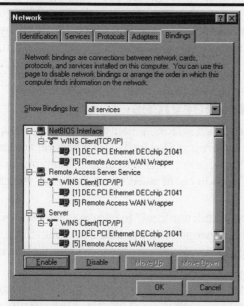

FIGURE 29.7: The Bindings tab of the Network Control Panel applet

Bindings are important in every network operating system, because they determine the order in which the installed components will be tried when making a network connection. In NT, bindings aren't really important for deciding how you will make a connection, because NT will attempt to make the connection with every installed protocol. The first protocol to respond is the one that you will use for the connection. But bindings are very important for deciding how your Server service will respond to a connection request from a client.

The binding at the top of the list in each section is the one that will be tried first when answering a request. This means that you can gain better performance by setting your most common protocol to be first on the list. Your computer won't waste time having to timeout on a protocol that no other computer uses before trying the one that all of the computers on your network support.

You can also improve performance by disabling a binding that you will not be using. For example, if you have two NICs in your computer, one attached to a network using NetBEUI and the other attached to your main network running TCP/IP, you could get better performance by disabling the bindings not in use. There will be a binding for the Server service through TCP/IP to both NICs by default. You could disable the binding from the Server service through TCP/IP to the NIC attached to the NetBEUI network. In this case, this method would ensure that you did not waste any time trying to use a protocol that would not get an answer.

Installing Network Services

Network services provide the actual functionality of NT on the network. Most services that you need are installed by default whenever you install network support, such as the Server, Workstation, and Computer Browser services. But others will need to be installed manually before you can use them.

Many people new to NT think it's "cool" to have many network services installed. These are the people who will install services just because they can. If you are one of these people, here are some reasons you might want to reconsider.

First of all, every service you install has an impact on the performance of your computer. Services take memory and processor time to run, some more than others. Some of the network services in NT also take up space on the hard drive to store their data files. Another reason to avoid adding more than you need is that many services will add to your already configured bindings, making the bindings more complicated. This will also add time to your connection attempts. Now that we've told you why you should resist adding too many services, here are some you may want to consider:

Dynamic Host Configuration Protocol   DHCP is a protocol and a server component that you can add to NT Server in order to dynamically provide TCP/IP addressing information.

Windows Internet Naming Service   WINS handles resolution of NetBIOS computer names to IP addresses in a dynamically addressed environment. It is a perfect complement to DHCP.

Domain Name System DNS is very similar to WINS except that it resolves *host* names to IP addresses. These are the names used for servers on the Internet.

Gateway or Client Services for NetWare GSNW or CSNW provide connectivity to NetWare servers from NT. They are native NetWare Core Protocol (NCP) speaking redirectors, or clients. GSNW is available on NT Server and has the added benefit of allowing NT to perform a gateway conversion between the NCPs used on NetWare networks to the Server Message Blocks (SMB) used by Microsoft networks.

The network environment in which you are installing NT will dictate the network services you choose to install. Just remember to use moderation when selecting services to obtain the best performance possible.

To install network services, you use the Network applet from the Control Panel again. To install a service, follow these steps:

1. Open the Control Panel and double-click the Network icon.

2. Click the Services tab. Figure 29.8 shows an example of the services listed in the Services tab.

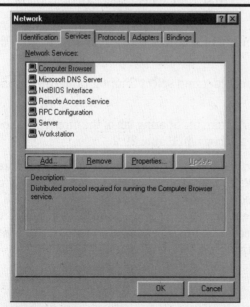

FIGURE 29.8: The Services tab of the Network Control Panel applet

Part iv

3. Click the Add button and select the desired service from the list of provided services. You may also install a third-party service by clicking the Have Disk button and directing NT to the installation files for the service.

4. Click OK to return to the Network applet.

5. Click OK to close the Network applet and install the service. You may be prompted for additional information depending on the service. You will most likely need to shut down and restart NT after installing the service.

Sharing Folders

One of the best reasons to install network support is to access shared resources on the network. NT also lets you share resources from your computer by creating shared folders. No one can connect to your computer to access data unless you first create a shared folder. Once the folder is shared, you assign permissions to control which users have access to the data contained in that folder.

There are a number of ways to share folders in NT. The easiest is to use My Computer or Explorer. To share a folder using Explorer, follow these steps:

1. Open Explorer and browse to the folder you wish to share on the network.

2. Right-click the folder and select Sharing from the context menu.

3. Select Shared As from the Sharing tab of the properties sheet for the folder, as shown in Figure 29.9.

4. Either use the name that NT suggests for the share or enter another name. If your network has MS-DOS or Windows for Workgroups computers, the name must conform to the 8.3 naming conventions. If the network consists only of computers that recognize long filenames, you are free to use a long, descriptive name for the share.

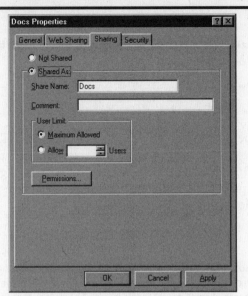

FIGURE 29.9: The Sharing tab of the Folder Properties dialog box

5. Click the Permissions button to set appropriate permissions for the share. Refer to the "Setting Permissions" section earlier in this chapter for more information about permissions.

6. Click OK to close the Permissions dialog box, then click OK again to close the folder properties sheet and create the share.

You can also create shared folders remotely using Server Manager in NT Server. In Server Manager, highlight the server where you wish to create the share and select Computer ➣ Shared Directories. The Shared Directories dialog box allows you to view existing shares or to create new shares. This method of creating shares will require administrator permissions.

PRINTING IN NT

Even though it seems that we take printing for granted, it is one of the most important business tasks. If you doubt that statement, just try turning off your office laser printer for a while and count how many complaints you receive. Unfortunately for most NT users, printing is also one of the least understood functions.

NOTE

For details on network and local printing, including a description of the NT print model, see Chapter 5.

Adding a Printer

It takes a high level of permissions and rights to add a printer to NT. Typically, only the administrator will add a printer, but any member of the Administrators, Print Operators, Server Operators, or Power Users groups has the ability to add a printer to the system. Essentially, what is required is Full Control permission for printing on the NT computer.

NOTE

According to Microsoft, a *printer* is the software and a *print device* is the hardware. A printer is the combination of driver, spooler, and support files that make up the printing software. A print device is the piece of hardware that takes up a portion of your desk. So when we talk about adding a printer, you may rest assured we are talking about adding and configuring the software that controls the hardware.

To add a printer to your NT computer, follow these steps:

1. Select Start ➤ Settings ➤ Printers to open the Printers window.

2. Double-click the Add Printer icon to start the Add Printer Wizard.

3. Follow the prompts of the Wizard to determine the connection to the print device, the make and model of the print device, and the driver to be used.

4. Decide whether the printer will be shared on the network.

5. Click Finish to complete the Wizard and install the printer.

Installing a printer in NT is similar to installing a printer in Windows 95/98. Simply start the Wizard and answer each question in turn. Once the Wizard is finished installing files, it will offer you the chance to print a test page. It is a good idea to print one to verify that the printer is communicating with the print device, but test pages are also useful for troubleshooting the printer later. When you print a test page, you verify that the printer can print in graphics mode (for the Windows logo) and text mode (for the text portion of the page). The text on the page contains a list of all of the details that make up the printer: the driver files, the name of the printer, and its location.

Having a test page printed out correctly tells you that the printer is properly installed; having a test page on hand when you have printer problems gives you a list of all the files to check for corruption.

Sharing a Printer on the Network

Most of the time, you will set up sharing a printer while you are installing it with the Add Printer Wizard, but sometimes you want to share an existing printer. Follow these steps to share a printer that has already been installed:

1. Select Start ➤ Settings ➤ Printers to open the Printers window.

2. Select the printer that you want to share and right-click its icon.

3. From the context menu, select Sharing.

4. On the Sharing tab of the Printer properties sheet, click Shared, as shown in Figure 29.10.

5. Type a name for the shared printer in the Share Name box. This is the name that others will use when connecting to your shared printer on the network.

6. Optionally, you can select the different operating systems to install printer drivers for them as well. This stores the driver for that operating system on the NT computer. When users connect to your shared printer using that operating system, they will automatically download the driver and configure it to match the setting you've given your printer. Microsoft calls this feature "Point and Print." It is only available for NT (all versions and platforms) and Windows 95/98.

Part iv

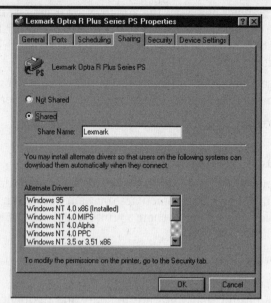

FIGURE 29.10: The Sharing tab of the printer properties sheet

7. Click OK to share the printer. If you opted to support Point and Print, you will be asked for the CD-ROM containing those drivers.

It is possible, and often a good idea, to create multiple printers that refer to the same print device. This enables you to set different properties for each printer and to schedule each printer's available times.

Administering Printers

Once you have installed and shared printers on your NT computer, you will find the need to administer them. As users start printing to your shared printers, you may run into situations where one document becomes much more important than another (like the boss's golf schedule).

Setting Permissions

Printing permissions are similar to share and NTFS permissions in the way they work, though perhaps just a little easier to work with since they don't combine with other types of permissions. Here are the four print permissions:

Full Control   Gives users the ability to print, to control their own and other's documents, to install print drivers, to take ownership of the printer, and to change the printer.

Manage Documents   Allows users to print, to manage their documents and other user's documents, and to clear the queue.

Print   Allows users to print documents on the printer and to manage their own documents. This is the default permission for the Everyone group.

No Access   Prevents access to the printer. Users have no granted permissions and will receive an Access Denied message when they try to connect to the printer.

Print permissions are cumulative, just like share permissions and NTFS permissions. When trying to determine the effective permission for a user, you must evaluate each group that user belongs to and the user's individual permission, if any. Once you have the permissions listed, simply add them together to find the effective permission. Remember that No Access overrides all other permissions.

To set permissions on a shared printer, follow these steps:

1. Open the Printers window.

2. Right-click the desired printer's icon and select Properties from the context menu.

3. Click the Security tab.

4. Click the Permissions button. You will see the dialog box shown in Figure 29.11.

5. Click Add to add new groups or users to the list of permitted accounts. Once you have selected the group or user, set the permission level in the Type of Access list box, then click OK to add the accounts.

6. Click OK to apply the new security settings and close the Printer Permissions dialog box.

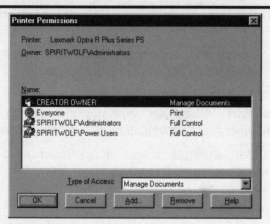

FIGURE 29.11: The Printer Permissions dialog box

Managing the Queue

Managing the queue means organizing the documents waiting in line to be sent to the print device. Remember that other users may be sending documents to your shared printer and you may be printing there also. From time to time, you may have a request to get a document printed as fast as possible. Perhaps it will be an invoice for a customer who is standing there waiting, or maybe it will be an urgent report for your boss.

To manage documents in the printer queue, you must have either the Manage Documents or Full Control permission. To rearrange print jobs in the queue, do the following:

1. Open the Printers window.

2. Double-click the desired printer icon to open the Print Manager window for the printer.

3. Select the document to manage by clicking once on the document name in the list.

4. Select the option you want from the Document menu. You can opt to delete the document by selecting Cancel, or you can Pause, Resume, or Restart the print job.

If you want to print one waiting document ahead of all others in the queue, you must pause all of the other documents. The desired document, being the only one not on pause, will then be free to print. You can also set priorities for each document to determine where it goes in the queue. Document priorities are set from 1 through 99, with 99 being the highest priority. In the queue, the highest priority documents will print first, then the lower priority. By default, document priorities are set to the lowest setting of 1.

TIPS ON TROUBLESHOOTING PRINTERS

Printing is perhaps the single greatest generator of support calls in the average corporate network. Very often, the anguished cry of "I can't print!" can be heard echoing through the halls as the person searches for a support technician worthy of the challenge. Well, that might be a little strong, but people do have a lot of printing issues.

Frequently, the problem is simple—the printer is not plugged in or it's turned off. Ever notice that the manufacturers of print devices are somewhat sadistic in the placement of the power switch? How many of the latest and greatest print devices have easily recognizable power switches placed where you can actually *see* them?

Sometimes the problem is more complex, occurring at the server itself and perhaps involving network issues.

The first place to start in any troubleshooting is with the simplest solutions. Check the cables from the print device to the printer and the power cable. Check *both* ends. Make sure the print device is turned on.

Next, ask yourself (or your customer, if you're providing support) whether this configuration has ever worked before. If the answer is no, then you need to go back and verify the simple things, and this time really look at the cables.

Reinstall the printer driver. Ask if there is an error message when you try to print, and if there is what is the error? Does anything come out on the print device?

Assuming that you have eliminated the simple things, and that the print device is connected and turned on, try printing a test document from Notepad. Notepad is the simplest form of printing you can do in NT. If this works, and another application fails to print, the problem is most likely that other application, or possibly the document you were trying to print.

CONTINUED ➡

Part iv

If the situation is that the queue is "stuck," and nothing at all will print on the print server, the first thing to try (maybe even before checking that the print device is plugged in and turned on) is to restart the Spooler service:

1. Open the Control Panel and double-click Services.

2. Scroll down the list of services until you find Spooler. Click the Spooler service to highlight it.

3. Click the Stop button and click Yes to confirm that you really want to stop the Spooler service.

4. After the service has stopped, click the Start button in the Services window. The Spooler service will restart.

If the documents in the queue do not start printing right after restarting the Spooler, you probably have a corrupted document blocking the queue. In this case, delete the first document in the queue. You may have to restart the Spooler again to make this work, but the queue should start printing immediately after you've deleted the document. If this works, have the user who submitted the offending document try it again. If the queue gets stuck again, have the user open the document in the program he or she used to create it, and use the Save As option to save a new copy of the document. Try the new copy, and it should print fine.

These techniques should resolve the most common printing issues. But if none of them resolve a stuck printer queue, try rebooting the print server. Consider the reboot to be a last-ditch effort before totally reinstalling the print drivers. In some cases, the problem can be resolved by installing a newer printer driver, preferably from the manufacturer of the print device. If you do install a new driver, be sure that it was written for your version of NT and is the correct hardware platform. Installing an Alpha driver on an Intel-compatible print server is not a good idea (and won't work).

EXTENDING NT

NT provides a wide array of features that allow you to perform tasks from the mundane to the phenomenal. But from time to time, you may need a feature that your system is lacking. Or, heaven forbid, you might run afoul of a bug in the operating system (what some people at Microsoft have been overheard calling an "undocumented feature"). This final section in the chapter discusses how to extend the capabilities of NT by adding new features or applying Service Packs.

Adding New Features

Many different vendors offer additional products and services for NT. Microsoft has several available from its Web site. Examples of these services include the following:

Routing and Remote Access Service   RRAS is an update to the Remote Access Service, which also installs advanced network routing support. RRAS (code named "Steelhead" during development) enables NT to compare favorably with hardware-based routers for performance, and it is available as a free download from Microsoft.

Distributed File System Server   Microsoft's Dfs is a service that lets you abstract the entire network from a user's point of view. For users, this means that they can connect to one network share and simply browse through a folder structure in that share to access resources located anywhere on the network. From the administrator's point of view, Dfs is a service that enables you to connect a series of network shares into a virtual file system that features fast access, ease of browsing, and built-in load balancing. The Dfs Server service can be downloaded from Microsoft and must be installed on NT Server 4. NT Server and Workstation 4 both have the Dfs client software built in, as does Windows 98. A Dfs client can be downloaded for Windows 95.

Windows NT Option Pack   The Option Pack includes several different server applications, but mostly it is known for providing Internet Information Server (IIS) 4. The Option Pack turns your mild-mannered NT Server into a powerhouse of Internet services. The Option Pack also includes the Microsoft Transaction Server (MTS) and the Microsoft Message Queue (MSMQ), both of which facilitate the development of transaction-based processing applications for data-aware Web sites and distributed applications.

Internet Protocol v6   IP6 is set to become the next generation of TCP/IP protocols sometime around the turn of the century. At the time of this writing, Microsoft has not revealed specific plans to provide support for this new protocol for NT 4, but word has it that it will be both a download for NT 4 and an integrated feature in Windows 2000. IP6 will provide a new addressing scheme that should ensure that we will have plenty of IP addresses well into the next century.

Each of these additions to NT's feature lineup can be easily installed either as services or as an individual program in NT Server and Workstation.

Installing Service Packs

We have yet to see a bug-free piece of programming, with the possible exception of computer viruses, which do exactly what they are intended to do. That being said, what do you do when you find some of the bugs in NT? Conventional wisdom says, "If it ain't broke, don't fix it." This is a good approach to take with something as complex as NT. What we're saying is, just because someone says there's a bug in NT doesn't mean that *you* have to fix it. If the bug doesn't cause you any problems, don't worry about it.

Bugs in software are really only a problem when they prevent you from doing something you need to do or when they cause unexpected and unpleasant effects. This section talks about how to go about updating NT with the latest bug-fixes from Microsoft and how to use them wisely.

What Is a Service Pack?

Service Packs are collections of patches and enhancements to NT. The lifespan of a Service Pack begins with customer calls to Microsoft Technical Support (MTS). When an MTS Support Engineer determines that the customer's issue arises from a bug in the NT code, the support person files a bug report for development to review. If the issue is urgent enough, a team of support professionals (each of whom has pretty extensive programming skills) takes over poring through the source code of NT to find out where the bug is caused. Then they write a patch for the bug. When it has been tested and found to work without blowing up some other piece of the operating system, the patch is collected with all the other patches, given an install program, and released as a Service Pack. It is not uncommon to see a new Service Pack for NT about every six months, though this can vary.

Microsoft also releases new features for the operating system as they are developed and frequently includes these in Service Packs as well. Service Packs will often contain changes to the Registry to compensate for bugs, control new features, or simply run things more efficiently. These changes to the Registry can often be the source of problems for some users who don't use Service Packs correctly.

Service Packs have specific versions, and they are intended for use only on the version of NT for which they were written. The good news is that Service Packs are inclusive; that is to say, they include all of the earlier versions in them. You only have to install the latest Service Pack to get all of the earlier Service Packs.

When Should I Install a Service Pack?

Unless you find that you are having a problem with NT that the latest Service Pack is known to fix, don't install the Service Pack. Even in the best light possible, Service Packs constitute a major change to the operating system. These changes should be avoided when possible and prepared for when they can't be avoided.

Some of the server applications that you may want to install in NT will require a specific version of Service Pack in order to run correctly. In this case, you don't have much choice, but you can prepare for the installation and minimize the chance of something going wrong. To summarize, these are the times when you should install a Service Pack:

When required by software   If a new application that you really want to run requires a certain level of Service Pack, then you will need to install that Service Pack or higher. Often the application will provide the Service Pack right on the CD-ROM.

When you are experiencing a specific problem   If you have one of the bugs listed as fixed in the Service Pack, you should install the latest Service Pack.

When you have tried everything else   If you've eliminated every other possibility in troubleshooting a problem, it may be worth the effort to install the Service Pack. This has been known to repair some very odd problems in NT. New bugs in NT are not very common. If you have a problem with NT, chances are that someone else has had the same problem before.

Part iv

Service Packs can be obtained in a variety of ways. They can be purchased on CD-ROM directly from Microsoft for a minimal charge (usually around $14, but this may change if the cost of production changes), or they can be downloaded for free from Microsoft's Web site. You may also receive the Service Pack on the installation media for an application. The Service Pack can be installed on either an NT Workstation or Server computer without any problems, because one Service Pack applies to both versions of NT.

When you install the Service Pack, you will probably notice that it gives you the option of backing up the files that will be replaced so you can uninstall the Service Pack if necessary. We recommend doing that if you have the hard disk space. In any case, you should have a newly made Emergency Repair Disk before applying the Service Pack at the very least, and preferably a full tape backup of your entire system, just in case. When evaluating a Service Pack in a network environment, install it on a test machine before deciding to roll out the Service Pack to the entire network.

One last caution: When you install a service, protocol, or other major component in NT, you should always be careful to reapply the Service Pack *before* rebooting the computer. Yes, NT will tell you that you must reboot in order for the changes to take effect, but it might be too late by then. Remember that we said that Service Packs make changes to the Registry? If the Registry is looking for a Service Pack version of a file and finds the original version instead, it may cause a blue screen error. Some of the blue screens caused in this fashion are almost impossible to recover from. If in doubt, read the setup release notes for the Service Pack; they will usually caution you where necessary.

What's Next?

This chapter reviewed the most common and important tasks in NT, ranging from installing NT itself to installing Service Packs. The next and final chapter in this book is a reference to NT commands, including their functions and syntax.

Chapter 30
COMMAND REFERENCE

I f you've used a graphical operating system long enough, you've no doubt encountered tasks that were easier to do from a command prompt. Or perhaps you have only recently started using Windows NT after using Unix for years. If so, you are very likely more comfortable at a plain, no-nonsense command prompt. Maybe you even detest these operating systems that dedicate so many CPU cycles to displaying pretty fluff, and just want to get down to work. Whatever your needs or reasons, this is the chapter for you.

In this chapter we'll take a close look at the common and not-so-common commands that you will use from the NT command prompt. It's true that you can accomplish nearly every task from the command prompt that you can from the GUI. It's also true that there are things that can be done only from one or the other. To be a master of NT, you should become comfortable with the command prompt.

To DOS or Not to DOS

Before we go any farther, we need to settle an old misconception. There is no MS-DOS in NT. There is *virtual DOS*, but that's a whole different animal. If you were to run a "DOS prompt," you would click on a shortcut (or use the Run command on the Start menu) to execute COMMAND.COM, which was the MS-DOS command interpreter and one of the core files that created MS-DOS. There just happens to be a version of COMMAND .COM provided in Windows, but if you run it, you will actually be starting a Virtual DOS Machine (VDM) and running *NT DOS*.

The command prompt that we will be talking about in this chapter is CMD.EXE, the 32-bit command-line interface to NT. This program is the Command Prompt you will find on the Start menu. You can also start CMD.EXE by selecting Start ➤ Run, typing in **CMD.EXE** in the Run dialog box, and clicking OK.

There is more than just a desire to nit-pick in pointing this out. The two command lines will operate differently in some important ways. Many of the commands in this chapter are 32-bit programs that will not run correctly in a VDM. The most common problems you will encounter involve long filenames. The VDM interface will usually (but not always) require you to place quotation marks around long filenames that include spaces. What's even more fun is that this behavior varies with each command. It's recommended that you always use CMD.EXE when administering NT from a command prompt. Leave COMMAND.COM to the 16-bit programs.

NT Command Summary

NT 4 supports most operations from the command line as well as the graphical interface. The command line of NT, CMD.EXE, supports nearly all of the commands available in MS-DOS 5. Learning to use these commands will add to your mastery of NT 4.

The remainder of this chapter provides a listing of the commands available in NT 4. Table 30.1 shows the commands that are represented by symbols, and an alphabetical listing of the commands follows it.

NOTE

The commands available in MS-DOS 5 will usually run in NT with the same functionality, and most are not listed here, since they are documented elsewhere. For complete details on the command syntax and available switches, refer to online help in NT.

TABLE 30.1: Command Symbols in NT

Symbol	Description	Syntax
>	Sends the output of a command to a file, program, or device that accepts command-line input	command1 > command2 command1 > lpt1:
<	Accepts input from another program or command and redirects it to the first command	command1 < command2
>>	Appends the output of a command to the end of a file without deleting any information from the file	command1 >> filename.txt
|	Redirects information to a *filter* command, such as more, sort, or find	command | filter
&	Allows you to group multiple commands for execution on one line	command1 & command2 & command3
^	Preceding a command symbol, forces the command line to see the character as text and to ignore its special meaning	command ^symbol
&&	Groups commands conditionally; the second command executes only if the preceding command was successful	command1 && command2
||	Groups commands conditionally; the second command executes only if the preceding command fails	command1 || command2

Append

The append command allows you to add another directory to the one you are working with. In effect, the data files in the appended directory appear to be in the same directory as the current directory. If you use the append command by itself, with no parameters, it will cancel any existing append operations on the current directory.

```
append [;] [[drive:]path[;...]] [/x:{on | off}][/path:{on | off}] [/e]
```

Arp

The arp command allows you to view and modify the arp cache. The Address Resolution Protocol (ARP) is used to resolve IP addresses to unique hardware addresses in TCP/IP networking.

```
arp -a [ip_addr] [-N [if_addr]]
arp -d ip_addr [if_addr]
arp -s ip_addr mac_addr [if_addr]
```

Assoc

The assoc command allows you to directly modify the program associations for each file extension.

```
assoc [.ext[=[filetype]]]
```

At

The at command schedules commands and programs to run on a computer at a specified time and date. The Schedule service must be running to use the at command.

```
at [\\computername] [[id] [/delete [/yes]]
at [\\computername] time [/interactive] [/every:date[,...] | /next:date[,...]] "command".
```

Attrib

The attrib command displays, sets, or removes the read-only, archive, system, and hidden attributes assigned to files or directories.

```
attrib [+r|-r] [+a|-a] [+s|-s] [+h|-h][[drive:][path] filename] [/s]
```

Backup

The backup command backs up one or more files from one disk onto another. You can back up files onto either a hard disk or floppy disk(s). Files can also be backed up from one floppy disk onto another, even if the disks have different numbers of sides or sectors. NT displays the name of each file it backs up.

```
backup source destination-drive: [/s] [/m] [/a][/f[:size
    ]] [/d:date [/t:time]][/l[:[drive:][path]logfile]]
```

Buffers

NT and the MS-DOS subsystem do not use the buffers command. It is provided only for compatibility with programs specifically written for MS-DOS. The command syntax is exactly as it is in MS-DOS 5.

Cacls

The calcs command displays or modifies access control lists (ACLs) of files.

```
cacls filename [/t] [/e] [/c] [/g user:perm] [/r user [...]]
    [/p user:perm [...]] [/d user [...]]
```

Call

The call command calls one batch program from another without causing the parent batch program to stop.

```
call [drive:][path] filename [batch-parameters]
```

Chcp

The chcp command displays the number of the active console code page or changes the active console code page that NT is to use for the console.

```
chcp [nnn]
```

Available code pages include:

437	United States
850	Multilingual (Latin I)
852	Slavic (Latin II)

855	Cyrillic (Russian)
857	Turkish
860	Portuguese
861	Icelandic
863	Canadian-French
865	Nordic
866	Russian
869	Modern Greek

NOTE

Only the OEM code page installed with NT will display correctly in a command prompt window using Raster fonts. Other code pages will display correctly in full-screen mode or command prompt windows that are using TrueType fonts.

Chdir or Cd

The chdir or cd command displays the name of the current directory or changes the current directory.

```
chdir [/d] [drive:][path] [..]
cd [/d] [drive:][path] [..]
```

Note that the /d switch allows you to change the drive and the directory in one command.

Chkdsk

The chkdsk command creates and displays a status report for a disk based on the file system used. Chkdsk also lists and corrects errors on the disk. If chkdsk cannot lock the drive, it will offer to check it the next time the computer reboots.

To issue the chkdsk command on a fixed disk, you must be a member of the Administrators group.

```
chkdsk [drive:][[path] filename] [/f] [/v] [/r]
```

Including the /f switch instructs chkdsk to correct any problems found.

Cls

The cls (Clear Screen) command can be used to clear the screen of all current output, leaving only a prompt and cursor in the upper-left corner of the command prompt window.

    cls

Color

The color command sets the default console foreground and background colors.

    color

If no argument is given, this command restores the color to what it was when CMD.EXE started.

    color bf

With these arguments, the command specifies color attributes of console output. *b* is a hex digit that sets the background color; *f* sets the foreground. *b* and *f* can have the following values:

0	Black
1	Blue
2	Green
3	Aqua
4	Red
5	Purple
6	Yellow
7	White
8	Gray
9	Light blue
A	Light green
B	Light aqua
C	Light red

D	Light purple
E	Light yellow
F	Bright white

If the foreground and background values are the same, `color` returns ERRORLEVEL 1.

Comp

The `comp` command compares the contents of two files or sets of files byte by byte. Comp can compare files on the same drive or on different drives, in the same directory or in different directories. As `comp` compares the files, it displays their locations and filenames.

```
comp [data1] [data2] [/d] [/a] [/l] [/n=number] [/c]
```

Compact

The `compact` command displays and alters the compression of files or directories

```
compact [/c] [/u] [/s] [/i] [/f] [/l] filename
```

Convert

The `convert` command converts FAT volumes to NTFS. You cannot convert the current drive. If `convert` cannot lock the drive, it will offer to convert it the next time the computer reboots.

```
convert [drive:] /fs:ntfs [/v] [/nametable:filename]
```

Copy

The `copy` command copies one or more files to another location. This command can also be used to combine files. When more than one file is copied, NT displays each filename as the file is copied.

```
copy [/a|/b] source [/a|/b] [+ source [/a|/b] [+ ...]]
     [destination [/a|/b]] [/v] [/n] [/z]
```

Date

The `date` command displays the date or allows you to change the date from your terminal or from a batch program.

```
date [mm-dd-yy]
```

Del

The del command deletes specified files.

```
del [drive:][path] filename [; ...] [/p] [/f] [/s] [/q]
    [/a[:attributes]]
```

Dir

The dir command displays a list of a directory's files and subdirectories.

```
dir [drive:][path][filename] [; ...] [/p] [/w] [/d] [/a[[:]
attributes]][/o[[:]sortorder]] [/t[[:]timefield]] [/s] [/b]
    [/l] [/n] [/x]
```

Diskcomp

The diskcomp command compares the contents of two floppy disks.

```
diskcomp [drive1: [drive2:]]
```

Diskcopy

The diskcopy command copies the contents of the floppy disk in the source drive to a formatted or unformatted floppy disk in the destination drive.

```
diskcopy [drive1: [drive2:]] [/v]
```

Diskperf

The diskperf command starts and stops system disk performance counters.

```
diskperf [-y|-n] [\\computername]
```

Doskey

The doskey command calls the Doskey program, which recalls NT commands, edits command lines, and creates macros.

```
doskey [/reinstall] [/listsize=size] [/macros:[all | exename]
    [/history] [/insert|/overstrike] [/exename=exename]
    [/macrofile=filename] [macroname=[text]]
```

Dosonly

The `dosonly` command prevents you from starting anything but 16-bit MS-DOS applications from the `COMMAND.COM` prompt.

```
dosonly
```

Echo

The `echo` command turns the command echoing feature on or off, or displays a message.

```
echo [on | off] [message]
```

Echoconfig

The `echoconfig` command is used to turn on the display of entries in the `CONFIG.NT` file. If this command is present, each line in `CONFIG.NT` will be displayed as it is executed.

```
echoconfig
```

Edit

The `edit` command starts MS-DOS Editor, which creates and changes ASCII text files.

```
edit [[drive:][path] filename] [/b] [/g] [/h] [/nohi]
```

WARNING

In order for the `edit` command to work, the file QBASIC.EXE must be present in the same folder as EDIT.COM.

Endlocal

The `endlocal` command is the complement to `setlocal`. It turns off the localization of environment settings.

```
endlocal
```

Erase

`Erase` is another name for the delete command (`del`).

```
erase [drive:][path] filename [; ...] [/p] [/f] [/s] [/q]
    [/a[:attributes]]
```

Exit

The `exit` command can be used to quit either `CMD.EXE` or `COMMAND.COM` sessions.

```
exit
```

Expand

The `expand` command expands one or more compressed files. This command is used to retrieve compressed files from distribution disks.

```
expand [-r] source [destination]
```

Fc

The `fc` command compares two files and displays the differences between them.

```
fc [/a] [/b] [/c] [/l] [/lbn] [/n] [/t] [/u] [/w] [/nnnn]
    [drive1:] [path1]filename1 [drive2:][path2]filename2
```

Find

The `find` command searches for a specific string of text in a file or files. After searching the specified files, `find` displays any lines of text that contain the specified string.

```
find [/v] [/c] [/n] [/i] "string" [[drive:][path]file-
    name[...]]
```

Findstr

The `findstr` command searches for strings in files using literal text or regular expressions. See the online help in NT for all of the wildcards that can be used with `findstr`.

```
findstr [/b] [/e] [/l] [/c:string] [/r] [/s] [/i] [/x] [/v]
    [/n] [/m] [/o] [/g:file] [/f:file] strings files
```

Finger

The `finger` command displays information about a user on a specified system running the Finger service. Output varies based on the remote system. This command is available only if the TCP/IP protocol has been installed.

```
finger [-l] [user]@computer [...]
```

For

The for command runs a specified command for each file in a set of files. You can use the for command within a batch program or directly from the command prompt. To use for in a batch program, use the following syntax:

```
for %%variable in (set) do command [command-parameters]
```

To use for from the command prompt, use the following syntax:

```
for %variable in (set) do command [command-parameters]
```

Forcedos

The forcedos command starts the specified program in the MS-DOS subsystem. This command is necessary only for those MS-DOS programs not recognized as such by NT.

```
forcedos [/d directory] filename [parameters]
```

Format

The format command formats the disk in the specified drive to accept NT files. You must be a member of the Administrators group to format a hard drive.

```
format drive: [/fs:file-system] [/v[:label]] [/a:unitsize]
    [/q] [/f:size] [/t:tracks /n:sectors] [/1] [/4] [/8]
```

Ftp

The ftp command transfers files to and from a computer running an FTP server service (also called a daemon). Ftp can be used interactively. This command is available only if the TCP/IP protocol has been installed.

```
ftp [-v] [-d] [-i] [-n] [-g] [-s:filename] [-a] [-w:window-
    size] [computer]
```

Ftype

The ftype command displays or modifies file types used in file extension associations.

```
ftype [filetype[=[command]]]
```

Goto

The `goto` command directs NT within a batch program to a line identified by a label. When NT finds the label, it processes the commands beginning on the next line.

    goto label

Graftabl

The `graftabl` command enables NT to display the extended characters of a specified code page in full-screen mode. Extended characters will not display in window mode.

    graftabl [xxx] [/status]

xxx specifies the code page that you want NT to modify in graphics mode. The following list shows each valid code-page identification number and its country or language:

437	United States
850	Multilingual (Latin I)
852	Slavic (Latin II)
855	Cyrillic (Russian)
857	Turkish
860	Portuguese
861	Icelandic
863	Canadian-French
865	Nordic
866	Russian
869	Modern Greek

Help

The `help` command displays online help for a command.

    help commandname

As an alternative, type:

    commandname /?

Hostname

If TCP/IP is installed on the computer, the hostname command displays the configured host name of the computer.

```
hostname
```

If

The if command performs conditional processing in batch programs. If the condition specified in an if command is true, NT carries out the command that follows the condition. If the condition is false, NT ignores the command.

```
if [not] errorlevel number command
if [not] string1==string2 command
if [not] exist filename command
```

Install

The install command loads a memory-resident program into memory.

```
install=[drive:][path] filename [command-parameters]
```

Ipconfig

The ipconfig command is a diagnostic tool that displays all (using the /all switch) current TCP/IP network configuration values. This command is of particular use on systems running the Dynamic Host Configuration Protocol (DHCP), allowing users to determine which TCP/IP configuration values have been configured by DHCP.

```
ipconfig [/all | /renew [adapter] | /release [adapter]]
```

Ipxroute

The ipxroute command displays and modifies information about the routing tables used by the IPX protocol. The command has different options for IPX routing and for source routing. Separate all options with spaces.

```
ipxroute servers [/type=x]
ipxroute stats [/show] [/clear]
ipxroute table
```

Keyb

The keyb command starts the Keyb program, which configures a keyboard for a specific language. Use keyb to configure a keyboard for a language other than United States English.

```
keyb [xx[,[yyy][,[drive:][path] filename]]] [/e] [/id:nnn]
```

In your CONFIG.NT file, use the following syntax:

```
install=[[drive:]path]keyb.com [xx[,[yyy][,[drive:][path]
    filename]]] [/e] [/id:nnn]
```

Label

The label command creates, changes, or deletes the volume label (name) of a disk. NT displays the volume label as part of the directory listing. If a volume serial number exists, NT displays this number as well.

```
label [drive:][label]
```

Loadfix

The loadfix command ensures that a program is loaded above the first 64KB of conventional memory, and runs the program.

```
loadfix [drive:][path] filename [program-parameters]
```

Lpq

This diagnostic utility is used to obtain the status of a print queue on a computer running the Line Printer Daemon (LPD) server. This command is only available if you are using the TCP/IP protocol.

```
lpq -SServer -PPrinter [-1]
```

Lpr

This connectivity utility is used to print a file to a computer running an LPD server. This command is only available if you are using the TCP/IP protocol.

```
lpr -SServer -PPrinter [-CClass] [-JJobname] [-O option]
    filename
```

Mem

The mem command displays information about allocated memory areas, free memory areas, and programs that are currently loaded into memory in the MS-DOS subsystem.

```
mem [/program|/debug|/classify]
```

Mkdir or Md

The mkdir or md command creates a directory or subdirectory.

```
mkdir [drive:]path
md [drive:]path
```

More

The more command displays one screen of output at a time. This command is commonly used to view long files. Enabling extended features activates commands that control the display.

```
commandname | more [/e] [/c] [/p] [/s] [/tn] [+n]
more [/e] [/c] [/p] [/s] [/tn] [+n] < [drive:] [path]
    filename
more [/e] [/c] [/p] [/s] [/tn] [+n] files
```

Move

The move command moves one or more files from one directory to the specified directory.

```
move [source] [target]
```

Nbtstat

This diagnostic command displays protocol statistics and current TCP/IP connections using NBT (NetBIOS over TCP/IP). This command is available only if the TCP/IP protocol has been installed.

```
nbtstat [-a remotename] [-A IP address] [-c] [-n] [-R] [-r]
    [-S] [-s] [interval]
```

Netstat

The `netstat` command displays protocol statistics and current TCP/IP network connections. This command is available only if the TCP/IP protocol has been installed.

```
netstat [-a] [-e] [-n] [-s] [-p protocol] [-r] [interval]
```

Net

The following sections document the full syntax of the `net` command because it is so important for the normal operation of NT.

Net Accounts

Can be used to view or modify the user accounts database on an NT computer or domain controller. You must have the NetLogon service running on the target computer.

```
net accounts [/forcelogoff:{minutes | no}] [/minpwlen:length]
    [/maxpwage:{days | unlimited}] [/minpwage:days]
    [/uniquepw:number] [/domain]
```

To force a full synchronization of the domain database, use the following:

```
net accounts [/sync] [/domain]
```

Net Computer

Adds or removes computers from the domain database. This command is available only on computers running NT Server.

```
net computer \\computername {/add | /del}
```

Net Config

Views the configurable services that are running or displays and modifies settings for a service.

```
net config [service [options]]
```

Net Config Server

Views or modifies settings for the Server service while the service is running.

```
net config server [/autodisconnect:time] [/srvcomment:"text
    "] [/hidden:{yes | no}]
```

Net Config Workstation

Views or modifies settings for the Workstation service while it is running.

```
net config workstation [/charcount:bytes] [/chartime:msec]
    [/charwait:sec]
```

Net Continue

Resumes paused services.

```
net continue servicename
```

Net File

Displays the names of all open files in shared folders on a server and the number of file locks, if any, on each file. This command can also close individual shared files and remove file locks.

```
net file [id [/close]]
```

Net Group

Adds, views, or modifies *global* groups in NT Server domain user account databases. This command is available for use only on NT domains.

```
net group [groupname [/comment:"text"]] [/domain]
net group groupname {/add [/comment:"text"] | /delete}
    [/domain]
net group groupname username[ ...] {/add | /delete} [/domain]
```

Net Help

Provides either a list of network commands or topics you can get help with. It also can provide help with a specific command or topic.

```
net help [commandname]
net commandname {/help | /?}
```

Net Helpmsg

Provides help information for NT network error messages.

```
net helpmsg message#
```

Net Localgroup

Views, adds, and modifies local groups on NT computers, both NT Server and NT Workstation.

```
net localgroup [groupname [/comment:"text"]] [/domain]
```

```
net localgroup groupname {/add [/comment:"text"] | /delete}
    [/domain]
net localgroup groupname name [ ...] {/add | /delete}
    [/domain]
```

Net Name

Displays and modifies the list of names (or aliases) the computer will accept messages for. The Messenger service must be running to use net name.

```
net name [name [/add | /delete]]
```

Net Pause

Pauses running NT services.

```
net pause servicename
```

Refer to the list of net start commands in Table 30.2 for applicable service names. Note that any service name that contains spaces must be enclosed in quotation marks for the command to work correctly.

Net Print

Displays and controls print jobs and available printer queues on the local or a remote computer.

```
net print \\computername\sharename
net print [\\computername] job# [/hold | /release | /delete]
```

Net Send

Can be used to send messages to individual users or computers, to a group name, or to an entire domain. The Messenger service must be running to receive messages.

```
net send {name | * | /domain[:name] | /users} message
```

Net Session

Displays or terminates the sessions between a local computer and the clients connected to it.

```
net session [\\computername] [/delete]
```

Net Share

Views, creates, and deletes shared resources on the local computer.

```
net share sharename
```

```
net share sharename=drive:path [/users:number | /unlimited]
    [/remark:"text"]
net share sharename [/users:number | unlimited]
    [/remark:"text"]
net share {sharename | drive:path} /delete
```

Net Start

Can display the currently running services on an NT computer as well as starting them if they are not running.

```
net start [servicename]
```

Refer to the list of **net start** commands in Table 30.2 for applicable service names. Note that any service name that contains spaces must be enclosed in quotation marks for the command to work correctly.

TABLE 30.2: Net Start Commands

COMMAND	DESCRIPTION
net start alerter	Starts the Alerter service, which is responsible for generating system alerts.
net start "client service for netware"	Starts the Client Services for NetWare on an NT Workstation computer.
net start "clipbook server"	Starts the ClipBook Server service.
net start "computer browser"	Starts the Computer Browser service, which supports browsing other computers on the network and announcing shared resources to the Browse List for the local network segment.
net start "dhcp client"	Starts the DHCP Client service, which is responsible for obtaining an IP address through the Dynamic Host Configuration Protocol (DHCP). Addresses are obtained during the client boot process.
net start "directory replicator"	Starts the Directory Replicator service that provides the mechanism for transferring data between computers. Used mostly between NT domain controllers for replicating logon scripts and policy files.
net start eventlog	Starts the Eventlog service that allows Event Viewer to gather and record system, application, and security log events.
net start "File Server for Macintosh"	Starts the Services for Macintosh to provide file support for Macintosh clients. Only available if the Services for Macintosh have been installed.

CONTINUED ➤

TABLE 30.2 continued: Net Start Commands

COMMAND	DESCRIPTION
net start "ftp publishing service"	Starts the FTP Publishing Service of Internet Information Server (IIS). Only available if IIS has been installed.
net start "gateway service for netware"	Starts the Gateway Service for NetWare on NT Server computers that interact with Novell NetWare.
net start lpdsvc	Starts the Line Printer Daemon service to host TCP/IP printing for UNIX hosts.
net start messenger	Starts the Messenger service, which provides support for pop-up messages throughout the network for users and computers.
net start "microsoft dhcp server"	Starts the DHCP Server service on an NT Server.
net start "net logon"	Starts the Net Logon service, which is responsible for logging users onto an NT domain, synchronizing the domain user database, and establishing and maintaining trusts between domains.
net start "network dde"	Starts the NetDDE service on NT.
net start "network dde dsdm"	Starts the NetDDE Server service.
net start "network monitor agent"	Starts the Network Monitor Agent service so the NT computer can assist in gathering data for another computer running Network Monitor (a network analyzer) or so the local computer can run Network Monitor.
net start "nt lm security support provider"	Starts the NT LM Security Support Provider service. Only available if the NT LM Security Support Provider has been installed.
net start "print server for macintosh"	Starts the Print Server for Macintosh service, permitting printing from Macintosh computers. Only available on computers running NT Server with Services for Macintosh installed.
net start remoteboot	Starts the Remoteboot service, permitting computers on the network to load their operating system from the server. Only available on computers running NT Server that have been configured for the Remoteboot service.
net start "remote access connection manager"	Starts the Remote Access Connection Manager service. Only available if Remote Access has been installed.
net start "remote access isnsap service"	Starts the Remote Access ISNSAP service. Only available if Remote Access has been installed.

Part iv

CONTINUED ➡

TABLE 30.2 continued: Net Start Commands

COMMAND	DESCRIPTION
net start "remote access server"	Starts the Remote Access Server service. Only available if Remote Access has been installed.
net start "remote procedure call (rpc) locator"	Starts the Remote Procedure Call (RPC) Locator service, which is the RPC name service for NT. The RPC Locator manages the RPC name service database. The server side of a distributed application registers its availability with the RPC Locator service. The client side of that same distributed application queries the Locator service to find available compatible server applications.
net start "remote procedure call (rpc) service"	Starts the RPC service, which is the RPC subsystem for NT.
net start schedule	Starts the Schedule service, which allows a computer to run programs or batch files at a specified time with the at command.
net start server	Starts the Server service, which provides the ability to share folders and printers across a network.
net start "simple tcp/ip services"	Starts the Simple TCP/IP Services service. Only available if TCP/IP and the Simple TCP/IP Services have been installed. The Simple TCP/IP Services include functions like the Character Generator, Daytime, and Quote of the Day normally found on UNIX systems.
net start snmp	Starts the SNMP service, which allows a server to report its current status to a SNMP management system on a TCP/IP network. Only available if TCP/IP and SNMP have been installed.
net start spooler	Starts the Spooler service, which provides the temporary storage for print jobs.
net start "tcp/ip netbios helper"	Enables the NetBIOS over TCP (NetBT) service. Only available if TCP/IP has been installed.
net start ups	Starts the Uninterruptible Power Supply (UPS) service. If this service won't start, check the polarity settings for the notification signals in the Control Panel UPS applet.
net start "windows internet name service"	Starts the Windows Internet Name Service (WINS), which provides dynamic NetBIOS name-to-IP address resolution for TCP/IP networking. Only available on NT Servers if both TCP/IP and WINS have been installed.
net start workstation	Starts the Workstation service, which is NT's network client redirector. This service allows NT to access network resources.

Net Statistics

Displays the statistics log for the local Workstation or Server service.

```
net statistics [workstation | server]
```

If no switches are added to the command, all of the services for which statistics can be displayed will be listed.

Net Stop

Allows you to stop an NT service from the command line. Its usage is identical to the net start commands listed in Table 30.2.

```
net stop servicename
```

Remember that all services that have spaces in their names must be enclosed in quotation marks for the command to work correctly.

Net Time

Synchronizes the computer's clock with that of another computer or domain. The /set switch allows you to synchronize your computer's system clock with another computer's clock on the network. Used without the /set option, net time displays the time for another computer or domain.

```
net time [\\computername | /domain[:name]] [/set]
```

Net Use

Connects a computer to or disconnects a computer from a shared resource, or displays information about computer connections. The command also controls persistent net connections.

```
net use [devicename | *] [\\computername\sharename[\volume]]
    [password | *]] [/user:[domainname\][username] [[/delete]
    | [/persistent:{yes | no}]]
net use devicename [/home[password | *]] [/delete:{yes | no}]
net use [/persistent:{yes | no}]
```

Devicename is the local drive letter you will assign to the mapping.

Part iv

Net User

Adds or modifies user accounts or displays user account information for both NT Workstation and Server.

```
net user [username [password | *] [options]] [/domain]
net user username {password | *} /add [options] [
    /domain]
net user username [/delete] [/domain]
```

Net View

Displays the browse list of domains, computers, or resources being shared by a specified computer.

```
net view [\\computername | /domain[:domainname]]
net view /network:nw [\\computername]
```

The /network:nw switch allows you to display server information for a NetWare network if you have the Client Services for NetWare or Gateway Services for NetWare installed.

Nslookup

This diagnostic tool displays information from Domain Name System (DNS) name servers. Before using this tool, you should be familiar with how DNS works. Nslookup is available only if the TCP/IP protocol has been installed.

```
nslookup [-option ...] [computer-to-find | - [server]]
```

Nslookup has two modes: interactive and noninteractive. If you only need to look up a single piece of data, use noninteractive mode. For the first argument, type the name or IP address of the computer to be looked up. For the second argument, type the name or IP address of a DNS name server. If you omit the second argument, the default DNS name server will be used.

If you need to look up more than one piece of data, you can use interactive mode. Type a hyphen (-) for the first argument and the name or IP address of a DNS name server for the second argument. If you omit both arguments, the default DNS name server will be used.

Ntbooks

The ntbooks command accesses online NT manuals. If they have been opened before, the path will be remembered. If not, you will be prompted for the path to the Online Books on the CD-ROM.

```
ntbooks [/s] [/w] [/n:path]
```

Ntcmdprompt

The ntcmdprompt command runs the NT command interpreter, CMD.EXE, rather than COMMAND.COM after running a TSR or after starting the command prompt from within an MS-DOS application.

```
ntcmdprompt
```

Path

The path command sets a search path for executable files. NT uses the path command to search for executable files in the directories you specify. By default, the search path is the current directory only.

```
path [[drive:]path[;...]] [%path%]
```

Pause

The pause command inserts a pause in the execution of a batch file, then displays the message "Press any key to continue."

```
pause
```

Pentnt

The pentnt command detects the floating-point division error, when present, in the Pentium chip, disables floating-point hardware, and turns on floating-point emulation.

```
pentnt [-c] [-f] [-o] [-?|-h]
```

Ping

The ping command verifies connections to a remote computer or computers. This command is available only if the TCP/IP protocol has been installed.

```
ping [-t] [-a] [-n count] [-l length] [-f] [-i ttl] [-v tos]
     [-r count] [-s count] [[-j computer-list] | [-k computer-
     list]] [-w timeout] destination-list
```

Popd

The popd command changes to the directory stored by the pushd command. Popd can be used only once to change directories; the buffer is cleared after the first use.

```
popd
```

Portuas

The portuas command merges a LAN Manager 2.x user accounts database into an existing NT user accounts database.

```
portuas -f filename [-u username] [-v] [/codepage codepage]
    [/log filename]
```

Print

The print command prints a text file while you are using other NT commands. This command can print in the background if you have an output device connected to one of your system's serial or parallel ports.

```
print [/d:device] [drive:][path] filename[ ...]
```

Prompt

The prompt command changes the NT command prompt. You can customize the command prompt to display any text you want, including such information as the name of the current directory, the time and date, and the NT version number.

```
prompt [text]
```

Pushd

The pushd command stores the current directory for use by the popd command, then changes to the specified directory.

```
pushd [path | ..]
```

Qbasic

The qbasic command can be used to write and run programs in the Basic language. This program is also necessary to run the EDIT.COM editor.

```
qbasic [/b] [/editor] [/g] [/h] [/mbf] [/nohi]
    [[/run][drive:][path] filename]
```

Rcp

The rcp (Remote Copy) command is used to copy files from an NT computer to one running the Remote Shell Daemon (RSHD). Typically, this command is used to copy files from one Unix computer to another without first downloading the file to the NT computer.

```
rcp [-a] [-b] [-h] [-r] source1, source2 … sourceN destination
```

Recover

The recover command attempts to recover readable information from corrupted data files. Any data held in bad sectors is lost. The recovery process is conducted on a sector-by-sector basis.

```
recover [drive:]]path] filename
```

Rem

The rem command allows you to insert comments into configuration files like SYSTEM.INI and CONFIG.NT, and also into user-defined batch files.

```
rem [comment]
```

Rename or Ren

The rename or ren command allows you to change the name of a file or directory, or even multiple files in one operation. It will not, however, allow you to perform the operation on multiple drives or network locations.

```
rename [drive:][path] filename1 filename2
ren [drive:][path] filename1 filename2
```

Replace

The replace command is used to overwrite files in a destination directory with files of the same name. It can also provide unique filenames to the destination folder.

```
replace [drive1:][path1] filename [drive2:][path2] [/a] [/p]
   [/r] [/w]
replace [drive1:][path1] filename [drive2:][path2] [/p] [/r]
   [/s] [/w] [/u]
```

Restore

The `restore` command restores files that were backed up by using the MS-DOS `backup` command.

```
restore drive1: drive2:[path[filename]] [/s] [/p] [/b:date]
    [/a:date] [/e:time] [/l:time] [/m] [/n] [/d]
```

Rexec

The `rexec` command executes commands on remote computers running the REXEC service. `Rexec` authenticates the username on the remote computer before executing the specified command. `Rexec` is typically used only on Unix computers where the user has a configured account and has been granted permissions. This command is available only if the TCP/IP protocol has been installed.

```
rexec computer [-l username] [-n] command
```

Rmdir or Rd

The `rmdir` or `rd` command removes an existing directory, provided the directory is already empty. All files and subdirectories must be removed prior to using the `rmdir` command.

```
rmdir [drive:]path [/s]
rd [drive:]path [/s]
```

Route

This command allows you to view and modify the routing table for the TCP/IP protocol (if installed). It is typically used only on multihomed computers (computers with more than one network interface) that are acting as routers.

```
route [-f] [-p] [command [destination] [mask subnetmask]
[gateway] [metric costmetric]]
```

Available commands for `route` include the following:

`print`	Prints a route
`add`	Adds a route
`delete`	Deletes a route
`change`	Modifies an existing route

Rsh

The rsh (Remote Shell) command is used to run commands on a remote computer that is running the Remote Shell Daemon (RSHD). The user must have configured permissions to use this command on a Unix computer across the network.

```
rsh computer [-l username] [-n] command
```

Set

The set command views and modifies environment variables in either NT or the MS-DOS subsystem. It is normally used in the AUTOEXEC.NT file to configure the MS-DOS environment.

```
set [variable=[string]]
```

Setlocal

The setlocal command begins localization of environment variables in a batch file. Each setlocal command must have an endlocal command to restore environment variables.

```
setlocal
```

Setver

The setver command sets the version number that the MS-DOS subsystem reports back to a program.

```
setver [drive:path] [filename n.nn]
setver [drive:path] [filename [/delete [/quiet]]
```

To display the current version table, use the following syntax:

```
setver [drive:path]
```

Shell

The shell command sets the path and name of an alternative command interpreter you want NT to use for the MS-DOS subsystem.

```
shell=[[drive:]path] filename [parameters]
```

Part iv

Shift

The shift command changes the position of variables within a batch file. For more information refer to online help in NT.

```
shift
```

Sort

The sort command receives input, sorts the data, and writes the results back to the screen, to a file, or to another device.

```
sort [/r] [/+n] [<] [drive1:][path1] filename1 [>
    [drive2:][path2] filename2]
[command |] sort [/r] [/+n] [> [drive2:][path2] filename2]
```

Stacks

The stacks command provides data stacks to dynamically handle hardware interrupts.

```
stacks=n,s
```

Start

The start command starts a separate window to run a specified program or command. Start can be used to run either a command-line program or a window program. This command provides one of the only ways to dynamically change the multitasking priority of a program.

```
start ["title"] [/dpath] [/i] [/min] [/max] [/separate]
    [/low] [/normal] [/high] [/realtime] [/wait] [/b]
    [filename] [parameters]
```

NOTE

A program started at an altered priority level only runs at that priority for the current session. The next time you run the program, it reverts back to its designed priority level. The start command can be used in a batch file if you want the appearance of a permanent alteration of the priority.

Subst

The subst command assigns a drive letter to a specific path.

```
subst [drive1: [drive2:]path]
subst drive1: /d
```

Tftp

The tftp (Trivial File Transfer Protocol) command is another TCP/IP utility for transferring data between computers. It is similar in function to FTP, but uses UDP to perform the transfer. Because of this, TFTP is slightly faster than FTP but does not produce a reliable communication.

```
tftp [-i] computer [get | put] source [destination]
```

Time

The time command is used to display or set the system clock on your computer.

```
time [hours:[minutes[:seconds[.hundredths]]][A|P]]
```

Title

The title command sets a custom title for the command prompt window.

```
title [string]
```

Tracert

The tracert (Trace Route) diagnostic utility determines the route taken to a destination by sending Internet Control Message Protocol (ICMP) echo packets with varying Time-To-Live (TTL) values to the destination. Each router along the path is required to decrement the TTL on a packet by at least 1 before forwarding it, so the TTL is effectively a hop count. When the TTL on a packet reaches 0, the router is supposed to send back an ICMP Time Exceeded message to the source system. Tracert uses this information to determine the route to the remote computer.

```
tracert [-d] [-h maximum_hops] [-j computer-list] [-w
    timeout] target_name
```

NOTE

Some routers silently drop packets with expired TTLs, so they will be invisible to tracert.

Part iv

Tree

The `tree` command displays a graphical view of the directory structure of a path or of the disk in a drive.

```
tree [drive:][path] [/f] [/a]
```

Type

The `type` command displays the contents of a text file without giving you the ability to alter the file. This command can be used to redirect output to a new file.

```
type [drive:][path] filename [...]
type [drive:][path] filename > filename2
```

Ver

The `ver` command displays current version information about NT.

```
ver
```

Vol

The `vol` command displays the disk volume label and serial number. A serial number is displayed for a disk formatted with MS-DOS version 4 or later, or with NT.

```
vol [drive:]
```

Winnt

This command is used to start the Windows NT Setup program from a 16-bit or 32-bit operating system other than NT.

```
winnt [/s:sourcepath] [/i:inf_file] [/t:drive_letter] [/x]
     [/b] [/ox] [/u[:script] [/r:directory]
```

This command is functionally identical to `winnt32`.

Winnt32

`Winnt32` is used to start the Windows NT Setup program from within NT only.

```
winnt32 [/s:sourcepath] [/i:inf_file] [/t:drive_letter] [/x]
       [/b] [/ox] [/u[:script] [/r:directory]
```

This command is functionally identical to `winnt`.

Xcopy

The xcopy command copies files and directories. Xcopy can be used to recursively copy all subdirectories in the same operation.

```
xcopy source [destination] [/w] [/p] [/c] [/v] [/q] [/f] [/l]
    [/d[:date]] [/u] [/i] [/s [/e]] [/t] [/k] [/r] [/h]
    [/a|/m] [/n] [/exclude:filename] [/z]
```

PART **V**

APPENDIX

Appendix

ANSWERS TO STUDY QUESTIONS

This appendix provides the answers to the sample study questions for the Windows NT Workstation exam (presented in Chapter 27) and the Windows NT Server exam (presented in Chapter 28).

SAMPLE STUDY QUESTIONS: WINDOWS NT WORKSTATION EXAM

1. Multiprocessing is

   A. running more than one process at a time on one microprocessor.

   B. having multiple processors on the network.

   C. using more than one microprocessor in the same computer.

   D. running more than one process at a time on one microcomputer.

   Answer: C

2. Windows NT divides memory into _____.

   A. user and protected

   B. conventional and expanded

   C. conventional and extended

   D. Windows NT does not segment memory

   Answer: A

3. What is the Sysdiff utility used for?

   A. It creates a mirror image of a hard drive onto another hard drive across the network.

   B. It creates difference files used to automate the installation of third-party applications onto NT Workstation.

   C. It creates users and groups, plus it established the low-level security for resource access.

   D. It is used to convert Windows NT 3.51 and Windows 95 Program Groups to Start Menu shortcuts.

   Answer: B

4. You currently have a computer with only a single hard drive that is already configured with a single partition. You want to install Windows 95 and Windows NT Workstation in a dual-boot configuration. You do not share this computer with anyone else, thus security is not important. Plus, you want to be able to access your data files from either operating system. Which of the following is your best option?

A. Back up any files currently on the computer. Reconfigure the drive with two partitions. Install Windows 95 onto one partition and restore your backed-up files to that partition. Format the other partition with NTFS and install NT Workstation on it.

B. Format the partition as FAT and install Windows 95. Then install NT Workstation into a different directory on the same partition.

C. Install Windows 95. Upgrade the Windows 95 installation to NT Workstation by installing into the same directory. Leave the partition formatted as FAT.

D. It is not possible to have both Windows 95 and NT Workstation on the same computer.

Answer: B

5. You are the administrator for a client-server network comprised of 28 Windows NT Workstation computers and three Windows NT Servers (one is the PDC). Some of your users use different clients each day. The users claim that when they change their password on one of the client machines, it is not automatically changed on any of the other computers. You have roaming profiles enabled. What is the problem and how can you resolve it?

A. The client machines are set to join a workgroup instead of a domain. Properly configure all of the computers to participate in the domain.

B. The previous passwords assigned to the user accounts have not expired. Deselect the Password Never Expires checkbox for these user accounts.

C. The user accounts are only local user accounts on the individual workstations. Create domain user accounts for everyone.

D. The User Cannot Change Password field has been checked for these users. Deselect this item on these accounts.

Answer: C

6. Your organization's security policy requires that notification be given at the time of logon to all potential intruders that unauthorized attempted access will be prosecuted to the full extent of the law. You must edit the LegalNoticeCaption and LegalNoticeText Registry keys to create such a message. What tools can you use to perform this task? Choose all that apply.

A. Performance Monitor

B. REGEDIT.EXE

C. Server Manager

D. REGEDT32.EXE

Answer: B, D

7. After installing a new hard drive in your Windows NT Workstation computer, you create a single FAT-formatted partition on it. Who has access to this drive and what permission level do they have by default?

A. Read for Everyone, Full Control for Administrators and the owner/creator

B. No Access for Everyone, Change for PowerUsers

C. FAT does not support any security restrictions, thus it has the equivalent of Full Control for Everyone

D. Full Control to Administrators, Change for PowerUsers, Read for Guests

Answer: C

8. When using the NT Backup utility that accompanies Windows NT Workstation, you can make backups of files stored on partitions formatted with which file system types?

    A. FAT

    B. NTFS

    C. HPFS

    D. CDFS

    Answer: A, B

9. NWLink is the protocol most commonly used by Windows NT Workstation clients to connect to or communicate with what types of servers or computer systems?

    A. MacOS

    B. NetWare

    C. Linux

    D. UNIX

    Answer: B

10. If your DNS Server address in your TCP/IP settings for your Windows NT Workstation client is defined incorrectly (in other words, you typed in the wrong IP address), then which of the following activities will be affected?

    A. Accessing NT-hosted directory shares and network printers

    B. Use of domain names for Internet-hosted Web resources

    C. Accessing an FTP server via IP address

    D. Saving files in your home directory

    Answer: B

11. Your network hosts a NetWare server in addition to the three NT Servers. You install CSNW on your Windows NT Workstation so you can gain access to the NetWare hosted resources. However, when you try to access those resources, your client is unable to locate the server. What is most likely the cause of this problem?

A. NetWare and NT are incompatible.

B. The NWLink frame type used by the NetWare server and NT are different.

C. The client is using a different subnet mask from the NetWare server.

D. A trust relationship has not been created between NetWare and NT.

Answer: B

12. You attempt to move a client from the SALES workgroup to the MARKETING domain. You log in to the Windows NT Workstation client. You open the Network applet and select the Identification tab. You select the Domain radio button and type in MARKETING in the blank field. After rebooting, you discover that the client cannot communicate with the domain. Why?

A. You must reinstall NT Workstation to change from a workgroup to a domain.

B. A computer account was not established in the domain for the NT client.

C. The browse list on the NT Workstation client has not been updated with the new resource list from the domain.

D. You did not select Domain from the Network Type menu in Server Manager.

Answer: B

13. The New Phonebook Entry Wizard is used to create what?

A. An entry containing contact information for your closest friends

B. A new dial-up connection definition for an outbound RAS session

C. Dialing property settings, such as area code, credit card, and call waiting, for a modem

D. A new user account to be used exclusively for RAS

Answer: B

14. You have been contracted by a publishing firm to author a multi-page article on the hobbies of dead presidents. You are required to submit the completed article on a floppy. However, they stipulated that the file should be a capture of printer output instead of a standard word processing document file. Since you are using Windows NT Workstation, you know you can accomplish this without any difficulty. Which tab of the printer's Properties dialog box is used to redirect a print job to a file?

A. General

B. Ports

C. Sharing

D. Device Settings

Answer: B

15. You have several utilities on your Windows NT Workstation computer that analyze data and perform complex calculations. The data from these utilities is saved in a text file. While the results of the utilities are important, they can take hours to complete. You notice that if you attempt to perform other normal activities such as check e-mail, type a document, and download files while these utilities are executing, the system is very slow. You need to be around while the calculations are performed, just in case the utilities encounter errors or require user interaction, but you also need to perform other work. You really can't afford to sit around and wait, so what can you do to improve your situation?

A. Increase the foreground priority boost on the Performance tab of the System applet.

B. Launch the utilities in a separate memory space.

C. Launch the utilities at a lower execution priority: start /low <application>.

D. Decrease the size of the paging file.

Answer: C

16. What methods can you use to launch Win16 applications so that if one fails the others are not affected?

   A. From Start ≻ Run, check the Run in Separate Memory Space option.

   B. Right-click the application's main icon (in Explorer, My Computer, or on the Desktop) and select Launch in Separate Memory Space from the pop-up menu.

   C. Edit a shortcut to the application, check the Run in Separate Memory Space box on the General tab.

   D. From a command prompt: start /separate <application>.

   Answer: A, C, D

17. You currently have Windows 95 installed on your computer. You install a second hard drive and install Windows NT Workstation in a dual-boot configuration. When your computer is first booted, the boot menu displays MS-DOS instead of Windows 95 as the selection to access Windows 95. What can you do to correct this?

   A. Use the System applet's Startup/Shutdown tab to edit the names listed in the boot menu.

   B. Reinstall Windows 95.

   C. Edit the BOOT.INI file, under the [operating systems] section so the line reads "Windows 95" instead of "MS-DOS".

   D. Use REGEDT32 to search for the string "BootMenuList" and edit the Value# item corresponding to "MS-DOS".

   Answer: C

18. Your Windows NT Workstation has a multimedia sound card installed. You download new drivers and install them through the Multimedia applet. To complete the installation, you need to reboot your computer. However, after the OS Loader displays the blue screen that lists the OS name and version, nothing else happens. What is the simplest method to restore the system so it will boot normally?

   A. When prompted, press the spacebar to access the Last Known Good configuration.

    B. Reinstall NT Workstation.

    C. Boot to DOS, execute the SETUPMGR.EXE program and remove the new multimedia driver.

    D. Create three new installation floppies using the WINNT /OX command, use these with the ERD to perform a repair of the boot areas.

    Answer: A

19. You currently have Windows 95 installed on your computer. You install a second hard drive and install Windows NT Workstation in a dual-boot configuration. Currently, Windows NT Workstation is the default OS and it takes 30 seconds for the boot menu to use the default selection. How can you change this?

    A. On the Startup/Shutdown tab of the System applet

    B. By using REGEDT32 to search and edit BootMenuList and BootMenuTimer

    C. By editing the BOOT.INI file

    D. By changing the PIF for WIN.COM

    Answer: A, C

20. Your Windows NT Workstation–based computer has two hard drives. One is an IDE drive formatted with FAT, the other a SCSI drive formatted with NTFS. NT Workstation is hosted on the SCSI drive. You replace your old no-frills non-BIOS SCSI controller with a new fast-wide, BIOS-enabled SCSI controller. When you attempt to boot your machine, you see the following error:

```
Windows NT could not start because the following file is
    missing or corrupt:
\<winnt root>\system32\ntoskrnl.exe
```

You try to boot again, but this time select to boot to DOS, which does succeed. What is the problem and how can you correct it?

    A. The ARC name listed in the BOOT.INI file points to the wrong partition. Edit the BOOT.INI file to change partition(1) to partition(0).

B. The ARC name listed in the BOOT.INI file for the NT Workstation boot partition is using a 'scsi' prefix instead of a 'multi' prefix. Edit the BOOT.INI file to use 'multi.'

C. You accidentally attached the IDE hard drive to the SCSI controller and the SCSI drive to the IDE controller. Switch the drive connectors back to the correct controllers.

D. NTDETECT is missing or corrupted.

Answer: B

21. Windows NT is not available for which of the following computers:

A. Intel 386 class machines

B. Digital Alpha–based computers

C. MIPS-based computers

D. PowerPC-based computers

E. VAX minicomputers

Answer: E

22. All of the following operating systems can be used in a peer-to-peer network (in other words, a network without a dedicated server), except for which one?

A. Windows NT Server

B. Windows NT Workstation

C. Windows 95

D. MS-DOS

Answer: D

23. Which process implements the security user interface when the computer is booted?

A. Account policy dialog box

B. WinLogon

C. Access token

D. Boot interface

Answer: B

24. You have attempted to remove NT Workstation from your computer, but each time you boot, the boot menu still appears. What step must you take to remove this?

A. Before removing NT Workstation, you need to set the Display Menu time to 0 (zero) on the Boot Options tab of the System applet and select Windows 95 as the default boot option.

B. Use the three NT Workstation setup floppies and select D from the menu to remove the boot loader.

C. Back up your system, reformat the hard disk, and then reinstall your operating system and restore your files.

D. At a command prompt from DOS or Windows 95, execute SYS C:.

Answer: D

25. At the end of each financial year, your organization spends the remainder of your equipment budget on purchasing large quantities of identically configured computers. You need to install NT Workstation on 100 identical Pentium computers, 80 identical 486DX100 computers, and 35 identical notebook computers. Instead of performing each install one at a time manually, how can you automate or simplify the installation procedure?

A. Create an unattended answer file for each computer type and a single uniqueness database file. Use these files as parameters of the Winnt setup utility launched from a network share.

B. Move the NT Workstation CD-ROM from one machine to the next as you complete each install.

C. Create one unattended answer file and a uniqueness database file for each computer type. Use these files as parameters of the Winnt setup utility launched from a network share.

D. NT Workstation cannot be installed onto notebook computers.

E. Create a single unattended answer file and a single unique-ness database file. Use these files as parameters of the Winnt setup utility launched from a network share.

Answer: A

26. To improve security, your organization has a security policy that states users can select their own passwords and should not share them with anyone, including the administrators. What setting on a user account will force users to change the temporary password an administrator provides when initially creating the account?

A. Check User Must Change Password at Next Logon in the New User window.

B. Check Account Disabled in the New User window.

C. Set Maximum Password Age to zero in the Account Policy window.

D. Check Users Must Log On in Order to Change Password in the Account Policy window.

Answer: A

27. On a Windows NT Workstation computer, what is the process for creating new user accounts?

A. Use the NET USER command line utility with the follow-ing parameters: NET USER /NEW /N:<username> /P:<password>.

B. Launch User Manager, Select User ➤ New User from the menu bar. Provide the requested information, then click OK.

C. Use the Users tab of the Environment applet.

D. Enter a new username and password at the logon prompt, NT Workstation will automatically create a new account for the unknown N/P pair.

Answer: B

28. You want to store all user profiles on a single computer within your network. However, your network is just a workgroup of 10 Windows NT Workstations. What can you do to store all profiles on just one of these machines?

A. Change the home directory path for each user to the UNC path to the destination directory on the specified Windows NT Workstation computer.

B. Change the User Profile path for each user to the UNC path to the destination directory on the specified Windows NT Workstation computer.

C. Profiles cannot be redirected within a workgroup; this can be performed only on a client-server network.

D. Enable roaming profiles for all accounts on the PDC.

Answer: B

29. A system administrator, named Elvis, left your organization. This user account was deleted by another SysAdmin. The president of your organization was able to convince Elvis to return and assume his previous responsibilities. Elvis' user account is re-created by the SysAdmin that deleted it. When Elvis tries to access certain files and resources that he had access to previously, he is unable to access them. Why?

A. Elvis' new account has a new SID, thus he is not the same user as he was previously.

B. The new account is not using a roaming profile.

C. Obviously, if Elvis cannot access a file or a resource, it was deleted when his account was deleted.

D. Elvis has forgotten his password.

Answer: A

30. What user accounts are created by default when Windows NT Workstation is installed? Choose all that apply.

A. Administrator

B. Supervisor

    C. Guest

    D. Superuser

    E. Everyone

    Answer: A, C

31. After installing a new high-performance video card in your Windows NT Workstation computer, the machine boots but the screen remains blank. What can you do to enable NT Workstation to properly use this new video card?

    A. Use the VGA Mode selection from the boot menu, and then install the correct driver through the Display applet.

    B. Boot into Safe Mode using the F8 Startup menu, and then install the correct driver through the Video applet.

    C. Boot using the Last Known Good configuration option (accessed by pressing the spacebar when prompted during bootup), and then install the correct driver through the Display applet.

    D. Use the VGA Mode selection from the boot menu, and then install the correct driver through the Video applet.

    Answer: A

32. You purchased a UPS to provide power protection for your Windows NT Workstation computer. What Control Panel applet is used to configure NT to communicate properly with the UPS?

    A. UPS

    B. System

    C. Devices

    D. Power

    Answer: A

33. Windows NT Workstation system services can be started, paused, and stopped through which Control Panel applet?

A. System

B. Network

C. Devices

D. Services

Answer: D

34. You have deployed a Windows NT Workstation machine to be used as the central repository for your company's financial data. To provide the most reliable storage possible on this computer, you want to implement a fault-tolerant drive configuration. How can you accomplish this?

A. Install three hard drives and use disk striping with parity.

B. Windows NT Workstation does not support fault-tolerant drive configurations.

C. Create a disk duplex with two drives, each on a separate drive controller.

D. Use partitions on four or more drives to create an expandable volume.

Answer: B

35. You performed a system-wide complete backup yesterday. Today, you have made changes to several new files, copied files from other machines to your local drive, and downloaded many new archives from a Web site. If you only want to back up the files that have changed or are new on your system since yesterday's backup, what type of a backup operation should you perform?

A. Normal

B. Copy

C. Incremental

D. Differential

Answer: C

36. After installing a new hard drive in your Windows NT Work-station computer, you create a single NTFS formatted partition on it. Who has access to this drive and what permission level do they have by default?

A. The owner/creator has Read.

B. The Everyone group has Full Control.

C. The Administrators group has Full Control.

D. The PowerUsers group has Change.

Answer: B

37. You have been hired to improve the operation of an existing network. The primary activity on the network is users accessing an NT Workstation–hosted database over NWLink. Unfortunately, three protocols are in use: TCP/IP (primary), NWLink, and NetBEUI. The NT Workstation hosting the database has a single 4GB SCSI drive that is almost full and whose performance is degrading fast.

Required result: Improve network access to the database.

Optional results: Improve the performance of the NT Workstation machine.

Solve the low storage space problem.

Implement fault protection for the database.

Solution: Bind NWLink as the primary protocol on the NT Workstation machine. Install an 8GB SCSI drive. Move the database to the new drive.

Which of the following is true?

A. The solution gives you the required result and all optional results.

B. The solution gives you the required result and two optional result.

C. The solution gives you the required result only.

D. The solution does not give you the required result.

Answer: B

38. PPTP or Point-to-Point Tunneling Protocol can be used by Windows NT Workstation to establish what?

  A. A communication link via a hollow pipe

  B. A remote-control connection with a server on another network

  C. A secure network connection over the Internet

  D. A community link where multiple users can interact directly over telephone lines

  Answer: C

39. The design department of your organization creates complex graphical architectural drawings. These drawings often take 15 minutes or more to print, even on your high-speed laser printer. You want to allow members of the DESIGN group to print, but don't want their print jobs to supercede the smaller print jobs of the rest of the company. Which of the following describes the proper steps you can take to establish such a system?

  A. Create two logical printers for the same printer—DESIGN-PRNT and ALLPRNT. Set DESIGNPRNT so it prints only after the entire print job is spooled and grant the DESIGN group Print access to this printer. Set ALLPRNT with a priority of 2 (one more than DESIGNPRINT) and set the DESIGN group permission to No Access.

  B. Grant the DESIGN group Print access to the existing printer. Grant the Everyone group Full Control.

  C. Create two logical printers for the same printer—DESIGN-PRNT and ALLPRNT. Set ALLPRNT so it prints only after the entire print job is spooled and set the DESIGN group permission to No Access. Set DESIGNPRNT with a priority of 2 (one more than ALLPRNT) and grant the DESIGN group Print access to this printer.

D. Create two logical printers for the same printer—DESIGN-PRNT and ALLPRNT. Set DESIGNPRNT so it prints directly to the printer, and grant the DESIGN group Print access to this printer. Set ALLPRNT with a priority of 2 (one more than DESIGNPRINT), and set the DESIGN group permission to No Access.

Answer: A

40. After returning from vacation, you boot your Windows NT Workstation computer. You allow the default boot menu item of NT Workstation to be activated. However, the following error message appears and continues to repeat:

```
I/O Error accessing boot sector file
multi(0)disk(0)rdisk(0)partition(1):\bootsect.dos
```

What could cause this error to appear?

A. The BOOT.INI file points to the wrong partition.

B. NTDETECT.COM is missing or corrupted.

C. NTLDR is missing or corrupted.

D. BOOTSECT.DOS is missing or corrupted.

Answer: D

SAMPLE STUDY QUESTIONS: WINDOWS NT SERVER EXAM

1. You have a Pentium 100 computer with 8MB of memory and a 1.2GB hard drive that you would like to turn into the server for your small network.

Required Result: The operating system you install must provide file system security for data stored on the server's hard drive.

Optional Result 1: You want your server to be able to provide print services.

Optional Result 2: You want your server to be able to provide file services.

Suggested Solution: Install Windows NT Server, implement NTFS and RAID on the hard disk drives, and create domain user accounts for network users. Share the printers attached to the server computer.

Which of the following is correct?

A. The suggested solution provides the required result and both of the optional results.

B. The suggested solution provides the required result and only one of the optional results.

C. The suggested solution provides only the required result.

D. The suggested solution does not provide the required result.

Answer: D

2. You are considering the purchase of a new computer for a server. You need to determine whether or not the hardware is compatible with Windows NT. The salesperson shows you Windows 95 running on the computer, but he doesn't have Windows NT. Which tools will help you determine whether or not this computer is capable of running Windows NT?

A. If it runs Windows 95, it will run Windows NT.

B. Run the HAL utility and check the HCL.

C. Run the NTHQ utility and check the HCL.

D. Run the HCL and check the HAL.

Answer: C

3. You have been tasked with establishing a multiple-domain Windows NT-based network for a company with a central office and five outlying branch offices. The branch offices are linked to the central office via leased lines. You must structure the network for centralized administration of user accounts and distributed administration of network resources.

Required Result: User accounts must be established and managed from one central location.

Optional Result 1: Resources must be controlled from the domains in which they reside.

Optional Result 2: Users must still be able to log on to the network even when the network link to the main office is down.

Proposed Solution: Create one domain for the central office and a separate domain for each of the branch offices. Configure each branch office domain to trust the central office domain. Create all user accounts on the central office domain. Configure the resources (file storage, printers, etc.) in the domains in which they reside.

Which of the following is correct?

A. The proposed solution satisfies the required result and both optional results.

B. The proposed solution satisfies the required result and one optional result.

C. The proposed solution satisfies the required result only.

D. The proposed solution does not satisfy the required result.

Answer: B

4. You have been asked to install computers and network software for an architectural firm with nine employees. They want a computer dedicated to storing files so that they have one place to back files up, but they are not interested in security (each user will have full control of their own computer). Which security role should the Windows NT Server computer play in this network?

A. Primary Domain Controller

B. Backup Domain Controller

C. Member Server

D. Stand Alone Server

Answer: D

5. Your company uses Microsoft SQL Server on a 180MHz Pentium Windows NT Server computer with 96MB of RAM. This server also runs several network software packages that are only available for the Intel platform. As your network has grown and new database clients have begun querying the central database, database performance has deteriorated. You have received funds to replace the SQL Server computer.

   Required Result: The new server must provide more than twice the computing power of the existing server in order to speed up the Microsoft SQL Server software.

   Optional Result 1: The server should support multiple processors to take advantage of Windows NT's multi-processor architecture.

   Optional Result 2: The server should support server-based applications compiled for the Intel microprocessor.

   Proposed Solution: Purchase a four processor 600MHz Digital Alpha workstation with Windows NT and the FX!32 software installed. Install SQL Server for the Alpha architecture.

   Which of the following is correct?

   A. The proposed solution satisfies the required result and both optional results.

   B. The proposed solution satisfies the required result and one optional result.

   C. The proposed solution satisfies the required result only.

   D. The proposed solution does not satisfy the required result.

   Answer: A

6. You must install the Windows NT operating system on 35 identically configured 266 MHz Pentium-II computers connected to your LAN. It is important that the software be installed quickly and without a lot of user intervention at the target computers during the install process.

   Required Result: Centralize the installation files so that the distribution media does not have to be physically present at each of the target computers and so that multiple installations can occur simultaneously.

Optional Result 1: Automate the installation process so that hardware-specific installation choices (video card settings, etc.) are not required at the target computers.

Optional Result 2: Automate the installation process so that installation-specific choices (computer name, etc.) are not required at the target computers.

Proposed Solution: Copy the Windows NT operating system installation files (the I386 directory) to a share on a file server. Create an unattended answer file for the computers. Create a boot disk for the target computers that maps a drive to the I386 server share and starts the Winnt program with the /u: option specifying the unattended answer file.

Which of the following is correct?

A. The proposed solution satisfies the required result and both optional results.

B. The proposed solution satisfies the required result and one optional result.

C. The proposed solution satisfies the required result only.

D. The proposed solution does not satisfy the required result.

Answer: B

7. You have purchased a 266MHz dual Pentium-II computer for use as the file server on your network. You installed four 9GB hard drives for the operating system and user file storage. It is important that user data not be lost in the event that a hard drive fails. The server should also provide file and directory security and respond as quickly as possible to file requests from network clients. You must configure the server computer appropriately.

Required Result: A single hard drive failure should not result in the loss of user data.

Optional Result 1: Disk access speed should be optimized.

Optional Result 2: The system administrator should be able to grant or revoke access to data on a file-by-file basis.

Suggested Solution: Divide each drive into a 512MB partition and a 8.5GB partition. Create a stripe set (RAID level 0) with the 8.5GB partitions and format it with NTFS. Store user data on this volume. Create a mirror set with two of the 512MB partitions, format it with Windows NT, and install the operating system to the resulting 1GB volume.

Which of the following is correct?

A. The proposed solution satisfies the required result and both optional results.

B. The proposed solution satisfies the required result and one optional result.

C. The proposed solution satisfies the required result only.

D. The proposed solution does not satisfy the required result.

Answer: D

8. You are installing a Windows NT Server computer in an IPX–based NetWare network. What transport protocol should you select for maximum interoperability between the NT and NetWare servers?

A. TCP/IP

B. AppleTalk

C. NWLink

D. NetBEUI

Answer: C

9. What tool do you use to add a network adapter driver to your Windows NT Server computer?

A. The Server Control Panel

B. The Services Control Panel

C. The Network Control Panel

D. A screwdriver

Answer: C

10. You have been tasked with establishing a multiple-domain Windows NT–based network for a company with a central office and five outlying branch offices. The branch offices are linked to the central office via leased lines. You must structure the network for centralized administration of user accounts and distributed administration of network resources.

Required Result: User accounts must be established and managed from one central location.

Optional Result 1: Resources must be controlled from the domains in which they reside.

Optional Result 2: Users must still be able to log on to the network even when the network link to the main office is down.

Suggested Solution: Create one domain for the central office and a separate domain for each of the branch offices. Configure each branch office domain to trust the central office domain. Create all user accounts at each branch office domain. Configure the resources (file storage, printers, etc.) in the domains in which they reside.

Which of the following is correct?

A. The suggested solution satisfies the required result and both of the optional results.

B. The suggested solution satisfies the required result and just one of the optional results.

C. The suggested solution satisfies the required result only.

D. The suggested solution does not satisfy the required result.

Answer: D

11. Rather than using cryptic usernames like hjtillman on your network you would like to create more readable usernames like Tillman, Henry J. Why won't User Manager for Domains let you create a user account name like this?

A. Spaces are not allowed in usernames.

B. That kind of name is too inconvenient to type every time you log on.

C. Usernames must be eight characters or less.

D. Usernames may not contain a comma.

Answer: D

12. What tool should you use to configure directory replication?

A. Server Manager

B. Event Viewer

C. User Manager for Domains

D. DHCP Manager

Answer: A

13. You are configuring RAS for your network. You have employees that work at home and that use Windows NT, Windows 95, Unix, and Macintosh computers. You would like to protect your network from intrusion and you want to provide the most bandwidth you can to dial-in users.

Required Result: All remote clients must be able to dial in to your network.

Optional Result 1: The dial-in connection should be secure.

Optional Result 2: The connecting user should be able to combine several dial-up lines.

Suggested Solution: Configure RAS to Require Microsoft Encrypted Authentication. Also select Require Data Encryption. Use the RAS callback feature. Allow dial-in clients to use the Multilink feature.

Which of the following is correct?

A. The suggested solution satisfies the required result and both of the optional results.

B. The suggested solution satisfies the required result and just one of the optional results.

C. The suggested solution satisfies the required result only.

D. The suggested solution does not satisfy the required result.

Answer: D

14. Internet Information Server provides which of the following Internet services? Select all that apply.

A. FTP

B. WAIS

C. HTTP

D. Gopher

Answer: A, C, D

15. You have configured your Windows NT Server computer to share a NetWare print queue as an NT printer. A user with sufficient privileges to administer printing on the Windows NT domain tried to stop printing to the printer but documents from NetWare clients continued to print. What is the problem?

A. You have the wrong printer driver installed on the Windows NT Server computer.

B. You have the wrong printer driver installed on the user's client computer.

C. The user's client software only has the ability to manage the software print share on the NT Server, not the actual NetWare print queue.

D. NetWare print queues cannot be stopped.

Answer: C

16. How do you limit the hours of operation of a specific printer?

A. Enter the hours of operation from the Hours button of the user's entry in the User Manager for Domains program.

B. Enter the hours of operation in the Hours tab of the Printer entry in the Services Control Panel.

C. Start and stop the printer service at regular intervals using the AT command.

D. Enter the hours of operation in the Scheduling tab of the Properties window of the printer.

Answer: D

17. What service would you install on your Windows NT Server computer to automatically configure the IP addresses of Microsoft networking clients on a TCP/IP network?

A. SNMP

B. DHCP

C. DNS

D. WINS

Answer: B

18. You have a single Windows NT Server computer on your 10BaseT Ethernet network as both a file and print server as well as an application server. You have doubled the number of client computers on your network in the last year and server performance has diminished. Using Performance Monitor, you determine that the file server is disk bound for file requests and memory bound for client access to the server-based application. Your top priority is to speed up access to files, but you would also like to speed up access to the server application.

Required Result: Significantly improve file access from network clients.

Optional Result: Significantly improve server-based application performance.

Suggested Solution: Install additional hard disk drives and create a RAID level 0 stripe set. Place files accessed by network clients on the RAID volume. Upgrade the network from 10Mbps Ethernet to 100Mbps Ethernet.

Which of the following is correct?

A. The suggested solution satisfies the required result and the optional result.

B. The suggested solution satisfies the required result only.

C. The suggested solution does not satisfy the required result.

Answer: B

19. You are evaluating a computer for use as a Windows NT Server on your network. You have just upgraded the memory, added a new hard drive, and installed a faster microprocessor. You want to make sure that these components work together. You would also like to be sure that the computer's other components (networking adapter, sound card, video adapter, etc.) are installed properly, without conflicts, and are compatible with Windows NT.

Required Result: Verify that the memory, microprocessor, and hard drive work.

Optional Result 1: Verify that the computer's components are installed correctly and without conflicts.

Optional Result 2: Verify that the components work with Windows NT.

Suggested Solution: Install DOS on the computer's hard drive and boot DOS.

Which of the following is correct?

A. The suggested solution satisfies the required result and both of the optional results.

B. The suggested solution satisfies the required result and just one of the optional results.

C. The suggested solution satisfies the required result only.

D. The suggested solution does not satisfy the required result.

Answer: C

20. Your Windows NT Server has reported several errors on startup. How do you view additional information about the errors?

A. Review the /etc/sys.log file in a text editor.

B. Click the System Events tab in Performance Monitor.

C. Select System from the Log menu of the Event Viewer.

D. Select Security from the Log menu of the Event Viewer.

Answer: C

21. Your boss tells you that he wants to convert the company's Sun Microsystems Sparc Ultra RISC-based server into a Windows NT Server. The machine has 10GB of disk space, 256MB RAM, and runs at 300MHz. This machine:

A. Won't work because the Sparc Ultra is not on the Hardware Compatibility List

B. Will work because it has adequate disk space, RAM, and processor speed

C. Won't work because Windows NT doesn't support the Sparc microprocessor

D. Will work because Sun is closely allied with Microsoft

Answer: C

22. Which of the following network client operating systems will Windows NT Server support? Choose all that apply.

A. MS-DOS

B. Windows 95

C. Macintosh

D. Windows NT Workstation

Answer: A, B, C, D

23. You are moving from a Windows 95–based workgroup to a Windows NT–based domain. You are upgrading a Windows 95 computer to Windows NT. Which of the following can you still use from Windows NT Server? Choose all that apply.

   A. 32-bit Windows (Win32) application software

   B. Simple DOS programs that do not communicate directly with the computer hardware

   C. Windows 95 device drivers

   D. OS/2 version 1.3 programs

   Answer: A, B, D

24. You are designing a network for a company that is concerned about the security and reliability of their network. The company will use a SQL database to track parts, production, and sales contacts. The budget will support two server computers and 37 client computers (as well as miscellaneous printers and network devices).

   Required Result: The network must provide centrally managed security, centrally stored user files, and SQL Server database support.

   Optional Result 1: Users should still be authenticated by the network even if the Primary Domain Controller goes down.

   Optional Result 2: Users should still have access to their files even if the Primary Domain Controller goes down.

   Proposed Solution: Install one Windows NT Server computer as a Primary Domain Controller for the domain and store all user files to this server computer. Install another Windows NT Server as a Backup Domain Controller and then install SQL Server on that computer.

   Which of the following is correct?

   A. The proposed solution satisfies the required result and both optional results.

   B. The proposed solution satisfies the required result and one optional result.

C. The proposed solution satisfies the required result only.

D. The proposed solution does not satisfy the required result.

Answer: B

25. Your medium-sized network has grown. You now have 2 Windows NT Server computers and 75 Windows 95 client computers. You have purchased another computer to store network data and to host server-based software. You do not want this computer to authenticate logon requests or maintain a copy of the domain security database. Which security role should the Windows NT Server computer play in this network?

A. Primary Domain Controller

B. Backup Domain Controller

C. Member Server

D. Stand Alone Server

Answer: C

26. You have a Member Server computer that you would like to promote to a Backup Domain Controller for your network. What must you do to enact this role change for this server?

A. Use the Server Manager program to promote the server from Member Server to Backup Domain Controller.

B. Use the Server Manager program to demote the Backup Domain Controller to Member Server. The Member Server computer will be promoted in the absence of a Backup Domain Controller.

C. Use the Service tab of the Network Control Panel to enable the Backup Domain Controller option.

D. Reinstall the operating system software.

Answer: D

27. Your file server uses a dual-Pentium motherboard but has only one Pentium microprocessor installed. As the network has grown, file server responsiveness to file requests has become sluggish. You must improve file request responsiveness. Also, file server applications could use more compute power, and a more responsive user interface on the file server would be appreciated.

Required Result: The server must be twice as quick in responding to network client's file access requests.

Optional Result 1: The server should be more responsive to a user at the file server console.

Optional Result 2: The server should provide more computing power to server-based applications.

Proposed Solution: Install a second 200MHz processor in the server computer.

Which of the following is correct?

A. The proposed solution satisfies the required result and both optional results.

B. The proposed solution satisfies the required result and one optional result.

C. The proposed solution satisfies the required result only.

D. The proposed solution does not satisfy the required result.

Answer: D

28. Which hardware component has the least impact on file server performance as observed from a network client?

A. Microprocessor

B. Hard drive

C. Video adapter

D. Networking adapter

Answer: C

29. You have a Windows NT Server 3.51 computer that you want to upgrade to Windows NT Server 4. You would like to keep the current configuration settings (networking protocols, computer name, etc.), and you do not intend to dual-boot between versions of the operating system. You would like version 4 of the operating system to replace version 3.51. How should you install version 4?

A. Install Windows NT Server to the same directory and select Upgrade.

B. Install Windows NT Server to a different directory in the same volume.

C. Install Windows NT Server to the same directory and select Replace.

D. Install Windows NT Server to a different volume.

Answer: A

30. You have created a uniqueness database file (UDF) containing unique information for each of the Windows NT computers you will install operating system software for on your network. What Winnt command line switch instructs the Winnt program to use the UDF file?

A. /O:

B. /U:

C. /UDF:

D. /OX

Answer: C

31. The file server on your network is the repository for large graphic files generated by computer animation software. It is important that the file server respond as quickly as possible to client file requests; fault tolerance for the data is less important (the images can always be recomputed). Fault tolerance is important for the operating system files, however, and users should not be able to access other user's files without the other user's permission. You are configuring a new computer to be the file server, and you have installed four

9GB hard drives to store operating system and user data. How should you configure this file storage?

Required Result: Disk access for user data must be as fast as possible.

Optional Result 1: Failure of a single hard drive should not cause the loss of operating system files or data.

Optional Result 2: Users should be able to set permissions on files and directories that they own.

Suggested Solution: Divide each drive into a 512MB partition and a 8.5GB partition. Create a stripe set (RAID level 0) with the 8.5GB partitions and format it with NTFS. Store user data on this volume. Create a mirror set with two of the 512MB partitions, format it with Windows NT, and install the operating system to the resulting 1GB volume.

Which of the following is correct?

A. The proposed solution satisfies the required result and both optional results.

B. The proposed solution satisfies the required result and one optional result.

C. The proposed solution satisfies the required result only.

D. The proposed solution does not satisfy the required result.

Answer: A

32. You are planning the disk configuration for your Windows NT Server computer. Which of the following file storage configurations provide fault tolerance?

A. Volume set

B. Stripe set

C. Mirror set

D. Stripe set with parity

Answer: C, D

33. You have installed a new 9GB hard drive in your Windows NT Server computer. You want to make the additional file space available to network users. You want users to be able to restrict who may have access to the files they place on this drive. What file system should you format the volume with?

A. DOS FAT

B. NTFS

C. HPFS

D. HFS

Answer: B

34. You are configuring a new network for a medium-sized company that has a traveling sales force equipped with laptops as well as several work-at-home professionals. The company has three branch offices linked to the main office by leased lines and routers. The main office and each branch office will have a server computer, but account information will be maintained on the central main office server computer. You must select a protocol for Windows NT and Windows 95 computers to use to connect to your Windows NT Server computers.

Required Result: All of the client computers must be able to connect to all of the server computers, regardless of which network the client computer is on or if the client computer is connected via dial-up networking.

Optional Result 1: The protocol should be efficient so that users connected to the network over dial-up lines or connecting to a server through a router and over a leased line are not penalized.

Optional Result 2: The protocol should be easy to configure.

Suggested Solution: Configure the servers and all of the client computers to use the NetBEUI transport protocol.

Which of the following is correct?

A. The suggested solution satisfies the required result and both of the optional results.

B. The suggested solution satisfies the required result and just one of the optional results.

C. The suggested solution satisfies the required result only.

D. The suggested solution does not satisfy the required result.

Answer: D

35. A router's primary function is at which layer of the OSI stack?

A. The physical layer

B. The logical link layer

C. The network layer

D. The session layer

Answer: C

36. Which Control Panel do you use to configure the screen saver?

A. Console

B. Display

C. Screen

D. Multimedia

Answer: B

37. Which of the following operations can you perform from the Display Control Panel? Select all that apply.

A. Set the resolution and color depth of the display.

B. Install a display adapter driver.

C. Select the mouse pointer icons.

D. Select screen fonts and window border colors.

Answer: A, B, D

38. What tool do you use to configure trust relationships in Windows NT Server?

A. Syscon

B. Server Manager

C. User Manager for Domains

D. Network Control Panel

Answer: C

39. You have two domains: CorpCentral and Subsidiary. You want users in the Subsidiary domain to be able to log on using accounts created in the CorpCentral domain, but not vice versa. How should you configure the two domains?

A. Configure CorpCentral as the trusting domain and Subsidiary as the trusted domain.

B. Configure both domains as trusting and trusted.

C. Configure Subsidiary as the trusting domain and CorpCentral as the trusted domain.

D. You cannot establish a one-way trusting/trusted relationship.

Answer: C

40. You want to connect your network to the Internet. What transport protocol must you use?

A. NWLink

B. OSI

C. TCP/IP

D. NetBEUI

Answer: C

INDEX

Note to the Reader: Throughout this index **boldfaced** page numbers indicate primary discussions of a topic. *Italicized* page numbers indicate illustrations.

G

H

I

P

ABOUT THE CONTRIBUTORS

Some of the best—and best-selling—authors have contributed chapters from their books to *Windows NT 4 Complete*.

James Chellis, an MCP, is president of EdgeTek, a national network training company and Microsoft Solution Provider specializing in Windows NT.

J. Scott Christianson, a networking and videoconferencing consultant, is co-author of *Virtual Classrooms: Educational Opportunity through Two-Way Interactive Television*. He is a CNA, MCSE, and Certified Videoconferencing Engineer.

Robert Cowart is one of the most well-known Windows authors in the world. He has written over 30 books on computer programming and applications, with 12 books on Windows, including *Mastering Windows 3.11*, *Windows NT Server 4: No experience required*, and the best-selling *Mastering Windows 95: Internet Edition*, all from Sybex. His articles have appeared in *PC Week*, *PC World*, *PC*, and *Microsoft Systems Journal*.

Lisa Donald is an MCSE, MCT, and MCNE. She has worked with numerous Fortune 500 companies and government agencies, including Digital, Apple, the U.S. Postal Service, and the U.S. Naval Academy, and is the author of the best-selling *MCSE: NT Server in the Enterprise Study Guide* from Network Press.

Peter Dyson has more than two decades of experience in engineering, software development, and technical support. His computer-related publications range from technical research papers to software user manuals. He has written more than a dozen books, including *The UNIX Desk Reference: the hu.man pages*, *The Network Press Dictionary of Networking*, *The PC User's Pocket Dictionary*, and *Mastering OS/2 Warp*, all from Sybex.

Ana Fajen researches and writes on education policy, and coordinated Missouri's statewide planning process for distance learning in higher education.

Barry Gerber is an IS consultant focusing on communications systems and networking technologies. He has worked in a variety of fields, including finance, law, and academia. A founding editor of *Network Computing Magazine*, he has served as Director of Social Sciences Computing at UCLA, Vice President of Distributed Data Processing at a major insurance company, and Computing Director for a federally funded healthcare program.

Peter D. Hipson is an author, consultant, and developer. When not writing computer books, he can be found teaching computer science. An avid Microsoft beta tester and C++ programmer, he reviews virtually every product developed by Microsoft. He has written several books on subjects such as Windows NT Server 4, Visual C++, and BackOffice.

Todd Lammle is an MCT with more than 15 years of experience designing and implementing LANs and WANs. He is president of GlobalNet Systems Solutions, Inc., a network integration and training firm based in Denver, and is the author of the best-selling *MCSE: TCP/IP for NT Server 4 Study Guide* from Network Press.

Mark Minasi has 25 years of experience in the computer business. He has been teaching professional seminars on networking since 1985 and has experience with IBM, Novell, and Microsoft-based networks. He is a columnist for *NT Magazine* and is currently the resident computer expert at CNN. Minasi's *The Complete PC Upgrade & Maintenance Guide* has sold nearly 1 million copies, and his *Mastering Windows NT Server 4* is the #1 best-selling NT book in the world.

Michael G. Moncur, MCSE and CNE, is co-author of three Network Press CNE Study Guides and owns Starling Technologies, a consulting firm specializing in internetworking and Internet connectivity for Windows NT and NetWare networks.

Charles Perkins, MCSE, is co-author of six Network Press MCSE Study Guides. Formerly director of Computing Services for the University of Utah College of Law, he is now a consultant specializing in Windows NT.

Todd Phillips is an MCSE+Internet and Certified Trainer. A former Microsoft Support Engineer, he has been teaching Microsoft operating systems and networking for several years.

Charlie Russel is a long-time systems administrator and a recognized expert on networking multiple operating systems. He is the co-author of many books on operating systems, including *Upgrading to Windows 95*, *OS/2 for Windows Users*, and *Murphy's Laws of Windows*.

Matthew Strebe, MCSE, began his career in the U.S. Navy, installing the Navy's first fiber-optic LAN aboard a ship. He is co-author of five Network Press MCSE Study Guides and is the owner of Netropolis, a network integration firm specializing in high-speed networking and Windows NT.

Boyd Waters is a software developer for Imana Corp. He often speaks at Windows NT and Macintosh networking conferences.

NT 4 NETWORK SECURITY
MATTHEW STREBE, CHARLES PERKINS, AND MICHAEL G. MONCUR

ISBN: 0-7821-2425-9
976 pages; 1 CD; 7.5" × 9"
$49.99 U.S.

Malevolent hackers, disgruntled employees, acts of nature—what could bring your NT network to its knees? Find out with the second edition of this comprehensive guide to NT security. Practical examples show you how to identify and defend against real security threats, whether your network handles two users or two thousand. Learn how to attack your own NT network and servers to identify weak links; inoculate your servers and clients against viruses; secure data against theft and corruption; and protect equipment from theft or malicious damage. This book includes special coverage of Internet- and intranet-related security issues. The CD is packed with essential demo utilities and share-ware, as well as a variety of hacker tools for testing your own network.

MASTERING MICROSOFT EXCHANGE SERVER 5.5
BARRY GERBER

ISBN: 0-7821-2237-X
912 pages; 7.5" × 9"
$44.99 U.S.

Microsoft Exchange is the backbone of Windows NT's e-mail and Internet access systems. Mastering Exchange Server 5.5 is essential reading for any administrator, consultant, or power user on a Windows NT network, or for anyone preparing to take the MS Exchange Server MCSE Certification Exam. Written by an Exchange authority who actually worked with the Microsoft development team, this third edition of the most comprehensive, respected Exchange Server 5.5 book on the market covers every aspect of this powerful messaging and groupware product.